A QUEST OF INQUIRIE

A QUEST OF INQUIRIE

Some Contexts of Tudor Literature

HOWARD C. COLE

Pegasus

A DIVISION OF

The Bobbs-Merrill Company, Inc., Publishers

INDIANAPOLIS   NEW YORK

This book is one of a series, Pegasus Backgrounds in English Literature, under the general editorship of John R. Mulder, New York University.

OTHER TITLES IN THE SERIES ARE

The Temple of the Mind: Education and Literary Taste in Seventeenth-Century England by John R. Mulder.

Allegory and Mirror: Tradition and Structure in Middle English Literature by James I. Wimsatt.

Loyalties and Traditions: Man and His World in Old English Literature by Milton McC. Gatch.

Copyright © 1973 by The Bobbs-Merrill Company, Inc.
Printed in the United States of America
Library of Congress Catalogue Number 73-91621

FIRST PRINTING
Designed by Tere LoPrete

Acknowledgments

The author is grateful to the following for permission to quote:

Houghton Mifflin Company: from *The Complete Poetical Works of Spencer*, edited by R. E. Neil Dodge, 1936.

Cambridge University Press: from *The Complete Works of Sir Philip Sidney*, edited by Albert Feuillerat, 1912–1926. Reissued 1962.

The Clarendon Press: from *Elizabethan Critical Essays*, edited by G. Gregory Smith, 1904. By permission of The Clarendon Press.

Wm. Collins and Co., Ltd.: from *Shakespeare: The Complete Works*, edited by Professor Peter Alexander, 1951.

Northwestern University Press and Longmans Green and Co., Ltd.: from J. H. Hexter, *Reappraisals in History*, 1963.

To Charles Tyler Prouty

who started me wading

Contents

Preface

But when after-times shall make a quest of inquirie, to examine the best of this Age, peraduenture there will be found
in the now contemned recordes of Ryme matter not vnfitting
the grauest Diuine and seuerest Lawyer in this kingdome. But
these things must haue the date of Antiquitie to make them
reuerend and authentical. For euer in the collation of Writers
men rather weigh their age then their merite, and *legunt*
priscos cum reuerentia, quando coaetaneos non possunt sine
inuidia.

—SAMUEL DANIEL, *A Defence of Ryme* (c. 1603)

Daniel's quiet confidence that future ages will judge much of his
own time's greatest literature more fairly than it has been by some
of his contemporaries is based on an axiomatic human truth: Men
are always reluctant to praise their fellows' achievements. But if
intervening centuries have given us that calmer perspective Daniel
longed for, they have also created self-evident notions about the
nature and end of art that would have baffled Tudor writers and
readers. A modern playwright's literary stature is no longer automatically diminished when his work is performed in a public theater. Today's novelist is expected to be original and "relevant," yet
hardly to provide explicit moral instruction. And the least of any
new poet's anxieties is whether he has properly imitated the best
ancient models, for how many citizens of the twentieth century
need "the date of Antiquitie" to make anything "reuerend and
authentical"? These are only a few of the many areas in which
sixteenth-century views about literature and life differ from our
own. The premise of this study is that if we would see the "merite"
of Tudor artists clearly as well as calmly, we must adjust our
anachronistic assumptions and "weigh their age" in a sense that
never occurred to the learned Daniel. Otherwise, we shall often
find ourselves trying to evaluate how well a thing was done without
really knowing what kind of thing was being attempted, or demon-

strating how certain Elizabethans speak to our time before being sure about what they were saying.

Chapters I and II therefore seek to re-create those literary, social, political, and historical contexts that yield the most helpful glosses upon some of the better known works written within them. *Twelfth Night*, for example, becomes all the more delightful on stage after we have spent enough time in Shakespeare's own "library" to recognize the clichés of romance, myth, courtliness, and rationalism he is burlesquing. Similarly, the "meanings" that the era assigned to Elizabeth Tudor, Rome, chivalry, the Earl of Essex, and voyages to the New World will help us see the extent to which the designs of Spenser, Donne, and Shakespeare were built upon commonplace opinion. For if the historian's major task is to render intelligible what men of another time dreamed, desired, and did, our responsibility is to measure the literary reflections of those dreams and desires against what they were, rather than against what we might logically expect them to have been.

Chapters III and IV deal mainly with literary practice as it followed or outran critical theory. Granted, some of the most fiercely contested issues of Daniel's day are more likely to inspire our pity than our terror. But the critics are in basic agreement about the kind of experience an Elizabethan anticipated as he sat down to read an elegy, satire, pastoral, or allegory. They also explain his expectation that even a love poem would be "right curious and artificial." They provide reasons why some of the time's most sensitive and sensible poets, including Sidney and Spenser, expended so much energy attempting to adapt English rhymes to Latin versification, and why its most inventive artists, including Shakespeare, sought to imitate creatively rather than be wholly original. Writers of any age are of course free to honor or reject contemporary literary theories, but no artist anxious to succeed prefers to work in critical darkness.

Finally, Chapters V and VI discuss influences and relationships that are more difficult to document and are, therefore, too often slighted. The former centers in the Elizabethan entertainments; it attempts to blur some of those fine but anachronistic distinctions that we tend to draw between drama and devising, and to erase altogether some erroneous yet logical ideas about what was obviously "caviary to the general." The latter is chiefly devoted to explaining how the materials of Greece, Rome, Italy, Spain, and medieval England were translated, transfigured, and mingled to produce a kind of literature found in the best and worst sixteenth-century writers, what the scholar might call "a loose containment of multitudes" and the student "a mixed bag." To illustrate the creative ferment so characteristic of the Renaissance, the works of genius are frequently placed alongside those of scholars and hacks; our inquiries begin with Shakespeare and conclude with some of the smaller fry who helped him set his stage.

In shaping these essays I have incurred more obligations than can ever be repaid. A large and long-standing debt is owed to Charles T. Prouty, who first showed me the imaginative possibilities of historical criticism and the differences between fanciful conjectures and responsible inferences. For suggestions as to which backgrounds need accenting, I wish to thank several past and present colleagues: Robert Ornstein, Leonard F. Dean, David Kay, and Michael Shapiro. And I am especially grateful to Gwynne B. Evans, Burton Milligan, Allan Holaday, Charles Shattuck, Marvin Vawter, and David Wiener, who have taken time from busy schedules to read various drafts of the manuscript and discovered errors of fact, style, and perspective. But my greatest obligation is to my wife, Elizabeth, whose good humor the lengthy preparation of this volume never managed to wither.

Champaign, Illinois
May, 1970

I

VISITORS OF OTHER SPECIES

The Relevance of Literary Backgrounds

When as perhaps the words thou scornest now
 May liue, the speaking picture of the mind,
 The extract of the soule that laboured how
 To leaue the image of her selfe behind,
 Wherein posteritie that loue to know
 The iust proportion of our spirits may find.

 .   .   .   .

O blessed letters that combine in one
 All ages past, and make one liue with all,
 By you we do confer with who are gone,
 And the dead liuing vnto councell call:
 By you th'vnborne shall haue communion
 Of what we feele, and what doth vs befall.
                    —SAMUEL DANIEL, *Musophilus* (1599)

The walls, where there was room, were well decorated with
calendars and posters showing bright, improbable girls with
pumped-up breasts and no hips—blondes, brunettes and red-
heads, but always with this bust development, so that a visitor
of another species might judge from the preoccupation of
artist and audience that the seat of procreation lay in the
mammaries.
                    —JOHN STEINBECK, *The Wayward Bus* (1947)

In view of the way Samuel Daniel manages his defense of "blessed
letters," it seems unlikely that he would have clearly understood

I

the rationale that underlies any book on the contexts of literature. The value of poetry is at issue, and since Daniel wishes to debate honestly, his learned spokesman, Musophilus, the lover of the muses, allows his worldly-wise opponent, Philocosmus, several concessions. The verses through which any upright poet naturally hopes to achieve immortality are just as naturally subject to the insolence of the "viperous Creticke" and the invincible ignorance of the "idle multitude." The English poet, moreover, faces a disadvantage unknown to his Continental fellows. The "walke of all [his] wide renowne" is only a "little point," a "scarce discerned Ile, / Thrust from ye world," whose "happier tongues" disregard a "speech vnknown." Worst of all, "how many thousands" of those who do speak his own "barbarous language" have never even "heard the name / Of *Sydney*, or of *Spencer*, or their bookes?" [1]

For all these rather bleak considerations, problems that Daniel himself must have pondered in his darker moments, Musophilus maintains the dignity of his role. Within this "wiser profit-seeking age" only the learned will value learning, and "for the few that onely lend their eare, / That few is all the world," a "Theater large ynow" (ll. 555 ff.). It is to an admittedly select audience that the English poet must entrust his present and future fame. Yet how much surer a foundation are one's literary efforts than children who may squander their inheritance, or a "proude title . . . / Written in yce of melting vanitie," or "aspiring pallaces" which even now are "leuell'd with th'earth, left to forgetfulnes" (ll. 123 ff.). Even "that wondrous *trophei*," seemingly immutable Stonehenge, counters Musophilus, is at best a "huge domb heap" whose silence has inspired the credulous to prate of Merlin's sorcery; "corrupted so with times despight," the once proud monument has "become a traitor" to those whose "faire art and cunning" erected it (ll. 337 ff.). In seeking to leave one's mark upon the world, then, literature is the answer. "Lines," not wealth, titles, or stones, become "the vaines, the Arteries, / And vndecaying life-strings" of communion between all ages (ll. 183 ff.).

Given only those difficulties honest Daniel admits, his solution seems sensible enough. But a twentieth-century Philocosmus—or even a modern Musophilus—might easily pose a more depressing question: Are you quite sure that Time will not eventually "corrupt" even that communion to which you appeal so confidently? The very suspicion undermines a premise Daniel and his even more learned contemporaries would have considered too self-evident to investigate. That "speaking picture of the mind," that artfully labored "extract of the soule," is not only the surest means of eternal conference, but an infallible index by which to measure exactly each era's "spirits." While making allowances for geographical and linguistic barriers, it hardly occurs to Daniel or his characters to acknowledge matters merely chronological; to admit time's power to turn "th'vnborne" into Steinbeck's "visitor of another species," misjudging latter-day Stonehenges; to appreciate, in short, the historical critic's insistence upon the value and often the necessity of placing any work within its cultural, intellectual, and aesthetic contexts before venturing a comment upon the exact or "iust proportion" of its author's concerns.

The relatively modern awareness of *Zeitgeist*, the realization that the intellectual and imaginative luggage of each age varies so markedly that the assumptions of one generation appear foreign to the second and impossible for the third or fourth wholly to recover, is a kind of learning Daniel does not consider. Yet it is precisely this kind of learning that provides a necessary frame of reference to explain his own seemingly curious optimism about literature, his strange (for us) trust in poetry's social and spiritual utility, his (apparently) self-centered belief that posterity will search his words with keen interest. Without this kind of learning, the modern reader is unable to proceed beyond his poem's subtitle, "CONTAINING A generall defence of all *learning*," without either damning Daniel's insufferable presumption or noting some hint of clever irony that, unfortunately, never materializes. Daniel and his contemporaries may have been presumptuous and were certainly at times ironic, but their first readers would never have used their (again for us) grandiose designs as evidence of either. "I have taken all knowledge to be my province," Francis Bacon writes to Lord Burleigh in 1592. Five years later patriotic Michael Drayton begins his fifteen-thousand-line *Poly-Olbion. or A Chorographicall Description of Tracts, Riuers, Mountaines, Forests, and other Parts of this renowned Isle of Great Britaine, with intermixture of the most Remarquable Stories, Antiquities, Wonders, Rarityes, Pleasures, and Commodities of the same: Digested in a Poem*, an ambitious project a quarter of a century in the making. Sage, serious, and essentially humorless Edmund Spenser dies in 1599 with but half of *The Faerie Queene* completed, and Sir Walter Raleigh, who undertakes nothing less than *The History of the World*, is executed in 1618, having finished less than one third of his proposed account, a mere 750,000 words.

To patronize Drayton's encyclopedic efforts or dismiss Raleigh's venture as naïve amateurism is clearly tantamount to censuring them for sharing one of their age's common "presumptions," to condemning them, in effect, for going about their business of being Elizabethans. Unconsciously affected by our own era's compartmentalized approaches to knowledge, in which a lecturer can not be expected to speak with authority outside his own "special field," even the aspirations of Marlowe's Dr. Faustus may at first strike us as more quaint than dangerous, and modern playwrights must give us men who play God in other, more convincing ways. And if Daniel appears too hasty in foreseeing posterity's acute interest in his contemporaries' deeds and desires, it is merely because the Elizabethans were almost as guilty as we are of thoughtlessly foisting upon past and future ages "truths" conveniently assumed to be eternally axiomatic. Like us, they were inclined to measure other periods from their own special vantage point, a moment in history toward which all time had obviously run. In other words, although their assumptions about many apparently self-evident values were different from ours, they at least shared our chronological snobbery. "They did not consider that future ages would look down on them with contempt, because they thought the world was not getting better, but worse. Rather they felt that it was the duty of their generation to give posterity something worthy of the veneration the future would feel for them." [2] They were naturally prone to fashioning both the past and future in their own image, and if we, with far less excuse, re-create them in ours, we are bound to be misled—less by them than by what Madeleine Doran aptly calls our own "anachronistic expectations." [3]

The more "self-evident" the assumption, the more "natural" the expectation—and the greater the difficulty in perceiving chronological snobbery under its guise of common sense. We naturally tend to explain things in terms of what lies about us, the readily familiar, what we take to be the obvious. When we sometimes catch ourselves casually reading our own everyday axioms into past literature, we do not regard ourselves as intellectually lazy but as charitably judging as we would be judged by. In confronting one of our most natural, modern assumptions, "that love should be the commonest theme of serious imaginative literature," C. S. Lewis notes that "a glance at classical antiquity or at the Dark Ages at once shows us that what we took for 'nature' is really a special state of affairs, which will probably have an end, and which certainly had a beginning. . . . It seems—or it seemed to us till lately—a natural thing that love (under certain conditions) should be regarded as a noble and ennobling passion: it is only if we imagine ourselves trying to explain this doctrine to Aristotle, Virgil, St. Paul, or the author of *Beowulf*, that we become aware how far from natural it is." [4] A more amusing instance is suggested by Steinbeck's "wide-hipped and sag-chested" Alice Chicoy, who worked among the beautiful calendar girls but "was not in the least jealous of [them]. . . . She had never seen anyone like them and she didn't think anyone else ever had." [5] Perhaps she was also sufficiently read in nineteenth-century pornography to realize how quickly even the "eternal and universal" standards of erotica can shift, and hopeful that after a dispensation of Twiggies her day would come.

Even after we realize the evils of judging as we would be judged by, chronological snobbery is further encouraged by the notion that whereas to err is human, pedantry is unforgivable. This notion is most often represented in the popular but unfairly forced antithesis between Shakespeare on the boards versus Shakespeare in the library, of art enriching and delighting as opposed to art hanged upon a gloss, disemboweled with a far-fetched analogue, and quartered by textual variants.[6] After all, as every frightened champion of the humanities never tires of pointing out, great art is immortal, which means, of course, that it speaks to every age; and this, in turn, is somehow supposed to mean that academic interpreters are closer to parasites than vital guides, that musty backgrounds obscure more often than illuminate literary beauties. And finally, it is often argued, since even those pallid antiquarians have never been able to agree completely over *the* sixteenth-century world view, much less one another's ideas about *the* typical Elizabethan, is it not safer to proceed simply upon modern assumptions than upon modern assumptions about Elizabethan assumptions?

The first of these objections is certainly the least justified, if only because it overlooks the surprising amount of "academic" knowledge that a responsible director usually brings to his lively production. Through his actors' voice inflections, gestures, costuming, positioning, and general "manner" (none but rarely indicated or even implied in the text), the director is necessarily the supreme interpreter of the responses Shakespeare wished to evoke, and if he appears to bear his knowledge easily, it is only because his glossing is completed before the audience arrives. Had we heard the troupe's silent partner during dress rehearsal, frantically correcting one poorly read phrase or slightly awkward movement, we should hardly have accused him of a pedantic obsession with trivialities, for minor slips ruin major scenes. We must keep the same sense of proportion in mind when judging academic interpretations; no activity that works toward the play as the final thing is trivial. The student of sources, for example, is engaged in antiquarian pastimes only if he becomes so entangled in his lists of Shakespearean indebtednesses that he fails to bother himself over the significance of Shakespearean additions and alterations.

At his imaginative best, then, the historical critic is motivated by concerns no less humane than the director's, and the sensitive spectator's dramatic pleasure usually varies directly in proportion to his awareness of the play's cultural and intellectual context, the background that the director is—or should be—also guided by but can only suggest. This is especially true in the case of most Shakespearean comedy. Aided only by native wit and a keen sense of humor, a modern audience is bound to miss all the fun that stems from Shakespeare's whimsical juggling of distinctly Elizabethan social proprieties and sentiments. Let us take *Twelfth Night* as an extreme example. Several years ago a company of players visiting the University of Illinois campus joyfully consented to join some of the faculty in discussing a play to be performed that evening. Attention eventually focused on how Shakespeare "went over" with different audiences—urban adults, boys in private schools, and so on. The moment that proved most disconcerting, at least to the "pedants," came when the actors enlarged on their statement that there was something in the playwright for everybody and insisted that a recent performance of *Twelfth Night* in the Northwest Territory for a largely Eskimo audience had been riotously successful.

Now the pedants were not against the right of Eskimos to enjoy Shakespeare; rather, they were somewhat dubious that any performance, no matter how superbly acted, could possibly communicate to so removed a culture every kind of comic situation and sentiment Shakespeare was exploiting. Realizing that all great art is *not* immortal (witness, for instance, the no longer extant plays of Xenocles, to whom Euripides at least once ran second), they reasoned that whatever great art has survived speaks to each age only because its themes and some of its characters are universal and therefore largely self-explanatory. In this special sense, *Twelfth Night* needs no interpreter. We hardly require a sophisticated sensibility or a keen awareness of backgrounds to enjoy watching well-laid plans going astray, mistaken identities, and selfless love rewarded, nor need we possess more than a dim conception of man as a basically rational and social animal to be diverted by Toby's drunken swaggering, cross-gartered Malvolio, or (though it would have baffled Plautus and his merry ancients, as C. S. Lewis reminds us) the prospect of Orsino in his gloriously self-annihilating, amorous-melancholic agonizings. Strictly in terms of stock themes and their concomitant stock characters, literature does enjoy that free communion between all ages of which Daniel speaks. Had all varieties of love and war been placed off limits during Homer's time, few of his successors would have had much to say. But if great art is thematically eternal, so is all poor art, and to appreciate the differences we must make more than thematic distinctions. How else can we justify our turning from television's spate of sex and violence to the sex and violence of Aeschylus and Arthur Miller, Aristophanes and Ionesco? We proceed beyond the changeless, immediately understandable themes shared by genius and hack, and focus upon the great artists' ever-changing and often not very obvious treatments and techniques. We become, in short, something like avid football fans, much more interested in how the game is being played than in which side eventually wins, and like them, we profit by explanations of offensive and defensive maneuvers.

Perhaps a few glances at *Twelfth Night*'s opening scenes will suggest what a deft game Shakespeare is playing as well as partially excuse the crusty impertinences of his academic commentators. "If music be the food of love, play on, / Give me excess of it. . . ." Thus the prostrate Duke ushers us into the romantic-realistic, faraway–near-at-hand, bittersweet-roistering realm of Illyria, and no reasonably proficient actor will find it difficult to implant in his audience the suspicion that the love upon which Orsino diligently surfeits is as "high fantastical" as his nourishing music and odoriferous violets. The sensible spectator, merely recollecting his own penchant for occasional heroic posturings and self-sentimentalizations, quickly senses that the good Duke is primarily in love with love and the pleasure of its pain, next to which his proud fair must run second. Less obvious, however, is Shakespeare's next move:

> *Cur.*   Will you go hunt, my lord?
> *Duke.*   What, Curio?
> *Cur.*   The hart.
> *Duke.*   Why, so I do, the noblest that I have.
>   O, when mine eyes did see Olivia first,
>   Methought she purg'd the air of pestilence!
>   That instant was I turn'd into a hart,
>   And my desires, like fell and cruel hounds,
>   E'er since pursue me.[7]

Why this intrusion of allegory? Solely in terms of plot, atmosphere, or theme, Orsino's outpouring seems dramatically gratuitous; in terms of character, it appears merely to confirm our impression that the Duke will take any instance of Olivia's beauty to underscore his own, more important suffering. "Do your utmost with the imagery," mutters the glosser; "unless you step outside the play for a moment, you will miss the fun going on inside it. Orsino is not allegorizing for the nonce, but belaboring one of the commonest Elizabethan literary and pictorial clichés, Ovid's tale of Actaeon and Diana: Returning from the hunt, he happened upon her while bathing and the naked goddess punished what she considered his effrontery by turning him into a stag, whose own dogs devoured him (cf. Arthur Golding's 1567 translation of *The Metamorphoses*, III. 150 ff.)." But why Ovid? The question is partly answered by Holofernes's learned query: "Ovidius Naso was the man. And why, indeed, 'Naso' but for smelling out the odoriferous flowers of fancy, the jerks of invention?" (*Love's Labor's Lost*, IV. ii. 116 ff.) And it was those "flowers" and jerks" for which the rhetorically oriented Elizabethans most often celebrated the Roman poet. Shakespeare's own early literary efforts were viewed by at least one of his admirers as an extension of Ovid's rhetorical prowess. "As the soule of *Euphorbus* was thought to liue in *Pythagoras*: so the sweete wittie soule of Ouid liues in mellifluous and hony-tongued *Shakespeare*, witnes his *Venus and Adonis*, his *Lucrece*, his sugred *Sonnets* among his priuate friends, &c." [8] Indeed, one of Shakespeare's earliest comedies pays this brief tribute to the amorous situations Ovid so eloquently narrates:

Pro. He after honour hunts, I after love;
He leaves his friends to dignify them more;
I leave myself, my friends, and all for love.
Thou, Julia, thou hast metamorphis'd me. . . .
(*The Two Gentlemen of Verona*, I. i. 63 ff.)

Ovid, then, is both amorous and exquisitely literary, a ready source for lovers' effusions, and through Orsino's mythological reference, Shakespeare assures us that the Duke, like his fellow fickle lover, Proteus, has been reading just the right kind of literature. The passage may also represent one of the playwright's many insistences that we recognize how literary-"romancey" are the materials he is amalgamating. If Orsino, aided by Ovid, dresses to formal rhetorical advantage his socially acceptable role of the disdained lover,[9] Olivia's equally acceptable part of the maiden forsaken is decked out with even more formal and splendid verbiage:

The element itself, till seven years' heat,
Shall not behold her face at ample view;
But like a cloistress she will veiled walk,
And water once a day her chamber round
With eye-offending brine; all this to season
A brother's dead love. . . .
(I. i. 26 ff.)

No doubt affected by the romantic formulas and stylized circumlocutions at least as much as by the mourning that ostensibly prompts them, Orsino replies in kind:

O, she that hath a heart of that fine frame
To pay this debt of love but to a brother,
How will she love when the rich golden shaft
Hath kill'd the flock of all affections else
That live in her; when liver, brain, and heart,
Those sovereign thrones, are all supplied and fill'd,
Her sweet perfections, with one self king!
(ll. 33–39)

"Eye-offending brine," "rich golden shaft"—characters who speak like this strain credulity. Yet it is mainly through our detection of Ovid the eloquent, artificial, and amorous that we adjust our expectations; instead of fruitlessly wondering how the mature

Shakespeare could handle romantic sentiments so unconvincingly, we begin to notice how deliberately, how *unromantically* he inundates Illyria with romantic truisms, making character, mood, and sentiment not merely quite incredible but quite comically incredible. The marvelous, rather than receiving realistic touches, is multiplied. Olivia vows fidelity for *seven* years, perhaps for no reason other than the romantic fact that "seven" sounds so nice, perhaps because she would serve Grief with the customary seven-year apprenticeship. And Orsino, never wishing to be half-safe, must have liver and brain, passion and intellect, as well as heart's affection. Finally, whereas the conventional romancer easily unveils his series of extraordinary circumstances with no visible self-consciousness, Shakespeare falters admirably:

> *Vio.*   And what should I do in Illyria?
>   My brother he is in Elysium.
>   *Perchance* he is not drown'd—what think you, sailors?
> *Cap.*   It is *perchance* that you yourself were saved.
> *Vio.*   O my poor brother! and so *perchance* may he be.
> *Cap.*   True, madam, and, to comfort you with *chance* . . .
>   (I. ii. 3 ff. Italics added.)

Although the third scene presents a far more realistic atmosphere, the full scope of its fun is also dependent upon our knowledge of literary ideals and conventions. Just as our Eskimos could vaguely enjoy but not pointedly appreciate Shakespeare's parody of romantic paraphernalia as simple romance, so an audience of almost any time and culture will no doubt find at least the appearance and sprightly stupidity of Sir Andrew Aguecheek rather amusing. But how much of Shakespeare's comic labor passes unnoticed without a pedantic gloss upon the Aguecheek first introduced through Sir Toby's eulogy: "He plays o' th' viol-de-gamboys, and speaks three or four languages word for word without book, and hath all the good gifts of nature" (I. iii. 23 ff.)? The function of this advertisement is not merely to provide a few specific accomplishments in which Aguecheek almost immediately proves himself woefully inept, but also to call to the audience's attention the whole elegant world of courtly behavior as outlined in Elizabethan courtesy books like Hoby's translation of Castiglione's *Il Cortegiano*, a world that will sit in comic judgment of both men throughout the play.

Moreover, as any student who has undergone the apparently dreary business of having Shakespeare's fun "explained" soon realizes, it is only as we assimilate the era's social baggage that we begin to respond spontaneously, that we come close to experiencing the immediacy of the comic moment instead of skipping between text and footnotes as if the play were some kind of crossword puzzle. The glosser is as anxious as the director to get Shakespeare out of the library, but the modern reader must cooperate. If in his hurry to get Shakespeare on stage he dismisses a prior knowledge of Elizabethan dance forms as irrelevant lore, for instance, he will fail to relish the incongruities suggested in Toby's commendation of Andrew's nimble legs: "Wherefore are these things hid? . . . My very walk should be a jig; I would not so much as make water but in a sink-a-pace" (I. iii. 117 ff.). And only if he is sufficiently familiar with Renaissance astrology to realize that Taurus governed the throat and neck will he appreciate the humorous irony underlying both knights' tipsy speculations:

Sir And.	Shall we set about some revels?
Sir To.	What shall we do else? Were we not born under Taurus?
Sir And.	Taurus? That's sides and heart.
Sir To.	No, sir; it is legs and thighs. Let me see thee caper. Ha, higher! Ha, ha, excellent!

(I. iii. 128 ff.)

Although the student of sources approaches the play on a slightly different tack, he can suggest other, less obvious but more cerebral, if not profound, comic dimensions. From the opening volley of chances and perchances in I. ii. to the play's closing moments, when Viola and Sebastian contemplate the singular fact that each had a parent with "a mole upon his brow," he notes how often the playwright underlines the romancers' clichés, and wonders if Shakespeare did not intend us to view *Twelfth Night*'s pervasive "midsummer madness" much as Fabian views the antics of "THE MADLY-US'D MALVOLIO": "If this were play'd upon a stage now, I could condemn it as an improbable fiction" (III. iv. 53, 121-123; V. i. 298). He observes how Shakespeare complements his characters' generally "mad" behavior—accusations of insanity, incidentally, echo throughout the play—with some rather madcap matings at the conclusion. Olivia hardly knows of Aguecheek's existence, spurns Orsino's suit, misunderstands Malvolio's, falls desperately in love with the disguised Viola, and hurries off to the altar her twin brother, who has innocently happened by. Only a few last-minute romantic plot manipulations convert Orsino from Viola's murderer to her husband, and the one remaining Illyrian lady, Maria, earns the title of Lady Belch solely for her ability to carry off a jest, her aid in gulling Malvolio (V. i. 349 ff.).

Even though Orsino, in two hundred lines, has sufficiently recovered from his unfounded jealousy and irrational hatred to draw the quasi-rational moral that he will marry his "boy" for her loving service, for the most part Shakespeare seems to accent the mindlessness of Cupid's labyrinthine ways. It is of course true that Shakespearean comedy almost always concludes with double or triple marriages; only in *Love's Labor's Lost* do we find a postponement of the inevitable. It is equally true that we are seldom encouraged to ask about his couples' future happiness; his heroines' intelligence quotients are usually twice those of their respective spouses, and their courtships have invariably proceeded more along the lines of emotional reactions than intellectual evaluations. But the "irrational" couplings in *Twelfth Night* are surely more than the customary consequences of conventional love-plotting; through its characters' often-expressed concerns about the madness of their fellows and fears for their own sanity, plot turns into theme. In Olivia's answer to Orsino's wooing, for example, Shakespeare is asking for more than a casual interest in loving for merit's sake:

> Your lord does know my mind; I cannot love him.
> Yet I suppose him virtuous, know him noble,
> Of great estate, of fresh and stainless youth;
> In voices well divulg'd, free, learn'd, and valiant,
> And in dimension and the shape of nature
> A gracious person; *but yet I cannot love him.*
> He might have took his answer long ago.
> (I. v. 241 ff. Italics added.)

Since few spectators, Elizabethan or modern, would expect romantic lovers to love rationally, in or outside of literature, why does Shakespeare worry the point? Again, we shall find it helpful to step outside the play, at least long enough to consider the following moralistic commentary:

> There is no child that is borne into this wretched worlde,
> but before it doeth sucke the mother's milke it taketh first
> a soope of the cupp of errour, which maketh us, when we

come to riper yeres, not onely to enter into actions of injurie, but many tymes to straie from that is right and reason; but in all other thinges, wherein wee shewe our selves to bee moste dronken with this poisoned cuppe, it is in our actions of love; for the lover is so estranged from that is right, and wandereth so wide from the boundes of reason, that he is not able to deeme white from blacke, good from badde, vertue from vice. . . .

If a question might be asked, what is the ground indeede of reasonable love, whereby the knot is knit of true and perfect freendship, I thinke those that be wise would answere—deserte: that is, where the partie beloved dooeth requite us with the like; for otherwise, if the bare shewe of beautie, or the comelinesse of personage might bee suffi- cient to confirme us in our love, those that bee accustomed to goe to faires and markettes might sometymes fall in love with twentie in a daie; desert must then bee (of force) the grounde of reasonable love; for to love them that hate us, to followe them that flie from us, to faune on them that froune on us, . . . who will not confesse this to be an erronious love, neither grounded uppon witte nor reason? Wherfore, right curteous gentilwomen,

concludes Barnaby Riche, you will find in my "historie," "Of Apolonius and Silla," [10] adequate evidence of the silly things which people who do not love according to merit are capable of. And here too, concludes Shakespeare's "librarian," you will find not only the major characters and events that appear in *Twelfth Night*, but the solemn attitude that at least partly inspired Shake- speare's theme of midsummer madness. The playwright, in other words, as well as burlesquing the rationalistic romancer's con- venient storms and shipwrecks, is having some fun with his slide- rule axiology. What sane person expects love to be initiated, di- rected, and controlled wholly by reason? If anyone in *Twelfth Night*, the highly proper Malvolio. According to Maria, the prim steward is "so cramm'd, as he thinks, with excellencies that it is his grounds of faith that all that look on him love him" (II. iii. 139 ff.). Although no character resembling Malvolio appears in prior treatments of the *Twelfth Night* story, it is quite possible that Shakespeare noticed this spoilsport's spirit lurking amidst Riche's anti-Illyrian preface, and deftly incorporated it into the play as a Puckish footnoting of indebtedness. [11]

Shakespeare, then, may become all the richer and more delightful on stage for having been drawn and quartered in the library, and his unique and sophisticated treatments of universal and elementary themes, profitably glossed with relevant backgrounds. Nevertheless, there remains the far more difficult problem implicit in chronological snobbery's preference for modern assumptions as opposed to modern assumptions possibly disguised as sixteenth-century assumptions. This kind of snobbery often makes a good deal of disconcerting sense. Far from actually snubbing chronology, it is sometimes more conscious of time's power than many self-designated historical critics, who first presume that a work's only meaning is the one it had for its original audience and then, by viewing that work solely through one contemporary document or another—each announced as a magical key, guaranteed to unlock all mysteries—arrive at different and often contradictory interpretations of that original audience's alleged response. In examining *Measure for Measure*, for instance, one historical critic assures us that although its Duke's manipulations may strike the modern reader as rather disingenuous, no member of Shakespeare's original audience would have taken such apparently dark-cornered doings more seriously than the conventions of those sources upon which Shakespeare drew. But this only increases the problems. No longer bothered by the Duke, we are left to wonder about Shakespeare, who must have entertained ethical and psychological problems so gratuitously, and about that odd audience, so safely abstracted from those scenes that underline the squalor and suffering of life in Vienna. Another historical critic admits the earnest atmosphere, and for the amorality of folk-tale conventions substitutes the overwhelmingly moral concerns of the morality play. We remain puzzled, for if this explains the pain, it ignores much of the plot, especially the resolution's exquisite juggling of wrath and reconciliation, a staginess that appears consciously at odds with the straightforwardness one expects of conventional morality frameworks. Shunted from "bedplots" to "bedrights," warned that what we properly despise in Polonius must be admired in Vincentio, overladen with obscure Renaissance treatises on justice, questionable Biblical parallels, and often a random Christ-figure in the bargain, our eventual cynicism as we ponder the relationship between our scraps of historical facts and the still essentially unexplained play is quite understandable.

Far more cautious than snobbish, we thus become aware of the ease with which the genuine problems and ambiguities of literature can be documented aside rather than honestly confronted, and we begin insisting that the special perspective we think we have gained by stepping outside the work be tested by making it square with whatever we encounter once we are back inside. We also attempt to distinguish between different kinds of backgrounds and the extent to which each may be used to "explain" the work, granting, for instance, both the accuracy and relevance of the glosser's treatment of "Taurus" because Taurus's domain is a demonstrable astrological "fact" and because the interpretation of the passage's dramatic function proceeds only on the relatively safe assumption that most of Shakespeare's audience were sufficiently acquainted with the zodiac to relish the joke played on Belch and Aguecheek. On the other hand, although we allow the glosser's identification of Orsino's "fell and cruel hounds," we are not convinced that through the mythological reference Shakespeare wished to stress more than the Duke's penchant for amatory fiction. Despite our commentator's demonstration of Ovid's reputation and popularity, both in and out of Shakespeare, in other words, he has really only suggested, not proved, the Roman poet's special relevance to *Twelfth Night*'s opening scene. Similarly, whereas we may accept the source hunter's contention that Shakespeare *could* have found Riche philosophically as well as dramatically inviting, we should also demand that he compare the point of view established in the tale "Of Apolonius and Silla" with the concerns illustrated in *Twelfth Night*'s many other sources and analogues. Perhaps Riche is being given too much credit, for it is one thing to say that a five-line passage has as its end a joke on Sir Toby, and quite another to imply that a joke on Riche, however delightful, is the final goal of the whole play. In focusing upon those moments in *Twelfth Night* that have significant parallels, the student of sources has told only that part of the story in which he is most interested. Since it is only part of the story, it may be critically misleading.

In moving from particular literary sources to more general backgrounds, snobbery's healthy skepticism becomes even more infectious. It makes us wonder whether one century's axioms are really possible for the next wholly to recover, whether the axioms of different generations within a single century may not vary markedly, and whether even one decade is not bound to include people with widely divergent views on some major points. Consequently, we begin reacting suspiciously to those who first isolate *the* thought of the period with convenient catchalls and then, without establishing the appositeness of their "key" frames of reference, confidently pronounce upon *the* response of *the* sixteenth-century reader to a given piece of literature. It is highly unlikely that we shall ever know enough about the Elizabethans to be fully confident that we are responding exactly as they did. And even when we wish to pretend that we have momentarily turned ourselves into Elizabethans, we should still have to decide *which* Elizabethans, for as Miss Doran notes, "*Hamlet* cannot have meant the same thing to Burleigh as to Burleigh's cook, or to Jonson the poet and critic as to Gresham the merchant." [12] Unfortunately, that "typical Elizabethan audience" to which we refer so casually always included men of equally different education, interests, and critical abilities. Had Shakespeare's friend and fellow playwright left us an essay on *the* meaning of *Hamlet*, we should still possess no more than one enlightened opinion concerning its author's intention, a viewpoint valuable because contemporary, but hardly infallible.

To make matters worse, we must not only admit how difficult it is merely to approximate those interests and attitudes shared by every Elizabethan and to determine even generally the degree to which carefully established backgrounds should be allowed to explain their literature. Our task is further complicated by the fact that what any period takes for granted is often either passed over in silence or "documented" by those purveyors of commonplaces who better represent, and therefore better explain, the ideas of their mediocre contemporaries than their artistic superiors. Although he skillfully employs historical methods himself, Professor Robert Ornstein has recently made us uncomfortably conscious of how they can be abused simply through confusing or limiting the meaning of great art with or to its fully, even carefully documented context. "If we do not see that the informing vision of a play transcends its explicit statements," he wisely remarks, "we will make a naïve equation not only between the thought of a dramatist and the ideas of his characters but also between the thought of a dramatist and the commonplace assumptions of his audience." [13] If we are willing to make what appear to have been the most popular books of Shakespeare's time the final measure of Shakespeare's thought, then we must be willing to "conclude that the key to the plays of Tennessee Williams and Arthur Miller lies in the works of Norman Vincent Peale, an ethical psychologist more widely read, more widely imitated, and, we must assume, more influential than were Charron, Coeffeteau or La Primaudaye." [14] Although Peale "sheds some light on the fates of Willy Loman and Blanche DuBois," and although there are often "startling resemblances between [his] ideas and those expressed by Williams' and Miller's characters," these playwrights' final views of life are hardly like his, and "it is disastrous . . . to assume that the Jacobean dramatists, who were superb observers of contemporary life, derived all their ideas, values, and knowledge of men from the books which their audiences read." [15] And finally, Ornstein queries, is Peale so popular because so many Americans actually share his faith in the power of positive thinking or because they, in an era of as much stress and anxiety as the late sixteenth century, "would like to believe that they can will themselves to happiness and security?" [16] To what extent, in other words, can we trust even the most "popular"—that is, the most extensively advertised—Elizabethan views as infallible indexes of what was not merely entertained but genuinely accepted? How do we separate hopeful fans from convinced disciples?

We may not wish to accept without further documentation Ornstein's suggestion "that Elizabethan uniformity of belief was frequently as mindless as modern conformity of belief and no doubt inspired by similar motives." [17] We might also argue that in the less philosophically pluralistic sixteenth century, it was much more possible for a great artist like Shakespeare and a widely admired theologian like Richard Hooker to share essentially the same views of men and things. But then we should also remember that the systematic thinker is primarily interested in making fully explicit and arguing for a point of view obviously his own, whereas the dramatist's central concern is often not even to pose, much less to justify, his personal philosophy. It seems wise, therefore, to keep Ornstein's facetious conjunction of Miller and Peale before us as a generally valid and timely warning. Even when sensibly and sensitively employed, literary backgrounds at best suggest what we might expect of the artist, what we should look for in his work, rather than what he was obliged to do, what should and therefore must be there.

As long as we realize that the fullest possible glossing of the work's context furnishes leading questions about, instead of automatic explanations of the work itself, and as long as these leading questions continue to lead but not restrict our interpretations, we shall at least be venturing from a sane point of departure and asking, if not always answering, the right critical queries. Since one of our major goals is to determine how well the work has been done, we must first ascertain what kind of work was attempted. And if our conjectures concerning where the artist finally stands in relation to the world he has created are to be more than anachronistic and irresponsible, imaginative but not fanciful, we must examine his handling of character, plot, atmosphere, theme, imagery, or idiom initially, if not exclusively, in the light of his own era's practices and influences. We dare not dismiss his contemporaries' attitudes and techniques simply because those of the great artist are manifestly more perceptive and skillful, for the nature as well as the extent of his superiority is revealed by pursuing the very comparisons we may at first consider odious. In other words, if it is absurd to rack genius upon its era's commonplaces, it is often helpful to keep them before us as assumptions ripe for genius to exploit, opinions so widely held as to invite important modifications, wholesale revisions, or ironic elaborations from those who thought or felt more profoundly. Rather than overlooking genius, we ask how it functioned, and to that end we endeavor to determine those phases of the creative process that may have been inspired, if not wholly dictated, by the traditions of art and thought in which the artist was usually expected to operate. Just as attempts to explain any work solely in terms of itself often produce little more than reiterated hypotheses, appeals to genius alone rapidly reach a point of diminishing returns.

Early in this century F. M. Cornford drew a similar relationship between the traditions and genius that shaped Greek drama: "Our argument does not suppose the original ritual drama or the degenerate folk-play which may have followed it to have contained, even in germ, either the wit of Aristophanes or the wisdom of Aeschylus, either the comic or the tragic perception of life." [18] It even admits, he continues, that "all these factors were needed, as independent and original forces," before that drama could develop. We must not, however, "offer the unknown in explanation of the known. That Aeschylus was a genius is patent enough; but to say that Tragedy owes its existence to that genius and its creative or inventive powers is to leave us no wiser than we were. It is certain, indeed, that such a statement must be in great measure true; but in what measure, we can only find out by discovering what Aeschylus did not invent." [19]

What Aristophanes rather than Aeschylus did not invent is of course Cornford's main concern, and if his efforts to interpret what happens in Aristophanes solely in terms of primitive seasonal pantomime often result in what his modern editor calls "a bizarre inconsistency," [20] it is probably because he wished to proceed immediately from what we *know* about ritual to what we *read* in the first extant Greek comedies. But Cornford's conscientious disdain for offering the unknown in what he terms "a scientific discussion of historic origins" [21] illustrates how easily one can get stuck simply by sticking to established evidence. Had he been content at least to make room for probabilities—sophistications of ritual patterns by unknown playwrights before Aristophanes, for instance—he would not have found it necessary to force so many Aristophanic characters and events into roles and functions of which they are obviously incapable. How uncomfortably, for example, Aristophanes's doddering field marshal of *The Birds*, Peisthetairos, rests upon Cornford's Procrustean bed of seasonal rites; yet as the final victor who marries Miss Sovereignty, Cornford reasons, he must be the bridegroom figure, primitive ritual's representative of the New Life or Order. As Theodore Gaster observes, Cornford also failed to recognize the importance of social innovations. He treats the *komos*, for instance, as "simply a survival of the bridal procession at the original Sacred Marriage," whereas by Aristophanes's time it "was really no more than a binge or a night on the town," a custom that is given "an amusing twist" in *The Clouds*, when Socrates, the unaccommodating "lady," has his whole house, not just his door, set on fire.[22]

In carrying ritual patterns into Aristophanes, then, Cornford necessarily moved from a discussion of origins to one of developments, and in attempting to piece together a very complicated puzzle, he realized he had but two large facts. One cannot be expected to analyze documents no longer extant, so Cornford, in his impatience with anything less than fact, treated Aristophanes as if all the facts were in, even though this sometimes necessitated reshaping his two pieces to make them completely congruent. One suspects, moreover, that Aristophanes often intended that his piece could be fitted only by turning it upside down, for a character like Peisthetairos—Mr. Win-friend, alias Mr. Blarney—seems closer to a comic inversion than a straightforward celebration of the hero-bridegroom of primitive pantomime. In any case, until we know more about what Aristophanes's predecessors attempted, we can only conjecture concerning the nature and extent of the playwright's originality.

Whereas Cornford's errors are basically sins of necessary omission, those who desire to trace the development of themes and techniques in Tudor literature confront a body of evidence so large, diverse, and sometimes contradictory that it is tempting to become impatient not, like Cornford, with the absence of facts, but with their superabundance, and consequently to sin, as Cornford never did, against ascertainable knowledge. With "lyfe so short" and "craft so long to lerne," we have good reason initially to wonder whether any "obscure" piece of commentary will significantly alter our general impressions, or to put it more directly, whether the slightly more accurate sense of perspective we may be able to bring to the great artists will ever fully repay those first dull hours with their "deservedly forgotten" contemporaries. If at the outset we resist the suspicion that we are being shortchanged, however, it is often not long before even relatively minor writers become exciting, less for their limited successes than for the energetic experimentation that obviously underlies their failures. In reading the small fry primarily as glosses upon the great, as points of reference to render our expectations more "chronistic" or to prepare ourselves to appreciate the wonderful and often unexpected uses to which their betters will later put them, we shall sometimes find them surprisingly interesting for their own sake: the remarkably disparate meanings they attach to the same stock theme, for instance; their varied attempts to articulate a speechless grief or joy; the great discrepancies between their professed aims and their actual performances; their desperate struggles for balance and design or their curious lack of concern in bringing to art the order they found everywhere in nature. Even when the goals these lesser figures sought and the ideas they elaborated upon are neither in themselves particularly fascinating nor eventually represented in a major writer, any student of intellectual and literary history will find it stimulating to observe the wheels in motion, the "coming-forthness" of what one Elizabethan called the "manifold varietie of inuention." [23]

But until such times as we may become excited by the prospects of tracking down ideas and techniques for their own sakes, quite irrespective of the profundity or literary stature of their representatives, we may profitably begin by selecting only those quaint and curious volumes that the century's greatest artists themselves undoubtedly read and either borrowed from or reacted against. "In small proportions we just beauties see," remarked Ben Jonson, in one of his finest classical moments, and certainly we shall receive truer, even though more limited, impressions of Elizabethan creativity by tracing the development of a single story through the Renaissance and into one of Shakespeare's plays or Spenser's poems than by launching directly into the highly selective (and therefore highly interpretive) fragments of a standard anthology, trusting its editor's introductory comments, glosses, and very arrangement of materials in the hope that some sense can finally be made of it all.

From the better anthologies, along with the aid of a skilled instructor and his carefully prepared lists of supplementary readings, we may of course get some valid "overviews" as well as random samplings; and even the worst anthology admittedly contains enough for us to measure the development of prose and poetic styles and the rise and fall of other literary ideals. But any anthology, whether arranged chronologically or according to genres, must remain fundamentally prescriptive and synthetic. Unless he decides upon the older-fashioned "shotgun" approach, nonprescriptive but also nonsensical, the anthologist must exclude some writers altogether and leave us from the outset merely free to discover those he thinks are worth reading, and only as much about them as his choice of snippets implies he believes worth revealing. Through the length and nature of the fragments he includes, he cannot help partially interpreting the author's achievements; and because he must exclude hacks and allow mediocre writers no more than short extracts, we are denied an experience that, if not altogether enjoyable, is usually instructive. Because he cannot grant respectable space to both dramatic and nondramatic prose and poetry, he is forced into distinctions that would probably have seemed far more arbitrary to the Elizabethans than to us, especially to those dramatists like John Lyly and Robert Greene, who brought to the private and public theaters the fruit of their earlier experiments in prose narrative. Even the anthologist wise enough to select and arrange according to themes and movements, who ignores rigid chronological and generic distinctions in order that we may not miss the period's sense of excitement and sudden outpouring of energy, has been forced to decide for us the character of those themes, energies, and excitements. We are in no position to determine whether the allegedly unifying movements are editorial conveniences, conscientious figments of his imagination, or wholly justified, for our only evidence has been furnished in his extracts and, more important, introduced through his sense of perspective.

However forbidding the suggestion may at first appear, the student who has read nothing in the sixteenth century other than a few of Shakespeare's plays will find the going both easier and more immediately rewarding by proceeding directly to a less conventional anthology, Professor Geoffrey Bullough's splendid seven-volume collection of the *Narrative and Dramatic Sources of Shakespeare*. Since each of Shakespeare's thirty-seven plays has at least one informative analogue, all but two or three at least one direct source, and many of his best known tragedies and comedies a large number of probable and possible sources and analogues, we may use any readily familiar play as a point of departure and then locate in Bullough the most important literary backgrounds Shakespeare had to work with. Like any other anthologist, of course, Bullough has been obliged to select, arrange, and thereby interpret. "To select is to oversimplify," he notes, "but that danger is inseparable from this undertaking." [24] He would no doubt appreciate our occasional desire that he might have included more of what he believes a significant extract. Nevertheless, Bullough has not been forced to exclude unquestionably relevant materials, and his volumes therefore provide an opportunity almost wholly lacking in standard anthologies: the chance to examine closely a series of widely varied sixteenth-century reactions to a particular human problem, a set theme or a central concern determined by the Elizabethans themselves rather than by a twentieth-century editor. As a result of Shakespeare's own extraordinarily eclectic reading tastes and penchant for tragical-comical-historical-pastoral play-wrighting, his creditors include both the great and mediocre, who freely carry the themes he eventually exploits across every generic boundary.

At least a half dozen years before Shakespeare turned to the theater, the puritanical Stephen Gosson complained "that the Palace of pleasure, the Golden Asse, The Œthiopian historie, Amadis of Fraunce, The Rounde Table, [and] bawdie Comedies in Latine, French, Italian and Spanish, [had] been throughly ransackt to furnish the Playe houses in London." [25] To these literary kinds Shakespeare added historians like Holinshed and Hall; martyrologists like Foxe; noble and ignoble Romans like Plutarch, Seneca, and Ovid; epic poets as unlike as Ariosto and Spenser; the treatises of high-minded Humanists like Elyot; the rationalistic morality plays as well as the moralistic exempla of *The Mirror for Magistrates;* the (for him) earliest English poets like Chaucer and Gower; courtesy books like Castiglione's; innocent farces and propagandistic interludes; and snippets of things as diverse as Bishop Cooper's *Thesaurus,* Scot's *Discoverie of Witchcraft,* ballads, and jest books. Even if we concentrated upon the literary types noted by Gosson and added to them only the stuff they inspired between 1582 and 1588—the translations, elaborations, and imitations of Whetstone, Young, Munday, Greene, Warner, Fraunce, Sidney, and Lyly, among others—we should perceive what plenty could have found its way to Stratford. To London, of course, Shakespeare also brought both idyllic and homespun vignettes of his Warwickshire countryside as well as a working knowledge of the classics, and in London he discovered not only the elegant and sordid realities of city streets but also the wonderful things Kyd had recently done with Seneca, Marlowe with Kyd and Seneca and Holinshed, and Peele with Holinshed and Marlowe and Sidney.

Rather than springing from the head of Zeus with startling innovations, Shakespeare's genius was content to borrow from his predecessors' works, and hence to follow their own imitative methods. He responded to the popularity of the chronicle plays by contributing nine histories in about as many years, first appropriating the revenge motifs taken from Seneca by Kyd and (especially for *Richard III*) Marlowe's technique of unifying the episodic incidents of history and fable through a single, incredibly domineering figure. Eventually he dismissed tragic ghosts and colossal villains, and in their stead injected into the political worlds of the chronicles the detailed urban scenes and humor characters that Ben Jonson was currently celebrating. Within the realm of comedy proper, Shakespeare began in a similar fashion, factoring out the essential ingredients of Roman situational comedy, farce, and pastoral romance and simply doubling or trebling them. Later, he capitalized upon his predecessors' world views as well as their plots and characters, whimsically examining the unexamined marvels of their romantic contrivances and underlining his realistic observation that only within the world of fiction can pain and evil be so neatly redressed.

In Shakespeare's experimentation with every kind of drama two characteristics seem to stand out: the promptness with which he reacted to his contemporaries' discoveries, from Lyly and Marlowe to Marston, Beaumont and Fletcher; and the progressively better uses to which he put them, from slavish imitation to criticism and burlesque to the creation of worlds that, for all their resemblances to those of his sources and rival playwrights, are essentially his own. Throughout his career, however, he remained as conventional as his fellows in his desire to exploit; he was unconventional only to the extent that he usually did an infinitely better job of it.

Although we can never turn ourselves completely into Elizabethans, from Bullough's easily accessible collections we can accurately infer a great deal about some of their writers' central concerns: the problems they found most worthy of posing, the vehicles they thought best suited to articulate them, and the kinds of authorities they appealed to in seeking solutions. And since Bullough has selected according to Shakespeare's often commonplace—i.e., normal or average Elizabethan—tastes and thematic interests, not his own or ours, we can be assured that our inquiry into any collection will be rewarded in at least three ways.

First, throughout each collection every contributor shares some common ground, either a comic motif, tragic moral, or the "meaning" of a certain king's reign. We are therefore guaranteed an opportunity to compare what Shakespeare, at least, considered like things, an especially valuable experience since by modern standards these like things may at first seem worlds apart. From each contributor's handling of character, plot, and mood, we induce his opinion of a popular story's special significance. By tracing the provenance of that narrative, we are able to experience at first hand some of the creative ferment so characteristic of the Renaissance; and by synthesizing the varied meanings that come to accrue about it, we arrive at a far more valid overview than we could have safely inferred from a standard anthology's prescriptive samplings. Secondly, because we are reading from Shakespeare's own library, we can be confident that our survey will eventually include at least one work of some artistic merit, the "chapter" he added to his precursors' pages. Finally, with all certain, probable, and possible treatments of the tale before us, we are in an ideal position to measure the quality and quantity of Shakespeare's indebtednesses and reactions, and thereby to evaluate the nature and often even the intention of his achievement.

We need not insist, of course, that every aspect of Shakespeare's handlings can be fully explained in terms of his predecessors' themes, treatments, and points of view. Shakespeare lived as well as read, and although we must never fall back upon those very probable joys and sorrows of his life to account for one play's sunniness and another's pessimism, there are sometimes incidents and characters and often informing atmospheres that have no literary prototypes. This fact underlines the importance of non-literary stimuli and the possibility that the playwright, at a happy or cynical moment in his career, went to his library to gather plots and personae adaptable to certain dramatic designs already partially conceived. We must also admit the likelihood that some of Shakespeare's most imaginative flights may have been influenced by experiences of which he was not completely conscious. While admitting the potential importance of both these stimuli, however, we must also remember that we know little about Shakespeare's life, much less concerning his personal feelings, and least of all about his subconscious. If in establishing a point of departure for examining Shakespeare's genius we focus almost solely upon the works he read, our excuse must be that these are the demonstrably relevant backgrounds, and that his art—at least the part that lends itself to an analysis of his artistry, not a psychoanalysis of his character—is, like our criticism, a wholly conscious thing.

Our second chapter will therefore begin with Shakespeare, still center stage, first reacting against backgrounds that are themselves pieces of literature and then reflecting nonliterary influences—interests and views confirming Ben Jonson's observation that his "gentle" friend was the "Soule of the Age" as well as " for all time." In moving out of one artist's library into every Elizabethan Englishman's England, our major concern will of course remain essentially the same: the adjustment of modern expectations. Just as we must first establish the alternatives open to Shakespeare before asking why he chose as he did, so we must also attempt to dismiss our often superior knowledge of what actually happened in the sixteenth century in favor of what the Tudors thought was happening; for literature is an expression not of facts but of assumptions taken as facts. Unless we honor this distinction, our backgrounds will not yield relevant contexts and our inquiries will become less and less apposite.

Notes to Chapter I

1. *Samuel Daniel: Poems and A Defence of Ryme*, ed. Arthur Colby Sprague (Cambridge, Mass., 1930), ll. 54, 176, 426 ff.
2. Roy Lamson and Hallett Smith, *Renaissance England* (New York, 1956), p. 13.
3. See Madeleine Doran, *Endeavors of Art* (Madison, Wis., 1964), p. v.
4. *The Allegory of Love* (London, 1953), p. 3. And, Lewis adds, "Even our code of etiquette, with its rule that women always have precedence, . . . is felt to be far from natural in modern Japan or India" (pp. 3–4). Since the first corrected edition of Lewis's book in 1938, "natural" Eastern ways have begun to change.
5. *The Wayward Bus* (New York, 1947), pp. 5–6.
6. "It is worth noting how successful Shakespearean works are when removed from the authority of the fearful pedants who strive so vigorously to remove the joy for hapless millions condemned to academic study of the plays." So one local reviewer moralized the Burton-Taylor production of *The Taming of the Shrew* (*Champaign-Urbana News Gazette*, August 20, 1967). But if we have been "swinging" with Burton and Taylor rather than Shakespeare, is our "joy" a measure of his success or theirs? Where the credit should go necessitates academic study.
7. I. i. 16–23. Citations from Shakespeare are to *The Complete Works*, ed. Peter Alexander (London, 1951).
8. Francis Meres, *Palladis Tamia, Wits Treasury* (1598), in *Elizabethan Critical Essays*, ed. G. Gregory Smith (London, 1904), II, 317.
9. See Joseph H. Summers's excellent article "The Masks of *Twelfth Night*," in *Shakespeare: Modern Essays in Criticism*, ed. Leonard F. Dean (New York, 1957), pp. 128–137.
10. From *Riche his Farewell to Militarie profession* (1581), in *Narrative and Dramatic Sources of Shakespeare*, ed. Geoffrey Bullough (London, 1957–), II, 345.
11. For several additional differences between Shakespeare and Riche, cf. Charles T. Prouty's introduction to his edition of *Twelfth Night* in *The Pelican Shakespeare* (Baltimore, 1958). The affinities between Riche and Malvolio were suggested (*supra* coffee) by Professor Roger Calkins of Mt. Allison University.
12. Doran, p. 4.
13. *The Moral Vision of Jacobean Tragedy* (Madison, Wis., 1960), p. 7.

14. *Ibid.*
15. *Ibid.*, pp. 7, 15.
16. *Ibid.*, p. 16.
17. *Ibid.*
18. *The Origin of Attic Comedy*, ed. Theodore H. Gaster (Garden City, N. Y., 1961), p. 166.
19. *Ibid.*
20. See Gaster, p. xxv.
21. *Ibid.*, p. 166.
22. *Ibid.*, p. xxiv.
23. Thomas Nashe, in his preface to Robert Greene's *Menaphon* (1589). See Smith, *Elizabethan Critical Essays*, I, 319.
24. Bullough, I, xii.
25. *Playes Confuted in Five Actions* (1582), as quoted by Bullough, I, v.

Suggestions for Further Reading

The most complete study of Elizabethan backgrounds is still that magnificent collection of thirty essays, *Shakespeare's England*, ed. C. T. Onions *et al.* (Oxford, 1916). The fifth printing (1950) is easily accessible. These two volumes were the most important, if not the only begetters of the following helpful discussions of Tudor life, lore, and literature.

Burton, Elizabeth. *The Elizabethans at Home*. London, 1958.

Byrne, M. St. Clare. *Elizabethan Life in Town and Country*. London, 1925.

Ford, Boris. *The Age of Shakespeare*. Baltimore, 1956.

Granville-Barker, Harley, G. B. Harrison, *et al. A Companion to Shakespeare Studies*. Cambridge, England, 1934.

Harbage, Alfred. *Shakespeare's Audience*. New York, 1941.

Holzknecht, Karl J. *The Backgrounds of Shakespeare's Plays*. New York, 1950.

Knights, L. C. *Drama and Society in the Age of Jonson*. London, 1937.

Pearson, Lu Emily. *Elizabethans at Home*. Stanford, Calif., 1957.

Sutherland, James, Joel Hurstfield, *et al. Shakespeare's World*. London, 1964.

Several eminently readable biographies focusing upon writers in their intellectual milieu are Marchette Chute's *Shakespeare of London* and *Ben Jonson of Westminster* (New York, 1949 and 1953) and John Buxton's *Sir Philip Sidney and the English Renaissance* (London, 1954). More specific studies of the same milieu are the well known accounts of E. M. W. Tillyard, Theodore Spencer, and Hardin Craig: *The Elizabethan World Picture* (London, 1943), *Shakespeare and the Nature of Man* (New York, 1942), and *The Enchanted Glass* (New York, 1936). Equally pertinent and valuable is Thomas Frederick Crane's lesser known *Italian Social Customs of the Sixteenth Century and Their Influences on the Literatures of Europe* (New Haven, Conn., 1920). Concise but very useful commentaries are also furnished by recent editors of Shakespeare and of Elizabethan anthologies:

Craig, Hardin. *The Complete Works of Shakespeare.* New York, 1951.
Harrison, G. B. *Shakespeare: The Complete Works.* New York, 1948.
Lamson, Roy, and Hallett Smith. *Renaissance England.* New York, 1956.
Rollins, Hyder E., and Herschel Baker. *The Renaissance in England.* Boston, 1954.

Among the many excellent studies of the relationship between literature and its backgrounds are:

Bullough, Geoffrey. *Narrative and Dramatic Sources of Shakespeare.* 7(?) vols. London, 1957–.
Doran, Madeleine. *Endeavors of Art.* Madison, Wis., 1954.
Lewis, C. S. *The Allegory of Love.* London, 1936.
Muir, Kenneth. *Shakespeare's Sources.* London, 1957.
Ornstein, Robert. *The Moral Vision of Jacobean Tragedy.* Madison, Wis., 1960.
Prouty Charles T. *The Sources of Much Ado about Nothing.* New Haven, Conn., 1950.
Tillyard, E. M. W. *Shakespeare's History Plays.* New York, 1946.
Whitaker, Virgil K. *Shakespeare's Use of Learning.* San Marino, Calif., 1953.

Finally, the opportunities to measure Shakespeare against specifically literary stimuli have been recently enhanced by the Signet Classic series, ed. Sylvan Barnet; each volume contains one play, a lengthy introduction, a generous extract from its source(s), and several critical essays. Also see:

Dean Leonard F. *A Casebook on Othello.* New York, 1962.
Griffin, Alice. *The Sources of Ten Shakespearean Plays.* New York, 1966.
Nicoll, Allardyce and Josephine. *Holinshed's Chronicles As Used in Shakespeare's Plays.* New York, 1955.
Satin, Joseph. *Shakespeare and His Sources.* Boston, 1966.
Soellner, Rolf, and Samuel Bertsche. *Measure for Measure: Text, Source, and Criticism.* New York, 1966.

II

COMMIT HIM WITH HIS PEERS

Some Backgrounds Imaginatively Applied

> My *Shakespeare*, rise; I will not lodge thee by
> *Chaucer*, or *Spenser*, or bid *Beaumont* lye
> A little further, to make thee a roome:
> Thou art a Moniment, without a tombe,
> And art aliue still, while thy Booke doth liue,
> And we haue wits to read, and praise to giue.
> That I not mixe thee so, my braine excuses;
> I meane with great, but disproportion'd [dissimilar] *Muses:*
> For, if I thought my iudgement were yeeres,
> I should commit [match] thee surely with thy peeres,
> And tell, how farre thou didst our *Lily* out-shine,
> Or sporting *Kid*, or *Marlowes* mighty line.
> —BEN JONSON, *To the Memory of My Beloued, . . .*
> *Mr. William Shakespeare: And What He Hath Left*
> *Vs.* (1623)

> I think you've got me hooked on this source stuff.
> —University of Illinois student (1967)

In approaching Shakespeare through what we *know* he read rather than through what we *think* he consciously or subconsciously experienced, we must again underscore the differences between solid foundations and stolid superstructures. It is possible to have a healthy respect for facts without being trammeled by them, and we can justify our identifications of Shakespeare's borrowings only by using them for imaginative ends. We list the characters and incidents he changed only in order to speculate as to why he changed them; we catalogue differences in theme, atmosphere, and point of view only as a means of seeking indications of new artistic designs and personal interests. The play, after all, is the thing that excites us, but we must earn our right to speculate within the realm of the gloriously subjective through our honest, often prosaic labor in the area of objective concerns. We must move, in other words, from the domain of what Arthur North Whitehead called "static thought," where one merely knows "exactly where Shakespeare bagged all his plots," [1] to the dimension of "active thought," which Whitehead, for good reason, found lacking in conventional studies of Shakespeare's borrowings. We must think, as Geoffrey Bullough reminds us, "as the Renaissance storytellers did, in terms ethical as well as mechanical, and regard Shakespeare as adapting incidents and characters to plot in accordance with a general, if undefined, idea implicit in the tale." [2] Even the admittedly pedestrian activity of ferreting out Shakespeare's slightest changes must be thoughtfully undertaken, for only when we are sure our list is accurate and complete are we prepared to ascertain which differences are truly significant. The smallest alteration may point up a passage in the source that served as a springboard for the playwright's imagination.

SHAKESPEARE AND SOME LITERARY STIMULI

Like all general backgrounds, even the most direct literary source provides leading questions about rather than a full explanation of the work itself; we examine it not for automatic answers, but to save ourselves the trouble of making irrelevant queries. The following examples should make it clear, however, that in sacrificing those inquiries inspired by assumptions not demonstrably relevant, we shall still possess a ready fund of suggestive questions. To what extent, for instance, should our interpretation of *Romeo and Juliet* be guided by the horrendous moralizations of its source, Arthur Brooke's *The Tragicall Historye of Romeus and Juliet*? Exhibiting a commonplace Elizabethan trust that history should—must, in fact, be made to—yield moral examples, Brooke prefaces his interminable poem with this dignified advertisement:

> And to this ende (good Reader) is this tragicall matter written, to describe unto thee a couple of unfortunate lovers, thralling themselves to unhonest [i.e., unchaste]

desire, neglecting the authoritie and advise of parents and frendes, conferring their principall counsels with dronken gossyppes, and superstitious friers (the naturally fitte instrumentes of unchastitie) attemptyng all adventures of peryll, for thattaynyng of their wished lust, usyng auriculer confession (the kay of whoredome, and treason) for furtheraunce of theyr purpose, abusyng the honorable name of lawefull mariage, [to] cloke the shame of stolne contractes, finallye, by all meanes of unhonest lyfe, hastyng to most unhappye deathe.[3]

Although Brooke's moralizing is less severe within the poem itself—his narrative gives far more credit to fickle Fortune than to youthful lust—the prefatory material at least promises to fulfill what we may assume to have been one reasonable expectation of the upright, anti-Catholic London citizen: History proves that disobedient children, especially those who resort to papistical subtleties, never prosper. Perhaps because Shakespeare followed Brooke's performance more closely than Brooke's professed designs, more likely because he also realized that unhappy endings characterize the greatest love stories, he rejects every premise of the advertisement but the last, the "hastyng," and upon this he constructs a theme similar to that of his fifteenth sonnet's opening quatrain:

> When I consider every thing that grows
> Holds in perfection but a little moment,
> That this huge stage presenteth nought but shows
> Whereon the stars in secret influence comment. . . .[4]

With the moral commonplaces of Brooke's preface before us, we cannot miss the dramatic functions of otherwise perplexing passages. Romeo's opening lines on the bittersweet nature of love, "Feather of lead, bright smoke, cold fire, sick health! / Still-waking sleep, that is not what it is!" may be misinterpreted as the unintentionally absurd wordplay of the young Shakespeare, who surrenders dramatic interest to verbal display. But Romeo, after asking whether his cousin will "not laugh" at this outburst, defines love as "a smoke rais'd with the fume of sighs," admits that he has "lost" himself, and finally confesses that—worst luck!—fair Rosaline will not "ope her lap to saint-seducing gold" (I. i. 181 ff.). This is the first of several instances where Shakespeare appears to enforce and then overturn his audience's expectations. Prepared to watch the consequences of "unhonest desire," we find Romeo—but surely not Shakespeare—unintentionally confusing lust with love, fuming with rhetorical inanities, and assuming that true love involves the loss of identity amid a formulated "siege of loving terms" and "encounter of assailing eyes." This sensual smoke, however, will only set off Juliet and real love more clearly, and it is interesting to note that the bawdiest lines in the play—Mercutio's attempts to conjure up Romeo by Rosaline's dainty parts—fall immediately between the real lovers' first meeting and their betrothal.

In underlining Brooke's view of the lovers' impetuousness, Shakespeare turns an affair of rebellious lust into one of frantic beauty. Juliet, finding their "contract . . . / . . . too rash, too unadvis'd, too sudden," trusts that the "bud of love, by summer's ripening breath, / May prove a beauteous flow'r" (II. ii. 117 ff.). There is also Friar Lawrence's warning that "violent delights have violent ends," and his advice to "love moderately" (II. vi. 9 ff.). But just as Shakespeare overturns our expectations of lust by proceeding from Rosaline to Juliet, so he appears to invite us to search for moral flaws only to underline the element of chance and to conclude that character is hardly the whole of one's destiny. His last plan having gone awry, Lawrence decides that "A greater power than we can contradict / Hath thwarted our intents" (V. iii. 153–154), and we are finally forced to see the wisdom of old age, as well as the ardor of youth, succumbing to a series of star-crossed incidents. These incidents, as well as the characters who are partially responsible for them, have been carefully arranged: the insolence of a hot-headed Tybalt, the ambition of Juliet's worldly parents, the ineffectiveness of an ecclesiastical messenger, a prince almost ready to put an end to an ancient quarrel. All these facts, which Shakespeare insists upon, make up the world of Verona, a violent world that does not understand "summer's ripening breath" and therefore does not allow the lovers to love—as if that were possible under any circumstances—in moderation. In absolving his couple not merely of lust but of almost all responsibility, Shakespeare lost a mediocre tragedy and several severely moral lessons; by relinquishing these dubious honors, however, he gained a very moving piece of pathos.

Even in his most mature plays, where the mysteries of evil and suffering are dramatized but never solved, Shakespeare continued to complicate his predecessors' relatively simple and often more optimistic world views. In concluding the Othello story, Giraldi Cinthio assures us that the Moor "was finally killed by Desdemona's kinsfolk as he deserved," and that in the consequent fall of his Ensign, tortured to death on the rack, we may see how "Thus did God avenge [her] innocence." [5] Neither Holinshed, Spenser, nor the anonymous *True Chronicle History of King Leir* leaves us with both Cordelia hanged and Lear dead of a broken heart. And Robert Greene appears to end his winter's tale with a careless shrug of the shoulders: "*Pandosto* [Shakespeare's Leontes] (calling to mind how first he betraied his friend *Egistus* [Polixenes], how his iealousie was the cause of *Bellarias* [Hermione's] death, that contrarie to the law of nature hee had lusted after his owne Daughter) moued with these desperate thoughts, he fell into a melancholie fit, and to close vp the Comedie with a Tragicall stratageme, he slewe himselfe. . . ." [6] None of Shakespeare's drastic alterations was necessitated simply by the requirements of staging prose narrative; instead, each represents the logical outcome of new thematic concerns and, especially in *The Winter's Tale,* the resolution of problems undreamed of by the writers who furnished Shakespeare's incidents and characters.

Equally suggestive are the leading questions that emerge when we compare Shakespeare's characters to those of Cinthio, *Leir,* and Greene. Like the explicitly providential world Cinthio's Ensign lives in, he is direct, honest, and one-dimensional in his villainy. Although Iago's "malignity" may not be so "motiveless" as Coleridge believed, how much safer we feel in the presence of the man who, "concerned not at all for his marriage vows nor for the friendship, allegiance and duty he owed the Moor, fell madly in love with Desdemona. . . . [B]ut her mind, occupied wholly with the Moor, had no thought for the Ensign or any other. And as all his stratagems proved useless, he fancied that this was so because she was smitten with the Captain [Shakespeare's Cassio], and he considered how he might be rid of him. The love he bore for Desdemona now turned to the most bitter hatred." [7] Cinthio's villain obviously overflows with consistent and clearly defined psychological motivations, whereas Shakespeare, often to the great dismay of modern readers, refuses to render Iago's motives less contradictory than evil itself. Shakespeare makes a similar "blunder" at the opening of *King Lear,* sacrificing Leir's thoroughly credible reasons for portioning out his kingdom in order to establish a less concrete, almost fairy-tale atmosphere, a context in which

Goneril's love may be defined thematically, as "Dearer than eye-sight," and not seem strained. How credible, for that matter, is Leontes's jealous outburst at the opening of *The Winter's Tale?* Greene tells us that Bellaria, "willing to show how vnfaynedly shee looued her husband by his friends intertainemĕt, vsed him likewise so familiarly, that her countenance bewraied how her minde was affected towardes him: oftentimes comming her selfe into his bed chamber, to see that nothing should be amis to mislike him." [8] Even after honoring the fine points of Renaissance etiquette, we must agree with Robert G. Hunter's observation that "it would be unnatural if 'sundry and doubtfull thoughts' did not enter the mind of a husband in such a case." [9] But again Shakespeare has rejected the credible for the mysterious or less readily explainable. We know that Leontes's monstrous thoughts were made to take shape with deliberate incoherence, for his speech is not only disjointed but contains no hint of Greene's easily accessible motivations.

Unless we are content to claim that Shakespeare simply bungled his predecessors' explicit leads, we should by now realize that our leading questions have taken us along an avenue of relevant inquiries toward several important conclusions. Regardless of how much we may differ as to why Shakespeare departed from his literary backgrounds—the reasons must be sought in the plays themselves, and they sometimes support partially conflicting conjectures—we must agree that since it is easier to follow than to change, such departures bespeak new, consciously chosen designs, and are therefore likely to prove more significant than mere borrowings. Secondly, once we agree that these changes were thoughtfully effected, we must also admit that although they do not directly establish exactly what Shakespeare was attempting, indirectly they tell us precisely what he did not care to attempt. Our questions, in other words, are becoming increasingly relevant and suggestive. They are also bringing us closer to the better-read members of Shakespeare's original audience, those whom he could depend upon startling with his uniquely pessimistic resolution of the Lear story or who, because they were familiar with one of Greene's most popular romances, would be even more amazed than we when Hermione's statue takes on life. Once again we see the importance of defining the kinds of backgrounds and traditions that invited the playwright's alterations. Although dramatic tone must always remain largely a matter of conjecture, the significant variations between source and play not only demonstrate the ways in which Shakespeare capitalized upon his predecessors' assumptions and exploited his audience's expectations, but make a great deal clearer the ethical and artistic interests that must have inspired such strategies.

Unlike his mature comedies and tragedies, Shakespeare's early histories more often simplify than complicate the views of his sources, in this case the political worlds of Edward Hall and Raphael Holinshed. In noting the demise of George, Duke of Clarence, for instance, Hall is far more ambiguous than Shakespeare's *Richard III:*

> IN the. xvij. yere of kyng Edward, there fel a sparcle of privy malice, betwene the king & his brother the duke of Clarence *whether* it rose of olde grudges before time passed, *or* were it newly kyndeled and set a fyre by the Quene, *or* her bloud which were ever mistrusting and prively barkynge at the kynges lignage, *or* were he desirous to reigne after his brother: . . . The fame was that the king *or* the Quene, *or* bothe sore troubled with a folysh Prophesye, and by reason therof began to stomacke & grevously to grudge agaynst the duke. The effect of which was, after king Edward should reigne, one whose first letter of hys name shoulde be a G. and because the devel is wont with such wytchcraftes, to wrappe and illaqueat [ensnare] the myndes of men, which delyte in such develyshe fantasyes they sayd afterward that the Prophesie lost not hys effect, when after kyng Edward, Glocester usurped his kyngdome. . . . *The king much greved* and troubled with hys brothers dayly querimonye [complaining], . . . caused hym to be apprehended, and cast into the Towre, where he beyng taken and adjudged for a Traytor, was prively drouned in a But of Malvesey [i.e., a barrel of malmsey wine].[10]

Like every other Tudor chronicler, Hall seldom approaches the objectivity of modern historians; here, however, he allows the reader to draw his own conclusions. Twenty-nine years later Holinshed rephrased Hall's account along similarly noncommittal lines, concluding that "George duke of Clarence was a goodlie noble prince, and at all times fortunate, *if either* his owne ambition had not set him against his brother, *or* the enuie of his enimies his brother against him." [11] Although *Richard III* overflows with "olde grudges," "barkynge," "querimonye," and "enuie of enimies," through Gloucester's opening soliloquy Shakespeare immediately clears up most of his chroniclers' ambiguities. There is no room for Clarence's ambition, and "enimies" is turned into a simple singular, the man "determined to prove a villain" with advertisements as subtle in meaning as in style:

> And if King Edward be as true and just
> As I am subtle, false, and treacherous,
> This day should Clarence closely be mew'd up—
> About a prophecy. . . .
>
> (36–39)
>
> Simple, plain Clarence, I do love thee so
> That I will shortly send thy soul to heaven. . . .
>
> (118–119)

Although Shakespeare thus credited Gloucester with more villainy than his predecessors dared or cared to provide, he must have found their accounts encouraging. Few sixteenth-century historians resisted the patriotic impulse to dwell at length upon Richard's monstrous wickedness. Holinshed is following the noble tradition of Robert Fabyan, Sir Thomas More, Polydore Vergil, John Rastell, Richard Grafton, and of course Hall himself when he describes Gloucester as "malicious, wrathfull, enuious," a "deepe dissembler, lowlie of countenance, arrogant of heart, outwardlie companiable where he inwardlie hated, not letting [hindering himself] to kisse whome he thought to kill," and concludes that "Friend and fo was much what indifferent" to Richard, especially "where his aduantage grew, [for] he spared no mans death whose life withstoode his purpose" (III, 362). And although Holinshed cannot be absolutely sure that "the duchesse his mother had so much adoo in hir trauell [travail], that she could not be deliuered of him vncut" or that "he came into the world with the feet forward" and "not untoothed" (III, 362), he does note that these biographical items are "for truth reported," most likely reasoning that if Richard did not enter the world so dramatically, history at least proves he should have. History also proved it expedient to keep the legend of Rapacious Richard alive; we must remember that with the exception of Polydore Vergil, all the contributors were subjects of the House of Tudor, which had saved the realm at Bosworth Field.

Although thus encouraged by the "truth" of history, it seems unlikely that Shakespeare "outmonstered" his literary backgrounds simply to demonstrate a more intense patriotism. As a playwright, he was obliged to reduce the major incidents of fifteen years (1471–1485) to a play of five acts, to glean from his episodic annals the most dramatic moments of Edward IV's reign and compress them into his stage's "two hours' traffic." More important, if the whole was to be significant, incidents had to be related, not merely fused; one scene should be made to comment upon as well as simply follow another. As artists of every time have known, if not admitted, there are great differences between life as directly experienced and life as represented and thereby interpreted in art. Real life is too full of unrelated fragments of sounds and furies to signify well-ordered, meaningful sequences, governing ideas, unifying principles. In this sense life is not ordered, yet in this same sense, art is nothing if not. What is left for the artist—even he who boasts of his pretended "slices of life"—but to exercise his craftsmanship, his ability to *wright* as well as write, and consequently to subvert real life (or "true history") for his own artistic ends? To represent is inevitably to select, compress, expand, omit, arrange, focus upon, relate, and thereby falsify.

As a historian with adequate space to recount and render intelligible all the events of Edward's reign, Holinshed's only excuse in coloring Richard so black was a happy subservience to unwarranted traditions; by modern historiographical standards, he was not thinking critically. But as a dramatist, seeking thematic and theatrically effective wholes among Holinshed's straightforward incidents, Shakespeare the apprentice was attempting to think very critically when he colored Richard even blacker, for "blackness" was his solution to a problem more structural than moral. Just as Kyd's *The Spanish Tragedy*, with its surplus of prophecies, curses, ghosts, bloody revenges, and heavy ironies furnished motifs by which to organize Holinshed's unrelated "facts," so Marlowe's *Tamburlaine* and *The Jew of Malta* each provided an incredibly domineering figure in whom all actions could be centered. It is no wonder, then, that the Richard who is successively dressed to political, moral, and finally dramatic advantage defies belief. Through one character's superhuman but unified evil, the inexperienced playwright achieves an unsophisticated unity of action. As the wheels of God and Seneca begin to grind, we discover in each scene either Richard manipulating or groups of characters responding to his machinations, gathered together simply to help or oppose him. By modern or even by Shakespeare's own maturer standards of psychological realism, their personalities, like Richard's, appear oversimplified. The monster's allies should have mistrusted him sooner; his foes had no grounds ever to trust him at all. We sense, however, that Shakespeare is far less interested in reflecting upon their naïveté than in demonstrating consummate villainy in action, an interest revealed not only in eminently theatrical and psychologically unconvincing language, but also by the extent to which he improves upon Holinshed's chronology. The first five scenes, for instance, quickly take us from 1477 back to 1471 and then forward to 1478 and 1483,[12] as Gloucester vows his brother's death, woos Anne of Warwick over her father-in-law's corpse, blames the Queen's kindred for Clarence's imprisonment, and after having him executed, adds his death to their crimes. Although Richard did in fact marry Anne in 1472, the wooing scene is wholly fictitious, and the exhumation of Henry VI's corpse, over which the lovers may plight their troth, is both bad history and grand theater. Again, however, we must remember that Gloucester's greatest defamer is dramatic compression: It took even Holinshed's monster thirteen years to accomplish what Shakespeare's seems to manage in a single day.

For the most part we should enjoy Shakespeare's tampering with history for the same reasons that we appreciate a modern novelist's ordering of life. The main difficulty is that whereas we immediately recognize how our contemporaries have artfully ordered our modern experiences, we often approach Shakespeare's political worlds to learn about English history rather than how he improved upon it. With Hall or Holinshed before us, we are forced to ask questions that may not be difficult to answer, but that otherwise we should never have thought of asking. In *Richard III*, for example, why has Shakespeare refused to follow Holinshed by having the Earl of Richmond invade England twice (1483, 1485)? (History, like life, is full of anticlimaxes.) Why does Queen Margaret, Henry VI's withered widow, hover about Edward's court, when Shakespreare knew she had returned to France in 1475?[13] (And let us lose a symbol of Fate, the curse upon the House of York and a prophecy of its fall? To underline the truth, invent a fiction; Shakespeare often lied, but never gratuitously.) Finally, Holinshed is quite clear that Richard, "manfullie fighting in the middle of his enimies, was slaine" (III, 444). The reason Shake-

speare has Richmond defeat Richard singlehandedly is as obvious
as why, at the Battle of Shrewsbury in *1 Henry IV*, he conveniently forgets that Hal's fiery young rival, Hotspur, was actually
pushing forty.

As necessary glosses upon Shakespeare's later histories, Holinshed
and Hall continue to be helpful, but the leading questions they suggest are less easy to answer. In sketching the background for *2
Henry IV*'s Gaultree Forest scenes, for instance, Holinshed clearly
credits the Earl of Westmoreland with the royalists' treacherous
victory. At the opening of his account, the presence of "the lord
Iohn of Lancaster the kings sonne" is duly registered, but it is the
Earl who "perceiued the force of the aduersaries, and that they laie
still and attempted not to come forward vpon him" and therefore
"subtillie deuised how to quaile their purpose" (III, 37). John is
merely represented as "those that were with" Westmoreland, who
assure the rebels of a fair hearing if they lay down their arms. In
concluding his account, Holinshed again focuses upon the Earl's

> vsing more policie then the rest: "Well (said he) then
> our trauell is come to the wished end: and where our peo-
> ple haue beene long in armour, let them depart home to
> their woonted trades and occupations: in the meane time
> let vs drinke togither in signe of agreement, that the people
> on both sides maie see it." . . . The people beholding such
> tokens of peace, . . . brake vp their field and returned
> homewards: but in the meane time, whilest the people of
> the archbishops side withdrew awaie, the number of the
> contrarie part increased, according to order giuen by the
> earle of Westmerland; and yet the archbishop perceiued
> not that he was deceiued, vntill the earle of Westmer-
> land arrested both him and the earle marshall with diuerse
> other.
>
> (III, 37–38)

Although Holinshed, admitting that "others write somwhat otherwise of this matter," includes a short account of how the rebels,
"being pursued, manie were taken, manie slaine, and manie spoiled,"
and although he adds that a certain "sir Iohn Colleuill of the Dale"
was later beheaded for treason at Durham, several items are con-
spicuously absent: the repeated appeal to "honour," a word that
reverberates throughout the later histories and is now further debased in meaning on the lips of John, whom Shakespeare substitutes

as the leading villain; "Colleuill's" confrontation with that most
worthy royalist officer, Sir John Falstaff, who appeals to "the word
of the noble" (IV. iii. 53) and concludes the forest scenes with a
eulogy upon "sherris-sack." Most obviously lacking is Holinshed's
unruffled tone:

West.	Of capital treason I attach you both.
Mowb.	Is this proceeding just and honourable?
West.	Is your assembly so?
Arch.	Will you thus break your faith?
P. John.	I pawn'd thee none:

        I promis'd you redress of these same grievances
        Whereof you did complain; which, by mine honour,
        I will perform with a most Christian care.

   .   .   .   .

        Strike up our drums, pursue the scatt'red stray.
        God, and not we, hath safely fought to-day.
                     (IV. ii. 109 ff.)

The effect of John's humble couplet is devastating, and our
realization that there is not a hint of such pious politeness in
Holinshed should encourage us to look throughout *2 Henry IV* for
similar elaborations upon the themes of (dis)honorable honor, false
report, and Christian responsibility, from Rumor's prologue through
Northumberland's definition of "honour" and Henry's discovery
of the meaning of "Jerusalem," to Hal's closing rejection of Falstaff.
But we must also notice that although Holinshed documents a
thematic alteration, he does not explain why John has replaced
Westmoreland. Our mere awareness of this fact, however, prompts
us to reason the need. We realize that this Shakespearean "lie" does
not materially affect the theme: Any leading royalist could have
broken faith. What about character? In defeating Hotspur at the
close of *1 Henry IV*, Hal not only saves the realm but loses his foil;
in his final speech we see Shakespeare again altering Holinshed in
order to establish another figure against which Hal's character
may be measured. Holinshed quickly concludes his account of the
Battle of Shrewsbury by noting that "the kings enimies were
vanquished, and put to flight, in which flight, the earle of Dowglas,
for hast, falling from the crag of an hie mounteine, . . . was taken,
and for his valiantnesse, of the king frankelie and freelie deliuered" (III, 26). By having the captured Douglas change hands

several times, Shakespeare gains an opportunity to resolve the theme of war as booty, to set Henry's opening references to "honourable spoil" and "gallant prize" (I. i.) into a nobler key, to comment for the last time in this play upon the theme of honor, and to anticipate the muted comparisons between John and Hal in *2 Henry IV*.

> *Prince.*   At my tent
> The Douglas is; and I beseech your Grace
> I may dispose of him.
> *King.*   With all my heart.
> *Prince.*   Then, brother John of Lancaster, to you
> This *honourable bounty* shall belong:
> Go to the Douglas, and deliver him
> Up to his pleasure, *ransomless and free;*
> His valours shown upon our crests to-day
> Have taught us how to cherish such high deeds
> Even in the bosom of our adversaries.
>   (V. v. 22–31. Italics added.)

Because Holinshed tells us, in effect, to watch for relationships that Shakespeare may draw between Henry's elder sons, we are also less likely to miss the significance of several otherwise minor passages: Henry warns Hal that his "place in council," "rudely lost," is now supplied by his younger brother (*1 Henry IV*, III. ii. 32–33),[14] and in the last act of *2 Henry IV*, Warwick naïvely wishes that Hal "had the temper" of the worst of his three brothers (ii. 14 ff.). Even Falstaff's entertaining description of the virtues of sack over "thin drink" originates from a comparison between Hal and John, though Falstaff, true to witty form, misinterprets his evidence. He will later discover that "hot and valiant" Hal can be cool and politic.

In justice to Falstaff, however, we should add that no character completely understands Hal's long-range purposes. Only toward the conclusion of *2 Henry IV*, when Hal publicly expresses his anticipated delight in mocking "Rotten opinion, who hath writ me down / After my seeming" (V. ii. 126 ff.), does the English court share the information we have gleaned from his first soliloquy (*1 Henry IV*, I. ii. 188 ff.), an ingenious rationalization that not only excuses his present behavior but assures us that he is an even subtler politician than his father, who, like everyone else, misunderstands him. By the end of *Henry V*, of course, not even the French can doubt Hal's dismissal of holiday. But does his sudden reformation result in a protagonist too perfect, antagonists too worthless, and a play that therefore lacks what all genuine drama demands, sufficient conflict? Holinshed certainly *offered* materials for epic drama, an era distinguished by its heroic king and his never-equaled conquests, a reign that the Elizabethans must have fondly recalled, for even the defeat of the Spanish Armada in 1588 was at most a defensive victory. How much greater those days when English armies had marched across the Continent under a man "of life without spot, a prince whome all men loued, and of none disdained, a capteine against whome fortune neuer frowned, nor mischance once spurned, whose people him so seuere a iusticer both loued and obeied. . . . [A] paterne in princehood, a lode-starre in honour, and mirrour of magnificence: the more highlie exalted in his life, the more deepelie lamented at his death, and famous to the world alwaie" (III, 133–134).

Amidst such unambiguous praise, however, Holinshed included an item that might well have proved attractive to the playwright who had already stressed his hero's jolly deviousness: "In time of warre such was his prouidence, bountie and hap, as he had true intelligence not onelie what his enimies did, but what they said and intended; of his [own] deuises and purposes few, before the thing was at the point to be done, should be made priuie" (III, 133). Judging from Holinshed's congratulatory tone, he could not have intended this side of Hal's character to jar against his epic portrait. However unwillingly, he may have nevertheless inspired Shakespeare's curiosity concerning the man under the conquering crown, whose personality, unlike the success of his military exploits, remains peculiarly ambiguous. Was it Holinshed's eulogy of Hal's secret "deuises" that led Shakespeare to continue his never-concluded investigation of Christian responsibility? Regardless of their sources, we cannot dismiss Shakespeare's less than heroic scenes: the murky politics of the ecclesiastical authorities; Hal's genius in disclaiming all responsibility for the bloodshed he knows will ensue; his God-inspired "retreat" from the English to the French throne; his charge that Harfleur is somehow "guilty in defence" (III. iii. 43); the analogies he strains to prove "his cause . . . just and his quarrel honourable" (IV. i. 127); and the alternating views of a campaign that both nourishes "horse-leeches" (II. iii. 55) and ostensibly reveals God's epic designs for Saints George and Harry.

Occasionally even Shakespeare's slightest changes are immensely

suggestive. If we were obliged to select the most curious lines of
Richard II's opening scene, for instance, we should certainly include Mowbray's strange reply to Bolingbroke's charge that he
plotted the murder of Thomas of Woodstock, Duke of Gloucester,
one of Richard's and Bolingbroke's uncles and brother to Gaunt
and York:

> For Gloucester's death—
> I slew him not, but to my own disgrace
> Neglected my sworn duty in that case.
>
> (132–134)

Despite their appeals to "rites of knighthood" and "chivalrous
design," apparently one of these eloquent knights is lying in his
throat; despite the fact that the King, God's anointed deputy, is
center stage, insuring the orderly observance of "oath and band
[bond]" and the formality and dignity of time-honored chivalric
values, surely something is essentially rotten in the ceremonious
state of England. Shakespeare soon makes us realize the irrelevance,
if not the total injustice, of Bolingbroke's accusation. In the next
scene his father, John of Gaunt, justifies his own inaction: "God's
is the quarrel," he explains to Gloucester's vengeance-seeking
widow, "for God's substitute, / His deputy anointed in His sight, /
Hath caus'd his death" (37–39). Immediately before his own death
he confronts Richard himself with the "witness good" that proves
"That thou [Richard] respect'st not spilling Edward's blood" (II.
i. 130–131), and even in the presence of Richard's Queen the
timorous York later cries:

> I would to God,
> So my untruth had not provok'd him to it,
> The King had cut off my head with my brother's.
>
> (II. ii. 100–102)

But if the play itself eventually affirms the Duke of Norfolk's
claim and implies that the judge, not the accused, should be on
trial, without Holinshed's readily available gloss Mowbray's reference to his neglect of "sworn duty" remains confusing. The
"truth" of the matter is as follows: Richard "sent vnto Thomas
Mowbraie . . . to make the duke [of Gloucester] secretlie awaie."
Mowbray "prolonged time for the executing of the kings commandement, though the king would haue had it doone with all

expedition, whereby the king conceiued no small displeasure, and sware that it should cost the earle his life if he quickly obeied not his commandement. The earle thus as it seemed in maner inforced, called out the duke at midnight . . . [and] caused his seruants to cast featherbeds vpon him, and so smoother him to death, or otherwise to strangle him with towels (as some write.)" (II, 837) From this vantage point we realize that Bolingbroke's charge contains an element of truth: Mowbray was indeed instrumental in causing Gloucester's death. At the same time we now also realize that Mowbray was a most unwilling instrument and, more important, that he wishes to *remind*, not inform, all parties concerned about his reluctance. Although it is possible that his "sworn duty" was to Gloucester, the prisoner he would normally be expected to protect, it is more likely that this phrase is a gage thrown at the feet of Richard, the party of the foremost part. Into the midst of these honorable, chivalric proceedings, so solemn, courtly, ceremonious—and so deftly avoiding the ugly truth—Mowbray casts his curt reminder: "I am actually in disgrace not for committing, but for forestalling murder."

What makes Mowbray's lines even more interesting is this: Although Shakespeare lifts most of his first scene directly out of Holinshed, the passage in question is entirely his own addition. Both chronicler and playwright have Bolingbroke accuse Mowbray first of having withheld funds for the troops at Calais, and secondly of having hatched all treason within the past eighteen years. Whether or not these charges are trumped up as decorative prefaces, the second is vague enough to be harmless, and the first, specific enough to be carefully refuted; Mowbray dismisses both with ease. The significant variance is between the historical and dramatic handling of the specific and very harmful final accusation. In Holinshed, Bolingbroke continues his grievances through an appointed spokesman: " 'By his false suggestions and malicious counsell, he hath caused to die and to be murthered your right deere vncle, the duke of Glocester, sonne to king Edward. Moreouer, the duke of Hereford saith, and I for him, that he will proue this with his bodie against the bodie of the said duke of Norfolke within lists.' *The king herewith waxed angrie*, and asked the duke of Hereford, if these were his words, who answered: 'Right deere lord, they are my woords; and hereof *I require right*, and the battell against him' " (II, 845. Italics added.) Richard has every reason to "wax angry." By seeking retribution for Gloucester's murder,

Bolingbroke has suddenly put aside vague or petty disloyalties; by insisting upon the almost sacred medieval sanction of trial by combat, he is forcing the hand of at least Richard's agent, if not that of the King himself. Holinshed's Mowbray, although he easily brushes aside the first and second charges, ignores the real case in point altogether: Calais remains strongly fortified, its troops well paid. For that matter, Mowbray insists, great sums of his own money have been spent in his other official capacities. Secondly, his treasonable acts are but one, "an ambush to haue slaine" John of Gaunt, to whom he has since been thoroughly reconciled. Further, however, the deponent saith not, either caught unprepared or having decided that before an angry king, discretion is indeed the better part of valor.[15]

Holinshed notwithstanding, Shakespeare's Mowbray refuses to ignore the charge; since he answers it so obliquely (his rebuttal is almost a parenthetical thirdly, set between his firstly and secondly), we may assume that Shakespeare is not so much interested in underlining Mowbray's indiscreet valor as in providing a dramatic equivalent for Holinshed's notice of Richard's wrath. God's deputy must maintain his dignity, but his audience, like Holinshed's reader, must be made to sense Richard's complicity; we are meant to be impressed by the scene's stately formalities, but we must also be given hints that the show is as hollow as it is brilliant. Surely this is the suspicion Shakespeare wishes to enforce as gages are hurled and knightly vows uncompromised. Neither contestant can recant, for as Mowbray explains, "Mine honour is my life; both grow in one; / Take honour from me, and my life is done" (I. i. 182–183). Moreover, the Anglo-Saxon preference for death before dishonor is clothed in medieval-chivalric dress. "I am disgrac'd, impeach'd, and baffl'd here," cries the anguished Mowbray. We immediately understand his disgrace and probably realize that by "impeach'd" he means "accused." By baffl'd," however, he does not mean "confused." He is saying, in effect, "I have been subjected as a perjured knight to public infamy,[16] my armor stripped away, the coat of arms painted on my shield reversed, my body or effigy hung upside down." [17] Even Richard, "not born to sue, but to command," must honor the right of trial by combat. Truth will out with sword and lance, he insists; "we shall see / Justice design the victor's chivalry" (202–203).

By the time we reach the lists at Coventry, Gaunt has given us enough of the real truth to make us relish the tension between

colorful appearances and sordid realities. Richard, the incorrigible
actor who eventually exchanges his crown for several choice lines
at Flint Castle, revels in Coventry's pageantry:

> Marshal, demand of yonder champion
> The cause of his arrival here in arms;
> Ask him his name; and orderly proceed
> To swear him in the justice of his cause.
>   (I. iii. 7–10).

The whole scene is close to Holinshed in detail, closer yet in
spirit, and it is likely that Shakespeare's company went to some
expense to adorn its actors as "richlie," "curiouslie," and "sump-
tuouslie" as the chronicler dresses his. The rest of Holinshed's
luxuries—"sumptuous scaffold," the "great companie of men apparelled in silke sendall, imbrodered with siluer," Richard's own
bodyguard of "aboue ten thousand men in armour" (II, 846–847)—
such magnificence could only be suggested by rich language, the
scene's superabundant references to knighthood, oaths, God, justice,
and truth, and by a structure as formal as the ceremony it describes.

But if Richard revels in Coventry's glitter, he evades its only
justifiable purpose. The combatants, after all, are on trial, not holiday, and just as beauty is about to become "truth," the warder is
dropped, the medieval-judicial machinery halted, and Richard
proceeds to make a mockery of the whole elaborate system by an-
nouncing that before the champions were armed, the justice of their
contradictory causes had been determined. In effect, justice had
been set aside. Is Shakespeare, along with his King, "baffling"
chivalry itself? Again we must notice a slight misrepresentation of
Holinshed. "The duke of Norfolke," reports the chronicler, "was
not fullie set forward, when the king cast down his warder, and
the heralds cried, Ho, ho. Then the king caused their speares to be
taken from them, and commanded them to repaire againe to their
chaires, *where they remained two long houres,* while the king and
his councell *deliberatlie consulted* what order was best to be had in
so weightie a cause" (II, 847. Italics added.) In reducing *"two
long houres"* to *"A long flourish,"* it is more likely that Shakespeare
is enforcing the theme of empty ritual than honoring dramatic
compression, and this motif of form without essence is repeatedly
complemented by instances of actions going nowhere: Trial by
combat to determine innocence is "answered" by mutual banish-
ment; the Welsh army was eager to engage—alas!—only yesterday;

Richard foresees thunder and lightning at Flint Castle, but later decides upon sentimental vignettes and regal rhetoric for a more moving scene; finally, at the opening of Act IV, as we anxiously await the outcome of the numerous gages thrown about Westminster Hall, we discover that Norfolk, like Godot, will never appear.[18]

Shakespeare and Some Social Influences

In noting Shakespeare's efforts to show how medieval ceremony could easily become empty, ineffective, and often arbitrary, we may find it easier to understand his point than to be assured that it had contemporary relevance; to be fully confident, in other words, that his own audience would not have thought he was belaboring the obvious or, like Falstaff, stabbing a corpse. In view of the frequent Tudor laments over the passing of the good old days, when, despite the Wars of the Roses, there was order to things and men knew their places, Shakespeare's equation of order to hollow formality may have been a point worth making. But the widespread nostalgia for old-fashioned charity and other homespun medieval virtues does not explain Shakespeare's thrusts at the specifically chivalric splendors of chivalry's last reign. Did not an audience at the close of the sixteenth century realize that the death of Richard's knightly fourteenth-century world was grimly celebrated at Agincourt in the early fifteenth century? This was an audience that should have noticed the rise of the Tudor state and the disappearance of the last feudal loyalties; it certainly had witnessed the development of modern mercantile systems and daily observed self-made and masterless men. Is it not likely that such an audience would have responded to Shakespeare's baffling of chivalric ceremony by echoing Horatio's rejoinder to Hamlet's self-evident discovery: "There needs no ghost . . . come from the grave / To tell us this" (I. v. 125–126)?

Again Holinshed proves helpful, for he not only shows us how, but suggests why, Shakespeare manipulated the "facts" of Richard's brilliant reign. The following account, although it cannot be strictly considered a dramatic source or analogue, may establish some common ground between the worlds of *Richard II* and Shakespeare's audience. It may also serve to remind us that people (and therefore a society) of any time are often prone to act upon assumptions felt as facts rather than upon premises continually re-shaped according to newly perceived political, scientific, and economic "realities." Certainly this incident should at least be thoughtfully considered before we conclude that Shakespeare's "modern" audience knew that chivalry was dead, realized that no man could be a citizen of both the Renaissance and the Middle Ages, and therefore viewed the undermining of medieval values in *Richard II* as unnecessarily slighting remembrances of things long past.

On June 18, 1571, Holinshed solemnly notes, Simon Low and John Kime appeared before the judges of the Court of Common Pleas at Westminster with a "writ of right" against Thomas Para-more, maintaining that the said Paramore had no just claim to "a certaine manour and demaine lands . . . in the Ile of Hartie" (IV, 261). The defendant, evidently suspicious of complicated legal processes, promptly "offered to defend his right by battell" and brought before the bench "one George Thorne, a big, broad, strong set fellow" as his champion. The plaintiffs, "offering likewise to defend their right . . . and to proue [it] by battell," accordingly introduced their man, Henry Nailer, "maister of defense, and seruant to the right honourable the earle of Leicester." The right of combat was granted, and the gauntlet duly thrown down and taken up. Each party seems to have been well satisfied. But "on the next morrow, the matter was staied." Elizabeth, having got wind of the proposed combat and "abhorring bloudshed," reconciled the opponents, granted manor and lands to Paramore, yet commanded him to post five hundred pounds "to consider the plaintifs, as vpon hearing the matter the iudges should award." Although the real quarrel was thus removed from the field of honor and returned to the court, there was no need to curtail the ceremony that had already been initiated.

> It was thought good, that *for Paramores assurance, the order should be kept* touching the combat, and that the plaintifs Low and Kime should make default of appearance; but that yet such as were suerties for Nailer their champions appearance, should bring him in; and likewise those that were suerties for Thorne, should bring in the same Thorne, *in discharge of their band*: and that the court should sit in Tuthill fields, where was prepared one plot of ground, of one and twentie yards square, double railed for the combat (IV, 261. Italics added.)

A "stage" was accordingly erected for the judges who composed the Court of Common Pleas, and "without the lists," scaffolds for the citizenry. On the morning of the battle Thorne appeared very early, retired to his tent, and impatiently awaited his foe's arrival. But Nailer was in no hurry to champion a cause already lost by default. Realizing that Tuthill Fields offered no glory, he reaped as much as possible in his splendid passage from London. About seven in the morning he proceeded through the city "apparelled in a dublet, and gallie gascoine breeches all of crimsin sattin, cut and rased, a hat of blacke veluet, with a red feather and band, before him drums and fifes plaieng." Also before him was Thorne's gauntlet, dangling from sword's point, while a yeoman of Her Majesty's Guard followed, bearing Nailer's shield. The odd procession paraded in great pomp from London to Westminster, "came backe into the Kings street, and so along thorough the Sanctuarie" and finally, some two hours later, emerged at Tuthill.

The next group of actors arrived about ten: the Lord Chief Justice and two associates, who made their way to the "stage" and "solemnlie" proclaimed that unless Low appeared, he would "lose his writ of right." Low, of course, was nowhere near Tuthill, but the champions and their sureties were nevertheless summoned and directed to prepare for battle. "Proclamation was made that none should touch the barres, nor presume to come within the same, except such as were appointed" (IV, 262). After "all this solemne order was finished," the Lord Chief Justice rehearsed the whole matter—neglecting, however, to mention the Queen's intervention—and then announced that "for default of appearance in Low," he was obliged to grant free title to Paramore, dismiss the champions, and "acquit . . . the suerties of their bands." But the ritual was not to be concluded no neatly.

> He also willed Henrie Nailer to render againe to George Thorne his gantlet. Whereto the said Nailer answered, that his lordship might command him anie thing, but willinglie he wold not render the said gantlet to Thorne except he could win it. And further he challenged the said Thorne to play with him halfe a score blowes, to shew some pastime to the lord chiefe iustice, and to the other there assembled. But Thorne answered, that he came to fight, and would not plaie. Then the lord chiefe iustice commending Nailer for his valiant courage, commanded them both quietlie to depart the field, &c. (IV, 262)

Had only Nailer and his whimsical kind been involved, the abortive combat so dutifully detailed by Holinshed might be quietly dismissed as simply a "shew" for "pastime," the holiday revelry of servant and apprentice. But the leading roles were played by the highest executive and judicial officers of the realm, by authorities not wont to answer "writs of right" with elaborate mockeries. Although Elizabethan justice sometimes strikes us as unduly harsh, it seldom seems arbitrary; [19] Henry VIII's vacillation was past and James I's yet to come. Although well aware of the outcome, the principals at Tuthill were not engaged in pastimes, nor was the essentially humorless Holinshed in sketching his chivalric vignette. Paramore had introduced the element of doughty deeds, and the Crown determined that for his "assurance, the order should be kept touching the combat." Paramore had set some of the judicial machinery of the Middle Ages in motion, and the Court of Common Pleas, taking its cue from one of Europe's most forward-looking princes, thought it wise to follow suit. Renaissance economic and political realities notwithstanding, the chivalric apparently remained as a respectable, even vital part of the social amalgam, and full-blown humanism yet honored the medieval gauntlet. Even before Tuthill's bourgeois audience, it is unlikely that either sprightly Nailer or dull Thorne represented the ideal champion. The seriousness of the occasion, however, had nothing to do with the combatants' characters or even with the value of Paramore's manor and lands. The real issue was one of "assurance . . . suertie . . . discharge of band," of responsibly following the proper procedures to guarantee order. If these procedures were sometimes old and sometimes new, so was the society they upheld.

We may be inclined to dismiss the Tuthill ritual as merely a temporary beclouding of Renaissance sunshine by lingering medieval shadows. We know, for instance, that by the days of the last Tudor, the old values were irrevocably lost. *But do we know that the Elizabethans shared our knowledge?* Without bothering to subject our own social conventions to the same scrutiny, we may appeal to logic. We realize that by the reign of Elizabeth feudalism was no longer a working military or social structure and therefore reason that chivalry, its ultimate expression, could hardly have been taken seriously. What sensible Elizabethan, keenly aware of the implications of the New Learning, the Reformation, and the rise of nationalism, would not have been amused by Tuthill's brave old world? But did such a person exist? And if he existed, is it realistic to assume that his sense of the mutually exclusive was keener than our own? Do our habits of thought more closely reflect present realities than the collective wisdom of the immediate past? When have customs themselves developed logically, quickly purging elements not vitally related to fresher and gradually predominating modes of thought? Our logic, in short, overlooks eternal cultural truths: native traditions unconsciously resisting newly acquired, practical knowledge; social and often even literary fabrics taking their basic patterns from outmoded warps.

The brilliant Dutch scholar, Johan Huizinga, in illustrating that fifteenth-century France and Holland were "still medieval at heart," points out that "the transition from the spirit of the declining Middle Ages to humanism was far less simple than we are inclined to imagine it. . . . We find it difficult to fancy the mind cultivating the ancient forms of medieval thought and expression while aspiring at the same time to antique wisdom and beauty. Yet this is just what we have to picture to ourselves." [20] The period during which the spirit of the "simpleness and purity of the ancient culture" was being assimilated, he concludes, "was intricate and full of incongruities." [21] The same intricacies and incongruities abound in sixteenth-century English minglings of the new and old in life, literature, and general outlook. Tuthill is the rule, not the exception, for as we shall later see, its lesson is spelled out in the fusions of disparate traditions or styles within Tudor art, architecture, drama, narrative poetry and prose, literary criticism—indeed, within whatever the sixteenth-century Englishman saw, heard, read, and consequently created.

Although much of what the Elizabethans read can be documented, and though a great deal of what they created has survived, what they really saw can only be inferred from the nature of their descriptions: the things they single out as especially noteworthy and the significances they attach to them, or the things we know were there for them to see that either pass unnoticed or at least inspire little commentary. This is perhaps the main reason why Holinshed and his fellows are most valuable when they least measure up to our expectations. Rather than worrying about what we might easily assume to have been their central concern, the rise of constitutional monarchy, within several folio pages they conclude a magnificent battle, proceed to the appearance of a strange sea creature off the Cornish coast, pass on to lament the death of a most worthy noble, turn to an account of a most foul murder in Yorkshire, reflect for a paragraph on how a stormy summer raised the price of grain, and finally report the birth of a two-headed calf in Kent. Documents are given no more prominence than gossip, rumor, and often weakly founded moralizations; each event is equally important and set down with complete seriousness.

Moreover, these chroniclers seldom seem even concerned about fulfilling what a modern historian considers his major tasks. Rather than a dispassionate arrangement of evidence, they provide colorful pageants, drums and trumpets, anecdotes, random speculations, and far from objective marginal commentaries. More important, instead of attempting to see past events through the eyes of the men who acted them, they watch a prior era unfold through the spectacles of their own current dilemmas and special interests. Thus they happily evade the responsibility of rendering intelligible *all* of their predecessors' aspirations, anxieties, and consequent decisions. Whatever part of the story yields no contemporary significance is hurried over, while the remainder, events suggesting lessons for the harried times, is shaped accordingly.

The result of such cavalier historiography is nowhere better illustrated than in Holinshed's coverage of the important events of 1215. Among King John's varied activities during that year, the chronicler does not begrudge a passing reference to his enforced subscription to Magna Charta (II, 321), but it hardly inspires anything like his enthusiastic editorializations upon the events of 1213, when, according to the marginalia, "England became tributarie to the pope" (II, 307). Like Shakespeare, whose *King John* never even alludes to Magna Charta, and very probably like any other intelligent, up-to-date Elizabethan, Holinshed obviously does not find the alleged foundations of English and American civil liberties very exciting. Had Elizabeth been beheaded, he would no doubt have discovered the Great Charter worth commenting upon or at least quoting. Instead, he leaves its interpretation to the "zealous seventeenth-century Parliamentarians," who sought "a precedent for their political reforms" and consequently discovered in it "meanings . . . that would have astonished the original drafters of the document," [22] and to J. R. Green, the great nineteenth-century historian, who transformed "the roughneck barons of Runnymede into harbingers of nineteenth-century democracy and nationalism." [23] As early as 1642 the splendid message of Magna Charta was so obvious to John Milton that he felt constrained to point out why the opportunistic "prelates in time of popery were sometimes friendly enough to [it]." [24]

Whether we watch Bishop William Stubbs "adding Victorian liberalism to the cargo that the Anglo-Saxons brought with them to England from their North German forests" [25] or notice Master Raphael Holinshed practically ignoring Magna Charta yet including every vile word of "The sawcie speech of proud Pandulph the popes lewd legat, to king Iohn, in the presumptuous popes behalfe" (II, 306), we are observing the meaning of the past being racked upon the terms and expectations of the present. Stubbs was not writing with conscious partiality when he discovered political liberalism where it never existed. Guided by the belief "that knowledge justifies itself only by a capacity to solve current problems," [26] he found imaginary parallels irresistible, and therefore explained the data of the past by invoking modern, readily available, yet anachronistic frames of reference. Similarly, when Holinshed, with equal sincerity, dwelled at length upon 1213 and gave short shrift to 1215, he was just as naturally viewing John's encounters through his own day's burning issues. The thought of deposing his Lord's Anointed to gain a healthier Commonwealth would have startled Holinshed, but in 1570 Elizabeth *had* been excommunicated and her loyal subject indignantly "interlace[s] some rorings" of Pius V's "pestilent bull" (IV, 252).

Any account of the past thus highlighted by dilemmas of the present, whether Holinshed's tendencies to read 1570 into 1213 or more recent inclinations to regard More as a socialist and Machiavelli as a proto-Fascist, is obviously bad history. A student of the thirteenth century would have as slight a chance of discovering the whole truth about King John in Holinshed as a student of the fifteenth in finding the real Richard III amongst Holinshed's prejudiced contemporaries. For the student of sixteenth-century literature, however, what actually happened in either reign is for the most part irrelevant. Only if we were more interested in Shakespeare's accuracy as a historian than in his craft as a playwright would the question of whether Richard actually murdered his nephews, for example, become apposite. To contrast what happens in Shakespeare to the whole truth would only prove what would hardly occur to any sensible person to deny: The playwright was no better a historical scholar than the chronicler. The questions to be asked, to paraphrase Falstaff, must distinguish between Shakespeare's deliberate and unintentional lies, must center in the variances between Shakespeare and the "truth" he exploited, not between him and the real truth both he and his creditors were ignorant of.

But "truth" is more useful than truth in a second way. As well as underscoring which lies the Elizabethan artists inherited and which they artfully invented, the bad history of the sixteenth century— simply because it is bad, because it often tells us more about its writers than their subjects—offers valuable insights into what the era's educated men considered current dilemmas. Their desire to discover in the past situations paralleling the present, although naïve, is symptomatic; and the ingenuity expended in relating dissimilar historical contexts is revealing. To see John's reign out of perspective is not to see it without any perspective but through the wrong and, for our purposes, far more important Elizabethan perspective. In this sense Holinshed's silence tells us as much as his indignant outbursts, and Elizabethan chroniclers increase in value as they diminish in objectivity. Their uncritical habit of treating the past in their own terms, in other words, is both a caution against treating them in ours and a great aid toward our treating them in theirs. Although remaining thankful that Holinshed has read 1570 into 1213, we should strive to keep the 1970s out of either period and thus render the task of the twenty-fourth-century historian of the twentieth century more difficult than our own.

THE LITERARY RELEVANCE OF TUDOR FACTS AND ASSUMPTIONS

No criticism is more flimsy than the kind that explains all literature either as a reflection of events that never happened (for instance, the ever-rising Tudor middle class and the ever-falling Tudor aristocracy [27]) or as an expression of events that happened but hardly ever seem to have been noticed (for instance, the demise of chivalry, the growth of the Tudor state). Since literature is rather an expression of assumptions felt as facts, our search for relevant backgrounds is better answered by the chronicles, journals, diaries, sermons, or even the ballads and jest books of the sixteenth century than by the constitutional or economic historians of the twentieth, however proud in their knowledge that they know more about what actually happened under Elizabeth than the Elizabethans. But even those modern historians who attempt to consider the past in its own terms may betray us with a knowledge too accurate and complete. As Professor Jack Hexter notes, the writer of what we may call "good" history should

> envisage events as the men who lived through them did. Surely he should try to do that; just as certainly he must do more than that simply because he knows about those events what none of the men contemporary with them knew; he knows what their consequences were. To see the events surrounding the obscure monk Luther as Leo X saw them—as another 'monks' quarrel' and a possible danger to the perquisites of the Curia—may help us understand the peculiar inefficacy of Papal policy at the time; but that does not preclude the historian from seeing the same events as the decisive step towards the final breach of the religious unity of Western Civilization. We may be quite sure however that nobody at the time, not even Luther himself, saw those events that way. The historian who resolutely refused to use the insight that his own peculiar time gave him would not be superior to his fellows; he would be merely foolish, betraying a singular failure to grasp what history is. For history is a becoming, an ongoing, and it is to be understood not only in terms of what comes before but also of what comes after.[28]

Since an important part of history is its writing as well as its acts, the literary historian can no more ignore the "becoming" or "ongoing" nature of his subject than Hexter's wise chronicler. Like the best Elizabethan dramatists, who adapted character to the demands of plot yet shaped plot to reveal character, neither historian can avoid alternating between inductive and deductive thinking, between what the "event" meant at the moment it happened, its intrinsic importance, and that meaning and importance it later enjoyed owing to unconnected events as well to the actions it influenced. There are moments, however, when the good literary-historical critic will find it advantageous to attempt to freeze time, to suspend his insight and temporarily rule out consequences. If we wished to treat Luther as a literary figure, for example, and read his sermons as dramatic monologues, would all our superior knowledge about "the final breach of the religious unity of Western Civilization" help our efforts to experience the urgency of his invective, the vitality of his confidence, the agony of his searching? Or would not considerations of what the West later lost and gained, appeals to incidents in a sixth act written by Luther's successors, only hinder the dramatic moment?

On the other hand, despite our attempts to make that moment contain all moments, we cannot help realizing that the words that *are* the obscure monk's *were* the words of Luther and the Reformation. Perhaps the wisest course is to alternate between employing and suspending our knowledge of the consequences. Like the historian, we first judge the event or work in terms of what it led to, the relative significance of the role it played in its own tradition. Although in this way we temporarily lose sight of the work's intrinsic importance, we profit from a larger perspective. If we pretended to know nothing of literature after 1592, for example, we might easily assume that the English hexameter had a brighter future than Shakespeare. In that year Gabriel Harvey admitted his desire to "be epitaphed, The Inuentour of the English Hexameter—whome learned M. Stanihurst imitated in his Virgill, and excellent Sir Phillip Sidney disdained not to follow in his Arcadia & elsewhere. . . ." [29] But because we *do* know more about what Hexter calls "a future that has already been," because we realize that nothing much ever came of the English hexameter, that Sidney is remembered for other accomplishments, and that Shakespeare transmuted "inventions" of no greater intrinsic worth than Harvey's into masterpieces, we examine the drama of the 1580's with more enthusiasm. Our inquiries are thus encouraged by an awareness that greatness lies around the corner.

Once our superior knowledge has justified the inquiry, however, we may then profit by our ignorance and view the work in terms of what it is rather than what it perpetuated. *And this is where the historical critic and the good historian must part.* As Hexter implies, when Conyers Read examined the diplomatic maneuvers of Mr. Secretary Walsingham, his research would not have been helped had he suspended his realization that such maneuvers would ultimately contribute to the defeat of the Spanish Armada in 1588.[30] Although we, too, deal with actions and reactions, historical and literary "events" are not entirely of the same nature. In order to see a series of literary events clearly, none must be obscured by the tradition it inspired or continued; otherwise we court dangers Read the historian never confronted. Seeking merely to compare or contrast a work to its successor, we tend to miss those aspects that appear to have inspired no reaction.

In restricting our examination to the area of obvious equivalents, immediately recognizable similarities and differences, we treat the first work simply in terms of what was done to it and risk over-looking all those other—sometimes great and perhaps even unique —things its writer was trying to do.

Moreover, tempted by later events and desiring to claim as much as possible for our own century, we begin collecting literary "firsts." Those that point backward are safe enough. When we claim *Ralph Roister Doister* (c. 1553) as the first "regular" English comedy and *Gorboduc* (c. 1562) as the first English tragedy, we may be asked to explain what we mean by "regular," "comedy," and "tragedy." This in turn will raise questions about classical, medieval, and early Tudor dramatic traditions and how Udall, Sackville, and Norton interpreted them. But such questions are profitable; they bring into our considerations a knowledge of what came before, a knowledge that these Tudor playwrights also possessed and that may, therefore, help us better understand the nature and extent of their achievements. When our literary "first" points forward, however, we gain at best a bare fact, at worst an irrelevant half-truth, and certainly no aid in seeing the "first" more clearly. A question not to be asked, for instance, is whether Gascoigne's *Adventures of Master F. J.* (1573) or Lyly's *Euphues* (1579) or Nashe's *Unfortunate Traveller* (1594) qualifies as the first English novel. This inquiry is doomed from the outset, for it will only end up obscuring the accomplishments of three rather different Elizabethan storytellers amid the altogether different aims, techniques, and successes of Samuel Richardson, and will usually also ignore a hundred and fifty years of intervening experiments in prose fiction that at least partially explain Richardson's superior achievements. Such wide-ranging speculations are better left to those profound minds who prove (or disprove) the obvious su-periority of Chaucer to Milton or find in the philosophy of theo-logians who flourished before *Beowulf* the key to Shakespeare's covert meanings. We shall get much farther if we first establish the alternatives open to men of a certain time and place and then ask why they chose as they did.

The importance of accurately establishing the options as each sixteenth-century writer saw them can hardly be exaggerated, for in effect all our previous worries about anachronistic expecta-tions and concerns in discovering truly relevant backgrounds amount to no more than this. As its title implies, George Sellery's helpful study of *The Renaissance: Its Nature and Origins* handles much larger problems, but the necessity of seeing the past in its own terms continually emerges. Through considerations of the epoch's economics, fine arts, inventions, politics, commercial enterprises, philosophy, and philology, Sellery argues that the Renaissance was not a revolution led by classical scholars but a slow, natural evolution, continually stimulated by the "energies, hopes, and activities of vigorous people all over Western Europe," whose discoveries of America and artillery, the printing press and pagan wisdom were not caused by, but constituted the Renaissance.[31] The older, far more dramatic views of Jacob Burckhardt and his followers, which envisioned medieval man throwing off the fetters of a thousand years, rejoicing to discover his political, social, and spiritual individuality, suddenly seeing his mind and flesh and the world about him as interesting, even beautiful, certainly no longer sinful—such lyricism, Sellery implies, both overlooks important aspects of the Renaissance and betrays a great ignorance of the Middle Ages. "Many of the so-called Renaissance characteristics—for example, individualism, love of nature, and secularism or the concentration of human interest upon the affairs of this world—are to be found in broad reaches of the Middle Ages; and . . . many of the so-called medieval characteristics—submissiveness to authority, supernaturalism or interest in the transcendental, and superstition—were common in Renaissance times." [32]

It is not difficult to undermine Burckhardt's revolution with numerous instances of the new amid the old and the old amid the new. The danger lies in first pushing the Renaissance back to the middle of the not-so-dark Dark Ages and then steadily "evolving" its historicity out of existence. Henry Thode and Carl Neumann were among those who took the former course, and Sellery certainly inclines toward the latter. In 1885 Thode argued that St. Francis of Assisi, "by his preaching of the human Christ and of flower-bedecked nature as a revelation of God to man, really inspired the artistic and poetical achievements of the Italian Renaissance, while the art of classical antiquity had merely contributed formal and technical aid." [33] Eighteen years later Neumann, after contrasting the "progressive civilization of Western Europe" to its unprogressive Byzantine neighbor, decided that "it was not the revival of antiquity but rather medieval Christianity and the realistic Teutonic 'barbarians' that had made possible the rise of true modern individualism." [34] Such quests for modernity's prime mover remind us of how very similar all different things are if one simply looks hard enough. But to regress through a chronological everywhere, in which vague anticipations are equated with actual performances and general rules blurred by rare exceptions, only leads to a logical nowhere: *The Renaissance, having more or less always happened, never happened.*

Although the historical Darwinist may thus rightly temper the exaggerated claims of his revolutionary colleagues, his tendency to see all things flowing inevitably and gently cannot explain those genuinely dramatic moments in history, events that even today appear sudden and, if foreseeable, hardly inevitable. In what amounts to a plea to cultivate our sense of the catastrophic, Hexter notes how the nineteenth-century historians used Darwin to evolve one large error out of two small facts. One fact is that the middle class and nationalism are first faintly discernible in the twelfth century; the other is that in the nineteenth, both attain unquestionable ascendancy. Nothing was "more natural for a historian committed to evolutionary gradualism than to connect" low ebb and high flood "by an ascending straight line," even though the beauty of such a construction "does not set historical facts in order." [35] In understanding the triumph of the English middle class in 1832, it may be more profitable to consider the far from inevitable, quite perceptible, hardly "oozing" developments across the Channel in 1789 than to glance back to Tudor England, where the middle class, like the aristocracy, daily rose and fell. What actually happened at the turn of the fifteenth century includes some wholly unpredictable events.

> Luther successfully defies the Pope; the conquistadors discover the precious metal hoards and mines of America. Within a few decades . . . the areas in which men can get along on the more-or-less type of decision shrink. The areas in which they have to face either-or decisions expand. As such decisions increase in number, they also increase in importance; both what decisions will have to be made next, and what their proximate consequences will be, become increasingly hard for contemporaries to predict, and the stream of happenings flows not with glacial majesty but with devastating violence. [36]

Once we have removed our evolutionary spectacles, then, some rather mountainous events begin to take focus amid the Darwinist's minute gradations of historical contours. And if we, removed and dispassionate, find these events truly catastrophic, how staggering must they have seemed to the men who had neither Darwin nor a certain knowledge of the consequences to moderate their hopes and fears. Did Henry VIII's subjects, along with Miranda, find mankind beauteous and their world entirely brave and new? If so, did their Elizabethan grandsons reply, with Prospero, " 'Tis new to thee"? The question is impossible to answer simply, if at all. Their answers would likely have depended upon whether they were Catholics or Protestants and which royal marriage seemed about to go forward, or whether Drake had recently landed, or Darnley been murdered, or Norfolk executed, or the Armada dispersed. The main thing to notice is that the evolutionary historian's detections of the old amid the new do not prove that the Elizabethans could never have believed their world essentially new, even unique, but merely that such views—if indeed they were held—would have often been unwarranted.

Despite the likelihood that the men who experienced such anxious days must have found the alternatives sudden and awesome, one searches in vain for a trustworthy witness's explicit claim that his event is as new and brave as Miranda's "creatures," that the world will now be profoundly changed and the course of human affairs irrevocably altered. The least ambiguous testimony is contained in the Tudor moralists' social criticism; with hardly an exception they not only denounce "climbing merchants, land-getting nobodies, and aristocrats who waste their substance or marry business fortunes" but also affirm that these evils are entirely modern, "that in the good old days nobles were liberal and hospitable but never prodigal; they did not sell their land. And merchants, industrious and honest, never greedy or grasping, did not seek to buy it, but were satisfied in the place to which God had called them." [37] But if their accusations ring loudly and clearly, their fellow moralists in the fourteenth and fifteenth centuries had lamented precisely the same "new" vices, and the history of medieval and Renaissance land transactions lends little support to what they see—or pretend to see—as outrageous novelties. Since as students of literature we are mainly interested in assumptions felt as facts, however, none of the Tudor moralists' claims can be rejected merely because it is unfounded. Perhaps, as Hexter conjectures, they really thought that they were honoring the facts of the past and that their grievances were new.

Their social ideal was the hierarchical society of fixed
social orders, and such a society they found in the 'histories' which were their regular diet—the romances of
chivalry. Here indeed was the society of the moralist's
dream, where knights were liberal and generous, town folk
industrious, humble, or preferably non-existent, peasants
docile and dutiful, a society above all without an economy, where there were no scarce goods, spending but no
getting. . . . This cloud-cuckoo land may be a world
of dreams to us; to many men up through the sixteenth
century it was no dream at all but a fact as living, more
living, than anything that had actually happened in the
days long before their birth. When Henry VII named his
first son Arthur he was not making a casual curtsey to a
lightly held fairy story; he was attaching his new dynasty
to that segment of the past which contemporary Englishmen most vividly knew.[38]

But in assuming that all sixteenth-century Englishmen recalled a
golden past, we have still not established that the moralist's readers
shared his professed convictions concerning a uniquely dismal present. Although both writer and reader vividly remembered what
had never happened, surely the social critic's exaggerated claims
about *contemporary* innovations would have been measured against
what his audience could not fail to observe: ruthless nobodies who
grasped and fell; merchants who went bankrupt; merchants who
succeeded and, for some mysterious reason, became liberal and
hospitable; recalcitrant aristocrats who refused to squander their
fortunes; foolish nobles, both the charitable and the niggardly, who
mismanaged their affairs and therefore decayed. If each group saw
the past in the moralist's terms of fixed social orders, the present
state of flux would probably have been regarded as new and evil,
or new and good, or new and challenging, or new and disheartening, and the responses would more likely have varied according to
each man's wit, abilities, temperament, previous fortune, and current successes than according to whether he had been meanly
or gently born. In our search for relevant backgrounds, then, the
danger lies not in accepting the moralist's dreams simply because
they were only dreams, but in assuming that all such dreams were
universally honored.

In the first four years of the 1580's, for example, Munday, Gos-

son, Field, Stubbes, and Babington tell their readers that the play-
houses outside London celebrate, and thereby inspire in their
audiences, riots, rapes, procuring, incest, murder, and treason. For
Munday, both a player and a playwright himself—and therefore,
one would expect, a trustworthy authority—the theaters are a
"schoole of Bauderie . . . the nest of the Diuel [devil], . . . sinke
of al sinne" and "a den of theeues and adulterers"; even death-
bed confessions are cited to prove what "filthie infections" are
daily communicated by the players' lascivious and "abhominable
speeches." [39] Although it may seem presumptuous to question such
eyewitness accounts, they hardly tally with several other facts.
First, none of the fifty-seven extant plays printed or entered for
printing between 1557 and 1580 supports Munday's accusations;
most are moral to the point of being tedious. Secondly, the players
were, as Munday himself complains, "Caterpillers," living off the
hard-earned wages of their *honest* audiences. It seems safe to assume, then, that the spectators were mainly responsible citizens
on holiday, continually demanding, paying for, and getting their
pleasures, but hardly at the cost of being robbed, murdered, de-
flowered, or otherwise contaminated by unspeakable lewdness. Had
London contained enough bawds and bullies to fill the theaters
continually, the actors might not have considered it advantageous
to run an honest business. Since things were quite the other way,
and since the players would have had royal as well as civic displeasure to reckon with if they had not been, we may dismiss
Munday's outcries as professional pamphleteering, the indignation of a hack who wrote for and against the stage with
more ease than conviction, whose muse is only sometimes moral
but always marketable.

If by way of evading the impossible question of what the era as
a whole considered new and brave we focus upon the life and
works of a single man, we still confront contradictory evidence.
At the other end of the century is a moralist of far greater education and stature than Munday, John Colet, one of the leading
first-generation Christian Humanists and the center, according to
his friend, Erasmus, of that small band of Oxford scholars and
reformers (including Grocyn, Linacre, and More) that flourished
about 1500.[40] Certainly the beauteous side of the ledger should include Colet's zeal for his own and others' education, his profound
belief in learning as an encouragement to piety, and his founding
and endowing of St. Paul's School, which John Milton attended

a century later. Under new and brave we might place Colet's humanistic, classical, and "existential" approach to Holy Writ. At Oxford in 1497 he delivered a series of public lectures on St. Paul's Epistle to the Romans; instead of a word-by-word scholastic and allegorical interpretation of Paul's letter, he employed a "free critical exposition of the obvious meaning of the text as a whole," illustrated the writer's personality, and compared his "references to the state of Roman society with Suetonius," a biographer who flourished shortly after Paul. Instead of treating his text as a series of infallible pronouncements, Colet rejected much of the doctrine of verbal inspiration, used Paul to support his own dissatisfaction with the condition of the Church, stressed the importance of loving rather than merely knowing God, and quoted not the medieval schoolmen but the Neo-Platonic philosophers of Cosimo de' Medici's Academy. For all his innovations, however, Colet remained a very conservative revolutionary. If his scriptural exegesis makes use of Suetonius, it also "often takes refuge in mystical subtleties." If he preaches Lollard sentiments before a convocation summoned to extirpate the Lollard heresy, it is "almost certain that the Lutheran Reformation, which he indirectly encouraged, . . . would have altogether exceeded his sense of the situation's needs" and that, had he lived, the man who publicly denounced Henry VIII's Continental wars in 1513 would have gone to the scaffold with his friend More in 1535.

The lives and works of men as unlike as Colet and Munday tell us something further about the relationship between literature and its backgrounds. Although it is only sensible to see history in its own terms, and usually helpful to place a piece of literature within that "chronistic" historical context, it is always dangerous to reverse our evidence and use the work as an infallible index of the assumptions that inspired it. "Moral outrage!" screams Munday, but is he moved by any crisis other than earning his daily bread? Colet, on the other hand, who had every reason to be one of the most anxious men of his time, and More, who faced awesome alternatives long before Henry's Act of Supremacy, temper their lives and writings with sweet reason and charity. While honoring Hexter's sense of the catastrophic, then, we must not always expect to find it expressed in the era's literature. Sometimes the crisis has been "filtered" through a revolutionary who justifies his leap forward with glances at the past, who wants his radical program to succeed enough to describe it as altogether proper, conservative, and traditional, while the pamphleteer, more interested in advancing himself than his ostensible cause, trumpets an important detection of the old, obvious, or nonexistent.

For the most part, writers throughout the century, regardless of education, social and literary stature, or religious and political orientation, freely mingle reflections of the old with anticipations of the new. The extent to which they are conscious that their "old" is fresh and their "new" traditional is often difficult to determine, but some of their most explicit claims must not be trusted. Notice, for example, the red herring within the very title of George Gascoigne's *Pleasant Fable of Ferdinando Jeronimi and Leonora de Valasco, Translated out of the Italian Riding Tales of Bartello* (1575). Pleasant or not, this *Fable* was first published anonymously in 1573 as *The Adventures of Master F. J.*, and celebrated a clandestine affair among some accomplished gentlefolk in a northern English manor. Because his first version of the story was condemned as immoral and—perhaps for good reason—suspected of containing current scandal, Gascoigne not only excised some of the allegedly improper material and added an apologetic foreword to "the reverend divines," but, while shifting his setting from England to Italy, conjured up a nonexistent Italian book and author in the bargain. Whether fearful of the "divines," the Queen, or a libel suit, the man who later called himself "Chaucer's boy [apprentice], and Petrarch's journeyman" [41] has simply adopted the characteristically Chaucerian pose of ascribing what is entirely original to "olde auctoritees."

We find this process reversed throughout Sir Philip Sidney's *Astrophel and Stella*, published in 1591 but written in the early 1580's. Few sixteenth-century sonneteers insist more explicitly, frequently, or convincingly that their careful artifice is personal, spontaneous, entirely original. "Let Dainty wittes cry, on the Sisters nine" (III), pleads the Starlover; "I Never dranke of *Aganippe* [the Muses'] well" (LXXIV). His verse flows smoothly not because he is a "Pickepurse of an others wit," but owing to Stella's kiss, which has inspired and sweetened his lips (LXXIV), and because he has followed his own muse's direction to "looke in thy heart and write" (I). Despite Astrophel's artful protests of artlessness, however, there was engraved upon that heart not only Stella's revivifying image, but the lines of lyric poets dating back to Petrarch. If in our misguided attempts to honor Sidney's "sincerity" we fail to recognize his themes as often trite and his pose as almost conventional, we are in no position to appreciate the new life he has breathed into them.

This brief cross-examination of Munday, Colet, Gascoigne, and Sidney appears to substantiate our earlier impressions. Whether the witness seems personally embroiled or dispassionate and reflective, whether the world he portrays is brave, new, sordid, or disheartening, his testimony may be only twenty-five per cent fact, twenty-five per cent genuine assumption, and the remainder "tainted" by influences as unlike as Munday's quest for lucre and Sidney's for artful design. The validity of each claim, in short, is roughly equal to the event plus the explicit meaning given that event by its reporter, both divided by his "ulterior" motives. Any portion of the writer's meaning that reflects an eccentric personality or an unconventional premise must of course be added to his "ulterior" motives, even though each may be quite sincere, for we must be sure that his claim is truly representative, and make allowances for a view that in its own time may have seemed merely propagandistic, fanatical, the mark of genius, or otherwise exceptional.

Perhaps several paragraphs from Holinshed will illustrate this formula. The first is his epilogue to the reign of Queen Mary (1553–1558); the second initiates "The Peaceable and Prosperous Regiment of Blessed Queene Elisabeth" (1558–1603); the third is taken from his eulogy of Edward Stanley, third Earl of Derby (1508–1572).

> Thus farre the troublesome reigne of Queene Marie the first of that name (God grant she may be the last of hir religion) eldest daughter to king Henrie the eight. (IV, 154)

> After all the stormie, tempestuous, and blustering windie weather of queene Marie was ouerblowne, the darkesome clouds, of discomfort dispersed, the palpable fogs and mists of most intollerable miserie consumed, and the dashing showers of persecution ouerpast: it pleased God to send England a calme and quiet season, a cleare and louelie sunshine, a quitsest [quittance or release] from former broiles, of a turbulent estate, and a world of blessings by good queene Elisabeth: into whose gratious reigne we are now to make an happie entrance as followeth. (IV, 155)

> His life and death deseruing commendation, and crauing memorie to be imitated, was such as followeth. His fidelitie vnto two kings and two queenes in dangerous times and

great rebellions, in which time, and alwaies as cause serued, he was lieutenant of Lancashire and Cheshire, and latelie offered ten thousand men vnto the queenes maiestie *of his owne charge* for the suppression of the last rebellion. His godlie disposition to his tenants, neuer forcing anie seruice at their hands, but due paiment of their rent. His *liberalitie to strangers,* and such as shewed themselves gratefull to him. His *famous housekeeping, and eleuen score in checkroll* [i.e., as his personal dependents], never discontinuing the space of twelue yeares. *His feeding especiallie of aged persons* twise a daie three score and od; . . . and euerie good fridaie . . . another two thousand seauen hundred, with meat, drinke, monie, and monie worth. . . . His yeerlie portion for the expenses of his house foure thousand pounds. His cunning in setting bones disiointed or broken, his surgerie and desire to helpe the poore, . . . and his ioie that he died in the queenes fauour. His ioifull parting this world, *his taking leaue of all his seruants by shaking of hands,* and his remembrance to the last daie. (IV, 320–321. Italics added.)

When these sentiments first appeared in 1577, how many of Holinshed's readers would have found them completely valid? Certainly none could have taken exception to the three facts contained in his accounts of Mary's exit and Elizabeth's entrance: Mary, Henry's elder daughter, died, and her sister succeeded her. But the objective portion is merely a point of departure for the chronicler's rhetoric: a pious parenthesis followed by a stream of richly connotative adjectives, metaphors, and value judgments—in effect, four-fifths of his "information." The most loyal Catholics would have resented "troublesome" and perhaps read no further. Holinshed's loyal-Catholic–loyal-English readers might have allowed "troublesome" and even "showers of persecution," for Elizabeth's reign had indeed been a relatively "peaceable and prosperous regiment." Unlike both Pope and Puritan, she insisted only upon outward conformity and left her subjects' consciences to God. While hardly concurring with the chronicler's parenthetical aside, then, many Catholics might have even been able to digest his "louelie sunshine."

But by 1577 the great majority of Englishmen thought of 1558 no more objectively than Holinshed; for them the most metaphori-

cal—to us, melodramatic—portions of his account came closest to
the real meaning of that truly blessed event. Whether London
craftsman, Cambridge professor, or courtier at Whitehall, they
shared Holinshed's sturdy Protestant assumptions and nationalis-
tic motives: a distrust of foreigners in general and papists like
Philip of Spain in particular; a horror of the needless persecution
and civil "broiles" that had almost destroyed England in the fifteenth century and were now bringing anarchy to France; a
reverence toward the Queen that often amounted to adoration. If
the description of Mary's reign supplied by the bourgeois Holinshed, a lowly translator for the London printing office of Reginald Wolfe, strikes us as bigoted and demogogic, we must remember that three years later Sidney, the intelligent aristocrat, the
perfect Elizabethan courtier, Humanist, and man of letters, told the
Queen that her splendid suitor, the French Duke of Anjou, was
"a Papist, in whom (howsoever fine wits may find further dealings
or painted excuses) *the very common people well know this*, that
he is the son of a Jezabel of our age, and that his brother made
oblation of his own sister's marriage the easier to make massacres
of our brethren in belief." [42] Sidney, of course, was recalling what
he saw in Paris on St. Bartholomew's Day (August 23), 1572, the
murder of several thousand French Protestants, and English indignation had not been soothed when medals commemorating this
"victory" were later struck in Paris and by the Pope.

And always fanning Protestant fears was Mary, the French
Catholic Queen of Scots, who had fled Scotland in 1568 and remained, until her execution in 1587, a prospective English queen
for Catholic Englishmen. Fifteen months after her death, Philip
launched his Invincible Armada, and it is unfortunate that Holinshed died too soon to hear his blessed Sovereign amid her troops
at Tilbury:

> My loving people, we have been persuaded by some
> that are careful of our safety, to take heed how we com-
> mit ourselves to armed multitudes, for fear of treachery.
> But I assure you, I do not desire to live to distrust my
> faithful and loving people. Let tyrants fear. I have always
> so behaved myself that, under God, I have placed my
> chiefest strength and safeguard in the loyal hearts and good
> will of my subjects; and therefore I am come amongst
> you, as you see, . . . to live or die amongst you all, to lay

down for my God, and for my kingdom, and for my people, my honour and my blood, even in the dust. I know I have the body of a weak and feeble woman, but I have the heart and stomach [courage] of a king, and of a king of England too.[43]

With some of her grandfather's political astuteness and a dash of her father's flair for the dramatic, Elizabeth thus entrusted herself to, and inspired trustworthiness in, her most loving subjects. If in 1558 even some Protestants were not completely convinced that they were on the threshold of countless blessings, by 1588, when the dramatists were setting Holinshed's scenes and sentiments on stage, even many Catholics had succumbed to the royal touch. Aided by papal blunders and Continental fanaticism, the Queen cultivated her chronicler's honest assumptions and publicly transmuted his value judgments into self-evident truths.

Holinshed's eulogy of the Earl of Derby reveals equally important though less controversial assumptions. He tells us nothing about Derby, the ward of Cardinal Wolsey, or about the Earl's strong opposition to religious reformation in the reign of Edward VI. Also absent is Derby's consequent joy at the accession of Mary, his being made a regular member of her Privy Council, a special commissioner for the trial of Lady Jane Grey, and a partner in the proceedings against heretics. And although Holinshed touches upon Derby's retention as a member of Elizabeth's Privy Council and his giving the government timely warning of the Catholic insurrection of 1569, he fails to note that the Earl's old "sympathies and connections rendered him an object of suspicion" to the Queen.[44] How easily Holinshed could have honored all the facts and proceeded from Derby, Mary's heretic hunter, to Derby, Elizabeth's chastiser of recusants, thereby turning "as cause serued" into "as time serued his cause." But in his portrait of the great and good old man, Holinshed skirts the controversial and enlarges upon those virtues that, irrespective of one's religious and political persuasions, craved "memorie to be imitated." When Derby's fidelity and charity were put in phrases like those italicized in the passage on page 67, who could gainsay them?

Now notice how profoundly medieval those unquestionably valid values are. Do "of his owne charge" and "eleuen score in checkroll" take us back to the great feudal barons of the thirteenth century? Or back only one year to Tuthill, when "it was thought good" to answer medieval judicial ceremony in its own language? In calling Derby's portrait "medieval," of course, we are not insisting that great hospitality and large private armies became extinct under Elizabeth. We are instead claiming that had Sir John Stanley (1350?–1414), the founder of the family fortunes under both Richard II and Henry IV, been eulogized by an early fifteenth-century chronicler, the same "timeless" virtues would have been stressed.

In a recent study of English chivalry we are told that "by the middle decades of the sixteenth century it was no longer possible for the intellectually alert Englishman to accept chivalric values as a system sufficient for the secular needs of the governing class," that having once "absorbed the New Learning" and "adjusted . . . to the truly national meaning of the Tudor state," he could return to chivalry "only in a spirit of nostalgia and in an atmosphere of romance." [45] But the development of chivalry-taken-as-fact to chivalry-known-to-be-fiction cannot be so precisely ascertained. The right of trial by combat, although circumvented by Elizabeth in 1571, was guaranteed under her successors until 1819.[46] And when Holinshed lamented the passing of great lords as if he were a lost retainer, unaware that his stay was in the Tudor state, there is no evidence that his readers were "intellectually alert" enough to regard his case as arrested development. On the contrary, in the middle decades of the sixteenth century the powerful northern Earls of Westmoreland and Northumberland, leaders of "men . . . reluctant to know any prince but a Percy or a Neville," [47] drove their armies south to liberate, in good fifteenth-century fashion, their rightful monarch, Mary of Scotland. When Northumberland and many of his liegemen were executed in the early 1570's, presumably none had even grasped, much less adjusted to, the Tudor state's "truly national meaning."

The "Meaning" of the Earl of Essex

Perhaps we should not expect intellectual alertness among the petty princes of the north, where the old faith and ancient habits and loyalties persisted. Let us therefore banish the backward third of Elizabeth's domain and try London itself, thirty years later, when that dashing Hotspur of the south, the Earl of Essex, attempted a similarly ill-fated uprising. Essex admittedly lacked both the calculating statesmanship of his adviser, Francis Bacon, and the political sophistication of his chief enemy, Sir Robert Cecil. His intellect, however, was probably as keen as that of his fellow conspirator, Shakespeare's patron, the Earl of Southampton, and his generosity, physical courage, courtly charm, and romantic flair inspired in both commoner and noble a popularity often equaling the Queen's. And although he no doubt lacked Sidney's sense of disinterested honor, when that knight whom Spenser considered "the president / Of noblesse and of chevalree" [48] died in 1586, Essex, who married Sidney's widow, also appears to have satisfied his country's need for a pattern of chivalry even more than his romantic rival, Sir Walter Raleigh.

We catch our first glimpse of his doughty deeds at Zutphen in September, 1586; Sidney is mortally wounded and Essex, only nineteen, created knight banneret for his boldness in the skirmish.[49] Three years later he sails with Norris and Drake to attack Lisbon. He is the first to wade through the surf to the Portuguese shore and later stands before the gates of the city, offering "to fight any of the Spanish garrison in the name of his mistress." [50] In 1591 he commands the siege of Rouen and challenges his rival general, Villars, to single combat. The offer, though unaccepted, does not pass unnoticed; it evokes a compliment on the knight-errantry of Englishmen from Cayet, a contemporary French chronicler. The next four years are relatively dull. Influenced by Bacon's injunction to abandon military ambition, Essex remains close to Court, impatiently resolved to secure "domestical greatness." But the "secular needs of the governing class," which Bacon must have kept before his young lord, are better answered by men like the Cecils, the faithful old Burleigh and his frail, hunchbacked son, Robert. In 1596 Essex, tired of closet diplomacy, leads three thousand men in the capture of Cadiz. At the order to enter the harbor, the youthful commander flings his heavily plumed hat into the sea, while Raleigh replies to the cannon shots from the Spanish fort with scornful fanfares of trumpets.

J. E. Neale finds in the Cadiz campaign "a perfect example of that dashing, careless bravery upon which Fortune was prone to smile. . . . The boyish competition to steal the lead and find a place in the bottleneck where the naval engagement took place; the reckless scaling of the town walls: all these were of a piece with the courtesy, humanity, and generosity of Essex in his treatment of the people of Cadiz after its capture. *They read like pages of a romance,* and even the Spaniards were moved to praise." [51] If not in fact, at least "in the popular mind this glorious and chivalrous youth [is] the victor of Cadiz, the personification of England at war." [52] He returns laden with spoil, the people's darling, the Queen's favorite, a national hero eulogized from the pulpit of St. Paul's; he also finds himself "braved by [Bacon's] little cousin," Robert Cecil, who has been appointed Elizabeth's secretary in his absence. Even worse, the following year his derring-do is much less successful: The Spanish treasure fleet returning from the Indies evades Essex's squadron, and it is a terrible thing to face a thrift-conscious Queen with little booty.

But England is yet unwilling to cashier its theme of honor and renown, and the Irish rebellion offers Essex another escape from the exacting pursuit of domestical greatness. Against so capable and subtle a man as Hugh O'Neil, Earl of Tyrone, failure is quite possible, but Essex cannot afford so great an honor passing to a rival. Perhaps even for him it is difficult to know where chivalry ends and jealous vanity begins. Does he not still possess an unrivaled military following, men whom he himself, to the consternation of the Queen and Burleigh, unwarrantedly knighted? Does he not also still enjoy the popularity of London, of the citizens whom he courted during his magnificent exits and entrances? Spenser's *Prothalamion* (1596) best illustrates the role Essex has always seemed to fit and is finally once more granted:

> Yet therein [Essex House] now doth lodge a noble peer,
> Great Englands glory and the worlds wide wonder,
> Whose dreadfull name late through all Spaine did thunder,
> And Hercules two pillors standing neere
> Did make to quake and feare.
> Faire branch of honor, flower of chevalrie,
> That fillest England with thy triumphes fame,
> Joy have thou of thy noble victorie, . . .
> That through thy prowesse and victorious armes
> Thy country may be freed from forraine harmes;
> And great Elisaes glorious name may ring
> Through al the world, fil'd with thy wide alarmes. . . .
>
> (ll. 145 ff.)

England, in short, expects another Cadiz, and when Essex departs from London in March, 1599, with the largest army that has ever left the realm during Elizabeth's reign, the very people who have been so sorely taxed for this fruitless expedition line the streets to cry their good wishes for Chivalry's Flower.

It is not only hack poets like Thomas Churchyard who wax eloquent over Essex's abilities to effect "A wished Reformation of Wicked Rebellion" (1598); the first performance of Shakespeare's *Henry V* can be dated by its Chorus's patriotic expectation of Essex's impending victory. Just as London celebrated Henry's return from Agincourt, so

> by a lower but loving likelihood,
> Were now the General of our gracious Empress—
> As in good time he may—from Ireland coming,
> Bringing rebellion broached on his sword,
> How many would the peaceful city quit
> To welcome him!
>
> (Prologue, V. 29–34)

But the most remarkable fanfare is sounded by John Hayward about one month before Essex's departure. There is nothing passing strange about a young Elizabethan lawyer's interest in applying past history to present problems. Hayward's *First Part of the Life and Reign of King Henry IV*, which chronicles Bolingbroke's rise as far as Richard II's deposition, can be simply interpreted as an extension of *Gorboduc*. During the Queen's first years Sackville and Norton had dramatized ancient "history" to illustrate the dangers of a realm divided against itself and of an unsettled succession, a sermon Elizabeth hardly needed; during her last years, *perhaps*, Hayward is merely seeking to remind England about impious rebellion and its cousin, anarchy. Nor need we find anything suspicious in his dedicating the book to Essex, the man Elizabeth herself had finally appointed to quell those notoriously rebellious Irishmen. The rubs lie in the terms with which he salutes the general, "You are indeed great, in present judgment and in the expectation of future time," and in the chronicle's preface, signed by one "A.P.," which points out that history reveals "not only precepts but lively patterns both for private direction and for affairs of state." [53] Is Hayward unaware that even as Essex prepares to battle Tyrone, he complains of leaving the Queen surrounded by evil counselors, and that those same evil counselors in turn maintain that he seeks to be a second Bolingbroke? If Hayward does not realize why the first three quartos of Shakespeare's *Richard II*

(1597, 1598, 1598) have been printed without the deposition scene, his subsequent imprisonment in the Tower will likely give him time to reflect.

Whereas Fortune turned recklessness into bravery at Cadiz, she now exposes it as dashing ineptitude. Against the Queen's express instructions, Essex postpones a confrontation with Tyrone in Ulster, dallies across Leinster into Munster, creates more knights, and refuses to dismiss Southampton as his General of the Horse. After two months of campaigning, Essex returns to Dublin "with a broken and weary army and no feat to boast of but the taking of a paltry castle," [54] while back home the Queen sarcastically notes that she is allowing him a thousand pounds a day to go on progress. Even worse than the ruinous expense is the fact that he is making "that base bush kern—Tyrone—to be accounted so famous a rebel." Almost five months after landing in Ireland, the "worlds wide wonder" finally confronts the "bush kern," but only to parley peace, not quell wicked rebellion. Tyrone sends word that if the Earl will follow his advice, he will make him the greatest man that ever was in England,[55] and Essex's enemies will later produce vague confessions of Irish retainers to prove that he "discussed the probability of his becoming king of England, and . . . promised in that case to make Tyrone viceroy of Ireland." [56] Neither the Queen nor her Council will ever be certain about Essex's understanding with Tyrone; even modern historians call the events of September 3–9, 1599, perplexing. But in August and September Essex continues to disregard orders, dubbing thirty-eight knights (and thereby creating new followers), getting his officers to subscribe to a resolution dissenting from the Ulster campaign (perhaps a reasonable procedure in modern eyes, but a strange piece of insolence then), formulating conditions of peace that almost amount to "Ireland for the Irish," and finally, despite the Queen's injunction not to desert his post, arriving in London with a " 'competent number' of choice men" on September 28.[57]

If such exploits give Essex's enemies new cause to murmur about a second Bolingbroke, the last seventeen months of his life make the parallel irresistible. During the first nine he is committed to the custody of Lord Keeper Egerton while Elizabeth plays a waiting game with public opinion. It is not difficult to understand why London is now crowded with knights, officers, and soldiers. Many have deserted the Irish expedition to answer their leader's need; most are possessed by a hatred of Cecil, Raleigh, and others of the opposite faction; all are driven by loyalty, "chivalry," vested military interests. But why such men are easily able to inflame the civilians of London cannot be so logically explained. Essex had wasted men, material, and money through stubborn disobedience and gross mismanagement. But the Earl is still their darling. They had flocked in "thousands to watch him at his recreations and shooting-matches," and he had obviously "taken infinite pleasure and pride in the sweet music of their praise." [58] They insist upon remaining loyal both to their hero and to their hero's Queen, and therefore vent their fury on Cecil. Villainous remarks about his character are scrawled even on the walls of the Court; over his door is written, "Here lieth the Toad." Essex falls ill, and some divines pray God to strengthen "noble Barak thy servant" and thus bring grief to "all wicked Edomites that bear evil will to Zion." [59] The moral is obvious: Essex keeps his armor, if not his honor, highly polished, while the far more competent Cecil devotes his life to the secular needs of the governing class. One evokes worship, even among the era's best poets; the other inspires only ugly graffiti.

But Essex's romantic nature now leads to his undoing. The Queen's postponements and eventual abandonment of Star Chamber proceedings indicate that she wishes a chastened, not a broken, servant; his cue is complete submission, and when he appears before a specially constituted court at York House on June 5, 1600, to be accused only of contempt and disobedience, not disloyalty, he appears to have mastered his passionate personality. Even some members of the select audience burst into tears when "Great Englands glory" is stripped of all offices. But both before and after the following August, when he is finally free to go anywhere save to the Court, Essex continues his intrigues. To Elizabeth go adulatory, seductive letters, requesting tokens of restored favor; from his close friend, Mountjoy, who now controls the Irish army, go secret missives to James VI of Scotland, promising that if James will prepare an army, Mountjoy will bring troops from Ireland, put Essex back in power, and declare James heir to the throne.[60] But the messenger returning with James's cautious answer is discovered and imprisoned, and Mountjoy answers Essex's renewed requests with proverbs about patience. In the autumn of 1600 his pleas to the Queen for at least one favor, a renewal of his highly lucrative lease of the customs on sweet wines, proves equally vain.

The desperate master of Essex House now throws its doors open to all his similarly desperate adherents. Zealous Puritans visit and preach; crowds of Londoners come to be instructed. Also in attendance is his sister, Lady Rich—Sidney's "sweet Stella," now as proud and resolute as Lady Macbeth. On Tuesday, February 3, the plot is hatched at Southampton's Drury House. Whitehall shall be seized, and Elizabeth forced to dismiss her "evil" counselors and summon a new Parliament. From almost every county Essex's "retainers" pour into London. On Friday, some attempt to inflame London further by having Shakespeare's company perform that by now ominous *Tragedy of King Richard the Second*. The players doubt that such an old play (six years at most!) will draw an audience. When Essex's friends swear to add forty shillings to the receipts, the actors consent, foolishly failing to mark the example of Master Hayward. On Saturday, Richard is deposed in the afternoon and Essex commanded to appear before the Council in the evening. His refusal inspires a deputation of Privy Councillors to appear Sunday morning in the name of the Queen. At first greeted by cries of "Kill them! Cast the Great Seal out of the window!" [61] they are held as hostages while Essex and two hundred of his liegemen hurry to raise London.

For once, however, the city that has always responded to the stuff of heroic poetry remains stolid, prosaic. Perhaps it is the herald, close upon the Earl's heels, proclaiming that awesome word, "Traitor." By now the gate he has entered is locked, the chained street blocked by armed men. His charge is repulsed. Having managed to regain Essex House by the Thames, he soon discovers his hostages gone and the Lord Admiral threatening to bombard his residence. He resolves to go forth alone and die fighting, then surrenders. The next day, February 9, Elizabeth issues a proclamation thanking the citizens for their loyalty. Shakespeare's company, evidently freed from suspicion, plays at Court two weeks later.[62] The following morning Essex finally enjoys a royal favor, a request that his execution for high treason be private, lest "the acclamation of the people might [be] a temptation unto [me]." [63]

The real truth of Essex's exploits, the plain facts of his attempted uprising, reveals the sordid designs of a vainglorious thirty-four-year-old adolescent. Many a modern *coup d'état* contains the same kinds of characters, incidents, and "patriotic" themes, echoes of Essex's cries as he charged up Ludgate Hill and along Cheapside: "For the Queen! For the Queen! A plot is laid for my life!" [64] But London did not shirk her self-seeking hero out of respect for such facts. The "truth" of Essex's bold chivalry, the assumption that this symbol of nobility would be victimized by the Toad and his fellow Court reptiles, was weighed against the "truth" of Gloriana, their most loving and merciful sovereign. It is unlikely that most citizens realized that the latter "truth" had a better foundation; it is extremely doubtful that any struggled through the crisis of Sunday morning fortified by reflections upon the national meaning of the Tudor state. One profoundly personal loyalty finally drove out the other.

Preposterous as it may seem to us (for we cannot experience Essex's "poetry" except through the praises of such excited witnesses as Spenser), many Englishmen were never quite sure they had made the right choice. The daring plot of several apprentices to raise a company of five thousand to free Essex and then storm the Court betrays, as Neale notes, "the romantic illusions of their class," [65] but if less given to wild schemes, other classes seem to have shared the equally romantic illusion of Essex's noble worth. His private execution did not prevent Derrick, the hangman, from being mobbed upon returning from the Tower; only the timely arrival of some sheriffs prevented his murder. The legend of Essex's ring, once sent by Elizabeth with the understanding "that she would pardon him any offence if he sent it her when in danger, and that just before his death he forwarded it to the Countess of Nottingham, who [wickedly] retained it," [66] underlines the common desire to provide a romantic epitaph for the man who died quietly, humbly, even devoutly. Tracts against entangling alliances with Spain (1624, 1642) were ascribed to the ghost of this sturdy champion, "sent from Elizium to the Nobility, Gentry, and Commonaltie of England"; the legend of the ring was elaborated upon throughout the seventeenth and eighteenth centuries. Under official instructions the preachers at St. Paul's Cross painted Essex black; the government published his treasons and as late as 1605 was suppressing all attempted exculpations, though one sympathetic treatment was printed at Antwerp and smuggled into England.[67]

The government had truth on its side, of course, and with our hindsight even we can perceive what Elizabeth probably foresaw: England's greatness was more dependent upon competent toads than a latter-day, perfidious St. George. But the people remained faithful to the "truth" they knew:

> Little Cecil trips up and down,
> He rules both Court and Crown,
> With his Brother Burghley Clown,
> In his great fox-furred gown;
> With the long proclamation
> He swore he saved the Town.[68]

The Crown could suppress pro-Essex tracts, but it could not keep the balladeers from composing or the people from singing their lamentable ditties.

> Sweet England's pride is gone!
> *welladay! welladay!*
>
> Brave honour graced him still [always],
> *gallantly, gallantly;*
> He ne'er did deed of ill,
> well it is known;
>
> But Envy, that foul fiend,
> whose malice ne'er did end,
> Hath brought true virtue's friend
> unto his thrall.

Eighteen months after Essex's execution, a German visitor was guided to the place where "the brave hero" was beheaded; at Whitehall he was shown the shields that the "great and celebrated noble warrior" had presented to the Queen when tilting;[69] and even her courtiers were found singing snatches of *Essex's Last Good Night*:

> All you that cry O hone [moan]! O hone!
> come now and sing O lord! with me.
> For why? our Jewell is from vs goone,
> the valient Knight of Chiualrye.
> Of rich and poore beloued was hee,—
> in tyme an honorable Knight—
> Who by our lawes condemnd was he
> and late [did] take *his last good-night*.[70]

After several stanzas celebrating exploits that must strike us as quixotic, the balladeer then includes the Earl's last blessing, a farewell to his "gracious Queene," "the Commons, great and small," and his own "Knights of chyvalrye."

Who was left to fill the role of "worlds wide wonder"? Raleigh, with his "bloody pride," or the unquestionably capable yet unquestionably unexhilarating Cecil? Elizabeth, although deeply grieved, never appears to have sickened with remorse, as the legend of Essex's ring maintains. In August, 1601, the Queen was perusing a descriptive account of the documents stored in the Tower, presented by the zealous antiquary, William Lambarde. Having come to the papers of Richard II's reign, she remarked, "I am Richard II. . . . He that will forget God, will also forget his benefactors. This tragedy . . . was played forty times in open streets and houses." [71] More medieval documents were leafed through before she again shared her thoughts with "good and honest Lambarde." "In those days force and arms did prevail; but now the wit of the fox is everywhere on foot, so as hardly a faithful or virtuous man may be found."

Even Elizabeth's nostalgic contrast between the "parfit gentil knyghts" of Chaucer's time and her own champions, who sometimes lacked both "trouthe and honour," does not bring us from chivalry-felt-as-fact to chivalry-known-to-be-fiction. Her voluntary identification with Richard and her concluding moral do not assume that chivalry is fictitious but that Essex's chivalry was false, not that the role of Chivalry's Flower was hopelessly antiquated but that he perverted its vital values. Obviously men no longer fought as they had in Richard's days. Even the balladeer who tells us of *Essex's Last Good Night* points out that "like a knight of chevalrye / . . . he persed [his enemies'] skinne" with "bullets," not sword or lance. To omit such realistic detail would be to engender an atmosphere of romance. An awareness of such superficial distinctions, however, did not prevent the Queen and her subjects from freely associating with their ancestors' feudal worlds. To outfit that knightly quest to Cadiz, Elizabeth "enforced the old feudal claim on seaports to provide ships for naval service," an appeal to charters like the one given by Henry II to Maldon, in the county of Essex, in 1171.[72]

The difficulties of translating the meaning of Essex's rebellion into modern terms should now be clear. G. B. Harrison is not exaggerating the importance of the Earl's fall when he claims that it "affected the nation more deeply than any event since the Great Armada. . . . With Essex's death vanished the last hope of a brave new world. It is more than coincidence that *Hamlet* as we know it was written in [his] last months."[73] Also seeing that piece of history in its own terms rather than as simply the biography of one man's folly and ruin, Neale comments, "Faction of the old heroic pattern died with its superb, its unsupportable exponent; and it almost seemed as if the soul of Elizabethan England also departed."[74] And it is the old feudal ties, the medieval sense of fealty underlying the old heroic pattern, that explain the profundity of Elizabeth's grief and England's despair. To us Essex seems merely proud, insolent, ungrateful; to the Elizabethans, a successful rebellion of Her Majesty's Earl Marshal, two inferior earls, two barons, and numerous noblemen's sons and brave gentlemen would have been a monstrous inversion of the whole order of things. This is why Essex's supporters insisted that he never meant to overthrow the Queen, but merely to remove the evil forces surrounding her. Many probably thought they were telling the truth, and if the balladeers are trustworthy witnesses, the public continued to think reverently of their hero's chivalry.

Just before Spenser's death in January, 1599, however, he is said to have refused "twenty pieces" sent by Essex,[75] who was still wrangling over his right to lead the Irish expedition. If the story is true, the impoverished Spenser must have already begun equating Essex not with the man celebrated in his *Prothalamion* (1596), but with those vain creatures whose chivalry is more apparent than real. As early as 1590 he had juxtaposed such seeming fellows against the upright Sir Satyrane, one of *The Faerie Queene*'s minor champions.

> Yt was a goodly swaine, and of great might,
> As ever man that bloody field did fight;
> But in vain sheows, that wont yong knights bewitch,
> And courtly services tooke no delight,
> But rather joyd to bee then seemen sich:
> For both to be and seeme to him was labor lich.
>
> (III. vii. 29)

Shakespeare's opinion is less open to question. Having inserted a complimentary allusion to Essex the rebellion-broacher in *Henry V*, he moves on to the melancholy Prince of Denmark, the unheroic, reflective man who, like Satyrane, insists upon "being" rather than "seeming." "Seems, madam! Nay, it is; I know not seems" (*Hamlet*, I. ii. 76). Next comes the strange history-comedy-tragedy of *Troilus and Cressida*, in which chivalry is not only baffled but savagely anatomized: a world whose "argument is a whore and a cuckold" (II. iii. 69); whose love is "hot blood, hot thoughts, and hot deeds. . . . [A] generation of vipers" (III. i. 125 ff.); whose theme is the nightmare of relativism, "What's aught but as 'tis valued?" (II. ii. 52). Cressida's conversion from Chaucer's mysterious, appealing heroine to Shakespeare's "daughter of the game" can be partly explained by intervening literary traditions; we dare not overlook, for instance, Robert Henryson's *Testament of Cresseid* (c. 1490), with her "fleshly foull affectioun" and "lustis lecherous." But it was Shakespeare's England in conjunction with his library that inspired Hector's pursuit of that anonymous Greek for his "goodly armour," Achilles's most unchivalric triumph, and the magniloquent knightly vaunts that, according to Achilles, "Maintain I know not what; 'tis trash" (V. viii. 2 ff.; II. i. 122). For in 1598 George Chapman had ironically related art to life by dedicating his translation of a part of Homer's *Iliad* to "the most honored instance of the Achilleian virtues, . . . the Earl of Essex."[76] Shakespeare did not exploit this opportunity to build a whole play upon the Earl's misadventures. Achilles is no more Essex than Ulysses, that public absolutist and private pragmatist, is Francis Bacon. The relationship is subtler than a one-for-one political allegory; the meaning of Essex's career permeates the play's mood, tone, and theme rather than being spelled out with specific caricatures. In other words, had Essex either triumphed over or been slain by Tyrone in the spring of 1599, *Troilus and Cressida* might well have premised a very different world.

Conclusion: History Versus Historical Criticism

Whether we attempt to gloss sixteenth-century literature with direct literary sources or indirect, nonliterary events, our principal responsibility seems obvious. Just as the historian's major task is to render intelligible what men of another time and place dreamed, desired, and did, so we must measure the reflections of those dreams and desires against what they were rather than what we might logically expect or wish them to have been. The meaning of our own Civil War affords an excellent analogy. Today a secondary-school student of American history is soon obliged to dismiss all romantic notions about the causes of that conflict. Juvenile enthusiasm for John Brown at Harpers Ferry, *Uncle Tom's Cabin*, and Julia Ward Howe's "Battle Hymn," and the odd grammar-school ideas that men fought to free slaves, preserve the republic, or resist Grant's "tyranny" are replaced by the dreary economic facts of southern agrarianism and northern industrialism. Thus the instructor who sees history in his own, or Karl Marx's, or Charles and Mary Beard's terms renders credible the enlistment of the Ohio farm boy and the motives of Whitman, who provides his epitaph.[77] Beard's truth may tell us why the North eventually won, but until time produces men so monstrously rational as to lay down their lives in acting out economic theses, it provides a rather pathetic explanation for any battlefield.

Garrett Mattingly's splendid account of that great battle of the sea in 1588 makes use of both kinds of truth. We are never allowed to forget that the Spanish Armada sailed with ill-stored provisions and confronted better ships and better guns. Only these facts can explain why the English won the battle before the Spaniards had any trouble with inclement weather. But Mattingly always interlaces such truths with that contemporary attitude so eloquently struck upon Elizabeth's Armada medals: "God breathed and they were scattered."[78] If England rejoiced in another visible display of Jehovah's Protestant sympathies, Spain solaced herself with the examples of defeated crusaders, chastised by God for fighting in His cause without proper humility; neither side appears to have thought of the outcome outside the context of God's winds and waves. To be sure, some Spaniards no doubt used the myth to excuse their own blunders; many probably found it less embarrassing to be defeated by God than by their mortal adversaries. But the English had no necessities to make virtues of. And when the Queen inspired her troops at Tilbury, Mattingly notes, perhaps

an objective observer would have seen no more than a battered, rather scraggy spinster in her middle fifties perched on a fat white horse, her teeth black, her red wig slightly askew, dangling a toy sword and wearing an absurd little piece of parade armor like something out of a

theatrical property box. But that was not what her subjects saw, dazzled as they were by more than the sun on
the silver breastplate or the moisture in their eyes. They
saw Judith and Esther, Gloriana and Belphoebe, Diana
the virgin huntress and Minerva the wise protectress and,
best of all, their own beloved queen and mistress, come
in this hour of danger, in all simplicity to trust herself
among them.[79]

Had we the means to capture that moment at Tilbury with
modern television coverage, "close-ups" of the scraggy spinster
would be a far less helpful background than her image caught in
her subjects' moistened eyes. The former shots would satisfy
antiquarian curiosities; the latter contains the stuff we need to
interpret literature. For over a century scores of Elizabethan
historians have tunneled through the Queen's ground with no
saner sense of perspective than that displayed by their subterranean
literary colleagues in their minute baggings of Shakespeare's baggings. Both groups, however, have furnished evidence that pleads
for imaginative employment. In availing ourselves of their discoveries, we need only distinguish between those that uncover
new facts about Elizabethan events and those that reveal new instances of Elizabethan attitudes. Both varieties of information
are valuable, but we must keep in mind which kind is being documented.

Several years ago, for example, F. W. Bateson rightly rejected
Walter Pater's definition of *The Renaissance* (1873), but for the
wrong reasons. To Pater, the Renaissance was "the name of a
many-sided but yet united movement, in which the love of the
things of the intellect and the imagination *for their own sake,*
the desire for a more *liberal* and *comely* way of conceiving life,
make themselves felt, urging those who experienced this desire
to search out first one and then another means of intellectual
or imaginative enjoyment, and directing them not only to the discovery of old and forgotten sources of this enjoyment, but to the
divination of fresh sources thereof—*new* experiences, new subjects
of poetry, new forms of art." [80] To Bateson, who is giving us "The
Approach to Renaissance Literature," [81] Pater's "crucial words"
—new, liberal, comely—reflect only the "brilliant surface" of the
English Renaissance and ignore "the historical context of the
Elizabethan achievement."

Unlike the Victorian aesthetes, we are uncomfortably
aware of the social matrix of the English Renaissance—a
continuous inflation (with the opportunities it provided the
new capitalism of enormous profits or total ruin), unprece-
dented technical progress (which included gunpowder as
well as the printing press), immensely efficient dictatorships, ruthless colonial exploitation (with syphilis, according to D. H. Lawrence, the most influential import of
all), a hysterical religious fanaticism, and an omnivorous
credulity (alchemy, astrology, and witchcraft flourished as
never before). *New* no doubt, scarcely *liberal*, not by any
means always *comely*.[82]

Against this impressive inventory of the muck beneath the diamonds we must lodge several objections. First, Pater uses "liberal"
and "comely" to describe neither Renaissance life nor the way it
was always viewed; he merely accounts for those men (none Elizabethans) who reflect *the desire* to conceive of life in brave-new-
beauteous-world ways. The more dunghills we uncover within
their social matrix, the easier it is to understand their disgust with
the old and desire for the new. Secondly, if we wish to apply
Pater's interpretation of Continental, pre-Elizabethan art to what
happened in Elizabethan England, the crucial and inaccurate words
are not "liberal" and "comely," but ones we might expect from
any Victorian aesthete: the love of things intellectual and imaginative "for their own sake." In Pater's attempt to divest art of all
overtly utilitarian, religious, and moral functions lies part of the
notion later popularized as art for art's sake. He naturally expected his artistic heroes to share his own interests. Perhaps some
of them did, but the Elizabethans (whom, Bateson implies, Pater is
describing) certainly did not. However lofty the Tudor artist's conception of his muse, she invariably inspired him to write either
for God's sake or for man's instruction and delight.

Finally, even if Pater had claimed that the Elizabethan always
saw his world as liberal and comely, we would need evidence of
another kind than that contained in Bateson's inventory to disprove him. As it stands, the inventory simply proves that Bateson
knows more facts than Pater, and has therefore provided additional
points of departure for solving the relevant problem of which
facts the Elizabethans also knew and how they reacted to them.
Whether we interview the Tudors chronologically, generically, or

according to themes, movements, and traditions, both men give us questions to ask them, but not their answers. With Pater in hand we approach sixteenth-century literature looking for expressions of liberal and comely strivings, discoveries of the old artistic enjoyments, divinations of the new. With Bateson's more specific but equally worthwhile inquiries, we cannot forget to search as well for explicit comments and concealed anxieties about things like inflation, technical progress, and dictatorships. But it is only the Tudors themselves who can tell us how comely and liberal life was for them. If they insist that their "immensely efficient" Queen is no dictator by Gloriana, we must be content. And if Her Majesty's voyagers lead no Elizabethan to think of "ruthless colonial exploitation," much less "syphilis," we shall have to await the discoveries of the eighteenth-century revolutionaries and D. H. Lawrence in the twentieth.

If we, like Pater, base our impressions upon the art men produced rather than the facts they may have failed to perceive, the Elizabethan world was usually—but not always—comelier than Bateson's list suggests. In his ode "To the Virginian Voyage" (1606), for example, Michael Drayton praises Elizabeth's greatest naval chronicler, "Industrious Hakluyt / Whose reading shall enflame / Men to seek fame." Now Richard Hakluyt's three-volume folio edition of *The Principall Navigations, Traffiques, Voiages, and Discoveries of the English Nation* (1598-1600) reveals not only enormous industry, but a conscientious zeal for the whole truth. Although Raleigh claims that his report of Sir Richard Grenville's last fight in the *Revenge* (1591) is given "without partiality or false imaginations," his own contradictions of "vainglorious [Spanish] vaunts" contain some remarkably pro-English exaggerations. Hakluyt patiently adjusts Raleigh's romantic statistics: The Armada of 1588 consisted of 140, not 240 ships; in 1591, the *Revenge* could not be taken by "above ten thousand" rather than "15,000" Spaniards; the enemy lost "well near one thousand," not "2,000" men.[83] Hakluyt, however, finds nothing to emend in Raleigh's sentiments, however bigoted and chauvinistic they may appear to us: "Thus it hath pleased God to fight for us and to defend the justice of our cause against the ambitious and bloody pretenses of the Spaniard, who seeking to devour all nations are themselves devoured."[84] A similar desire to report the whole truth is evident in Hakluyt's editing of Edward Hayes's account of Sir Humphrey Gilbert's second voyage (1583). Having been separated from the fleet by fog, the sailors manning the *Swallow* became pirates; a grim delight underlies the account of how "God's justice did follow the same [English] company, even to destruction," for He "more sharply took revenge upon them . . . [who] went under protection of his cause and religion." [85] Such renegades had clearly tainted Hayes's and Hakluyt's patriotic and holy cause: "to take possession of those lands to the behalf of the Crown of England and the advancement of Christian religion in those paganish regions." [86]

For the poets of Hakluyt's time, the voyagers' heroic quests through unchartered worlds offered brave new facts to stimulate widening imaginative horizons. Fearing lest that sometime, nowhere "happy land of Faery" be condemned as the "painted forgery" of "an ydle braine," Spenser prefaces Sir Guyon's adventures with reminders of other romantic lands recently discovered.

> But let that man with better sence advize,
> That of the world least part to us is red [known]:
> And daily how through hardy enterprize
> Many great regions are discovered,
> Which to late age were never mentioned.
> Who ever heard of th' Indian Peru?
> Or who in venturous vessell measured
> The Amazons huge river, now found trew?
> Or fruitfullest Virginia who did ever vew?
>   (II, Prologue, 2)

If dreams have been proved realities by the "hardy" and "venturous," Spenser concludes, how dare "witlesse man" presume that "nothing is, but that which he hath seene?" John Donne, on the other hand, presents a less idealistic set of reasons which send men a-voyaging:

> Whether a rotten state, and hope of gaine,
> Or to disuse mee from the queasie paine
> Of being belov'd, and loving, or the thirst
> Of honour, or faire death, out pusht me first,
> I lose my end: for here as well as I
> A desperate may live, and a coward die.
>   ("The Calme," 39–44)

Or in speaking "To His Mistris Going to Bed," Donne can set Hakluyt's heroic quests into a delightfully bawdy key:

> Licence my roaving hands, and let them go,
> Before, behind, between, above, below.
> O my America! my new-found-land,
> My kingdome, safeliest when with one man man'd,
> My Myne of precious stones, My Emperie,
> How blest am I in this discovering thee!
> (*Elegie XIX*, 25–30)

But Donne in his most cynical or sensual moments cannot manage a witty reference to colonial exploitation, nor is Spenser, when apostrophizing the "tradefull merchants" who seek the "most pretious things" of "both the Indias" (*Amoretti, XV*), thinking in terms of venereal disease.

In reflecting upon other aspects of their rich and anxious lives, however, the Tudors appear to disavow Pater's views, and tell us, with Bateson, that things are indeed "scarcely liberal, not by any means always comely." Early in the century (c. 1520) John Skelton's *Colin Clout* surveys contemporary (chiefly ecclesiastical) abuses and bids farewell to "benignitie . . . simplicitie . . . humilitie . . . good charitie!" [87] For simple Colin, Bateson's "hysterical religious fanaticism" is "Luther's wark" and the "devilish dogmatista" (rhymes with "Wicliffista") of "Hussians . . . Arians . . . Pelagians.[88] A century later Donne finds that "We'are scarce our Fathers shadowes cast at noone," worries about the "new Philosophy" (of Copernicus, among others) that "calls all in doubt," and seems as aware as any modern political theorist of economic exploitation: "He that purchases a Mannor, will thinke to have an exact Survey of the Land: But who thinks of taking so exact a survey of his Conscience, how that money was got, that purchased that Mannor? We call that a mans meanes, which he hath; But that is truly his meanes, what way he came by it" ("An Anatomy of the World," ll. 144, 205 ff.; "Sermon of Dec. 12, 1626," 2). For Spenser, as for Hamlet, "the world is runne quite out of square" and "growes daily wourse and wourse" (*Faerie Queene*, V, Prologue, 1). In his "Litany," the usually effervescent Thomas Nashe concludes that "Heaven is our heritage, / Earth but a player's stage," and the swashbuckling Raleigh, in his *History of the World*, notes that "the long day of mankind

[is] drawing fast towards an evening and the world's tragedy and time near at an end." [89] By the turn of the century, it appears, anxieties as strong as Skelton's, although quite different in nature, become more pronounced: The world is running down. But as soon as we seem to be on solid, pessimistic ground, we confront the richest literature of the decade, Shakespeare's romances, with actions controlled by "great creating nature," optimistic celebrations of man's ability to create, revivify, forgive—Perdita's, if not Miranda's, "brave new world." Terrestrial nature in upheaval, which has formerly reflected man's unnatural acts, is now the handiwork of "blessed Apollo" and "good Prospero"; *Lear*'s storm yields to *The Tempest*'s.

In seeking *the* thought of *the* period, then, we must not expect different men with different artistic goals in different times, situations, or places to answer each of our questions in the same way. Perhaps the only generalization we may safely operate upon is that Tudor England, more than any other time and place, expresses the rich diversities Walt Whitman found in himself:

> Do I contradict myself?
> Very well then I contradict myself,
> (I am large, I contain multitudes.) [90]

Within some diversities, however, there is widespread, if not complete, uniformity. Although Hakluyt's navigators inspire many meanings, they do not suggest all (modern) meanings, and the idea of the Queen is fairly constant. Although Ulysses, like many a modern demagogue, prefers to manipulate men's illusions rather than guide them according to the objective standards he so eloquently outlines, few Elizabethans would have quarreled with his speech on order and degree (*Troilus and Cressida*, I. iii. 75 ff.). Nor did they yet have cause to argue against "that incestuous, that adulterate beast," King Claudius, when he draws upon those concepts of order and degree to reason: "There's such divinity doth hedge a king / That treason can but peep to what it would" (*Hamlet*, I. v. 42; IV. v. 120–121). Similarly, Jonson, Burleigh, and Burleigh's cook no doubt found different things in the play to admire, but they all appreciated the comparisons Hamlet makes in his observations upon man, that marvelous "piece of work." And if every Elizabethan did not subscribe to the idea that man is the measure and therefore the measurer of all things, few would not have "seen," along with Marlowe's wretched Faustus, "where Christ's blood streams in the firmament" and none failed to experience, with his Chorus, the tragic sense of what could have been: "Cut is the branch that might have grown full straight." For if man does not completely control, he at least partially directs his destiny and is therefore responsible for his actions. Hence the importance of history as a *Mirror for Magistrates* and their subjects, a series of lessons illustrating deeds to follow or avoid, and the moral impulse underlying even the most entertaining art.

Finally, and for our purposes most important, the Elizabethan artists and literary critics shared a great many views about the nature of art that are quite different from ours; what it meant to create *and* imitate, translate *and* transfigure, be original *and* artificial. Although we normally think of creation-imitation as an either-or phenomenon, for example, it does not seem to have been so conceived by sixteenth-century writers and reviewers. One theme of George Peele's *Arraignment of Paris* (c. 1584) is a classical commonplace, Paris's judgment of Venus as fairer than Juno or Pallas. And the awarding of the golden ball had been often employed before Peele's time to flatter reigning goddesses, among them Elizabeth's mother, Anne Boleyn. From the moment Ate flourished her prize (Prologue, I), any half-versed courtier amongst Peele's select audience would have been able to supply the resolution: Sooner or later the "bane of Troy" would rest in Elizabeth's hands. Despite such evidence of Peele's filching, however, Thomas Nashe sees in this old device the playwright's "pregnant dexteritie of wit and manifold varietie of inuention, wherein . . . hee goeth a step beyond all that write." [91] Nashe is certainly aware of what we would call Peele's "plagiarism." In committing Peele with his peers, he reveals an orthodox aesthetic assumption: Wit and creativity are displayed by going "a step beyond," not by starting from scratch. An old theme, Paris's judgment, is rounded off with a new, his arraignment before the gods for partiality; an old motive to flatter royalty provides the chance to experiment with new verse forms; old mythic characters are intermingled with recent English rustics, "stolen" from Spenser's *The Shepheardes Calender;* pastoral scenes that had delighted the Queen during her summer progresses are brought indoors, related, and put on the boards, lush descriptions partially compensating for the loss of natural sylvan backdrops.

But why Peele did not exercise all of his inventive powers and give us an entirely original fable must be reserved for the next two chapters, essays on sixteenth-century literary theories and practices. After once again adjusting our expectations, we may still, of course, find fault with both Tudor aesthetic assumptions and the art these assumptions inspired; but let us hope that we shall at least be wiser even about what we do not like. If we remain unexcited by Sidney's *Arcadia*, for instance, we shall not be betrayed by one nineteenth-century critic's anachronistic assumptions and call it "one of the greatest monuments of the abuse of intellectual power upon record." [92] Nor shall we have much patience with that eighteenth-century chronological snob who saluted Pope for "giving harmony to [John Donne,] a writer more rough and rugged than even any of his age." [93] What a pity Donne had allowed his "vast fund of sterling wit, and strong sense" to be "degraded and deformed . . . by the most harsh and uncouth diction"! What waste in that poet "who profited so little by the example *Spenser* had set, of a most musical and mellifluous versification"! In judging the literature of their own time, both Hazlitt and Warton were fairly acute; their downfall lay in their insistence upon measuring the achievements of Tudor art solely in terms of their self-evidently pure and eternally axiomatic artistic standards. Accustomed to the often "rough and rugged" poetry of the twentieth century, we are more likely to dismiss "mellifluous" Spenser than the "harsh" man who reacted against him. But we, too, may misinterpret Elizabethan achievements by failing to understand their excitement over the "artificial" or ignoring their concept of creative imitation. And then what shall we do with that most flagrant filcher of them all, Will Shakespeare, who often lacked even the decency to disguise his booty? In artistic as well as historical matters, we must distinguish between (and decide upon the relative importances of) truth and "truth."

Notes to Chapter II

1. Lucien Price, *Dialogues of Arthur North Whitehead* (1954), as quoted by Kenneth Muir, *Shakespeare's Sources* (London, 1957), p. xiii.

2. *Narrative and Dramatic Sources of Shakespeare*, ed. Geoffrey Bullough (London, 1957–), II, 73.

3. Bullough, I, 284 ff.

4. Citations from Shakespeare are to *The Complete Works*, ed. Peter Alexander (London, 1951). The similarity has been noted by Margaret Webster, *Shakespeare Without Tears* (New York, 1955), p. 114.

5. *Hecatommithi* III, 7 (1565), trans. Leonard F. Dean and Joseph B. Cary, in *A Casebook on Othello*, ed. Leonard F. Dean (New York, 1962), p. 264.

6. *Pandosto: The Triumph of Time* (1588), in *The Life and Complete Works in Prose and Verse of Robert Greene*, ed. Alexander B. Grosart (London, 1881–1886), IV, 317.

7. Dean, p. 256.

8. Grosart, IV, 237.

9. *Shakespeare and the Comedy of Forgiveness* (New York, 1965), p. 187.

10. *The Union of the Two Noble and Illustre Famelies of Lancastre & Yorke* (1548), ed. Geoffrey Bullough, III, 249–250. Italics added.

11. *The Chronicles of England, Scotland and Ireland*, 2nd ed. (London, 1587), ed. H. Ellis (London, 1807–1808), III, 362. Italics added. Holinshed's epitaph for Clarence epitomizes Hall's, who in turn was quoting from Sir Thomas More's *Life of Richard III*; see Bullough, *Sources*, III, 252. Since Bullough does not include all the portions of Holinshed that I consider significant, all my citations from Holinshed are to the Ellis edition.

12. See Karl J. Holzknecht's helpful table of historical events treated or alluded to in *The Backgrounds of Shakespeare's Plays* (New York, 1950), pp. 319–320.

13. Holzknecht lists these and many other Shakespearean "lies" on pp. 307 ff.

14. Although "thy younger brother" could refer to Thomas or Humphrey, they do not exist, dramatically speaking, until *2 Henry IV;* it is more likely that Shakespeare intended a comparison between Hal and John.

15. Probably the latter. Holinshed later notes that the exiled Mowbray "at the last came to Venice, where he for thought and melancholie deceassed: for he was in hope (as writers record) that he should haue beene borne out in the matter by the king, which when it fell out otherwise, it greeued him not a little" (II, 848). Richard, in fact, may have owed his liberty, if not his life, to Mowbray's disclosure of Gloucester's intended *coup*, an attempt to imprison the King, York, and Gaunt and execute "all the other lords of the kings counsell . . ." (II, 836).

16. See the *Oxford English Dictionary*, which cites Spenser's *Faerie Queene*, VI, vii, 27.

17. See G. B. Harrison's footnote to I. i. 170, in his edition of *Shakespeare: The Complete Works* (New York, 1952).

18. Cf. E. M. W. Tillyard, *Shakespeare's History Plays* (New York, 1962), pp. 280 ff.: "First, the very actions" of the play "tend to be symbolic rather than real" (p. 280). "Second, in places where emotion rises, where there is strong mental action, Shakespeare evades direct or naturalistic presentation and resorts to convention and conceit" (p. 281). "We are," Tillyard concludes, "in a world where means matter more than ends, where it is more important to keep strictly the rules of an elaborate game than either to win or to lose it" (p. 287).

19. Among the events of the year preceding the Tuthill episode, Holinshed includes Elizabeth's charge to her judges: "Have care ouer my people. You haue my place. Do you that which I ought to doo. They are my people. Euerie man oppresseth them, and spoileth them without mercie. They cannot reuenge their quarrell, nor help themselues. See vnto them, see vnto them, for they are my charge. I charge you euen as God hath charged me. I care not for my selfe, my life is not deare to me, my care is for my people" (IV, 253). The royal subscription to Shakespeare's doctrine of responsibility is obvious.

20. Johan Huizinga, *The Waning of the Middle Ages* (Garden City, N. Y., 1956), pp. 323, 335.

21. *Ibid.*, p. 335.

22. Holzknecht, p. 309.

23. J. H. Hexter, *Reappraisals in History* (New York, 1963), p. 2.

24. *The Reason of Church Government Urged Against Prelaty*, in *Complete Poems and Major Prose*, ed. Merritt Y. Hughes (New York, 1957), p. 685.

25. Hexter, p. 2.

26. *Ibid.*, p. 1.

27. See Hexter's excellent chapter on "The Myth of the Middle Class in Tudor England," pp. 71–116.

28. Hexter, pp. 11–12.

29. *Foure Letters and certaine Sonnets*, in *Elizabethan Critical Essays*, ed. G. Gregory Smith (London, 1904), II, 230–231. The widespread admiration for and attempts to imitate this classical six-foot verse are discussed in Chapter III.

30. Hexter, pp. 10–11.

31. George Sellery, *The Renaissance: Its Nature and Origins* (Madison, Wis., 1965), p. 260.

32. *Ibid.*, p. 6. See also Douglas Bush's helpful essay on "Modern Theories of the Renaissance," in *The Renaissance and English Humanism* (Toronto, 1968), pp. 13–38.

33. Sellery, pp. 6–7.

34. *Ibid.*, p. 7.

35. Hexter, pp. 38–39.

36. *Ibid.*, p. 39; cf. also p. 116.

37. *Ibid.*, p. 81.

38. *Ibid.*, p. 82.

39. Anthony Munday, *A second and third blast of retrait from plaies and Theaters* (1580), quoted in E. K. Chambers, *The Elizabethan Stage* (Oxford, 1923), IV, 208–210. For similar "blasts" see Chambers's "Documents of Criticism," IV, 208–225.

40. See the *Dictionary of National Biography* (hereafter *DNB*), IV (London, 1908), 777–784. In the last years of Elizabeth's reign Thomas Campion celebrates the accomplishments of these men in terms explicitly brave and new: "Learning, after the declining of the *Romaine* Empire and the pollution of their language through the conquest of the *Barbarians*, lay most pitifully deformed till the time of *Erasmus, Rewcline* [Reuchlin], Sir *Thomas More,* and other learned men of that age, who brought the Latine toong again to light, redeeming it with much labour out of the hands of the illiterate Monks and Friers. . . ." See Smith, II, 329. Again, however, how trustworthy is our witness? The following year Samuel Daniel's *A Defence of Ryme* (c. 1603) found in Campion's particular variety of chronological snobbery "a most apparant ignorance, both of the succession of learning in *Europe* and the generall course of things. . . ." See Smith, II, 368 ff. The often quoted Tudor remarks concerning the abysmal ignorance of their ancestors usually amount to little more than complaints against medieval interests in "lewd" romances and rhymed verses, and the fact that they were sometimes composed by the Catholic clergy.

41. *The Grief of Joye* (1576), stanza 4.

42. See John Buxton, *Sir Philip Sidney and the English Renaissance* (New York, 1965), p. 54. Italics added.

43. In J. E. Neale, *Queen Elizabeth I* (Garden City, N. Y., 1957), pp. 308–309.

44. See the *DNB*, XVIII (London, 1909), 938.

45. Arthur B. Ferguson, *The Indian Summer of English Chivalry* (Durham, N.C., 1960), pp. 26, 102. Ferguson rightly allows for a lapse in time between fact and recognition of fact: "Contact between the ideal and the actual in the world of affairs," he notes, "was maintained in the mind of the English gentry for a long time after the conditions of English society no longer warranted it" (p. xvii). I am merely suggesting that the actions of many practical men *throughout* the sixteenth century seem irrational unless we extend chivalry's Indian summer beyond the days of Malory and Caxton, even beyond "the revolutionary events of the thirties" (p. 26).

46. See Arthur Underhill's chapter on "Law," in *Shakespeare's England*, ed. C. T. Onions *et al.* (*Oxford*, 1916), I, 390.

47. Neale, p. 179.

48. "To His Booke," *The Shepheardes Calender* (1579), in *The Complete Poetical Works of Spenser*, ed. R. E. Neil Dodge (Cambridge, Mass., 1936), p. 4.

49. See the *DNB*, V (London, 1908), 876.

50. *Ibid.*, p. 877.

51. Neale, pp. 353–354. Italics added.

52. *Ibid.*, p. 355.

53. Cited by Harrison, p. 433.

54. Neale, p. 371.

55. *Ibid.*, p. 374.

56. *DNB*, V, 885.

57. Neale, pp. 375–377.

58. *Ibid.*, p. 378.

59. *Ibid.*, pp. 379–380.

60. *Ibid.*, p. 383.

61. *Ibid.*, pp. 387 ff.

62. See Chambers's "Court Calender," IV, 113.

63. Neale, p. 390.

64. *Ibid.*, p. 387.

65. *Ibid.*, p. 388.

66. *DNB*, V, 887.

67. *Ibid.*, pp. 888–889. Among the poems censured in James I's reign was Samuel Daniel's "Philotas."

68. This lampoon and the ballad that follows are reprinted in Neale, pp. 394–395.

69. Neale, p. 397.

70. *The Shirburn Ballads,* LXXIX, ed. Andrew Clark (Oxford, 1907), pp. 328 ff.
71. Neale, p. 398.
72. Clark, p. 177.
73. *Ibid.,* p. 24.
74. *Ibid.,* pp. 396–397.
75. *DNB,* V, 889.
76. Cited by Harrison, p. 974.
77. I.e., Whitman's "Come Up from the Fields Father."
78. *The Armada* (Cambridge, Mass., 1962), p. 390.
79. *Ibid.,* p. 349.
80. Quoted by Bateson in *A Guide to English Literature* (Garden City, N. Y., 1965), p. 46. Italics added.
81. So his chapter is entitled.
82. Bateson, p. 47.
83. See the helpful commentary furnished by Roy Lamson and Hallett Smith, *Renaissance England* (New York, 1956), pp. 492, 497–498.
84. *Ibid.,* p. 499.
85. *Ibid.,* p. 466.
86. *Ibid.,* p. 467.
87. *The Complete Poems,* ed. Philip Henderson (London, 1931), p. 300.
88. *Ibid.,* p. 299.
89. See Lamson and Smith, p. 516.
90. *Song of Myself,* stanza 51.
91. Preface to Robert Greene's *Menaphon* (1589); see Smith, I, 319.
92. William Hazlitt, quoted by Lamson and Smith, p. 234.
93. Joseph Warton, *An Essay on the Genius and Writings of Pope,* 5th ed. (London, 1806), II, 348.

Suggestions for Further Reading

Most of the studies listed at the conclusion to Chapter I are at least indirectly concerned with the imaginative employment of backgrounds. Perhaps the best way of getting into a sufficiently Elizabethan frame of mind is to invest several hours leafing through Holinshed's folio volumes, ed. H. Ellis (London, 1807–1808), paying special attention to the marginalia. Another means of adjusting modern expectations is to compare several sixteenth-century views upon a central topic. To what extent, for example, are the problems of man, the social animal, as illustrated in Sir Calidore's quest of Courtesy (*Faerie Queene*, Book VI), also reflected in Shakespeare's maturer comedies or in Sir John Harington's translation and comments upon Ariosto's *Orlando Furioso?* Generous selections from Harington have recently been made available by Rudolph Gottfried, *Ariosto's Orlando Furioso* (Bloomington, Ind., 1963), and Graham Hough's very readable *Preface to The Faerie Queene* (New York, 1963) is recommended for the student intimidated by Spenser's bulk or learning.

For a short, helpful account of Renaissance historiography, see Herschel Baker's *The Race of Time* (Toronto, 1967). J. H. Hexter's *Reappraisals in History* (London, 1961) is an invaluable aid toward seeing history in *its* terms, not ours. Also distinguishing between truth and "truth" are:

Bush, Douglas. *The Renaissance and English Humanism.* Toronto, 1939.

Ferguson, Arthur B. *The Indian Summer of English Chivalry.* Durham, N. C., 1960.

Huizinga, Johan. *The Waning of the Middle Ages.* London, 1924.

Jenkins, Elizabeth. *Elizabeth the Great.* New York, 1958.

Mattingly, Garrett. *The Armada.* Boston, 1959.

Neale, J. E. *Queen Elizabeth I.* London, 1934.

Read, Conyers. *Mr. Secretary Cecil and Queen Elizabeth.* London, 1955.

Rowse, A. L. *The England of Elizabeth.* London, 1950.

Finally, for intellectual and cultural contexts of the Renaissance, see:

Cassirer, Ernst. *The Individual and the Cosmos in Renaissance Philosophy.* New York, 1963.

———, Paul Oskar Kristeller, and John Herman Randal, Jr. *The Renaissance Philosophy of Man.* Chicago, 1948.

Ferguson, Wallace K., *et al. The Renaissance.* New York, 1953.

Kristeller, Paul Oskar. *Renaissance Thought.* New York, 1961.

———. *Renaissance Thought II.* New York, 1965.

Roeder, Ralph. *The Man of the Renaissance.* New York, 1958.

Sellery, George Clarke. *The Renaissance: Its Nature and Origins.* Madison, Wis., 1950.

Werkmeister, William H. *Facets of the Renaissance.* New York, 1963.

III

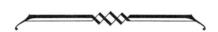

LAWS OF
WRIT AND LIBERTY

Literary Theory Versus Literary Practice

The best actors in the world, either for tragedy, comedy, history, pastoral, pastoral-comical, historical-pastoral, tragical-historical, tragical-comical-historical-pastoral, scene individable, or poem unlimited [any play observing or disregarding the unities of time and place]. Seneca cannot be too heavy nor Plautus too light. For the law of writ and the liberty [plays honoring or ignoring critical rules], these are the only men.

—*Hamlet*, II. ii. 392–397

I would hartily wish you would either send me the Rules and Precepts of Arte, which you obserue in Quantities [the rules by which you lengthen or shorten the pronunciation of syllables in your English imitations of classical, quantitative versification], or else followe mine, that M. Philip Sidney gaue me, being the very same that M. Drant deuised, but enlarged with M. Sidneys own iudgement, and augmented with my Obseruations, that we might both accorde and agree in one, leaste we ouerthrowe one an other and be ouerthrown of the rest. . . . Nowe, my *Dreames* and *Dying Pellicane* being fully finished, . . . I wil in hande forthwith with my *Faery Queene*.

—Edmund Spenser to Gabriel Harvey, in *Three Proper and wittie familiar Letters* (1580)

The experts summoned to the courts of England, Portugal, and Spain remained skeptical, but Christopher Columbus clung to his belief that the wealthy lands of Marco Polo and "Sir John Mandeville" lay within a short and easy voyage across the Ocean Sea. From old Portuguese sailors he had gathered reports of strange objects thrown upon the coasts of the Azores by western gales: oddly carved wood, reeds never seen in Europe, bodies of men with strange faces.[1] Toscanelli, a Florentine geographer, assured him that if the need arose, he could always break his voyage at the Antilia, those well-known but unfortunately mythical islands that map-makers for centuries had used to decorate the unknown. Best of all, he had both ancient and modern scholarship on his side: the cosmographical studies of Aeneas Sylvius, finished after he had become Pope in 1458; Cardinal Pierre d'Ailly's *Imago Mundi* (c. 1410) and his later pamphlets, inspired by Ptolemy's *Geography*. The more than one thousand notes Columbus entered in the margins of the *Imago Mundi* indicate how carefully he read this great compilation of compilations. It revealed Aristotle's opinion that between western Spain and eastern India the sea is small, and Seneca's judgment that with favorable winds it could be navigated in a few days. The Old Testament Esdras clearly states that only one seventh of the earth is covered by water; and although its reasoning is more involved, Pliny's most unnatural *Natural History* draws a similar conclusion. So accessible was the eastern edge of Asia, the authorities argued or implied, that one wonders why they did not attempt a western voyage themselves. Instead, they merely supported what the Genoese sailor knew from his "scientific" calculations: Only twenty-four hundred nautical miles separated Japan from the Canary Islands.[2] Encouraged by ancient and medieval cosmographical errors, and by his own miscalculations of about four hundred and fifty per cent, Columbus missed the famous Antilia, caught the more substantial easterly trade winds, and found the West precisely where he had determined the East should begin.

In our first frustrated efforts to relate Elizabethan literary criticism to Elizabethan literature, the frequent disparities between theories and performances may often remind us of the man who blundered upon the New World. How paltry or irrelevant most of the era's critical pronouncements appear when measured against its marvelous accomplishments. Observations on the art of English poesy rarely lead us to anticipate anything as fine as the poetry that soon emerges, and instructors in versifying seem seldom aware of the splendid examples already at hand. With good reason we expect intentions to run alongside or slightly ahead of achievements, and we are startled to discover deeds apparently outstripping professed designs. Had every line of Elizabethan literature been lost, should we not have in contemporary criticism convincing evidence that the loss could not have been very great? And would all the age's theorizing adequately indicate even the nature, much less the success, of its artistic endeavors? We must not expect much from fussy rhetoricians turned critics, but is it not strange that when artists like Sidney and Spenser touch upon the present and future state of English letters, they pay little attention to the creative ferment about them, and seem to have "but careless ears for the immortal music of contemporary verse; that they find the measure of dramatic excellence in Buchanan's *Jephthes* or Watson's *Absolon*, or the secret of English poetry in hobbling hexameters?" [3]

Our initial impression that theory utterly fails to explain or even tally with performance may encourage either of two uneasy suspicions. Our first discomforting conjecture is that if Tudor creativity sailed with the same assumptions and goals explicitly advertised in most Tudor criticism, only blind chance saved it from shipwreck. The artists, in other words, did not guide themselves to success, but like Columbus simply stumbled upon lands far richer than those they sought. We of course reject this analogy, for it leads us from an improbable geographical truth to a wholly incredible aesthetic hypothesis. This way lies madness, absurd intimations of the legendary monkey at its typewriter, haphazardly punching out another *King Lear*. Far better to yield to our second suspicion that the keenest critical thinking of the period was never published and probably never written, and that we must therefore not expect to find the most relevant critical backgrounds neatly outlined in the era's formal definitions. The theories that shaped and best explain the art of *Hamlet*, for example, are implicitly recorded within the play itself; its skillful characterization, articulation of theme, and very structuring certainly prove that at least one Elizabethan thought more profoundly, if less explicitly, about the nature of tragedy than any of his fellow theorists would ever suggest.

TRAGEDY IN THEORY AND PRACTICE

We have already noted how great art may be abused when its meaning is confused with or limited to the meanings of its *literary* backgrounds. We need only commit Shakespeare with his more theoretical peers to see that racking genius upon *critical* common-places is equally dangerous. The following commentaries are as close as contemporary critics came to defining the tragic play-wright's means and ends. If we were to approach *Hamlet* with only their expectations, how much of its grandeur might pass unnoticed? In his *Defence of Poetry* (1579) Thomas Lodge notes that even the ancient tragedians "set forth the sower fortune of many exiles, the miserable fal of haples princes, the reuinous decay of many countryes." [4] Also attempting a brief history of drama, William Webbe's *Discourse of English Poetrie* (1586) reveals that "Tragedy wryters" eventually related "onely sorrowfull and lament-able Hystories, bringing in the persons of Gods and Goddesses, Kynges and Queenes, and great states, whose partes were cheefely to express most miserable calamities and dreadful chaunces, which increased worse and worse, tyll they came to the most wofull plight that might be deuised" (I, 249). Such historical considera-tions lead Webbe to "comprehende" under the "Tragicall" even nondramatic poetry: "all dolefull complaynts, lamentable chaunces, and what soeuer is poetically expressed in sorrow and heauines."

Instead of providing helpful glosses upon *Hamlet*, Lodge and Webbe furnish us with questions that are almost misleading. Like Richard II, they simply "talk of graves, of worms, and epitaphs," those "sad stories of the death of kings" which most medieval narrators considered the essence of tragedy. The Canterbury pil-grims hardly needed to be told by Chaucer's Monk that

> Tragedie is to seyn a certeyn storie,
> As olde bookes maken us memorie,
> Of hym that stood in greet prosperitee,
> And is yfallen out of heigh degree
> Into myserie, and endeth wrecchedly.[5]

Even less do we need all of the Monk's gloomy examples to realize that in a world capriciously regulated by Dame Fortune, a man's character and deeds are both grandly irrelevant to his destiny. Seventeen times the jolly Monk spins Fortune's grim wheel; seven-teen times we watch great princes—both the vicious and the vir-tuous—dashed to earth. To qualify for the role of tragic hero, one need only be caught at the height of prosperity. If amid utter wretchedness one maintains a bare existence, there is always the comforting possibility that the wheel will be given another half-turn. Generally, however, Fortune's amoral behavior elicits a more moral reaction: a scorn for the slippery ways of this finite, transitory world, the Christian Stoicism of *The Knight's Tale*, with its repeated reminder that

> It is ful fair a man to bere hym evene,
> For al day meeteth men at unset stevene.
>   (I, 1523–1524)

But men who bear themselves with equanimity in the face of "unset" appointments are hardly the stuff of tragedy. Their composure is more likely to inspire the boring heroism of Addison's *Cato*.

Not all Elizabethan critics were willing to describe tragedy as simply the fall of the great. Like Lodge and Webbe, George (?) Puttenham provides in his *Arte of English Poesie* (1589) a short account of the development of poetic genres, and at first he also honors their medieval notions of tragedy. "Besides those Poets *Comick* there were other who serued also the stage, but medled not with so base matters, for they set forth the dolefull falles of infortunate & afflicted Princes, & were called Poets *Tragicall:* such were *Euripides* and *Sophocles* with the Greeks, *Seneca* among the Latines" (II, 27). Four chapters later, however, Puttenham introduces another aspect of tragedy, which allows its inclusion, along with satire and Old and New Comedy, among the "foure sundry formes of Poesie" not only *"Drammatick"* but "reprehensiue" (II, 36). After the earliest poets had composed hymns to their gods, they "chiefly studied the rebuke of vice, . . . for as yet for lacke of good ciuility and wholesome doctrines there was greater store of lewde lourdaines [louts] then of wise and learned Lords" (II, 32). To protect themselves from reprisals and to make their "most bitter inuectiue against vice and vicious men . . . seeme grauer and of more efficacie," these poet-priests disguised themselves as rural gods—satyrs or sylvans—and recited "verses of rebuke" out of bushes and briars. Having proved insufficiently persuasive, the biting sermons of these *"Satyristes"* gave place to the comic playwrights' more lively reprehensions, at first "sharpe and bitter after the nature of the *Satyre"* but eventually "more ciuill and pleasant a great deale, and not touching any man by name, but in a certaine generalitie glancing at euery abuse." Finally, Puttenham concludes, when all men were no longer social equals and sovereignty tempted the mighty into "all maner of lusts," the poets were granted nobler vices to castigate. As these princes died and "posteritie stood no more in dread of them, their infamous life and tyrannies were layd open to all the world, their wickednes reproched, their follies and extreme insolencies derided, and their miserable ends painted out in playes and pageants, to shew the *mutabilitie of fortune, and the iust punishment of God* in reuenge of a vicious and euill life" (II, 35. Italics added.)

In tracing the growth of "Poesie *Drammatick* [and] reprehensiue," Puttenham dates major developments according to the relationships he sees within different poetic genres instead of through historical documentation, thereby reckoning the passage of time with "logic" rather than chronology. And because these relationships center in the progressively nobler uses to which poetry's moral efficacy was put, his whole argument works toward a definition of tragedy as the representation of "iust punishment." The closing reference to Fortune's mutability, on the other hand, is unanticipated, illogical, and an apt tribute to the persistence of medieval views. But faint reminiscences of Fortune's wheel are even found amid the sophisticated Aristotelian criticism of Sidney's *Apologie for Poetrie* (c. 1583, printed 1595). When it is rightly used, Sidney reminds his poet-hating opponents, none can find fault with "high and excellent Tragedy, that openeth the greatest wounds, and sheweth forth the Vlcers that are couered with Tissue; that maketh Kinges feare to be Tyrants, and Tyrants manifest their tirannicall humors; that, with sturring the affects of admiration and commiseration [i.e., fear and pity?], teacheth the vncertainety of this world, and vpon how weake foundations guilden roofes are builded" (I, 177). Of all Elizabethan critics, only Sir John Harington seems wholly untouched by the medieval insistence that tragedy celebrate the transitoriness of life. In the first part of his *Briefe Apologie of Poetrie* (1591), at least half of which is taken from Sidney, he notes that tragedy is wholly free from "lightnes & wantonnes," representing "onely the cruell & lawlesse proceedings of Princes, mouing nothing but pitie or detestation" (II, 209).

The prime mover behind this shift in emphasis from "dreadfull chaunces" to "lawlesse proceedings" is impossible to determine. Although medieval and early Tudor plays and playwrights are hardly ever referred to in Elizabethan criticism, the still popular moralities could have suggested an Everyman who chose wrongly and, therefore, a glimpse of the tragedy of character. An earlier transition from blind Fortune to sinful man was made by Chaucer's contemporary, John Lydgate (c. 1370–c. 1451). Drawing upon some of the same materials used by the Monk, this stern moralist regards complaints against Fortune as idle words "which foolis vsen in ther aduersite for excusacioun." After all, he explains,

> It is nat she that pryncis gaff the fall,
> But vicious lyuyng, pleynli to endite.[6]

There were also Lydgate's numerous and equally moralistic offspring. The most famous, *The Mirror for Magistrates* (1559; expanded in 1563, 1578, and 1587), was in fact originally designed as an appendix to Lydgate's didactic handling of Boccaccio's *De Casibus Virorum Illustrium* (c. 1350). Its general editor, William Baldwin, expresses his astonishment that Boccaccio forgot "among his myserable princes, such as wer of our nacion, whose numbre is as great, as their aduentures wunderful. . . . But seinge the printers mynde is to haue vs followe where *Lidgate* left," the authors will begin with the reign of Richard II and continue "vnto this presente time," treating "suche as Fortune had dalyed with here in this ylande: whiche might be as a myrrour for al men . . . to shewe the slyppery deceytes of the waueryng lady, and the due rewarde of all kinde of vices." [7] Here again are Puttenham's apparently contradictory alternatives: external mishap and internal misrule. But once Baldwin and his fellows allow the ghosts of these fallen princes to make their laments, "due rewarde" is stressed. Regretfully but repeatedly the shades admit that they were Fortune's fools only in the sense of having freely and wrongfully succumbed to the wavering lady's tempting deceits. Thus the authors achieve the goal implicit in their title, edification through illustration, and thus they reflect what is popularly termed the Renaissance conception of man, the shaper of his own end, a conception that was of course shared and partly shaped by their medieval model.

Classical and Continental ideas and practices must have also influenced Elizabethan theories of tragedy. Roger Ascham concludes the Second Book of *The Scholemaster* (published posthumously in 1570) with a discussion of "the trew vse of perfite Imitation," and fondly recalls the days at Cambridge when he, Sir John Cheke, and Master Watson "had many pleasant talkes togither, in comparing the precepts of *Aristotle* and *Horace de Arte Poetica* with the examples of *Euripides, Sophocles,* and

Seneca. Few men, in writyng of Tragedies in our dayes, haue shot at this marke. Some in *England,* moe in *France, Germanie,* and *Italie* also, haue written Tragedies in our tyme: of the which not one I am sure is able to abyde the trew touch of *Aristotles* preceptes and *Euripides* examples, saue onely two that euer I saw, *M. Watsons Absalon* and *Georgius Buckananus Iephthe*" (I, 23–24). Although Ascham never explains the exact nature of those precepts and examples—his interests, to judge from the immediate context, lie in form rather than content—each classical critic or dramatist he cites either argues for or lends indirect support to the tragedy of character: despite an allowance for external mishap and an insistence upon the world's slippery ways, Seneca's carefully prepared and most violent retributions; Sophocles's and Euripides's plots, spun by the passions of men and gods; Aristotle's demand that the "action" that tragedy imitates spring from two natural causes, character and thought. Implicit approval could even be found in Horace's frequently quoted comments on the poet's didactic end, paraphrased by Webbe as "He misseth nothing of his marke which ioyneth profitt with delight, as well delighting his Readers as profiting them with counsell" (I, 250). Aristotle's *Poetics* had of course been translated into Italian and discussed by Italian critics in the first half of the century, and Sidney, whose *Apologie* is "a veritable epitome of the literary criticism of the Italian Renaissance," is the first Englishman to reflect their neo-Aristotelian theories in a more than incidental and allusive manner.[8]

Although native, classical, and European writers may have all aided in undermining the notion of Fortune's wheel, we must also allow for nonliterary influences. Like the men who designed the *Mirror,* the Elizabethan critics were nourished by sermons illustrating the wages of sin, and must have heard as well the historians' and philosophers' rival claims to pre-eminence as teachers of virtue, the very assertions, in fact, against which Sidney measures the accomplishments of his "peerelesse Poet" (I, 164). The conception of history as a series of examples to follow or avoid underlies even the power politics of Machiavelli's *The Prince* (1532; written in 1513): If Lorenzo de' Medici will but "tread the footsteps" of those ruthlessly efficient and duplicitously successful heroes whose careers he has outlined, Italy shall be united and her barbaric conquerers expelled.[9] In view of what can only be described as "in the air," it would be absurd to see the artists alone catching that "air" directly and leaving the critics to experience it only through their readings. Although Puttenham, for example, refers to Lydgate or *The Falls of Princes* a half-dozen times, we should not insist that the critic who occasionally interlaces his theories with reminders of superior Christian concepts and duties (e.g., II, 29, 60) needed Lydgate or his successors to conceive of tragedy as a revelation of God's just punishment. Similarly, had Seneca's revenge and Everyman's conscience never been displayed, Hamlet would nevertheless have grappled with "To be, or not to be," though perhaps a little differently.

Whichever the major influences, one conclusion seems inescapable: Elizabethan theories of tragedy were rarely influenced by Elizabethan tragedies. If Aristotle often reminds us of a Monday morning quarterback, reflecting upon the ways in which the weekend's games were and should have been directed, the Tudor critics almost invariably imply that no significant matches were played. We can forgive Ascham for his vague and sketchy treatment of contemporary tragedy because his primary concern is to exemplify successful imitation within poetry as a whole. What to him are first things must come first, in this case Watson's mastery of classical versification. Secondly, before 1568, when Ascham died, the "some" English tragedies written with or without his touchstones were very few indeed. It would be another eight years before the first English playhouse, the Theatre, was erected by James Burbage, and there was even less common ground between the learned Cambridge lecturer and the strolling players, with their renditions of bombastic stuff like Thomas Preston's *A Lamentable Tragedie, mixed full of pleasant mirth, containing the life of Cambises King of Percia* (c. 1565).

The only plays Ascham might have thought significant, yet ignores, are of one type, the rather free translations of Seneca's *Troas* (1559), *Thyestes* (1560), and *Hercules Furens* (1561) by an Oxford student, Jasper Heywood, and the Inns of Court tragedies like Sackville and Norton's *Gorboduc* (acted, 1562) and Gascoigne and Kinwelmersh's *Iocasta* (acted, 1566), both of which follow Heywood's cue in attempting to out-Seneca Seneca. Although little action takes place on stage, *Gorboduc*'s bloody events are vividly recalled by the messengers who hurry in and out, and the "argument" or plot summary neatly outlines its series of atrocities:

> *Gorboduc* king of Brittaine, diuided his realme in his life time to his sonnes, *Ferrex* and *Porrex*. The sonnes fell to

discention. The yonger killed the elder. The mother that
more dearely loued the elder, for reuenge killed the
yonger. The people moued with the crueltie of the fact,
rose in rebellion and slew both father and mother. The
nobilitie assembled and most terribly destroyed the rebels.
And afterwardes for want of issue of the prince whereby
the succession of the crowne became vncertaine, they fell
to ciuill warre, in which both they and many of their
issues were slaine, and the land for a long time almost desolate and miserably wasted.[10]

Even in translating Seneca the Elizabethans could rarely resist
improving upon the Roman's melodrama, violence, and sententious
moralizing. The "Faythfully Englished" *Thyestes,* for instance,
concludes with a scene "Added to the Tragedy by the Translatour," [11] Heywood's opportunity to reveal how he has mastered
what Sidney will later term "the height of *Seneca* his stile" (I, 197).
Having been tricked by his brother, Atreus, into feasting upon his
sons' flesh, the English Thyestes must now step forth for sixty-two
lines, first summoning all the monsters of hell and then repeatedly
recollecting the whole gory business:

> I my sonnes, alas, have made my meate.
> I could thy famyne better beare, my paunch is now repleate
> With foode: and with my children three, my belly is extent.
> O filthy fowles and gnawyng gripes, that Tytius
>   bosome rent
> Beholde a fitter pray for you, to fill your selves uppone
> Then are the growing guts of him: foure wombes
>   enrapt in one
> This paunche at once shall fill you all. . . .[12]

All that remains is *Iocasta: A Tragedie vvritten in Greeke by
Euripides.* Although its subtitle would appear to take us back to
Ascham and his "trew touch" of great tragedy, the play is more
English, Italian, and Roman than Greek, more Senecan than
Euripidean, for Gascoigne and Kinwelmersh actually translated
Lodovico Dolce's *Giocasta,* itself a free version of a Latin render-
ing of Euripides's *Phoenissae.*[13] Moreover, to judge from the man-
ner in which they handled Dolce, "the principal charm of
Giocasta probably lay in its close resemblance to the ideals of
Seneca." [14] That the translators also had one eye on *Gorboduc*

is indicated by their use of blank verse and dumb shows, and by Gascoigne's marginal notation to Oedipus's closing reflections: "A mirrour for Magistrates." [15]

Just as Ascham had found in tragedy "the goodliest Argument of all" (I, 19), yet not one in English that shot at the right mark, so Sidney, about fifteen years later, surveys the potentialities of "high and excellent Tragedy" with enthusiasm, only to conclude that they have yet to be realized. No English tragedy, he laments, can "iustly bring forth [the] diuine admiration" evoked by the Latin plays of George Buchanan (I, 201). But Sidney alters two of his predecessor's touchstones. Whereas Ascham included Seneca among his examples, he insisted that "the *Grecians Sophocles* and *Euripides* far ouer match our *Seneca* in Latin, namely in Οἰκονομία *et Decoro* [arrangement and propriety (of words?)]," even though Seneca's "elocution and verse be verie commendable for his tyme" (I, 19). Sidney appears to reverse this criterion. Although Euripides is later used as *an* example (I, 198), Seneca is *the* model. In one of the few passages of Elizabethan criticism that carefully examines contemporary literature, Sidney congratulates the authors of *Gorboduc*. "Full of stately speeches and well sounding Phrases," it climbs "to the height of *Seneca* his stile" (I, 196–197). It is, moreover, "full of notable moralitie, which it doth most delightfully teach," thereby obtaining—and here every critic, especially Ascham, would concur—"the very end of Poesie." Only one flaw, in fact, prevents *Gorboduc* from remaining "an exact model of all Tragedies": It is "faulty both in place and time, the two necessary companions of all corporall [corporeal] actions. For where the stage should alwaies represent but one place, and the vttermost time presupposed in it should be, both by *Aristotles* precept and common reason, but one day, there is both many dayes, and many places, inartificially imagined" (I, 197).

Here is Ascham's second touchstone, altered even more than the respective merits of Euripides and Seneca. For whatever Aristotle's precepts meant to Ascham, they could hardly have signified the unities of time and place that Castelvetro formulated the same year that *The Scholemaster* was published, and which Sidney now holds up as Aristotle pure and undefiled.[16] Aristotle's sole "precept" regarding unity is his plea for art as an organic whole, a structural and perhaps thematic oneness, a unity of action that the poet achieves by admitting only those incidents with necessary or probable connections (*Poetics*, VIII). And if Sidney's Italianated

Aristotle is too refined, his "common reason" is too hasty. As Shakespeare's Theseus, caught amid a play as "tedious brief" and full of "tragical mirth" as Preston's *Cambises,* charitably observes, "The best in this kind are but shadows; and the worst are no worse, if imagination amend them."¹⁷ Unlike Sidney, Shakespeare realized that the same amending imagination that allows us to see a single, faraway time most vividly can also help us turn "th' accomplishment of many years / Into an hour-glass;" and that if "the quick forge and working-house of thought" aids us in pretending that a relatively bare stage is really a London tavern in one scene, it will serve as well to change the tavern into "the vasty fields of France" a few moments later (*Henry V,* Prologues I, V).

In all fairness to Sidney, however, we must also admit that when Theseus suggests that imagination can amend the "shadows" before them, his Queen replies, "It must be your imagination then, and not theirs," the "hempen homespun" players' and playwright's. Shakespeare would have agreed with Sidney that it argues no facility in the playwright to tax his audience's imagination unduly, and had the usually far from dogmatic critic lived to see Shakespeare artfully violate his unities, he probably would have emended them. If Sidney judges native drama by standards more stringent than Aristotle's, in other words, it is because his Euripides has not yet written, and he has, therefore, no glorious exceptions to check "common reason's" formulation of rules. Sidney is simply drawing upon the best examples available when he complains that the "inartificially imagined" *Gorboduc* is nevertheless incomparably better than the popular stage's absurd derring-do. Instead of one place being represented, in these plays

you shal haue *Asia* of the one side, and *Affrick* of the other, and so many other vnder-kingdoms, that the Player, when he commeth in, must euer begin with telling where he is, or els the tale wil not be conceiued. Now ye shal haue three Ladies walke to gather flowers, and then we must beleeue the stage to be a Garden. By and by, we heare newes of shipwracke in the same place, and then wee are to blame if we accept it not for a Rock. Vpon the backe of that, comes out a hidious Monster, with fire and smoke, and then the miserable beholders are bounde to take it for a Caue.

(I, 197)

Such romantic devisings are even more liberal with time, for in "two hours space," prince and princess "fall in loue. . . . She is got with childe, deliuered of a faire boy; he is lost, groweth a man, falls in loue, and is ready to get [beget] another child."

Fortunately, enough of this wild stuff has survived to justify Sidney's classical indignation. Anyone who thinks his censures too severe should be sentenced to a two-hour reading of *Sir Clyomon and Clamydes* (c. 1570) or *Common Conditions* (c. 1576), preferably in a facsimile reprint without full stage directions. If the reader remembers to forget *The Winter's Tale*, he will be as convinced as Sidney that no dramatic good can come of these haphazard adventures. If, on the other hand, he brings his fuller knowledge into play and finds *Sir Clyomon* whispering "On to Shakespeare," he will at least not be surprised to hear Sidney saying, "Back to the ancients!" The same distinction applies to his discussion of mood. We smile when Sidney singles out the "mingling [of] Kings and Clownes" as evidence of "grosse absurdities," plays that "be neither right Tragedies, nor right Comedies" (I, 199). But he is correct in claiming that the ancients "neuer, or very daintily, match Horn-pypes and Funeralls," and no play of his time has survived to contradict the charge that "neither the admiration and commiseration, nor the right sportfulnes, is by their mungrell Tragy-comedie obtained." Unlike some of the best French and worst English classicists of the succeeding century, Sidney never places great rules before great art. Toward the end of his essay he explains why "diuers smally learned Courtiers" often show "a more sounde stile" than some "professors of learning"(I, 203). It is because "the Courtier, following that which by practise hee findeth fittest to nature, therein (though he know it not) doth according to Art, though not by Art: where the other, vsing Art to shew Art, and not to hide Art (as in these cases he should doe), flyeth from nature, and indeede abuseth Art." In view of Sidney's preference for what is "fittest to nature," it may be that his point concerning the contemporary mingling of kings and clowns is not that it cannot or should not be done, but that it has neither been nor is likely to be done successfully. If "the matter so carrieth it," if the clown is not simply "thrust in . . . by head and shoulders," and if that clown is less a country bumpkin than a fool—and yet "not altogether fool" (*King Lear*, I. iv. 150)—then he might "play a part in maiesticall matters" with both "decencie" and "discretion" (I, 199).

Prior to Sidney, the only extensive commentary upon contemporary practice is offered by a playwright to justify his own
superior dramaturgy. In his dedicatory letter to *The right excellent and famous Historye of Promos and Cassandra* (1578),
George Whetstone explains why his play has ten acts. He was
forced to divide "the whole history into two Commedies, for that,
Decorum vsed, it would not be conuayed in one" (I, 58). Since the
action of both parts is set upon the streets of the city of Julio
(obviously London), the decorum honored here is the unity of
time; the events that Shakespeare elaborates upon in the first four
acts of *Measure for Measure* are conveyed in *Promos, Part I*, while
the incidents he indecorously adds in Act V are correctly reserved
by Whetstone for *Part II*. After complaining that Italian, French,
and Spanish comedies are much too lascivious, and that German
comedies are but sermons in disguise, Whetstone turns upon the
Englishman's romantic offerings, all "most vaine, indiscreete, and
out of order" (I, 59). By the same standards and in very similar
terms, he condemns the same popular stuff that grieved Sidney five
years later. Having first grounded "his worke on impossibilities,"
the popular playwright runs breathlessly through "the worlde,
marryes, gets Children, makes Children men, men to conquer
kingdomes, murder Monsters, and bringeth Gods from Heauen, and
fetcheth Diuels from Hel" (I, 59). Worst of all, he will do anything for a laugh: "Manye tymes (to make mirthe) they make a
Clowne companion with a Kinge; in theyr graue Counsels they
allow the aduise of fooles; yea, they vse one order of speech for
all persons: a grose *Indecorum* . . ." (I, 59–60). To judge from
his detailed stage directions, Whetstone intended *Promos* to be performed, and probably in order to raise his audience's literary tastes
as much as their moral standards. In 1582, however, he notes that
Promos was "yet never presented upon stage," and by 1584 he is
attacking "Stage-plays (unproperly called, Tragedies, Comedies,
and Morals), as the springs of many vices, and the stumbling-
blocks of godliness and virtue." [18]

As far as tragedy is concerned, then, up to 1583 theory is only
occasionally influenced by practice. Neither the critics' slight
awareness of nor their usually negative responses to the popular
drama is surprising. Quite startling, however, is the fact that as
we move through the last twenty years of Elizabeth's reign, as
the popular stage attracts the genius of Kyd, Marlowe, and Shakespeare, critical comment diminishes. Whereas a good share of the

worst Elizabethan literature, the drama of the sixties, seventies, and
early eighties, receives some careful, if disapproving notice, in
other words, the drama succeeding it, by which roughly half of the
greatness of the Elizabethan literary achievement must be measured, is almost ignored. If Kyd's extremely popular *Spanish
Tragedy*, for example, was on the boards by 1585, as many scholars insist,[19] Webbe does not consider the event worth mentioning in 1586. Whether Whetstone is accounted worthy to "weare the
Lawrell wreathe" (I, 244) because of his *Promos and Cassandra*
is not clear, but when Webbe's references are obviously to the
drama, his praise is reserved for plays equally decorous and academic. It is "the learned company of Gentlemen Schollers and
students of the Vniuersities and Innes of Courte" that inspires his
admiration. Among the important writers placed next to Whetstone is Robert Wilmot, who had about twenty years before col-
laborated with four other Inner Temple gentlemen to turn
Boccaccio's tale of Tancred and Ghismonda (*Decameron*, IV, 1)
into the thoroughly Senecan *Gismond of Salerne* (acted, 1568).
And when Wilmot brought out a second edition of his tragedy in
1591, "polished according to the decorum of these daies" (that is,
with decasyllabic quatrains now cast in blank verse), Webbe's prefatory epistle commended his "pains in disrobing [it] of [its]
antique curiositie, and adorning [it] with the approved guise of our
stateliest English terms." [20] From this we may gather that Webbe
was a very earnest student of the drama, or at least of the kind
of drama that remained correct, classical, and therefore statically
Senecan for more than a quarter of a century. The only other
"dramatists" saluted in 1586 are the translators like Jasper Heywood, those "laudable Authors of *Seneca* in English" (I, 244), not
The Spanish Tragedy, which did a far better job of "translating"
Seneca into a modern Elizabethan than the relatively pale academic
imitations.

By 1589 and 1591, when Puttenham and Harington discuss the
best English tragedies, Marlowe's *Tamburlaine* (c. 1587), *Dr.
Faustus* (c. 1588–1591), and *The Jew of Malta* (c. 1589) join the
critics' list of plays to be snubbed. Puttenham discusses the origin
and nature of tragedy in some detail (II, 27, 31–36), but the only
tragic playwrights he mentions are "the Lord of Buckhurst &
Maister *Edward Ferrys*," who "for such doings as I haue sene of
theirs, do deserue the hyest price" (II, 65). Buckhurst is of course
Thomas Sackville, who contributed to *The Mirror for Magistrates*

and, along with Thomas Norton, wrote the stately *Gorboduc*. Edward Ferrys is probably George Ferrers, who also contributed to *The Mirror* and helped devise entertainments for the courts of Edward VI and Elizabeth; if his tragical "doings" are other than his verses for *The Mirror*, however, none has survived. And such vague criticism is the best Puttenham can manage in a section expressly devoted to describing that "crew of Courtly makers" who "in her Maiesties time that now is are sprong vp" (II, 63). "Makers" outside the court are obviously not even worth a passing glance. Puttenham's awareness of their existence is reflected only in chance remarks illustrating proper and improper rhyming. There is no "fowler fault" than to rhyme with words "fetched from the Latine inkhorne [pedantic neologisms drawn from the scholar's study] or borrowed of strangers [unnaturalized foreign loan words]," for their use is "nothing pleasant, sauing perchaunce to the common people, who reioyse much to be at playes and enterludes, and, besides their naturall ignoraunce, haue at all such times their eares so attentiue to the matter, and their eyes vpon the shewes of the stage, that they take little heede to the cunning of the rime, and therefore be as well satisfied with that which is grosse, as with any other finer and more delicate." [21]

Harington must have shared Puttenham's sentiments. To prove that "Tragedies well handled be a most worthy kinde of Poesie" (II, 210), he furnishes a more up-to-date example: *"Richard the 3."* Unfortunately, however, it is the *Richard III* "that was played at S. *Johns* in Cambridge," Thomas Legge's Latin tragedy, performed in 1579.[22] Similarly frustrating is the apparently happy prophecy of Gabriel Harvey in *Pierce's Supererogation*. Scornfully turning from the "phantasticall bibble-bables" of his enemy, Pierce Penniless (alias Thomas Nashe), and other clownish scribblers, he announces that "the winde is chaunged, & there is a busier pageant vpon the stage" (II, 261). At last, in 1593, something significant! But Harvey is speaking metaphorically; The busy players are Gilbert, Drake, Frobisher, Raleigh, and Essex. Harvey, in short, takes no notice of Kyd or Shakespeare, and Marlowe serves only to point up obvious folly: Nashe's "gayest floorishes" are merely Robert Greene's "crankes, or Marlowes brauados; his iestes but the dregges of common scurrilitie, or the shreds of the theater, or the of-scouring of new Pamflets . . ." (II, 266).

Throughout the last decade of Elizabeth's reign the story is much the same. The classical playwrights are frequently celebrated, their academic or courtly translators and imitators often praised, and the popular dramatists usually ignored or brushed aside in terms like Puttenham's or Harvey's. In stressing *The Excellency of the English Tongue* (c. 1596), for instance, Richard Carew notes how "apt and forcible" this language is "for expressing our passions" (II, 287). How easily he could have proved his point with what Jonson later called *"Marlowes* mighty line." Instead, he quibbles over the relative superiority of English interjections: "Findeinge ourselues sometimes somewhat agreeued, wee cry *Ah;* yf more deeply, *Oh;* when we pittie, *Alas;* when wee bemone, *Alacke;* neither of them soe effeminate as the Italyane *Deh* or the French *hélas.*" About 1603, Samuel Daniel manages a successful *Defence of Ryme* against Thomas Campion, and graciously confesses that his "Aduersary hath wrought [only] this much vpon me, that I thinke a Tragedie would indeede best comporte with a blank Verse and dispence with Ryme, sauing in the *Chorus,* or where a sentence [that is, a maxim or precept] shall require a couplet" (II, 382). For Daniel at least, the blank verse of Kyd, Marlowe, and Shakespeare was not so convincing as the least absurd of Campion's attacks on rhyme in the *Obseruations in the Art of English Poesie* (1602).

The Professional Playwright's Literary Status

It is not until about 1596 that we discover popular dramatists admitted into the company of respectable writers, and even then through what may seem to us a back door. To prove that "what soeuer grace any other Languadge carryeth, in Verse or Prose, in Tropes [figures of speech] or Metaphors, . . . maye all be liuely and exactly represented in ours," Carew honors the Elizabethan method of cataloguing ancients and moderns according to literary kinds. "Will you haue *Platos* vayne? reede *Sir Thomas Smith.* . . . Will yow reade *Virgill?* take the *Earll of Surrey: Catullus? Shakespheare,* and *Marlowes* fragment: *Ovid? Daniell: Lucane? Spencer.* . . . Will yow haue all in all for prose and verse? take the miracle of our age Sir *Philip Sydney*" (II, 293). Obviously both dramatists are being celebrated for their likeness to Catullus, the Roman lyric, erotic, and epigrammatic poet; for their *literature,* in other words, not their *plays.* Shakespeare's credentials were *Venus and Adonis* (1593) and *The Rape of Lucrece* (1594), and Marlowe's, the unfinished translation-transfiguration of Musaeus's *Hero and Leander*, published posthumously in 1598. Shakespeare's worth is similarly measured in *The Returne from Parnassus, II*, the last of three plays written and acted at St. John's College, Cambridge, between 1598 and 1603. Presumably its sprightly, academic author concurs with his character, "Iudicio," when he comments upon Shakespeare's place in modern literature. Who does not admire "*Adonis* loue or *Lucre's* rape," Judicio queries, for Shakespeare's "sweeter verse containes hart robbing life [heart throbbing life, or line?]." [23] Overlooking nonliterary trifles like *1 Henry IV* (published in 1598), *Julius Caesar* (acted in 1599), and perhaps even *Hamlet* (entered for publication in 1602), the critic offers only one suggestion for improvement: "Could but a grauer subiect him content, / Without loues foolish languishment." Although Judicio has clearly related Marlowe to the stage only a moment before, Shakespeare's name is not besmirched until the ignorant and insolent Will Kemp makes his boast: "Few of the vniuersity pen plaies well, they smell too much of that writer *Ouid*, and that writer *Metamorphosis*, and talke too much of *Proserpina* & *Iuppiter*. Why heres our fellow *Shakespeare* puts them all downe. . . ." [24] Small wonder, then, that after Kemp departs, one of the impoverished students he has interviewed as a prospective playwright for the Lord Chamberlain's Company laments, "And must the basest trade yeeld vs reliefe?" [25]

The scholar's sense of degradation is founded upon three clearly defined Elizabethan views regarding all literary activity: To write verses is commendable, to live by them is base, and to write professionally for professionals is basest of all. Because "the authors owne purpose . . . is to make of a rude rimer a learned and a Courtly Poet" (II, 164), Puttenham never contemplates the horrors of the Muses being prostituted. But some courtiers, he complains, are either too modest or too fearful that their fashionable versifying will be taken as more than the outgrowth of a gentlemanly cultural avocation. "It is so come to passe that they haue no courage to write, &, if they haue, yet are they loath to be a knowen of their skill. So as I know very many notable Gentlemen in the Court that haue written commendably, and suppressed it agayne, or els suffred it to be publisht without their owne names to it: as if it were a discredit for a Gentleman to seeme learned and to shew him selfe amorous of any good Art" (II, 22). We would see how many "haue written excellently well," he later laments, if only "their doings could be found out and made publicke with the rest" (II, 63). Some forty years after, Michael Drayton concludes his criticism with a similar apology. He can but comment upon those "few men" who have published their "numbers,"

> For such whose poems, be they nere so rare,
> In private chambers, that incloistered are,
> And by transcription daintyly must goe;
> As though the world unworthy were to know,
> Their rich composures, let those men that keepe
> These wonderous reliques in their judgement deepe,
> And cry them up so, let such Peeces bee
> Spoke of by those that shall come after me. . . .[26]

As Puttenham makes clear, some excellent "doings" are dramatic. A gentleman-scholar could write closet drama or plays to be performed by his fellow students at the Inner Temple or Oxford without being stigmatized. These plays almost always imitated classical models and would therefore be considered legitimate literary exercises. If they were just for fun, like the *Parnassus* trilogy, they were at least respectably uncommercial, free from the charge another Cambridge satirist had recently leveled:

> Shame that the Muses should be bought and sold,
> For every peasant's brass, on each scaffold.[27]

When his revised version of *The Tragedie of Tancred and Gismund* appeared in 1591, Robert Wilmot excused the indecorum of publishing a play by the example of Buchanan's *Jephthes*.[28] Although Daniel, on the other hand, was never reluctant to publish his works, he clearly dissociated himself from any "peasant's brass." His "verse respects nor Thames nor Theaters," he tells his *Delia*, his patroness, the Countess of Pembroke; "God forbid I should my papers blot, / With mercynary lines, with seruile pen. . . ." [29] Two years later he honored his promise with the very classical *Cleopatra* (1594), inspired by Lady Pembroke's "well grac'd *Antony*," not by the base motive of having it performed. Although his *Philotas* (1604) was eventually performed, it was presented in a private theater, not upon the common stage; and even then he explains that it was originally intended to be acted "by certaine Gentlemens sonnes, as a private recreation," and speaks with some embarrassment about being "driven by necessity to make use of my pen, and the Stage to bee the mouth of my lines, which before were never heard to speake but in silence. . . ." [30] His best excuse is that he thought "so true a History, in the ancient forme of a Tragedy, could not but have had an unreproveable passage with the time, and the better sort of men; seeing with what idle fictions, and grosse follies, the Stage at this day abused mens recreations." [31]

Perhaps no writer better expresses orthodox literary attitudes than Donne's friend, Sir Richard Baker, in his *Chronicle of the Kings of England* (1643). Like Holinshed, Baker sums up the greatness of each reign in terms of its most famous men. For Elizabeth's age he notes statesmen like Burleigh and Walsingham, sailors and soldiers like Raleigh, Drake, and Essex. The "literary" figures are mainly theologians, however, and Baker concludes his account with what may strike us as damningly faint praise:

> After such men, it might be thought ridiculous to speak of Stage-players; but seeing excellency in the meanest things deserve remembring, and *Roscius* the [Roman] Comedian is recorded in History with such commendation, it may be allowed us to do the like with some of our Nation. *Richard Bourbidge* [Burbage] and *Edward Allen*, two such actors as no age must ever look to see the like: and, to make their Comedies compleat, *Richard Tarleton*, who for the part called the Clowns Part, never had his match, never will have. For Writers of Playes, and such as had been Players the[m]selves, *William Shakespeare* and *Benjamin Johnson*, have specially left their Names recommended to posterity.[32]

Sir Richard clearly admired "the meanest things." When the acrid Puritan leader, William Prynne, attacked the theater in 1633 with his enormous *Histrio-Mastix*, Baker countered with *Theatrum Redivivum, or the Theatre Vindicated*. But his ungrudging admiration did not betray him into anything so foolish as speaking of a great sermon and *King Lear* in the same breath. Nor does the Puritan education of Sir Thomas Bodley (1545–1613) wholly explain his pious desire that the great library he was founding at Oxford should never house "baggage books," plays in quarto or folio volumes.[33]

With such a host of respectable witnesses to correct modern expectations, it should now be easier to understand why the popular stage, even as it approaches greatness, is ignored by Webbe and Harington, and used by Puttenham and Harvey only as illustrations of self-evident worthlessness. To any impartial observer, by 1603 it must have been obvious that "the basest trade," maintained by "every peasant's brass," would leave posterity a far richer legacy than the height of Wilmot and Daniel their styles. But we cannot find any record of fact triumphing over theory, and very little evidence to qualify Professor Holzknecht's claims that however profitable, "plays could add nothing to a man's literary reputation," or that "works meant to be read were literature; those designed for the mouths of actors were art of another kind, ephemeral products of no permanent literary value." [34] To judge from his own behavior, Shakespeare would have found nothing strange in Daniel's, Carew's, or the *Parnassus* playwright's oversight of his own plays. The only writings Shakespeare seems to have been interested in having published—at least the only things he bothered to write dedications for—are the very pieces that Carew and "Iudicio" consider his sole literary credentials: *Venus and Adonis* and *The Rape of Lucrece*. And beneath the former's title appears the telltale Latin posy: "Let the vulgar admire vile things; for me may golden-haired Apollo provide cups full of water from the Castalian spring [that is, from the fountain whence the Muses drank inspiration]." [35] Did Shakespeare therefore silently concur with the sentiment of his fellow dramatist, Thomas Heywood, when he confessed, "It never was any great ambition in me to be in this kind voluminously read"? [36] Some of Shakespeare's greatest plays were only in manuscripts and carelessly printed quartos when he died in 1616; perhaps many would have been permanently lost had not his former partners, Heminge and Condell, carefully and lovingly gathered the scraps together and published the First Folio seven years later. Certainly they did not intend to slight their friend's memory when they begged the Earls of Pembroke and Montgomery "to descend to the reading of these trifles," and observed that the "meanest of things are made more precious, when they are dedicated to Temples." Had not their friend himself admitted to his patron, the mysterious "Mr. W. H." of the sonnets, that he was "sham'd by that which I bring forth, / And so should you, to love things nothing worth"? [37] E. K. Chambers notes that of the more than 280 plays recorded by Philip Henslowe as produced or commissioned by the companies for which he acted as banker between 1592 and 1603, only 40-odd have survived. [38] If all 280 were "things nothing worth" by Elizabethan standards, how many of the lost 240 would have been by ours?

To every rule there are of course a few exceptions. Driven by the odd notion that his plays were literature, Jonson saw his dramatic efforts through the press in 1616 and dignified the collection with the title, *The Workes of Beniamin Jonson*. By "Workes," Jonson was obviously encouraging the public to think of his writings in terms of his much admired classical authors' *Opera*, literary works, works of art. Playwrights like Thomas Heywood were indignant, but contemporary wiseacres facetiously asked for explanations. "Pray, tell me, Ben," queried one wit,

> where does the mystery lurk,
> What others call a play you call a work? . . .
> The author's friend thus for the author says
> Ben's plays are works, when others' works are plays,

and despite its humble preface, the rationale underlying Heminge's and Condell's labor of love inspired similar merriment.[39] Aside from Jonson, in fact, the only Elizabethan dramatists who acknowledge an interest in and often an enthusiasm for the common stage are two of the bohemian playwrights, Nashe and Greene. Nashe's *Pierce Penilesse* (1592) proves popular playwrighting a "rare exercise of vertue" in that "our forefathers valiant acts (that haue line [lain] long buried in rustie brasse and worme-eaten bookes) are reuiued, and they themselues raised from the Graue of Obliuion . . . to pleade their aged Honours in open presence . . . to these degenerate effeminate dayes of ours." [40] If the *Harry the Sixth* that Henslowe records as having been first performed on March 3, 1592, is Shakespeare's *1 Henry VI*, the honor of being the first to take note of Shakespeare as a dramatist probably goes to Nashe, for his examples of patriotic dramaturgy begin with the following rhetorical question: "How would it haue ioyed braue *Talbot* (the terror of the French) to thinke that after he had lyne two hundred yeares in his Tombe, he should triumphe againe on the Stage, and haue his bones newe embalmed with the teares of ten thousand spectators at least (at seuerall times), who, in the Tragedian that represents his person, imagine they behold him fresh bleeding." [41] And because the common stage shows "the ill successe of treason, the fall of hastie climbers, the wretched end of vsurpers, the miserie of ciuill dissention, and how iust God is euermore in punishing of murther," Nashe plans to eternize in Latin those deserving actors like famous Ned Allen.[42]

Nashe's friend, on the other hand, effects a balance between Pierce's uncommon, perhaps rebellious praise and the *Parnassus* playwright's conventional disdain. *Greene's Groatsworth of Wit* (1592) includes an interesting letter to his "fellowe Schollers about this Cittie," a warning *"To those Gentlemen his Quondam* [former] *acquaintance, that spend their wits in making Plaies,* [whom] R. G. *wisheth a better exercise, and wisdome to preuent his extremities."* [43] First the "famous gracer of Tragedians" (very likely Marlowe) is cautioned not to abuse his "excellent wit," God's gift, with atheism and Machiavellianism. Then "young *Juuenall,* that byting Satyrist, that lastlie with mee together writ a Comedie" (probably Nashe, but perhaps Lodge) is advised not to censure too severely. Finally, there is one "driuen (as my selfe) to extreame shifts" (probably Peele), whose example brings the impoverished Greene to his main point: Write no more lines for "those Puppits . . . that speake from our mouths," those clowns

> garnisht in our colours. Is it not strange that I, to whom they al haue beene beholding: is it not like that you, to whome they all haue beene beholding, shall (were ye in that case that I am now) be both at once of them forsaken? Yes trust them not: for there is an vpstart Crow, beautified with our feathers, that with his *Tygers heart wrapt in a Players hide,* supposes he is as well able to bumbast out a blanke verse as the best of you; and being an absolute *Johannes fac totum,* is in his owne conceit the onely Shake-scene in a countrie. O that I might intreate your rare wits to be imployed in more profitable courses: & let those Apes imitate [i.e., act out] your past excellence, and neuer more acquaint them with your admired inuentions. . . . For it is pittie men of such rare wits, should be subject to the pleasures of such rude groomes.[44]

If contemporary critical opinion accurately reflects enlightened Elizabethan attitudes, few educated Englishmen would have quarreled with Greene's conclusion. In his pitiful spectacle of "rude groomes" exploiting "rare wits," the Cambridge Master of Arts anticipates one of the major themes of the *Parnassus* trilogy, performed a decade later. What is exceptional is the argument leading to the predictable conclusion, for Greene insists that despite the rudeness of its actors—clods, clowns, mere puppets and apes—the popular stage has produced great art, "past excellence, . . . admired inuentions." The rareness of their university wits has, in fact, so beautified one Johnny-come-lately that he supposes himself a Johnny-do-all. Having finally realized that his success as an actor is owing to the majesty of their verse, he now presumes to write plays as well as act them! But Greene need hardly point out to his fellow scholars that if the muse is to be prostituted, they should be hired to do it. Arrogant "Shake-scene," without the advantages of an Oxford or Cambridge education, will inspire only parody. Take that goodly stuff in *Harry the Sixth*, for example:

> Thou are as opposite to every good
> As the Antipodes are unto us,
> Or as the south to the septentrion.
> O tiger's heart wrapp'd in a woman's hide!
> (*3 Henry VI*, I. iv. 134–137)

Along with Nashe, then, Greene shares the honor of first noticing Shakespeare. Even though his evaluation is apparently determined by factors more economic than aesthetic, at least part of Greene's bitterness arises from a not wholly warranted but unquestionably sincere pride in his own "past excellence." He takes one aspect of "the basest trade," in other words, as seriously as Nashe, who four years later claimed that for "plotting Plaies," Greene "was his crafts master." [45]

Aside from Jonson's and his bohemian predecessors' efforts to justify their own craft, the only critic who does not treat the common stage as the meanest of things is Francis Meres. But in attempting to be encyclopedic, *Palladis Tamia, Wits Treasury* (1598) is exceptionally vague and uncritical, even by Elizabethan standards. It is the most commonplace of the era's commonplace books, put together with scissors, much paste, and little thought, for in arranging his pearls, Meres is so anxious to offend none that he salutes whoever passes. His "Comparatiue Discourse of Our English Poets with the Greeke, Latine, and Italian Poets" (II, 314–324) is usually comparative only in the sense of illustrating set topics, claims to fame, with sweeping roll calls. The comparisons begin with Chaucer, Gower, and Lydgate. Rather than contrast these very different medieval writers, Meres is content to lump them together simply because they are (for him) England's "three auncient poets," and

they in turn resemble Orpheus, Linus, and Musaeus, if only because these were the three Greek poets of greatest antiquity (II,
314). Ovid chronicled the beginning of the world to his own time,
and so did Hardying; Homer and *Piers Plowman* each adorned his
language without the "curiositie of rime"; Antipater Sidonius,
Ovid, and Tarleton were all very witty; Achilles tortured Hector's corpse, and Harvey showed the same inhumanity to Greene.
Meres's world is so charged with the grandeur of similes that his
"comparisons" are often not only strained or trivial, but wholly
erroneous: "As Anacreon died by the pot: so George Peele by the
pox. . . . As the poet Lycophron was shot to death by a certain
riual of his: so Christopher Marlow was stabd to death by a bawdy
Servingman, a riual of his in his lewde loue" (II, 324). Perhaps
Meres should be given some credit for recommending *The Faerie
Queene* as England's most "excellent or exquisite Poem" (II, 316)
and Shakespeare as "most excellent in both kinds for the stage" (II,
318). The critic who at first appears unusually liberal and perceptive, however, lists "*Henry the 4*" among Shakespeare's tragedies,
singles out Doctor Legge's "two famous tragedies" for special commendation, notes that Anthony Munday is "our best plotter" in
comedy, and among those sonneteers "most passionate among vs to
bewaile and bemoane the perplexities of loue," sets Whetstone and
Churchyard next to Spenser and Shakespeare (II, 318–321). By
dealing only in superlatives and by designing his topics to admit
every writer he had read, seen, or heard of, Meres was bound to hit
the mark occasionally.

SHAKESPEARE'S RECALCITRANCE

In attempting to explain Elizabethan theories of tragedy, we have so
far found it necessary to draw upon two kinds of backgrounds.
The first comprises all of those critical "truths" honored by the
critics, facts as factual as Lydgate's and Baldwin's moral designs,
as exaggerated as Euripides's Senecan accents, as false as Aristotle's
unities. The second background is a set of social premises to which
the critics pay even louder tribute, the incomparably bad taste of
popular audiences and the ignorance of the lewd men who entertain
them, "truths" again both true and false, probably true enough
for Sidney's time but obviously not wholly for Shakespeare's. We
need not quarrel with the critics' errors or even bother separating
them from the truth, however, for our purpose is not to render

their formulations accurate but their conclusions intelligible. Critical pronouncements are simply another part of history, a past that must always be interpreted first in its own terms. Just as we found it valuable to take the sometimes outrageously prejudiced Holinshed at his word, so we must now suspend a modern disbelief in the professional playwright's lack of social and literary status if the critics are to make any sense at all. To have founded their theories of tragedy upon what the basest trade itself considered the meanest of things would have been as incredible as for them to have disregarded their schoolmasters' interpretations of classical models.

But if their own backgrounds prove the critics sensible, how useful is the background of critical comment that they in turn pass on to us? Paradoxically enough, our main interest in their theories is directed by the realization that they are often wrong, that the meanest of things, for instance, are far from "nothing worth." To demonstrate the relevance, not the "rightness," of critical opinion, we must prove that practice honored theory at least more often than theory honored practice. In order to see artistic history, the creative process, in its own terms, let us review the three axioms that must have crossed Shakespeare's mind in the years leading up to the writing of *Hamlet*.

(1) *Get thee to an Inn of Court!* Or at least betake thyself to Oxford, and from there, as Daniel, to a patroness or, as Lyly, to the Court itself. Whenever Shakespeare first conceived an interest in the making of plays, he must have also immediately realized that an artist could not write for the common stage without surrendering all literary pretensions. The critics told him that it meant forfeiting critical notice and settling for the praise of boors. The Statutes of the Realm told him that it meant consorting with men who, without proof of "belonging to any Baron of this Realme," should be "taken adjudged and deemed Roges Vacaboundes and Sturdy Beggers," a felony sometimes punishable by death.[46] And observation must have taught what Greene and Peele later confirmed: Playwrights received but a small share of the peasants' brass. If, on the other hand, Shakespeare's first interest was in acting, as Greene implies, it argues even baser aspirations in a man descended from landowners and gentlefolk.

(2) *Better late than never!* Perhaps Shakespeare's first error was unavoidable. At twenty, Lyly, Greene, Marlowe, Nashe, and Peele

were gathering Oxford and Cambridge degrees; at the same age, Shakespeare was supporting a wife and three children. Further formal education and a chance to make the right connections were apparently out of the question. His next "blunder," however, must have been deliberate, and increases our suspicion that even if he had gained full academic honors, he would have made Greene's mistake anyway. For in 1593 Shakespeare turned from subliterary endeavors like "Harry the Sixth," *The Comedy of Errors,* and *Titus Andronicus,* asked the Earl of Southampton to "let the vulgar admire vile things," and dedicated to this glittering youth "the first heire of my invention," [47] *Venus and Adonis,* handsomely printed by Richard Field and sold by one of London's major publishers, John Harrison, men who did not ordinarily traffic in the basest trade's cheap little quartos. Its rich imagery and sensual descriptions pleased more than its beautiful patron. By 1616 it had gone through ten editions and been lavishly quoted in anthologies. Only *The Rape of Lucrece,* dedicated to Southampton the next year, seems to have been more successful; four editions were called for in its first six years.[48] And the dedication to Shakespeare's second piece of literature implies that he had quickly won what Greene and Peele would die seeking. The general tone suggests that *Venus and Adonis* had found favor; mention is made of "the warrant" the poet now has of his lordship's "disposition" or regard.[49] The cynic might point out that the plague had kept the London theaters closed from the fall of 1592 to the spring of 1594, and that sheer economic necessity forced the young playwright's risky excursion into literature. But what explains Shakespeare's return to the theater? It was certainly not to gain the good opinion of people whose opinions did not matter. Nor was it for money, unless we assume that in 1594 Shakespeare was looking forward to 1599, when he became a shareholder in his own company. Marchette Chute rightly emphasizes this turning point in his career:

> The success of his two poems found Shakespeare in an enviable position in the spring of 1594. No poet, especially a beginning poet, could have asked for more. He had a wealthy, influential and satisfied patron who was one of the highest noblemen in the land. He had a publisher who was one of the most important men in his profession and who was obviously deeply interested in his career. He was beginning to get a chorus of commendation from the critics

... and his position in the eyes of posterity, if he had kept on as he had begun, was assured. ...

There was nothing in this to prevent Shakespeare continuing with his profession as an actor, but it gave him no special incentive to go on writing plays. The average play did not bring its author more than six pounds, and the approval of Harrison and Southampton would have guaranteed him much more than that for a new narrative poem.[50]

Among the most important "qualities that make a writer great," Chute concludes, "is his instinct for avoiding a pitfall that can destroy him." Had Shakespeare not returned to the "vile things" so loved by the "vulgar," had he continued to offer up to Southampton and "golden-haired Apollo," he would have merely "gone on writing handsome ornate poems that were as rich in detail as a well-made tapestry. . . . [But] when the special Renaissance cult that produced such poems receded at the end of the decade, Shakespeare's work would have receded with it; he would have become one of the many minor Elizabethan writers. . . ."[51]

(3) *Bring Aristotle to the Bankside!* Shakespeare's rejection of the first two axioms may help to explain his apparent indifference to the third. A writer who argued with success, evidently turning his back upon both literature and a "Baron of this Realme" at the same time, a writer who had no "reason" to put much thought into something to be vended upon "each scaffold" and left his plays to prove that he did—such a writer must have had "reasons" never entertained by contemporary critics: an instinct for seeking a less restrictive form than that with which he had already twice delighted them, glimpses of an art more expansive, intellectually and emotionally rewarding, and hence more "correct" than the critics could have imagined, and a quiet conviction that he would realize this unconventional goal. This is not to say that Shakespeare was wholly scornful of critical theory or preferred to work in critical darkness. Whether or not he and his fellow dramatists meditated by night upon the precepts of Aristotle and the Italian critics, they could not have escaped, as Madeleine Doran notes, "the traditional concepts of tragedy and comedy as formulated by the grammarians, and they could not have avoided acquaintance with Senecan tragedy and Roman comedy."[52] We must also realize, she continues, that

what may seem to us a rejection of classical precedent may actually
be an earnest imitation of what they took that precedent to be.
Conversely, of course, the dramatists must have sometimes thought
they were rejecting classical precedent when they were actually
rejecting medieval or contemporary Italian glosses upon it. It is
highly unlikely, for instance, that if Shakespeare knew Aristotle, he
knew him in a purer form than Sidney did. Hamlet's injunction that
the visiting players observe "the purpose of playing, whose end . . .
was and is to hold, as 'twere, the mirror up to nature; to show
virtue her own feature, scorn her own image, and the very age
and body of the time his form and pressure" (III. ii. 22 ff.)
suggests Shakespeare's familiarity with a definition ascribed to
Cicero by an essay on drama in turn ascribed to Aelius Donatus, a
fourth-century grammarian.[53]

Just as Shakespeare knew that rival playwrights were often
attracting large audiences simply by tearing "a passion to tatters,
to very rags, to split the ears of the groundlings," just as he surely
must have known that much of *Hamlet* would be "caviary to the
general," so he would no doubt have welcomed both "the law of
writ and the liberty" to help any "honest method" (*Hamlet*, II. ii.
396 ff.; III. ii. 10 ff.). It is inconceivable that a writer who never
disdained even a trivial tale when it could be shaped to dramatic
advantage would not also have desired to profit by contemporary
critical insights. Assuming that he sought, was there anything in
what he found that could possibly have been as helpful as the
meanest of his sources so often were? Certainly nothing that could
be termed a springboard for any dramatist's imagination. By combining the theories of tragedy we have already noticed, adding to
them as much classical and medieval commentary as these theories
even faintly suggest, and finally including the definitions furnished
in Tudor dictionaries,[54] we may have more, but certainly not less,
than what Shakespeare had to work with: Tragedy is a lofty,
solemn kind of poetry representing the cruel, miserable, frightening, or pitiful doings of historical or fabled kings or heroes, whose
fall from felicity to ruin reflects Fortune's treachery or God's just
judgment, and thereby inspires the reader or audience to fear evil,
to scorn the evildoer, to pity the oppressed, and to realize the
uncertainty of this world.

Now it is quite true that with much patience and mental dexterity, we could show how every line in *Hamlet* works to fulfill
some part of this definition; even the gravediggers' "poetry," how-

ever lacking in loftiness, advances solemnity and underlines this world's uncertainty. And since any era's best art is always so much grander than even the best criticism that follows and attempts to explain it, we should hardly expect the theroists *preceding* Shakespeare to furnish critical keys to *Hamlet's* mystery. What we might expect and do not get from them, however, are theories of tragedy that become increasingly incisive. Fond as the critics are of repeating "the classical doctrine that originality of real worth is to be achieved only through creative imitation," despite their scorn for slavish, secret, or superficial copying and their admiration for the poet who adapts, reinterprets, and improves upon the best available models, ancient and modern,[55] the methods they expect the writer to follow are usually lacking in their treatises upon his work. Such servility may well have disappointed Shakespeare. Had the critics imitated Sidney more originally, had they profited by, not merely repeated, his ideas concerning "Arte, Imitation, and Exercise" (I, 195), they would, for example, have developed his definition of tragedy and thereby glossed for us (and perhaps for Shakespeare) Sidney's passing reference to tragedy's "sturring the affects of admiration and commiseration" (I, 177).

The reference is first of all far clearer out of context than in. Taken out of context, it immediately reminds us of Aristotle's *Poetics*, XIII: The fall of the protagonist evokes pity as well as terror or fear—fear because we see ourselves in this man; pity because he is rather frail than vicious or depraved, and his misfortune is not wholly merited. Placed in context, however, the reference to these two "affects" is puzzling, for Sidney celebrates tragedy first as an exposer of hidden evil (it "sheweth forth the Vlcers that are couered with Tissue" and makes "Tyrants manifest their tirannicall humors"), next as a severe moralizer (it "maketh Kinges feare to be Tyrants"), then as an inspirer of wonder and pity, and finally as the traditional instructor of this world's mutable glories. Perhaps tragedy's different roles are not mutually exclusive, but if it is *always* a severe moralizer, dealing with kings like Aeschylus's Agamemnon, whose vices admit no mere frailties and whose "misfortunes" are indeed merited, how is commiseration stirred? Is it a compassion for those oppressed by "tirannicall humors" rather than for the tyrant himself, and do we therefore see ourselves in his victims? Or is our pity reserved for the protagonist in that other kind of tragedy, which teaches "vpon how weake foundations guilden roofes are builded"? Harington, the only critic who takes note of Sidney's tantalizing reference, does not help matters when he speaks of "the Tragicall . . . as representing onely the cruell & lawlesse proceedings of Princes, mouing nothing but pitie or detestation" (II, 209). Here we do not even have Fortune's wheel to fall back upon. And if Harington's pity is evoked even more mysteriously than Sidney's, his "detestation" takes us farther from Aristotle than his predecessor's "admiration." Although Aristotle does not wish the catastrophe to shock our moral sense— the spectacle of a wholly virtuous man being ruined—neither does he wish to satisfy it completely with the downfall of an utter villain. He is clearly interested in tragedy's psychological effects, the momentary influence of pity and terror upon the audience's mind, not in a tragedy of ethical directives—go thou and do not do likewise.[56] Since Sidney tells us that *Gorboduc* attains "the very end of Poesie" because "it doth most delightfully teach . . . notable moralitie" (I, 197), and since Harington insists that from the earliest times all true poets wrote "to soften and polish the hard and rough dispositions of men, and to make them capable of vertue and good discipline" (II, 197), it would seem that for them, where destiny is related to character, the protagonist is rewarded with remorseless poetic justice, and pity is reserved for his victims; and where destiny is related to Fortune rather than character, we pity the hero and fear his antagonist.

Behind this odd business probably lie the finely confused Italian hands of Daniello, Cinthio, Scaliger, and Minturno, all of whom contradict Aristotle as well as one another when they explain what the *Poetics* really says or what tragedy is really all about.[57] It is certainly preferable to believe that the wise and witty Sidney and Harington knew Aristotle secondhand, than that they knew him directly and then wrote nonsense. Their moralized Aristotle is not so surprising when we refer back to Scaliger's view that the tragic poet must always reward virtue and punish vice,[58] or read Puttenham's account of tragic poets first arising to reprehend rising tyrants (II, 35), or realize that for the Renaissance, Sophocles's *Oedipus Rex*, despite Aristotle's lengthy analyses, represented the "Grecian" concern to illustrate as a lesson to the mighty the fall of a dangerously ambitious man.[59] Minturno, it is true, did not allow his conception of tragedy's ethical aim to blind him to the fact that by *catharsis*, the purging of fear and pity, Aristotle was speaking of an emotional or psychological rather than a moral effect. Nor did Milton, in his preface to *Samson Agonistes*.[60] However, when Pope tells us, in his prologue to Addison's *Cato* (1713), that "the tragic Muse first trod the stage" in order "To make mankind in conscious virtue bold," we are much closer to what the English critics told Shakespeare; and had he listened, his tragedies would have been as "correct" and ineffective as those of the eighteenth century. Twenty years before *Cato*, Thomas Rymer had pondered the catastrophe of "*Othello:* A Bloody Farce," and with the same moral expectations as Pope, had asked, "If this be our end, what boots it to be Vertuous?" [61]

If our interpretations of Sidney's and Harington's fear and pity are correct, it would seem that *Hamlet* was written not because of or even in ignorance of the era's best theories, but in spite of them. Shakespeare did not need the critics for ideas as commonplace as comedy's happy and tragedy's unhappy conclusions, the tragic protagonist as a man of high degree who always fell, or the justice of God, the uncertainty of the world, the fickleness of Fortune, and the viciousness of vice. Such views are part of the period's intellectual baggage, unnecessarily labored in the homilies he heard, the sources he exploited, and except for the popular stage's occasional use of a commoner as hero, the plays he saw. And the less commonplace elements the critics offered—a moralized Aristotle, a triply-unified Aristotle—he consciously rejected. If Shakespearean tragedy honors the theorists' misinformation about the *Poetics* at all, it is in following their conclusion that when Aristotle mentions tragedy representing men as better and comedy as worse than in actual life (II), his essential distinction is between social classes rather than (as the context certainly indicates) the relative greatness and meanness of character.[62] But again Shakespeare's sources afford an easier explanation. If in his tragedies a prince remains a prince, in his comedies a duke remains a duke, all class-conscious Aristotelians notwithstanding.

And so the Bankside audience was given a tragedy that both critics and playwright must have assumed decidedly out of accord with the *Poetics*: a plot unified only by organically related incidents and themes, not by place, even less by time; a protagonist whose greatness of character counts far more toward making his fall tragic than any considerations of his princely status; a tragedy overflowing with ethical directives (many of the most explicit offered by its fops and villains), but surely not stirring the kind of fear and pity Sidney and Harington seem to have had in mind, nor answering in any sense their moral expectations. What self-respect-ing tyrant would not be confirmed in his "humors" rather than frightened from them by *Hamlet's* example? "Taint not thy mind," concludes the Ghost, after revealing a story so sordid that only the callous would not sicken (I. v. 42 ff.). "Report me and my cause aright," concludes Hamlet, "th' occurrents, more and less, / Which have solicited—the rest is silence" (V. ii. 331, 349–350).

Between challenge and reply we have a "hero" without conventional heroic stature, who weighs the merits of action and inaction by "Whether 'tis *nobler* in the mind," even though he realizes that "the *name* of action" may be lost amidst "the pale cast of thought" (III. i. 56 ff. Italics added.) We ask why Hamlet does not act, and Hamlet asks about the significance of action. Encouraged by Elizabethan criticism, we go flaw-hunting and discover a man undone by his nobility, and his creator evoking our sympathy for him not because of what he does but because of what is done to him, the ugly events that have "solicited." Hamlet's reactions against a world that places its highest premium on appearances, on the value, practicality, and prudence of fair seeming, can be easily reported by his one friend, Horatio. Perhaps the "rest," which must remain silent, are those internal battles so unlike Fortinbras's and Laertes's, actions of far grander "pitch and moment" than those that "honour" finds in eggshells, but which as events of "being" rather than "seeming" are not documentable, were not seen, cannot be reported, and therefore never "happened." In any case, Shakespeare's critical backgrounds gave him no incentive to keep from his audience the comforting and profoundly nontragic implication that destiny is wholly a result of character, and not a hint of what A. C. Bradley has so eloquently defined in "The Substance of Shakespearean Tragedy": the painful mystery "of a world travailing for perfection, but bringing to birth, together with glorious good, an evil which it is able to overcome only by self-torture and self-waste." [63] For that matter, the critics gave Shakespeare every reason to stick to something as solidly moral as *Richard III.* Shakespeare's final blunder was the most fortunate of all.

In view of Shakespeare's refusal to write tragedy "correctly," of what use are his age's literary theories? Like the meanings his contemporaries gave to the literature he read and the history he experienced, critical backgrounds at best furnish leading questions about rather than automatic explanations of his work. The only difference between these backgrounds is that whereas Shakespeare wrote *against* the first two, accepting and adding to the meanings of literature and history almost as often as changing them, he usually wrote *over* the last, and we therefore rarely find critical glosses leading us to perceptions we should not have inferred from the plays themselves. In other words, if after our fifth careful reading of *Richard II* and *Troilus and Cressida* as modern poems, divorced from their historical context, we bring into play Essex's bold chivalry, we shall get a great deal more mileage out of our sixth reading; by taking stock of critical commentary between our readings of *Hamlet*, on the other hand, our awareness of Shakespeare's dedication to his art may increase, but nothing more. The evidence of a carefully wrought play, for instance, is now supplemented by the knowledge that to write it, Shakespeare had been forced to reject a promising "literary" reputation and a less exacting, more lucrative employment. But this puts us in no better position to interpret specific cruxes within the play itself.

Sometimes, however, a knowledge of critical backgrounds will help to corroborate our responses to specific passages. A good example is suggested as we attempt to determine the many ways in which Hamlet and Shakespeare employ the visiting players. For Hamlet, their chief contribution is to act "The Murder of Gonzago," a device whose dramatic function is specifically and explicitly structural. He quickly turns their most fortunate arrival into "The Mouse-trap," an opportunity to "catch the conscience of the King" and thereby discover whether Claudius's past deeds or his own present "imaginations are as foul / As Vulcan's stithy" (II. ii. 601; III. ii. 81–82). In his reflections upon these visitors, of course, Hamlet also helps his creator enforce some of the play's central concerns. The theme of human ingratitude is given two surprising twists when the medieval Danish prince hears that "the tragedians of the city" are now out of fashion, notes that the "little eyases" who "so berattle the common stages" will soon "grow themselves to common players . . . if their means are no better," and compares the boys' success with Claudius's sudden popularity among the very courtiers who recently mocked him (II. ii. 325 ff.). And the prevailing distinction between seeming and being is lengthily underlined as Hamlet marvels over the First Player's convincing, convulsive grief

> ... for nothing!
> For Hecuba!
> What's Hecuba to him or he to Hecuba,
> That he should weep for her? What would he do,
> Had he the motive and the cue for passion
> That I have?
>
> (II. ii. 550–555)

For Shakespeare, however, the play's official actors serve an additional function that Hamlet perceives but faintly, if at all. What indeed *would* the First Player do had he a genuine "cue for passion," were he not a mere actor enacting "a fiction . . . a dream of passion," but a "real" person with "real" pain like Hamlet's? Since this man can speak and gesture so movingly "for nothing," reasons Shakespeare's hero, in real grief he would "drown the stage with tears, / And cleave the general ear with horrid speech"; drive the guilty mad and terrify the innocent. Despite his later cautions about a delivery that "out-herods Herod," the inhuman bellowings of actors who have "imitated humanity so abominably" (III. ii. 14 ff.), Hamlet certainly seems to admire the First Player's acting. Similarly, although Hamlet does not think much of "The Mouse-trap," his admiration for the Hecuba speech is beyond question. This passage, he tells us, comes from an unsuccessful play, performed but once at most, for the common herd could not digest a delicacy so excellent (II. ii. 428 ff.). Prepared to welcome popular, romantic devisings of adventurous knights, ladies, kings, and clowns (II. ii. 317 ff.) and quick to exploit the equally popular, more sensationalistic Italianate tragedy of revenge and intrigue, the Wittenberg student properly reserves his complete approval for drama employing a loftier kind of poetry, closer to "scene individable" than "poem unlimited."

> Out, out, thou strumpet, Fortune! All you gods,
> In general synod, take away her power;
> Break all the spokes and fellies from her wheel,
> And bowl the round nave down the hill of heaven,
> As low as to the fiends.
>
> (II. ii. 487–491)

To Polonius's complaint that all "this is too long," Hamlet retorts that without "a jig, or a tale of bawdry, . . . he sleeps." These lines are without "sallets" to incite the lascivious, without phrases to indict their author of affectation; like the play itself, "well digested in the scenes, set down with as much modesty as cunning," Hecuba's plight is described honestly, orderly, and elegantly (II. ii. 435 ff.). Of all this the Prince is confident, since "others whose judgments in such matters cried in the top of mine" (II. ii. 433–434), probably the same "judicious" spectators whose "censure . . . must . . . o'erweigh a whole theatre of others" (III. ii. 29–31), also found the play excellent. Small wonder, then, when the critically oriented Hamlet concludes that if the First Player's grief were real, he would "cleave the general ear with horrid speech," with lines even more bombastic than the Senecan stuff that we, like Polonius, find a bit tedious.

A decade earlier Shakespeare would have sided with Hamlet. Rising to the height of Kyd's style,

> O eyes! no eyes, but fountains fraught with tears;
> O life! no life, but lively form of death;
> O world! no world, but mass of public wrongs,
> Confus'd and fill'd with murder and misdeeds!
> O sacred heavens! . . .
> How should we term your dealings to be just,
> If you unjustly deal with those that in your justice trust? [64]

York's withered, wan widow wails her weighty, wasting woes:

> Dead life, blind sight, poor mortal living ghost
> Woe's scene, world's shame, grave's due by life usurp'd,
> Brief abstract and record of tedious days,
> Rest thy unrest on England's lawful earth,
> Unlawfully made drunk with innocent blood.
>   (*Richard III*, IV. iv. 26–30)

"Hungry for revenge"—so the young playwright excuses his own hunger for rhetoric—Queen Margaret follows with similar verbal gymnastics. Between 1592 and 1600, however, Shakespeare learned that such demonstrations of rhetorical prowess not only hinder characterization but the very mood of sorrow and despair they ostensibly seek to evoke, and that when his Duchess rounds off a hundred and twenty-five lines of speechless grief by asking "Why should calamity be full of words?," Elizabeth's answer that

"they ease the heart" is, for the dramatist, an unsatisfactory
apology.

Although *Richard III*'s most self-consciously rhetorical lines,
the Player King's and Queen's turgid couplets, and the First
Player's heavy, elaborate narrative all have their own diction and
rhythm, it would be difficult to determine which fails most effectively to communicate grief. Since Hamlet finds the Hecuba
passage without affectation, he probably thinks it "artificial" in
the most complimentary Elizabethan sense, "wrought with great
skill or artifice," whereas we find the passage as stagy and unnatural—"artificial" in our sense—as "The Murder of Gonzago." But
since Shakespeare reserves "horrid speech" for seeming grief, and
enforces the reality of his larger piece of fiction through his leading
actor's comments on the dexterity of a good actor, it appears that
Hamlet elaborates upon the relationships between art and life
with a method learned by experience rather than from the critics.
In 1592 Shakespeare, like Kyd, was guilty of what Sidney had
called "vsing Art to shew Art, and not to hide Art"; how often
Richard III "flyeth from nature, and indeede abuseth Art" (I, 203).
But by the end of the century his tragic heroes do not "cleave the
general ear," nor is "calamity," at least in the Duchess's sense, "full
of words." His comic protagonists, meanwhile, discover that the
truer their love, the more difficult it is to express. About the time
Hamlet is admiring the First Player's "broken voice, and his whole
function suiting / With forms to his conceit" (II. ii. 549–550),
Benedick surveys "a whole bookful of these quondam carpet-mon-
gers [in Cupid's army], whose names yet run smoothly in the even
road of a blank verse, . . . [but] were never so truly turn'd over
and over as my poor self in love. Marry, I cannot show it in
rhyme" (*Much Ado about Nothing*, V. ii. 29 ff.). His heroes' in-
ability with "forms," whether Benedick's unwritten sonnets or
Hamlet's un-Senecan sorrow, illustrates Sidney's alternative to
"vsing Art to shew Art": Far better for the writer to follow "that
which by practise hee findeth fittest to nature" and "therein
(though he know it not) [write] according to Art" (I, 203).

But Shakespeare finally takes a third road. Unlike Sidney's courtier, he knows very well that he writes "according" to art. Unlike
Sidney himself, however, he realizes that sometimes life can be
represented most artfully through a juxtaposition of art concealed
and art displayed, the "rogue and peasant slave" who relishes

dramatic caviar, but whose own agony pushes him off blank verse's "even road," and therefore curses himself for "cursing like a very drab, / A scullion!" (II. ii. 582–583). Just as Hamlet's self-vilification actually vindicates his nobility, so his self-reproach that he "can say nothing" (that is, nothing comparable to the First Player's high-flown lines) only reminds us of Shakespeare's less "literary," more moving power. Nor should Hamlet's marked preference for "the law of writ" obscure the fact that in creating him, Shakespeare preferred "the liberty." About seven years later, when Shakespeare had gained even more confidence in his ability to manipulate illusions, he had the boy who played Cleopatra resolve to die in Alexandria, lest in being taken to a Roman theater she "see / Some squeaking Cleopatra boy my greatness / I' th' posture of a whore" (V. ii. 218–220).

In seeking the uses to which Shakespeare put the city tragedians, we have drawn all "conclusive" evidence from the play itself, the players' immediate context, and all "supporting" evidence from external glosses, the context in which *Hamlet* was written. Had we confused these contexts and attempted to establish, rather than confirm, the meaning of the Prince's situation or the function of the First Player's speech by reference to Benedick's plight or *Richard III*'s rhetoric, we should have been violating *Hamlet*'s artistic integrity. Like any piece of art, this play is a self-contained whole, and it would be as critically dangerous for us to conclude by external gloss as for the logician to rest his case upon an analogy. As long as glosses are not offered in place of proofs, however, they are wonderfully convenient things, especially when our self-contained whole seems hardly self-explanatory, and we should be thankful for any evidence from without that substantiates conjectures based upon evidence within. Our use of Sidney's observations on art tells us something more. When our gloss comes from the criticism of Shakespeare's contemporaries instead of from analogies between *Hamlet* and his other plays, it is not only critically dangerous but quite unnecessary to conclude with confirmations. The First Player's lines, for example, are surrounded by a great deal of explicit commentary concerning "scene individable, or poem unlimited," all prefaced by Hamlet's promise that "the lady [player] shall say her mind freely, or the blank verse shall halt for't" (II. ii. 321–322). Add to this the fact that Hamlet's own "verse" frequently halts and often degenerates into plain prose, and it becomes obvious that we hardly require Sidney's comments to see how carefully Shakespeare was thinking about rules, art, life, and what indeed is "fittest to nature."

The same goes for another piece of confirming evidence, a gloss from a rather surprising quarter. Nashe's preface to *Menaphon* (1589), one of Robert Greene's eighteen imitations-combinations of Lyly's *Euphues* and Sidney's *Arcadia,* is ostensibly written to insure that "the Gentlemen Students of Both Vniuersities" will welcome the artistic endeavors of their fellow "scholler-like Shepheard" (I, 307). But Nashe is characteristically unable to stick to his subject or forgo any chance for a sarcastic aside. And so we get much more about presumptuous ignorance than his "sweet friend['s] . . . *Arcadian Menaphon,*" and as many examples of false as of true eloquence: "the seruile imitation of vainglorious tragoedians, who contend . . . to embowell the clowdes in a speach of comparison; thinking themselues more than initiated in poets immortalitie if they but once get *Boreas* by the beard, and the heauenlie bull by the deaw-lap" (I, 308). Counting on the prejudices of his academic audience and anticipating Greene's attack on Shakespeare in the *Groatsworth of Wit* (1592), Nashe next turns upon the companies' playwrights, "their idiote art-masters, that intrude themselues to our eares as the alcumists of eloquence, who (mounted on the stage of arrogance) think to outbraue better pens with the swelling bumbast of a bragging blanke verse," commit "the digestion of their cholerick incumbrances to the spacious volubilitie of a drumming decasillabon," and thus "repose eternitie in the mouth of a player . . ." (I, 308). After a few rapid shots at those who feed upon the crumbs that fall from the translators' plates, the plodding knaves who strut in Ovid's and Plutarch's stolen plumes and plunder sheets of similitudes from Pliny, and an ignorant public as likely to honor a trivial tale as the best of Tasso, Nashe returns to his first censure with a cannonade at Kyd:

> It is a common practice now a daies amongst a sort of shifting companions, that runne through euery arte and thriue by none, to leaue the trade of *Nouerint* [the opening word of a scrivener's document; hence, scrivener or public copyist], whereto they were borne, and busie themselues with the indeuors of Art, that could scarcelie latinize their necke-verse if they should haue neede; [65] yet English *Seneca* [*Seneca His Tenne Tragedies,* ed. Thomas Newton, 1581]

read by candle light yeeldes manie good sentences, as
Bloud is a begger, and so foorth; and, if you intreate him
faire . . . , he will affoord you whole *Hamlets,* I should say
handfulls of tragical speaches. But O griefe! . . . what's that
will last alwaies? The sea exhaled by droppes will in con-
tinuance be drie, and *Seneca* let bloud line by line and page
by page at length must needes die to our stage: which
makes his famisht followers to imitate the Kidde in *Aesop,*
who, . . . forsooke all hopes of life to leape into a new
occupation, and these men . . . to intermeddle with Italian
translations. . . . [W]hat can be hoped of those that thrust
Elisium into hell, and haue not learned . . . the iust measure
of the Horizon without an hexameter. Sufficeth them to
bodge vp a blank verse with ifs and ands, & other while for
recreation . . . spend two or three howers in turning ouer
French *Doudie,* where they attract more infection in one
minute than they can do eloquence all dayes of their life. . . .

(I, 311–312)

But what do all these puzzling snarls have to do with Shakespeare's *Hamlet?* Let us first note how Kyd epitomizes (for Nashe)
all that is plodding, impertinent, and slovenly. For "trade of
Nouerint," read Thomas Kyd, a London scrivener, and his father,
Francis; for "necke-verse," see Nashe's earlier complaints about
"those that neuer ware gowne in the Vniuersitie" (I, 309). This
may explain the ignorance that thrusts Pluto upon "the fair Ely-
sian green" (*The Spanish Tragedy,* I. i. 73), and ignorance in turn
explains his usually mediocre imitations and translations: In 1588
"the Kidde" leaped into Tasso's *Padre di Famiglia* and produced
The Householders Philosophie; his "turning over French *Doudie,*"
the neoclassical tragedies of Robert Garnier, resulted in *Cornelia*
(1594); and Virgil's hexameters (*Aeneid,* Book VI) yielded the
horizon's exact measurements for *The Spanish Tragedy*'s pictures
of the lower world.[66] Nashe pretends to find Kyd's presumption
inexplicable, and *The Spanish Tragedy*'s success probably explains his genuine indignation. Of greater interest to us, however, is Nashe's plea for an imitation more creative, a warning
that Seneca's bloody well is rapidly running dry. Kyd no doubt
perceived this and turned to Garnier, perhaps with one eye upon
Wilton, where Daniel and his Delia were reading their Garnier-
inspired tragedies at one another.

Nashe's gloomy forecast, of course, neither concludes nor confirms what happens in *Hamlet*. It does not even prove that Kyd
wrote that famous, no longer extant "Ur-Hamlet," which has attracted so much detailed discussion. It does indicate that when
Shakespeare arrived in London, about the same time Nashe was
introducing *Menaphon*, the popular stage offered him handfuls of
Hamlets. It corroborates our earlier observation that Shakespeare
was never overruled by critical commentary; 1594 saw the printing
of *Titus Andronicus* as well as *Cornelia*, and Seneca once again set
a-bleeding. But if Nashe's warning anticipates some of the young
Shakespeare's affectations, his plea for originality and true eloquence looks forward to new uses of old Hamlets. Although his
moral was to abandon Seneca altogether, Nashe lived long enough
to hear Pistol's "drumming decasillabon," and may have even survived to watch Shakespeare successfully "repose eternitie in the
mouth of [one] player" by committing to *another* "the swelling
bumbast of a bragging blanke verse."

Some Theories of Poetry:
Alehouse Rhyme and Roman Numbers

Unfortunately, criticism even as indirectly helpful as Nashe's does
not turn up very often. How frequently we discover the obvious
labored, general "truths" repeated, individual writers not con-
trasted, nor even compared, but simply lumped together in the
manner of Meres's "Comparatiue Discourse." After darkly explaining how Ovid, among other classical poets, should be "moralized
according to his meaning," Webbe comes "to our English Poets, to
whom I would I were able to yeelde theyr deserued commendations" (I, 238–239). First, he knows of "no memorable worke
written by any Poet in our English speeche vntill twenty yeeres
past" (that is, 1566), partly because, one assumes, the Middle Ages
"conuerted the naturall property of the sweete Latine verse" into
"this tynkerly verse which we call ryme" (I, 239–240). Webbe
therefore gives all poets before Gascoigne rather short shrift. We
hear only of Gower's learning and Lydgate's "good proportion . . .
meetely currant style" and superstitious concerns. As the "God of
English Poets," Chaucer brings "delight and profitable knowledge,"
a style that may now seem "blunte and course" but in his time "a
delightsome vayne," allowing him to "gyrde at the vices and abuses

of all states . . . so learnedly and pleasantly" that he escaped political censorship, and therefore answers to Webbe's idea of "a true picture or perfect shape of a right Poet" (I, 241). But prior to the merry, sharp-witted nipper of Henry VIII's reign, John Skelton, he has heard of no other save that "harshe and obscure" yet very "pithy" fellow, *Piers Plowman,* and because he wrote "without the curiosity of Ryme," Webbe somehow concludes that Langland was the first to make English verse run upon classical feet.

Since he humbly wishes Gower's works "were all whole and perfect among vs," and since even Spenser and Sidney had earlier foreseen a brave new world of English hexameters, we may forgive Webbe for his hurried, misleading picture of medieval literature and his strong prejudice against rhyme. More difficult to excuse are those imprecise treatments of his contemporaries. The best he can do for Gascoigne is to acknowledge his wit and then quote Master E.K., who also finds him witty, full of "naturall promptnes" if not learning (I, 242). Next come a dozen writers ranging from Surrey to Churchyard, an ambiguous "Haiwood" (John or Jasper?) to an inexplicable "S.Y.," whose couplings are justified only by Webbe's vague conclusion: "to speake of their seuerall gyfts and aboundant skyll shewed forth by them in many pretty and learned workes woulde make my discourse much more tedious" (I, 242–243). That Surrey's and Churchyard's gifts were indeed "seuerall" no one would deny, but we should prefer some term more revealing, however inaccurate or tedious. Our frustration, in other words, arises from a sense of helplessness, not disagreement. We hardly expect analyses as eclectic and incisive as the best of the twentieth century; a Sam Johnson of the eighteenth or even a Ben Jonson of the seventeenth would serve our turn. At their most wrong-minded moments they would have at least told us *how* Langland "obserued the quantity of our verse" (I, 242), or *why* Chaucer is "yet not altogether so poetical" as Virgil and his Italian imitators (I, 263). Like Falstaff's Hostess, Webbe's criticism is a thing "a man knows not where to have." And excepting Meres, none better illustrates Smith's observation that the critics constantly borrow from each other and from overseas opinion, often verbatim, and that their theories are often but "shreds of Horatian tradition or patchwork of Renaissance commentary" (I, xxi, lxvii).

With no one's help, Webbe astutely discerns Spenser's "excellent skyll and skylfull excellency" (I, 263). He then defends this

acute perception by comparing *The Shepheardes Calender* with
Virgil's eclogues: Both covertly praise a reigning monarch; both
contain a "braue coloured complaint of vnstedfast freendshyppe"
and "pretty Pastorall contentions." Next, he quotes E.K.'s celebration of the New Poet's witty devising, pithy utterances, lovely
plaints, pleasing descriptions of pleasure, pastoral rudeness, moral
wisdom, and " 'his due obseruing of *decorum* every where, in personages, in season[s], in matter, in speeche, and generally in all
seemely simplicity of handling hys matter and framing hys
wordes' " (I, 263). Finally, Webbe notes the more obvious morals
to be drawn from the poem and leaves it to the reader to "picke out
much good sence" among the obscurer parts, only insisting,
along with E.K., that there is no pederasty among Spenser's
shepherds. But as Webbe hurries on to his main purpose of disin-
fecting English verse from the barbarous custom of rhyming, he
leaves unnoticed what we probably find one of the most interesting
aspects of *The Shepheardes Calender*, Spenser's youthful experimentation with a multitude of rhyme schemes. To be sure, Webbe
later allows a momentary confrontation between theory and fact.
The "rightest English poet that euer I read" (I, 245) is eventually used to furnish examples of verses differing in length, rhyme,
or stanzaic pattern (I, 270 ff.), and there is even one hint that
Spenser's skill in rhyming may have something to do with his skill
as a poet: "The third kynd is a pretty rounde verse, running
currantly together, commonly seauen sillables or sometime eyght
in one verse [that is, single line], as many in the next, both
ryming together: euery two hauing one the like verse after them,
but of rounder wordes, and two of them likewyse ryming
mutually. That verse expresseth, notably, light and youthfull talke,
such as is the thyrde *Aeglogue* betweene two Sheepheardes boys
concerning loue.

> *Thomalin*, why sitten we so,
> As weren ouerwent with woe
> Vpon so fayre a morrowe?
> The ioyous time now nigheth fast,
> That wyll allay this bitter blast
> And slake the Winter sorrow."
>   (I, 270–271)

But we get only brief glimpses of theory wedded to practice.
The sweetly varied lengths of Spenser's lines, not his rhyme

schemes, usually catch the critical eye, and Webbe soon becomes impatient even with these. There are, he concludes, as many kinds of verse as dancing measures or tunes, "which euerie Fidler knowes better then my selfe . . ." (I, 272). Obviously for Webbe the "rightest English poet" would have been even righter without rhyme. That "rude kinde of verse . . . borrowed from the *Barbarians*" and "ingraffed by custome, . . . I may not vtterly dissalowe . . . least I should seeme to call in question the iudgement of all our famous wryters. . . . I can be content to esteeme it as a thing the perfection whereof is very commendable, *yet* so as wyth others I could wysh it were by men of learning and ability *bettered, and made more artificiall,* according to the woorthines of our speeche" (I, 266–267. Italics added.) And Webbe modestly leads the way by trying to turn Colin's song of Elisa (*Shepheardes Calender,* "April," 37–153) into Sapphic stanzas (I, 287 ff.). To determine which is worthier of our speech, one example should suffice.

Spenser: Shewe thy selfe, Cynthia, with thy silver
          rayes,
          And be not abasht:
          When shee the beames of her beauty displayes,
          O how art thou [i.e., Apollo] dasht!
                                        (82–85)
Webbe: Shew thy selfe now, *Cynthia,* with thy cleere
          rayes,
          And behold her: neuer abasht be thou so:
          When she spreades those beames of her
              heauenly beauty,
          how
                              thou art in a dump dasht?

Although we should not wish to hold up either piece as an example of great poetry, notice the respective prices each poet pays for displaying his artifice. Spenser exhibits his skill with a concord of sound, length, rhythm, and meaning. Neither the rhyme (*a b a b*), nor the alliteration of accented syllables ("be . . .-basht," "beames . . . beauty," and perhaps "Shew . . . Cyn-"), nor the repetition of lengths of lines (10, 5, 10, 5 syllables), nor even the echoing of rhythmic patterns—both *a* lines have two dactyls (/– –), a trochee (/–), and an iamb (–/), and both *b* lines, an iamb, and an anapest (−−/)—obscures Spenser's tribute to Majesty's transfiguring glances, the relationship between chaste Cynthia and his Virgin Queen. Despite earlier complaints about how often rude poets rhyme without reason, wrenching syntax and thereby sense in their search for like sounds (I, 274), Webbe proceeds to make Spenser "more artificiall" at the cost of the lyric's meaning, Sappho's versification, and received English pronunciation. The graceful turn of Spenser's compliment is effected by the implication that Elizabeth's beauty is not only triumphant but modest; Cynthia would never have outshone Phoebus had he not contested her brightness and had her loving subject not encouraged her awesome epiphany. But in Webbe, the relationship between winsome self-effacement and resplendent conquest is obscured. Whether Cynthia or Phoebus should be "neuer abasht" is unclear, for instead of following Spenser by addressing two lines to Cynthia and two to Apollo, Webbe speaks one line to the moon, turns to the sun with three words, returns to the moon with five, and then puts to the sun an awkwardly phrased question.

Such confusion is the result of forcing English words to run upon classical feet, and Webbe himself realizes—is, in fact, proud of—the difficult task he undertakes. Sapphic verse, he explains, presents the poet with the "troublesome and tedious" obligation of framing "in our speeche" three lines with the same pattern of lengthened and shortened syllables: the first foot a trochee (/−), the second a spondee (//), the third a dactyl (/−−), and the fourth and fifth both trochees (I, 286). Moreover, after every third line, he has decided to "sette one *Adonium* verse," a dactyl followed by a spondee. Webbe's concern about how to "frame" and "sette" makes his distortion of Spenser's ideas easier to understand. Whereas Spenser's imagination leaped from Elizabeth, modesty, and beauty to Cynthia, chastity, and supernal loveliness to garish Phoebus, Webbe's hobbled from his model to the exacting demands of a more artificial framework.

As well as suggesting all that Spenser sees, Elizabeth must also be this:

```
/-  //  /--  /-  /-
/-  //  /--  /-  /-
/-  //  /--  /-  /-
                /--  //
```

And except for the "how," which floats between Webbe's third and fourth lines, the Queen is measured as exactly as he has promised. This is not to imply that Spenser thought of Elizabeth in an "unformed" way, as simply matter without meter. Even as he drew his relationships between spectator, sun, and moon, Spenser was equally anxious about the feet in which his message had to run:

$$/-- \quad /-- \quad /- \quad -/$$
$$-/ \quad --/$$
$$/-- \quad /-- \quad /- \quad -/$$
$$-/ \quad --/$$

As Webbe himself notes, the difference is not between matter expressed with and without artifice, but between the relative exquisiteness of each man's artificiality. His is more difficult to attain, "more troublesome," and Spenser's comes more easily. An initial glance at both metrical schemes appears to justify Webbe's claim. That "the naturall course of most English verses seemeth to run vppon the olde Iambicke stroake" (I, 273), he has already observed. What flows more naturally than Marlowe's "Come *live* with *me* and *be* my *love*"? Since our everyday conversation overflows with iambs, it argues no great artifice to employ them, Webbe implies. Spenser uses two, Webbe none: Score one point for Webbe. Give him another for repeating his metrical scheme twice, since Spenser echoes but once. Because trochees (*Give* me *back* the *pastry which* was *stolen*), dactyls (*Give* me the *thief* who has *sto*len the *man*nikin), and anapests (I shall *steal* what I *can*) take no special skill unless run on at great length, and then usually to the delight only of the feeble-minded, Webbe does not outdo Spenser here. Least common in our daily speech are spondees, for monosyllabic words tend to rise and fall except in moments of great excitement (like mad Lear's challenges on the heath: "*Blow, winds* . . . *rage, blow*" and "*Singe my white head*"), and polysyllabic words rarely receive two equal stresses except in compounds (*Bright-eyed childhood's heyday!*). Because Webbe speaks of his "*Adonium* verse" as "this addition" (I, 286), it seems that he is intentionally altering Sappho's last line (a dactyl and a mere trochee) to a dactyl and—Oh brave new artifice!—a final spondee. Since Spenser has no spondees and even Sappho only three (the second foot in each of her first three lines), Webbe's poetical supererogation should gain him at least ten additional points.

Upon more careful consideration, however, we wonder about Webbe's victory. In the first place, spondees composed of two lengthened syllables (for instance, *gli-ding*) are much easier to find than those of two accented syllables (*child-hood*, not *gli*-ding). Secondly, Webbe's fourth spondee is, after all, but a "dump dasht," and his second is attained at the cost of bringing Apollo in too soon and thus obscuring the meaning. And we need only read his first line to sense that something else is wrong. Surely in his everyday pronunciation even an exquisitely artificial poet did not stress, either by accenting or lengthening, all the italicized syllables in "*shew* thy *selfe now*, Cyn*thia, with* thy *cleere* rayes." Webbe's answer is partly implicit in his work's subtitle, *Together with the Authors iudgment, touching the reformation of our English Verse*, anticipated in his "Preface to the Noble Poets of Englande," and made clear in the *Discourse* proper, where he explains how orthography and received pronunciation "must needes be a little wrested" (I, 282) if we are to write true verse. We shall later consider some of those intricate rules of classical prosody that every Elizabethan schoolboy became familiar with as he scanned his Virgil and Horace. For the present, it is more important to understand the general rationale behind Webbe's apology: Since we must choose between everyday custom (which almost invariably produces bad poetry) and attempts to imitate the obviously superior verse of the Greek and Latin poets, what sane man will not elect the latter?

We must place ourselves in Webbe's time to see that like the visions of more important men, his dreams are grounded upon valid reasons sensibly employed. Sidney had hardly foreseen anything higher than the height of Seneca when he sailed with information as faulty as Columbus's. Webbe also voyages with the "wrong" assumptions and goals, but his motives are equally commendable. The rich mines of Homer, Sappho, and Virgil lie across an Ocean Sea of imitation and exercise or practice. Unlike Columbus, however, he was traveling toward a land far poorer than that he sought, an Antilia that never quite materialized. To us he seems too pessimistic about contemporary practice, too optimistic about English verse being fitted into classical measures, too quick to conclude that bad rhymed verse is bad because it rhymes, and too hasty in assuming that custom must be completely overthrown rather than reformed from within. If, as he has already admitted, "all our famous wryters . . . haue wonne eternall prayse by theyr memorable workes compyled in that verse" which rhymes and is accented rather than lengthened, why must rhyme's barbaric pedigree still cause uneasiness among "men of learning and ability"? That small "yet," upon which Webbe turns his discussion from present perfection to a future, even more perfect way, once again illustrates contemporary critical stubbornness, a conscious refusal to allow the very best facts to hinder the development of even better theories, formulations that are superior to practices not because rules precede deeds, but because new rules are bound to lead the way to infinitely finer practices. Whereas we can sometimes explain the discrepancies between tragic theories and practices in terms of the social prejudices that led to critical ivory towers, Webbe's stand, though equally militaristic, is better informed. He knows his adversaries, from captains like the anonymous New Poet, whom he respects, to the rank and file, "the vncountable rabble of ryming Ballet makers and compylers of sencelesse sonets, who . . . can frame an Ale-house song of fiue or six score verses, hobbling vppon some tune of a Northen Iygge, . . . whole swarmes of . . . pottical, poeticall (I should say), heades . . . gorgiously garnished with fayre greene Barley, in token of their good affection to our Englishe Malt" (I, 246).

But Webbe was not the only Elizabethan critic who pleaded for a reformation, who nailed his scholarly theses to the alehouse doors of red-nosed rhymers. The controversy raged throughout the period, involving some of England's better scholars (Sir John Cheke, who died in 1557, then Ascham, finally Harvey) and best poets (Sidney, Spenser, Campion, and Daniel, who attacked Campion about 1603). Among these seven sensible men only Daniel, it appears, was not at some time in accord with most of Webbe's theories. And they were all practical people, far too busy to fight for lost causes. Although the quantitative versifiers rarely attained anything as good as Campion's "Rose-cheekt *Lawra*, come" (1602; II, 348), neither the fine poetry written without classical rules nor the usually bad verse written with them could quite convince the critics that their cause would not soon be vindicated by a poetical breakthrough. A war need not be won in order to be informative, even exciting. In attempting to render intelligible this piece of a future that has already been, we shall at least receive a clearer idea about the Elizabethan obsession with the "artificial," a term that fell upon evil days only in the early nineteenth century. A brief account should also furnish nondramatic examples of theory versus practice to supplement what we learned by measuring *Hamlet* against all the rules for proper tragedy. Finally, since Spenser faced this battle even as *The Faerie Queene* was "in hande forthwith" (I, 100), it certainly has literary relevance. What if Campion had been born early enough to substantiate theory with successful practice by 1580, and perhaps prevented Spenser's defection to the rude rhymers? The mind boggles at the prospect of the Knights of Faerie being celebrated in thirty-five thousand lines of epic hexameters or pseudo-Chaucerian English tripping upon dainty Sapphics.

Ascham is the first Elizabethan to wish that his countrymen "would acknowledge and vnderstand rightfully our rude beggerly ryming, brought first into Italie by *Gothes* and *Hunnes,* whan all good verses and all good learning to[o] were destroyd by them, and after caryed into France and Germanie, and at last receyued into England by men of excellent wit in deede, but of small learning and lesse iudgement in that behalfe" (I, 29–30). Now that we have the best and worst models to imitate, he pleads, "surelie to follow rather the *Gothes* in Ryming than the *Greekes* in trew versifiyng were euen to eate ackornes with swyne, when we may freely eate wheate bread emonges [amongst] men" (I, 30). If we join such observations to Ascham's earlier comment that "the prouidence of God hath left vnto vs . . . onelie in the *Greke* and *Latin* tong, the trew preceptes and perfite examples of eloquence" (I, 22), the choice takes on even religious overtones. But how are we to avoid becoming infidel swine? Here Ascham reveals that he has grasped, if not solved, the main problem. The real villains are not the Goths, but their rude brothers, the Angles and the Saxons; the enlightened poet must repel barbaric custom with a fundamentally barbaric language. Ascham is of course too patriotic to put the case so bluntly, but this is what his admission amounts to: "In deed, our English tong, hauing in vse chiefly wordes of one syllable which commonly be long, doth not well receiue the nature of *Carmen Heroicum* [heroic verse, that is, epic hexameters], bicause *dactylus,* the aptest foote for that verse, conteining one long and two short, is seldom therefore found in English; and doth also rather stumble than stand vpon *Monasyllabis*" (I, 30).

Because the critics all agreed that epic and tragic poets celebrated the loftiest matters, and that Homer and Virgil were among the greatest, most eloquent artists, an English mastery of the classical hexameter was a duty as solemn and patriotic as the

Lord Admiral's control of the high seas. And Ascham's conclusion that his poetical navy must venture out with leaky ships is repeatedly demonstrated by its failures to capture the eloquence of the *Iliad* or *Aeneid*. With a vocabulary rich in polysyllabic words, Virgil encountered no great difficulty in opening his epic with a line scanned by Puttenham (II, 123) as follows:

*ar*ma ui *rum*que ca *no tro ie qui pri*mus ab *o*ris.

As Webbe points out, this "most famous verse of all the rest," the dignified "*Hexametrum Epicum*, . . . consisteth of sixe feete, whereof the first foure are indifferently either *Spondoei* or *Dactyli*, the fift is euermore a *dactyl*, and the sixt a *Spondoe*" (I, 282–283). We should only add that the fifth foot might be a spondee and the sixth a trochee. But the proof is in the practice, and if we read *aloud* the best examples Webbe is able to produce, crippled spondees as well as maimed dactyls become obvious. First, Webbe's own:

> *Ty*terus *happily thou liest tumbling vn*der a
> *beetchtree.*

And then Master Watson's famous distich, "which for the sweetnes and gallantnes therof in all respects doth mat[c]h and surpasse the Latine coppy of *Horace* . . .

> *All* traue*llers doo glad*lie re*port great praise* to
> *Vlisses,*
> *For* that he *knew* manie *mens maners, and saw* many
> *citties.*"
>
> (I, 283)

Because Webbe claims that a thorough examination will reveal Watson's verses attaining "the very perfection" of poetry by honoring "all the rules and obseruations of the best versifying" (I, 283), it is necessary to understand a few finer points of classical prosody as they were applied by the critics to English measures. We must first ask, in other words, what Watson and his admiring critical audience were trying to do, and only then inquire as to how well they did it. These two questions should be sympathetically entertained, if only in order that we may not feel too uncharitable when we answer the third and most important: Was all this really worth doing? Since even some Elizabethan stomachs were unable to digest an imitation so often servile and an art so very artificial, we need not feel too snobbish when suspended disbelief begins to fray. A remarkably high tolerance is certainly required when theorists like Webbe, Puttenham, and Spenser discuss poetry as if it were something to be seen and not heard, or at least two removes from English as spoken in any place at any time.

The first remove is usually taken for granted. Webbe is merely rehearsing schoolboy stuff when he notes that the "speciall poyntes of a true [that is, classical] verse are the due obseruations of the feete and place of the feete," that the "foote of a verse is a measure of two sillables, or of three, distinguished by time which is eyther long or short," and that the "place of the feete is the disposing of them in theyr propper roomes. . ." (I, 280). All but one word in Webbe's definition would also serve for modern, "false" verse. With or without rhyme, poetry is always a rhythmical arrangement of words, and rhythm is attained by setting like measures in like places. The difference between true and false verse, according to Webbe, depends on how we stress a given foot. We may feast with the ancients and measure by "time," or feed with the Goths and emphasize by accent. To gain the glories of Greece and Rome, in short, we must versify by quantities and ignore rude custom's "qualities." When practiced by a master, this theory need not dishonor everyday pronunciation, for the rude, usually long monosyllables which Ascham complains about have many varying quantities: *fit, fat, fond, fault,* and *faith* increase in length, and *foil,* especially when we emphasize its importance (Give me the foil!), comes close to "foyall." The careful ear of Campion, a musician as well as a poet, heard every distinction. Notice how often he relies upon diphthongs in lengthening the right syllables:

> *Iust* be*gui*ler,
> *Kin*dest *loue,* yet *only chas*test,
> *Roy*all *in* thy *smooth* de*ny*als,
> *Frow*ning *or* de*mure*ly *smil*ing,
>   *Still* my *pure* de*light.*
>   (II, 348)

Rather than wrenching received pronunciation, Campion exploits it. Whether our scansion is determined by each word's rhetorical importance, its place in the line's grammatical structure, or the time we would hold it irrespective of its context, the italicized syllables remain the same. This kind of artifice we can appreciate. All other things being equal, is it not more artful to accent "foil" than "fit"?

This happy coinciding of proper quantities, comprehensible syntax, and the stresses that aid in communicating the verse's sense are quite exceptional, however. Usually we get something as far removed from real speech as Watson's "perfectly versified" distich, or Campion's patriotic desire that Elizabeth may *"Liue long with triumphs to blesse thy people"* (II, 347). To help make their meanings clear, we must emphasize that Ulysses knew *"many men's manners,"* not "manie mens maners," and that the Queen should live "with *triumphs*" or "with *triumphs*" but surely not "*with* triumphs." Whether rhetorical importance is conveyed by time or accent is immaterial. But we feel even farther from poetry as something heard when we realize that as well as stressing the wrong rhetorical points, Watson has no quantitative justification for making both syllables of "manie" short and both syllables of "*maners*" long, or that simply in terms of the time we hold our words, Campion's line should be scanned as *"Liue long with triumphs to blesse thy people,"* for each stressed word at least partially glides.

For these unquantitative quantities Campion and Webbe have no reasons, merely rules—dozens of them. Hearkening back to Ascham, among others, Webbe admits that English words "are nothing resemblaunt in nature" to the classical masters', and "therefore not possible to bee framed with any good grace after their vse" (I, 279). The answer is to imitate the Latins as the Latins imitated the Greeks, altering "the cannon of the rule according to the quality [that is, pronunciation] of our worde, and where our wordes and theyrs wyll agree, there to iumpe with them, [and] where they will not agree, there to establish a rule of our owne. . . ." Moreover, if any learned poet should publish "some famous worke, contayning dyuers formes of true verses, fitting the measures according to the matter, it would of it selfe be a sufficient authority, without any prescription of rules, to the most part of Poets for them to follow and by custome to ratify" (I, 279). So far Webbe exhibits good sense: True poets make the right rules even as they fit form to content, adopt the old when possible, adapt it when necessary, and continually experiment with a flexible language. He next lists each of poetry's measures with one example, information his readers would

have taken as commonplace but which gives our ears a moment
to tune out accents and tune in quantities: spondee (*goodnesse*),
pyrrhic (hyther), iambus (dy*ing*), trochee (*glad*ly), molossus
(*forgiueness*), tribrachys (merylie), dactyl (*h*appily), anapest
(trauel*ers*), bacchius (re*membrers*), palimbachius (*accor*ded),
creticus (*daun*ger*ous*), amphibrachus (re*ioy*ced). Or, as the mathe-
matician (another artificial fellow) would say, the permutations
and combinations are simply $2^2 + 2^3 = 12$.

Even as we adjust to syllables lengthened and shortened, however, we become uneasy. "*Goodness*," "hither," and "*glad*ly"
present no difficulties, but what about "dy*ing*" and "trauel*ers*"?
"Now as for the quantity of our wordes," confesses Webbe, "therein
lyeth great difficultye, and the cheefest matter in this faculty" (I,
281). Since his argument assumes too many unfamiliar premises, let
us turn to Campion, sometime student of law, for a clearer presentation. In observing "the quantity of their sillables," he begins
his defense, the Greeks took far greater license than the Latins; and
we English, because our language "stands chiefely vpon mona-
sillables, which . . . are of a heauy cariage," must take greater
license than either (II, 351). And with such classical precedent for
support Campion next makes each part of his case clear, but the
whole rather muddied. Notice how often he twists and turns between poetry heard and poetry read.

But aboue all the accent [that is, the lengthening and
shortening] of our words is diligently to be obseru'd, for
chiefly by the accent in any language the true value of the
sillables is to be measured. Neither can I remember any
impediment except position that can alter the accent of
any sillable in our English verse. For though we accent
the second of *Trumpington* short, yet is it naturally long,
and so of necessity must be held of euery composer.
Wherefore the first rule that is to be obserued is the nature
of the accent, which we must euer follow.

The next rule is position, which makes euery sillable
long, whether the position happens in one or in two words,
according to the manner of the *Latines*, wherein is to be
noted that *h* is no letter.

Position is when a vowell comes before two consonants,
either in one or two words. In one, as in *best*, *e* before *st*
makes the word *best* long by position. In two words, as in

setled loue, e before *d* in the last sillable of the first word and *l* in the beginning of the second makes *led* in *setled* long by position.

A vowell before a vowell is alwaies short, as *flīing, dīing, gŏing,* vnlesse the accent alter it, in *dĕnīing.*

The diphthong in the midst of a word is alwaies long, as *plaīing, deceīving.*

In the twenty-two paragraphs that follow and treat of even finer points, we find the same alternation between the claims of England and Rome, the imperative we discover so often among the "position poets": *Always* honor the word's natural length *except*———. With some difficulty we dismiss all natural inclinations to stress a syllable in order better to communicate the sense of its line or to honor customary pronunciation, as in *Trum*pington. But having managed to assign "true values" to all syllables by regarding them as distinct entities, and thus realizing the truth and "naturalness" of Trum-*ping*-ton, we are told that "best" must be held as long as "boil," and that "-led" is lengthened for "settled love" and shortened for "settled hate," since "h" is no letter. Campion, in short, is asking us to exchange one kind of position for another. Whereas we are prone to stress the position occupied by a word or syllable of great rhetorical importance, to punctuate the proper places as we see a series of syllables begetting an idea, we are now reminded to forget ideas, words, and even syllables, and to concentrate upon consonants. Enlightened by these rules for true versifying, we see why Webbe's Tyterus lies so awkwardly, yet artificially *"tumbling vn*der" his tree. Like Watson's famous "traue*llers,*" he is doing his thing "according to the manner of the *Latines*" and that is, at least for the position poets, an artful exception to their own natural patterns of speech.

The natural as regulated by Rome could easily degenerate into a game of orthographical manipulations. To judge from printers' spellings, at least, Elizabethan orthography was not sufficiently normalized to hinder the typesetter's search for even margins; hence the frequent variations within one page of prose: "bless," "blesse," and "bles." [67] Moreover, as any elementary schoolboy learning to read by phonics soon discovers, there is no logical justification for our different pronunciations of "rough," "cough," "dough," and "through." Campion seems aware of both problems, for he restricts the license invited by position. Because "our English

Orthography (as the French) differs from our common pronunciation, we must esteeme our sillables as we speak, not as we write;
for the sound of them in a verse is to be valued, and not their letters,
as for *follow* we pronounce *follo;* for *perfect, perfet;* for *little,
littel;* for *loue-sick, loue-sik;* for *honour, honor;* for *money, mony;*
for *dangerous, dangerus;* for *raunsome, raunsum;* for *though, tho;*
and their like" (II, 352). But Campion's sudden return to the
everyday is qualified by further comments on position: If in a
word of two syllables the second has "a full and rising accent that
sticks long vpon the voyce," the first is always short "vnlesse
position, or the diphthong, doth make it long..." (II, 353). Because
"an infinite number of sillables both among the *Greekes* and
Romaines are held as common," shortened or lengthened at will, he
excuses his shortening of syllables ending in "u" (virtue, rescue)
which the Latins always held. At times we suspect that he is more
affected by received pronunciation and rhetorical importance than
he realizes. When he prays that Elizabeth may live long "to *blesse*
thy *peo*ple," for example, he is not stressing "peo" because of position (the two consonants that follow), for he disclaims "littel"
pronounced as "little." The sound to be valued is clearly "pee-pul,"
and the only rule that justifies lengthening "pee" appears to be
this: "Words of two sillables that in their last sillable mayntayne a
flat or falling accent, ought to hold their first sillable long, as
rĭgŏr, glōrĭe, spīrĭt, fūrĭe, lābŏŭr, and the like: *ăny, mănы, prěty,
hŏly,* and their like are excepted" (II, 353). In view of "fūrie,"
it would seem that Campion could have found a "falling accent"
in "pul-pee" as well as "pee-pul."

None of Ascham's sons labored more diligently than Campion to
restore true versifying to England. Other than asking all civilized
Englishmen to select and imitate the best models with care and
learning, however, Ascham had not accompanied his challenge with
helpful suggestions. To rhyme is rude, to write epic hexameters is
difficult, if not impossible, and the number of times the Cambridge
Professor of Greek suddenly veers from specific instructions is
amazing: English verse stumbles upon monosyllables—Quintilian
says much the same about Latin monosyllables—in the same place
he rails against rhyme—if you dislike my invective against rhyme,
you must dislike Quintilian—but I am sure our tongue will receive iambic verse—yet people are too ignorant or lazy to attempt
it—and so we whall continue to drown in rude and lewd rhymes—
which some excuse by invoking Chaucer and Petrarch—worthy wits,

of course, despite faults like rhyme—but to follow what is worst in the best amounts to imitating that half-wit who thought himself like Sir Thomas More, simply because he wore his gown awry —any classical poet who rhymed was hissed—Surrey did well to avoid it when he translated part of the *Aeneid*—but his feet did not observe true quantities—even learned Italians presently avoid Petrarch's rhyming—and, be it spoken to poor England's glory, we began seeking to amend this fault first (I, 30–34). But precisely how we are to amend it is never suggested. At the other end of Elizabeth's reign stands Campion, equally aware of the "hardly intreated *Dactile*," more aware of the "passing pitifull successe" of those who attempt hexameters "altogether against the nature of our language," and therefore prepared to abandon that Antilia of heroic verse and build new quantitative schemes upon mere iambs, trochees, and position (II, 333).

Thirty-two years of woeful examples have not dampened the theorist's enthusiasm. Campion's subtitle explains that English will nevertheless "receiue eight seuerall kinds of numbers, proper to it selfe" and there is a strain both heroic and pathetic in his dedication to Lord Buckhurst, the man who had given England the glories of *Gorboduc* forty years before: "For this end haue I studyed to in-duce a true forme of versefying into our language: for the vulgar and vnarteficiall custome of riming hath, I know, deter'd many excellent wits from the exercise of English poesy" (II, 327). The sting is not in "vulgar," or common, but "vnarteficiall," or slovenly. Since man excels all other creatures in two things, reason and speech, "in them by how much one man surpasseth an other, by so much the neerer he aspires to a celestiall essence," which is, after all, what the Lord of Creation had intended. No literate subject of Elizabeth or James I would have quarreled with Campion's goal of making the artificial vulgar. In beautiful Jacobean English, David had sung:

When I consider thy heavens, the work of thy fingers, the moon and the stars, which thou hast ordained;

What is man, that thou art mindful of him? and the son of man, that thou visitest him?

For thou hast made him a little lower than the angels, and hast crowned him with glory and honour.

Thou madest him to have dominion over the works of thy hands; thou hast put all things under his feet. . . .[68]

Although the psalmist's "things" are "sheep and oxen, yea, and the beasts of the field," for any patriotic English poet man's dominion included the dutiful husbanding of reason and speech, yea, even the trochees of his verse. To all poets, even the red-nosed rhymers, it was equally obvious that the "world is made by Simmetry and proportion, and is in that respect compared to Musick, and Musick to Poetry." For whether the Elizabethan lyric flows with the elegant simplicity of Campion's quantitative hymns to Laura or Shakespeare's rhymed, accented songs of his Warwickshire countryside, whether it hobbles upon some alehouse jig or limps as lamely after Sappho, it asks, with Campion, "What musick can there be where there is no proportion obserued?" (II, 329).

The only disagreement centered in the kinds of proportion and artifice the poet might legitimately employ. Campion assumes that he must elaborate upon the antirhymers' tired complaints before introducing his eight new numbers. Once more we hear about the barbarians, "pollution of . . . language," and learning "most pitifully deformed"; chronological snobbery reaches its acme when Erasmus, More, and Reuchlin are honored for bringing "the Latine toong again to light, redeeming it with much labour out of the hands of the illiterate Monks and Friers" (II, 329). Thirty-two years of increasingly successful experimentation with rhyme are ignored as Campion dismisses his adversaries as cavalierly as Ascham. He who demonstrates "the imperfections of Rime must encounter with many glorious enemies," but the glorious turn out to be the same straw men scorned by Ascham, people who "can if neede be extempore (as they say) rime a man to death" (II, 329–330). The sonnets of Sidney and Spenser, the couplets of Marlowe, Hall, and Marston, and *Lucrece*'s and *Rosamond*'s rhyme royal are conveniently overlooked as Campion likens poets created by "the facilitie and popularitie of Rime" to flies bred under a hot summer's sun. No evidence can deter him "from a lawful defence of perfection," make him consent "to that which is lame and vnbeseeming," or shake his conviction that "things naturally imperfect can not be perfected by vse."

Judged with or without reference to his particular time, much of Campion's attack seems nonsensical. The more we know about that background of great poetry the critic himself ignores, the stranger his words sound. The mystery increases when we realize, as the baffled Daniel put it, that Campion's own "commendable Rymes" had already given "to the world the best notice of his worth" (II,

358). To Daniel, at least several things were certain. First, Campion's contempt for native traditions, especially those uncharitable references to accent as "a ridiculous and vnapt drawing of . . . speech" and rhyme as a "childish titillation" (II, 331), was damnably unpatriotic. My adversary, mused the usually gentlemanly Daniel, wrote merely to exhibit his own skill, and "so he might well haue done without doing wrong to the fame of the liuing, and wrong to *England*, in seeking to lay reproach vpon her natiue ornaments, and to turne the faire streame and full course of her accents into the shallow current of a lesse vncertaintie, cleane out of the way of her knowne delight" (II, 379). Always anxious lest our own prejudices render Campion's unintelligible, in this instance we discover that modern frustrations are not wholly owing to anachronistic expectations, for Daniel shares them. The historical critic has no "context" that fully explains Campion's attack. The wisest course is to admit that he was operating upon premises most of his fellow theorists no longer honored, and to note the sincere, misguided patriotism that inspired them: "What honour were it then for our English language to be the first that after so many yeares of barbarisme could second the perfection of the industrious *Greekes* and *Romaines?*" (II, 332). Similarly strange is the insistence that rhyme and accent can never "be perfected by vse." This is the argument of a revolutionist, not a reformer: All must be leveled, and not one old timber shall go into the new, stately mansion. Again, Daniel seconds our impressions. Campion's "great discouery of these new measures, threatning to ouerthrow the whole state of Ryme in this kingdom, I must either stand out to defend, or els be forced to forsake my selfe and giue ouer all" (II, 358). And again, it is Campion's lines, not his times, that assure us of his radical conservatism, a desire to conserve the development of the finest poetry, temporarily arrested by a millennium of Gothic antics.

Through Daniel, however, the historical critic can provide one valuable gloss. If Daniel's response confirms our first impression that Campion is a disloyal, ungrateful revolutionary, it also tells us not to regard his attack too lightly. So far removed from this battle, we are likely to assume that Campion's contemporaries would have merely smiled at his idle fantasies. How can he admit "the vnaptnes of our toongs and the difficultie of imitation," but ask why "old customes, if they be better, . . . should . . . not be recald," and then describe "numerous poesy" as a "yet florishing custome. . . ." (II, 330)? But Daniel finds the attack dangerous as well as ridiculous, not less "threatning" merely because it is silly. His *Defence of Ryme* was, in fact, originally conceived as a "priuate letter, . . . a defence of mine owne vndertakings" in rhyme, "to a learned Gentleman, a great friend of mine, then in Court," both to "confirm my selfe in mine owne courses, and to hold him from being wonne from vs" (II, 356).

Perhaps Daniel's claim that he had no "desire to publish the same to the world" is a scholarly attempt at *sprezzatura*, that "easy manner" or "studied carelessness" celebrated in Hoby's translation of Castiglione's *Book of the Courtier* (1528, 1561). As Campion had asked Buckhurst "to take in worth so simple a present, which by some worke drawne from my more serious studies I will hereafter endeuour to excuse" (II, 327–328), so his opponent would make it clear that these twenty-nine pages of careful analyses were but a piece of passing correspondence. In the grand volume that Castiglione claims he "accomplished a fewe dayes," it is prescribed that the courtier observe "in everye thing a certaine disgracing to cover arte withall, and seeme whatsoever he doth and saith, to doe it without paine, and (as it were) not minding it." [69] Such a graceful, calculated spontaneity inspires Sidney's *Apology*. Honoring his own observations upon art written according to yet concealing art, Sidney opens with convivial chat, closes with humorous descriptions of the rewards and punishments awaiting poetry's lovers and haters, and characterizes himself as "hauing slipt into the title of a Poet" who, "sick among the rest, [desires] to shewe some one or two spots of the common infection growne among the most part of Writers" (I, 150, 203–204, 206–207). For all Sidney's self-deprecating asides—"this incke-wasting toy of mine" (I, 206)—and attempts to make his classical oration appear to amble —"I finde already the triflingnes of this discourse is much too much enlarged" (I, 205)—we perceive his solemn, studied, carefully organized purpose. The same can be said of Ascham's "pleasure . . . to play and sporte with my Master *Tully*" (I, 34), Gascoigne's perception that "this poeticall licence is a shrewde fellow" (I, 53), and Whetstone's advertisement that *Promos* was one of those "vnregarded papers" he planned to leave "disparsed amonge my learned freendes, at theyr leasure to polish" (I, 58). After reading his "lyttle somewhat," we may agree with Webbe that much of it was indeed "sifted out of . . . [a] weake brayne" (I, 229), but this is not the response his modest disclaimer was intended to evoke. Into "so simple a present" Campion had put the best of his similarly misguided energies, and the easy manner that initiates Daniel's counterattack gives way to increasingly sterner metaphors: Let no rhymer "be any way discouraged in his endeuour by this brave allarum, but rather animated to bring vp all the best of their powers, and charge with all the strength of nature and industrie vpon contempt. . . . Let the Aduersary that thought to hurt vs bring more profit and honor by being against vs then if he had stoode still on our side" (II, 380).

Campion's and Daniel's quarrel over the limitations of artifice and proportion is best explained simply in terms of their different responses to the claims of the classics, "all that insolent *Greece,* or haughtie *Rome* / Sent forth, or since did from their ashes come," as Jonson remarked in his estimation of Shakespeare. Campion was as confident as Jonson that he knew what those wonderfully industrious and disciplined ancients were talking about. "Some eares accustomed altogether to the fatnes of rime may perhaps except against the cadences" of my new numbers, Campion warns, but a judicial examination will reveal that "they close of themselues so perfectly that the help of rime were not only in them superfluous but also absurd" (II, 350). Daniel's ear was as sensitive, his classical knowledge as good, but his native pride and eclectic temperament led him to see a more enlightened Middle Ages and a less forbidding Rome. Campion's *Observations* are grandly irrelevant, for "euerie Grammarian in this land hath learned his *Prosodia,* and alreadie knowes all this Arte of numbers," and if the ignorant now turn into "true" versifiers, "wee are like to haue leane Numbers instead of fat Ryme" (II, 379).

In wooing his friend from Campion, Daniel repeatedly spices abstract argument with homespun practicalities, and continually asks whether man was made for the Sabbath or the Sabbath for man. Custom precedes law, nature precedes art, and both have always worked upon man to frame his words within certain measures "differing from the ordinarie speach, and introduced, the better to expresse mens conceipts, both for delight and memorie" (II, 359). Aristotle supports this anthropological-aesthetic truth; even in his time men perceived that *rhythmi,* or frames of words, were common to all nations, and we see that they occur as naturally in English as artifice could ever make them, "being such as the Eare of it selfe doth marshall in their proper roomes" (II, 360). The ear, in fact, must govern all. Words out of natural rank grate upon it, whereas rhyme gives "both to the Eare an Echo of a delightful report, and to the Memorie a deeper impression of what is deliuered therein." You need only apply your own observations with common sense, Master Campion, to see that rhyme is merely a more recent fashion to honor that symmetry, proportion, and music you talk so much about. And is not this rhyme an "excellencie added . . . a Harmonie farre happier than any proportion Antiquitie could euer shew vs," and affording "more grace . . . then euer bare numbers, howsoeuer they be forced to runne in our slow language, can possibly yeeld"? Classical verse stands upon the number and quantity of syllables, English upon measure and accent. If the ancients strictly observed the correct number of quantities, we "most religiously respect the accent." Since each system attains "harmonie in the best proportion of Musicke," why not admit that both reveal that "hereditary eloquence proper to all mankind" (II, 360), be he Greek or Goth, Homer or Hun? We are bound to get farther by taking the best from each time and place. "Suffer then the world to inioy that which it knowes, and what it likes: Seeing that whatsoeuer force of words doth mooue . . . the affections of men, in what Scythian sort soeuer it be disposed or vttered, that is true number, measure, eloquence, and the perfection of speech" (II, 363).

In parrying theory with theory, in developing what Touchstone calls the Retort Courteous, however, Daniel occasionally pauses to level a Quip Modest, Reply Churlish, or Reproof Valiant. He doubts that quantities will ever thrive "in our Climate, if they shew no more worke of wonder than yet we see"; notes that if we follow his opponent's "new lawes of words," we shall not "better our imperfections" but merely "put off these fetters to receiue others"; and insists that since "imitation wil after, though it breake her necke," idle wits will simply turn from qualitative to quantitative scribbling (II, 362–363). Next comes a sensible Countercheck Quarrelsome, a challenge to the tailor who "hath but found other clothes to the same body, and peraduenture not so fitting as the former." We admire the ancients "not for their smooth-gliding words, nor their measures, but for their inuentions; which treasure if it were to be found in Welch and Irish, we should hold those languages in the same estimation" (II, 364). To them, of course, "their owne *idioma* was naturall; but to vs it can yeeld no other commoditie then a sound." Since "it is matter that satisfies the iudiciall, appeare it in what habite it will," why pursue their sounds at the cost of our sense?

For both Campion and his ancients there is finally the Lie Direct. Daniel dares to suggest that the Greeks and Romans "thanke their sword" for making "their tongues so famous and vniuersall," since their verse is often "a confused deliuerer of their excellent conceits" (II, 364). They torture their words, violate their own laws, and in striving to vary the measures of their odes, write "as if Art were ordained to afflict Nature." Some English rhymers, especially the sonneteers, also exhibit a presumption beyond their ability; others, however, employ rhyme with such skill that "so farre from hindering their inuentions, . . . it hath begot conceit beyond expectation, and comparable to the best inuentions of the world" (II, 365). It all depends on whether we make rhyme our master or servant. In carping at our quatrains, Campion would have us believe that rhyme automatically enforces a poet "to abiure his matter" or handle "his subiect as tyrannically as *Procrustes* . . . his prisoners" (II, 331). But "in an eminent spirit, whome Nature hath fitted for that mysterie, Ryme is no impediment to his conceit"; it "rather giues him wings to mount, and carries him, not out of his course, but as it were beyond his power to a farre happier flight" (II, 365). Thinking of sonneteers in terms like Meres's—"these are the most passionate among vs to bewaile and bemoane the perplexities of loue" (II, 320)—Daniel notes that the poet's imagination is "an vnformed *Chaos*" which must be "wrought into an Orbe of order and forme" (II, 366). The "certaine limit obserued in Sonnets" is rather inspired and blessed by Nature than prescribed by Procrustes, for the "conceit" or idea is not mutilated, but measured so as to underline its essentially lyrical character; it is reduced, in other words, to a "iust forme, neither too long for the shortest proiect, nor too short for the longest, being but onely imployed for a present passion." Since our real "passions are often without measure" and since "Nature . . . desires a certaintie and comports not with that which is infinite," artifice offers rhyme as an intermediary.

For a modern opponent, Daniel might have had to answer different charges: How can "the most passionate . . . bewaile and bemoane" so artfully? Is it really natural for the distraught to proportion their syllables and sounds with such patent cunning? Has not a calculated artificiality undercut an allegedly immediate, real, and therefore spontaneous and sincere outburst? Like his contemporaries, however, Campion never asks whether, but in what ways, the natural and the artificial should go hand in hand. It is therefore sufficient for Daniel to point out, not defend, the sonnet's *inspired* craftsmanship and *natural* artifice in terms that would serve as well for the circumscribed worlds of Jane Austen's novels: "Besides, is it not most delightfull to see much excellentlie ordred in a small roome, or little gallantly disposed and made to fill vp a space of like capacitie, in such sort that the one would not appeare so beautifull in a larger circuite, nor the other do well in a lesse? which often we find to be so, according to the powers of nature in the workman" (II, 366).

With these premises in mind, the rest of Daniel's case is easily predictable. He first attacks Campion's chronological snobbery. Men of all times and places are "children of nature," enjoy "the same Sunne of Discretion," have an equal "portion of the same virtues as well as of the same vices" (II, 366–367). Why then must we build "by the square of *Greece* and *Italie*"? It is, moreover, neither their trochees, poetry, nor philosophy but "that great booke of the world and the all-ouerspreading grace of heauen" that shall grant our writings more wisdom. To hold this nation barbarous or that time rude is both arrogant and ignorant. Gothic laws and customs are yet honored, that most civilized state of China has never heard of anapests, and Europe abounded with learned men long before that rhymer, More. It is really only "the clowds gathered about our owne iudgement that makes vs thinke all other ages wrapt vp in mists, and the great distance betwixt vs that causes vs to imagine men so farre off to be so little in respect of our selues" (II, 370). From the man who has such trust in poetry to "combine in one / All ages past, and make one liue with all," [70] and from an age so confident in its opinions about past and future, it is remarkable now to hear that history is merely "a Mappe of Men," telling us no more concerning "times, men, and maners, iust as they were" than a "superficiall Card" reveals "the true Substance of Circumstances" to the navigator, whose coast "always proues other to the eye than the imagination forecast it" (II, 370). We must not assume there were no Caesars and Catos "borne elsewhere then at *Rome*"; we must realize that the time of Erasmus, More, and Reuchlin bred no profounder theologian than Aquinas, no greater lawyer than Bartolus, no acuter logician than Duns Scotus; and we must admit that history does illustrate the malignant effects of that viper, innovation, "borne with reproch in her mouth," promising much, performing little, disgracing all.

"Perfection," concludes Daniel, "is not the portion of man," and we shall never even come close "if wee be euer beginning" (II, 374). Men of good will therefore seek to adorn, not deface, the present. Had Campion actually demonstrated a better way, we should all have admired him. But a proper attempt "to raise the glory of our language" has produced only "a few loose and vncharitable Epigrammes." We are told to imitate the classics and then shown how to disobey them, lengthening their short syllables and shortening their long by "imperfect rules, weake proofs, and vnlawful lawes" (II, 375). Campion tortures words that are naturally obedient and racks received pronunciation; his eight new numbers, "had they come in their kinde and naturall attire of Ryme, wee should neuer haue suspected that they had affected to be other, or sought to degenerate into strange manners, which now we see was the cause why they were turnd out of their proper habite, and brought in as Aliens, onely to induce men to admire them as farre-commers" (II, 377-378). If Campion is adamant about rhyme as something naturally imperfect, Daniel is equally unyielding about accent, that "chiefe Lord and graue Gouernour of Numbers," and even more insistent that "our ydle Arguments," not rhyme, have debased modern verse. Posterity "shall make a quest of inquirie" and separate wheat from chaff; our responsibility is to "looke the better to our feete, . . . matter, . . . maners," to embrace rhyme "as the fittest dwelling for our inuention," and to experiment with earnest humility. For "if this right or truth" be nothing other than self-love or proud affectation dictates, "we shall shape it into a thousand figures, seeing this excellent painter, Man, can so well lay the colours which himselfe grindes in his owne affections, as that hee will make them serue for any shadow and any counterfeit" (II, 383).

More Practical Criticism:
A Truer Art for God and Country

It is fitting that Daniel, in this first piece of Jacobean criticism,[71] should share the moral and patriotic concerns of so many of his Elizabethan predecessors. It is also fitting that through the course of his *Defence* he should reflect the spirit in which their arguments were conceived and conducted; like them, he is occasionally indignant, often humble, and usually both earnest and informal. Above all, he epitomizes their basically sensible perspective. For though the sixteenth-century theorists' learning is sometimes pon-

derous and their citations from authorities lengthy and abstruse,
their main reason for writing is generally as practical as Daniel's
and just as clearly expressed: Good criticism furnishes guidelines
for better art and is thereby indirectly helpful in bringing honor
to God, profit and delight to man, and praise to England. Even the
oddest notions these men advance as truths and the quaintest fictions
they labor under should not obscure the picture they paint of
themselves, struggling alongside the practicers, quick to aid and
slow to condemn. If some of them were misleading in their encouragement to capture the finest points of Roman artifice, every
critic is motivated by similar concerns and works in different ways
toward the same general ends.

When we take the Elizabethan theorists simply as people, the
first thing we notice is the frequency with which they evince
religious interests. God never enters as an afterthought; His
presence is often central to the thesis. Daniel reveals an unassuming
but profoundly Christian orientation in his specific references to
"the all-ouerspreading grace" and "awe of heaven" (II, 367), in his
metaphor of the imagination as "an vnformed *Chaos*, . . . without
day" being wrought "by the diuine power of the spirit" into "an
Orbe of order," and perhaps even in his closing admission that
"the law of time" will soon make "al that for which we now contend *Nothing*" (II, 384). His precursors, however unlike their
personalities and qualities of scholarship, are often more explicit.
Ascham warns that without "the trewe doctrine of Gods holie
Bible," his beloved Plato, Aristotle, and Cicero "be but fine edge
tooles in a fole or mad mans hand" (I, 7). Lodge stoutly defends
the theater against his Puritan opponent, but must praise him for
reprehending the players' profanation of the Sabbath, and urges the
civil authorities to take appropriate measures (I, 84). On a more
abstract plane, Sidney argues for poetry as a moral aid, a means by
which "erected wit" may overcome "infected will," the result of
"that first accursed fall of *Adam*" (I, 157). Those critics who
share Sidney's desire to demonstrate "that Incke and Paper cannot
be to a more profitable purpose employed" than in writing poetry
also follow his logic: The best learning is both moral and practical,
and none teaches and moves us to virtue better than poetry (I, 184).
Most also seem to imply, with Sidney, that to the extent that art
is immoral, it is not art. Webbe entertains the idea that to the
impure, all things are impure, assuring us that Chaucer's merriest
tales and the ancients' "vainest trifles" contain some "profitable

counsaile," and that only those who "tread downe the fairest flowers and wilfullie thrust their fingers among the nettles" will find Ovid, Catullus, and Martial wholly harmful (I, 251–252). But he never insists that all true or "very Poetrie" is pure, or that to the purest it will always seem so. Some gardens should be closed to children. It were better for an adult to see no part rather than all of Lucian's. And despite his differences with Sidney, he is thankful that whereas lascivious writers gained passage among the ancients "for their Arte sake," Christian England is less tolerant (I, 255). Merry, scoffing Nashe is anxious lest "we dwell . . . so long in Poetry that wee become Pagans, or that we make . . . such proceedings in Aristotle that we prooue proficients in Atheisme" (I, 337). Rehearsing the kinds of ancient poetry we may wish to imitate, Puttenham stipulates that "we Christians are forbidden to vse" imprecatory verse, the "*Dirae*" practiced by Virgil and Ovid (II, 60). Harington brings forth his Ariosto with the concession that "to vs that are Christians, in respect of the high end of all, which is the health of our soules," poetry and "al other studies of Philosophy are in a manner vaine and superfluous" (II, 197).

As Smith makes clear, some of the odd tactics employed by poetry's apologists are explained by the nature of the poet-whippers' attacks,[72] but we must not mistake the concerns listed above for disingenuous, *ad hominem* argument. Since the Puritans, for example, had produced a disarming array of citations against poetry and plays by combing ancient and medieval authorities and wresting the Church Fathers to their own ascetic pleasure, Sidney no doubt found a special enjoyment in noting those places where "the holy scripture . . . and euen our Sauiour Christ vouchsafed to vse the flowers" of poetry (I, 166–167, 174, 181). Neither here nor in his discussion of "infected will," however, do we find a secular spirit playing with theology or adopting a theistic stance to win a Christian audience from his more sincerely religious opponents. The Puritan penchant for argument by testimonial explains the critics' dreary roll calls of pro's to counter con's. Their sometimes documented instances of the theater's social and political abuses, and of poetry's lewdness, partly explain why the critics must attack bad poets as well as poet-haters. Without the Puritans, the critics might have been less severe with alehouse wits and rude rhymers, might not have insisted so strongly upon literature's instruction as opposed to its delight, and might have found England, before the advent of bawdy Italy's customs and art, not so innocent. All such ammunition for poetry's suppression was turned into arguments for its improvement. How often the critics follow Sidney's lead, underlining their disdain both for the evil men who abuse art and for the well-meaning men who abuse men and art by preaching that art abuses man. Had the Puritans not appealed so often to Plato's charge that poets are liars and to his desire to bar them from the perfect commonwealth, Lodge would probably never have remarked upon the philosopher's bad theology: "Your Plato in midst of his presisnes [Puritanism] wrought that absurdite that neuer may be redd in Poets, to make a yearthly creature to beare the person of the creator, and a corruptible substance an incomprehensible God!" (I, 67). Nor would Sidney have descended from gentility to bid his adversaries read Plato's *Symposium* and consider "whether any Poet doe authorize [such] abhominable filthines" as this philosopher, or to point out that *The Republic* could not have expelled poets "for effeminate wantonnes," since its writer "alloweth communitie of women" and "little should . . . Sonnets be hurtfull when a man might haue what woman he listed" (I, 190–191).

But the critics did not need the Puritans to undervalue the Middle Ages, to conclude with the Protestant courtier, Puttenham, that "in writing of rymes and registring of lyes was the Clergy of that fabulous age wholly occupied" (II, 15), or to agree with the bohemian, Nashe, that they should resist the efforts of "bable bookemungers . . . to restore to the worlde that forgotten Legendary licence of lying, to imitate a fresh the fantasticall dreames of those exiled Abbie-lubbers" (I, 323). Since Nashe also warns against those who would "repaire the ruinous wals of *Venus* Court," and since his own *Choise of Valentines* answers to these pornographic endeavors, we must be cautious in speaking of sincerity. The evidence, however, usually indicates that the critics shared their opponents' religious and moral principles, but were also genuinely convinced that such principles had been misapplied.

Throughout Elizabethan criticism we discover as well Daniel's interest in bettering art for England's glory. Censuring the bad teaching and ignorant writing "of our Diuinitie dunces," Nashe asks how "such bungling practitioners . . . shuld euer profite the Common wealth"; and modern romancers, who resurrect "the feyned no where acts of Arthur of the rounde table," are also scorned for yielding "no Commonwealth commoditie" (I, 314,

323). Four years later, Harvey attempted to establish Nashe's own worthlessness by reference to the same patriotic premises. In a sarcastic tribute to Pierce Penniless's "Aqua fortis" muse, far superior to "the trickling water of Helicon," Harvey celebrates "a new-found land of confuting commodities discouered by this braue Columbus of tearmes . . . that detecteth new Indies of Inuention" (II, 246). The recent "flourishing transplantation" of the "most noble Commonwealthes vpon Earth" into "these remote parts of world," the flowing of Tiber into Thames and removal of Athens to London, was but faintly heralded by those violets of March, Sidney and Spenser; for the rich harvest we must look to Nashe, "the onely life of the presse and the very hart-blood of the Grape" (II, 248–249). However bitter Nashe's and Harvey's quarrel, it was fought on common ground. Nashe would have seconded Harvey's request that every man, regardless of his craft, "be respected according to the vttermost extent of his publique seruice or priuate industrie" (II, 280), and had it not been issued by Nashe, Harvey would have applauded that challenge to "diuine Master *Spencer*, the miracle of wit, to bandie line for line . . . in the honor of *England*, gainst *Spaine, France, Italie,* and all the world" (I, 318).

Critical patriotism is as explicit as the title of Carew's tract, *The Excellency of the English Tongue;* its author was but one of many who urged his countrymen to exploit the aptness, preciseness, ease, sweetness, and copiousness of their native language (II, 285 ff.). Greek and Latin, which Carew uses "as touchstones," are themselves the result of "filching." The Greeks robbed the Hebrews, the Latins stole from the Greeks, all Christendom from the Latins, and Englishmen may now "(like bees) gather the honye," or like merchants "the rarest Iewelles" of Spain, Italy, France, and Germany, "and leaue the dreggs to themselfes" (II, 286, 293). Within the critical ranks there is again some disagreement. Just as Nashe and Harvey differed as to whose muse profited the realm more, but not about the value of public service, and just as the rhymers and position poets went their own equally patriotic ways, so E.K. honors Spenser for avoiding what Carew will later call "a Iust Legitimation of . . . bastard wordes . . ." (II, 291). Carew welcomes all foreigners to his already copious English garden: "wee graffe vppon Frentch wordes those buddes to which that soyle affordeth noe growth." E.K., on the other hand, is angry at those who have "patched up" English "with peces and rags of other languages, borrowing here of the French, there of the Italian, euery where of the Latine. . . . So now they haue made our English tongue a gallimaufray or hodgepodge of al other speches" (I, 130). Vested interests are of course at stake. His "one special prayse" for the New Poet is that "he hath laboured to restore, as to theyr rightfull heritage, such good and naturall English words as haue ben long time out of vse and almost cleane disherited," and he realizes that the "patchers," who are not "so wel sene in the English tonge as perhaps in other languages, if they happen to here an olde word, albeit very naturall and significant, crye out streightway that we speak no English, but gibbrish" (I, 129–130). A fig for those willing to be counted strangers to "their own mother tonge," a second for their ignorant censures, and a third for the most shameful of all, who not only refuse "to garnish and beautifie" ancient English, "but also repine that of other [tongues] it should be embellished."

Sidney remained unimpressed. To be sure, *The Shepheardes Calender* contained much good poetry, but "that same framing of his stile to an old rustick language I dare not alowe, sith neyther *Theocritus* in Greeke, *Virgill* in Latine, nor *Sanazar* in Italian did affect it" (I, 196). Besides, the modern "hodgepodge" nature of our speech gives it strength; "some will say it is a mingled language. And why not so much the better, taking the best of both the other?" (I, 204). For Sidney, the most enlightened patriotism is much less concerned with restoring lost words than with using the new "gallimaufray" skillfully. Had Spenser remembered that each pastoral master respected his own audience's idiom, he would have come even closer to demonstrating that English equals "any other tongue in the world" for "vttering sweetly and properly the conceits of the minde, which is the end of speech" (I, 204).

The precise nature of idiomatic English remained undefined, however, and the battle of diction, like that of rhyme, raged throughout Elizabeth's reign. In 1557 Sir John Cheke warns that as English is "euer borowing and neuer payeng, she shall be fain to keep her house as bankrupt"; being imperfect, she must occasionally import foreigners, but let her borrow with great "bashfulnes," and only after making sure that she has not overlooked "old denisoned [naturalized] wordes" (I, 357–358). Daniel says much the same in 1603, defining affectation as that "vnkinde and vnnaturall" desire for "disguising or forging strange or vnusuall wordes . . . onely vpon a singularitie, when our owne . . . would expresse vs more familiarly and to better delight . . ." (II, 384). Cheke's compromise was generally followed. Although Puttenham, for example, does not deem "eloquence" too outlandish—Cheke had preferred "welspeakinges"—he will not allow *"facunditie"* (II, 153). Quite aware that his "mother speach" or *"Idioma"* was once something like Cornish or Welsh, then Anglo-Saxon, and now Norman English, he insists that after any "speach is fully fashioned to the common vnderstanding, & accepted by consent of a whole country, . . . it . . . receaueth none allowed alteration but by extraordinary occasions, by little & little, as it were insensibly, bringing in of many corruptions that creepe along with the time" (II, 149).

Throughout the earlier portions of his treatise Puttenham implies that English words are far too precious for any man to play William the Conquerer with. He first justifies his title. There *can* be an Arte of *English* Poesie since our language is "no lesse copious, pithie, and significatiue" than the ancients', our ideas are as good, our wits no less apt, our industry to fashion proper procedures is as patient, and we have, moreover, inherited "twentie other curious points in that [poetical] skill more then they euer had, by reason of our rime and tunable concords or simphonie, which they neuer obserued" (II, 5–6). Because Webbe holds rhyme to be "within compasse of euery base witt" (I, 278), he is not interested in such "curious points." But the severe reformer also praises the "royall dignitie and statelie grace" to be found in our language, and is equally proud of "the exquisite excellency in all kindes of good learning nowe flourishing among vs, inferiour to none other nation . . ." (I, 228). In Thomas Phaer's translation of the *Aeneid*, Webbe claims, English attains "the verye maiesty of a ryght Heroicall verse," and he urges others to enlarge "the credite of their natiue speeche" (I, 256, 278–279). Unlike Webbe, Puttenham does not reserve his compliments for contemporary writers. Some poets of "the first age," especially "the most renowmed" Chaucer, have "by their thankefull studies so much beautified our English tong as at this day it will be found our nation is in nothing inferiour to the French or Italian" in copy, subtlety, good method, and proportion (II, 62–64). But as much as we may admire Chaucer, and however grateful we should be for our medieval legacy, we must not imitate a language "now out of vse" (II, 150). The courtly "maker" is in fact advised to avoid all speech except that presently spoken at Court or by the better people in London "and the shires lying about London within lx. myles, and not much aboue" (II, 150). The language of coastal towns is corrupted by foreign merchants, "vplandish" villages by poor rustics, and universities by their scholars' "peeuish affectation of words out of the primatiue languages." The lower-class Londoner speaks in "strange accents or ill shapen soundes," and "the purer English Saxon" of the northern aristocracy is as unacceptable as the "far Westerne mans speach." The young poet must even be careful to reject the "inkhorne termes" he reads and the "many darke wordes" he hears at Court (II, 151).

Lest he appear too presumptuous, Puttenham concludes by apologizing for his own "many straunge and vnaccustomed" words: *scientificke* (to designate the kind of artifice that draws upon science—that is, knowledge—as opposed to the kind that works with concrete objects, the *mechanicall;* the difference, for example, between a play*wright* and a ship*wright*); *politien* (which combines our "political scientist" and "politician"); *conduict* (a little boy may lead, but only a great leader "conduicts"); and so on. We can hardly spare other fine words like *numerositee, placation, assubtiling,* and that brand-new term, *impression,* but we should avoid *audacious* (for bold) and *compatible* (for agreeable in nature). Other dangerous neologisms that today seem quite tame are *conscious, ingenuitie, artificiallite, negotiation,* and *extensiuely emploid,* which Nashe must dutifully "scum off . . . as the new ingendred fome [foam]" of Harvey's "ouer-rackt" diction (II, 242). Even Chaucer's authority may not excuse Harvey's awkward "balductums." In the springtime of English poetry, art "was glad to peepe vp through any slime of corruption, to be beholding to she car'd not whome for apparaile, trauailing in those colde countries," but there is now no reason why "shee, a banisht Queene into this barraine soile, hauing monarchized it so long amongst the Greeks and Romanes, should . . . still be constrained . . . to weare the robes of aduersitie" or dishonor her "new prosperitie" by donning Harvey's "old rags" (II, 242–243). It took Harvey less than a year to reply in kind. Among Nashe's "mishapen rablement of absurde and ridiculous wordes," Harvey finds both *declamatorie stiles* and *hermaphrodite phrases,* a *ratifying of truthable and eligible English* as well as *the horrisonant pipe of inueterate antiquitie* (II, 275–276). There is nothing logically wrong or unapt about Harvey's *precious Traynment* or Nashe's *fictionate person,* nor anything inherently fine about Shakespeare's *milk of human kindness,* and *eaten me out of house and home.* It is their greater contexts that have made the latter more popular, hence more familiar, and thus more "fitting" or "natural."

Regardless of the principles or prejudices the critics reveal in seeking a proper English idiom, they make it clear that Elizabeth's subjects, like Navarre's, had partaken of "a great feast of languages and stol'n the scraps" (*Love's Labor's Lost*, V. i. 33–34). Amid this new world of words, Shakespeare's humbler countrymen might have concluded with Costard that "remuneration" is simply "the Latin word for three farthings," and "guerdon," some " 'leven-pence farthing better" (III, i. 130, 161). The affected, like Armado, that "man of fire-new words, fashion's own knight," no doubt enjoyed saluting "the posteriors of this day; which the rude multitude call[ed] the afternoon" (I. i. 176; V. i. 75–77). And many sensible Rosalines must have guided their ardent Berownes from "Taffeta phrases, silken terms precise, / Three-pil'd hyperboles" and "Figures pedantical" with a dainty "Sans 'sans', I pray you" (V. ii. 406 ff.). Shakespeare is usually merry with "fire-new" phrases. That most fashionable Illyrian knight, Sir Toby Belch, asks whether courtly "Cesario" will "encounter the house."

	My niece is desirous you should enter, if your trade be to her.
Vio.	I am bound to your niece, sir; I mean, she is the list of my voyage.
Sir To.	Taste your legs, sir; put them to motion.
Vio.	My legs do better understand me, sir, than I understand what you mean by bidding me taste my legs.
Sir To.	I mean, to go, sir, to enter.
Vio.	I will answer you with gait and entrance. But we are prevented [*Enter* OLIVIA *and* MARIA.] Most excellent accomplish'd lady, the heavens rain odours on you!
Sir And.	That youth's a rare courtier—'Rain odours' well!
Vio.	My matter hath no voice, lady, but to your own most pregnant and vouchsafed ear.
Sir And.	'Odours', 'pregnant', and 'vouchsafed'—I'll get 'em all three all ready.

(Twelfth Night, III. i. 72 ff.)

But courtly jargon is represented less pleasantly in Osric, the "water-fly," with his "carriages" and "soft society" (*Hamlet*, V.

ii. 83 ff.), and in Kent's anatomy of Oswald, the "whoreson zed" (*King Lear*, II. i. 57 ff.). We also have both the comic wordplay of Feste, who insists he is not Olivia's "fool, but her corrupter of words" (III. i. 33–34), and the more sinister corruptions of men like Edmund, who adjust the meanings of older words—"bond," "bastard," and "natural"—to the special needs of each situation (for example, *King Lear*, I. ii. 1 ff.; II. i. 44 ff.). And when we remember what Prince John will soon make of "honour" at Gaultree Forest, Doll Tearsheet's indignant retort to Mistress Quickly's "good Captain Pistol" takes on more somber hues: "A captain! God's light, these villains will make the word as odious as the word 'occupy'; which was an excellent good word before it was ill sorted. Therefore captains had need look to't" (*2 Henry IV*, II. iv. 138 ff.).

Francis Bacon "looked to it" by translating his *Essays* and *History of Henry the Seventh* into Latin, for, as he explained to Buckingham, "I do conceive that the Latin volume of them (being in the universal language) may last as long as books last." [73] Although such a formidable task would have been as easy for that accomplished Latinist, Ben Jonson, he entrusted his *Workes* to English and implied that one of his rival playwrights, John Marston, should have done the same. Toward the end of the *Poetaster* (acted, 1601), Horace (alias Jonson) administers an emetic to Crispinus (alias Marston), who vomits up words as un-English as *inflate, clutcht, strenuous, clumsie, retrograde,* and *reciprocall.*[74]

In very different ways, then, Tudor writers reflect the critics' concern over the instability of native speech, and they illustrate even more extensively the patriotism that inspired the critical quest for normalized idiom. In his commemoration of Wyatt, for example, Surrey proceeds from the poet's craftsmanship ("hammers bet styll in that liuely brayn / As on a stithe"), to his patriotism ("where that some work of fame / Was dayly wrought, to turne to Britaines gayn"), to his poetry ("A hand, that taught what might be sayd in ryme"), to his place in English literature ("That reft Chaucer the glory of his wit"), to his public service ("A toung, that serued in forein realmes his king"), to his morality ("Whose courteous talke to vertue did enflame"), and finally to that "Witnesse of faith" he left behind.[75] Surrey is probably listing Wyatt's virtues in what he considers an ascending order; Wyatt's stature is meant to grow as we note his services to art, Henry VIII, and God. Surrey is in turn conceived by Drayton as finding "no cause, nor . . . reason why / My Countrey should give place to *Lumbardy*" in natural beauty, and though in language

> to the *Tuscans* I the smoothnesse grant,
> Our Dialect no Majestie doth want,
> To set thy [Geraldine's] praises in as high a Key,
> As *France*, or *Spaine*, or *Germanie*, or they.[76]

Rosamond is similarly confident that her *Complaint* will prove to posterity that "Thames had Swannes as well as euer Po," and Musophilus, another of Daniel's agents, notes that

> our accents equall to the best
> Is able greater wonders to bring forth:
> When all that euer hotter spirits exprest
> Comes bettered by the patience of the North.[77]

With such critical and poetic expressions of patriotism before us, we better understand why Raleigh proceeds so obliquely in his "Vision upon This Conceipt of the Faery Queene." The height of compliment is attained not through specific, direct notices of Spenser's greatness, but by detailing the stir his poem has caused in the poets' heaven. Having first envisioned the grave of Petrarch's famous Laura,

> Whose tumbe faire Love, and fairer Virtue kept,
> All suddeinly I saw the Faery Queene:
> At whose approch the soule of Petrarke wept,
> And from thenceforth those graces were not seene.
> For they this Queene attended; in whose steed
> Oblivion laid him downe on Lauras herse:
> Hereat the hardest stones were seene to bleed,
> And grones of buried ghostes the hevens did perse:
> Where Homers spright did tremble all for griefe,
> And curst th' accesse of that celestiall theife.[78]

Along with Daniel, then, the Elizabethan critics are earnest, careful, and almost devout about seeking an art and language that disgraces neither God's designs nor England's name. But again like Daniel, they approach their subjects and air their views with an easy informality and winsome self-effacement; the seriousness of their undertakings never makes them pompous or sterile. That "studied carelessness" recommended by Castiglione no doubt influenced both organization and style, but it does not wholly explain the critics' candid asides, reluctance to prescribe any infallible rule, spirited dissent, and often racy idiom. In Sidney's reference to his "incke-wasting toy," for instance, we perceive a courtly, artful concealing of art. In his vignette of the poet enticing children from play and old men from chimney corners (I, 172), on the other hand, we sense a natural enthusiasm for the homespun. Similarly, when Sidney exemplifies his own "barbarousnes," he is not so much honoring Italian *sprezzatura* as that native English habit of stopping by the wayside for friendly chat: "I neuer heard the olde song of *Percy* and *Duglas* that I found not my heart mooued more then with a trumpet; and yet is it sung but by some blinde Crouder, with no rougher voyce then rude stile" (I, 178). In Richard Stanyhurst's dedication to *Thee First Foure Bookes of Virgil his Aeneis* (1582), he claims for his translation the loftiest of goals: "too aduaunce thee riches of oure speeche" by the "making of verses in such wise as thee *Greekes* and *Latins*" (I, 138, 141). His scholarly aspirations and the learned nature of his argument, however, do not prevent him from describing Virgil as "telling as yt were a *Cantorburye tale*," from claiming that "*Ennius* his ragged verses . . . sauoure soomwhat nappy of thee spigget," or from characterizing the "*peale meale*" rhymer as a "simple *Tom Towly*" (I, 136–137, 140). And he discusses his method with equal informality: "I purpose not too beat on euerye childish tittle that concerneth *Prosodia*" nor attempt "too chalck owt any lines or rules too oothers, but too lay downe too thee reader his view thee course I tooke" (I, 144).

Although the critics are sometimes sure that a particular writer, work, or technique is bad, they usually introduce new and better ways as working hypotheses, not pontifications. Gascoigne furnishes no *Summa*, simply *Certayne Notes of Instruction* (1575). At the other end of the period Daniel is still searching. He is "not so farre in loue" with his own "mysterie" (that is, craft) of rhyming that he will not admit how "verie tyresome and vnpleasing" those "continuall cadences of couplets" echo in his ear (II, 382). Occasionally, in fact, "to beguile the eare with a running out, and passing ouer the Ryme, as no bound to stay vs in the line where the violence of the matter will breake thorow, is rather gracefull then otherwise." But long series of couplets "to another may seeme most delightfull," and he will certainly never condemn any man's enjoyment of what "stuffs . . . rather then intertaines" his own hearing. He freely admits, in other words, both his "neede to learne of others" and the possibility that some dislikes are the result of personal "daintinesse" (II, 382). In *Ane schort Treatise . . .* [on] *Scottis Poesie* (1584), which is dedicated simply "to the docile bairns of knawledge," the royal hand of James VI is discernible only in the caution for poets to "be war of wryting any thing of materis of commoun weill, or vther sic graue sene subiectis" (I, 221). For the most part, this King would suggest, not demand. Elizabeth's sprightly godson, Harington, worries lest those who allow poetry and like Ariosto fall upon his translation, for "where the hedge is lowest, there doth euery man go ouer" (II, 195). Equally inelegant is the simile served up by George Chapman, the scholarly translator of Homer. Purists such as E.K. are likened to "a broode of Frogs [croaking] from a ditch, to haue the ceaselesse flowing riuer of our tongue turnde into their Frogpoole" (II, 305). And when Harvey, the Cambridge don, matches "the songes of Priapus" with "the rymes of Nashe," and comments upon the "ruffianisme" of the latter's "brothell Muse," he is gathering the choicest flowers of Eastcheap rhetoric: "Cannot an Italian ribald vomit out the infectious poyson of the world but an Inglishe horrel-lorrel must lick it vp for a restoratiue. . . ?" (II, 259, 261).

Harvey's less than informal denunciation is in turn explained by practical as well as patriotic concerns, for like most critics he holds that the best art comes from a marriage of genius and hard work. A dozen years earlier he had published several letters on reformed versifying that had recently passed between Spenser and himself. Spenser had concluded one epistle by modestly confessing that the "singular paines" of "Master *Holinshed* hath muche furthered and aduantaged" his nearly completed piece of quantitative verse, "a worke, beleeue me, of much labour . . ." (I, 100). When Harvey later insisted that no writer should "dreame of perfection that emproueth not the perfectest Art with most perfect industrie" (II, 237), he enforced his point with an ironic contrast between the "singular paines" always taken by careful, old-fashioned workmen like Spenser, and the modern methods of creatures like Nashe, "our new-new writers, the Loadstones of the Presse. . ." (II, 238). These modernists are "fine men" indeed, with "many sweete phrases" and a "dainty stile . . . far surpassing the stale vein of *Demosthenes* or *Tully*, . . . *Sidney* or *Spencer*." Conscientious artificers quickly perceive, however, that this "only new fashion of current Eloquence in Esse" is a product of the ass and the calf, ignorance and inexperience. With "the common sort of studentes, [it] may please a little, but profiteth nothing." In essence it is not eloquence but a verbal game, a test rather of agility than learning, a mere fencer's "snatch and away" (II, 237), or what that fop, Armado, calls "a quick venue of wit—snip, snap, quick and home" (V. i. 52–53). Next to such rhetorical glitter the Cambridge Humanist places the solid fruit of "pretious Trainement, . . . the foundation of all priuate and publike good."

> To excell, ther is no way but one: to marry studious Arte to diligent Exercise: but where they must be vnmarried, or diuorced, geue me rather Exercise without Arte then Arte without Exercise. Perfect vse worketh masteries, and disgraceth vnexperienced Arte. Examples are infinite, and dayly display themselues. A world without a Sunne; a Boddy without a Soule; Nature without Arte; Arte without Exercise—sory creatures. Singular practise the only singuler and admirable woorkeman of the world.
>
> (II, 236)

Whether praising Holinshed or damning Nashe, both critics suggest a world in which poems are "made" and plays "built" or "wrighted." Spenser, one of Elizabeth's most "inspired" poets, has obviously been "grinding things out." His friend, who cherishes poetry as much as any man, discusses the creative process with what may strike us as almost crude practicality. He argues informally, invoking everyday metaphors instead of abstract principles, and making small allowance for what we should term "sudden flashes of genius." Of course Nature (the created world, including men who would in turn create) requires Art (rules, precedent). The "quickest capacity . . . needeth Methode, as it were the bright Moone, to illuminate the darkesome night" (II, 236). But the theorist has no more patience with mere theory than with an irreverent originality. Genius—if that is what Harvey means by "quickest capacity"—must first humble itself before the Moon of Method, and then dutifully proceed to "Practise," the "bright Sun" and "only . . . admirable woorkeman." If Spenser's reference to helpful Holinshed reminds us of the greater uses the chronicler will soon serve, the progress of Harvey's poet from apprentice to journeyman to master craftsman tells us how Shakespeare's audience would have explained the differences between *1 Henry VI, Richard II,* and *1 Henry IV.* No man was too good to serve his craft. Daniel has his "mysterie," Surrey celebrates Wyatt's "hammers" and "stithe," and Jonson, probably the proudest poet of all, employs the same homely metaphors in honoring Shakespeare's "sweat."

> Yet must I not giue Nature all: Thy Art,
> My gentle *Shakespeare,* must enioy a part.
> For though the *Poets* matter, Nature be,
> His Art doth giue the fashion. And, that he,
> Who casts to write a liuing line, must sweat,
> (Such as thine are) and strike the second heat
> Vpon the *Muses* anuile: [79] turne the same,
> (And himselfe with it) that he thinkes to frame;
> Or for the lawrell, he may gaine a scorne
> For a good *Poet's* made, as well as borne.[80]

Lest we assume that Jonson is merely confusing his own painstaking manner with Shakespeare's, there is Sidney's similar gloss upon poetical genius. As Astrophel, Sidney has never drunk of Helicon, nor been a "Pickepurse of an others wit," nor understood that strange talk about the "Poets fury." [81] As an apologist for poetry, Sidney frequently refers to those first inspired makers who brightened an ignorant world with "highest knowledge" (I, 152), notes the versified oracles of Delphos and David's "diuine Poem," and concludes that careful artifice, combined with a wide-ranging imagination, must bespeak some poetical fury: "For that same exquisite obseruing of number and measure in words, and that high flying liberty of conceit proper to the Poet, did seeme to haue some dyuine force in it" (I, 154). But when the poet and apologist finally confronts the very bad state of poetical affairs surrounding him, when he admits that "the very true cause of our wanting estimation is want of desert" (I, 195), he insists that Parnassus shall never be taken by the merely furious. The proverb about the orator being made, and the poet born, is in one sense quite true. "Poesie must not be drawne by the eares; it must bee gently led, or rather it must lead." That is what the ancients meant when they spoke of it as "a diuine gift, and no humaine skill: sith all other knowledges lie ready for any that hath strength of witte: A Poet no industrie can make, if his owne *Genius* bee not carried

vnto it" (I, 195). Harvey's "pretious Trainement," in other words, is
an exercise that will profit only those with natural ability. But
after this necessary qualification—or is it simply an anticipation of
Harvey's "quickest capacity"?—Sidney counts upon genius no
more than Harvey. And like Jonson, he suggests that what is
actually born is not a poet, but a poetic potential, which will
never be realized without conscientious husbanding.

> Yet confesse I always that as the firtilest ground must bee
> manured, so must the highest flying wit haue a *Dedalus* to
> guide him. That *Dedalus* . . . hath three wings to beare it
> selfe vp into the ayre of due commendation: that is, Arte,
> Imitation, and Exercise. But these, neyther artificiall rules
> [i.e., rules of artifice] nor imitatiue patternes, we much
> cumber our selues withall. Exercise indeede wee doe, but
> that very forebackwardly: for where we should exercise to
> know, wee exercise as hauing knowne: and so is oure
> braine deliuered of much matter which neuer was begotten
> by knowledge. For, there being two principal parts, matter
> to be expressed by wordes and words to expresse the
> matter, in neyther wee vse Arte or Imitation rightly.
> (I, 195–196)

It was of course a similarly practical quest for "artificiall rules"
and the best "imitatiue patternes" that drove the position poets
toward their never realized Indies. As some of the poetry in the
Arcadia shows, Sidney thought quantitative versification a worthy
exercise. After all, "the greatest part of Poets have apparelled their
poeticall inuentions in that numbrous kinde of writing which is
called verse" (I, 159). Anticipating Daniel, however, Sidney refuses to mistake the clothes for the body. Verse is "but an ornament and no cause to Poetry," for many excellent poets have never
versified, and our age swarms with versifiers who do not perceive
that a lawyer dressed in armor is not a soldier. The "right describing note to know a Poet by," despite the fact that "the Senate
of Poets hath chosen verse as their fittest rayment," is the "fayning
[of] notable images of vertues, vices, or what els, with that delightfull teaching" (I, 160). One form or another is absolutely necessary, since poets never let their "words . . . chanceably fall from
the mouth," but which form depends solely upon the "dignitie of
the subiect."

It would be unfair to call those with narrower definitions of poetry "impractical." Indeed, our modern insistence that true verse always employ rhythm puts us closer to the position poets than the apologist, who champions all imaginative literature (including Xenophon's history and the Alexandrian prose romances) under the title of poetry. Nor were people like Watson impractical in their attempts to run upon borrowed feet. The exciting ferment so characteristic of the Renaissance was inspired by a willingness to attempt all things, to entertain multitudes. In that "sweete tyme" of "pleasant talke" fondly recollected by Ascham (I, 29), when he, Cheke, and Watson discussed the best methods of serving God, country, Cambridge, and art, conscientious men formulated and applied their theories of poetry according to the best available lights. If we weigh the evidence *they* possessed, their "prejudices" are as logical and their "errors" as intelligent as those that led one of our own century's greatest scholars into designating *Fulgens and Lucrece* a "Tragedy on Classical Model(?)." In 1903, when E. K. Chambers published his monumental two-volume study of *The Mediaeval Stage*, there was no reason to think that the two-page fragment of a "Play concerning Lucretia" was not severely moral, tragic, and classical.[82] Sixteen years later, when the complete text came to light, its authorship (Henry Medwall) and probable first performance (before the Spanish and Flemish ambassadors during the Christmas festivities of 1497) were established.[83] More important, we now possess a fifteenth-century anticipation of Greene's, Lyly's, and Shakespeare's romantic comedies, England's first—perhaps!—wholly secular play.

We shall assure the early Elizabethan critics a fair hearing only by suspending a knowledge of those consequences that they themselves partially shaped. Until we see all things within a historical present, knowing nothing of tomorrow and only as much about yesterday as they did, we shall hardly experience their enthusiasms and anxieties, and their apparently strange decisions will consequently continue to seem unintelligible, if not downright stupid. How easily looking backward becomes looking downward, with hasty, patronizing glances at experiments that bore no fruit and a careful study only of those that did. The danger of measuring the whole of one era solely in terms of those parts the next found to its liking has been well illustrated by Madeleine Doran. We have paid too much attention, for example, to the "school-driven logic and formalism" reflected in the sixteenth-century Italian formulations of Arsitotle's unities, sought too earnestly for indexes of a later and purer classical temperament, and not sufficiently heeded an obvious and "genuine enthusiasm . . . for the variety and multiplicity characteristic of the age they live in." [84] Led astray by a superior knowledge of their severely classical successors, we fail to note that the manner in which they defend and elaborate upon Aristotle's "single action" reveals an acceptance of much action, some even extraneous. "As with the history of science," Miss Doran wisely cautions, "where there is always a tendency to distort the state of things in a given period by singling out for emphasis those attitudes and ideas which were fruitful for later developments, so in the history of criticism we have tended to distort the position of the renaissance critics in relation to their own times by seeing them primarily as forerunners of the rigid doctrines of the neo-classical period." [85] Subtler distortions are found in modern displays of the fine and applied arts. One room of our museum houses "A Typical Augustan Drawing Room," and another, "Representative Edwardian Painters." For all its scholarly accuracy, the first is likely to give the impression that when Queen Anne ascended the throne, the typical eighteenth-century aristocrat promptly discarded his finest Carolean furnishings. This is a room that certainly should have been, but probably never was. The second is as truly unrepresentative, and in a more insidious way. The painters are all Edwardian, to be sure, but they stand less for their time as a whole than for one special group of that time, a school whose techniques most closely approximate those of contemporary art. And through this looking glass of Narcissus, we see most darkly indeed.

CRITICAL CURIOSITIES COMPREHENDED AND APPLIED

A detailed history of sixteenth-century English criticism is of course beyond our scope. But even as we have touched on a few places where theory seems most at odds with practice, let us hope that we have made some sense of the discrepancies without turning the critics into pedants or visionaries, or the artists into inspired disdainers of rules and precious "trainement." Despite great differences over means and sometimes even ends, we find no theorist so impractical nor any practitioner so impertinent as to attempt "the ayre of due commendation" wholly without Sidney's three-winged Daedalus. The most academic critics, like Harvey, "loue Method, but honour Practise" (II, 235); none suggests that rules are as important as exercise. And among the artists, who obviously had the critics' encouragement to experiment freely, we seldom find a work without at least several extant "imitatiue patterns," models that it tried to improve upon. Aside from the truly alehouse rhymers and itinerant playwrights, it is likely that each writer did his best to use art and imitation rightly.

The differences between good theory and better practice are most easily explained simply in terms of Sidney's warning about exercising "very forebackwardly." For Sidney, something in addition to genius must be put into practice; the most gifted athlete will not excel on the field without the finest coaching, physical conditioning, and equipment. We "exercise to know" by knowing what has already been done, and then seeing what we can do with it. Only after the best models have been thoroughly digested— "deuoure them whole, and make them wholly" yours (I, 202)— may we use art to hide art, pretending, for instance, that we know nothing of Helicon. "Forebackward" exercise, on the other hand, is writing too much without having read enough, proudly presuming that our grounds of endeavor are so naturally fertile that they will burgeon without being manured by the proper rules and examples. The argument is eminently practical, but the practitioners may well have differed as to how much reading was enough, which examples were really proper, or the extent to which precedent should obtain in attempting new literary kinds. Certainly in some cases what appeared to the critic as evidence of exercising forebackwardly was the result of an orthodox use of art and imitation. Twenty lines after noting how "oure braine [is] deliuered of much matter which neuer was begotten by knowledge," for instance, Sidney condemns Spenser for "framing . . . his stile to an old rustick language," despite the examples of Theocritus, Virgil, and Sannazaro; and ten lines after this, *Gorboduc* is complimented for its Senecan rhetoric and condemned for its failure to follow Aristotle's unities.

Like Nashe and Harvey on patriotism, Campion and Daniel on proportion, reformed and unreformed versifiers on artifice, or reformed and unreformed Christians on the value of poetry of any kind, the authors of *The Shepheardes Calender*, *Gorboduc*, and the *Apology* agree in principle and differ as to application. E.K. points out that the New Poet is new in his use of old words for rustic yet decorous effects, and relatively new in his carefully wrought structure, "well grounded, finely framed, and strongly trussed up together" (I, 128, 131). But his adoption of the lowly name, Colin, and the pastoral form, "so base for the matter and homely for the manner," shows him humbly "following the example of the best and most auncient Poetes. . . . So flew Theocritus. . . . So flew Virgile, as not yet well feeling his winges. So flew Mantuane, . . . Petrarque . . . Boccace . . . Marot, Sanazarus . . . whose foting this Author euery where followeth." [86] A spokesman for Sackville and Norton could have pointed to Grafton's *Chronicle* (1556), *The Mirror for Magistrates* (1559), and Heywood's early translations of Seneca (1559, 1560, 1561), and might well have asked Sidney whether these were not enough for one work to exercise with. In giving "trainement" their blessing, in other words, the critics had made room for new combinations of old forms, and the mixtures sometimes displeased them: Colin's use of Chaucer's diction for rustic pastoral; King Gorboduc's subjects speaking Senecan, but appearing at many times in many places, as characters in English chronicles and plays had so often been prone to do.

In adapting the best to their own designs, writers naturally took greater and greater liberties with the "law of writ." Few "poems unlimited," however, seem to have been written in ignorance, neglect, or scorn of Daedalus; like the critical treatises, most make it clear that the third wing of the creative process comes last but takes us highest. The poets thus indicate that poetry is in the making, while the critics openly insist that this is equally true of criticism. When we weigh the respective merits of theory and practice, of course, the practitioners have one great advantage, that of sheer numbers. The era overflows with literary deeds, and most of us have been guided only to the best, which have in turn been guided by their authors' own acute critical forethoughts. Even after several months of careful study, we have tasted only the finest vintage. Two weeks with the Elizabethan critics, on the other hand, gives us time for all the embarrassing dregs. This does not mean that the best theorist is as good as the best performer, but that the silliest criticism has many literary counterparts, and that when we measure only the most successful practices against *all* the theories, our judgment is bound to be distorted.

Like Shakespeare's most trivial sources, Elizabeth's silliest critics can be put to profitable use. If we cheat the theorists by not taking careful notice of their forgotten prejudices and least practical instructions, we end up cheating the artists, for we are in no position to appreciate how many wrong things they rejected in working their way toward what we may hastily assume to have been inevitable. Nor dare we even assume that the artists immediately saw contemporary instructions as impractical, wrong, or misguided. Practice outstripped theory not because writers decided the time had come to drive out bad hypotheses with good facts, but because patient workmen started with what seemed to them perfectly respectable theories, indeed the very best available, and in the course of their trials hammered out happier ways. What we are inclined to see as a rejection of the wrong was probably for them a replacement of the good by the better. And when that "sun of practice" outshines even the brightest "moons of method," when we get something much finer than what we should have expected, we have an eloquent argument for the Elizabethan literary achievement. That argument, however, is only as eloquent as it is solid. We must first be quite sure about what we really should have expected, carefully reconstructing all those options open to the writer, both the methods and models the critics advanced and, most important, any "reasons" they may suggest for their selections. Against this usually explicit testimony we must next place all evidence indicating the options elected by the writer as implicitly recorded in his work. Only then will our conjectures as to which "reasons" were actually new, and why they replaced the old, be imaginative and not merely fanciful.

We must not of course pretend that those considerations will ever carry us farther than the realm of responsible inference. The first half of this chapter, for example, has merely worked toward a full gloss of its first epigraph. How were the kinds of tragic "scene individable, or poem unlimited" represented to Shakespeare? Which theories supported the notion that Seneca "cannot be too heavy"? What did "clyming to the height of *Seneca* his stile" and Aristotle's precepts mean to Sidney and his academic fellows? The options open to Shakespeare, as well as the critics' reasons for offering them, are usually demonstrable. With these critical backgrounds in mind, we may then reason the need for *Hamlet*'s different unities and un-Senecan aspects, confident that the right questions should center in such Shakespearean replacements, and assured that our speculations will be well founded. Just as we used these considerations to infer that Shakespeare found Seneca too light for his Prince and just heavy enough for his players, so we could have measured comic theory against *The Comedy of Errors*, Shakespeare's closest

imitation of Plautus. Even in this early play we should have discovered plenty of evidence that the English playwright found his
Roman predecessor much too light. And already there are signs that
he also thought the critics' instructions too heavy: their insistence,
for instance, upon stock characters, everyday "realistic" situations,
"deedes, and language, such as men doe vse"; their assumption
that "laughter hath onely a scornful tickling"; their concern that
comedy act as a social corrective and deal only with "the common
behauiours" of "the meaner sort of men," not the lofty doings of
dukes.[87]

The second half of this chapter has also worked toward a gloss
of its epigraph, and along similar lines of critical testimonial. But
this epigraph is itself merely another piece of criticism, not a
portion of practice in which theory is simultaneously entertained
and transmuted. "Here are the playwright's options," announces
Polonius, within a play that has already demonstrated a mastery of
those his creator has elected. "Either send me the poet's options as
you see them," Spenser begs Harvey, "or else follow those devised
by Drant, enlarged by Sidney, and augmented by myself. Your
quantities are perplexing, and how shall we escape overthrowing
one another, and eventually being overthrown by the rest, if we
cannot even agree over the rules for a system as relatively closed
as classical versification? And now that I have finished my
Epithalamion Thamesis, Dreames, and *Dying Pellicane* [none of
which has survived, at least under these titles], let me get back to
work on my *Faerie Queene*." We know very little about what
Spenser had planned for his great poem when he wrote in April,
1580.[88] And no amount of critical glossing can fully explain why,
six months earlier, he had found himself "of late, more in loue wyth
my Englishe Versifying than with Ryming" (I, 89). We do know
that he must have regained his former love fairly soon, for the first
half of *The Faerie Queene* (1590) and at least two of his nine
Complaints (1591) were written or revised in the 1580's. And
because of that renewed love, the second half of this chapter has
nothing as grand as *Hamlet* to work toward. Probably it would not
have had anyway. But even a tale of what never quite came to pass
can be revealing. Why critical mountains trembled only to engender, at best, Campion's mice, is obvious. The position poets are
themselves practical enough to list—and sometimes enthusiastic
enough to revel in—the difficulties they face. And their excitement
over the skillfully manufactured, which led them to underestimate

those difficulties, was shared by their "less artificial" opponents. Their concerns are also as patriotic. Let our English tongue be the first to restore Greece and Rome! Their story is simply another celebration of Daedalus, and leads to the same moral: With *which* methods and materials do we exercise, and *how far* shall wondrous precedent obtain?

It is a curious tale, but not told by idiots nor signifying nothing. It is rich with reasons why Spenser, at twenty-eight, could have seen in true versifying a new and better way. Only one year before, he had cast his lot with rhyme of almost every variety. *The Shepheardes Calender* (1579) works with ballads and roundelays, sestinas and quatrains, regular and irregular accentual verse. But the New Poet's fledgling exercise is carefully qualified by E.K. Having noted Spenser's "finely framed" or organized "knitting of sentences," he feels it necessary to "scorne and spue out the rakehellye route of our ragged rymers (for so themselues vse to hunt the letter) which without learning boste, without iudgement iangle, without reason rage and fome, as if some instinct of Poeticall spirite had newly rauished them aboue the meanenesse of commen capacitie" (I, 130–131). Aside from telling us that all *bad* poetry is the spontaneous overflow of powerful feelings, E.K. is in effect asking two questions. First, what good has come of alliteration, that horrid hunting of the letter? Great good, we should answer, beginning with Caedmon and *Beowulf*, *The Seafarer* and *The Wanderer*, and adorning even Chaucer's time: *Sir Gawain and the Green Knight* and *The Pearl*, among others. Along with our Anglo-Saxon examples, however, we must remember Puttenham's description of Chaucer and Gower as poets of "the first age" (II, 62), and against those fine examples of the northern alliterative revival we must place Webbe's humble wish that the works of Gower "were all whole and perfect among vs" (I, 241).

The critics, in short, are both proud of and argue by appealing to a precedent they know only in very small part. Even Puttenham, probably the most broad-minded Elizabethan, will not tolerate the artifice of a heavily alliterative verse. Aside from "writing of rymes and registring of lyes," the medieval clergy "had leasure . . . to deuise many other knackes . . . whereof one was to make euery word of a verse to begin with the same letter" (II, 15). Although in his own time, for example, the poem by "*Hugobald* the Monke" was "thought no small peece of cunning, . . . in truth it were but a phantasticall deuise, and to no purpose at all more then to make

them [that is, words] harmonicall to the rude eares of those barbarous ages" (II, 15–16). Astrophel scorns sonnets with "rymes,
running in ratling rowes," [89] and Sidney notes that this cursed
"coursing of a Letter" reveals the poet's determination "to followe
the method of a Dictionary" (I, 202). Catching himself referring
to Spenser's "long, large, lauish, Luxurious, Laxatiue Letters,"
Harvey asks, "now, a Gods name, when did I euer in my life hunt
the Letter before?" (I, 93). All the time, "good *Gilgilis Hobberdehoy*," replied Nashe, "and abusing the Queenes English without
pittie or mercie." [90] The context of Campion's remark about "that
absurd following of the letter amongst our English so much of late
affected, but now hist out of Paules Churchyard" (II, 330), indicates that he speaks of verse, not *Euphues*'s prose. Only one
English critic, Gascoigne, will allow alliteration, and then but
sparingly: Look that you do not "hunte a letter to death." [91] With
monkish Hugobald rather than the *Pearl* Poet for evidence, it was
proper to assume that letter-hunting had never attracted a "right
artificial maker." This assumption about the past was substantiated,
moreover, by the present practices of witless fellows. Finally, there
was the judgment of Chaucer himself (actually his Parson):

> But trusteth wel, I am a Southren man,
> I kan nat geeste 'rum, ram, ruf,' by lettre.[92]

Gascoigne, another southern man, begins his *Instruction* by insisting that a good poem must be "grounde . . . upon some fine
inuention," for "it is not inough to roll in pleasant woordes, nor
yet to thunder in *Rym, Ram, Ruff* by letter (quoth my master
Chaucer)" (I, 47). Of all the "Elizabethans," only that most
northern King of Scots tells us that "the maist pairt of your lyne
sall rynne vpon a letter," at least "sa far as may be, quhatsumeuer
kynde" of verse one attempts (I, 218).

E.K.'s second implicit question—How much bad has come of
rhyming itself?—was of course frequently asked by the position
poets. In the early 1580's even Sidney, the rhymer, can find but few
accomplishments to support his defense of "euer-praise-worthy
Poesie," or to illustrate that "our tongue is most fit to honor" it
(I, 205); with little practice to aid brave theories, he must be
content to destroy poetry's detractors ("the blames laid against it
are either false or feeble") and to draw necessary distinctions ("the
cause why it is not esteemed in Englande is the fault of Poet-apes,

not Poets"). Sidney's *Anthology of English Literature: 700–1580* begins with nondramatic poetry: (1) Chaucer, who has "great wants," yet saw clearly for his "mistie time"; (2) *The Mirror for Magistrates*, "meetely furnished of beautiful parts"; (3) Surrey's *Lyrics*, "tasting of a noble birth, and worthy of a noble minde"; (4) *The Shepheardes Calender*, with much real poetry spoiled by a rustic style. "Besides these, doe I not remember to haue seene but fewe (to speake boldely) printed, that haue poeticall sinnewes in them" (I, 196). Then comes English drama: (1) *Gorboduc;* (2) "Al the rest," too inane to merit more than a footnote.

Nor does Sidney's *Anthology* become much larger when we put all the Queen's critics together. There are now five pre-Tudor poets: (1) John Hardying, whose *Metrical Chronicle* was first published in 1543 by Richard Grafton, along with his own continuation.[93] He is mentioned only four times by two writers: Puttenham calls him "a Poet Epick or Historicall" who "handled himselfe well according to the time and maner of his subiect" (II, 64); and Meres, in one of his few apparently original moments, notes "his maner of old harsh riming" (II, 314). (2) *"Pierce Ploughman,"* Webbe's "harshe and obscure, but . . . very pithy wryter" (I, 242), who is joined by Meres to Lodge and Hall as "best for Satyre" (II, 320). With more sophistication, Puttenham refers to "that nameles, who wrote the *Satyre* called Piers Plowman," but then proceeds to congratulate this "malcontent" for prophesying the fall of the Roman clergy (II, 62, 65). Most interesting is the fact that in these three critics' six notices of William Langland (?), not one mentions his alliteration. We should expect Puttenham to have placed hunting the letter next to Piers's "loose meetre, and . . . termes hard and obscure." Webbe, on the other hand, sees only what he wants to see. Because Piers avoided "the curiosity of Ryme," he wrote in classical quantities.

More frequently mentioned are (3) Lydgate and (4) Gower (each ten times by five critics) and of course (5) Chaucer, who is alluded to by fourteen critics on thirty-two occasions. Like Hardyng and Piers, however, they usually receive at best patronizing compliments: Despite being culturally disadvantaged, these men did fairly well. Against Petrarch and Tasso, the patriotic Nashe would "oppose *Chaucer, Lidgate, Gower*, with such like, that liued vnder the tirranie of ignorance" (I, 318). And even when praise is not faint, it is largely uncritical, often approaching the impreciseness of Webbe's notice of Spenser's "excellent skyll and

skylfull excellency." There is first Lydgate, Chaucer's "worthy
scholler" (I, 127), with a verse of "good proportion" and a style
"meetely currant," at least "as the time affoorded," but too "oc-
cupyed in supersticious and odde matters then was requesite in so
good a wytte" (I, 241–242). Puttenham attacks Lydgate on two
other grounds. Although his verse is good, he was "a translatour
onely, and no deuiser of that which he wrate" (II, 64). When
Puttenham takes a later look at that good verse, however, he finds
ill-proportioned caesuras. That very necessary pause in a longer
line's rhythmical flow is used "either very seldome, or not at all, or
else very licentiously" (II, 79). But Lydgate enjoys good company.
Chaucer's caesuras are equally careless, and his *Troilus and Criseyde*, like *The Falls of Princes*, was merely "translated, not deuised" (II, 69). Gower fares no better. Webbe simply notes that he
probably deserved Chaucer's admiration (I, 241), and Puttenham, in
one of Elizabethan criticism's rare moments of preciseness, condemns all of Gower save his morality. His poetry "was homely
and without good measure, his wordes strained much deale out of
the French writers, his ryme wrested, and in his inuentions small
subtillitie: the applications of his moralities are the best in him, and
yet those many times very grossely bestowed" (II, 64).

Chaucer is of course ranked first, but first "in a barbarous age,"
when "riming writers . . . were graue morall men but very homely
Poets" (II, 86). Despite the frequency with which this god of
English poets is alluded to, on the basis of what is actually said
about his work one would hardly suppose him the most often
imitated native model of the sixteenth century. His most loyal sons
call him "father," "master," "the Loadestarre of our Language," the
chief architect in making English "a Treasure-house of Science"
(I, 47, 50, 127, 152). Among poetry's most famous "speaking
picture[s]," Sidney celebrates "the *Terentian Gnato* and our
Chaucers Pandar so exprest that we nowe vse their names to signifie
their trades" (I, 166). In warning potential patrons that "it is not
your lay Chronigraphers, that write of nothing but of Mayors and
Sheriefs, and the deare yeere, and the great Frost, that can endowe
your names with neuer dated glory," Nashe points out that "not so
much but *Chaucers* host, *Baly* in Southwarke, & his wife of Bath,
. . . shalbe talkt of whilst the Bath is vsde, or there be euer a bad
house in Southwark." [94]

For the most part, however, Chaucer's praise is qualified by
three complaints or anxieties. The first is that he is sometimes

wholly lacking in originality. This charge need not be taken too seriously, for only Puttenham, who begins carping at mere translators in his treatise's opening paragraph (II, 3) and is vehemently refuted by Harington (cf. II, 196–197, 218–219), seems concerned that "many of his bookes be but bare translations out of the Latin & French" (II, 64). Chaucer's delightful pretense of historical objectivity and literal accuracy—"For as myn auctour seyde, so sey I" [85] —was probably taken by Ascham with equal seriousness, but like Harington, he does not think of translation and creativity as mutually exclusive. Chaucer and other more recent writers went "as farre to their great praise as the copie they followed could cary them" (I, 30). For Ascham, Chaucer's mistake was in not being directed by the best examples, and therefore versifying as a "Gothian." The critics' second concern is related to Nashe's notice of Bath's famous Wife and Southwark's bad houses. Lodge insists that "Chaucer in pleasant vein can rebuke sin vncontrold; and, though he be lauish in the letter, his sence is serious" (I, 69). Webbe sees him as a "bolde spyrit," taxing the time's enormities "eyther in playne words, or els in some prety and pleasant couert" (I, 241). With similar uneasiness, Harington explains away Ariosto's ribaldry by invoking "our *Chawcer,* who both in words & sence incurreth far more the reprehension of flat scurrilitie, as I could recite many places, not onely in his millers tale, but in the good wife of Bathes tale, & many more, in which onely the decorum he keepes is that that excuseth it and maketh it more tolerable" (II, 215). In an age when moral instruction was at least as necessary as delight, the wisest strategy was to point out the propriety with which the poet matched indecent words with indecent characters.

But Chaucer's chief failing is his want of artifice. Sidney grants him "poeticall sinnewes," given his "mistie time," yet both rhymers and antirhymers condemn his proportions. Among the latter, we find Ascham's advice to imitate Chaucer's virtues and scorn his vices, a distinction that those who "neuer went farder than the schole of *Petrarke* . . . abroad, or els of *Chaucer* at home" are unable to grasp, and who will, therefore, "wander blindlie still" in their "foule wrong way" (I, 31, 33). Perhaps the same concern underlies Webbe's cryptic comment about Chaucer as "yet not altogether so poeticall" as his pastoral predecessors (I, 263). Aware of the changing nature of pronunciation and syntax, both camps try to appreciate a style that now seems "blunte and course to many fine English eares" (I, 241; II, 150). With sprightly inconsistency, Nashe first appeals to and then challenges Chaucer's precedent in order to attack Harvey's quantities and diction. To prove that *"our english tongue is nothing too good,* but too bad *to imitate the Greeke and Latine,"* Nashe asks whether Chaucer and Spenser, England's Homer and Virgil, "were farre ouerseene that they wrote not all their Poems in Hexamiter verses also" (II, 240). But just in case Master Hobberdehoy should use the same authority to excuse his own rhetorical rags, Nashe confides that had Chaucer "liu'd to this age, I am verily perswaded hee would haue discarded the tone halfe of the harsher sort" of his words (II, 242).

Finally, at least two of the rhymers themselves slight some of Chaucer's rhyming. Among his many recommended rhyme schemes, Gascoigne almost forgets to include "a notable kinde of ryme, called ryding rime," the couplets "suche as our Mayster and Father *Chaucer* vsed in his Canterburie tales, and in diuers other delectable and light enterprises"; they serve "most aptly to wryte a merie tale," just as "Rythme royall is fittest for a graue discourse" (I, 56). Puttenham also finds Chaucer's rhyme royal or "meetre Heroicall," at least in the *Troilus,* "very graue and stately" (II, 64). This "chiefe of our ancient proportions," however, argues very little facility in its maker, for the "staffe" or stanza (*ababbcc*) is concluded with a couplet "concording with none other verse that went before, and maketh but a loose rime" (II, 68, 93). The scheme or "band" lacks "cunning," in other words; the conclusion hath been but pasted on. Puttenham entertains *The Canterbury Tales* with similarly mixed feelings. They are all, so Puttenham supposes, of Chaucer's "owne inuention," and therefore show "more the naturall of his pleasant wit" than his "bare translation" of *Troilus;* here too we find "similitudes, comparisons, and all other descriptions . . . as can not be amended" (II, 64). Unfortunately, many of the *Tales'* verses "be but riding ryme," and although these well become "the matter of that pleasaunt pilgrimage," the scheme lacks the "wide distance" that satisfies the learned ear (II, 64, 89, 91). It delights "the rude and popular" sensibility, passing "so speedily away and so often return[ing] agayne, as their tunes are neuer lost" (II, 89, 91). It is, in short, the meanest kind of harmony; it simply jogs along. When Puttenham adds to this Chaucer's use of "such vnshapely wordes as would allow no conuenient *Cesure,"* his habit of simply allowing "rymes [to] runne out at length . . . till they came to the end," he is reminded of that modern maker of "ryme dogrell," who must "be tyed to no rules at all, but range as he list, [and] may easily vtter what he will" (II, 79).

When we realize that poetical valor was proved upon such fields of choicest artifice, and when we find even the rhymers so apologetic about native barbarousness, E.K.'s embarrassment over old ways and Spenser's excitement over the new come as no surprise. An examination of Webbe's, Puttenham's, Carew's, and Meres's lengthy roll calls of more recent makings (I, 242–247; II, 62–66, 293–294, 314–324) reveals an awareness that most are mediocre; the relatively few that are lifted above anonymity and given hearty plaudits are usually seen as attempts to rise to sundry ancients' high styles and matters. Literature, criticism, and language itself are in the making, and when one must decide between Homer and Chaucer, or which of Virgil and which of Surrey, the learned must at least hesitate. What do all your Gascoignes, Goldings, and Wyatts amount to alongside eloquent Demosthenes or Theocritus, Tully or Horace? Acknowledging that despite his title he has discoursed as much about the classics as the works of his own countrymen, Webbe trusts that "the courteous Readers wyll pardon me, considering that poetry is not of that grounde and antiquity in our English tongue, but that speaking thereof only as it is English would seeme like vnto the drawing of ones pycture without a heade" (I, 247). Only a hack was free to range where he listed and utter what he would. A poet of any pretensions voluntarily circumscribed his area of exercise with art and imitation; he would go forward, in other words, only by looking backward.

In walking backward, men are of course often prone to stumble. First, having decided that the past holds the keys to the future, they may assume that they know that past almost perfectly. To the extent that their discoveries of medieval rudeness are based on faulty records, the critics can be excused. They seem to know nothing of the *Pearl* Poet or the Wakefield Master, any one of whose works is as good as anything produced in England between 1500 and 1590. To the extent that charges of barbarism stem from different standards of artifice or from Protestant antipathies toward a ribald, rhyming, ignorant Catholic clergy, however, the critics cannot be defended, merely understood. Men of every age tend to test past art against standards as irrelevant as contemporary taste or political and religious rightmindedness. Secondly, upon that imperfect knowledge they may hastily reason that what has not already been done well holds no promise. What would Puttenham have said about lowly riding rhyme as handled by those exquisitely artificial makers of the Restoration and eighteenth century, or even about Marlowe's *Hero and Leander*, which appeared a few years after his condemnations? Since Chaucer could not convert him from his belief in "wide distances," perhaps he would have stood upon his concords, and begged Pope to quit wasting time and compose *canzoni*. Thirdly, whether looking upon the past or present, and regardless of their time, men usually see what they are predisposed to see. Despite Ariosto's *Orlando Furioso*, for instance, Harvey betrays the same antimedieval, antiromantic prejudices as his enemy, Nashe, when he returns to Spenser an early portion of the "Eluish Queene" with the following caution: "But I wil not stand greatly with you in your owne matters. If so be the Faerye Queene be fairer in your eie than the Nine Muses, and Hobgoblin runne away with the Garland from Apollo, . . . fare you well, till God or some good Aungell putte you in a better minde" (I, 115–116).

Another example is noted by Smith. The critics do not seem to realize that "in their efforts to be rid of the jingle of English metres they were working for the recognition of blank verse, and were in reality justifying it on the side of theory" (I, xlix). Like many theories and models, blank verse seems to have been an Italian import. In 1534 the Fourth Book of Virgil's *Aeneid* was translated into *versi sciolti* (literally, verses free, loose, or unconstrained; that is, by rhyme). Twenty years later, William Owen published another version of the same book, only this time "translated into English, and drawn into a straunge metre, by Henry late Earl of Surrey."[96] Evincing the same enthusiasm for classical versifying that led him to celebrate Langland's quantities, in 1586 Webbe looks upon this first instance of blank verse and honors Surrey for giving England her first epic hexameters, even though "without regard of true quantity of sillables" (I, 283). But what should we have called it, or compared it to? If this shows what Smith terms a "stumbling Webbe" (I, xlix), then we must allow for a stumbling Ascham, since this far greater scholar also reads into the absence of rhyme an attempt at "perfite and trew versifying," and proceeds to demonstrate how poorly it scans (I, 32–33).

Dare we place Webbe and Ascham in an ivory tower because they lacked Owen's critical nonchalance and wished to see into which tradition Surrey's "straunge metre" could best be fitted? Even as late as 1586, Webbe also had good reasons to observe that

the most popular rhyme was the "fourteener," that dreary couplet of seven iambs marching across each line, and to admit that
"our aunciente Chroniclers and reporters of our Countrey affayres"
were the best things England had to rival the "Heroycall workes"
of Homer and Virgil (I, 255, 269). Not until 1590 did Spenser give
him a better example of "that princelie part of Poetrie, wherein
are displaied the noble actes and valiant exploits of puissaunt
Captaines." The next year, Wilmot gave him a play newly cast
into blank verse, and Webbe appreciated such "commendable
pains" (I, 412). If he had ignored Kyd's equally commendable
pains in 1586, it was because he wished to discuss literature, not
plays, and we have already seen how many popular playwrights
shared this ivory tower.

If Webbe stumbles at all, it is when he concludes one paragraph by noting that "all our famous wryters . . . haue wonne
eternall prayse" with rhymed, accented syllables, and begins the
next with the wish that the "very commendable . . . were by men
of learning and ability bettered" (I, 266–267). Here he ignores not
what he has no reason to know, but a past that clearly registered
the most dismal exercises. By 1594 it was clear to another new poet,
George Chapman, that

> sweet poesie
> Will not be clad in her supremacie
> With those straunge garments (Romes Hexameters)
> As she is English: but in right prefers
> Our natiue robes, put on with skilfull hands
> (English heroics) to those antick garlands.[97]

Although eight years later Campion would still insist that people
like Chapman lacked both fortitude and fine ears, the tide had
already begun to turn. Exercise had proved some art irrelevant,
some imitation impossible. What had started as a movement to exploit Rome for England's glory came to be seen as a plot to uphold
Rome at England's cost. And one is struck by the honesty of those
who tried to remain loyal to both. For Ascham, in 1570, there is
little hope for the hexameter, but a patriotic optimism for the iambic (I, 30). Although Gascoigne (1575) recommends rhyme, the
whole poem must be grounded "upon some fine inuention" or good
idea, and "do you alwayes hold your first determined Inuention,
and do rather searche the bottome of your braynes for apte wordes
than chaunge good reason for rumbling rime" (I, 47, 52). The

letters exchanged by Harvey and Spenser in 1579 and 1580 reveal
a Cambridge don weaning a young poet *from* pedantry *to* practicality. Spenser, to be sure, claims that had he followed Harvey's
counsel, he would "long since" have preferred versifying to rhyming (I, 89), but the versifying taking place at Leicester House
raises a rebuttal from Trinity Hall.

Spenser writes of Sidney, Dyer, and Archdeacon Drant, those
brave Areopagites who have "drawen mee to their faction." Part of
their program Harvey must have admired: "a generall surceasing
and silence of balde Rymers." But "their whole Senate" has also
"prescribed certaine Lawes and rules of Quantities of English
sillables for English Verse," and it is upon those laws that Spenser
challenges Harvey's own quantities (I, 89–90). Harvey has—God
save the mark!—dared "once or twice [to] make a breache in Maister DRANTS Rules." Within a fortnight Cambridge replies. First,
Spenser's own verses, which he had enclosed, are good, but far from
perfect. Perhaps, Harvey queries, the errors "may rather proceede
of his Master M. DRANTES Rule than of himselfe"? (I, 96). Secondly, Harvey's own alleged violations: "I knowe not what
breache" I have made "in your gorbellyed [corpulent] Maisters
Rules: which Rules go for good, I perceiue, and keepe a Rule,
where there be no better in presence. My selfe neither sawe them,
nor heard of them before . . ." (I, 97). Despite his friend's quan-
dary, Spenser's answer does not include Drant's gospel. In the
course of his rather indirect and apologetic remarks, however,
enough is said to confirm Harvey's suspicions that the "gorbellyed"
Archdeacon's school is versifying by position. You have often
said, Spenser begins, that the hexameter is "neither so harde, nor
so harshe, that it will easily and fairely yeelde it selfe to oure
Moother tongue" (I, 98). The only major difficulty lies in accent,
"whyche sometime gapeth . . . ilfauouredly, comming shorte of
that it should, and sometime exceeding the measure of the Number,
as in Carpenter the middle sillable, being vsed shorte in speache,
when it shall be read long in Verse, seemeth like a lame Gosling
that draweth one legge after hir." The solution is suggested by
precedent. "For why, a Gods name, may not we, *as else the
Greekes*, haue the kingdome of oure owne Language, and measure
our Accentes by the sounde, reseruing the Quantitie to the Verse?"
(I, 99. Italics added.)

In effect Spenser reasons that to write artificially, one must assign to each syllable an artificial value: "Rough words must be sub-

dued with Vse." As the exercises of Webbe and Campion later proved, Spenser was quite correct; one must eventually fall back upon position. But as Daniel's treatise makes clear, Harvey was also correct. There are limits to artifice, and what exceeds those limits will never take permanent hold. In 1593, he will speak of how little "Dranting of Verses, and Euphuing of sentences, did edifie" (II, 272). But to Spenser, in 1580, he can only elaborate upon what Gascoigne has said five years earlier: "And in your verses remember to place euery worde in his natural *Emphasis* or sound, that is to say, . . . as it is commonly pronounced or vsed" (I, 49). Both Spenser and his friend are attempting something more artificial than Gascoigne's rhyming poetry, yet Harvey predicts that there will be no "more regular and iustifiable direction, eyther for the assured and infallible Certaintie of our English Artificiall Prosodye particularly, or generally to bring our Language into Arte and to frame a Grammer or Rhetorike thereof, than first of all vniuersally to agree vpon ONE AND THE SAME ORTOGRAPHIE, in all pointes conformable and proportionate to our COMMON NATURAL PROSODYE." [98] Harvey would still "gladly be acquainted with M. DRANTS Prosodye"; he would not yet "dare geue . . . Preceptes, nor set downe any CERTAINE GERNERAL ARTE" (I, 102–103). Only about one specific matter is he confident. "By the faith I beare to the Muses, you shal neuer haue my subscription or consent (though you should charge me wyth the authoritie of fiue hundreth Maister DRANTS) to make your *Carpēnter*, our *Carpēnter*, an inche longer or bigger than God and his English people haue made him (I, 117). It is not, Harvey concludes, "either Position, or Dipthong, or Diastole [lengthening], or anye like Grammer Schoole Deuise that doeth or can indeede either make long or short," but only the "Maiestie of our speach: which I accounte the only infallible and soueraigne Rule of all Rules" (I, 119, 121).

For many "Dranters," Harvey's rhetorical question—"Is there no other Pollicie to pull downe Ryming and set vppe Versifying but you must needes correcte *Magnificat* . . . ?" (I, 117)—remained open and worthy of serious discussion. Only sufficient exercise would prove the best really best, or *Magnificat* "uncorrectable," and some workmen were unreasonably patient. Stanyhurst (1582), for instance, will not "attribute greater prerogatiue too thee Latin tongue than reason wyl affurd, and lesse libertye too oure language than nature may permit" (I, 142). Englishmen should no more "cramp" their mouths with Latin rules than the Romans did

"fetter theyre speeche . . . wyth thee chaynes of thee Greeke preceptes." Some of Harvey's examples of English words "straying
from thee Latin preceptes" are then cited (I, 143). Despite his concern that "nothing may bee doone or spoaken agaynst nature," and
his desire not to be "stieflie tyed too thee ordinaunces of thee Latins" (I, 141, 144), however, the very length of Stanyhurst's explanation of his prosody makes it clear that he will not consistently
honor "nature" or "ordinaunces." "Leaves," for example, is long
when pronounced as a monosyllable, short when divided into two
syllables. And although we are reminded that the ear, not
orthography, "must decyde thee quantitye as neere as is possible,"
immediately before this we are told that "*passage* is short, but yf
you make yt long, *passadge* with D would bee written" (I, 145–
146). Webbe (1586) is at least less devious, first openly championing position and then allowing for orthographical manipulations—
sometimes the spellings of syllables "must needes be a little
wrested" (I, 282)—to achieve the position desired. Although he
treats of much larger problems, Sidney (c. 1583) finds time to
observe that English may better accommodate ancient versification
than any other modern tongue. Italian overflows with vowels;
German, with consonants; French and Spanish have no words with
antepenultimate accents (an*ti*cipate, *gar*dener), "and, therefore,
very gracelesly may they vse *Dactiles*" (I, 205). Sidney's anxiety
about graceful, normally accented dactyls indicates that either his
loyalty to Drant's rules was weaker than Spenser's letters suggest,
or that between 1580 and 1583 he had come to agree with Harvey.

By 1589, the same year that Raleigh brought Spenser and the
first three books of *The Faerie Queene* back from Ireland, two
critics discuss quantitative versifying as an exercise no longer
intellectually respectable. Nashe laments the fact that "epitaphers
and position Poets haue wee more than a good many, that swarme
like Crowes to a dead carcas, but flie, like Swallows in the Winter,
from any continuate subiect of witte," and parodies the "hexameter furie" that "infired" Master Stanyhurst:

> Then did he make heauens vault to rebounde,
>   with rounce robble hobble
> Of ruffe raffe roaring, with thwick thwack
>   thurlery bouncing.
>
>   (I, 315–316)

Such "Thrasonical huffe snuffe" really argues no greater artifice than that of the alehouse rhymers, whom Nashe next attacks. Two years later Nashe employs the same principle of guilt by association, linking the euphuists who sail with "their fraught of spangled feathers, golden Peebles, Straw, Reedes, Bulrushes" to their artificial cousins, "so hardly bested for loading that they are faine to retaile the cinders of *Troy*" (II, 226). Finally, two years before Chapman renounces Rome's "straunge garments," Nashe begs all "HEATHENISTS and Pagan Hexamiters" to "come thy waies down from thy *Doctourship*, & learne thy Primer of Poetry ouer againe" (II, 239). Gabriell Howliglasse, that proud father of the English hexameter, should realize that in "this Clyme of ours" his child "cannot thriue. . . . Our speech is too craggy for him to set his plough in; hee goes twitching and hopping . . . vp the hill in one Syllable, and downe the dale in another, retaining no part of that stately smooth gate which he vaunts himselfe with amongst the Greeks and Latins," as Nashe's own "Hexamiter interrogatory very abruptlie" proves:

> *But ah!* / *what* newes do / *you* heare of / *that good* /
>   *G*abriel / *huffe snuffe,* /
> *Knowne* to the / *world* for a / *foole, and* / *clapt*
>   in the / *Fleete* for a / *Rimer?*
> (II, 240–241. Scansion added.)

But we must not read into Nashe's twitching celebration of Harvey's art more than a disdain for *bad* artifice, *irrelevant* methods, and *foolish* imitations. To Harvey's charge that his rhetoric smacks of clownish Tarleton, queasy Greene, and stale *Euphues*, Nashe retorts, "Wherein I haue borrowed from *Greene* or *Tarlton*, *that I should thanke them for all I haue?* Is my stile like *Greenes*, or my ieasts like *Tarltons?* Do I talke of any counterfeit birds, or hearbs, or stones, or rake vp any new-found poetry from vnder the wals of *Troy?*" (II, 243). And though "*Euphues* I readd when I was a little ape in Cambridge, . . . to imitate it I abhorre, otherwise than it imitates *Plutarch*, *Ouid*, and the choisest Latine Authors." Neither Nashe nor Harvey claims originality; neither attacks the other for what we should call plagiarism. To vilify one's enemy, one pointed to the bad uses he made of bad models, and the uselessness of his exercise.

Puttenham's more courteous condemnation of English quantities proceeds upon the same premises. Since he would examine *The Arte of English Poesie*, and since "Poesie is a skill to speake

& write harmonically" (II, 67), Puttenham must show every possible harmony or proportion the poet may use: (1) staff or stanza, a set number of lines repeated throughout; (2) measure or meter, a set number and pattern of feet (for the ancients) or syllables (for the moderns) repeated throughout; (3) concord, symphony or rhyme, a kind of music that the modern maker may offer in place of that "delicate running" of classical feet (II, 81); (4) situation, the "placing of euery verse in a staffe or ditty by such reasonable distaunces as may best serue the eare for delight" (II, 88); this proportion yields two harmonies, of course, for both the "tune" of the last syllable(s) in each line, and the lengths of the lines themselves, may be variously patterned; (5) figure, the only proportion premising a reader rather than a listener, since our meters are "by good symmetrie reduced into certaine Geometricall figures" or shapes. The seventy-five pages Puttenham devotes to these proportions and the great care with which he unmasks a faulty caesura, diagrams the seven possible rhyme schemes to be gained from a seven-line stanza, and illustrates figures like "The Taper reuersed" or "The Lozange rabbated" clearly reveal a mind transported by artifice. His concluding chapters on quantitative versifying, however, are offered "for the information of our yong makers, and pleasure of all others who be delighted in noueltie, and to th'intent we may not seeme by ignorance or ouersight to omit any point of subtillitie, materiall or necesarie to our vulgar arte" (II, 117). And so he proceeds—dutifully, impatiently, halfheartedly. We are frequently reminded that our ears must not be too dainty (II, 117, 122, 124, 125, etc.), asked whether "it be somewhat too late to admit a new inuention of feete and times that our forefathers neuer vsed" (II, 124), always invited to consider the possibilities of position, but finally told that "the pleasant melody of our English meeter" will be much better served by accent and rhyme than those "mincing measures, which an idle inuentive head could easily deuise" (II, 134).

Whether silently dismissed by Spenser, reduced to Trojan cinders by Nashe, or killed with kindness by Puttenham, "true" versifying had been conscientiously weighed before it was found wanting. Like every other literary theory of the sixteenth century, it was tried by a jury of craftsmen, and according to those laws of Daedalus that every court upheld. Seen in terms of our time, it presents a story without a conclusion and a striking example of theory jarring against practice. Viewed in terms of its own time, however, it becomes an important chapter of a far larger tale, into whose conclusion *Hamlet*, as well as the hexameter, may easily be fitted. Only as working hypotheses and potentially adaptable models do we gather and then select the best "artificiall rules" and "imitatiue patterns." Next we experiment, giving our laws of writ the liberty of exercise.[99] With so many methods and models to adopt, adapt, and fuse, new shapes and kinds are inevitable. As the ranks of experimenters grow, deeds outstrip designs and specific theories seem more and more paltry or irrelevant. But these facts only confirm what the theorists themselves insist is the rule of all rules: "Perfect vse worketh masteries." The cornerstone of theory, in other words, allows for continual discrepancies between what we might expect and what we actually get. At the close of Elizabeth's reign the theorists' grand imperative is illustrated positively by a tragedy that not only partly rejects, but sometimes re-enforces, replaces, or improves upon tragic rules and patterns. At the very opening of James's reign, the same imperative is given a negative twist when Daniel charges us no longer to practice with what practice has already shown to be impracticable. "Trainement" is no more "pretious" in revealing how to travel than in registering closed avenues.

The emphasis of this chapter has also been primarily negative. Perhaps that emphasis is unavoidable, since we found it necessary to confront several relevant but essentially negative impressions: Theory does *not* apparently tally with practice; critics of the drama do *not* appear excited about the right things; so much theorizing about past and present poetry seems *neither* founded upon fact, *nor* developed within a sensible perspective, *nor* concluded with practical instructions. If a reconstruction of the critics' own backgrounds has helped us see their judgments as sometimes "wrong," sometimes "right," but almost invariably reasonable and proper, we have at least partially bridged the gap between literary ideas and deeds. Not only was the critics' general charge to exercise by imitating always honored, but the good reasons supporting their more specific recommendations, advice that may today seem misguided, usually commanded the artists' respect. As Spenser's defection from the Dranters makes clear, however, to bridge the gap between ideas and deeds completely we must not merely demonstrate that the practitioner respected the theorist's recommendations. We must also show where that respect motivated successful endeavors, instances of exercise finding the theoretically good actually helpful and proving it valid. So far we have seen little evidence of this happy concord. In the case of the English hexameter, where no permanent facts ever materialized, our critical backgrounds provide excellent glosses upon what is in and of itself rather insignificant. In the case of *Hamlet*, where respectable theories are more often transmuted than followed, the literature is rich and the gloss not very helpful, rarely leading us to perceptions we should not have inferred from the play itself. Fortunately, our choice is not always restricted to the insignificant or irrelevant. There are moments when a great writer appears to have had one eye upon a specific critical observation, and we have good reason to wonder whether he would have proceeded exactly as he did without it. There are other pieces of criticism that may not have directly influenced the writer but certainly represent concerns he shared, and therefore clarify the nature of his attempts. As examples of good practice honoring sound theory, however obliquely, both provide critical backgrounds of great literary relevance, sometimes confirming our impressions of the writer's goals, sometimes underlining an aspect of the work we might otherwise have missed. To some of these more helpful critical observations we shall now turn.

Notes to Chapter III

1. George Clarke Sellery, *The Renaissance: Its Nature and Origins* (Madison, Wis., 1965), pp. 241 ff.
2. *Ibid.*, pp. 239–241.
3. G. Gregory Smith, *Elizabethan Critical Essays* (London, 1904), I, xi.
4. In Smith, I, 80. Unless otherwise noted, all citations from Elizabethan criticism are to Smith's two-volume anthology.
5. *The Poetical Works of Chaucer*, ed. F. N. Robinson (Cambridge, Mass., 1933), "The Prologue of the Monk's Tale," VII, 1973–1977. All citations from Chaucer are to this edition.
6. *The Falls of Princes*, Prologues to VI, 282–283, and to II, 45–46, as cited by Karl J. Holzknecht, *The Backgrounds of Shakespeare's Plays* (New York, 1950), p. 326.
7. "*William Baldwin* to the *Reader*," in *The Mirror for Magistrates*, ed. Lily B. Campbell (New York, 1960), pp. 68–71.
8. J. E. Spingarn, *A History of Literary Criticism in the Renaissance* (New York, 1963), p. 170.
9. See his closing chapter, "An Exhortation to Free Italy from the Barbarians."
10. In *Early English Classical Tragedies*, ed. John W. Cunliffe (Oxford, 1912), p. 4.
11. In *The Tudor Translations*, Second Series, XI, ed. Charles Whibley (London, 1927), I, 53, 93 ff.
12. *Ibid.*, I, 94.
13. Frederick S. Boas, *An Introduction to Tudor Drama* (Oxford, 1933), p. 35.
14. Charles T. Prouty, *George Gascoigne: Elizabethan Courtier, Soldier, and Poet* (New York, 1942), p. 145.
15. Cunliffe, p. 157.
16. For a brief discussion of the development of "the Three Unities," see Smith, I, 398, and Spingarn, pp. 61–63.
17. *A Midsummer Night's Dream*, V. i. 56–57, 209–211. All citations from Shakespeare are to *The Complete Works*, ed. Peter Alexander (London, 1951).
18. See E. K. Chambers, *The Elizabethan Stage* (Oxford, 1923), III, 512; IV, 227.
19. See Chambers's discussion, III, 395–396.
20. Smith, I, 412; cf. Chambers, III, 514.

21. Smith, II, 86. Puttenham later warns the courtier-poet not to use "these maner of long *polisillables*, . . . for they smatch more the schoole of common players than of any delicate Poet, *Lyricke* or *Elegiacke*" (II, 132).

22. See Smith, II, 424.

23. Ed. John S. Farmer (London, 1912), sig. B2ᵛ.

24. *Ibid.*, sigs. B2ᵛ, G2ᵛ.

25. *Ibid.*, sig. G3ᵛ.

26. "To . . . Henery Reynolds Esquire, of Poets and Poesie," ll. 187–194, in *The Works of Michael Drayton*, ed. J. William Hebel, III (Oxford, 1932), p. 231. In 1586, Webbe speaks of "our late famous English Poet who wrote the *Sheepheards Calender*," whoever he may be, and is certain that "if his other workes were common abroade, which are as I thinke in the close custodie of certaine his freends, we should haue of our owne [English] Poets whom wee might matche in all respects with the best" (I, 232). He also knows of other "verie daintie peeces of worke, among some of the finest Poets this day in London, who for the rarenesse of them keepe them priuelie to themselues and wil not let them come abroad" (I, 277).

27. Joseph Hall, *Virgidemiarum* (1597), Book I, Satire 3, ed. Thomas Warton (London, 1824), p. 12.

28. Chambers, III, 514.

29. Sonnet XLVIII, in *Samuel Daniel: Poems and A Defence of Ryme*, ed. Arthur Colby Sprague (Cambridge, Mass., 1930).

30. Chambers, III, 275.

31. *Ibid.*, III, 275–276.

32. Cited by Charles T. Prouty, introduction to facsimile edition of First Folio of *Shakespeares Comedies, Histories, & Tragedies* (New Haven, Conn., 1954), p. ix.

33. See Holzknecht, p. 344.

34. *Ibid.*, pp. 344, 346.

35. As trans. by G. B. Harrison in his edition of *Shakespeare: The Complete Works* (New York, 1952), p. 1546.

36. Cited by Prouty, *Shakespeares Comedies, Histories, & Tragedies*, p. ix.

37. *Sonnet LXXII.* What the poet brings forth could of course also be the sonnets themselves, the "verse so barren of new pride" noted in *LXXVI*. But cf. Holzknecht, p. 344, and *Sonnets CXI, CXII*.

38. III, 182.

39. *Wit's Recreations* (1640) and R.C.'s *Conceits, Clinches, Flashes and Whimsies* (1639), cited by Holzknecht, pp. 346–347.

40. *The Works of Thomas Nashe*, ed. Ronald B. McKerrow (London, 1904–1910), I, 212.

41. *Ibid.*

42. *Ibid.*, I, 213, 215.

43. *The Life and Complete Works in Prose and Verse of Robert Greene, M. A.*, ed. Alexander B. Grosart (London, 1881–1886), XII, 141.

44. *Ibid.*, XII, 144.

45. *Haue With You to Saffron-Walden* (1596), McKerrow, III, 132.

46. See Chambers, IV, 270.

47. See Alexander, p. 1268.

48. Marchette Chute, *Shakespeare of London* (New York, 1949), pp. 116–117.

49. Alexander, p. 1284.

50. Chute, p. 118.

51. *Ibid.*, p. 119.

52. Madeleine Doran, *Endeavors of Art: A Study of Form in Elizabethan Drama* (Madison, Wis., 1964), p. 147.

53. *De Tragoedia et Comoedia;* see Smith, I, 369, and Doran, pp. 106–109.

54. See Doran, pp. 382–384.

55. Harold Ogden White, *Plagiarism and Imitation During the English Renaissance* (New York, 1965), pp. 118–119, 202.

56. See Spingarn, p. 52, and Doran, p. 105.

57. See Spingarn, pp. 52–53.

58. *Ibid.*

59. Doran, p. 126.

60. Spingarn, p. 51.

61. Included in Leonard F. Dean, *A Casebook on Othello* (New York, 1961), p. 123.

62. See Doran, p. 117.

63. *Shakespearean Tragedy* (New York, 1958), p. 40. By Jacobean times, criticism appears to have partly acknowledged the practice that yielded plays like *Hamlet*. See L. G. Salingar, "Tourneur and the Tragedy of Revenge," *The Age of Shakespeare*, ed. Boris Ford (Baltimore, 1964), pp. 334–354. In Fulke Greville's *Life of Sidney* (c. 1610), Salingar notes (p. 334), "there is a striking comment on Renaissance tragedy. Ancient tragedy, according to Greville, had been ultimately rebellious; it had sought 'to exemplify the disastrous miseries of man's life, . . . and so out of that melancholic vision, stir horror, or murmur against Divine Providence'. Modern tragedy, on the contrary, was dominated by moral law; it sought 'to point out God's revenging aspect upon every particular sin, to the despair, or confusion of mortality'. . . . In emphasizing the moral consciousness of tragedy and the notion of rigorous divine punishment, Greville was completely in agreement with the majority of Elizabethan critics. . . . But Greville's statement also hints unconventionally at possible contradictions in interpreting the moral law. . . . And whichever

dramatists Greville may have had in mind, his reference to 'the despair, or confusion of mortality' might well be taken as the keynote of many of his contemporaries."

64. *The Spanish Tragedy,* III. ii. 1–5, 10–11, in *English Drama: 1580–1642,* ed. C. F. Tucker Brooke and Nathaniel Burton Paradise (Boston, 1933).

65. I.e., these men with literary aspirations scarcely have the knowledge to save their own necks. But in Nashe's time this was not a mere figure of speech. Medieval clergymen arraigned for a felony enjoyed the privilege of exemption from trial by a secular court. The ability to read, however, which was originally merely the accused's means of proving his "clergy" or clerical position, eventually became the ground instead of the test of this privilege. Hence, "benefit of clergy" in the sixteenth century often amounted to "benefit of scholarship," and every literate person could plead exemption from the sentence upon his first conviction of certain crimes. Women were excluded under James I, but the old law was not completely abolished until 1827. Neck-verse was a line of Latin verse, usually the beginning of Psalm LI, placed before the cleric or scholar who claimed the exemption. When Ben Jonson killed a fellow actor in a duel in 1598, he saved his neck in this way. See the *Oxford English Dictionary.*

66. See Smith, I, 424–426; and Chambers, III, 394–397; IV, 234.

67. See Ronald B. McKerrow, *An Introduction to Bibliography for Literary Students* (Oxford, 1928), pp. 246 ff.

68. Psalm 8: 3–6.

69. Ed. W. H. D. Rouse (London, 1956), pp. 8, 46.

70. See first epigraph to Chapter I.

71. Daniel's treatise (c. 1603) is dedicated "To All the Worthie Louers and Learned Professors of Ryme Within His Maiesties Dominions," II, 356.

72. See his sections on "The Puritan Attack" and "The Defence," I, xiv–xxxi.

73. *The Essays or Counsels, Civill and Morall* (1625), in *The Works of Francis Bacon,* ed. James Spedding (Boston, 1840), XII, 77.

74. V. iii. 465 ff., in *Ben Jonson,* ed. C. H. Herford and Percy Simpson, IV (Oxford, 1932).

75. *A Third Tribute to Wyatt,* in *The Poems . . . of Surrey,* ed. Frederick Morgan Padelford (Seattle, 1928), pp. 98–99.

76. *Englands Heroicall Epistles: Henry Howard, Earle of Surrey, to the Lady Geraldine,* ll. 11–14, 227–228, in *Works,* ed. Hebel, II (Oxford, 1932), pp. 277 ff.

77. *The Complaint of Rosamond,* l. 728; *Mvsophilvs,* ll. 953–956; in Sprague.

78. The first of many commendatory verses to *The Faerie Queene,* in

The Complete Poetical Works of Spenser, ed. R. E. Neil Dodge (Cambridge, Mass., 1936), p. 138.

79. Shakespeare uses the same image to underline the tragedy of Richard II's life. The man who would always rather speak than do, emote than analyze, who uses words to evade responsibilities, and who finally exchanges his crown for several choice lines at Flint Castle (III. iii. 176 ff.) is last seen at Pomfret Castle, determined to use words to get at realities, to "hammer . . . out" relationships (V. v. 5), to take his murderers with him and die royally.

80. "To the Memory of . . . Shakespeare," in Prouty, *Shakespeares Comedies, Histories, & Tragedies,* sig. A4ᵛ.

81. *Sonnet LXXIV,* in *The Complete Works of Sir Philip Sidney,* ed. Albert Feuillerat, II (Cambridge, 1922), p. 272.

82. See Chambers (London, 1903), II, 443, 458.

83. See Boas, pp. 3–5.

84. Doran, p. 265.

85. *Ibid.*

86. I, 131–132. *The Shepheardes Calender* itself honors the conventional concept of poetry as "inspired imitation." The "Argument" for "August," for example, tells us that the poem has been "made in imitation of that in Theocritus: whereto also Virgile fashioned his third and seventh Aeglogue." But "October" is prefaced by the observation that poetry is "no arte, but a divine gift and heavenly instinct, not to bee gotten by labour and learning, but adorned with both, and poured into the witte by a certain . . . celestiall inspiration." See Dodge, pp. 36, 44. Webbe (I, 232) similarly insists upon the poet's "celestiall instinction" and within a dozen lines praises Spenser for the way he "narrowly immitateth" his models.

87. See Whetstone, I, 59–60; Lodge, I, 80–82; Jonson, II, 389; Sidney, I, 199; Puttenham, II, 27 ff. In very different ways both *As You Like It* and Jonson's *Volpone* dishonor Sidney's dictum that "Comedy is an imitation of the common errors of our life, which he [the playwright] representeth in the most ridiculous and scornefull sort that may be; so as it is impossible that any beholder can be content to be such a one" (I, 176–177).

88. In "October," Piers urges Cuddie to sing of bloody Mars, jousts, knights, and "fayre Elisa."

89. *Sonnet XV,* in Feuillerat, II, 248.

90. *Strange Newes,* in McKerrow, I, 261, 299.

91. I, 52. From Gascoigne's *The Steel Glasse* and *The Mirror for Magistrates* through *The Faerie Queene* and the sonneteers of the 1590's, all poets use some alliteration. It is therefore likely that by "hunting" or "coursing" the letter, the critics usually mean *excessive* alliteration. If so, Gascoigne is not broader minded, merely

more explicit, and even he does not make clear how far the poet may go.

92. "The Parson's Prologue," in Robinson, X, 42–43.

93. H. S. Bennett, *English Books & Readers: 1475 to 1557* (Cambridge, 1969), p. 129.

94. *Pierce Penilesse His Supplication to the Diuell*, in McKerrow, I, 194.

95. *Troilus and Criseyde*, II, 18, in Robinson.

96. Cited by Tucker Brooke, "The Renaissance (1500–1660)," p. 344, in *A Literary History of England*, ed. Albert C. Baugh (New York, 1948).

97. "Hymnvs in Cynthiam," ll. 86–91, in *The Poems of George Chapman*, ed. Phyllis Brooks Bartlett (New York, 1941).

98. I, 102. By "COMMON NATURAL PROSODYE," Harvey of course means what we should call "received pronunciation." One extant copy of Gascoigne's treatise is filled with marginal comments in Harvey's hand. Over Gascoigne's *"Emphasis"* (see preceding quotation), Harvey wrote the word "Prosodie." See Smith, I, 359.

99. Every critic insists upon this. The proof of the pudding is always in the eating. When critics as unlike as Sidney, Webbe, Nashe, Harvey, and Puttenham speak about the priorities of art, imitation, and exercise, it is only their styles that distinguish them.

Suggestions for Further Reading

Although I have attempted to allow the Elizabethan critics to tell their own stories through frequent and direct citations, it has sometimes been necessary to paraphrase freely. Even more dangerous is the very organization of this chapter, which allows the critics to speak only to those points I consider most relevant to our understanding of what they and their fellow artists were seeking. This superimposition of order should not create the impression that they always spoke in concert, that they did not often ignore one another's views on some particular issues, or that in many cases their arguments do not go off on curious tangents. There is, in short, no substitute for the critics themselves, however tangled their presentations may be. The student should begin with Sidney's very lucid exposition, and then measure his interests against those underlying Puttenham's more specific observations. He will also find it helpful to watch how Nashe and Harvey attempt to destroy one another; whether their accusations are justified is not so important as that body of self-evident truth upon which both base their charges.

The best (and still easily accessible) collection of treatises is G. Gregory Smith's two-volume *Elizabethan Critical Essays* (Oxford, 1904). This may be supplemented with Roger Ascham's *English Works*, ed. William Aldis Wright (London, 1904), and *Wilson's Arte of Rhetorique, 1560*, ed. G. H. Mair (Oxford, 1909). The student especially interested in dramatic criticism should consult the "Documents of Criticism" and "Documents of Control" cited or summarized in E. K. Chambers's *The Elizabethan Stage* (Oxford, 1923), IV, 184–345. Healthy portions of criticism from Caxton through Milton, as well as a helpful introduction and general bibliography, are furnished in *English Literary Criticism: The Renaissance*, ed. O. B. Hardison, Jr. (New York, 1963).

Although not exclusively devoted to discussing critical contexts, C. S. Lewis is at his best in "New Learning and New Ignorance," the introductory chapter of his *English Literature in the Sixteenth Century* (Oxford, 1954). Madeleine Doran's *Endeavors of Art: A*

Study of Form in Elizabethan Drama (Madison, Wis., 1954) is one of the most exciting critical studies ever written. Also valuable are:

Atkins, J. W. H. *English Literary Criticism: The Renascence.* London, 1951.

Baldwin, Charles Sears. *Renaissance Literary Theory and Practice.* New York, 1939.

Baldwin, T. W. *William Shakspere's Five-Act Structure.* Urbana, Ill., 1947.

Farnham, Willard. *The Medieval Heritage of Elizabethan Tragedy.* Berkeley, Calif., 1936.

Hathaway, Baxter. *Marvels and Commonplaces: Renaissance Literary Criticism.* New York, 1968.

Herrick, Marvin T. *The Fusion of Horatian and Aristotelian Literary Criticism, 1531–1555.* Urbana, Ill., 1946.

Holzknecht, Karl J. *The Backgrounds of Shakespeare's Plays.* New York, 1950.

Spingarn, J. E. *A History of Literary Criticism in the Renaissance.* New York, 1899.

Whitaker, Virgil K. *The Mirror up to Nature.* San Marino, Calif., 1965.

Wimsatt, William K., Jr. and Cleanth Brooks. *Literary Criticism: A Short History.* London, 1957.

IV

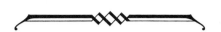

WADING FARTHER

More Relevant Critical Backgrounds

And whereas . . . the unnoble . . . have a want of provocation and of feare of slaunder, . . . they reckon not them selves bound to wade any further than their ancestors did before them. . . .

Therefore will I have our Courtier . . . set all his delight and diligence to wade in everie thing a little farther than other men, so that he may be knowne among all men for one that is excellent. . . .

And even as the Bee in greene medowes fleeth alwaies about the grasse, choosing out flowers: So shall our Courtier steale his grace from them that to his seeming have it, and from eche one, that parcell that shall be most worthie prayse. . . .

Sometime I would have him take certaine wordes in an other signification than that is proper to them, and wrasting them to his purpose (as it were) graffe them like a graffe of a tree in a more luckie stocke, to make them more sightly and faire. . . .

Neither would I have him to sticke to forge new also [refrain from inventing new words as well], and with new figures of speach, deriving them featly from the Latins, as the Latins in old time derived from the Grecians. . . .

I know not then how it will stand well, in steade of enriching this tongue, . . . to seeke to shut it up into so narrow a roome, that everye man should bee compelled to follow onely Petrarca and Boccaccio. . . .

And truely it should bee a great miserie to stop without wading any further than almost the first that ever wrote: and to dispaire, that so many and so noble wits shall never finde

out any moe than one good manner of speach in the tongue
that unto them is proper and naturall.

> —CASTIGLIONE's *Book of the Courtier* (1528),
> translated by HOBY (1561)

Now in his parts, kindes, or *Species* (as you list to terme
them), it is to be noted that some Poesies haue coupled together two or three kindes, as Tragicall and Comicall, wher-
vpon is risen the Tragicomicall. Some in the like manner haue
mingled Prose and Verse, as *Sanazzar* and *Boetius*. Some haue
mingled matters Heroicall and Pastorall. But that commeth
all to one in this question, for, if seuered they be good, the
coniunction cannot be hurtfull.

> —SIR PHILIP SIDNEY, *An Apologie for Poetrie*
> (c. 1583)

INCIDENTAL CRITICAL RELEVANCIES: THE CASE AGAINST HOLOFERNES

We have already noticed that one of *Hamlet*'s most helpful glosses
comes from a very unlikely source, Thomas Nashe's preface to
Greene's *Menaphon* (1589). Nashe should be praising Greene; instead, within several pages he is attacking Kyd, who reads "English
Seneca . . . by candle light" to gain "whole *Hamlets*, I should say
handfulls of tragical speaches." [1] Nashe should be commending a
pastoral romance, but less than halfway through his opening paragraph he is already snarling at "the seruile imitation of vain-glori-
ous tragoedians" and those "idiote art-masters" who "repose eternitie in the mouth of a player" (I, 308). At least a decade before
the *Hamlet* we know was written, and probably a few years before
Nashe had even heard of Shakespeare, criticism pleads for an
eloquence truer than "the swelling bumbast of a bragging blanke
verse" and an imitation more creative than "*Seneca* let bloud line
by line and page by page." Practice had to discover the wisdom of
such criticism on its own: *Titus Andronicus* (c. 1594) is gorier than
the goriest scenes of Seneca or Kyd. And although Shakespeare's
"indeuors of Art" eventually hit upon a tragedy Nashe could have
admired, they neither abandoned Seneca altogether, as the critic
seems to have hoped, nor worked with him in a way the critic
had anticipated. The relationship between gloss and artifact is
therefore in one sense quite tenuous. We use Nashe's remarks as

a commentary upon a play and playwright he was not speaking about, the artistic strategies of a maker who appeared later and then either refused to follow or was ignorant of his critical counsel. What justifies our making this critic serve a use he never intended is that experience must have soon led Shakespeare to ask the same question Kyd's example had already raised for Nashe: Since handfuls of Hamlets have bled Seneca dry, would it not be wise to avoid this tired stuff? Nashe's gloomy forecast of 1589, in short, does not tell us what is happening in *Hamlet*, but it does increase the likelihood that Shakespeare asked the above question, and thus indirectly prepares us for new uses of old Hamlets and a refurbished Seneca.

A great many helpful critical comments at first seem equally "happenstance," thrown off at odd moments in casual asides, and certainly not directed toward the work we are attempting to gloss. In making such random notes and queries relevant almost in spite of themselves, however, we are simply building upon several assumptions: (1) Critical commentary is a generally accurate index of received opinion concerning matters of art and knowledge; (2) the artist, whether or not he shares these views, is prone to exploit them; (3) the value of incidental critical remarks is established when they bring us closer to the meaning a specific literary event or character had for its original audience. To illustrate the usefulness of this procedure, let us measure the apparently formidable learning of Holofernes, the opinionated schoolmaster of *Love's Labor's Lost*, against what the theorists reflect as received opinion.

Our first witness knows nothing of Holofernes; he rather deals with the invincible ignorance of enemies all too real. In the third of *Foure Letters and certaine Sonnets: Especially touching Robert Greene, and other parties, by him abused* (1592), Gabriel Harvey interrupts his invective against Greene to rail upon that "mad hooreson," his "sworne brother," Master Nashe. "The summe of summes" concerning Pierce Penilesse, Harvey concludes, is that "he tost his imagination a thousand waies, and, I beleeue, searched euery corner of his Grammer-schoole witte (for his margine is as deepelie learned as *Fauste precor gelida*) to see if he could finde anie meanes to relieue his estate; but all his thoughtes and marginal notes consorted to his conclusion that the worlde was vncharitable, and he ordained to be miserable" (II, 233). To complement abject poverty with abject ignorance, the Cambridge don provides a sure instance of his upstart enemy's shallow knowledge. Pierce's "mar-

gine" (the "marginal notes" to Nashe's *Pierce Penilesse his Sup-*
plication to the Diuell [1592] [2]) reveals a mind that has mastered
mere grammar-school materials like *Fauste, precor gelida,* the
opening words of the first of Mantuan's Latin *Eclogues,* a prescribed text for contemporary schoolboys. Perhaps Harvey is even
implying that some of *Pierce's* marginalia were taken from
volumes as commonplace and elementary as Mantuan's, for early
editions of the *Eclogues* are heavily annotated.[3] In any case, since
Harvey wished to be understood as well as witty, we may assume
that had a literate Elizabethan wished to exemplify his scholarship, he would have offered something far more "deepelie learned"
than this Latin tag. And it is precisely this tag that Holofernes
offers.[4]

Now we need no critics come from their graves to tell us that
Holofernes is an intellectual fop. The play itself, from the schoolmaster's first sweet utterances, makes this abundantly clear: "The
deer was, as you know, sanguis, in blood; ripe as the pomewater
[large apple], who now hangeth like a jewel in the ear of caelo, the
sky, the welkin, the heaven; and anon falleth like a crab on the
face of terra, the soil, the land, the earth" (IV. ii. 3 ff.) And when
his cultured confederate, Sir Nathaniel, the parish curate, replies,
"Truly, Master Holofernes, the epithets are sweetly varied, like a
scholar at the least," we wonder whether the souls of Navarre's
citizens are not in as perilous a state as their minds. Berowne later
takes comfort in the fact that the Show of the Nine Worthies will be
played by "the pedant, the braggart, the hedge-priest, the fool,
and the boy" (V. ii. 538–539); such stock fools guarantee a spectacle even more absurd than that which the King and his court
have unintentionally presented throughout the play. "Though my
mocks come home by me," resolves Dumain, "I will now be merry,"
and he promptly turns to rallying Hector, alias Armado (V. ii.
626 ff.). In defense of Nathaniel, we should at least note his concern
over how Holofernes will "find men worthy enough to present"
the Worthies, and that although he is "soon dash'd" in playing
Alexander the Great, he remains "a marvellous good neighbour,
faith, and a very good bowler; but for Alisander—alas! you see
how 'tis—a little o'erparted" (V. i. 109; V. ii. 575 ff.). For Holofernes, on the other hand, we need only realize that the ridiculous
pageant is entirely his idea, that he sees in it an opportunity to
represent three of the Worthies himself, and that as Judas Mac-

cabaeus, he plays into the hands of his audience by refusing to be outfaced.

To appreciate some of the less obvious though equally amusing heights of Holofernes's affectations, however, we must alternate between his comments and those of the critics, for in his initial, rather brief appearance he misrepresents or misapplies their learning at least a half dozen times. There is first his opening celebration of the deer just slain by the Princess, lines that Nathaniel finds full of "epithets . . . sweetly varied" and scholarly displayed. Strictly speaking, the speech contains no epithets, no adjective or adjectival phrase expressing some quality or attribute considered characteristic of a person or thing (for instance, "*summer-ripened* apple," not "apple which has been ripened under a summer sun," and certainly not "a deer ripe as an apple," in which the deer's maturity is described with a simile, a directly expressed comparison, and a silly one at that). But both Renaissance and modern usages allow a looser sense of "epithet." It can mean "any significant appellation." We speak of Ivan the Terrible, and in 1579 Harvey spoke against christening things "by names and epithites nothing agreable or appliante to the thinges themselves." [5] Finally, as misused by moderns, an epithet can be "any apt term, phrase or expression," a sense that Shakespeare sometimes honors. Iago alludes to Othello's bombastic phrases, "Horribly stuff'd with epithets of war" (I. i. 14), and when Beatrice asks her reluctant suitor "for which of my good parts did you first suffer love for me?," Benedick replies, "Suffer love—a good epithet! I do suffer love indeed, for I love thee against my will" (*Much Ado about Nothing*, V. ii. 56 ff.). But if these examples show that Nathaniel has good reason to call Holofernes's comparisons and synonyms "epithets," they also indicate that he has no reason at all to think them sweetly and scholarly varied. Whether adjective, noun phrase, title, or merely a striking expression, the epithet must be, as Harvey says, "agreable or appliante." There is nothing especially apt about designating the sky as caelo, welkin, or heaven, however impressively varied the terms may be, and we must sacrifice sense as well as significance to give that sky an ear in order to hang upon it a jewel, relate the welkin's red earring to a large apple dangling from a tree, and compare that fruit to the bloody deer for their common redness, ripeness, juiciness, and fatal fall upon "terra, the soil, the land, the earth."

Since *Love's Labor's Lost* seems to have been performed before a select courtly audience about 1593, let us also set Holofernes's speech against several warnings given a few years before to the same kind of audience by George Puttenham: (1) Avoid the speech of "Vniuersities where Schollers vse much peeuish affectation of words out of the primatiue languages" (II, 150); (2) The "high stile is disgraced and made foolish and ridiculous by all wordes affected, counterfait, and puffed vp, as it were a windball, carrying more countenance then matter" (II, 159); (3) "Figuratiue speech is a noueltie of language euidently (and yet not absurdly) estranged from the ordinarie habite and manner of our dayly talke and writing, and figure it selfe is a certaine liuely or good grace set vpon wordes, speaches, and sentences to some purpose"; although "our figures be but transgressions of our dayly speech, yet if they fall out decently to the good liking of the mynde or eare and to the bewtifying of the matter or language, all is well; if indecently, and to the eares and myndes misliking (be the figure of it selfe neuer so commendable), all is amisse" (II, 165, 174–175); (4) "Some of our vulgar writers take pleasure in giuing Epithets, and do it almost to euery word which may receiue them, and should not be so, yea though they were neuer so propre and apt, for sometimes wordes suffered to go single do giue greater sence and grace than words quallified by attributions do" (II, 169).

It is equally unlikely that Puttenham or the courtiers he addressed would have preferred Holofernes's "Dictynna" to Nathaniel's "Phoebe, . . . Luna" or Dull's "moon." Like "haud credo," Dictynna is one of those "many straunge and vnaccustomed wordes" (II, 151) that the pedant uses to lord it over Navarre's humbler subjects. They guarantee Dull's "barbarous intimation," an "insinuation, as it were, in via, in way, of explication; facere, as it were, replication, or rather, ostentare, to show, as it were, his inclination, after his undressed, unpolished, uneducated, unpruned, untrained, or rather unlettered, or ratherest unconfirmed fashion" (IV. ii. 13 ff.). Having drawn heavily upon those "inkhorne termes so ill affected brought in by men of learning as preachers and schoolemasters" (II, 151), Holofernes next undertakes an "extemporal epitaph on the death of the deer." Unlike "epithet," "epitaph" appears to have had only one meaning. Puttenham defines it as "the report of the dead persons estate and degree, or of his other good or bad partes, to his commendation or reproch, . . . an inscription such as a man may commodiously write or engraue

vpon a tombe in few verses, pithie, quicke, and sententious, for the
passer-by to peruse and iudge vpon without any long tariaunce"
(II, 58). Under the first Tudor, merry John Skelton had written a
eulogy for a sparrow named Philip. In a more sentimental era,
Coleridge, with terrible seriousness, could call a young ass "Poor
little Foal of an oppressèd race!" and hail it *"Brother*—spite of the
fool's scorn!"⁶ But in an age of Gascoigne's *Noble Arte of
Venerie or Hunting* (1575) and Turberville's *Booke of Faulconrie
or Hauking* (1575), when a most merciful Sovereign shot with a
crossbow at enclosed deer while the royal musicians played,⁷ it is
doubtful that any animal was thought human enough to be honored
with an epitaph. Holofernes, to be sure, does not attempt to
humanize the spectacle in the vein of Duke Senior and the
melancholy Jaques (*As You Like It,* II. i), but his use of "epitaph"
must have seemed comically incongruous to men like Puttenham,
for whom the word suggested "large tables [tablets] . . . hanged vp
in Churches and chauncells ouer the tombes of great men" (II, 59).

The epitaph itself is a precious piece of artifice. "I will something affect the letter," notes the Schoolmaster, "for it argues
facility."

> The preyful Princess pierc'd and prick'd a pretty pleasing
>   pricket [young buck].
> Some say a sore [older buck]; but not a sore till now made
>   sore with shooting.
>
> (IV. ii. 52 ff.)

As we have observed in reference to E.K.'s "rakehellye route of
our ragged rymers" (I, 131), such stuff argued no facility whatsoever; even Gascoigne, the only Englishman who allows that alliteration, "(beyng modestly vsed) lendeth good grace to a verse,"
cautions not to "hunte a letter to death" (I, 52). To judge from
critical complaints, nothing could be farther from the truth than
Nathaniel's claim that this kind of verse exhibits "a rare talent!"
Long before he argues with Nashe, in fact, Harvey thinks it epitomizes all those "meere fooleryes, vices taken vpp for virtues,
apish deuices, friuolous boyishe grammer schole trickes" (I, 126).
And against the critics' repeated advice to write and act in a
natural, easy manner, we should place Holofernes's immediate response, a rather ungraceful attempt at *sprezzatura:* "This is a gift
that I have, simple, simple; a foolish extravagant spirit, full of forms,

figures, shapes, objects, ideas, apprehensions, motions, revolutions. These are begot in the ventricle of memory, nourish'd in the womb of pia mater, and delivered upon the mellowing of occasion. But the gift is good in those in whom it is acute, and I am thankful for it" (IV. ii. 63 ff.). Then Nathaniel touches upon another common critical concern. Under Holofernes, his parishioners' sons "are well tutor'd . . . and their daughters profit very greatly. . . . You are a good member of the commonwealth." And again we note a discrepancy. "If their daughters be capable," comes the bawdy reply, "I will put it to them" (IV. ii. 71 ff.)

Jaquenetta then enters, greeting Parson Nathaniel as "Master Person" or "pers-one." Holofernes instantly rejects what is to him a mispronunciation, just as he will later criticize Armado's strange accents. "I abhor . . . such rackers of orthography, as to speak 'dout' . . . when he should say 'doubt'; 'det' when he should pronounce 'debt'—d, e, b, t, not d, e, t. He clepeth [calls] a calf 'cauf', half 'hauf'; neighbour vocatur [is called] 'nebour'; 'neigh' abbreviated 'ne'. This is abhominable—which he would call 'abbominable' " (V. i. 17 ff.). Armado's fault, in other words, is in following received sixteenth-century pronunciation, and the manner in which Holofernes grimaced his way through a precisely orthographical pronunciation of "neighbor" must have been entertaining. There can be no doubt as to whose side the critics would have chosen. Campion warns that "because our English Orthography (as the French) differs from our common pronunciation, we must esteeme our sillables as we speake, not as we write" (II, 352). Harvey urges us "to agree vpon ONE AND THE SAME ORTOGRAPHIE, in all pointes conformable" to received pronunciation (I, 102). One of Harvey's examples is especially interesting. We use the sound, "*ayer*, bothe *pro aere* [Latin, "for air, atmosphere"] and *pro haerede* ["for heir"], for we say not *Heire* but plaine *Aire* for him to[o]" (I, 120). Harvey is mainly interested in justifying the slight differences in the spellings (and, presumably, the pronunciations) of *aire* and *ayer* or *aier*, but he is also careful to reject a sounded *h* simply because *heir* comes from the Latin *haeres* or *heres*. Because of his willingness to "be epitaphed, The Inuentour of the English Hexameter" (II, 230), a role Nashe never let the world forget, Harvey's name suggests to us the depths of Elizabethan pedantry. The real pedants were the men he opposed, creatures like Holofernes, who, to the later dismay of George Bernard Shaw, managed to get many English words to follow the spellings of their Latin originals, and then tried, with less success, to have our pronunciations reflect those spellings. From the thirteenth through the sixteenth centuries, *heir* is usually spelled *eir, eyr, ayr,* or *aire.* The fourteenth provides the first instances of these forms prefaced by a dimly relevant Latin *h.*[8] Chaucer's scribes cannot make up their minds: *ayr, eyr,* and *heir* alternate. Like *heir, debt* and *doubt* come from the Old French (*det* or *dette,* and *dute, dote,* or *doute*). In Chaucer, we find *dette* and *doute.* The *h*'s which Holofernes insists we honor, are there only because learned clerks decided these words should reflect their indirect Latin origins: *debere,* to owe; *dubitare,* to waver in opinion. Sometimes these clerks overreached themselves. From the fourteenth through the sixteenth centuries *abominable* is regularly spelled *abhominable* and explained as *ab homine,* "away from man," inhuman, or beastly; the word actually comes from *abominari,* to deprecate as an ill omen. Shakespeare may have been no more aware of such faulty etymologizing than he was of the fact that Chaucer introduced his parson as "This Persoun." Like the critics, however, he prefers racking orthography to racking the pronunciation he knows, regardless of how it had come to him.

After championing a pronunciation neither etymologically correct nor physiologically possible, Holofernes displays "his Grammer-schoole witte" with a line from Mantuan. Professor Craig notes the possibility of an additional blunder. Both the quarto (1598) and folio (1623) texts have the pedant say "Facile," not "Fauste."[9] Was the error Holofernes's or the printers'? If the former, how would Shakespeare's knowledgeable audience have reacted to a schoolmaster who misquotes even schoolboy stuff and then complacently observes, "Old Mantuan, old Mantuan! Who understandeth thee not, loves thee not"? Or who next peruses Berowne's competent sonnet and, despite his own verses upon the "pretty pleasing pricket," finds it lacking in "the elegancy, facility, and golden cadence of poesy" (IV. ii. 115–116)? In Holofernes's and Costard's wordplay with "Person," "pers-one," and "pierc'd" (pronounced *pursd,* as in Nashe's penniless "purse"), Craig also sees possible verbal echoes of Nashe and Harvey. "Piercing a hogshead!," for example, may come from Harvey's *Pierce's Supererogation* (1593), in which Nashe is referred to as "the hogges-head of witt."[10] The play certainly abounds with inexplicable topical allusions. If Shakespeare went so far for the entertainment of his courtly audience as to shape his dialogue in accordance with recent backchat, it is possible that Holofernes's *"Fauste, precor gelida"* was inserted *because* Harvey had used it to pierce Nashe.

But we need not prove direct borrowings in order to argue the relevance of critical backgrounds. Whether or not Shakespeare knew how Harvey had used Mantuan, he could count upon his audience to know what Harvey had assumed in his. We in turn know that he could, because Harvey tells us as much. Our enjoyment of Holofernes and his academic folly would not be materially enriched by an exact knowledge of which phrases came from which sources. Critical glosses are more helpful in a less direct way. They tell us what Shakespeare's audience considered elegant and trite, new- and old-fashioned, and what really argued facility, and thereby provide one aspect of that social context against which any comic playwright measures the virtues and vanities of man, the social animal. As Sir John Harington realized, social proprieties change more rapidly than human values. "Ouid gaue precepts of making loue, and one was that one should spill wine on the boord & write his mistresse name therewith. This was a quaynt cast in that age; but he that should make loue so now, his loue would mocke him for his labour, and count him but a slouenly sutor" (II, 215). Men of every age love and laugh, but they express their love in different ways and laugh at different things. New mannerisms pursue new manners, always affording high comedy new instances of "what fools these mortals be!" Backgrounds give us the correct perspective to distinguish between sentiment and sentimentality, actions and posturings. They usually make clear which things each era's social animals are likely to affect, which things their contemporaries would have considered self-evidently absurd, and which customs are "more honour'd in the breach than the observance." In Holofernes's case, they tell us that he is too obvious a fool to pose a threat to society.[11]

THE DOCTRINE OF CREATIVE IMITATION

The usefulness of critical backgrounds is best illustrated when we confront the Schoolmaster's final blunder. For the "golden cadence of poesy," which Berowne's sonnet lacks, Holofernes holds up Ovid as "the man," that Ovidius Naso (cf. Latin *nasus*, nose) so adept at "smelling out the odoriferous flowers of fancy, the jerks of invention. Imitari [to imitate] is nothing: so doth the hound his master, the ape his keeper, the tired horse his rider" (IV. ii. 115 ff.). The modern reader may find in this praise of "invention" or originality and dispraise of imitation Holofernes's most sensible utterance, whereas Shakespeare intends it as evidence of his greatest folly. The man who cultivates his conversation with Latin scraps and forces English words into Latin forms completely misunderstands the Latin theories of art, imitation, and exercise, not to mention his own era's views, which were based upon them. As Harold Ogden White's study of *Plagiarism and Imitation During the English Renaissance* [12] clearly demonstrates, "Imitari" was far from "nothing" to the Romans and their sixteenth-century admirers; properly understood, it was almost everything. A summary of White's conclusions will explain why Berowne can plead,

> Small have continual plodders ever won,
> Save base authority from others' books,

and then pen a sonnet no more "original" than a dozen other English imitations of Petrarch (I. i. 86–87; IV. ii. 100 ff.); why Nashe can attack the "seruile imitation" of some writers, claim that "the vaine which I haue . . . is of my owne begetting, and cals no man father in England but my selfe," and then grant that he may have imitated *Euphues* insofar as it imitates "the choisest Latine Authors" (I, 308; II, 243); or why Sidney can insist that "the highest flying wit" must be borne up by imitation and, seven pages later, ask the "diligent imitators" of Cicero and Demosthenes to throw away their "*Nizolian* Paper-bookes [thesauruses] of their [model authors'] figures and phrases" (I, 195, 202). However frequently the literary theorist and practitioner seem to be operating upon different premises, they are in perfect agreement about the meaning of originality.

They received that meaning from the classical and Continental ideas about imitation, and White cites Quintilian, Longinus, Cicero, Lucian, Isocrates, Horace, Macrobius, Plautus, Terence, and many others to this effect: Imitation is essential; fabrication, dangerous; subject matter is common property. To the ancients, "combining old material with new and expressing the combination in an original manner constituted originality. This originality was achieved by a composite process which may for convenience be divided into three steps: selection, reinterpretation, and improvement" (pp. 6–8). One first *selects* only the best features of the best writers;

most ancients hold that few writers who have stood the test of time do not have something worthy to be imitated. Secondly, one must *reinterpret* his selections, putting old ideas into a contemporary idiom and exemplifying them with personal experiences and observations. In its best—perhaps it would be more accurate to say at its most modern—moments, reinterpretation involves transformation. When Seneca uses the figure of the bee, he is asking the writer for more than an ancient topic in new dress. As the bee turns the nectars of varied flowers into honey, the writer should "so blend . . . whatever [he has] gathered from a varied course of reading . . . into one delicious compound that, even though it betrays its origin, yet it nevertheless is clearly a different thing from that whence it came." [13] Another popular analogy is that drawn between the digestion of literal and literary food. What is merely memorized or copied has not been digested and will not nourish. "Our mind," concludes Seneca in his eighty-fourth letter, "should hide away all the materials by which it has been aided, and bring to light only what it has made of them." Fifteen hundred years later, Sidney wishes that Cicero's imitators would "deuoure" his "figures and phrases . . . whole, and make them wholly theirs," rather than cast "Sugar and Spice vpon euery dish that is serued" or, "like those Indians, not content to weare eare-rings at the fit and naturall place of the eares, . . . thrust Iewels through their nose and lippes, because they will be sure to be fine" (I, 202). When C. S. Lewis tells us that Seneca's *Epistles* "are at least as important to the student of the sixteenth century as his tragedies," [14] he is speaking of the noble Roman's philosophy, but the remark is equally apt in understanding Sidney's view of an imitation both decorous and creative.

Finally, having selected and reinterpreted or transformed his models, the writer is expected to *improve* upon them, not merely changing, but changing for the better. One therefore asks to be compared to his predecessors and challenged by his successors. Isocrates's aim is to "speak better" on his topic than anyone before him, and he desires his contemporaries to "center [their] rivalry" upon his theme in order to "study how [they] may surpass [him] in speaking on the same question." [15] In accordance with this conception of circumscribed originality, the Romans regarded Latin adaptations from the Greek (whether of form, of content, or of both) as *new* works, and "the first adapter of any type of literature claimed honors more or less equivalent to those awarded its 'inventor'" (p. 12). There is therefore nothing strange about Terence's terming three of his plays "new" while naming the Greek originals of each, or Virgil's claim that he treads "untouched" fields in his *Georgics.* Open piracy, on the other hand, is roundly denounced. Martial is the first writer to use *plagiarius,* literally "kidnaper," for literary thievery; a certain "Fidentinus" had tried to pass off Martial's children as his own. Secret or perverse borrowing is also condemned, the former because any attempt to conceal an indebtedness indicates that the writer is not proudly imitating and openly challenging his models, the latter because it selects the best authors' vices rather than their virtues. By far the most common complaints are against servile or superficial imitators, those who may have selected wisely but "failed to transform what they have borrowed. So Horace warns . . . not . . . [to] copy slavishly. . . . A mere copy, even of the merits of a model, is to Quintilian a lifeless shell" (p. 17). And therefore, White concludes, the classical attitude toward imitation is best represented by two figures; Horace's "strutting crow, for the superficial, mechanical imitator, and [Seneca's] busy bee, for his assimilating, transforming opposite" (p. 18).

In sixteenth-century Italy and France, the story is much the same. Between 1535 and 1595, Daniello, Muzio, Giraldi Cinthio, Minturno, Tasso, and Pontanus reiterate the ancient doctrine that "true originality is achieved through an imitation which selects its models carefully, reinterprets them personally, and endeavors to surpass them gloriously" (p. 30). Among so much critical warfare we might expect some champions of invention in its more modern romantic sense. But of the four Italians who disdain the busy bee, three elect the crow. As early as 1512 Pico rightly defines, and encourages Bembo to accept, the truly classical view. In his reply (1513) Bembo agrees about the imitation of matter, but holds little hope for bettering Virgil's and Cicero's styles (pp. 19-20). Scaliger later (1561) turns Bembo's servility into idolatry. The poet has no freedom, for Virgil, "who alone is worthy of the name of poet," who "seems not so much to have imitated Homer as to have shown us how Homer should have written," has given us a work in which "nothing has been omitted," and to which "nothing remains to be added, . . . except by the stupid" or "changed, except by the impudent." [16] Vida (1527), on the other hand, admires the manner by which the crow disguised himself in peacock feathers. He turns the ancient doctrine that all literary matter is common property into the unclassical idea that one should transform to deceive rather than to outdo (p. 21).

The only critic who satisfies modern expectations is Castelvetro. For the first time (1570) original invention, fabrication of the wholly new, becomes the essence of poetry. We need only accept this radical's major premises to appreciate the remorseless logic that follows. Because any poem's excellence depends upon the difficulties overcome in its creation, and because "whoever takes from another employs no labor in invention," imitators as respectable as Plautus, Terence, Seneca, Virgil, Boccaccio, Petrarch, and Ariosto are all lazy thieves, crows with stolen plumage, "mere versifiers or translators only, notwithstanding that without merit of their own they have usurped the title of poet," and intelligent men "should debase and scorn them." [17] To avoid turning crow, in short, the bee must produce the flowers as well as the honey. The true poet "neither follows the examples already set forth, nor does what has already been done . . . but makes a thing wholly different from anything that has been done before"; he must avoid treating of actual happenings, either past or present, for then "he will not have labored at all in inventing them, and will be no poet"; finally, of course, "that which a man has invented is his very own." [18] More surprising than Castelvetro's explosion, however, is the fact that no one paid it much heed. The seven critics who follow him denounce servility, admire invention, but still think of originality in terms of figures like Muzio's (1551) and Minturno's (1563): Writings should "exhale their previously absorbed odor, like a garment preserved among roses"; the author's borrowed flowers should "appear to have grown in his own garden, not to have been transplanted from elsewhere" (pp. 22, 26). In 1594, Tasso and Pontanus are still honoring Seneca's bee and the common classical analogy of digestion. As a whole, the French are even more orthodox. Du Bellay at first approaches the servility of Bembo, raises a storm of protest, and rectifies his errors. We find no hint of a Gallic Castelvetro.

Sixteenth-century England also runs true to classical form. The heretics exaggerate in the direction of Bembo and Scaliger, not Castelvetro. Under the Tudors and early Stuarts, the great medieval reverence for authority is challenged by the classical safeguards for a limited originality. English literary liberty moves forward as men look backward and come to understand that those wonderful ancients really expected to be outdone as well as admired. Slavish, superficial, perverse, and secret borrowing receive increasingly severe denunciations. Beyond the freedoms allowed by the Romans, however, the Tudors do not venture. "Only three minor writers [actually four: an anonymous Puritan tract (1580), Thomas Churchyard (1593), John Taylor (1612), and George Wither (1613)] made imitation, correctly practised, the object of censure. Not only were Englishmen from 1500 to 1625 without any feeling analogous to the modern attitude toward plagiarism; they even lacked the word until the very end of that period" (pp. 201–202). Granted, the critics' own definitions are sometimes misleading. In the first English treatise upon *The Art or Craft of Rhetoric* (c. 1530), for example, Leonard Cox places "Invencyon" first among the creator's requirements and discusses nothing else, but his discussion in turn reveals that by this term he means the ability to find apt quotations and to use them to the best advantage (p. 38). Most of the other early theorists and practitioners advocate, or imply an acceptance of, the classical doctrine of a freer, more creative imitation: Wilson (1553), Hawes (1509), Lupset (1535), Elyot (1531), Ascham (1545), Palsgrave (1540), Cranmer (1551), pre-Elizabethan poets like Barclay and Skelton, Hoby's translation of Castiglione (cf. this chapter's first epigraph), Ascham (1570), Wilson (1570), Harvey (1577), Gascoigne (1573, 1575), Whetstone (1577), Googe (1577), Painter (1566, 1567), and Pettie (1576).[19]

Imitation in theory and practice from Sidney to Jonson enlarges upon but does not essentially change the basic story. If White's book has by now become a bit tedious, it is only because his witnesses continue to testify along similar lines. Taken individually, almost every one gives the lie to Holofernes; none thinks of "imitari" in terms as ignoble as his "hound," "ape," and "tired horse." Taken together, they create a context of prevailing opinion against which to measure the nature and extent of dissent; most exceptions to the rule are only apparent, and the real are usually intelligible. Early in his treatise, for example, Sidney tells us that the truest poets are those who "most properly do imitate to teach and delight, and to imitate borrow nothing of what is, hath been, or shall be: but range, onely rayned with learned discretion, into the diuine consideration of what may be, and should be" (I, 159). Here White provides a valuable observation: "Elizabethan literary theorists, like their Continental teachers, continually employ the word 'imitation,' without distinction, for following nature (*mimesis*) and for following other writers" (p. 61 n.). Several para-

graphs earlier Sidney himself notes that "Poesie therefore is an
arte of imitation, for so *Aristotle* termeth it in his word *Mimesis*,
that is to say, a representing, counterfetting, or figuring foorth: to
speake metaphorically, a speaking picture" (I, 158). When Sidney
admires the psalmist who "did imitate the inconceiuable excellencies
of God," scorns "the meaner sort of Painters (who counterfet
onely such faces as are sette before them)," and insists that "right
Poets" range beyond 'was' and 'is' to the realm of 'may be' or
'should have been,' he is obviously using imitation in the sense of
representation. When he checks that wide, imaginative ranging
with the reins of "learned discretion," he is probably anticipating
a later usage of imitation, the second wing of Daedalus, whose
"ayre of due commendation" is the final resting place of Seneca's
wise, practical, energetic bee. Unlike Castelvetro, Sidney allows
the poet to use "the best of the Historian," for "whatsoeuer
action . . . the Historian is bound to recite, that may the Poet
(if he list) *with his imitation make his own;* beautifying it both for
further teaching, and more delighting, as it pleaseth him: *hauing
all,* from *Dante* his heauen to hys hell, *vnder the authoritie
of his penne*" (I, 169. Italics added.) Both kinds of imitation offer
a freedom and responsibility the historian may not accept. In representing life, the poet is free to use events that never happened or
improve upon those that did, but his "speaking picture" must speak
more instructively and delightfully than the chronicler's. Similarly,
the poet has greater liberty in selecting his sources, but the historian is not obliged to beautify his borrowings, much less make
those documents "his own."

By now it should be obvious that Astrophel's contempt for the
"Pickepurse of an others wit" (Sonnet LXXIV) can mean both a
great deal less and a little more than we might otherwise suspect.
That it would have been taken in a properly classical spirit by
James VI, Webbe, Puttenham, and Harington, White clearly shows.
Although each critic emphasizes different aspects of ancient doctrine and omits some altogether, there is no hint that they are not in
substantial agreement with one another, with Sidney, and with foreign tradition (pp. 78–79). The same may be said of the attitudes
toward originality revealed in the heated battles between Harvey
and Nashe, "Martin Marprelate" and his Anglican opponents, and
the detractors and defenders of the stage. The first Englishman
to attack imitation correctly practiced is the anonymous author of
the second part of *A Second and Third Blast of Retreat from Plays*

and Theaters (1580). Simply to call its author stupid may not make this first exception to the rule any more intelligible, but what sense can be argued for a complaint about the playwrights' habits of giving familiar stories "a newe face" and making "that seeme new which is old"?[20] The only other sixteenth-century exception is more understandable. *Churchyard's Challenge* (1593) reveals the mind of a frustrated egomaniac, certain that all his rivals are stealing from his garden, too proud to take anything from theirs (pp. 115–118). The quality of his poetry makes it difficult to believe that those nameless thieves could have been even tempted. We might well wish that his flowers were as original as he claims, for nothing would have better illustrated the helpfulness of creative imitation. From practitioners as unlike as Spenser and Lyly in 1579 to Daniel, Hall, and Jonson at the turn of the century, we get an entirely different response: None but an idiot seeks a "scratch" to start from rather than a great model to rival and hopefully improve upon. And when Joseph Hall finally (1598) introduces Martial's figurative use of *plagiarius* to the English language, he is abusing "a plagiary sonnet-wright" who will "filch whole pages at a clap, for need, / From honest Petrarch, clad in English weed." A decade later the same man explains how his *Characters of Virtues and Vices* was written: "As one . . . that, in worthy examples, holds imitation better than invention, I have trod in their [his model authors'] paths, but with an higher and wider step; and out of their tablets have drawn these larger portraitures."[21]

To appreciate Hall's sentiments fully, the ancients would require a modern gloss upon "sonnet" and "Petrarch." For our two terms they would, in exchange, easily interpret the rest for us. Our notions about originality and plagiarism, which chronological snobbery would assume to have been formulated by the inventors of the alphabet, are very recent indeed. In this respect the distance between the first and seventeenth centuries is much smaller than that between the seventeenth and twentieth, and we may conclude our summary of White's findings by citing two of his most apt late Elizabethan depositions. A maxim that is probably Francis Bacon's likens writers who go no farther than what they have read "to pismires; they only lay up and use their store." But those who are truly original, who write without reading (by 1798 they will prefer "one impulse from a vernal wood"), are less than ants, mere "spiders; they spin all out of their own bowels." Praise is reserved for the bee, "gathering from abroad, . . . digesting that

which is gathered by his own virtue" (p. 195). Donne expresses
the same spirit more eloquently in his preface to *The Progress
of the Soul* (1601): "Now when I beginne this booke, I have no
purpose to come into any mans debt; how my stocke will hold out
I know not; perchance waste, perchance increase in use; if I doe
borrow any thing of Antiquitie, besides that I make account that
I pay it to posterity, with as much and as good: You shall still
[always] finde mee to acnowledge it, and to thanke not him
onely that hath digg'd out treasure for mee, but that hath lighted
mee a candle to the place" (p. 127). But he who works common
lodes without acknowledgments of gratitude, or leaves behind no
treasure at least as rich as that he has appropriated, must suffer
Donne's witty logic: that man

> is worst, who (beggarly) doth chaw
> Others wits fruits, and in his ravenous maw
> Rankly digested, doth those things out-spue,
> As his owne things; and they are his owne, 'tis true,
> For if one eate my meate, though it be knowne
> The meate was mine, th'excrement is his owne.[22]

The manner in which Hall treads old "paths" is related to
another Elizabethan figure for creative imitation, one almost as
common as the bee and digestion. To proceed with Hall's "higher
and wider step" is to "wade farther." Peele's *Arraignment of Paris*,
according to Nashe, "might plead to your opinions his pregnant
dexteritie of wit and manifold varietie of inuention, wherein . . .
hee goeth a step beyond all that write" (I, 319). That Peele has
shown himself wittier, brighter, more inventive and facile than
most means that he is excellent. That Peele has gone "a step beyond" may also mean that he has reached that excellence *through
imitation*, since several pages earlier Nashe uses the same figure less
ambiguously. For his adaptation of Ariosto's *I Suppositi*, "Master
Gascoigne* is not to bee abridged of his deserued esteeme, who
first beate the path to that perfection which our best Poets haue
aspired too since his departure; whereto he did ascend by comparing the Italian with the English, as *Tullie* did *Graeca cum Latinis*"
(I, 315). In the first epigraph to this chapter, Castiglione is equally
clear about avenues to every courtly excellence. His ideal courtier
must "wade in everie thing a little farther than other men," a little
farther than the best horseman, at least as far as the foremost

Italians in tilting, best Frenchmen in swordplay, greatest Spaniards in "running at Bull" and "casting of Speares and Dartes." [23] In other words, Castiglione continues, reverting to an older figure, the courtier must fly as an international bee, determine which man or nation represents the flowering of a particular accomplishment, steal only the best from each best, and—so we must infer—redeem these thefts by transforming himself into a masterpiece, something wholly new, the Perfect Courtier, to be reverenced with capital letters, as any Platonic Idea. Naturally he will excel in speaking and writing as much as in wrestling, vaulting, dancing, and singing, and naturally he will attain these "graces" in the same way, "wrasting" or "grafting" old words to an original "purpose," coining new words and figures, not limiting his models to Petrarch and Boccaccio but experimenting with all, and wading as far as his own "noble wits" may carry him.[24] After all, "if Virgill had *altogether* followed Hesiodus, hee should not have passed him, nor Cicero Crassus, nor Ennius his predecessors." [25]

Difficult as it may be to find something wholly new under the sun, Castelvetro's modern approach offers a securer way. Bacon's spider, which spins everything out of its "own bowels," risks neither being censured for selecting the wrong models nor rebuked for failing to outdo the right ones. To create with absolute originality—as if that were possible—is at once to create the work and the standards by which it must be judged. The Elizabethan "higher and wider step" may at first seem to us a convenient, perhaps even lazy shortcut within the creative process. But if it offered the writer a head start and a chart by which to sail, it also automatically evoked great expectations in his readers, for they had watched others cross the same sea. The writer was free only to choose the tradition he would essay. That decision obliged him to honor his worthiest predecessors, for wading farther than the least of his chosen kind argued no achievement. The better his models, the more intimidating his standards of excellence and, if he navigated successfully, the greater his accomplishment. In its own time the "step beyond" must have been viewed as anything but a ready and easy way. It was accepted as a critical necessity that only the greatest could make a virtue of. The young makers, both good and bad, must have quickly sensed that one could easily tread old paths to one's destruction.

Once that perilous way had been well managed, the writer or critic was anxious that no man think success had come cheaply.

He even invited those inevitable comparisons. So E.K. would make it clear that "this Author euery where followeth" the paths or "foting" of Theocritus, Virgil, "and also diuers other excellent both Italian and French Poetes" (I, 132) and then, throwing down the New Poet's gauntlet, concludes, "yet" he has imitated "so as few, but they be wel sented, can trace him out." Only the ignorant, in other words, will find *The Shepheardes Calender* too servile *or too original* to qualify as properly creative. And only those who were unsuccessful in their own time seem to have looked forward to ours. In praising their own originality, however, Churchyard, Taylor, and Wither are not quite championing "starting from scratch" as a high, abstract standard.[26] Their pleas are more personal, something closer to the complaint of the man who has lost and wishes to change the rules: "If I am not very good, at least I am different; I have not imitated anyone." And this is a readier way of turning necessity to a virtue. Students who wish that Shakespeare had been ambitious enough to invent his own plots are thus, in effect, criticizing his failure to take what his audience would have considered the easier alternative, avoiding the obligation to step *beyond* by mapping his very own path.

The Doctrine Applied

The concept of wading farther also explains what must strike us as a critical obsession. Whether praising or blaming, the theorists continually appeal to earlier models and proceed by interminable comparisons. In this respect Ascham appears to have been the most influential critic. Imitation is first defined as "a facultie to expresse liuelie and perfitelie that example which ye go about to folow" (I, 5). Only he who has "neither will to do good him selfe, nor skill to iudge right of others," who condemns

> by pride and ignorance, all painfull diligence and right order in study, will perchance say that I am to precise, to curious, in marking and piteling thus about the imitation of others; and that the olde worthie Authors did neuer busie their heades and wittes in folowyng so preciselie, either the matter what other men wrote, or els the maner how other men wrote. They will say it were a plaine slauerie, and iniurie to, to shakkle and tye a good witte, and hinder the

course of a mans good nature, with such bondes of seruitude, in folowyng other.

Except soch men thinke them selues wiser then *Cicero*
for teaching of eloquence, they must be content to turne
a new leafe.

(I, 10)

We may enjoy Ascham's witty rejoinder to indolent genius,
but we also wonder how fast the critic himself would "shakkle"
us in the "bondes of seruitude," especially when he sets sarcasm
aside and openly admires the way "*Tullie* did . . . purposelie and
mindfullie, bend him selfe to a precise and curious Imitation of
Plato" (I, 11). Unless "precise" means something less than "exact,"
such imitation does not seem to satisfy his initial definition, that
"facultie to expresse" one's models in a "liuely" manner. Here
Ascham probably overstates his case. Indignant at those who exaggerate the freedom of "good witte, and . . . nature," he in turn
exaggerates his respect for authority and comes close to upholding
"plaine slauerie."

Between his opening remarks and angry reply, however, we get
an excellent summary of "all the necessarie tooles and instrumentes,
where with trewe *Imitation* is rightlie wrought withall in any
tonge" (I, 8–9). There is none of Scaliger's servility in Ascham's
introduction of the chief problems. Instead of telling the young
maker that Cicero is the alpha and omega of prose and Virgil of
poetry, Ascham would have him first determine which writers he
will follow, "which way to folow; . . . in what place; by what
meane and order; by what tooles. . . ; by what skill and iudgement
ye shall trewelie discerne whether ye folow rightlie or no."
Erasmus's desire that learned men would "write out and ioyne
together where the one [Cicero] doth imitate the other [Demos-
thenes]" is in fact described as "good, but surelie . . . not good
enough," for "onelie to point out and nakedlie to ioyne togither
their sentences, with no farder declaring the maner and way how
the one doth folow the other, were but a colde helpe to the en-
crease of learning" (I, 8–9). For the writer who will, as Ascham
later puts it, "do good him selfe," or the critic who wants "skill
to iudge right of others" (I, 10), the careful cataloguing of similar
passages is only a means to a far greater end.

But if a man would take his paine also, whan he hath
layd two places of *Homer* and *Virgill* or of *Demosthenes*

and *Tullie* togither, to teach plainlie withall, after this sort:
    1. Tullie reteyneth thus moch of the matter, thies sentences, thies wordes:
    2. This and that he leaueth out, which he doth wittelie to this end and purpose.
    3. This he addeth here.
    4. This he diminisheth there.
    5. This he ordereth thus, with placing that here, not there.
    6. This he altereth and changeth, either in propertie of wordes, in forme of sentence, in substance of the matter, or in one or other conuenient circumstance of the authors present purpose.

(I, 9)

Were we to substitute Holinshed for Demosthenes, and Shakespeare for Tully, Ascham's insistence upon a thorough and imaginative comparison between "imitations" and models would but echo those claims for the relevance of literary backgrounds we have registered in earlier chapters. *For what purpose* has this been retained, that omitted, added, diminished, reordered, or altered? The demanding nature of source study receives further notice when Ascham censures Bartolommeo Ricci's superficial comparisons between Virgil and poets ancient and modern. Instead of providing random instances of several recent Italian imitations of Virgil, and one example of Virgil's own borrowing from Catullus, Ricci would have told us more about Virgil (and thereby how best to imitate him) had he "declared where and how, how oft and how many ways, *Virgil* doth folow *Homer*" (I, 14). Here Ascham suggests a half-dozen incidents both epics share, "and other places infinite mo, as similitudes, narrations, messages, discriptions of persons, battels, tempestes, shipwrackes, and common places for diuerse purposes, which be as precisely taken out of *Homer* as euer did Painter in London follow the picture of any faire personage" (I, 15). We must begin, in short, by working closely with specific, acknowledged borrowings rather than using one writer as a convenient point of departure for discussing literature past and present. The Aschams of our day complain as bitterly about books like *Crime and Punishment in Shakespeare and Sartre*, wherein they "like better [the author's] diligence and order of teaching than his iudgement in choice of examples" (I, 14).

Writers were also challenged for their choice of examples. In Harvey's *Letter Book*, composed during a period from 1573 to 1580, "those that hunte the letter" are placed alongside other fools, whose "triflinge and childishe . . . verses . . . represente the form and figure of an egg, an ape, a winge, and sutche ridiculous and madd gugawes and crockchettes" (I, 126). "Nothing so absurde and fruteles," sighs the weary critic, "but beinge once taken vpp shall haue sume imitatoures." And nothing better summarizes Harvey's attack upon Greene and Nashe a dozen years later. Theirs is a "liuely and frisking thing of a queint and capricious nature, . . . that scorneth to be a booke-woorme, or to imitate the excellentest artificiality of the most renowned worke-masters that antiquity affourdeth" (II, 277). Whatever Harvey's primary motive for censuring Greene—it was probably more personal than literary—it suffices to ask the reader to compare the "fooleries" of this "Scriuener of Crosbiters" with "*Tullies* sweete Offices; or *Isocrates* pithy instructions; or *Plutarches* holesome Morrals; or the delicate Dialogues of *Xenophon* and *Plato;* or the sage Tragedies of *Sophocles* and *Euripides*" (II, 231). For a critic bent on destruction and as widely read as Harvey, odious comparisons come easily enough. And they include modern as well as ancient classics. "Euen *Guicciardines* siluer Historie and *Ariostos* golden Cantoes grow out of request, & the Countesse of Pembrookes Arcadia is not greene inough for queasie stomackes; but they must haue *Greenes* Arcadia, and, I beleeue, most eagerlie longed for *Greenes* Fairie Queene." Nashe, too, must be told that "Right artificiality . . . is not mad-brained . . . but admirable; not according to the fantasticall mould of *Aretine* or *Rabelays,* but according to the fine model of *Orpheus, Homer, Pindarus,*" Spenser, Buchanan, Watson, and Daniel (II, 234). Harvey, in short, blames the present evil state of letters upon three factors. Those writers who do follow the bee visit only "mad-brained, or ridiculous, or absurd, or blasphemous, or monstrous" flowers (II, 234). Or, to change the figure, "young Euphues hatched the egges that his elder freendes laide" (II, 268). Those who do not imitate the wrong models do not imitate at all. Like Bacon's spider, the "witt of this & that odd Modernist is their owne; & no such minerall of richest Art as praegnant Nature, the plentifullest woombe of rare Inuention. . . . Whuist Art! and Nature aduaunce thy precious Selfe. . . . Desolate Eloquence and forlorne Poetry . . . lye prostrate at thy dainty foote, and adore the Idoll-excellencey of thy monstrous Singularity!" (II, 277–278).

Finally, there is that green public, which knows no more of "right artificiality" and "the most renowned worke-masters" of antiquity than the authors it supports.

But if Harvey sometimes compares in order to censure, he also salutes what is best by the same method. To praise some of Spenser's early sonnets, he first sets up alternative models. "Amorous Sonnets" are all too often "but . . . iunkets of a wanton liuer, or buddes of an idle head" and, of course, "Aretine's muse was an egregious bawd, & a haggishe witch," whose "ribald vomit" Nashe has already been accused of "lick[ing] vp for a restoratiue" (II, 259). But "Petrarckes Inuention is pure Loue it selfe," and his "Elocution pure Bewty it selfe: his *Laura* was . . . a delitious Sappho, not a lasciuious Lais," and his muse "confined Loue within the limits of Honour, Witt within the boundes of Discretion, Eloquence within the termes of Ciuility." The stage now carefully set, Spenser is allowed to enter as the "Inglishe Petrarck." But this is nothing next to the elaborate comparisons reserved for the *Arcadia*. From Master Asteley, "our Inglish Xenophon," Harvey proceeds to Sidney, our English almost-everything. His "gallant Legendary, full of pleasurable accidents and proffitable discourses," is a "written Pallace of Pleasure" (Painter's palaces had begun to appear in 1566) or a "printed Court of Honour" (Castiglione's was translated by Hoby in 1561). The terms in which Harvey first summarizes the book's four virtues do not make it sound especially formidable. One learns from and enjoys its "amorous Courting (he was young in yeeres)," its "sage counselling (he was ripe in iudgement)," its "valorous fighting (his soueraine profession was Armes)," and its "delightfull pastime by way of Pastorall exercises" (II, 263). The *Arcadia* certainly had this wide popular appeal; all the realm's courtiers and scholars could not alone have supported fourteen editions within its first century. We must also remember that when the "hard rocks of Predestination" sometimes appear to mar the idealized landscape, English Calvinism was the "very latest thing," just as "modish as the shepherds and goddesses." [27] But this does not prevent Harvey from appreciating how much art and imitation have gone into Sidney's exercise. "Liue euer, sweete Booke, . . . and euer notify . . . that thy Writer was the Secretary of Eloquence, the breath of the Muses, the hoony-bee of the dayntiest flowers of Witt and Arte" (II, 264–265). To list all those flowers would have taxed Ascham's ingenuity. Harvey is content to compare the Arcadian knights to those in the *Iliad, Odyssey,* and

Aeneid, and its author's descriptions of character and incident to the "veine of Salust, Liuy, Cornelius Tacitus. Iustine, Eutropius" and other more recent, "most sententious Historians." He might also have included the more romantic worlds of late classical Alexandria, of medieval French, Spanish, and English chivalry, and of Renaissance Italian pastoral.

Shakespeare was certainly at least as popular as Sidney and, to judge from the disparate literary kinds he exploited, probably as widely read. Holofernes's obviously wrong views about "Imitari," however, is as close as Shakespeare came to an explicit comment on wading farther. To this we might add that refusal to step in the wrong direction with "new-found methods and . . . compounds strange," and contentment with "dressing old words new" (Sonnet LXXVI). Unlike Spenser, Shakespeare never invited a friendly E.K. to point out whose great paths he had traced. Unlike Sidney, he never turned critic to assure us that he knew the importance of treating one's models in an original and personal manner. Unlike Jonson's *Sejanus*, his history plays are not ornamented with hundreds of scholarly footnotes to indicate how decorously he had handled his sources. He left behind some friends who thought his works worth publishing, and their worth, in turn, has inspired readers from the time of Mrs. Lennox (*Shakespear Illustrated*, 1753) to our own day to provide for him the glosses that many of his contemporaries provided for themselves. The results consistently demonstrate that if Shakespeare wished for an originality more modern than Sidney's, Spenser's, or Jonson's, he never gave that desire any expression except, perhaps, in *Love's Labor's Lost* and *The Tempest*. For these we may have lost the literary originals. In his other thirty-five plays and nondramatic poetry, we find an increasingly better argument for the greatness that can be achieved by imitating creatively. Some of his "actions," in fact, speak more clearly than the theorists' many words or learned footnotes.

Shakespeare's awareness of that necessary higher and wider step may be inferred from two other kinds of evidence. First, he surely must have realized that his manner of composition agreed with what the critics were recommending and his rivals practicing. It is also inconceivable that as he looked about for a ready-made plot and confronted several handlings of the same tale, he did not ask Ascham's questions about the "conuenient circumstance of [each] authors present purpose" and tried to shape those purposes to his own. Like the critics, in other words, Shakespeare was forced to

make comparisons and to judge which contributors had carried a
common story forward, which backward, and which sideways.
How far back into each tradition he went is often not possible to
establish. Certainly that "small Latin" Jonson allowed him was
respectable by modern standards. Scholars usually grant him some
French and Italian as well. The main point is that the farther he
retraced old steps, the more obvious the obligation to make common property richer must have appeared. He would have noticed
this not only in each writer's elaborations, but sometimes in the
comments that accompanied or followed specific works. *The Taming of the Shrew* (c. 1594), for example, takes its less farcical,
more conventionally romantic subplot from Gascoigne's *Supposes*
(1566). With his great fondness for romantic story, it is probable
that Shakespeare read one of Greene's best novelle, *Menaphon*
(1589), along with Nashe's preface celebrating Gascoigne's wading farther in his translation of Ariosto's *I Suppositi*. And if
Shakespeare was especially interested in how Gascoigne "first
beate the path to . . . perfection . . . by comparing the Italian with
the English," as Nashe had claimed (I, 315), he might have done
some "comparing" on his own. The prose version of Gascoigne's
model [28] makes this rather large and encouraging claim:

> And in this [switching of identities] the author confesses
> having followed both Plautus and Terence, one of whom
> had Chaerea switched with Dorus, and the other, Philoc-
> rates with Tyndarus, and Tyndarus with Philocrates, the
> one in the *Eunuch*, the other in the *Captives*. For he [the
> author] desires to imitate the ancient and celebrated poets
> to the best of his ability, not only in their manners, but also
> in the plots of their stories. And as they followed Menander
> and Apollodorus and other Greeks in their Latin comedies,
> so he does not wish to shun the Latin writers' customs and
> methods in his Italian plays. So I tell you, he has abstracted
> from Terence's *Eunuch* and Plautus's *Captives* part of the
> plot of his *Switched Ones*, but so modestly that Terence
> and Plautus themselves, if they heard about it, would take
> it kindly, and call it poetic imitation sooner than theft.[29]

Had Shakespeare wished to retreat and compare even further,
he would have found Ariosto's claims supported by Terence in
the prologue to his *Eunuch*. Mindful of the critic who is complain-

ing that Terence's flattering parasite and swaggering soldier have been stolen from Naevius and Plautus—that critic has himself "by translating well but writing badly . . . made feeble Latin plays out of good Greek ones"—the Prologue admits that both characters were originally Menander's, but that if the author may not therefore use them, "why should he be any more allowed to describe a slave running, or to put on the stage virtuous matrons, vicious courtesans, . . . old gentlemen tricked by their slaves, love, hatred, or suspicion? In short, nothing is said now that has not been said before; you ought to reflect upon this, and pardon us new writers if we practice the same tricks as the old ones." [30] The last sentence could have been spoken by Ariosto, Udall, Gascoigne, Shakespeare, Jonson, Massinger, Wycherley, or Sedley, each of whom wades in different directions with either the *Eunuch*, the *Captives*, or both. When in our own century Jean Giraudoux entitled his adaptation of another Plautine comedy *Amphitryon 38*, he was acknowledging his thirty-seven predecessors. We might hope his reckonings included not only Dryden, Moliere, and Shakespeare, but also the anonymous *Jack Juggler* (c. 1555), which turns Sosia into Jenkin Careaway, Mercury into the clever Vice, and Jack's appropriation of Jenkin's identity into what is probably a subtle attack upon the papists' juggling doctrine of transubstantiation. [31]

The other piece of evidence suggesting Shakespeare's awareness of wading farther is offered by some of his own comic characters. Here we should first notice how often they remind us that their world is a literal stage, a society ruled by dramatic as well as social conventions. "Nay, then, God buy you [God be with thee; that is, farewell] an [if] you talk in blank verse" (*As You Like It*, IV. i. 29); "If this were play'd upon a stage now, I could condemn it as an improbable fiction" (*Twelfth Night*, III. iv. 121–122). Notice, too, that neither character respects the convention he calls our attention to. Although the melancholy Jaques's most memorable lines ("All the world's a stage," II. vii. 139 ff.) are in blank verse, he will not suffer such patently stagy speech from his fellow players. Similarly, Fabian, who really "exists" only to help gull Malvolio, is confident that no playwright would include an incident so improbable. Although by the end of *Love's Labor's Lost* Berowne should sense that his world has been steadily shifting from artifice toward reality, he is unhappy with the play's "artless" resolution.

> *Ber.* Our wooing doth not end like an old play:
> Jack hath not Jill. These ladies' courtesy
> Might well have made our sport a comedy.
> *King.* Come, sir, it wants a twelvemonth an' a day,
> And then 'twill end.
> *Ber.*   That's too long for a play.
>   (V. ii. 862 ff.)

Through his own characters' objections to life being represented as more or less orderly than it either is or should be, Shakespeare dares us to overlook or take exception to the manner in which he has imitated customary dramatic practices.

More interesting, however, are those moments when his characters relate life not only to art in general (language, incident, plot) but to some of the specific literary conventions of the worlds from which Shakespeare drew them. Berowne, whom an Elizabethan audience would have taken as a character from real life, the contemporary French Marshal de Biron, has no right to expect real life immediately to yield a convenient Jill for every Jack. Within a romantic dream upon Midsummer Night, on the other hand, Lysander and Hermia may properly catalogue and gloss the time-honored conventions of romantic love-plotting.

> *Lys.* Ay me! for aught that I could ever read,
> Could ever hear by tale or history,
> The course of true love never did run smooth;
> But either it was different in blood——
> *Her.* O cross! too high to be enthrall'd to low.
> *Lys.* Or else misgraffed in respect of years——
> *Her.* O spite! too old to be engag'd to young.
> *Lys.* Or else it stood upon the choice of friends——
> *Her.* O hell! to choose love by another's eyes.
> *Lys.* Or, if there were a sympathy in choice,
> War, death, or sickness. . . .
>   (I. i. 132 ff.)

Or Puck, or "sweet bully Bottom," we might add, for these are the unexpected crosses and spites with which Shakespeare wades beyond his genre's conventional antagonists. With the possible exception of one of his earliest comedies, *The Two Gentlemen of Verona*, he finds something comic within the very romantic patterns he exploits. Through Lysander's solemn rehearsal, we are reminded of what we have all read and heard; through Hermia's exaggerated responses, we are told to expect all this and something more.

Finally, through lovers more sophisticated than Lysander and Hermia, Shakespeare makes us aware that it is the playwright, not the plot he imitates, that directs our responses to romantic story. Lorenzo and Jessica, for instance, pass a magical night at Belmont by "outnighting" one another with examples of loves which ended unhappily.

> *Lor.*   In such a night,
>   Troilus methinks mounted the Troyan walls,
>   And sigh'd his soul toward the Grecian tents,
>   Where Cressid lay that night.
> *Jes.*   In such a night
>   Did Thisby fearfully o'ertrip the dew,
>   And saw the lion's shadow ere himself,
>   And ran dismayed away.
>   (*The Merchant of Venice*, V. i. 3 ff.)

Obviously neither the incidents nor the personae of the Troilus or Thisbe story need make it tragic, but the mood and tone in which that story is conceived. Shakespeare will later turn what Lorenzo offers as fuel for comedy into a world of nightmare, and had he not already assigned the part of Thisbe to Flute, the bellows-mender, we might find her tale as potentially tragic as the remarkably similar misfortune of Juliet. A handbook of plot summaries can never distinguish the sunniness of *As You Like It* from the unpleasantness of *All's Well*, nor indicate why we feel that *Measure for Measure* is much "darker" than *Much Ado*. Occasionally a character even implies that the plots beyond which Shakespeare stepped, the apparently confining areas in which he exercised his originality, were for him (and remain for us, when merely outlined) generically neutral. The most amusing scenes of *Twelfth Night* and the most tragic or pitiful of *Othello* are both wrought by disguise. When Viola realizes how her "outside" has "charm'd" Olivia, she acknowledges what Othello discovers too late:

> Disguise, I see thou art a wickedness
> Wherein the pregnant enemy does much.
>   (II. ii. 25–26)

Having then proceeded to redefine, within a serious context, all those relationships that we have enjoyed as merrily confused, she can only conclude by invoking a disguised Shakespeare.

> O Time, thou must untangle this, not I;
> It is too hard a knot for me t' untie!
> (38–39)

Messrs. Belch and Aguecheek now appear, reminding us that we are still in Illyria. Their scene assures us that naught shall go ill; coupled with Viola's, however, it tells us that all could easily go ill had not Fortune, Time, or whatever other alias the playwright goes under already decided otherwise. With Iago's numerous references to the problems he faces in "wrighting" *Othello*, Shakespeare again keeps before us how his own "Muse labours, and thus she is deliver'd" (II. i. 127).

There appears to be only one essential difference between Shakespeare's comic and tragic treatments of neutral romantic story. That difference cannot be explained simply in terms of the conventions he follows. Some of the love stories he elaborates upon end unhappily (*Romeo and Juliet*, "Pyramus and Thisbe," *Othello, Antony and Cleopatra*), some happily (the early comedies, the "romantic" comedies). One kind of resolution is no more conventional than the other, for the world of romance yields a Tristram and Isolde for every Aucassin and Nicolette. Moreover, whether his source dictates that the lovers proceed to the altar or the grave, Shakespeare is equally anxious to remind us that they are pieces of his fiction. Proper staging and probable character motivation is a recurrent theme in Iago's soliloquies, and one of Cleopatra's last concerns is that

> the quick comedians
> Extemporally will stage us, and present
> Our Alexandrian revels; Antony
> Shall be brought drunken forth, and I shall see
> Some squeaking Cleopatra boy my greatness. . . .
> (V. ii. 215 ff.)

But if tragic lovers are as inclined as their happier cousins to see their stories as plots men might act out, they never suggest, as their comic counterparts so frequently do, that their romance is merely a variation upon a common theme, that it is, in any sense, conventional.

Intentionally or not, lovers from Berowne to Orsino make romance self-conscious about the formulas it is following; they all proclaim, "Here we go again." Lecturing Orlando against the folly of wasting in despair, the disguised Rosalind not only turns romantic legend inside out, but gives the lie direct to its most basic premise.

> The poor world is almost six thousand years old, and in all this time there was not any man died . . . in a love-cause. Troilus had his brains dash'd out with a Grecian club; yet he did what he could to die before, and he is one of the patterns of love. Leander, he would have liv'd many a fair year, though Hero had turn'd nun, if it had not been for a hot midsummer-night; for, good youth, he went but forth to wash him in the Hellespont, and, being taken with the cramp, was drown'd; and the foolish chroniclers of that age found it was—Hero of Sestos. But these are all lies: men have died from time to time, and worms have eaten them, but not for love.
>
> (*As You Like It*, IV. i. 83 ff.)

Of course men die for love, but not in a world where wooing is by the book, like Orlando's, or dying is by the book, like Pyramus's. The delicious comedy of Rosalind's last few sentences does not center in the foolishness of the chroniclers, but in the fact that love has been so often chronicled; not in "died . . . not for love," but in "died from time to time."

Unhappy loves may be equally conventional, but we never get that impression from the plays themselves. "Here we go again" is replaced by "Lo, nothing like this ever happened before." Romeo and Juliet both indirectly echo Marlowe's (and anticipate Phebe's) "Who ever lov'd that lov'd not at first sight?," but on their lips tired old refrains seem fresh, even spontaneous, and therefore truly lyrical. Phebe, on the other hand, deflates the lyrical and enforces the traditional by registering the sentiment as a quotable quotation: "Dead shepherd, now I find thy saw of might" (*As You Like It*, III. v. 80). Through Mercutio's catalogue of lovers, to be sure, we come close to seeing tragic romance as a well-patterned, highly stylized game. Expecting a Romeo "without his roe, like a dried herring," a Romeo enervated by a night with or in pursuit of "that same pale hard-hearted wench, that Rosaline," Mercutio merrily muses:

> O flesh, flesh, how art thou fishified! Now is he for the numbers that Petrarch flow'd in; Laura, to his lady, was a kitchen-wench—marry, she had a better love to berhyme her; Dido, a dowdy; Cleopatra, a gypsy; Helen and Hero, hildings and harlots; Thisbe, a gray eye or so, but not to the purpose.
>
> (II. iv. 4, 37 ff.)

But we know Rosaline is no longer "his lady," and that Mercutio's patterns, comparisons, and later bawdy gloss (88 ff.) are themselves "not to the purpose." Petrarch no doubt flowed into that "siege of loving terms" with which Romeo once attempted to seduce fair Rosaline (I. i. 210). He certainly endeavors to idealize his new love with Petrarchan terms during the balcony scene. Juliet, however, will not be proud fair, lacks the "cunning to be strange," bids "compliment" farewell, and cashiers Petrarch in the bargain. Mercutio's sentiments are grandly irrelevant because Romeo's real lady has already appropriated the book by which he would woo. His remarks are dramatically relevant, though, for in confusing an exception with the general rule, Mercutio unknowingly clarifies the beauty of that exception.

But if in employing Mercutio to hold up the same patterns as Lysander, Lorenzo, and Rosalind Shakespeare is again forcing us to note the playwright's presence, he is now saying something different about his role: "This is a road I could have taken, but not here, where love must create a world within the world of the play, a society of two, bound to be misinterpreted as conventional by the other characters." Similarly, when the "real" Cleopatra's greatness is eventually "boyed," her "infinite variety" will remain as fundamentally mysterious for Caesar's audience as it has been for us and the Romans within the play. Mysterious is the last thing we should call her happier sisters or their stories, for the comic heroines' fellow characters, whether in or out of love themselves, know exactly what to expect from romance because of their frequent readings in Shakespeare's library. Long before we know exactly how the knot will be untied, we sense that romance is proceeding comically or tragically, and that sense is in turn based upon either one of two illusions that Shakespeare cultivates as he wades farther. In his romantic *comedies,* he presents himself as a snapper-up of time-honored formulas, dutifully following the patterns of love in the prescribed way and showing a characteristically Chaucerian (ir)reverence for "auctoritee." In his romantic *tragedies,* he gives the impression that he has found no source to imitate, and therefore draws from life itself. Whether we are offered the "same old thing" (or, more accurately, an entirely original parody of the same old thing) or something immediate and "real," there is a marked similarity between the characters who seem to love and the dramatist who seems to write, with or without book.

By now it should be obvious that both the masterpieces of Elizabeth's artists and many of the most trifling comments of her critics were partly shaped by a common subscription to the doctrine of creative imitation. Whether admitting that the story has been often told and whimsically stressing its conventionalities or feigning that his tale is unique because he would make it tragic, Shakespeare always dresses old stuff to new advantage and thus steps beyond. The wonderfully surprising directions in which he finally waded should not obscure the fact that he began just as the thorniest theorists, by appealing to earlier models and comparing each author's purpose. He too, in short, was guilty of interminable comparisons, but destroyed all the evidence except that implicitly recorded within his plays. Those endless similes that Francis Meres uses to string his observations together reveal a habit of mind as commonplace as the observations themselves, an attitude that "tainted" even the genius of his contemporaries. Meres has his faults, to be sure. Shakespeare knew his fellow playwrights well enough to have caught several of the critic's biographical errors. Harvey would certainly have objected to Meres's inclusion of popular plays as literature. And the scholarly Ascham would likely have disdained the mindlessness and prosaic style of his wearisome *as*'s and *so*'s. But to each of these very different men, Meres's approach to literature was fundamentally sound. "As Virgil doth imitate Catullus in the like matter of *Ariadne* for his story of Queene *Dido:* so Michael Drayton doth imitate Ouid in his *England's Heroical Epistles.* . . . As Plautus and Seneca are accounted the best for Comedy and Tragedy among the Latines: so Shakespeare among the English is the most excellent in both kinds for the stage" (II, 316–318). To criticize well, whether as an end in itself or as a preface to writing skillfully, one must proceed by comparisons, and happy is the writer who can even kill or be killed by good ancient precedent: "As Achilles tortured the deade bodie of Hector, and as Antonius and his wife Fuluia tormented the liuelesse corps of Cicero: so Gabriell Haruey hath shewed the same inhumanitie to Greene, that lies full low in his graue. . . . As Anacreon died by the pot: so George Peele by the pox" (II, 323–324).

These biographical comparisons no doubt struck most Elizabethans as carrying the doctrine of creative imitation too far, but there is no critic who weighs a work without reference to its kind, and in describing the creative process, few do not employ the metaphor of wading farther or eventually fall back upon concealed similes. Stanyhurst, for example, prefaces his translation of the *Aeneid* by warning that the "ignorant wyl imagin that thee passage was nothing craggye, in as much as M. *Phaere* hath broken thee ice before mee" (I, 137). They should realize that Phaer's pains have only increased his own. Few can match him, "none, I am wel assured, ouergoe hym: yeet hee hath rather dubled than defalckt oght of my paines, by reason that, in conferring his translation with myne, I was forced too weede owt from my verses such choise woordes as were forestald by him, vnlesse they were so feeling as oothers could not countreuaile theyre signification" (I, 138). Four years later (1586), Webbe notes that the success of Phaer's "most gallant verse" was partly owing to his model, that "best peece of Poetry whereon [he] sette" it (I, 243). Virgil of course also merits our attention as a moral and political guide: "Vnder the person of *Aeneas* he expresseth the valoure of a worthy Captaine and valiaunt Gouernour, together with the perrilous aduentures of warre, and polliticke deuises at all assayes" (I, 237). But his works are equally valuable as poetical guides, "greate helpes and furtheraunces to the obtayning of good Letters." And they not only serve as best pieces whereon to set our own, but show us how to do it, for he "performed the very same in [his] tongue" which the Greeks managed in theirs, "or rather better, if better might" be possible. "As he immitateth *Homer* . . . so doth he likewyse followe the very steps of *Theocritus*, . . . and likewyse *Hesiodus* . . . but yet more grauely, and in a more decent style" (I, 237–238).

Since the critics all reveal essentially similar expectations about the roles of art and imitation, and since they all appear to honor the same ground rules when approving the good, we might expect them to find the same things bad and to furnish similar reasons. Here, however, we discover that one critic's food is another's poison. Although there is, by modern standards, only one "school of criticism," the schoolmasters differ as widely over whether the right rules have been *rightly applied* as the writers vary in the extent to which they *creatively* imitate. The very freedom that the practitioners were expected to exercise in choosing, combining, and wading in different directions with their models automatically insured that they would get mixed reviews from theorists of the same school. No one disagrees with Puttenham's picture of Wyatt and Surrey and their "new company of courtly makers . . . as nouices newly crept out of the schooles of *Dante, Arioste,* and *Petrarch*" (II, 62). But it did not necessarily follow that in "imitating . . . their Maister *Francis Petrarcha*," they had imitated him "in all [ways] . . . very naturally and studiously" (II, 65). After comparing the novices with their master, an Elizabethan could have legitimately questioned Puttenham's assertion that "their conceits were loftie, their stiles stately, their conueyance cleanly, their termes proper, their meetre sweete and well proportioned." Although agreeing with Puttenham about the nature of Wyatt's and Surrey's goals, models, and methods, contemporary critics would not have needed C. S. Lewis's twentieth-century standards to find their poetry sometimes "drab." But most are too grateful to these "first reformers of our English meetre and stile" (I, 63) to notice that they were not always lofty, stately, or even "cleanly." The sole complaint is Ascham's, who wishes "soch good wittes and forward diligence had bene directed to follow the best examples," had gone "farder than the schole of *Petrarke* and *Ariostus* abroad, or els of *Chaucer* at home" (I, 30, 33).

Essentially like-minded critics are much farther apart in their evaluations of *Euphues* and *The Shepheardes Calender*. Webbe concludes his *Discourse* with a translation of "the Cannons or generall cautions of Poetry, prescribed by Horace, [and] first gathered by *Georgius Fabricius*," an Horatian commentator (I, 290 ff.). No Elizabethan critic would have argued against the rightness or relevance of the following points:

> 42. An immitation should not be too seruile or superstitious, as though one durst not varry one iotte from the example: neyther should it be so sencelesse or vnskilful as to immitate thinges which are absurde and not to be followed.

43. One should not altogether treade in the steppes of others, but sometime he may enter into such wayes as haue not been haunted or vsed of others. *Horace* borrowed the *Iambick* verse of *Archilocus*, expressing fully his numbers and elegantly, but his vnseemely wordes and pratling tauntes hee moste wyselye shunned.

(I, 298)

With such Horatian principles for support, Webbe may claim that "Master *Iohn Lilly* hath deserued moste high commendations, as he which hath stept one steppe further therein then any either before or since he first began the wyttie discourse of his *Euphues*" (I, 256). "Let the learned examine and make tryall," challenges Webbe, and they will find *Euphues* matchless in "all the partes of Rethoricke, in fitte phrases, in pithy sentences, in gallant tropes, in flowing speeche, in plaine sence." Nashe and Harvey, on the other hand, although (perhaps *because*) they are equally aware of Horace's commandments, frequently use *Euphues* as an example of wading into a morass. For Nashe, euphuistic ornament, those "gallant tropes" so admired by Webbe, is but a "fraught of spangled feathers, golden Peebles, Straw, Reedes, Bulrushes" (II, 226); for Harvey, "Euphues Similes" or like "morsels of fly-blowne Euphuisme" may serve the same "puling stomackes" as "Scoggins tales, . . . Tarletons trickes, Eldertons Ballats, [or] Greenes Pamflets" (II, 272–273). As an indirect answer to Webbe's "partes of Rethoricke," Harvey insists that the "loosest period [sentence] in M. Ascham" is rhetorically superior to "the tricksiest page in Euphues," that the booksellers now (1593) "finde more gaine in the lillypot blanke [blank sheets of paper watermarked with "lily-pots"] then in the lillypot Euphued" (II, 274–275). All this does not merely indicate that *Euphues* had become unfashionable; it also shows that different personalities at different times, although aware of the same rules and authorities, differ greatly over what is pre-eminently and self-evidently elegant and absurd. The same differences of opinion are registered in Webbe's and Sidney's reactions to Spenser. Following E.K.'s cue (I, 132), Webbe bids readers of *The Shepheardes Calender* to "Take *Virgil* and make some little comparison betweene them, and iudge as ye shall see cause" (I, 263). In Webbe's judgment, such comparisons prove that Spenser "may well . . . steppe before the best of all English Poets." About three years earlier, however, Sidney dared not allow "that same framing of his stile to an old rustick language" since no pastoral master, including Virgil, "did affect it" (I, 196).

That comparisons could prove whatever the critics wanted them to is best illustrated by the treatment that Webbe's peerless ancient, Virgil, receives in the causes championed by Chapman and Harington. If Webbe uses Virgil to document Spenser's excellence, Chapman abuses him to enforce Homer's "more then Artificiall and no lesse then *Diuine Rapture*" (II, 297). Although he would "not be thought so ill created as to bee a malicious detracter of so admired a Poet as *Virgill*," Chapman has been ravished with "the whole drift, weight, & height of" Homer: "the maiestie he enthrones and the spirit he infuseth into the scope of his worke so farre outshining *Virgill*, that his skirmishes are but meere scramblings of boyes to *Homers*; the silken body of *Virgils* muse curiously drest in guilt and embrodered siluer, but *Homers* in plaine massie and vnualued gold" (II, 299).

For Harington, on the other hand, Virgil, Homer, and even Aristotle may be honored insofar as they will serve Ariosto's turn. To defend the art of *Orlando Furioso*, he first selects the *Aeneid* as "some other Poeme that is allowed and approued by all men," and then begins to "compare them together" (II, 211). A carefully chosen set of similarities leads to Harington's blanket claim that "there is nothing of any speciall obseruation in *Virgill* but my author hath with great felicitie imitated it, so as whosoeuer wil allow *Virgil* must *ipso facto* (as they say) admit *Ariosto*" (II, 211–212). But Harington's case is not simply that "whatsoeuer is prayseworthy in *Virgill* is plentifully to be found in *Ariosto*." The *Orlando* adds to Virgil God's Christian plenty, "infinit places full of Christen exhortation, doctrine, & example" (II, 213). This brings him to Ariosto's bawdy, which he now asks us to pardon, then excuses as something "ment . . . to breed detestation," now allegorizes, then illustrates as no more lascivious than Virgil's, now denies altogether, and finally upholds as having been done or spoken in character and, therefore, decorously (II, 214 ff.). Harington next confronts those who, "reducing all heroicall Poems vnto the methode of *Homer* and certain precepts of *Aristotle*," vow that Ariosto lacks art, and again the defender cleverly deploys his examples. Those who find the *Orlando* episodic are sent to Homer, not Aristotle; those who believe that the epic should be grounded upon a short space of history are sent to Aristotle and Ariosto, not Homer. Those who find in Aristotle that "nothing

should be fayned vtterly incredible" (II, 216) are asked to compare
the miracles in the *Orlando* with the teachings of the Church;
those who dislike Ariosto's habit of breaking "off narrations verie
abruptly" are referred to Sidney's excellent *Arcadia*. Whereas all
critics prove by comparisons, none is better able to invoke the right
references at the right times.

Always behind this special pleading is Harington's sincere love
for the Italian poet. It is most apparent when he concludes by
defending his master's most lovable fault—"he speaketh so much in
his own person by digression" (II, 217). Obviously "neither *Homer*
nor *Virgill* did it. Me thinks it is a sufficient defence to say,
Ariosto doth it." Perhaps insufficient, but certainly more honest
and sensible. Eight years later, Jonson's well instructed Cordatus
summarizes the innovations of ancient playwrights and can "see
not then, but we should enjoy the same licence, or free power, to
illustrate and heighten our inuention as they did; and not bee tyed
to those strict and regular formes, which the nicenesse of a few
(who are nothing but forme) would thrust vpon vs." [32] It seems
likely that the last and most "romantic" of Harington's defenses
would have struck Jonson as sufficiently "classical."

THE CONCEPT OF SPONTANEOUS ARTIFICIALITY

Prefacing Harington's defense of his chosen poet is a brief apology
for poetry itself, a section borrowed from Sidney and revealing
a far more classical temperament. If the critic is modern and
romantic enough to praise a great exception to an otherwise great
body of precedent, he is thoroughly Elizabethan and unromantic
in speaking of "both parts of Poesie [as] inuention *or* imitation
and verse" (II, 207. Italics added.) Despite our previous notice of
all the creativity that could go into wading farther, it may still
seem farfetched to grant "imitation" the same dignity as "inuention." But this equation is not a slip on Harington's part.
Central to his later defense is that "my author hath with great
felicitie imitated" every "speciall obseruation" in a piece "approued by all men." Even after allowing for "great felicitie," we
should prefer Harington to be speaking about something more
mechanical, less "inspired," than poetry. His claims for Ariosto's
art make art appear too calculating, too artificial, and (probably
most unsettling) both unoriginal and impersonal.

Perhaps Harington speaks only for the epic, a kind of poetry that rarely strikes us as spontaneous, impulsive, or unpremeditated. Surely Harington's frigid definition of poetry does not apply to Ben Jonson's simple songs. Would we dare question, for example, the warmth and sincerity of the lover who tells his mistress:

> I sent thee late a rosy wreath,
>   Not so much honouring thee
> As giving it a hope, that there
>   It could not wither'd be.

Or that manly resolve to have done with mere formality:

> Give me a look, give me a face,
> That makes simplicity a grace;
> Robes loosely flowing, hair as free:
> Such sweet neglect more taketh me
> Than all the adulteries of art;
> They strike mine eyes, but not my heart.

Making allowances for poetic diction, what man has not at some time deeply felt and at least tried to say much the same? And because we are personally affected, we may respond less to these poems as manufactured things (quatrains and couplets, diction, tactics employed in organizing content) than to the personality of the man behind the poem. If scholarly rudeness prevails and these beautiful lyrics be burdened with footnotes, let the glosses tell us about the Celia to whom Jonson sings, or about those too artful ladies who never caught his heart.

The real facts are less emotionally pleasurable. A genuine Celia must remain conjectural. But if we do not know to *whom* Jonson was singing, we certainly know *what* he was singing from. The outburst against "the adulteries of art" is based upon an anonymous late Latin poem, and the celebration of lovely Celia turns out to be a series of paraphrases of passages from the letters of a Greek rhetorician.[33] We may of course prefer to take these lyrics entirely on their own and enjoy them simply for what they say. If we dismiss the gloss that reveals rapture or indignation as an exercise and invention as imitation, however, we must also notice that the verses themselves encourage no special interest in the man who composed them. The complaint against always being neat is managed very neatly; both poems give general situations graceful turns. It is not Jonson but we who have made "sincerity" an issue, who have unconsciously brought into the songs the romantic premises that "all good poetry [and especially the lyric] is the spontaneous overflow of powerful feelings," that poetry "takes its origin from emotion recollected in tranquillity." [34]

The poems themselves, in short, tend to encourage one kind of historical gloss and discourage another; they are more inclined to bespeak the poet's personal involvement with poetic art and traditions than the tranquil recollection of an emotionally surcharged, private experience. Whereas the romantic poet implies something like "this is how it affected *me*," the Elizabethan says "look at how I'm doing *it*." We cannot prove that Wordsworth's "Lucy Gray" was not an imaginary character, but the very suspicion pales before such "obviously real" grief as:

> She lived unknown, and few could know
>   When Lucy ceased to be;
> But she is in her grave, and, oh,
>   The difference to me! [35]

How relatively restrained Jonson's last couplet *On My First Daughter:*

> This grave partakes the fleshly birth,
> Which cover lightly, gentle earth.

And if we insist upon salvaging Jonson's humanity by reading his poetry in Wordsworth's terms, what shall we make of that "callous brag" spoken over the grave of his young son:

> Rest in soft peace, and asked, say, "Here doth lie
> Ben Jonson his best piece of poetry."

Despite the fact that Jonson puts his name into one line, and despite our awareness that this was his own child, we find a more direct reflection of Wordsworth the man in the anonymous "me" lamenting a pseudonymous "Lucy."

In warning us that "the Elizabethan mind was interested in the poet behind the poem hardly at all," that even a lyric was for him "a *thing*, an object created, like a cathedral or bridge," Professors Lamson and Smith wisely insist that we rid ourselves of "lurking tendencies" to attribute too much value to the poet's originality or the extent to which he reveals himself.[36] "The typical Elizabethan poem," observes Miss Agnes Latham, "contains no jot of personal emotion: as often as not it is translated from a Frenchman, who had it from an Italian, who found it in Plato, and the author is perhaps a literary hack, like Robert Greene, living squalidly—and for all that the poem is as fresh as a flower." [37] Many Elizabethan flowers are of course far from fresh, but when the sixteenth-century poet fails, his badness is of a kind different from his romantic successors. Webbe's "Tȳtĕrŭs hāppĭly̆ thōu līest tūmblīng v̆ndĕr ă bēetchtrēe" (I, 283), for example, is wrought with an artifice too apparent; it errs in the direction of the traditional or conventional. When Wordsworth claims that sometimes his "heart with pleasure fills, / And dances with the daffodils" [38] or Keats begins a sonnet with that striking claim, "Oh! how I love," [39] on the other hand, it is not too much artifice against which we react, but an excess of the personality and passion that Webbe altogether lacks. We need not take sides when we contrast the artistic premises of different times. It suffices to use them as partial explanations for the particular virtues and vices of their respective writings. Because the Renaissance put a large premium on imitation, its worst poets are often unbearably trite; because the early nineteenth century stood upon originality, even its best poets are sometimes unbelievably silly.

Nothing better illustrates the kind of involvement Wordsworth expected from his readers than the personal way in which he evidently read the Renaissance sonneteers.

> Scorn not the Sonnet; Critic, you have frowned,
> Mindless of its just honors; with this key
> Shakspeare unlocked his heart; the melody
> Of this small lute gave ease to Petrarch's wound;
> A thousand times this pipe did Tasso sound;
> With it Camöens soothed an exile's grief.[40]

And so on, from Dante through Spenser to Milton. For the poet committed to "the spontaneous overflow of powerful feelings," the narrow limits prescribed by the sonnet form had to be defended either as epitomized ecstasy or, during more tranquil moments, when "Me this unchartered freedom tires," in terms of a "convent's narrow room" where "nuns fret not":

> In truth the prison, unto which we doom
> Ourselves, no prison is: and hence for me,

In sundry moods, 'twas pastime to be bound
Within the Sonnet's scanty plot of ground;
Pleased if some Souls (for such there needs must be)
Who have felt the weight of too much liberty,
Should find brief solace there, as I have found.[41]

Even as he becomes self-conscious about artifice—his genre's
"scanty plot"—Wordsworth must triumph over it by unlocking his
heart and drawing the world-wearied reader into his fourteen-line
refuge.

In the sixteenth century the critics frowned or smiled upon the
sonnet, and the poets defended and exploited it, for entirely different
reasons. Meres at first seems to strike a romantic note when he
salutes Wyatt, Surrey, Sidney, Spenser, and others as "the most
passionate among vs to bewaile and bemoane the perplexities of
loue" (II, 320). Passionate they may sometimes appear, but hardly
seen by Meres as original in the romantic sense, for his list of
Englishmen concludes a catalogue of more than a dozen Greeks
and Latins also "famous . . . for Elegie." And when he celebrates
Shakespeare's sonnets, he applies an adjective that would have
been as odious to Wordsworth as "sonneteer." Notice that it is
neither Shakespeare's originality nor his passion but his artifice that
Meres upholds: "As the soule of Euphorbus was thought to liue in
Pythagoras: so the sweete wittie soule of Ouid liues in mellifluous
and hony-tongued Shakespeare, witnes his *Venus and Adonis*, his
Lucrece, his sugred *Sonnets* among his priuate friends, &c." (II,
317). One begins to wonder whether Wordsworth and Meres are
speaking about the same poems; sonnets as vents to overcharged
hearts and sonnets as sweetmeats are worlds apart. The different
readings cannot be explained in terms of Wordsworth's superior
sensibility and Meres's admittedly commonplace mind, but by
reference to the two centuries that separate them. From Meres's
far more sensitive contemporary, Daniel, we get an even more
"mechanical" approach. Noting the "certaine limit obserued in
Sonnets," the critic frets not over "the weight of too much liberty."
It rather occasions a rhetorical question: "Is it not most delightfull
to see much excellentlie ordred in a small roome, or little gallantly
disposed and made to fill vp a space of like capacitie, in such sort
that the one would not appeare so beautifull in a larger circuite,
nor the other do well in a less? which often we find to be so, according to the powers of nature in the workman" (II, 366).

Besides making a sonneteer look like an engineer, Daniel is rich with other examples of sixteenth-century gospel and nineteenth-century heresy. It would be both amusing and instructive to imagine any romantic poet poring over this Elizabethan *Defence of Rhyme*. How unjust to honor the sonnet for "reducing" the "conceit" to a "iust forme," and how heartless to speak of the form as "neither too long for the shortest proiect, nor too short for the longest, being but onely imployed for a present passion" (II, 366). And how would the author of the Preface to the *Lyrical Ballads* have reacted to "our imagination being as an vnformed *Chaos* without fashion," or a "Nature, that desires a certaintie and comports not with that which is infinite," or the very image of the craftsman, ordering, gallantly disposing, inflating, and deflating raw stuff as if the "circuite" were more important than the experience to be communicated? Wordsworth himself realized that his poems were "so materially different from those upon which general approbation is at present bestowed," and bad reviews led him to criticize his audience's "known habits of association," to plead that the relationship between writer and reader, "must in different eras of literature have excited very different expectations."[42] For all that, his view of the sonnet's "just honors" would have baffled an Elizabethan. "Vse *Sonet* verse," commands James VI, "for compendious praysing of any bukes, or the authouris thairof, or ony argumentis of vther historeis, quhair sindrie sentences and change of purposis are requyrit," and he refers us to the two that preface and summarize his own treatise (I, 223). Equally cold-blooded is the manner in which he surveys all amorous verse. If "ye speik of loue, be warre [how] ye descryue your *Loues* makdome, or her fairnes" (I, 220). Triteness must be avoided, lest "it will appeare ye bot imitate, and that it cummis not of your awin *Inuentioun*, quhilk is ane of the cheif properteis of ane Poete." And therefore,

> gif your subiect be to prayse your Loue, ye sall rather prayse hir vther qualiteis, nor [not] her fairnes or hir shaip; or ellis ye sall speik some lytill thing of it, and syne [afterwards] say that your wittis are sa smal, and your vtterance sa barren, that ye can not discryue any part of hir worthelie; remitting alwayis to the Reider to iudge of hir, in respect sho matches, or rather excellis, *Venus*, or any woman, quhome to it sall please yow to compaire her.
>
> (I, 220)

Gascoigne, from whom James VI freely borrows, will not pontificate over the exact form of the sonnet. Although "some thinke that all Poemes (being short) may be called Sonets," he "can beste allowe to call those Sonnets whiche are of fouretene lynes, euery line conteyning tenne syllables." [43] Unlike James, however, he insists that sonnets may "serue aswell in matters of loue as of discourse" (I, 57), and when the "fine inuention" (upon which the maker must always "grounde" his poem) is amorous, Gascoigne knows exactly what to advise. First, "if I should vndertake to wryte in prayse of a gentlewoman, I would neither praise hir christal eye, nor hir cherrie lippe, etc. For these things are *trita et obuia*" (I, 48). What was trite and obvious for the critic in 1575 could have hardly seemed very fresh to Shakespeare, twenty years later, when he had Demetrius cry,

> O Helen, goddess, nymph, perfect, divine!
> To what, my love, shall I compare thine eyne?
> Crystal is muddy. O, how ripe in show
> Thy lips, those kissing cherries, tempting grow! [44]

Thisbe's beauties also include "cherry lips," perhaps to complement her lover's "cherry nose" (V. i. 188, 322). In any case, Gascoigne's comment substantiates our impression that the noble lovers who laugh at the conventions of the mechanicals' presentation are themselves presented as conventionally as possible.

But Gascoigne does not simply tell us what to avoid. "I would either finde some supernaturall cause wherby my penne might walke in the superlatiue degree, or els I would vndertake to aunswere for any imperfection that shee hath, and thereupon rayse the prayse of hir commendacion" (I, 48). One might, in other words, exploit the conventional, as Shakespeare manages to do so effectively in Sonnet CXXX, noting that his "mistress' eyes are nothing like the sun," that her lips are far from coral red, her breasts less white than snow, her cheeks without roses, voice not altogether musical, hair quite black,

> And yet, by heaven, I think my love as rare
> As any she belied with false compare.

The imperfections mutiply only to "rayse the prayse" of a "she" too "rare" to tally with Petrarchan expectations.

I grant I never saw a goddess go—
My mistress when she walks treads on the ground.

Or one could play the game straightforwardly, premising a cause as "supernaturall" as Spenser's *Amoretti* XXII or LXVIII. In the first, the Lenten season inspires the poet's "devotion" to his own "sweet saynt," as well as other religious metaphors from the tradition of courtly love. The second takes place on Easter, and with the help of a French model (Desportes) and several Biblical echoes, Spenser brings us from the love that triumphed in the Resurrection to a partially secular conclusion:

So let us love, deare love, lyke as we ought:
Love is the lesson which the Lord us taught.

It is of course always possible that a Delia, Diana, Phillis, Licia, Fidessa, or Stella was as beloved as her respective cycle insists. But whether the adored one was a real woman or a convenient organizing principle, an abstract "theme of honor and renown," the sonneteer had to take his art seriously. The more real his passion, the greater the reason to honor it with his best artifice. Hence the amazing number of strategies to circumvent the triteness inherent in a common problem, to prove that whereas others feigned, "I *really really* love." When the sonnet reached its vogue in the 1590's, each man experimented in one or more of the areas suggested by Gascoigne: "If I should disclose my pretence in loue, I would eyther make a strange [unfamiliar, strikingly different] discourse of some intollerable passion, or finde occasion to pleade by the example of some historie, or discouer [reveal] my disquiet in shadowes *per Allegoriam,* or vse the couertest meane that I could to auoyde the vncomely customes of common writers" (I, 48). No doubt some of those "vncomely . . . common writers" really loved their real mistresses, but to succeed, wit had to control heart, and Mistress Art take precedence over the lady in question. The more perceptive poets must have realized that if genuine passion motivated the attempt, the same sincerity might hinder a successful realization; the real lover is, alas, often inarticulate, if not wholly dumb. When Sidney censures "that Lyricall kind of Songs and Sonnets" that "come vnder the banner of vnresistable loue," it is because the singers have failed to convey the *illusion* of sincerity. "But truely . . . if I were a Mistres, [they] would neuer perswade

mee they were in loue; so coldely they apply fiery speeches, as men
that had rather red Louers writings, and so caught vp certaine
swelling phrases, which hang together like a man which once tolde
mee the winde was at North West, and by South, because he would
be sure to name windes enowe,—then that in truth they feele those
passions, which easily (as I think) may be bewrayed [revealed] by
that same forciblenes, or *Energia* (as the Greekes cal it), of the
writer" (I, 201). How easily Sidney could have gone to what we
might think the heart of the matter. "Your speeches are frigid
because your passion is cold. Get thee to a mistress!" Instead, he
asks us to look better to our diction. The fault is not in "apply[ing]
. . . speeches" but in applying them coldly and carelessly, not in
not feeling "those passions," but in not making our mistresses
feel we feel. The warning falls between the passage on the three
wings of Daedalus (I, 195 ff.) and his encouragement to devour and
make wholly ours the "figures and phrases" of others (I, 202 ff.)

Nashe certainly interpreted Sidney's own sonnets in this spirit.
The first edition of *Astrophel and Stella* (1591), which revived an
interest in the sonnet form unknown since Henry VIII's courtly
makers and which was soon to inspire whole cycles of imitations,
was heralded by Nashe as an excellent piece of theater. There are
no autobiographical expectations in the introductory request that
the reader "turn aside into this Theater of pleasure, for here you
shal find a paper stage streud with pearle, an artificial heau'n to
ouershadow the fair frame, & christal wals to encounter your curious eyes, while the tragicommody of loue is performed by starlight" (II, 223). The "chiefe Actor," in fact, is neither Sidney nor
his persona, Astrophel, but Melpomene, the Muse of tragedy,
"whose dusky robes, dipt in the ynke of teares, as yet seeme to
drop when I view them neere. The argument [theme] cruell chastitie, the Prologue hope, the Epilogue dispaire." The anguish of the
starlover for the star is seen as a thing of pearl and crystal,
glittering by starlight, excellently adorned, gallantly disposed, curiously wrought. The despair is only as real as the inky tears that
"seeme to drop." But if Nashe expects the sonnet to furnish actors
and artifice, real life (or the literature that attempts a more authen-
tic reflection of real life) may yield an entirely different picture.
Jack Wilton, *The Vnfortunate Traueller* (1594), takes this "realistic" notice of a sonnet in the making:

> Now would he kneele & kisse the ground as holy ground
> which she vouchsafed to blesse from barrennes by her

steppes. Who would haue learned to write an excellent passion, might haue bin a perfect tragick poet, had he but attended halfe the extremitie of his lament. Passion vpon passion would throng one on anothers necke, he wold praise her beyond the moone and starres, and that so sweetly and rauishingly as I perswade my self he was more in loue with his own curious forming fancie than her face; and truth it is, many become passionate louers onely to winne praise to theyr wits.

He praised, he praied, he desired and besought her to pittie him that perisht for her. . . . From prose hee would leape into verse, and with these or such like rimes assault her.

> *If I must die, O, let me choose my death:*
> *Sucke out my soule with kisses, cruell maide,*
> *In thy breasts christall bals enbalme my breath,*
> *Dole it all out in sighs when I am laide.*

.   .   .   .

Sadly and verily, if my master sayde true, I shoulde if I were a wench make many men quickly immortall. What ist, what ist for a maide fayre and fresh to spend a little lipsalue on a hungrie louer? My master beate the bush and kepte a coyle and a pratling, but I caught the bird: simplicitie and plainnesse shall carrie it away in another world. God wot he was *Petro Desperato*, when I stepping to her with a dunstable tale made vp my market. A holy requiem to their soules that thinke to wooe a woman with riddles.[45]

Although the sonnet of Jack's master is more riddle-ridden than most of Nashe's contemporaries', the critic-novelist leaves little doubt as to which means best suit which ends. Where does the "lover's" passion really lie? Would he seduce the wench or the reader? A maid of either the sixteenth or the twentieth century might prefer more than "simplicitie and plainnesse," but at least a "dunstable tale" does not create the suspicion that her lover is "more in loue with his own curious forming fancy than her face." Jack Wilton is of course only one side of Thomas Nashe. It is likely that Jack, who traffics exclusively in "real" women, would have also rejected Astrophel's artifice as "a coyle and a pratling." Thomas, however, knows how to appreciate art as well as life, realizes that sonnets are written neither to catch the bird nor to soothe one's grief if it escaped, but "to winne praise to [one's] wits" by "sweetly and rauishingly" feigning both.

In a similar vein Sidney concludes his *Apology* with this curse upon poet-haters: "While you liue, [may] you liue in loue, and neuer get fauour for lacking skill of a *Sonnet;* and when you die, your memory die from the earth for want of an *Epitaph*" (I, 207). The context is not wholly serious, for the curse is prefaced by exaggerated promises of the rewards awaiting poet-lovers and patrons. "Thus doing, your name shal florish in the Printers shoppes; thus doing, you shall bee of kinne to many a poeticall Preface; thus doing, you shall be most fayre, most ritch, most wise, most all; you shall dwell vpon Superlatiues" (I, 206). The curses are equally exaggerated. Surely Sidney realized that many men achieved lasting fame without epitaphs, that even more wooed and won without a line of poetry, and that notwithstanding his half-humorous wish, sensible Elizabethan ladies would continue to regard their suitors' anguished rhymes as indexes of fertile minds, not overcharged hearts. Among them was his own sister, the Delia of Daniel's sonnets. Had the Countess of Pembroke gone to the poet instead of the traditions behind the poems, Daniel would have undoubtedly lost his patronage. Yet no poet insists more urgently that he is indeed unlocking his heart: "Heere I vnclaspe the booke of my charg'd soule"; "To saue thine owne, stretch out the fayrest hand";

> These lines I vse, t'unburthen mine owne hart;
> My loue affects no fame, nor steemes [esteems] of art.[46]

The grandest lie of all—had Delia

>   not beene faire, and thus vnkinde,
> My Muse had slept, and none had knowne my minde
>   (VI)—

was similarly appreciated for the manner in which it elaborated upon the conventional. The real heart of the real Daniel is revealed in his dedicatory preface "To the Right Honourable the Ladie *Mary,* Countesse of Pembroke." "I desire onely to bee graced by the countenance of your protection: whome the fortune of our time hath made the happie and iudiciall Patronesse of the Muses. . . . And if my lines heereafter better laboured, shall purchase grace in the world, they must remaine the monuments of your honourable fauour." [47]

Even when information external to the cycle assures us that the poet and his mistress were real lovers, the sonnets themselves remain generally impersonal. One of the *Amoretti*, to be sure, tells us that Spenser received a third kind of love and "grace" from the last of the three Elizabeths in his life (LXXIV); history provides his fiancée's surname, Boyle. Sonnet LX reveals that he is approaching his forty-second year, mainly to anticipate an astronomical conceit, "The spheare of Cupid fourty yeares containes." Preceding and succeeding references to New Year's days (IV and LXII), and the claim of the subtitle of the *Amoretti* and *Epithalamion*, published together in 1595 and "written not long since," make it likely that Sonnet LX was written late in 1593 and that Spenser was therefore born in 1552, a date that tallies with a document revealing his entering Cambridge in 1569.[48] But beyond these explicit references we must venture with extreme caution. Although Spenser could hardly have remained uninspired by the sweet and bitter moments of his eighteen-month courtship, and although all indications of passing holidays and seasons are chronologically consistent, we shall encounter numerous difficulties if we read his other eighty-six sonnets as true narrative or personal confessions, the diary of a lover published by Ponsonby. Did Spenser expect the world to believe that when he first wooed, his lady was "lyke to yse," her "hart frosen cold," and that at forty-one this only made him "burne much more in boyling sweat" (XXX)? Or that he was so blinded by love that he could not distinguish the gold of her hair from the "net" that enclosed it (XXXVII)? And if Elizabeth Boyle did not mind being pictured as "the tyrannesse" who "doth joy to see / The huge massacres which her eyes do make" (X), would she not have resented that highly personal inventory of her charms, concluding with "Her nipples lyke yong blossomd jessemynes" (LXIV), and perhaps pointed out that her fiancé later admits (LXXVI) that only his "sweet thoughts" have lodged in that "bowre of blisse"?

For the Elizabethans, Spenser's mistress included, these were changes rung upon the notes of Petrarch and his French imitators, as conventional as the Bacchus who appears at the Anglican wed-

ding reception in the *Epithalamion* (l. 255), and not necessarily
more realistic than those little Irish boys who allegedly ran up and
down the streets crying "Hymen, Iö Hymen" (ll. 137 ff.). We
may take Spenser's address to his friend, Lodowick Bryskett, and
his anxiety about the completion of *The Faerie Queene* (XXXIII,
LXXX) as direct autobiography. Nor is it harmful to see the
Amoretti's most realistic incidents as having been partly drawn
from life. It would be unfair, for instance, to deny that an angry
Elizabeth actually burned one of Edmund's letters simply because
the heroines of romantic fiction frequently considered this good
form, or because the poet moralizes upon that cruel action so wittily (XLVIII). But had Miss Boyle read the whole cycle as the
history of a genuine courtship, with all its lyrical ups and passionate downs, she might well have suspected her future husband
of an acute emotional instability.

It would of course be impossible to prove that a few sonneteers did not occasionally write primarily to unlock their hearts.
The more widely we read, however, the more we sense that such
a motive was the last thing their readers would have suspected.
The critics discuss the sonnet either as a form or a stance, something "excellentlie ordred" within a specified "circuite," "sugred"
with "pearle . . . & christal," and varied less by content than by
shifting personae entertaining stock situations with "the couertest
meanes" invention can muster. The practitioners all accept the
dozen-or-so available themes, insisting, as Shakespeare, that "I will
not praise that purpose not to sell" (XXI), or "As he [Time] takes
from you, I engraft you new" (XV), or

> If this be error, and upon me prov'd,
> I never writ, nor no man ever lov'd.
>   (CXVI)

Throughout the century some poets die for love and some do not;
most manage to do both, easily ranging from deep devotion to
cynical scorn, from righteous indignation to witty earthiness, sometimes from sonnet to sonnet, occasionally within the space of one.
Reading no more than a few sonnets daily may satisfy existential
expectations; reading several cycles at one sitting forces us to
notice how a game is being played. By examining more than the
very best featured in anthologies, we begin to see that excellence is

wholly a matter of making the trite seem fresh and personal, the
calculated spontaneous and sincere. The greatest and poorest exploit the same themes, follow the same models, attempt the same
covert strategies. The ladies are all celebrated for the same perfections or imperfections; the lovers all experience the same grace or
disdain; even the images and conceits fall into set patterns. To
read the sonnets for content, story, or profound and original reflections upon life is tedious and disappointing; all the events and
ideas of every cycle could be summarized in one paragraph of
prose. When Surrey concluded that "Sweet is the death that taketh
end by love," he was adapting, strengthening, and passing on a
Renaissance commonplace. In his *Sonetto in Vita*, XCI, Petrarch
had decided "Che bel fin fa chi ben amando more," which Wyatt
followed with a vaguer "For goode is the liffe ending faithfully." [49] There was no reason for Surrey to say the same thing unless he could say it better. He no doubt intended that his friends
at Court would recognize the model and compare his imitation to
Wyatt's. Of course the matter was stale. What really important
ideas have not already been expressed? Because they are important,
they are worth refurbishing; because they are old, their new dress
is all the more conspicuous. In these senses alone Surrey would
have stressed the importance of content.

If it is impossible to disprove sincerity, it is equally impossible
to prove it. The very attempt to find the poet behind his poetry
brings us to the varied personae Gascoigne recommends. We
may easily reconcile the personality revealed in *The Prelude* with
that reflected in any of Wordsworth's other poems, but who
would imagine that the author of *Tamburlaine* also wrote *The
Passionate Shepherd to His Love*? Or that when Surrey cried,

> Bryght ys her hew, and Geraldine shee highte;
> Hampton me tawght to wishe her furst for myne

(thus begetting a love story treated sometimes facetiously by
Nashe's *Unfortunate Traveller* and always reverently in Drayton's
England's Heroical Epistles), the real Geraldine (Elizabeth Fitz-
gerald) was only nine years old? [50] Depending upon which direction the sonneteer wished to wade, he needed a Laura or an anti-
Laura, a Stella or a Dark Lady, and what life failed to provide had
to be conjured. In view of Sidney's comments upon the artful

concealing of art, and the businesslike manner in which he discusses how to reveal our passions with "forciblenes, or *Energia*" (I, 201–203), it is quite possible that the real Astrophel was pleased to discover that the real Stella had married a man with a name as promising as Rich.

By the turn of the century, Drayton vows that throughout his cycle, *Idea,*

> No farre-fetch'd Sigh shall ever wound my Brest,
> Love from mine Eye a Teare shall never wring,
> Nor in *Ah-mees* my whyning Sonnets drest,
> (A Libertine) fantastickly I sing,

for his

> Muse is rightly of the *English* straine,
> That cannot long one Fashion intertaine.[51]

About the same time John Donne, that most facile role-player, can at one moment praise and the next condemn

> That loving wretch that sweares,
> 'Tis not the bodies marry, but the mindes;

can ask a very unconventional sun—"Busie old foole," "Sawcy pedantique wretch"—a very conventional, Petrarchan question, whether "her eyes have not blinded thine"; can sometimes smoothly and tenderly plead,

> Sweetest love, I do not goe,
> For wearinesse of thee,

and at other times rasp about that "spider love, which transubstantiates all," or undercut Petrarch by querying,

> Alas, alas, who's injur'd by my love?
> What merchants ships have my sighs drown'd?
> Who saies my teares have overflow'd his ground?
> When did my colds a forward spring remove?[52]

We may say that Donne's idiom is more immediate, cerebral, vital, virile, and passionate than Spenser's, and in these senses it is more "personal" but hardly more "self-revealing." The same can be said of Shakespeare's sometimes anguished, sometimes cynical or even bawdy responses to that faithless dark wanton who haunts his final sonnets. Reactions to literary conventions are themselves literary and soon become equally conventional. Petrarch inverted argues wading farther, not the reality of a Mary Fitton.

And if the sonnets cannot be read as the autobiographies of their makers, even less can they be used as the biography of the age. We should expect the era's responses to evolve toward cynicism, to find Petrarch first honored, then questioned, and finally satirized. But the darkest responses to Petrarchan idealism are full-blown at least two decades before Donne, a fact that indicates that Spenser was not blindly following the only avenue open, but registering a preference. Petrarch had caught his first glimpse of the divine Laura on Good Friday, the day both courtly and Christian lovers might expect grace to abound.

> Blessed may be the day, the month, the year,
> And the season, the time, the hour, the point,
> And the country, the place where I was joined
> By two fair eyes that now have tied me here.
> And blessed be the first sweet agony
> That I felt in becoming bound to Love,
> And the bow and the arrows piercing me,
> And the wounds that go down so deep to move.[53]

In recounting the most amorous of *The Adventures of Master F.J.* (1573), Gascoigne appropriated this blessed experience to celebrate the protagonist's seduction of his host's wife:

> After he grew more bold & better acquaynted with his Mistresse disposition, he aduentured one Fryday in the morning to go unto hir chamber, and theruppon wrote as followeth: which he termed a Frydayes Breakefast.
>
> G. T.

> That selfe same day, and of that day that hower,
> When she doth raigne, that mockt Vulcane the Smith:
> And thought it meete to harbor in hir bower,
> Some gallant gest for hir to dally with.
> That blessed hower, that blest and happie daye,

I thought it meete, with hastie steppes to go
Unto the lodge, wherein my Lady laye,
To laugh for joye, or ells to weepe for wo.
And lo, my Lady of hir wonted grace,
First lent hir lippes to me (as for a kisse:)
And after that hir body to embrace,
Wherein dame Nature wrought nothing amisse.
What followed next, gesse you that knowe the trade,
For in this sort, my Frydayes feast I made.[54]

Surely a blessed meal, a breakfastful of grace, next to which Drayton's flippancy, Donne's "I can love any, so she be not true" ("The Indifferent"), or Shakespeare's "belied with false compare" (CXXX) seems innocent. The cynicism of Gascoigne's final couplet is matched only in the opening and closing scenes of *Troilus and Cressida*, where Pandarus describes the progress of love as "the kneading, the making of the cake, the heating of the oven, and the baking" (ll. 23 ff.) and finally salutes those "Good traders in the flesh" among the audience that has witnessed his fall (45 ff.).

When viewed without romantic spectacles, then, the most lyrical Elizabethan literature can be praised by some, condemned by others, but at least recognized by all for what it was designed to be: artfully artless, passionately contrived, spontaneously artificial, a series of "conceited" variations upon impersonal themes. For better or worse, even the sonneteers work within a tradition; fly with Daedalus's art, imitation, and exercise; look in their hearts to discover foreign models as well as saintly images. Taken individually, they may sometimes convince us that their lines are unpremeditated outcries, that their responses have not even been "recollected in tranquillity." When read collectively, however, they suggest a world of literary actions and reactions, of experiments both imaginative and craftsmanlike, "inspired" by concerns as practical as James's "Reulis and Cautelis" or the tricks of the trade:

Gif your purpose be of loue, to vse commoun language, with some passionate wordis.
Gif your purpose be of tragicall materis, to vse lamentable wordis, with some heich, as [if] rauishit in admiratioun.
Gif your purpose be of landwart [rustic, probably pas-

toral] effairis, to vse corruptit and vplandis wordis.

(I, 218)

How easily James passes from one literary kind to the next, decorously, yet almost mechanically matching specific goals with correct procedures.

THE ELIZABETHAN POET AND HIS OPTIONS

Puttenham is far more careful than James in listing and defining
the poet's options, but his expectations concerning each genre are
just as rigid and formal. Most of his first book "Of Poets and
Poesie" has in fact been written to "set forth . . . very briefly all
the commended fourmes of the ancient Poesie, which we in our
vulgare makings do imitate and vse" (II, 61). Obviously for Puttenham the artistic process begins as the writer selects any legitimate area of exercise and adapts himself to the conditions imposed
by that choice. A survey of those "commended fourmes" should
help us put the sonnet in a proper sixteenth-century perspective; it
may also give us a better idea of what peculiar excellences an
Elizabethan reader anticipated when he sat down to a piece labeled
"satire," "elegy," or the like. To insure that Puttenham's responses
are truly representative, each of his treatments will be supplemented by the opinions of his contemporaries.

(1) *Poetry in general.* "To myne intent," Puttenham explains,
"Poesie" is any "wittie and delicate conceit of man meet or worthy
to be put in written verse, for any necessary vse of the present
time, or good instruction of the posteritie" (II, 25). Regardless of
the genre they essay, in other words, all poets must face two questions. First, is the idea, relationship, thought, or "conceit" worthy
to be dignified by verse? Fourteen years before, Gascoigne had
warned that the "first and most necessarie poynt . . . meete to be
considered in making of a delectable poeme is this, to grounde it
upon some fine inuention. For it is not inough to roll in pleasant
woordes . . . nor yet to abounde in apt vocables or epythetes" (I,
47). Although Sidney insists that "it is not riming and versing that
maketh a Poet" (for Heliodorus's "sugred inuention of that picture
of loue in *Theagines* and *Cariclea*" makes his prose poetic), his

whole defense of poetry assumes that the poem has something
vitally important to say, that the most beautiful flesh is justified
only by a skeleton of profitable thought (I, 160). The second concern shared by all makers is whether the idea is as useful as it is
fine, and here Puttenham lists in descending value the three "matter[s] or subiect[s]" of poetry. Quite naturally the "chief and
principall" matter has always been "the laud, honour, & glory
of the immortall gods" (II, 25). The second most valuable body is
secular, yet thoroughly didactic and uplifting: "the worthy gests
of noble Princes, the memoriall and registry of all great fortunes,
the praise of vertue & reproofe of vice, the instruction of morall
doctrines, the reuealing of sciences naturall & other profitable Arts,
the redresse of boistrous & sturdie courages by perswasion, the
consolation and repose of temperate myndes." Running a distant
third are kinds that seem merely secular, for earthly delight:
"finally, the common solace of mankind in all his trauails and
cares of this transitorie life; and in this last sort, being vsed for
recreation onely, may allowably beare matter not alwayes of
the grauest or of any great commoditie or profit, but rather in
some sort vaine, dissolute, or wanton, so it be not very scandalous
& of euill example."

In an era that would never have understood, much less approved
of, "art for art's sake," Puttenham's poetic hierarchy is very orthodox. The courtier and instructor of courtiers will conclude with
"posies," a line or two "for the nonce" printed on "banketting
dishes of suger plate," or painted on wooden trenchers, or inscribed
"as deuises in rings and armes and about such courtly purposes"
(II, 60), but as a practical Christian he knows that all art is for
man's sake, and that the most useful is for man's spiritual sake.
Such self-evident priorities—God's honor, society's instruction, and
man's everyday solaces—even color Puttenham's "history" of
literary genres. An unknown past is first seen in terms of what
ought to have happened, new poetic kinds emerging to meet man's
spiritual, moral, and recreational needs, and then described as an
indisputable course of events, as if the historian had documents as
well as "logic" on his side.

Assured that his own premises obtained among the earliest
societies, Puttenham announces that hymns to the gentile gods
comprised "the first forme of Poesie and the highest & the stateliest,
& they were song by the Poets as priests, and by the people or

whole congregation, as we sing in our Churches the Psalmes of *Dauid*" (II, 31). The historian is equally confident about the manner in which the second "subiect" or body of poetry developed. "Some perchance would thinke that next after the praise and honoring of their gods should commence the worshippings and praise of good men. . . . But it is not so, for before that came to passe the Poets or holy Priests chiefly studied the rebuke of vice, . . . for as yet . . . there was greater store of lewde lourdaines then of wise and learned Lords" (II, 31–32). Satire, comedy, and tragedy, the "three kinds of poems reprehensiue," answered this purpose; only then were the poet-priests "in conscience & credit bound next . . . to yeeld a like ratable honour to all such amongst men as most resembled the gods by excellencie of function," often deifying with hymns of praise contemporary figures like Bacchus, Hercules, and Theseus (II, 36–37). Moral discipline also found oblique expression in pastoral and epic poetry about the same time. Finally, there is Puttenham's third matter or area of poetry, "the common solace of mankind." Here his transition is less clearly marked. From epic or "historicall poesie" he proceeds to "some litle dittie, or Epigram, or Epitaph," those "slight poemes" in which "inferiour persons with their inferiour vertues haue a certaine inferiour praise to guerdon their good with, & to comfort them to continue a laudable course in the modest and honest life and behauiour" (II, 45). We have now evidently reached the meanest of kinds. But his next chapter discusses "The Forme Wherein Honest and Profitable Artes and Sciences Were Treated," clearly a "matter" included among the second category. And surely the "formes" that follow—amorous affections, rejoicings, lamentations—could and often did instruct and uplift. Of the dozen lesser kinds, in fact, only the "posie" seems to serve "for recreation onely."

If we gloss Puttenham's definitions with his examples, we discover that poetry's three basic kinds are not godly, moral, and amoral, but godly, moral-universal, and moral-particular-occasional. All men will always profit by satire, comedy, tragedy, pastoral, and the praise of heroes in myth or epic, whereas only certain men in special circumstances require epigrams, epitaphs, posies, or "a thousand delicate deuises, odes, songs, elegies, ballads, sonets, and other ditties" (II, 47) to celebrate birth and death, love and marriage, a monarch's coronation or his army's victory. If "this last sort" may also "allowably beare matter . . . dissolute, or wanton," the critic furnishes no instances. The least of the least are courtly trifles, like posies, or those epigrams by "which euery mery conceited man might, without any long studie . . . make his frend sport, and anger his foe, and giue a prettie nip, or shew a sharpe conceit" (II, 56). From heavenly psalms to ale-house epigrams, then, poetry decreases in moral-universal intent, and therefore profit, and therefore value. We could reply that one beautiful stanza of "pure poetry" might outweigh a dozen poor epics, but this would be to answer a question Puttenham never asks.

Neither do Sidney and Harington, the only other critics who anatomize poetry by its "speciall kindes, to see what faults may be found in the right vse of them" (I, 175). Whether we read the *Apologie* or Harington's summary and elaborations upon it, we find a hierarchy of functions and values similar to Puttenham's. Except to point out that "Poetrie is of all humane learning the most auncient and of most fatherly antiquitie, as from whence other learnings have taken theyr beginnings," that "it is so vniuersall that no learned Nation dooth despise it, nor no barbarous Nation is without it," and that "both Roman and Greek gaue diuine names vnto it" (I, 180), Sidney does not support his priorities with a pseudo-chronological survey of emerging genres. His specific defenses of particular kinds, however, are carefully anticipated by a series of value judgments, the most basic of which is that "the ending end of all earthly learning [is] vertuous action," "well dooing and not . . . well knowing onely" (I, 161). Like Puttenham, in other words, he proceeds upon a strictly utilitarian aesthetic; divorced from what Puttenham calls "any necessary vse of the present time, or good instruction of the posteritie" (II, 25), neither learning nor beauty is its own excuse for being. But whereas Puttenham turns the poet's accomplishments into historical periods, Sidney measures them against those of his competitors.

Partly in order to justify poetry's ancient and universal esteem, partly to ensnare the poet's rivals, Sidney first moves rather obliquely. "There is no Arte deliuered to mankinde that hath not the workes of Nature for his principall obiect, without which they could not consist, and on which they so depend, as they become Actors and Players, as it were, of what Nature will haue set foorth" (I, 155). We shall entrap ourselves by taking this claim in a roman-tic sense and having Sidney say, "All fine arts, from painting and sculpture to music and literature, seek to emulate the beauties of terrestrial nature." In the first place the "artists" he lists include astronomers, philosophers, historians, lawyers, physicians, and grammarians; in the second, the poet's "arte" never depends solely upon "the workes of Nature," for he, being "lifted vp with the vigor of his owne inuention, dooth growe in effect another nature, in making things either better then Nature bringeth forth, or, quite a newe, formes such as neuer were in Nature, as the *Heroes, Demigods, Cyclops, Chimeras, Furies,* and such like: so as hee goeth hand in hand with Nature, not inclosed within the narrow warrant of her guifts, but freely ranging onely within the Zodiack of his owne wit" (I, 156). To understand Sidney's strategy, we must understand his initial distinctions, and these will be only as clear as his terms. By "workes of Nature" he means a far larger "landscape" than romantic poetry customarily focuses upon, a universe of all things created by God—angels, stars, men, dogs, plants, and stones—and, in the case of men, all things that God has ultimately set in motion—mortal thoughts, decisions, deeds, history. Like Spenser, he sees God as "this worlds great workmaister," who once "did cast / To make al things such as we now behold." [55] In defending something even more important than poetry, *The Trewnesse of the Christian Religion* (1587), Sidney concludes that "the whole world . . . is a plaine booke laide open to all men, yea even unto Children to reade, and (as yee would say) even to spell God therein," for "Thou madest all things, and whole nature is nothing els but an image of thee." [56]

With God as the Great Craftsman and all of Nature's works as pieces of His artifice, the sense in which the astronomer, lawyer, and physician are artists becomes clearer. Like the poet, they are created things. Unlike the poet, however, they do not themselves create, but imitate, record, catalogue, or otherwise work with and within an area of other created things. The Workmaster is obviously greater than all His works, but when Sidney speaks of these artists as "Actors and Players . . . of what Nature will [desires to] haue set foorth," Nature becomes God the Playwright, joyfully observing His script being properly performed. The "lines" furnished the actor-astronomer are the stars, by which he "setteth downe what order Nature hath taken therein. . . . So doth the Musitian in times tel you which by nature agree, which not. . . . The Lawyer sayth what men haue determined. The Historian what men haue done" (I, 155–156). Whether it is the physician considering the nature of man's body, or the moral philosopher his passions, or the grammarian his speech, each artist is but wading after, not farther than, his Creator. For Sidney, in short, all arts are performing arts, wholly dependent upon and solely consisting of what one of Nature's works, man, can make out of any other. The critic's contemporaries would have added to his list of artists men who might today pass for artisans: jewelers, dressmakers, and carpenters, skilled workmen whose "principall obiect[s]" are inanimate; they would also have admitted those who wrought upon living stuff: farmers as well as landscape architects, trainers of horses and hounds, and drill instructors. We are in a world where the medieval view of arts as crafts, professions, "qualities," or "mysteries" still obtains. Hawking and sailing and managing the great horse in the tournament "all use the materials of nature but exploit the ingenuity of man's mind." [57] Many arts were worthy of a gentleman's attempts, few beneath his interest. Sidney himself versified the divine imperative of Psalm 8:5–6 as,

> For though in lesse then Angells state
>   Thou planted hast this earthly mate:
>   Yet hast thou made ev'n hym an owner
>   Of glorious crown, and crowning honor.
>
> Thou placest hym upon all landes
>   To rule the workes of thine own handes:
>   And so thou hast all things ordained,
>   That ev'n his feete, have on them raigned.[58]

The mark of the artist, then, is the skill with which he shapes his materials, not the character of the stuff itself. Ascham's *Scholemaster* reminds parents and educators of what is "but common in all natures workes. Euery man sees . . . new wax is best for printying: new claie, fittest for working: newshorne woll aptest for sone and surest dying: new-fresh flesh, for good and durable salting" and naturally (or 'nature-like-ly') the "pure cleane witte of a sweete yong babe, is like the newest wax, most hable to receiue the best and fayrest printing." [59] Like fresh wax, clay, and babes, new land is eminently workable. Edward Hayes's account of Gilbert's second voyage to Newfoundland, included among Hakluyt's *Principal Navigations*, at first displays a modern conservationist's enthusiasm for virgin wilderness: "nothing appeared more than nature itself without art, who confusedly had brought forth roses abundantly, wild, but odoriferous, and to sense very comfortable." [60] Within several pages, however, God, Hayes, and Nature are all pleading for artists to turn fertile confusion into order and profit.

> We could not observe the hundredth part of creatures in those unhabited lands, but these mentioned may induce us to glorify the magnificent God, who hath superabundantly replenished the earth with creatures serving for the use of man, though man hath not used a fifth part of the same, which the more doth aggravate the fault and foolish sloth in many of our nation, choosing rather to live indirectly and very miserably to live and die within this realm pestered with inhabitants, than to adventure as becometh men, to obtain an habitation in those remote lands, in which nature very prodigally doth minister unto men's endeavors, and for art to work upon.[61]

Hayes cannot be blamed for encouraging what was to become an ecologist's nightmare. Newfoundland had been created chiefly for man's service and mastery. It is a mark of Hamlet's noble mind to reason: "What a piece of work is a man! . . . How infinite in faculties! . . . in apprehension, how like a god! the beauty of the world! the paragon of animals!" (II. ii. 303 ff.). And it is only his feigned madness or sincere melancholy that forces him to see "this brave o'erhanging firmament" as "no other . . . than a foul and pestilent congregation of vapours." As God's principal and most beautiful work, there was every reason for man to take delight in and husband the rest of His artifice. Castiglione's most eloquent courtier, Peter Bembo, has no difficulty relating what we would term things natural and artificial. In one breath he praises "the beautifull heaven, beautifull earth, beautifull sea, beautifull rivers, beautifull woodes, trees, gardens, beautifull cities, beautifull churches, houses, armies," for "this comely and holy beautie is a wondrous setting out of everie thing." [62] God's delight in design is first revealed by celestial bodies, knitted "together of an order so necessarily framed, that with altering them any one jotte, they should be all lowsed [loosed], and the world would decay." [63] Consider also "the shape of man, which may be called a litle world: in whom every parcell of his bodie is seene to be necessarily framed by arte and not by happe, and . . . the forme altogether most beautifull. . . . The like may bee saide of all other living creatures." But when Bembo proceeds to what he who was "framed by arte" has in turn by his own art framed, we are given a surprising imperative: "Leave *nature*, and come to arte." [64]

If we have read Sidney, Ascham, and Hayes carefully, however, we shall see that Bembo has not confused his terms. God's finished products, the results of His art, *is* Nature, and it is only natural and therefore divinely designed that man should instinctively seek "a wondrous setting out of everie thing," whether his art aims at ordering land, babes, speech, temples, or armies. Between Artist and artist there is no jealous rivalry, only harmony. It is likely that Ascham's readers would have taken the waxen imprint as well as the wax itself as parts of "natures workes," for God, through the bee and then the man, made both. Sometimes what the romantic poets find most natural is celebrated by the Elizabethans as exquisitely artificial. Keats, for example, hears the nightingale, only to be reminded that the world is too much with him: "Still wouldst thou sing, and I have ears in vain— / To thy high requiem become a sod." [65] For Drayton, on the other hand, there is no tension, no longing for release. A Tudor nightingale suggests a consort of viols or madrigals, for she "moduleth her tunes so admirably rare, / As man to set in Parts, at first had learn'd of her." [66] Conversely, of course, what the romantics would condemn as most artificial and therefore highly "unnatural" is honored for matching or outdoing Nature. With very different ends in view, Marlowe can praise Hero's veil of "artificiall flowers and leaues, / Whose workmanship both man and beast deceaues," [67] and Spenser speak of "faire pictures" in which "oftimes we Nature see of Art / Exceld, in perfect limming every part." [68] If this is rivalry, it is most friendly, natural, even God-inspired. The representation by Spenser's artist, like those of Sidney's, makes Nature clearer or more orderly than she might otherwise at first appear, and Hero's veil, like Sidney's musician, renders Nature the tribute of imitation.

By romantic standards the most impertinent artist is the trimmer and pruner invoked by Hayes. But Hayes has God's Word that not all His works are perfect. Even before man fell, God had commanded him to "replenish the earth, and subdue it: and have dominion . . . over every living thing" (Genesis 1:29); after the Fall, the ground was cursed and brought forth thorns and thistles

(3:17–18). The Elizabethans glorified the good earth as much as Wordsworth, but never expected any "impulse from a vernal wood" to teach them "more of man, / Of moral evil and of good" than the sage who wrote Genesis. After Eden, for man or ground to do what came naturally might result in wildness, a disorder never intended. Elizabethan babes do not enter "trailing clouds of glory" but stained with original sin, and children must be tenderly molded, not revered as prophets. To "Heaven lies about us in our infancy" they reply, "Early pricks the tree that will prove a thorn." Noble Tudor savages are Shakespeare's Caliban and Spenser's rapists. So great is Mowbray's hatred that he would dare encounter Bolingbroke even on "the frozen ridges of the Alps," and it is part of Richard II's tragedy that he has not followed the example of his gardener, "old Adam's likeness," in rooting out "the noisome weeds" that choke England, "our sea-walled garden" (I. i. 64; III. iv. 29 ff.). If Cordelia honors the bonds of "nature," so does Edmund; we do not get very far into *King Lear* without expanding the definitions Wordsworth assigns to that word.

Such commonplace assumptions about the interplay between art, artist, and Nature must be kept before us if we are to appreciate the role Sidney claims for the poet. Even in his most inspired moments the mere artist simply improves upon Nature's works, thereby revealing his Maker's own delight in making. Shakespeare spells out this harmony in horticultural terms when Polixenes answers Perdita's refusal to tamper with nature. Man's own artifice, he admits, has played its part in producing "carnations and streak'd gillyvors"; obviously there is "an art which in their piedness shares / With great creating nature" (*The Winter's Tale*, IV. iv. 82 ff.). But there is nothing illegitimate in the desire or act of crossbreeding, for

> nature is made better by no mean [method]
> But nature makes that mean; so over that art,
> Which you say adds to nature, is an art
> That nature makes. You see, sweet maid, we marry
> A gentler scion to the wildest stock,
> And make conceive a bark of baser kind
> By bud of nobler race. This is an art
> Which does mend nature—change it rather; but
> The art itself is nature.

Clearly God, or Apollo, or Great Creating Nature, enjoys the prospect of art (man) responding to art (Himself), and by art (artifice) changing art (works of Nature). And certainly Polixenes's gardener, although "inclosed within the narrow warrant of [Nature's] guifts," comes close to growing "in effect another nature." Perhaps Sidney would have placed him alongside the apprentice poet, who exercises with "artificiall rules" and "imitatiue patternes" in order someday to imitate creatively, and who realizes that before "freely ranging onely within the Zodiack of his owne wit," the "highest flying wit [must] haue a *Dedalus* to guide him" (II, 156, 195). But even if the gardener occasionally rivals the poet with "formes such as neuer were in Nature," Nature's works remain his "principall obiect" and, more important, his carnation never incites virtuous action.

The poet, moreover, mends or changes Nature not by minor graftings but with wholesale and wholly unrealistic representations. Nature never set forth trees so fruitful, nor friends so constant, nor warriors so valiant (I, 157). When the poet wades beyond writing as a craft or art, he leaves behind all "Actors . . . of what Nature will haue set foorth" and becomes the sole rival of God the Playwright. Lest this claim be thought blasphemous, "too sawcie a comparison to ballance the highest poynt of mans wit with the efficacie of Nature," Sidney returns us to Genesis. His comparison has rather rendered

> right honor to the heauenly Maker of that maker, who, hauing made man to his owne likenes, set him beyond and ouer all the workes of that second nature, which in nothing hee sheweth so much as in Poetrie, when with the force of a diuine breath he bringeth things forth far surpassing her dooings, with no small argument to the incredulous of that first accursed fall of *Adam:* sith our erected wit maketh vs know what perfection is, and yet our infected will keepeth vs from reaching vnto it.
>
> (I, 157)

Couple this to his earlier remark that whereas Nature's "world is brasen, the Poets only deliuer a golden" (I, 156), and it becomes clear that Sidney is undermining the very foundations of his poet-hating opponents. Poetry, to be sure, is unrealistic; it bespeaks a discontent with the way things are because God has instilled in us a yearning for the way things should be, and once were, in the golden world of Eden. All poetry is "a representing, counterfetting, or figuring foorth" (I, 158), and of its "three seuerall kindes," the "chiefe both in antiquitie and excellencie" is that which represented "the inconceiuable excellencies of GOD," from the songs of David and Solomon to those of "a full wrong diuinitie," the hymns of Orpheus, Amphion, and Homer. The man who holds "the holie Ghost in due holy reuerence" dares not speak against the poetry He inspired in the Old Testament. The bad theology of Moses's and David's pagan contemporaries, on the other hand, proves that their wits were at least "erected" enough to seek to know, if not truly grasp, "what perfection is." Whereas certain Jews and Christians have recorded special revelations, all nations reflect in their poetry the evidence of God's common grace: a delight in His still lovely though partially flawed earth; an imagination that, though partly tainted itself, is yet capable of remembering a time when the rose had no thorns, and only gold was real and natural.

By encouraging this common desire to redeem Nature, then, the true poet not only makes us all the more conscious of our "infected will," but helps to disinfect it. Among the earliest body of writers, both Orpheus and the author of Job represented the excellence of God in order to teach and delight; both were therefore genuine poets. A second group, however, followed rather than outdistanced Nature's works; it includes moral philosophers like Cato, historians like Lucan, and even the Virgil of the *Georgics*, a natural philosopher. Although instructive and delightful, "thys second sorte is wrapped within the folde of the proposed subiect" (I, 158), borrows from "what is, hath been, or shall be." The third group, the "right Poets," whose defense Sidney is chiefly interested in, are men who "range, onely rayned with learned discretion, into the deuine consideration of what may be, and should be" (I, 159). In this sense some painters qualify as poets rather than mere artists, for when we see a Lucrece whom the painter saw only in his mind's eye as an idea of "vertue" to be realized with "outwarde beauty," we have a more imaginative representation than those of "the meaner sort of Painters (who counterfet onely such faces as are sette before them)." Neither kind of painter, of course, has a place among Sidney's list of the "most notable" of poetry's "speciall denominations": "*Heroick, Lirick, Tragick,*

Comick, Satirick, Iambick, Elegiack, Pastorall, and certain others"
(I, 159). But Sidney is so determined in discounting verse and other
ornaments, so anxious to include imaginative prose, so insistent
that "the right describing note to know a Poet by" is the "fayning
[of] notable images of vertues, vices, or what els, with that
delightfull teaching," that one suspects he would sooner invent a
new genre to save Lucrece than admit a single prosaic rhymer.

Having made such all-important "supra-generic" distinctions,
Sidney proceeds to a more detailed argument. He will "first . . .
waigh this latter [the third] sort of Poetrie by his works" (what
the poet and his rivals each accomplish, I, 160–175); "then by his
partes" (what each of the poet's kinds specifically accomplishes,
175–181) and, finally, as a "counter-ballance," against the claims of
poet-haters ("obiections . . . worthy eyther of yeelding or answering," 181–207). The first victory is Sidney's from the outset. He
need only remind us that what we call "learning" is the "purifying
of wit, . . . enritching of memory, enabling of iudgment, and en-
larging of conceyt," and that its ultimate goal is obviously "to lead
and draw vs to as high a perfection as our degenerate soules,
made worse by theyr clayey lodgings, can be capable of" (I, 160).
It follows that some disciplines "are but seruing Sciences," at best
helping us toward "well knowing," not "well dooing." Mathematics,
for example, attracts some by its "certainty of demonstration," but
he who has mastered the art may still "draw foorth a straight line
with a crooked hart." Similarly, we have observed the astronomer
falling into a ditch while gazing upward and the philosopher who
lacks self-knowledge. In a roundabout way the proper use of any
science or body of knowledge contributes to virtuous action: The
saddler makes a good saddle, which advances the "nobler facultie"
of horsemanship, and thus skillful soldiery, and thus great deeds.
But which man moves us most directly, skillfully, and irresistibly?

Surely not the poet's principal challengers. The moral philosopher
approaches with "a sullen grauity," teaching without delighting,
"setting downe with thorny argument the bare rule, . . . so hard of
vtterance, and so mistie to bee conceiued, that one . . . shall wade
in him till hee be olde before he shall finde sufficient cause to bee
honest" (I, 164). The historian, on the other hand, insofar as
his "old Mouse-eaten records" are not "built vpon the notable
foundation of Heare-say," is too involved with particular truths to
handle general reasons (I, 162, 164). Restricted to "his bare *Was*,"

he must often attempt to satisfy us with disconnected, incoherent events; at other times, when cause can be documented and events put in series, his accounts are plainly "a terror from well dooing, and an incouragement to vnbrideled wickednes" (I, 168, 170). His examples may move us more than the philosopher's precepts, but in which direction? Because the lawyer's concern is with public rightness, not private virtue, and because Sidney, "with all reuerence," excludes the divine, for he deals not with earthly learning ground-plot of a profitable inuention" (I, 185). Granted, the poet but supernatural revelation,[69] only the poet (or those philosophers and historians who are essentially poetical) remains. The poet attacks man's "imaginatiue and iudging powre": in our mind's eye we see Ulysses longing for Ithaca or hear old Anchises crying amid the destruction of Troy, and we have a picture that speaks more movingly about love of country than the philosopher's abstract definitions or historian's bare facts. Christ realized that His parables "would more constantly . . . inhabit both the memory and iudgment" than "morall common places" or literal truths (I, 166–167). After all, whether or not men understand the philosopher's terms, they know what is good and bad, and that it is good to do good. The real problem is in making them desire both to practice the good they already know, and to seek it further. The poet, who "holdeth children from play, and old men from the chimney corner," traps even "those harde harted euill men who thinke vertue a schoole name," for they, too, are "content to be delighted, which is al the good felow Poet seemeth to promise" (I, 172–173). Sidney's hero, in short, is a confidence man working on the angels' side.

With the same ease, spirit of fair play, and even more relish, Sidney turns from those who challenge the poet to those who merely hate him. Some automatically scorn all rhyming and versifying, forgetting that many poets do neither, and many nonpoets do both. Even assuming that all verse is poetry, however, is there nothing noble in the attempt to gain harmony, order, and proportion in our speech, seeing that "Speech next to Reason, bee the greatest gyft bestowed vpon mortalitie"? (I, 182). Besides, if "reading bee foolish without remembring," and knowledge useless if forgotten before it has been applied, the lowliest rhyme is an aid to memory. But there are other "false or feeble" complaints. Of those who contend that the poet's time should be more profitably employed, Sidney simply asks for an end higher than moving men to virtue. Those who call poetry "the mother of lyes" forget that it speaks of what should or should not be, not of what was or is. Obliged to affirm the truth on the basis of incomplete knowledge, the historian can hardly escape lying. From the poet, on the other hand, even a child expects something more essentially true than the literal truth, the truth of holy Nathan's fable about David and Bathsheba, or of Aesop's tales, fiction that serves "as an imaginative groundplot of a profitable inuention" (I, 185). Granted, the poet sometimes gives his inventions historical names like Cyrus (and Aeneas!), but this is to make his "picture the more liuely," to show "what men of theyr fames, fortunes, and estates should doe," certainly "not to builde any historie" (I, 185–186).

This is one of the few places where the *Apologie* could be better organized. Sidney's example of the bishop on the chessboard supports his contention that the poet must also name his players, but not that a prince of Cyrus's fame be named Cyrus. He could have escaped the appearance of special pleading by a reminder of how the poet builds *upon* history (I, 169). More important is the apparent evasion or oversight in his command not to "giue the lye to things not affirmatiuely but allegorically and figuratiuelie written" (I, 185). However he feigns or improves upon the "bare *Was*," the poet affirms the truth of "should have been," and must be censured for false visions, *mis*representations of the nature of men and things, lack of figurative verisimilitude, or for trying to make the world golden by denying that brass exists. Here again the critic might well have included a summary of his earlier remarks. "What Philosophers counsell can so redily direct a Prince, as the fayned *Cyrus* in *Xenophon*? . . . or a whole Common-wealth, as the way of Sir *Thomas Moores Eutopia*? I say the way, because where Sir *Thomas Moore* erred, it was the fault of the man and not of the Poet, for that way of patterning a Common-wealth was most absolute, though hee perchaunce hath not so absolutely perfourmed it: for the question is, whether the fayned image of Poesie or the regular instruction of Philosophy hath the more force in teaching" (I, 166). For Sidney, there is no such thing as amorality, and art is not art if immoral. His distinction between More the poet's "way" and More the man's (and probably thinker's) "fault" indicates an awareness of truthful affirming as well as imaginative feigning, and a tolerance for the man unable to manage both.

Sidney's earlier insistence that he speaks of "the Arte, and not of the Artificer" [70] reappears in his last rebuttals, and in his concluding explanation for the bad poetry that presently inundates England. If poetry is not the "mother of lyes," it surely seems "the Nurse of abuse, infecting vs with many pestilent desires" and encouraging effeminacy. The worst evil, of course, is a perversion of the best good. Poetry does not abuse but is abused by man's wit. Painters may similarly produce "wanton shewes," heretics distort Holy Writ, and if a darning needle poses less danger than a sword, it also offers less help. As for effeminacy, poetry has always been "the companion of the Campes" (I, 188), and the Sphinx cannot remember that allegedly blessed time when men delighted only in doing and not imagining. There remain only those who cry, "as if they out shot *Robin Hood*, that *Plato* banished [poets] out of hys Common-wealth." Sidney is not the only apologist who admits that his "burthen is great; now *Plato* his name is layde vpon mee" (I, 190). Nashe's claim that recent artists are reviving poetry, "though it were executed ten thousand times, as in *Platos*, so in Puritanes common wealth" (I, 319), suggests how readily precisian poet-haters exploited the *Republic* and its author's reputation. Whereas Sir Thomas Hoby had given England the beautiful world of Castiglione's *Courtier* (1561), his son's tastes evidently ran along severer lines; the thirty-fifth chapter of Matthieu Coignet's *Politique Discourses on trueth and lying*, translated by Sir Edward in 1586, begins not unexpectedly:

> PLATO wrote that Poetrie consisted in the cunning inuention of fables, which are a false narration resembling a true, and that therein they did often manifest sundrie follies of the gods; for this cause he banished and excluded them out of his common wealth, as men that mingled poyson with honie. Besides thorough their lying and wanton discourses they corrupt the manners of youth, and diminish that reuerence which men ought to carrie towards their superiors and the lawes of God, whom they faine to be replenished with passions & vice. And the principall ornament of their verses are tales made at pleasure, & foolish & disorderly subiectes, cleane disguising the trueth & hystorie, to the end they might the more delight; and for this cause haue they bin thrust out of sundry cities.
>
> (I, 341)

Whether or not such a Plato is real, it was the Plato Sidney faced, and as usual his strongest allies were Italian, not English.[71] Nashe himself simply agrees that no "politique Counsailour . . . will ioy or glorie . . . in that some stitcher, Weauer, spendthrift, or Fidler hath shuffled or slubberd vp a few ragged Rimes," claims that only "such kind of Poets were they that *Plato* excluded," and then proceeds to discuss poetry as "a more hidden & diuine kinde of Philosophy, enwrapped in blinde Fables and darke stories" (I, 327–328). Lodge makes no greater headway, attacking Plato's foolish theology and overturning both Gosson's and Plato's "presisnes" with other authorities and a similar lecture on allegory (I, 65–77). To see how large a shadow Plato the puritan cast upon feigning poets, we need only note how often Renaissance writers either insist that their stories contain dark conceits and are not to be taken literally, or support their "true histories" by citing firsthand witnesses or reliable informants, or wade farther with what strikes us as sheer invention but which they see (or pretend to see) as elaborations upon commonly received facts, additional truths their predecessors neglected to mention. For all his earlier remarks on the kind of truth poetry affirms, even Sidney reveals some anxiety. In his opening paragraphs he accuses Plato of being a poet in disguise, beautifying the bones of philosophy with the comely skin of invention, "for all standeth vpon Dialogues, wherein he faineth many honest Burgesses of Athens to speake of such matters, that, if they had been sette on the racke, they would neuer haue confessed them" (I, 152). Twenty pages later we are again reminded that Plato was imaginative enough to employ the "flowers" or "masking rayment of Poesie."

When he confronts Plato the expeller of poets, however, Sidney balances uneasily between grudging admiration and Nashe's mode of invective. He is first amazed that this "most poeticall" philosopher would "defile the Fountaine out of which his flowing streames haue proceeded" (I, 190). Is this because he, like other philosophers, made "a Schoole-arte of that which the Poets did onely teach by a diuine delightfulnes," and "like vngratefull Prentises, . . . not content to set vp shops for themselues, . . . sought by all meanes to discredit their Maisters"? Surely, thinks Sidney, "a man might maliciously obiect" that Plato's hatred proceeded from jealousy. Many Greek cities claimed Homer, many "banished Philosophers as not fitte members to liue among them"

(I, 190). Next, Sidney lodges a few of his own malicious objections. The commonwealth from which Plato banished poets was one in which he allowed "communitie of women," and elsewhere he authorizes that "abhominable filthines" of homosexuality. Only after such sharp parrying does Sidney proceed to make peace with his adversary, reminding us that Plato meant to rail upon the abuse of poetry, that the poets nourished but did not invent superstition while the philosophers replaced it with atheism, that Plato's *Ion* gives "high and rightly diuine commendation to Poetrie," and that his "Lyons skin" has been wrongfully used by poet-haters to justify their "Asse-like braying" (I, 192).

Having discovered that the real lion granted to "Poesie more then my selfe doe, namely, to be a very inspiring of a diuine force, farre aboue mans wit," we wonder whether Sidney did not intend his earlier hostility to be taken ironically. Although irony may cover a multitude of critical sins, it is the ironist's responsibility to assure us, however indirectly, of where his values finally lie. To find that Plato is, after all, our friend, does not quite take the sting out of "vngratefull Prentises" or "abhominable filthines," and when Sidney concludes with a Lodge-like summoning of poetry's admirers, his attitude still seems ambiguous: "And euen the Greek *Socrates* . . . is sayde to haue spent part of his old tyme in putting *Esops* fables into verses. And therefore, full euill should it become his scholler *Plato* to put such words in his Maisters mouth against Poets" (I, 192). How should we take the critic's "should"? Harington, who paraphrases Sidney, offers no help here (II, 203–204).

Probably because he is less confused himself, Sidney is much easier to follow in his closing survey of contemporary literature (I, 193–207) and in his intermediate commentary on poetic genres (I, 175–181). Although "our tongue is most fit to honor Poesie," the main reason "it is not esteemed in Englande is the fault of Poet-apes, not Poets" (I, 205). Whether good wits who remained idle or idle wits who became busy were ultimately responsible, bad money is presently driving out or at least intimidating the potentially good. Poetry needs men possessed of both great natural ability and a craftsmanlike patience in mastering the proper rules and models. Art, imitation, and exercise must guide inspiration; without the latter men will not fly, and without the former they will but fly awkwardly. Genius must stoop in order to conquer, and even *The Shepheardes Calender* and *Gorboduc* leave room for improvement. Exercising "forebackwardly" has resulted in tragedies absurdly ordered, comedies that confuse delight with laughter, and lyrics foundering under frigid rhetoric. The gloomy scene Sidney finally paints is brightened only by those "smally learned Courtiers" who follow what practice has taught as "fittest to nature," and therefore write "according to Art, though not by Art," and by the great poetic potential he finds in the "mingled" nature of his mother tongue (I, 203–204). But he is similarly optimistic in his earlier survey of the excellent "parts, kindes, or *Species*" that classical and Continental models now offer as areas in which Englishmen may exercise forwardly. No matter that some of these genres—tragic and comic, prose and verse, epic and pastoral—are often as "mingled" as the English language itself; "if seuered they be good, the coniunction cannot be hurtfull" (I, 175). And no matter, we should add, that the critic tells us that he is "perchaunce forgetting some, and leauing some as needlesse to be remembred." He has earlier (I, 159) listed eight kinds "and certaine others." We must not be tripped up by Sidney's calculated informality. His detailed examination deals only with the same eight genres previously noted, and treats them in a precisely reversed order. His list, moreover, closely parallels Puttenham's, whose order we shall follow.

(2) *Epic poetry.* Since Puttenham catalogues poetic "matters" or "subiects" according to their spiritual, moral, and recreational usefulness, and since Sidney rests his whole case upon the poet as the foremost inciter of virtuous action, it should not surprise us to find both critics ranking heroic or epic poetry as the noblest of secular kinds. In his chapter "Of Poemes and Their Sundry Formes," Puttenham first honors "Poets *Heroick*," those who "gaue themselues to write long histories of the noble gests of kings & great Princes entermedling the dealings of the gods, halfe gods, or *Heroes* of the gentiles, & the great & waighty consequences of peace and warre" (II, 26). Chief and most ancient among the Greeks was Homer, and among the Latins, Virgil. But it is not until his "chronological" survey allows him to treat "Of Historicall Poesie" that he explains why the heroic poem "is of all other next the diuine most honorable and worthy, as well for the common benefit as for the speciall comfort euery man receiueth by it" (II, 40–41). To establish this literary kind's "benefit" and "comfort," Puttenham of course reasons anthropologically and ethically rather than aesthetically. Next to man's reason and will, nothing is "more

noble or more necessary to the actiue life then memory," for when he is able to compare the present with the past, he may well consider the future and be resolved as to "the best course to be taken in all his actions and aduices in this world" (II, 41). To all this Machiavelli would have subscribed, and we wonder if Puttenham really intends to justify the epic by reference to the Renaissance commonplace that the study of history is practical.

It soon becomes obvious, however, that "history" simply means virtue-inspiring examples. The memory may be stored with what was only if this coincides with what should have been. Probably glancing at Sidney's remarks about the poet building upon history, he tells us that "these historical men . . . vsed not the matter so precisely to wish that al they wrote should be accounted true, for that was not needeful nor expedient to the purpose, namely to be vsed either for example or for pleasure" (II, 42). To Puttenham, then, "historicall" never means more than "set in the past"; our modern definition is incidental and almost irrelevant. The differences between Thucydides's "worthy and veritable historie" and Xenophon's "fained and vntrue" biography are not nearly so important as the fact that both men wrote "to one effect, that is for example and good information [that is, good informing or shaping] of the posteritie" (II, 43). We are similarly expected to profit not only by Musaeus's "true treatise of the life and loues of *Leander* and *Hero*," but from Homer's "fabulous or mixt report" of the *Iliad* and *Odyssey* (II, 42). But if "historicall poesie" may include matters feigned and in prose, it should always center in "great and excellent persons & things, that the same by irritation of good courages (such as emulation causeth) might worke more effectually" (II, 43). It should also employ a high style; hence the poets who used the hexameter for its "grauitie and statelinesse."

Puttenham's admiration of the epic is characteristic. Webbe calls it "that princelie part of Poetrie, wherein are displaied the noble actes and valiant exploits of puissaunt Captaines, expert souldiers, wise men, with the famous reportes of auncient times" (I, 255). And he too cites the "Heroycall workes of *Homer* . . . and the heauenly verse of *Virgil*" as "the summe and grounde of all Poetrie." Harington follows a similarly moral line. "By all mens consent," the "chiefe of all" poetry is the heroical, "allowable . . . to be read and studied without all exception" (II, 210–211). To be sure, Harington admits, with a glance at Sidney's own notice of the romantic epic (I, 186), "*Cupido* is crept euen into the Heroicall

Poemes," but "of all kinde of Poesie the Heroicall is least infected therewith" (II, 209), and he need only show that Ariosto's muse is even more chaste than Virgil's. Evincing a better sense of strategy, Sidney saves the epic for his last and most telling arguments. "There rests the Heroicall, whose very name (I thinke) should daunt all back-biters; for by what conceit can a tongue be directed to speake euill of that which draweth with it no lesse Champions then *Achilles, Cyrus, Aeneas, Turnus, Tideus,* and *Rinaldo?*" (I, 179). That which teaches and moves men "to the most high and excellent truth," makes justice and magnanimity "shine throughout all misty fearefulnes and foggy desires," and decks out Virtue "to make her more louely in her holyday apparell" is obviously "the best and most accomplished kinde of Poetry." As the image of each action stirs and instructs the mind, so the lofty image of each Worthy "most inflameth the mind with desire to be worthy, and informes with counsel how to be worthy."

From the above we may safely gather several "chronistic" expectations. When an Elizabethan sat down to a piece labeled "heroicall," he anticipated above all an educational experience, instruction perhaps more delightful and compelling than Elyot's *Gouernour* or Ascham's *Scholemaster,* and certainly more adventurous than Hoby's *Courtier,* but equally devoted to what we should call "character guidance." He would also expect a grave and stately style, whether in prose or verse, but not simply because decorum demanded that "waighty consequences" be loftily articulated. Behind the artistic desire to match matter with meter there seems to have been an even more fundamental concern about subordinating high matter to high morality. The epic is primarily a thing to challenge and cure our ignoble desires. The pill itself is, for example, the precept that Virgil meant to represent in Aeneas. The sugar coating is the exciting narrative, the great deeds that Virgil had Aeneas perform in order to exemplify those virtues. The majestic language, as well as all epic similes, catalogues, descriptions, roll calls, and such furniture, merely form a bottle of sufficient dignity to house so noble a pill. Puttenham admittedly asks that the hero be of high social station "because the actions of meane & base personages tend in very few cases to any great good example" (II, 43). His ultimate reason for this requirement, however, is not social but ethical. The higher a man's degree, the more means he has to serve his own appetites with impunity. Since "continence in a king is of greater merit then in a carter" (II, 44), a monarch's chastity is more heroic. All this insistence upon the instructive would not of course have prevented many readers from hoping for an interesting story, and some for beautiful ornament. But when they turned to the greatest Elizabethan epic, they would have found nothing odd in its author's straightforward and solemn confession of purpose:

> The generall end therefore of all the booke is to fashion a gentleman or noble person in vertuous and gentle discipline: which for that I conceived shoulde be most plausible and pleasing, being coloured with an historicall fiction, the which the most part of men delight to read, rather for variety of matter then for profite of the ensample, I chose the historye of King Arthure.[72]

(3) *Lyric poetry*. Some ancient poets, continues Puttenham, were "more delighted to write songs or ballads of pleasure, to be song with the voice, and to the harpe, . . . [and] were called melodious Poets (*melici*), or, by a more common name, *Lirique* Poets: of which sort was *Pindarus, Anacreon,* and *Callimachus,* with others among the Greeks, *Horace* and *Catullus* among the Latines" (II, 26). Next to the lofty designs of the epic, pleasant "songs or ballads" seem small things, and we might expect the critic to encounter some difficulty in measuring them against his standards of high moral seriousness. This difficulty is temporarily circumvented, however, for the only songs Puttenham at first mentions are those hymns of praise gentile poets offered to their noble princes —paragons like Bacchus, Ceres, Perseus, Hercules, and Theseus —"who thereby came to be accompted gods and halfe gods or goddesses" (II, 37). Puttenham's genres, in short, developed analogically as well as practically. Poets first celebrated the gods' glories, next taxed the vices of the great and mean with Satire, Old Comedy, New Comedy, and Tragedy, and then, having reprehended evil, thought it only reasonable to reward virtue by returning to songs of commendation (II, 36). And when we realize that the commendations were for "honorable and iust conquests" as well as marriages and the making of "wholsome lawes," we can see how "epic" the lyric can be. Puttenham, in fact, concludes his account of "heroicall" or "historicall poesie" by noting the "Hymnes & *Encomia* of *Pindarus* & *Callimachus,* not very histories, but a maner of historicall reportes" (II, 43).

Those *"Ditties* or *Odes"* that Campion believes he "may call *Lyricall"* (II, 346) bring us closer to the songs the Elizabethans actually composed and sung than the highly instructive epic strains at first heard by Puttenham. Defending metrics rather than morality, Campion is free to illustrate how one form of verse "will excellently fit the subiect of a *Madrigall,"* and how his "voluble" (and languishing) trochees are "fit to expresse any amorous conceit" (II, 348–349). Three of his four examples, and especially the song to "Rose-cheekt *Lawra,"* tally with our sense of the lyric, its melody, subjectivity, warmth, and disarmingly simple mood, a thing that more delights than teaches, obviously capable of beautifying even immorality. Puttenham might have been able to defend Campion's encomium of Queen Elizabeth, "Faiths pure shield, the Christian *Diana"* (II, 347), but only by ignoring the final stanzas, which paint a picture and advance a mood rather than a precept. His other three songs clearly deal with "amorous conceits," that "wantonnes and loue and toying" that Harington confesses are "many times" found in the pastoral and epigram as well as the sonnet (II, 209). It is significant that Harington does not follow Sidney's lead in defending the lyric. Perhaps the intervening eight years had produced too much beauty to argue against, had driven him to a weaker stand: "yet euen the worst of them may be not ill applied, and are, I must confesse, too delightfull."

For Sidney, of course, the purpose to which the song is sung is the central issue, and lyrics "ill applied" are simply not admitted. "Is it the Liricke that most displeaseth, who with his tuned Lyre, and wel accorded voyce, giueth praise, the reward of vertue, to vertuous acts? who giues morrall precepts, and naturall Problemes, who sometimes rayseth vp his voice to the height of the heauens, in singing the laudes of the immortall God" (I, 178). Pindar proved this "kinde most capable and most fit to awake the thoughts from the sleep of idlenes, to imbrace honorable enterprises," and if he also sometimes praised "victories of small moment, matters rather of sport then vertue," it was the fault of the poet, not his genre (I, 179). Clearly a sporting Pindar, for all his "gorgeous eloquence," runs far behind the rough voice and rude style of the blind minstrel's "olde song of *Percy* and *Duglas."*

In weighing this allegedly hurtful species of poetry, Sidney does not even suggest an awareness of "amorous conceits." Negative implications are obvious, however, and we may wonder whether the critic is not undermining his own sonneteering. Perhaps Sidney would have answered that whereas Astrophel does not always move us to virtuous action, a proper reading of *Astrophel and Stella* will; the poet as confidence man must play many roles. Later in his treatise he does entertain the charges that "Comedies rather teach then reprehend amorous conceits. . . . [T]he Lirick is larded with passionate Sonnets: The Elegiack weepes the want of his mistresse" (I, 186). The apology comes by way of apostrophe. "Alas, Loue, I would thou couldest as well defende thy selfe as thou canst offende others." Grant love of beauty to be a beastly fault (though beasts themselves do not have it), grant that lovely Love deserves our hate (though moral philosophers have set forth its excellence), and grant that some poems inspire "not onely loue, but lust, but vanitie, but . . . scurrilitie," and we have still only proved that men abuse poetry, not the reverse. But we have also left unsolved what kinds of passion the lyric may rightfully be "larded with." At the conclusion of his survey, Puttenham is more explicit. The lyric developed quite decorously. The first songs were for the gods, the second deified noble princes, and the third celebrated human love. But whether "amorous affections and allurements were vttered" as "odes, songs, elegies, ballads, sonets" or any other of the "thousand delicate deuises" and "ditties," those affections were chaste, "honest. . . . [C]ommendable, yea honourable . . . loue well meant" (II, 46–47). The lyric, in short, still honors "laudable things," even though it has lost its epic affinities.

(4) *Elegiac poetry*. Since Puttenham concludes his discussion of amorous utterances by casually joining the lyric's "songs or ballads" to elegies and sonnets, it may at first seem odd that his initial survey of forms establishes elegiac poetry as an independent genre and ignores the sonnet altogether. Besides "melodious . . . or . . . *Lirique* Poets," there "were an other sort, who sought the fauor of faire Ladies, and coueted to bemone their estates at large & the perplexities of loue in a certain pitious verse called *Elegie*, and thence were called *Elegiack*: such among the Latines were *Ouid*, *Tibullus*, & *Propertius*" (II, 26–27). Surely, we should conclude, Puttenham would have us place the sonnet under elegiac poetry, not among "songs or ballads of pleasure." Supporting this impression is Meres's notice of Wyatt, Surrey, Sidney, Spenser, Daniel, Drayton, and Shakespeare as "famous . . . for Elegie, . . . the most passionate among vs to bewaile and bemoane the perplexities of loue" (II, 320–321). For Harington, on the other hand, it is the

pastoral, sonnet, and epigram that may "sauour of wantonnes and loue and toying" (II, 209). He evinces no anxiety about the elegy; it is simply "still [always] mourning." And from Sidney, we should gather that for wooing fair ladies elegies are about as suitable as the Lamentations of Jeremiah. Let us reverence "the lamenting Elegiack, which in a kinde hart would mooue rather pitty then blame, who bewailes . . . the weakenes of mankind and the wretchednes of the world: who surely is to be praysed, either for compassionate accompanying iust causes of lamentation, or for rightly paynting out how weake be the passions of wofulnesse" (I, 176).

Puttenham and Meres, in other words, see the elegy and, by implication, the sonnet primarily as love plaints, whereas Harington and Sidney speak of elegiac verse as a mournful, contemplative, and compassionate response either to this world's real wretchedness ("iust causes of lamentation") or to man's less than justified (and unheroic?) reactions to that world (rightly representing "the weakenes of mankind" and his sorrows). Of all Elizabethan definitions, Sidney's "compassionate accompanying iust causes of lamentation" comes closest to our own, an expectation nourished by the most anthologized elegies of the seventeenth (Milton's *Lycidas*), eighteenth (Gray's *Elegy Written in a Country Churchyard*), and nineteenth (Shelley's *Adonais*) centuries. Whether what is lost is a particular person or human potential, and whether the grief is personal or philosophical, we know that the loss is great, that it is fitting to lament it, and that it has nothing to do with "the perplexities of loue." But we must not exaggerate the differences between Puttenham and Sidney. The former speaks of elegists bemoaning "their estates at large" as well as seeking female favors, and the latter's reference to frail man's frailer sorrows could include the amorous. Puttenham first defines and much later defends the elegy; Sidney is first defending it with a rather special definition, and only after he has weighed every part of poesy does he confront that elegist who but "weepes the want of his mistresse" (I, 186). We are bound to encounter contradictions when we compare one man's cataloguing of forms with another's defense of a particular kind.

We have already glossed one of Sidney's transitions (from the lyric as a trumpet call to brave deeds to the lyric as larded with passionate sonnets) by noting Puttenham's stipulation that our songs, if amorous, be chaste. His final comment on man's varied responses to love may again be used to complement Sidney's different reactions to the elegy. For Puttenham, love is not less "puissant and passionate," nor its course less smooth, simply because it is true and honest. To reflect this aspect of human experience, the poet therefore "requireth a forme of Poesie variable, inconstant, affected, curious, and most witty of any others, whereof the ioyes were to be vttered in one sorte, the sorrowes in an other" (II, 46–47). Puttenham, in short, not only tells us the extent to which Sidney would have allowed the loss of one's mistress as a just cause for lament. He also suggests the reason why we find the sonnet listed under both lyric and elegy. When the sonneteer is "laughing, reioysing, & solacing the beloued," he is writing lyrics; when he is "sorrowing, weeping, lamenting," or even "railing, reuiling, and cursing," he is writing elegies. Obviously the skillful maker will vary his cycle with both genres.

Both the sonneteer and his kindred dealers in amorous conceits had, moreover, logic and tradition to support their definition of the elegy as a love plaint. Love is surely a fundamental part of that often lamentable human condition. Our more restricted sense of this kind as fit only to mourn and praise the dead had not yet evolved. The Elizabethans, glancing upon classical models as potential areas of exercise, saw the elegy first as a form especially suited to certain subjects. "The next verse in dignity to the *Hexameters* is the *Carmen Elegiacum*," notes Webbe, "which consisteth of foure feete and two od sillables, viz: the two first feete, eyther *Dactyli* or *Spondoei* indifferent, the[n] one long sillable, next two *Dactyli* and an other long sillable" (I, 285). Whether the first two feet are dactyls or spondees, the two "long" or lengthened syllables make the verse run slowly:

$$// \quad // \quad / \quad /-- \quad /-- \quad /$$
$$// \quad /-- \quad / \quad /-- \quad /-- \quad /$$
$$/-- \quad /-- \quad / \quad /-- \quad /-- \quad /$$

and classical poets therefore used it for subjective meditations, reflections upon death, love, war, and real or mythological scenes.[73] The three ancients Puttenham mentions—Ovid, Tibullus, and Propertius—were all chiefly known for their love-elegies, and after maintaining that the elegy "serueth especially to the handling of loue and dalliances," Webbe cites two lines from Ovid's *Amores*. From the elegy, then, the Elizabethan reader expected a certain mood and tone, but no special subject; under this kind he could have easily fitted some of the *Amoretti* and many of Spenser's

Complaints ("Containing Sundrie Small Poemes of the Worlds Vanitie") as well as *Astrophel*, Spenser's "Pastorall Elegie upon the Death" of Sidney.

(5) *Comic poetry* and (6) *Tragic poetry*. Since a large portion of the preceding chapter has examined dramatic theories and practices, we need only briefly note the nature and applicability of Puttenham's opening remarks concerning those poets who "wrote onely for the stage" (II, 27). "*Comicall* Poets," from Aristophanes to Terence, sought "to recreate the people with matters of disporte" and therefore "set forth in shewes [and] pageants, accompanied with speach, the common behauiours and maner of life of priuate persons, and such as were the meaner sort of men." "*Tragicall* Poets" like Euripides, Sophocles, and Seneca, on the other hand, "medled not with so base matters, for they set forth the dolefull falles of infortunate & afflicted Princes." But whether the poet handled private persons or public figures, dealt with common or special behavior, and worked toward "disporte" or dole, his chief end was to reprehend, and the first third of Puttenham's survey is devoted to showing how Old Comedy, then New Comedy, and finally tragedy were used by satirists seeking more effective social correctives. Sidney's and Harington's expectations are equally severe. The latter finds tragedy "representing onely the cruell & lawlesse proceedings of Princes, mouing nothing but pitie or detestation" (II, 209), and the former watches the comic playwright imitating "the common errors of our life . . . in the most ridiculous and scornefull sort that may be; so as it is impossible that any beholder can be content to be such a one" (I, 176–177).

We have already observed the dangers of racking tragedies like *Hamlet* upon contemporary critical notions. Since the great art of any era often subverts commonplace expectations, we did not restrict Shakespeare's means or ends to those his first audience probably anticipated. To appreciate how the artist enriched or at least changed those meanings, however, we also found that we could not ignore the context in which he worked, including the traditions and expectations against which he reacted. By measuring *Hamlet* against, rather than restricting it to, tragic theories, we were, in effect, basing a relevant method of inquiry upon often irrelevant ideas and forcing critics like Sidney to gloss a kind of tragedy they could hardly have foreseen. We could have employed the same method to arrive at similar conclusions about the disparities between comic theories and practices. "Naughtie Play-makers and Stage-keepers haue iustly made [the comic] odious," cries Sidney, but when this kind is not abused, we shall imme-diately recognize and eventually be cautioned from the actions "of a nigardly *Demea*, of a crafty *Dauus*, of a flattering *Gnato*, of a vaine glorious *Thraso*" (I, 177). So far Shakespearean comedy is at least sometimes correct. For Terence's stern, stingy father, Shakespeare gives us Silvia's parent, the Duke of Milan, who pre-fers rich Thurio to either gentleman of Verona; for the crafty Roman slave, flattering parasite, and braggart soldier, we need only notice how Falstaff compounds and outdoes all three.

Generally speaking, however, Shakespeare abuses comedy. We may not "be content to be such a one" as Falstaff, or Costard, or Bottom, but because their creator has not presented them "in the most ridiculous and scornefull sort that may be," we find their "common errors" a source of amusement,[74] all-too-human frailties that we would no more wish to change than the humorous eccen-tricities of the neighborhood philosopher. Comedy rightly de-signed, according to Sidney, is bound to evoke the proper re-sponse: "There is no man liuing but, by the force trueth hath in nature, no sooner seeth these men play their parts, but wisheth them in *Pistrinum* [that is, sentenced to hard labor, "on the rockpile"]: although perchance the sack of his owne faults lye so behinde hys back that he seeth not himselfe daunce the same measure; whereto yet nothing can more open his eyes then to find his own actions contemptibly set forth" (I, 177). It is difficult to find many Shake-spearean characters to whom we may respond so "properly." The great majority are affected, often foolish, but rarely vicious. For every "melancholy Jaques" or Malvolio, we get a dozen like Holo-fernes, or Berowne, or Aguecheek. And since the social fabric has not been seriously threatened, our final reaction is something like Dumain's as he enters the Show of the Nine Worthies: "Though my mocks come home by me, I will now be merry" (V. ii. 626-627). These sprightly, cerebral, yet partly sentimental worlds have as their touchstone, "as all is mortal in nature, so is all nature in love mortal in folly" (*As You Like It*, II. iv. 51-52). The most recurrent vice is taking one's self too seriously, not a very deadly sin but perhaps wider spread today than those more obvious faults Sidney would punish so severely. Even the more classical and satirical Ben Jonson is tainted by a charitable good humor, especially in his earlier, Elizabethan moments. By the mid-

seventeenth century, it is Frenchmen like Moliere who best practice Sidney's preachment that "Laughter hath onely a scornful
tickling" (I, 199).

These obvious differences between *dramatic* theories and facts
suggest two limitations to the method we have followed in our
examination of other genres. First, the audience did not always
get what it anticipated. Secondly, that audience, especially in the
case of drama, may well have had anticipations other than those
the critics mention. Our method has forced us to equate the expectations of a large silent majority with a very small and articulate
minority. Although every spectator at the Globe might have understood Sidney's artistic views and professed his moral concerns,
they had also been nourished by those rougher plays the critic
despised, worlds in which clowns jostled kings and "Horn-pypes"
accompanied "Funeralls" (I, 199). Such theoretically indecorous
minglings of moods and social stations Shakespeare cultivated, giving his audience what stage tradition had led them to anticipate,
but in surprisingly new forms. Cleopatra does receive "all joy of
the worm," as the Clown intends, for its "biting" proves truly
"immortal" (V. ii. 245 ff.). For nondramatic genres, on the other
hand, the critics are probably a better index of received opinion.
The man who read an English epic was likely to have read the
classics and been aware of critical ideas and ideals. The reader
who sat down to *The Faerie Queene*[:] *Disposed into Twelve
Books, Fashioning XII Morall Virtues* no doubt received more
delight than either its forbidding subtitle or contemporary definitions of the epic promised. There is nothing moral about a good
yarn well spun, but Spenser realized that "the most part of men,"
even those who disdained "naughtie Play-makers," read "rather for
variety of matter then for profite of the ensample."

To determine the extent to which the lyric and elegy were
read for the right critical reasons, we should first have to decide
whether the right reasons are those the critics usually employ to
defend these kinds, or those which slip in by way of aside; then
we should have to separate our "average" reader into the same
variety of general temperaments and special moods that we today
also see and experience. Above all, we must be careful not to
equate the popular with the low, or the high with the educated
and refined. The "great fault" of the popular playwrights, according to Sidney, "is that they styrre laughter in sinfull things"
(I, 200). In addressing a far more cultured audience than the

average theatergoer, Harington not only insists that the "lasciuious"
episodes in Ariosto's epic were "ment . . . to breed detestation"
(II, 214). He also believes he sees some readers "searching already for these places of the booke, and you are half offended
that I haue not made some directions that you might finde out
and read them immediately." A volume that ran through many
editions was popular, but popularity does not stamp it as solely
bourgeois. Ascham tells us, for example, that he found Lady Jane
Grey "in her Chamber, readinge *Phoedon Platonis* in Greeke, and
that with as moch delite, as som ientlemen wold read a merie tale
in *Bocase* [Boccaccio]." [75]

(7) *Pastoral poetry.* After touching on poets heroic, lyric,
elegiac, comic, and tragic, Puttenham notes still "others who
mounted nothing so high as any of them both [the dramatists],
but, in base and humble stile by maner of Dialogue, vttered the
priuate and familiar talke of the meanest sort of men, as shepheards, heywards [herdsmen], and such like: such was among the
Greekes *Theocritus,* and *Virgill* among the Latines; their poems
were named *Eglogues* or shepheardly talke" (II, 27). Despite its
humble style and apparently mean matter, however, the pastoral
came "long after the other *drammatick* poems" (II, 40). To be sure,
Puttenham grants his mistaken opponents, that "which we commonly
call by the name of *Eglogue* and *Bucolick*" celebrates a primitive
society, and even imitates that "first familiar conuersation, . . .
babble and talk vnder bushes and shadie trees" (II, 39). We consequently hear refrains similar to what must have been the "first
disputation and contentious reasoning, and their fleshly heates
growing of ease the first idle wooings, and their songs made to their
mates or paramours either vpon sorrow or iolity of courage the
first amorous musicks." For all such evidence of primitive innocence, though, pastoral poetry was written by highly sophisticated men, "not of purpose to counterfait or represent the rusticall
manner of loues and communication, but vnder the vaile of homely
persons and in rude speeches to insinuate and glaunce at greater
matters, and such as perchance had not bene safe to haue beene
disclosed in any other sort" (II, 40). Surely, reasons Puttenham,
Virgil meant to shadow forth or "treat . . . by figure matters of
greater importance than the loues of *Titirus and Corydon,*" and
pastoralists like Mantuan have continued thus "to containe and
enforme morall discipline."

From Sidney and Webbe we get much the same. The former
expects poet-haters to attack the pastoral first, for "where the
hedge is lowest they will soonest leape ouer" (I, 175). Sidney's
defense is primarily to demonstrate how high a hedge they have
actually undertaken. The "poore pype . . . of *Melibeus*" reveals
"the miserie of people vnder hard Lords or rauening Souldiours";
that of Tityrus, "what blessednes is deriued to them that lye lowest
from the goodnesse of them that sit highest." And often "vnder the
prettie tales of Wolues and Sheepe" we eventually discover "whole
considerations of wrong dooing and patience." Webbe similarly
observes what we should call the pastoralist's stance and setting:
"vnder these personnes, as it were in a cloake of simplicitie," poets
of "great pythe and learned iudgment" either "sette foorth the
prayses of theyr freendes, without the note of flattery, or
enueigh grieuously against abuses, without any token of bytter-
nesse" (I, 237, 262). Virgil's *Eclogues* and Spenser's *Shepheardes
Calender*, for example, both yield like incitements to moral discipline: gallant, yet oblique praises of their respective sovereigns;
complaints against fickle friends; "pretty Pastorall contentions."
But Webbe is equally enthusiastic about concerns in Spenser that
he has not found in Virgil, those parts that inveigh against "the
loose and retchlesse lyuing of Popish Prelates" or "shame and dis-
prayse . . . idle and ambitious Goteheardes" (I, 264). Naturally
many denuciations are "vttered somewhat couertly, especially the
abuses of some whom he would not be too playne withall," but
although unsure of "hys speciall meaning," Webbe knows the
general matter is "so skilfully . . . handled, as any man may . . .
picke out much good sence in the most obscurest of it."

The Greek and Roman models to which all three Elizabethans
allude are of course long on love and very short on satire. Theocritus and Virgil would have been amazed at Harington's anxiety
over the pastoralist's inclusion of "loue and toying," and almost as
baffled by the Renaissance desire to make rustic scenes yield veiled
commentaries upon political and ecclesiastical corruptions. Under a
far from covert allegory, Virgil admittedly reveals a personal
grievance against the military for expropriating his land, hence
Sidney's reference to "the miserie of people vnder . . . rauening
Souldiours." But his principal end is not, as Puttenham claims and
Sidney and Webbe imply, "to containe and enforme morall discipline." The transition from urbane shepherds to reforming pastors
was chiefly inspired by a fifteenth-century Italian, Battista Spag-

nuoli, whom Erasmus entitled "The Christian Virgil" ("*Christianus Maro*").[76] It is this second Mantuan who stands behind the religious debates of the May, July, and September portions of *The Shepheardes Calender*, months that "The Generall Argument" defines as neither "plaintive" nor "recreative," but "moral, [and] which for the most part be mixed with some satyrical bitternesse." [77] And it is probably this same later Mantuan who led contemporary critics to overemphasize the detections of abuses in the earlier.

Another reason why even the almost wholly amorous Theocritus had "to insinuate and glaunce at greater matters" is that all art was ultimately defended on moral grounds. For the strange notion that the end of poetry is wholly to delight, we must go to a small minority of Italians like Castelvetro and Robortelli.[78] The English critics, on the other hand, all argue that each literary kind serves a specific ethical or spiritual use. When the genre inclines toward realistic representation (for instance, always comedy, often tragedy and epic, and sometimes lyric and elegy), the theorists assume that it must have been intended as either a positive incitement to virtue or a negative, usually satiric warning from vice. Although it is likely that Plautus and Terence, for example, enjoyed the realistic pranks of their "crafty Dauus" as much as we, Sidney vows that all right-minded men will wish him chained to the mill. Conversely, when the literary kind inclines toward scenes as "unrealistic"—or at least as morally unpromising—as the "prettie tales of Wolues and Sheepe," the critics contend that it could not have been written merely to describe, speculate upon, or entertain. Hence the worthiness of the piece must be salvaged in good medieval fashion. We assume that the delightful is but an allegorical coating to sweeten the kernel of truth, that pastoral woodnotes must contain some satiric or otherwise instructive burden.

The penchant to moralize upon each ancient's spectacle is almost universal. Like every Elizabethan critic, Stanyhurst knows that "thee chiefe prayse of a wryter consisteth in thee enterlacing of pleasure wyth profit," and since Virgil's *Aeneid* and Ovid's *Metamorphoses* have "so wisely alayed" these elements, the "shallow reader may bee delighted wyth a smooth tale," while the "diuing searcher may bee aduantaged by sowning [sounding, examining] a pretious treatise" (I, 136). Stanyhurst obviously considers himself one of those "reaching wyts" who realize "what deepe and rare poynctes of hydden secrets *Virgil* hath sealde vp" in Aeneas's adventures, and who will therefore proceed beyond "gnibling vpon thee outward ryne of a supposed historie" to the more important task of "groaping thee pyth that is shrind vp wythin thee barck and bodye." Webbe similarly upholds the Ovidian mysteries. Granted, the *Metamorphoses* consists of "fayned Fables . . . and poeticall inuentions, yet beeing moralized according to his meaning, and the trueth of euery tale beeing discouered, it is a worke of exceeding wysedome and sounde iudgment" (I, 238).

The deep meanings under the pretty myths of Amphion and Orpheus are as apparent to the courtiers, Sidney and Puttenham, as they are to the schoolmaster, Webbe. The bark or body is that Amphion built the walls surrounding Thebes by charming the stones into place with his lyre; the pith or kernel is that an early lyric poet, using sweet and eloquent persuasion, soothed and unified his contemporaries' hard hearts and ushered in cities and civilization. Orpheus accomplished much the same among wild beasts, "figuring thereby," according to Puttenham, the education of his own "rude and sauage people" (II, 6; cf. also I, 151–152, 234). Critics as unlike as Sidney and Nashe agree that poetry enshrines divers secrets, and envelops all-important truths. The courtier concludes his case by asking the reader "to beleeue . . . that it pleased the heauenly Deitie, by *Hesiod* and *Homer*, vnder the vayle of fables, to giue vs all knowledge, Logick, Rethorick, Philosophy, naturall and morall," and that "there are many misteries contained in Poetrie, which of purpose were written darkely, least by prophane wits it should bee abused" (I, 206). The bohemian is no less insistent that poetry is "a more hidden & diuine kinde of Philosophy, enwrapped in blinde Fables and darke stories," pearls of precepts "that delight more if they be deeper sette in [the] golde" of sweet verse and varied invention (I, 328–329). Just as "in Vines the Grapes that are fayrest and sweetest are couched vnder the branches that are broadest and biggest, euen so in Poems the thinges that are most profitable are shrouded vnder the Fables that are most obscure." And it is exactly such "grapes" that Lodge throws at his poet-hating opponent, Stephen Gosson: "you remember not that . . . vnder the shadow of byrds, beastes, and trees the follies of the world were disiphered; you know not that the creation is signified in the Image of Prometheus, the fall of pryde in the person of Narcissus; these are toyes, because they sauor of wisedome which you want" (I, 65).

Despite frequent allegorizings to justify literature on the side of morality, the critics rarely attempt to justify allegory itself, to explain how this mode may enrich the writer's art and the reader's aesthetic experience. Would Puttenham's ancient pastoralists have used "the vaile of homely persons" if they had been assured political security? Was Webbe's Spenser concerned about art as well as personal safety when he refused to be "too playne withall"? And did Sidney's Hesiod and Homer write darkly only because they feared profane wits? Nashe's simile seems symptomatic. Allegorical poems are likened to vines not in order to emphasize the similarity of their fruit, but to show that the best of each plant is equally difficult to harvest. We are not searching for the "fayrest and sweetest" when we struggle to get underneath the poem's broadest "branches"; the reward we expect is medicinal rhubarb rather than succulent grapes. There is of course something especially delightful about allegory, for while plain fables excite the senses, obscure ones also bring the intellect into play. The allegorist, in other words, is a teacher who doubly delights; he first tempts us, as any other poet does, with the beauty of the rind, and then offers to the "diuing searcher" the additional enjoyment of "groaping thee pyth." One wonders, however, whether the richer experience of the diver can really be called aesthetic. Stanyhurst's "shallow reader" is at least responding to beauty, whereas his "reaching wyts," who exchange a "smooth tale" for a "pretiouse treatise," seem to be unraveling a riddle. More important, having broken down the code, having discovered what Virgil really meant to say, they are content. Their responses could have been artistic, and not merely intellectual, if they had only tried to see whether the pith is not more meaningful, as well as more attractive, *because* of its rind; whether the allegorist's code is not an essential part of his meaning rather than a sweet covering. Since beauty is not its own excuse for being, and the imagination is distrusted, the critics hasten to assure us that the fable $(x + y + z)$ is exactly equal to the moral $(1 + 2 + 3)$. And since Amphion is no more than a mathematical equation, we are free to cancel out the beautiful letters as mere ornaments, concessions to our fallen condition, and retain only the numbered precepts. The emphasis, in short, is on the meaning of the whole as no more than the sum of the moral meanings of each of its parts. We forget that the allegorist's part may be "$y + 2$," not "$y = 2$," and that the meaning of his whole might be radically altered by rearranging the parts.

Perhaps the best indication of the common critical reluctance to defend allegory on the side of art appears in Puttenham's discussion "Of Figures and Figuratiue Speaches" (II, 159 ff.). Here allegory, "a duplicitie of meaning or dissimulation vnder couert and darke intendments"—it is later christened the "Figure of False Semblant" (II, 169)—joins metaphor, "an inuersion of sense by transport," "*Ironia*, or the Drie Mock; *Sarcasmus*, or the Bitter Taunt; . . . *Hiperbole*, or the Ouerreacher, otherwise the Loud Lyer" and dozens of other devices that the poet employs "to inueigle and appassionate the mind" (II, 160, 169). All these figures, Puttenham acknowledges, are "in a sorte abuses or rather trespasses in speach, because they passe the ordinary limits of common vtterance," and are deliberately used "to deceiue the eare and also the minde, drawing it from plainnesse and simplicitie to a certaine doublenesse, whereby our talke is the more guilefull & abusing." For these reasons the critic believes that before courts of law arguments should be stated as literally as possible; the "straite and vpright mind of a Iudge" must not be beguiled by "such manner of forraine & coulored talke" (II, 160). The poet, on the other hand, is "a pleader . . . of pleasant & louely causes and nothing perillous, such as be those for the triall of life, limme, or liuelyhood," and his "doublenesse" is directed at gentlewomen and courtiers rather than severe judges. In this safer context, figurative utterances will "tende but to dispose the hearers to mirth and sollace by pleasant conueyance and efficacy of speach," and only such as displease our sense of decorum, decency, or proportion will not be allowed.

For Puttenham, then, allegory, metaphor, or any other figure is at best a delightful ornament, something entirely external, "a certaine liuely or good grace set vpon wordes, speaches, and sentences" (II, 165). What we should call the language of poetry is merely the literal truth dressed to a decorously guileful advantage. Puttenham never appears to suspect that some poets immediately see a thing as "$y2$"; instead, they first fasten upon a "2" with the mind of a judge and then, having moved outside the more perilous, practical affairs of the court, substitute a "y" for poetic effect. More important, Puttenham is no readier to defend "y" for its own sake than Sidney, for the most skillful representation of a merely harmless "2" will delight but not instruct. Both critics, in short, seem to celebrate the imagination only as a useful moral tool. The poet's responsibility is to turn the message into a fable; the reader's, to work in reverse. One darkly suspects that Puttenham, for all his lists of figures, does not see that in the best poetry of his own time, form is part of the meaning. He could easily have catalogued the "trespasses" with which Shakespeare deceives our senses when Richard II's Queen addresses her deposed husband:

> thou most beauteous inn,
> Why should hard-favour'd grief be lodg'd in thee,
> When triumph is become an alehouse guest?
> (V. i. 13–15)

He would have recognized the personifications: that unwelcome guest, Grief, with his sour features, and that lodger whom any host gladly entertains, Triumph or Success. He would also have noticed the metaphors: courtly, refined Richard is an elegant hotel; Cousin Bolingbroke, a cheap tavern. The Queen is using "the Loud Lyer" to offer Triumph "the Bitter Taunt." Had her "inuersion of sence by transport" been lengthened, we would have encountered "False Semblant," for what is allegory except extended metaphor? But would Puttenham have noticed that something other than delight had been lost in his paraphrase? To judge from his definitions of poetry (any idea "meet or worthy to be *put in* written verse") and poetic figure ("good grace *set vpon* . . . speaches"), it seems unlikely.[79]

The longest and most explicit discussion of the nature and function of allegory is offered by Harington. He is conventional in his belief that those myths that record the gods' "fowle deeds, . . . contentions, . . . adulteries, . . . [and] incest" were originally intended to rebuke the "enormous faults" of historical princes (II, 213–214). Puttenham similarly treats Jupiter's amorous adventures as a "figuratiue & misticall" application of "some part of an historie," the real lusts of a real ruler figuratively reprehended (II, 29). Like the other critics, Harington is also quick to show how many great teachers preferred to speak obliquely, from Demosthenes, Nathan, and Christ to Henry VIII's recalcitrant prelate, Bishop Fisher, each of whom feigned either to delight or to evade being punished for a direct reprimand. Finally Harington displays a characteristically Elizabethan facility for "groaping thee pyth." The story of Tantalus, who "sits vp to the chinne in water, and yet is plagued with thirst," obviously "signifies the selfe same man . . . that wallows in plentie, and yet his miserable minde barres him the vse of it" (II, 208). The example of a miserly magistrate of London is then brought in to support the gloss. Consequently, we no longer have the Tantalus of Homer and Pindar, punished with poetic justice for stealing from the gods the food that bestowed immortality. The myth now comes closer to the moral of Dyer's "My Mind to Me a Kingdom Is."

It is only when Harington singles out the myth of Perseus that he becomes uncharacteristically precise and helpful. The creative process remains the same; the allegorist is still seen placing one meaning upon or within another. In analyzing the process, however, Harington gives us two rinds and several possible cores.

> First of all for the litterall sence (as it were the vtmost barke or ryne) they set downe in manner of an historie the acts and notable exploits of some persons worthy memorie: then in the same fiction, as a second rine and somewhat more fine, as it were nearer to the pith and marrow, they place the Morall sence profitable for the actiue life of man, approuing vertuous actions and condemning the contrarie. *Manie times* also vnder the selfesame words they comprehend some true vnderstanding of naturall Philosophie, *or somtimes* of politike gouernement, *and now and then* of diuinitie: and these same sences that comprehend so excellent knowledge we call the Allegorie.
>
> (II, 201–202. Italics added.)

With these expectations Harington is able to see why *"Perseus* sonne of Iupiter is fained by the Poets to haue slaine *Gorgon,* and, after that conquest atchieued, to haue flown vp to heauen." In the outer, historical-literal rind, we first learn that a great warrior, "by the participation of *Iupiters* vertues which were in him, or rather comming of the stock of one of the kings of Creet, . . . slew *Gorgon,* a tyrant in that countrey *(Gorgon* in Greeke signifieth earth), and was for his vertuous parts exalted by men vp vnto heauen." And from the inner, and therefore more hidden, moral rind, we discover that a very wise man, "endewed with vertue from aboue, slayeth sinne and vice, a thing base & earthly signified by Gorgon, and so mounteth vp to the skie of vertue."

Even though he has yet to penetrate the domain of allegory, Sir John's method has already led him astray. "Gorgon" has nothing to do with earth or things earthly; *gorgos* is simply the Greek word for "terrible" or "fierce," an apt title for both the snaky-haired

Gorgo-Medusa whom Perseus killed and her two immortal sisters who pursued him, the Gorgons Sthenno and Euryale. For Perseus's ascent to the sky of fame (historical sense) or of virtue (moral), on the other hand, the interpreter need not strain. At her death Medusa gave birth to the winged horse, Pegasus, whom her conqueror promptly mounted. But Harington certainly appears arbitrary when he turns the literal Jupiter into a king of Crete, and overingenious when he likens the moral Jupiter's visit to Danaë in a shower of gold to the endowing of Perseus "with vertue from aboue." Even greater wonders are in store, however, for the myth also yields three allegorical readings. First, the "natural allegory," *natural* in the sense that "man [is] one of the chiefe works of nature" (II, 202): "the mind of man being gotten by God, and so the childe of God killing and vanquishing the earthlinesse of this Gorgonicall nature, ascendeth vp to the vnderstanding of heauenly things, of high things, of eternal things, in which contemplacion consisteth the perfection of man." Next comes "a more high and heauenly Allegorie, that the heauenly nature, daughter of *Iupiter*, procuring with her continuall motion corruption and mortality in the inferiour bodies, seuered it selfe at last from these earthly bodies, and flew vp on high, and there remaineth for euer." Finally there is "also another Theological Allegorie: that the angelicall nature, daughter of the most high God the creator of all things, killing & ouercomming all bodily substance, signified by *Gorgon*, ascended into heauen" (II, 202–203).

Under Harington's guidance, Perseus has become an Everyman, even an Everything: the terror of tyrants, the slayer of sin, the aspiring mind or Platonic contemplator, the soul freed from its bodily prison, and finally an exemplum verging on the New Testament exhortation to be crucified with Christ. A determined allegorist cannot be denied, and we are inclined to accept Harington's brag that "the like infinite Allegories I could pike out of other Poeticall fictions, saue that I would auoid tediousnes" (II, 203). It was probably a fear of being tedious that led him to gloss only a small part of Perseus's story. Surely the man who could squeeze so much pith out of so little rind had the dexterity to explicate Medusa's head and Andromeda's rescue on at least five different levels. As each layer of meaning is stripped away only to reveal another even more marvelous, we may feel that Harington is simply playing a rather involved joke upon the Perseus he really saw, and upon any reader who accepted his multiple equations. If he is allegorizing only in jest, however, his humor remains as dry and subtle as the apparently humorless Stanyhurst's. The "principall cause" why "men of greatest learning and highest wit in the auncient times did of purpose conceale these deepe mysteries of learning, and, as it were, couer them with the vaile of fables and verse" was not a fear that profane wits would rashly abuse their science, nor the realization that precepts are better remembered when cast into verse. The main motivation for both coverings, verse as well as fable, was to produce "one kinde of meate and one dish . . . to feed diuers tastes. For the weaker capacities will feede themselues with the pleasantnes of the historie and sweetnes of the verse, some that haue stronger stomackes will as it were take a further taste of the Morall sence, a third sort, more high conceited then they, will digest the Allegorie" (II, 203).

For the reader who had finished Virgil's *Eclogues* still assuming that a sheep is a sheep is a sheep, or had left the *Metamorphoses* with the shallow notion that these were fleshly, not spiritual, adventures, the glosses of Puttenham, Sidney, Stanyhurst, Webbe, and especially Harington must have been intimidating. What man will confess himself so weak-stomached as to have been led astray by the *Aeneid*'s pleasant fable and sweet verse, so low conceited that he had allowed its art to encourage a subliterary response? If Astrophel's disclaimer may be trusted, the tendency to allegorize was found even among the readers of lyric and elegy.

> You that with allegories curious frame
> Of others children changlings use to make,
> With me those paines for God-sake doe not take,
> I list not dig so deepe for brasen fame.
> When I see *Stella*, I doe meane the same.[80]

Sidney realizes that we need not always allegorize to uncover a moral, that his sonnets can incite virtuous action without turning a real woman into an abstract principle. Many a critic, however, seems to allegorize as if he believes that his poet's morality can be saved in no other way, and he becomes so distracted by the task of proving that his poet should be allowed that he forgets to convince us that he should be read.

The widespread uneasiness over the sweet outer rind, the customary haste to get under the poem's branches, and the common claim that this poet is, down deep, as instructive as that philosopher may tell us why the Puritans, with equal sincerity, enjoyed Ovid as well as the Song of Solomon, and why they eventually produced many more Bunyans than Miltons. And if we require no Elizabethan commentary to be assured of *The Faerie Queene*'s morality, certainly Harington tells us something about the way in which Spenser's allegory was and should still be read. Even so facile an allegorist as Sir John does not expect all levels of every fable always to obtain. We may count upon Spenser always to delight the "weaker capacities" with sweet verse and a pleasant history or "litterall sence," and also to offer to "stronger stomackes" precepts "profitable for the actiue life" within the second, moral rind. But we should not expect the allegorical core(s) to remain consistent. "Manie times" we shall detect "naturall Philosophie," "somtimes" affairs of state, and "now and then" even theological matters. There is no better caution for the "high conceited" modern reader who would "digest the Allegorie" whole, and who therefore insists that political and theological meanings must lurk under every literal-moral episode.

(8) *Satiric poetry.* "There was yet another kind of Poet," Puttenham continues, "who intended to taxe the common abuses and vice of the people in rough and bitter speaches, and their inuectiues were called *Satyres*, and them selues *Satyricques:* such were *Lucilius, Iuuenall,* and *Persius* among the Latines, & with vs he that wrote the booke called Piers plowman" (II, 27). And it is these "Satyricques" who play a leading role in the critic's survey of developing genres, for he is certain that after the earliest "Poets or holy Priests" had honored their gods with hymns, they looked upon men, found "much to reproue & litle to praise," and therefore "chiefly studied the rebuke of vice" (II, 32). The results of their efforts to "make the people ashamed," to "carpe at the common abuses, such as were most offensiue to the publique and priuate," were the "foure sundry formes of Poesie *Drammatick* reprehensiue": first satire, next Old and then New Comedy, and finally tragedy (II, 32, 36).

> And the first and most bitter inuectiue against vice and vicious men was the *Satyre:* which, to th'intent their bitternesse should breede none ill will, either to the Poets, or to the recitours . . . , and besides to make their admonitions and reproofs seeme grauer and of more efficacie, they made wise as if the gods of the woods, whom they called *Satyres* or *Siluanes,* should appeare and recite those

verses of rebuke, whereas in deede they were but disguised
persons vnder the shape of *Satyres*, as who would say,
these terrene [earthly] and base gods, being conuersant
with mans affaires, and spiers out of all their secret faults,
had some great care ouer man, & desired by good ad-
monitions to reforme the euill of their life, and to bring
the bad to amendment by those kinde of preachings;
whereupon the Poets inuentours of the deuise were called
Satyristes.

(II, 32–33)

With such "history" as his evidence, it is easy to understand why
Puttenham considers satire not merely "reprehensiue," but the only
begetter of all *"Drammatick"* kinds. Old Comedy arose, in fact,
only as a better means of achieving the same end: "But when
these . . . recitals of rebuke, vttered by the rurall gods out of bushes
and briers, seemed not to the finer heads sufficiently perswasiue,
nor so popular as if it were reduced into action of many persons, or
by many voyces liuely represented," the poet-priests produced a
form "somewhat sharpe and bitter after the nature of the *Satyre*,
openly & by expresse names taxing men [so] maliciously and impudently" that the actors disguised themselves for fear of reprisals
(II, 33–34). The association of satires with satyrs also explains why
Puttenham, at the outset, characterizes the satirists' invectives as
"rough," not simply "bitter." When Harington calls his enemy
"a Satire, a quipping fellow," he is probably reflecting the same
etymological confusion.[81] Even Shakespeare (Sonnet C) assumes
that to "make Time's spoils despised everywhere," one must "*be*
a satire to decay" (italics added). Clearly, treating mutability
satirically means treating it as a satyr would. And when poets like
Donne and Marston deliberately commit metrical violence, occasionally offering lines that "defy scansion altogether," they are writing "under the influence of the old blunder which connected
satira with *satyros* and concluded that the one should be as
shaggy and 'salvage' as the other." [82]

Just as the examples of Renaissance pastoralists led the critics to
exaggerate the detections of abuses in Virgil's *Eclogues*, so the
image of the hairy satyr appears to lie behind Stanyhurst's odd
rejection of the relatively smooth Latin satirists. The most rugged
of Ennius's verses are hardly as "ragged . . . nothing current" or
drunken ("nappy of thee spigget") as Stanyhurst claims (I, 136).

And surely this champion of Virgil is overstating his case when he dismisses the verses of Juvenal, Persius, and even Horace for running "harshe and rough," for performing "nothing in matter but biting quippes, taunting Darcklye certeyn men of state that liued in theyre age, beesprinckling theyre *inuectiues* with soom moral preceptes aunswerable too thee capacitye of eurie weake brayne" (I, 137). Perhaps another part of Stanyhurst's resentment stems from his belief that although these shaggy Romans taunted darkly, they never offer those "hydden secrets *Virgil* hath sealde vp in his . . . *Aeneis*," those "rare poynctes" that the "diuing searcher" may "ferret owt" and crow over.

From Sidney and Harington, on the other hand, the satirist receives only praise. For the latter, it is the pastoral, sonnet, and epigram that may "now and then break . . . the rules of Poetry, [and] go into plaine scurrilitie"; the satiric is "wholly occupied in mannerly & couertly reprouing of all vices" (II, 209). Similarly, when Sidney illustrates how man's wit abuses poetry, his examples are drawn from comedy, lyric, elegy, and epic, but not satire (I, 186). His satirist, in fact, is as well-intentioned as Puttenham's satyr, but without that creature's roughness and bitterness. He makes us "feele how many headaches a passionate life bringeth vs to" yet his barbs are delivered "sportingly"; he never gives over until he gets a man "to laugh at folly, and, at length ashamed, to laugh at himselfe; which he cannot auoyd, without auoyding the follie" (I, 176).

To judge from these varied comments, the Elizabethan reader's expectations were as diverse as our own. He knew the satirist would reveal a critical attitude, take a strong stand, and either openly or indirectly suggest how the crooked could be made straighter. He was not sure whether the attack would be made with "most bitter inuectiue," "maliciously and impudently," or with laughter, "sportingly," even "mannerly." The enemy might be a particular fool, "certeyn men of state," or a general kind of folly, or, like Decay, an aspect of the human condition one feared and therefore scorned but could not change. And the challenge could be either leveled directly and dramatically, as if an honest satyr had sprung from his bush to deliver a sermon, or sent through a second and worded almost as darkly as allegory. To complicate matters further, Ronsard and Spenser sometimes make the satyr an idyllic figure, a child of uncorrupted nature, a savage more civil than our vicious civilization usually displays. Hence we find one misconception displacing another in William Rankins's *Seven Satires* (1598); his satyr is no hairier than Goldsmith's Chinaman, and its songs are therefore smooth and gentle.[83] Although Sidney takes no notice of metrics, his definition of the satirist's function is interlaced with lines from Persius and Horace, two of the Romans Stanyhurst disdains as "harshe and rough." Since Sidney in citing these men as authorities as well as illustrations, we may assume that he did not agree with Stanyhurst. Even farther from Stanyhurst's "harshe" and "biting quippes" is Harington's "mannerly . . . reprouing." Finally, if C. S. Lewis is correct in claiming that Samuel Rowlands was the only Elizabethan satirist who "grasped the fact that it is useless to attack knaves unless you entertain readers, that neither moral purpose nor personal malice will do instead of comic power," [84] we must honor Sidney's anticipation of that fact in his vignette of the sporting gadfly, who makes man laugh at himself. In an age of such ferocious moralizing, it was all too easy for theorist, practitioner, and general reader to settle for a kind of satire long on vituperation and short on comic art. Although often given to mere railing himself, Harvey realizes that "Inuectiues by fauour haue bene too bolde, and Satyres by vsurpation too presumptuous . . . and I must needes say Mother Hubbard in heat of choller, forgetting the pure sanguine of her sweete Feary Queene, wilfully ouer-shott her malcontented selfe" (II, 229). Thus Harvey, in 1592, complains against one of the nine *Complaints* published by Spenser the preceding year. In June, 1599, however, the Privy Council hoisted Harvey with his own petar. All of his works, but none of Spenser's, were among those books of satires that the ecclesiastical authorities ordered to be collected and burned.

(9) *The eighth kind.* So far all the critics who care to venture opinions about the number and nature of the genres that the modern poet may worthily imitate are in essential agreement. Having descended to less important kinds, they now differ either as to the options remaining, or nomenclature, or both. Only Puttenham provides more than eight "formes." Along with the satirists, there were other poets "of a more fine and pleasant head [who] were giuen wholly to taunting and scoffing at vndecent things, and in short poemes vttered pretie merry conceits, and these men were called *Epigrammatistes*" (II, 27). The critic then concludes his chapter "Of Poemes and Their Sundry Formes, and How Thereby

the Auncient Poets Receaued Surnames" with "Poets *Mimistes*" and the "*Pantomimi.*" It is probably Puttenham's characteristic desire to be as thorough as possible which keeps him from subsuming the ancients' mimes and pantomimes under comedy and tragedy. The same attention to detail is revealed later (II, 47 ff.), when he takes one part of lyric poetry, the "Forme of Poeticall Reioysings," and breaks that part down into songs "*Triumphal*" ("for . . . victorie and peace"), "*Encomia*" ("carols of honor"), "*Epithalamies*" ("songs nuptiall"), and "*Genethliaca*" ("songs natall").

But if Puttenham is uncharacteristically thorough in listing two genres his contemporaries do not mention, he is typically Elizabethan in the manner in which he stresses their moral or harmlessly recreational nature. His ignorance of the Roman *mimus* may of course be sincere. Its generally topical, farcical, and indecent fare is seen as being offered "for the peoples good instruction," speeches "of short and sententious meetres, very pithie and of good edification" (II, 27). For such a portrayal Puttenham has no evidence, only a piece of ingenious logic: Certain poets were surnamed "*Mimistes*, as who would say, imitable and meet to be followed for their wise and graue lessons." Thus we are free to proceed beyond the literal meaning of *mimus*, "an actor or playlet that mimics," and an era of the theater in which even fornication was both mimed and actually performed, to those upright poets who did not mimic, but advocated the mimicking of straight and narrow paths. Probably a similarly confused meaning underlies his unhistorical description of the "*Pantomimi*," players who entertained a weary or restless audience by appearing between the acts of a comedy or tragedy and "conuerting all that which they had hard [heard?] spoken before to a certaine derision by a quite contrary sence" (II, 28). A *pantomimus* was a male dancer who *played all the parts* by changing costumes and masks, not a member of a cast that *parodied all things* within the play proper.[85]

Puttenham is less confused about his eighth kind, and when he later details the epigrammatist's domain, we understand how that poet's "taunting" differs from the satirist's. Originally they shared the same attitudes and goals. If the satirist "intended to taxe the common abuses and vice of the people," his cousin was "giuen wholly to . . . scoffing at vndecent things" (II, 27). The first epigrammatists simply used different means, "short . . . pretie [and] merry conceits" rather than long, "rough and bitter speaches." Unlike the solemn satyr, they proceeded with a keen sense of humor, bristles gaily trimmed, and at their sides hung rapiers, not clubs. The element of cut and thrust is underlined in Puttenham's later explanation of how "euery mery conceited man might, without any long studie or tedious ambage, make his frend sport, and anger his foe, and giue a prettie nip, or shew a sharpe conceit in few verses" (II, 56). The result is what we should call versified graffiti, "for this *Epigramme* is but an inscription or writting made as it were vpon a table, or in a windowe, or vpon the wall or mantell of a chimney in some place of common resort, . . . where many merry heades meete, and scrible with ynke, with chalke, or with a cole, such matters as they would euery man should know & descant vpon." It was only afterward, in the days of Martial, that this kind became literary and less reprehensible, including "messages of mirth" and "frendship" as well as of "defiaunce." But whether scribbled on a wall or printed in a book, whether biting foes or praising friends, the epigram must always appear spontaneous, occasional, "short and sweete (as we are wont to say)" (II, 56). And when Puttenham proceeds to the epitaph as "a kind of Epigram," he is stressing their single common denominator: "an inscription such as a man may commodiously write or engraue . . . in few verses, pithie, quicke, and sententious" (II, 58–59). He scorns those ignorant "bastard rimers," whose so-called epitaphs "exceede the measure of an Epigram"; they "might better call them Elegies." The smoothest, merriest, and most conceited satirist who entitled his four-score verses of rebuke an epigram would no doubt have been censured for a similar confusion of terms.

Puttenham's fellow critics, on the other hand, seem to agree on only one point: There are not ten kinds of poetry, as he alleges, but eight. As to the name and nature of the eighth kind, however, they differ with him and with one another. Immediately before asking how the sporting satirist could offend any but those who love their follies, Sidney queries, "Is it the bitter but wholsome Iambick, which rubs the galled minde, in making shame the trumpet of villanie with bolde and open crying out against naughtines?" (I, 176). Harington, who usually follows Sidney closely, also surveys eight kinds, but substitutes sonnet for lyric, and epigram for iambic. He notes, moreover, that the epigram sometimes tends toward wantonness or scurrility, and uses several verses from Martial to support his confession that "euen the worst" may become "too delightfull" (II, 209). If these men are speaking about the same thing, we have a genre always bitter and mostly merry, never impure, usually pleasant, and occasionally ribald. Campion returns us to at least part of Puttenham's description when he analogizes, "What epigrams are in poetry, the same are airs in music: then in their chief perfection when they are short and well seasoned." [86] Another element of Puttenham's characterization, the "prettie nip," appears in Coignet, but the latter chooses Sidney's term: "He which first inuented the *Iambique* versifying, to byte and quippe, was the first that felt the smart" (I, 342). And our confusion is furthered when we recollect that "quipping" is precisely the term Harington uses to describe his odd "fellow," the Satire.

The acme of critical bewilderment is reached by that cautious scavenger, Francis Meres. He first reasons that "as there are eight famous and chiefe languages, . . . so there are eight notable seuerall [separate] kindes of Poets, Heroicke, Lyricke, Tragicke, Comicke, Satiricke, Iambicke, Elegiacke, and Pastoral" (II, 319). Drawing upon previous commentary, Meres is able to furnish a lengthy list of authors or titles, ancient and modern, for all except his "iambical" poets. As examples of those who excel in iambics, he is content to list two Greeks (Archilochus Parius and Hipponax Ephesius) and two Englishmen (Harvey and Stanyhurst) "bicause I haue seene no mo in this kind." But Meres is even more perplexing as he proceeds from vagueness to contradiction. Having exhausted his "eight notable" varieties of poets, he concludes with a ninth, the epigrammatists, including the Romans, Martial and Catullus, as well as modern makers like "wittie Sir Thomas Moore," John (?) Heywood, and Davies.

Before patronizing such critical confusion, however, we must realize that each theorist could have supported his comments with examples from ancient practice. Even Meres's difficulties with his "eight—or is it nine?" genres is understandable once we ourselves understand that among the Greeks and Romans, iambic and epigrammatic poems are sometimes identical, sometimes closely related, and often utterly different. The very term "iambus" is first used by Meres's Archilochus (c. 700 B.C.), evidently to refer to his own satirical verse written in iambic meter. Rhythm that so nearly approximates that of everyday speech, Archilochus tells us, is well suited to satire and ridicule, but he also expresses personal likes and dislikes in trochaic tetrameter, and even those short poems about war or wine, which employ the far slower elegiac line (/-- /-- / | /-- /-- /), are "remarkable for their strongly

personal note." [87] Even more colloquial and abusive is Meres's
Hipponax (c. 550), alleged to have nipped two of his enemies so
skillfully that they committed suicide. It is probably this latter
iambic versifier Coignet has in mind when he speaks of its inventor
being "the first that felt the smart" (I, 342), for Hipponax was
attacked, caricatured, and finally banished from Ephesus. In any
case, one suspects that the Elizabethans would have found their
eighth kind easier to deal with had it not been for this very minor
poet's rather slight innovation. For the first five feet of the old
six-foot iambic trimeter he retained the easy iamb; in place of the
last iamb, however, he substituted a spondee. The strategy is to
pause and thereby emphasize the ridicule or hatred that has
hitherto flowed so naturally. Hipponax's successors called his invention the *scazon* ("the limper," or "that which halts") or *choliambus*
(freely translated, "lamed iambic trimeter"), and the iambic line,
in both its pure and crippled forms, proceeded on a generally
vituperative path down to early Christian times.

To a rather frustrated Webbe, such innovations only prove that
"a Poet must not vse too much licence or boldnes. The auncient
writers in *Iambick* verses vsed at first pure *Iambicks*: Afterwards
Spondoeus was admitted into *Locos impares* [places unfitting],
but at last such was the licentious custome, that they woulde both
Spondoeus where they listed, and other feete without regarde." [88]
A more typically Elizabethan response is found in Campion, who
regards ancient license as a cue to wade farther, and hence illustrates
his *Observations* with "Th' English *Iambick* licentiate" as well as
"English *Iambicks* pure" (II, 334 ff.). Campion is of course interested in how "our English verses" may "hold pace with the
Latines" (II, 335), not in weighing what Sidney calls poetry's
"parts, kindes, or *Species*" (I, 175). At what point does license
become anarchy and the iambic lamed beyond recognition? For
"our *Iambick* licentiate," Campion demands iambs only in the
third and fifth feet; the other places of a five-foot line may be supplied by spondees, iambs, dactyls, tribrachs (– – –) and occasionally anapests (II, 335). Another "part of the *Iambick*, which is
our most naturall and auncient English verse," Campion explains, is
the "Iambick Dimeter," one odd syllable preceded by two feet,
neither of which need be iambic (II, 338). Finally, when Campion
mingles these two varieties of "iambic" lines to produce "The
English Elegeick Verse," and illustrates it with one elegy and nine
"*Epigrams*, in Elegeick verse" (II, 344–345), we are back to Meres's
iambic and/or epigrammatic poets.

If the Elizabethans found the ancient iambists not always iambical in form, they could at least count upon a characteristic subject and mood. Although some later iambists put their verse to new uses—descriptions of plants, literature, foreign lands, for example—they usually followed the satirical lines noted by Sidney, rubbing galled minds and trumpeting villainy. From the Greek and Roman epigrammatists, on the other hand, one could expect any meter, topic, and treatment suitable to a short poem. Puttenham is on solid classical ground when he calls the epigram "but an inscription," and includes under it poems as different as posie and epitaph. That which is inscribed (the literal meaning of *epigramma*) must be clear, pointed, concise—nothing else. The first verse-epigrams (c. 700 B.C.) appear on tombstones and votive offerings and are cast in elegiac couplets, one or more hexameters, or even in iambics. Within several centuries, however, "epigram" came to be applied to any verse that one could, but never would, carve upon a tomb or tablet: poems of dead animals, works of art, country scenes, love, wine, enemies. Although the Romans imitated each variety, the invective epigram was especially popular, and it was the witty, satirical Catullus and Martial who in turn especially appealed to the sometimes genuine, sometimes merely fashionable moral fervor of the Elizabethans. Something pointed need not pierce with abuse. Hence, Ben Jonson's epigrammatic epitaphs, reflections, neatly turned compliments, and verse epistles. Hence, too, Daniel's dismay at Campion's "vncharitable Epigrammes" (II, 375). But Puttenham seems more typical. He knows that the Romans, including Martial, used the epigram for "ordinarie missiues [letters]" and "frendship" (II, 56). He nevertheless prefers the taunting side of Martial, those "priuy nips or witty scoffes." Whether we expect something more dignified, like Sidney's "wholsome Iambick," or tending toward scurrility, like Harington's epigram, our orientation remains essentially satirical.

Why the eighth kind was given different names may have partly depended on how freely each critic was willing to define iambic meter. Very few of Martial's abusive epigrams, for example, employ the pure iambic; by far the most are in elegiac meter. For the critic who wished to stress Martial's iambical spirit, however, there are seventy-seven poems that honor Hipponax's *scazon*. Lamed iambic trimeters are also used by Martial's epigrammatic master, Catullus, yet the latter's references to his own "iambi" appear to signify the critical nature of his attacks rather than a particular meter. We must also remember that even when one critic borrows from another, he gives his argument a personal emphasis. Harington, for instance, is certainly no more ignorant of the iambic than Sidney is of the epigram. Sidney carefully examines each part, "for, if seuered they be good, the coniunction cannot be hurtfull" (I, 175). Had he been asked why he omitted the epigram, he could have appealed to this principle: You will find that kind listed under both "lamenting Elegiack" and "wholsome Iambick." Harington, on the other hand, must defend Ariosto and his own translation as well as poetry. He therefore simplifies. Let "Sonnet" stand for "Liricke," and "Epigramme" for any short piece with a witty, satirical, and often scurrilous point. What comes soonest to mind, the chief meanings, replace Sidney's fuller, more accurate definitions. Sidney is again on safer ground when he treats not the elegy, but those poets who used elegiac verse to bewail man's weaknesses as well as the world's wretchedness. The elegy, in short, may be used for reproof, "for rightly paynting out how weake be the passions of wofulnesse" (I, 176). Yet Harington's convenient oversimplification—"the Elegie is still mourning" (II, 209)—comes closer to our own not wholly classical expectations. Similarly, it is a well-informed classicism that inspires Campion to compose elegiac epigrams, and prevents Puttenham from labeling all epigrammatic poets "iambical."

CONCLUSION: AN UNNOTED INDECORUM

Here, then, are the options, the best paths to follow in stepping beyond, as the Elizabethans saw them. If most of those dramatic and metrical "laws of writ" outlined in the preceding chapter make the critics appear naïve, impractical, or misguided, this chapter has emphasized their more apposite comments. And in this second area, where theorist and practitioners share the same premises, where fact is therefore more inclined to complement opinion, the critics clarify the nature of the artists' endeavors. It was of course the Tudor writers who decided the fate of all critical observations; which ones could be validated by successful practice, which would remain episodes in a story of unfulfilled promises. It was only their failures that make some theories seem strange and visionary today, only their triumphs that allowed other views to become for us truly relevant backgrounds. If we would know more about the writer, we cannot refuse the offices of any critic he indirectly endorsed. The criticism he acted upon tells us how to take Holofernes's scorn of imitation and E.K.'s praise of Spenser's servility. Wordsworth notwithstanding, we realize that Shakespeare's heart will be no sooner unlocked by his sonnets than his plays. We become less puzzled over the roughness of Donne's "satyrs," and when we sit down to his elegies, our first question is not "Who died?" We are less disturbed when we finish an episode of *The Faerie Queene* without finding a theological or political meaning; Harington suggests it may not exist. In such diverse ways Elizabethan theories become the modern reader's practical tools.

Concerning one of the most characteristic Tudor literary practices, however, the critics remain almost silent. We cannot read very long before being struck by the era's tendency to produce a "mixed bag," a fusion of disparate literary worlds or traditions. Sidney admittedly notes that "some Poesies haue coupled together two or three kindes, as Tragicall and Comicall" (I, 175). Others "in the like manner haue mingled Prose and Verse" or "matters Heroicall and Pastorall." Why Sidney believes that it "commeth all to one in this question," why he is sure that "the coniunction cannot be hurtfull," is because his question is moral. If each part of poetry moves a man to virtuous acts, how can any combination be harmful? When Sidney later admits that "euen to the Heroical *Cupid* hath ambitiously climed" (I, 186), the indecorum remains essentially moral; the central question, at least, seems no more aesthetic than what immediately precedes it: "The Elegiack weepes the want of his mistresse." Occasionally Sidney's responses to his contemporaries' incongruous mixtures take an aesthetic turn: Spenser has wrongly framed his style to an old rustic language, thereby violating a pastoral propriety; *Gorboduc* incorporates too much time and too many places; "with neither decencie nor discretion," popular playwrights are given to "mingling Kings and Clownes" (I, 196–199). Sidney is typical in his cautions against these varieties of indecorous fusions. "To entermingle merie iests in a serious matter is an *Indecorum*" (I, 48), says Gascoigne, and so are "obscure and darke phrases in a pleasant Sonet." Dramatists "vse one order of speach for all persons: a grose *Indecorum*" (I, 60), complains Whetstone, and they have not been "entermingling all these actions in such sorte as the graue matter may instruct and the pleasant delight." E.K. celebrates his New Poet for "dewe obseruing of Decorum euerye where, in personages, in seasons, in matter, in speach," and for resisting those who "haue made our

English tongue a gallimaufray or hodgepodge of al other speches" (I, 128–130). Stanyhurst similarly praises Virgil for his "similitudes so aptly applyed" (I, 137), and James urges "a mutuall correspondence" between each poem's subject and ornament (I, 219).

At least half of Puttenham's lengthy study is principally concerned with illustrating "*decorum* and good proportion in euery respect," since decorum or "decencie is . . . the line & leuell for al good makers to do their busines by" (II, 155, 173). With characteristic and often wearisome attention to detail, Puttenham devotes his "Second Booke" (II, 67–141) to "Proportion Poetical," and the opening paragraph of his "First Booke," subtitled "Of Poets and Poesie," tells us why. "A Poet is as much to say as a maker. . . . Such as (by way of resemblance and reuerently) we may say of God; who without any trauell to his diuine imagination made all the world of nought" (II, 3). Unlike God's imagination, of course, the poet's usually follows a "paterne or mould," and therefore "Poesie [is] an art not only of making, but also of imitation." But whether poets create "by instinct diuine or naturall," "experience," or a "president or paterne layd before them," they certainly do not share the lunatics' and lovers' "seething brains" and "shaping fantasies," as Shakespeare's Theseus supposes (V. i. 2 ff.). Only "barbarous ignoraunce" finds the poet "a light headed or phantasticall man" (II, 19). If the "vicious disposition of the braine hinders the sounde iudgement and discourse of man with busie & disordered phantasies," that is one thing. If the intellect is so "well proportioned, and so passing cleare, that by it . . . are represented vnto the soule all maner of bewtifull visions, whereby the inuentiue parte of the mynde is so much holpen [helped] as without it no man could deuise any new or rare thing," that is quite another. Theseus, in short, is "not making difference betwixt termes"; without thoughts "that apprehend / More than cool reason ever comprehends," there "could be no politique Captaine, nor any witty enginer or cunning artificer" (II, 19–20).

Puttenham obviously intends his books on proportion and ornament to discipline but not blind "the poet's eye," all too often "in a fine frenzy rolling." As he illustrates how those poetical proportions of staff, measure, concord, situation, and figure may be most cunningly blended, he may seem to us a mere statistician, an actuary poring over mortality tables. But we cannot get very far into his most "trivial" stuff without recollecting some great art that reflects the same concerns. Do not the delicately patterned lengths of the *Prothalamion*'s lines and the seven rhymes or concords that bind each eighteen-line staff or stanza together come to mind when Puttenham praises the "wide distances" and "sundry lengths" that characterize the verses of Petrarch's *canzoni?* For us, the sophisticated harmonies of that "Spousall Verse Made by Edm. Spenser" may be easily overlooked. For Puttenham, "all that can be obiected against this wide distance is to say that the eare by loosing his concord is not satisfied. So is in deede the rude and popular eare, but not the learned" (II, 91). Whether reading the Italian *canzone* or the longer interwoven form Spenser derived from it, with Puttenham's help we now "must thinke he doth intende to shew himselfe more artificiall then popular" (II, 87). We also notice the exquisite artifice of the bond or "band giuen to euery staffe . . . by one whole verse running alone throughout the ditty or ballade" (II, 93): "Sweete Themmes, runne softly, till I end my song."

The darker sides of imitation, artifice, and blending are, to be sure, also represented in Puttenham: poetry by position, or "reduced into certaine Geometricall figures" like the "egge displayed" or "Lozange rabbated" (II, 95 ff.); the language of poetry likened to a lady's richest dress, or to the pearls that embellish an embroidery (II, 142 ff.). But all the merely technical points that compose his work's middle sections must be balanced against its philosophical beginning and end. His conclusion, which illustrates how art imitates, aids, alters, and finally outdoes Nature, is as thoughtful as the best of Sidney's criticism. The only rationale for wading is to go farther, to make all borrowings one's own; hence he leaves us with that poet who is "most admired when he is most naturall and least artificiall" (II, 192). But we must first possess the art before disguising, disgracing, or "naturalizing" it. The "graue and naturall eloquence" of men like Sir Nicholas Bacon, for example, may "be naturall to them or artificiall (though I thinke rather naturall), yet were they knowen to be learned and not vnskilfull of th'arte when they were yonger men" (II, 145). So, too, the development of the critic's audience, those young courtier-poets who would write effortlessly, yet well. Puttenham would not have been the least embarrassed over our analogy between learning how to write sonnets and drive cars; with practice, the "proportions" of clutch, shift, and accelerator come more easily. The context in which the Elizabethans experimented, for better or worse, is perhaps best represented by a happening among Puttenham's circle, and by his closing reflections:

Make me, saith this writer to one of the companie, so many strokes or lines with your pen as ye would haue your song containe verses; and let euery line beare his seuerall length, euen as ye would haue your verse of measure. Suppose of foure, fiue, sixe, or eight, or more sillables, and set a figure of euerie number at th'end of the line, whereby ye may knowe his measure. Then where you will haue your rime or concord to fall, marke it with a compast stroke or semicircle passing ouer those lines, be they farre or neare in distance. . . . And bycause ye shall not thinke the maker hath premeditated beforehand any such fashioned ditty, do ye your selfe make one verse, whether it be of perfect or imperfect sense, and giue it him for a theame to make all the rest vpon. If ye shall perceiue the maker do keepe the measures and rime as ye haue appointed him, and besides do make his ditty sensible and ensuant to the first verse in good reason, then may ye say he is his crafts maister. For, if he were not of a *plentiful discourse,* he could not vpon the sudden shape an entire dittie vpon your imperfect theame or proposition in one verse. And, if he were not *copious in his language,* he could not haue such store of wordes at commaundement as should supply your concords. And, if he were not of a *maruelous good memory,* he could not obserue the rime and measures after the distances of your limitation, keeping with all grauitie and good sense in the whole dittie.

(II, 94–95. Italics added.)

To Puttenham, such offhand improvisation is neither cheap theater nor the mark of dilettantism. Measure the italicized words against Hamlet's appreciation of man as the Creator's best "piece of work," "noble in reason" and "infinite in faculty," and the virtuoso's strivings seem to honor the God of order, design, and artifice.

In all of Puttenham's cataloguing of poetical kinds, proportions, and figures, and in all of Sidney's references to mingling and decency, however, we find no awareness of that special indecorum that underlies the best and worst Tudor literature. Of all Elizabethan critics, only Harvey appears to glance upon it when he characterizes an unfinished draft of *The Faerie Queene* as "HOBGOBLIN runne away with the Garland from APOLLO" (I, 116). Does the muse of "HOBGOBLIN" have something to do with the disparate worlds Spenser fuses: the Redcrosse Knight, for instance, being overcome by a medieval giant, haughty Orgoglio, when he lays aside the armor of St. Paul's Ephesians; or Pride, this time christened Lucifera, being given Pluto and Proserpina for parents? [89] Harvey's dislike of the "Eluish Queene" may simply reflect that classical quest for more unified times, places, and episodes. To the very end of his romantic epic Spenser admits sailing across a sea of adventure in an apparently rudderless vessel.

> Like as a ship, that through the ocean wyde
> Directs her course unto one certaine cost,
> Is met of many a counter winde and tyde,
> With which her winged speed is let and crost,
> And she her selfe in stormie surges tost;
> Yet making many a borde, and many a bay,
> Still winneth way, ne hath her compasse lost:
> Right so it fares with me in this long way,
> Whose course is often stayd, yet never is astray.[90]

Unlike the majority of his contemporaries, however, Spenser is careful to point out that his labyrinth is the result of conscious choice.

> Now turne againe my teme, thou jolly swayne,
> Backe to the furrow which I lately left;
> I lately left a furrow, one or twayne,
> Unplough'd, the which my coulter hath not cleft:
> Yet seem'd the soyle both fayre and frutefull eft,
> As I it past, that were too great a shame,
> That so rich frute should be from us bereft.[91]

But if Harvey is mainly lamenting neither the romantic fable, the main roads of faerie, nor romantic formlessness, those byways Spenser cannot resist, "Hobgoblin" may typify what he later calls Nashe's "Methode, . . . a hotch-pott for a gallymafry" (II, 253). Like Nashe, in other words, Spenser not only *goes*, but *takes from* here and there; his method or principle of composition reminds Harvey of a cook, hashing up odds and ends to produce a heterogeneous stew.[92] Spenser himself acknowledges in his introductory letter to Raleigh that he has not only drawn from the springs of Homer and Virgil, but drunk deeply of the classical epic as transfigured by Ariosto, that mad weaver of Ferrara. Like the renowned

Renaissance bee, which produced sweet honey from both weeds and flowers, he has appropriated the fond tales of paganism, the bold bawdy of medieval romance, and the urbane laughter of sixteenth-century Italy to compose his edifying picture of spiritual conditions. No dish is too removed for his moral feast.

It is not really *The Faerie Queene*'s length or interwoven episodes that make us frequently ask where we are, but the multiple worlds it blends together. We are similarly "lost" amid the *Epithalamion*'s far shorter space. Within 433 lines we proceed from Helicon to the even more "heavenly tabernacles" of the "blessed saints." In between we encounter Orpheus and the Irish water "nymphes of Mulla"; Aurora bidding farewell to Tithonus against a medieval chorus of birds; Elizabeth Boyle being adorned by the Three Graces, and Hymen heralded by the little boys of Cork. There is time to relate what excellent "trouts and pikes" swim in Mulla, to describe the minstrels' thoroughly Gaelic instruments, "the pipe, the tabor, and the trembling croud." And it is not merely the lark, thrush, and "mavis" who "all agree, with sweet consent, / To this dayes merriment" (ll. 80 ff.). The stout Protestant poet renews his devotion to Phoebus, yet rehearses his love's Petrarchan charms with echoes of Old Testament imagery (ll. 121 ff., 148 ff.). The Platonic observations of the eleventh strophe yield to the concrete details of the twelfth and thirteenth, where "a small Protestant church becomes a Salomonic or even a pagan temple and at the same time a great cathedral of the old religion with high altar, roaring organs, and crowds of hovering angels." [93] It is an Irish midsummer; hence the "yong men of the towne" are invited to dance and sing about their bonfires, while "the Pouke" and "other evill sprights" are charmed into silence. It is also the summer solstice; hence the presence of Bacchus among the Anglican guests, and Juno, to "patronize" the "lawes of wedlock," and Genius, the pagan god of fertility. It is finally St. Barnabas's Day; hence the closing hope that the children of this marriage may see the Lord's salvation.

This is *The Faerie Queene*'s "methode" in miniature. Although Spenser proclaims he has "followed all the antique poets historicall," not to mention Aristotle's "twelve private morall vertues," and although he weaves into his arras many figures from ancient myth, neither the highways and byways of his plot, nor his treatment of subject matter, evinces an interest in, or perhaps even a knowledge of, classical discipline and unity. Apollo might believe in chivalry, *or* Calvin, *or* Ovid, *or* Plato; Hobgoblin is a syncretist. For these reasons the greatest Elizabethan poem takes its place among the group that Douglas Bush calls "a 'Gothic' and edifying tapestry into which are woven more and more silver threads from Ovid and threads of gilt from Italy. Such poetry, heavily encrusted with Renaissance brocade, is obviously seldom 'classical'."[94] If this is also the gist of Harvey's criticism, it is, for his era, quite exceptional; a few pages after lamenting "hotch-pott" methods, even he becomes syncretic: Petrarch's Laura is "a sauing Hester, not a destroying Helena" (II, 259). The great majority of critics, for all their references to decorum, seem unaware of the mixed worlds or literary themes their contemporaries are continually producing. The usually caustic Nashe praises Greene's *Menaphon* for its "extemporall . . . inuention," and Peele's *Arraignment of Paris* for its "pregnant dexteritie of wit and manifold varietie of inuention" (I, 309, 319). Is this because, or despite, or aside from, the facts that the former is a hodgepodge of shepherds, knights, oracles, and pirates, and that the latter's cast ranges from Helen of Troy to Elizabeth of England, Jupiter and Ate to Hobbinol and Diggon? About the time Sidney denounces the marriage of hornpipes and funerals, he is also busily rewriting the *Arcadia* with "matters Heroicall and Pastorall" before him: Heliodorus, Ariosto, Sannazaro's *Arcadia*, the Spanish Peninsular Romance, and probably Malory and the *Amadis*.

Not all Elizabethan imitations mingle traditions so obviously or straightforwardly. Some writers adhere to the basic plots and characters of a single source, choosing to wade farther with merely verbal embellishments. However circumscribed such areas of exercise, invention will out; instead of coupling two or more worlds, they freely inject new concerns into one old theme, and the result is almost equally hybrid. Even when one wished, like Stanyhurst, to follow his original faithfully, to reveal "thee pyth that is shrind vp wythin thee barck and bodye of so exquisit and singular a discourse" (I, 136), he invariably creates a new world, usually because he misconceives the very spirit he is attempting to capture. In his effort to put Virgil "intoo English Heroical Verse," Stanyhurst neither grafts nor crossbreeds; he is about the wholly serious business of translation proper. But in carrying Maro across the Channel, he cannot forgo racy language and rich proverbial expressions: Fame, "First lyke a shrimp squatting for feare," musters courage to noise abroad Dido's "rutting bitcherye," news "as wild as a marche hare," and the Queen of Carthage, fearing she will be left "lyke a castaway milckmadge," warns Aeneas, "I wyl, as hobgoblin, foloa thee" [95]—all this despite Stanyhurst's scholarly appreciation of Virgil's "similitudes so aptly applyed" (I, 137). Whether mingling, grafting, or merely extracting the "pyth," the Tudor poet handles his materials no more impersonally than his rarely objective rival, the historian. In a long didactic poem (c. 1560) five times the length of its source, an anonymous Englisher of Ovid's story of Narcissus (*Metamorphoses*, III, 342–510) informs his readers,

> I meane to shewe, accordying to my wytte
> That Ouyd by this tale no follye mente
> But soughte to shewe, the doynges far vnfytte
> Of soundrye folke.[96]

He consequently discovers in the story of Narcissus and Echo—"the callynge Ympe"—a sermon against pride, and promptly roams through numerous worlds to find complementary examples: Lucifer, Goliath, Samson, Dives, Cressus, Milo, Darius, Philomela, Absalom, Clytemnestra, and Cleopatra. A similarly "medieval" desire to reconcile the profane with the sacred can be found throughout Arthur Golding's translation (1567).

To see Dido as a forlorn milkmaid or Narcissus rubbing elbows with Lucifer and Absalom is at least partly to understand the attitudes of the Renaissance weavers. Their classicism often comes in by way of romantic adornment, a brighter and sometimes exotic woof to enrich the native warp, which itself frequently ran at curious angles. Does this mean that the New Learning simply provided new decoration and no clearer comprehension of what those disciplined Romans were talking about? It is occasionally difficult to tell whether a great comic artist is consciously exploiting or simply ignorant of the incongruities of the traditions he fuses. Chaucer's cultivated audience probably took the minglings in "The Merchant's Tale" as a whimsical parading of matters known to be mutually exclusive. Ovid's Pluto and Proserpina, decked out as the King and Queen of "Fayerye" and deposited within a garden in Lombardy, comment on May's assignation with January's squire, and engage in an involved debate concerning woman's faithlessness, during the course of which "Salomon," "Jhesus, *filius Syrak*," Christian martyrs, and Roman "geestes" are duly cited.[97] Against this facetious fusion stands the wholly serious world of "The Knight's Tale," a mixture of classical Athens, medieval derring-do, courtly love, and Boethian philosophy. Neither Chaucer nor his Knight seems aware of any incongruities here; they are both too busy holding up Palamon and Arcite as perfect flowers of Greco-Roman chivalry and underlining their Christian-Stoic moral. With two centuries of classical scholarship to profit by, Shakespeare simply brings his Athens up to date. Chaucer's dukes, squires, and pages give way to an Elizabethan Master of the Revels, a Warwickshire Puck, and those London mechanicals who would have puzzled the "real" Theseus more than his Minotaur.

The discoveries of several generations of humanists have not really changed Hobgoblin's method. It is not a Virgilian or even an Ovidian Dido before whom Chaucer's Aeneas kneels,

> And tolde hire al his herte and al his wo,
> And swore so depe to hire to be trewe,
> For wel or wo, and chaunge hire for no newe,
> And as a fals lovere so wel can pleyne,
> That sely [innocent] Dido rewede on his peyne.[98]

It is an equally unclassical Dido, however, who

> In such a night
> Stood . . . with a willow in her hand
> Upon the wild sea-banks, and waft her love
> To come again to Carthage.
> (*The Merchant of Venice*, V. i. 9–12)

Shakespeare's context is admittedly comic. Lorenzo and Jessica obviously realize that their catalogue of classical-medieval lovers who ventured all, were all poorly paid. But what is for us perhaps the deftest touch of humor, that willow in Dido's hand, was hardly intentional. We cannot of course prove that no one at the Globe laughed for the right, classical reasons. We can, however, show that if such laughter arose, it did not necessarily come from the formally educated or more aristocratic members of the audience. Our next chapter focuses upon those programs with which the citizen both greeted and instructed his visiting Sovereign and the far more romantic entertainments the courtier offered his Gloriana. It should further illustrate some of those political, historical, and literary backgrounds noted in the first two chapters, and certainly add to our knowledge of the critical contexts discussed in the third and fourth. Above all, it seeks to blur some of those fine but anachronistic distinctions that we tend to make between drama and devising, and to erase altogether some erroneous yet logical expectations about what was obviously "caviary to the general." Many of Elizabeth's "Princelye pleasures" featured scenes as "tragical-comical-historical-pastoral" as the rudest popular stage. A few of the most Gothic were written by the very critics who seem so keen about decorum. Others, which reveal all the fanciful longings of bourgeois escapism, were produced by earls and privy councilors. At least two of the Queen's romantic "pageantwrights" were also dramatists proper. In following the royal path across "this enchanted Isle of Albion," they must have found hints for their removed, Arcadian, yet recognizably English worlds, in which knights and nymphs mingle with magicians, milkmaids, and palmers.

Notes to Chapter IV

1. In *Elizabethan Critical Essays*, ed. G. Gregory Smith (London, 1904), I, 312. Unless otherwise noted, all citations from Elizabethan criticism are to Smith's two-volume collection.
2. The margins of Nashe's work are in fact decorated with scores of commentaries and summaries. See *The Works of Thomas Nashe*, ed. Ronald B. McKerrow (London, 1904–1910), I, 149–245.
3. Smith, II, 428–429.
4. IV. ii. 89. All citations from Shakespeare are to *The Complete Works*, ed. Peter Alexander (London, 1951).
5. For these usages and examples, unless otherwise noted, see the *Oxford English Dictionary* (hereafter *OED*).
6. "To a Young Ass" (1794).
7. E. S. Turner, *The Court of St. James's* (New York, 1959), p. 90.
8. See *OED*.
9. See his note to IV. ii. 95–97, in his edition of *The Complete Works of Shakespeare* (New York, 1951), pp. 114–115.
10. *Ibid.*, p. 114.
11. After their first reading of the play, my students, at least, usually speak of Holofernes as a tyrant. Before he can be enjoyed, the quality of his apparently formidable learning must be properly glossed.
12. Boston, 1935.
13. *Letters*, lxxxiv, 3, 5; cited in Harold Ogden White, *Plagiarism and Imitation During the English Renaissance* (Boston, 1935), p. 10.
14. C. S. Lewis, *English Literature in the Sixteenth Century* (Oxford, 1954), p. 54.
15. *Panegyricus*, 8, 188; cited by White, p. 11.
16. *Poetics*, cited by White, pp. 23–24. This idolatry inspired George Chapman's impudent apostrophe: "But thou soule-blind Scalliger, that neuer hadst anything but place, time, and termes to paint thy proficiencie in learning, nor euer writest any thing of thine owne impotent braine but thy onely impalsied diminuation of *Homer* . . ." (II, 301).
17. In his commentary on Aristotle's *Poetics*; cited by White, p. 26.
18. *Ibid.*; cited by White, pp. 26–27.
19. Discussed in this order by White, pp. 38–59.
20. Cited by White, p. 80.

21. Cited by White, pp. 121, 124.

22. "Satyre II," ll. 25–30, in *The Complete Poetry and Selected Prose of John Donne*, ed. Chârles M. Coffin (New York, 1952).

23. *The Book of the Courtier* (1528), trans. Sir Thomas Hoby (1561), ed. W. H. D. Rouse (London, 1928), p. 41.

24. *Ibid.*, pp. 45, 58, 63.

25. *Ibid.*, p. 61; italics added.

26. See White, pp. 117, 190–191.

27. Lewis, p. 43.

28. See C. T. Prouty, *George Gascoigne: Elizabethan Courtier, Soldier, and Poet* (New York, 1942), p. 160: "Gascoigne did not, however, merely translate Ariosto's prose comedy; he combined the original prose and a later verse rendition, which was composed between 1528 and 1531, and in so doing he demonstrated a very real dramatic ability."

29. From the "Prologo," in *Ludovico Ariosto: Opere Minori*, ed. Cesare Segre (Milano, n. d.), p. 298; translation, mine.

30. In *The Complete Roman Drama*, ed. George E. Duckworth (New York, 1942), II, 254–255; translator, anonymous.

31. See Frederick S. Boas, *An Introduction to Tudor Drama* (Oxford, 1933), p. 27.

32. Induction to *Every Man Out of His Humor*, ll. 266 ff., in *Ben Jonson*, ed. C. H. Herford and Percy Simpson, III (Oxford, 1927).

33. Both the songs and their sources are given in *Seventeenth-Century Prose and Poetry*, ed. Robert P. Tristram Coffin and Alexander M. Witherspoon (New York, 1946), pp. 43, 49.

34. Preface to the second edition of *Lyrical Ballads* (1800), in *Anthology of Romanticism*, ed. Ernest Bernbaum (New York, 1948), pp. 301, 308.

35. "She Dwelt Among the Untrodden Ways," in Bernbaum, p. 204.

36. Introduction to *Renaissance England*, ed. Roy Lamson and Hallett Smith (New York, 1956), p. 11.

37. Cited by Lamson and Smith, p. 12.

38. "I Wandered Lonely As a Cloud," in Bernbaum, pp. 228–229.

39. "Oh! How I Love," in Bernbaum, p. 751.

40. "Scorn Not the Sonnet," in Bernbaum, p. 295.

41. "Ode to Duty" and "Nuns Fret Not at Their Convent's Narrow Room," in Bernbaum, pp. 221, 230.

42. Preface to *Lyrical Ballads*, in Bernbaum, p. 300.

43. I, 55. Gascoigne is correct in thinking of "sonnet" as "a diminutiue worde deriued of *Sonare.*" *Sonare* or *suonare* means "to ring, sound, or play," and *sonetto* once meant "little sound or tune" as well as "sonnet." For the Elizabethans, "sonnet" could simply indicate any little song. In Lodge's *Rosalynde* (1590), for ex-

ample, not one of the dozen so-called "sonnets" or "sonnettoes" agrees with what Gascoigne may best allow. They range from ten to thirty-six lines; the closest is one "sonnet" with two fourteen-line stanzas, yet each begins with a line of ten syllables, follows with twelve lines of six, and concludes with one line of twelve.

44. *A Midsummer Night's Dream*, III. ii. 137–140. Relationship noted *supra* coffee by Professor Sanford Golding, sometime colleague.
45. McKerrow, II, 262–263.
46. Sonnets I, IV, XXXVIII, in *Samuel Daniel: Poems and A Defence of Ryme*, ed. Arthur Colby Sprague (Cambridge, Mass., 1930).
47. *Ibid.*, p. 9.
48. See *The Complete Poetical Works of Spenser*, ed. R. E. Neil Dodge (Boston, 1936), pp. xi–xii, 716.
49. See *The Poems of Henry Howard Earl of Surrey*, ed. Frederick Morgan Padelford (Seattle, 1928), pp. 50, 57, 208.
50. Padelford, p. 219.
51. "To the Reader of These Sonnets," in *The Works of Michael Drayton*, ed. J. William Hebel, II (Oxford, 1932), p. 310.
52. "Loves Alchymie," "The Sunne Rising," "Song," "Twicknam Garden," "The Canonization," in Coffin, pp. 31, 11, 16–17, 23–24, 13–14.
53. *Sonetto in Vita*, LXI, in *Petrarch: Sonnets & Songs*, trans. Anna Maria Armi (New York, 1946), p. 97.
54. George Gascoigne: *A Hundreth Sundrie Flowres*, ed. C. T. Prouty, The University of Missouri Studies, XVII (Columbia, Mo., 1942), p. 74. See p. 250 for note on Petrarch.
55. "An Hymne in Honour of Beautie," ll. 29–30, in Dodge, p. 747.
56. In *The Complete Works of Sir Philip Sidney*, ed. Albert Feuillerat, III (Cambridge, 1923), p. 272. Feuillerat assigns this part of the translation of Philippe de Mornay's treatise to Sidney (see III, ix).
57. Lamson and Smith, p. 8.
58. Feuillerat, III, 194.
59. Ed. Edward Arber (London, 1870), p. 45.
60. In Lamson and Smith, p. 468.
61. *Ibid.*, p. 472.
62. Rouse, p. 310.
63. *Ibid.*, p. 309.
64. *Ibid.*, p. 310; italics added.
65. "Ode to a Nightingale," ll. 59–60; in Bernbaum, pp. 818–819.
66. *Poly-Olbion*, "Song XIII," ll. 70–71, in Hebel, IV, 277.
67. *Hero and Leander*, I, 19–20, in *The Works of Christopher Marlowe*, ed. C. F. Tucker Brooke (Oxford, 1910).
68. "An Hymne in Honour of Beautie," ll. 82–84; in Dodge, p. 747.

69. So I infer from Sidney's note that the Divine's "scope" is "as far
    beyonde any of these [rivals] as eternitie exceedeth a moment"
    (I, 163). When he later entitles his poet the "Monarch" of "all
    Sciences," he reminds us that he "speaks still of humane [knowl-
    edge], and according to humaine conceits" (I, 172).

70. I, 169. Whenever Sidney turns from poetry in theory to poetry as
    it should be practiced, he treats the poet as a kind of artist, and
    imitation becomes the process of following models rather than
    representing what never was. The first half of the *Apologie* is
    mainly theoretical, the second largely practical.

71. See Smith's notes on Minturno, Scaliger, Fracastorius, *et al.*; I, 395–
    397.

72. Spenser's letter to Raleigh, "Expounding His Whole Intention in the
    Course" of *The Faerie Queene;* in Dodge, pp. 136-138.

73. See *The Oxford Classical Dictionary* (Oxford, 1966), "Elegiac Po-
    etry, Greek," and "Elegiac Poetry, Latin." Also helpful is the
    briefer entry in William Flint Thrall and Addison Hibbard's
    A Handbook to Literature (New York, 1936). In *The Enduring
    Monument: A Study of the Idea of Praise in Renaissance Literary
    Theory and Practice* (Chapel Hill, N. C., 1962), O. B. Hardison
    presents a much more detailed analysis of the elegy and kindred
    genres.

74. In *Shakespeare's History Plays* (New York, 1962), however, E. M. W.
    Tillyard warns against not taking Falstaff scornfully enough. The
    "school of criticism that furnished him [Falstaff] with a tender
    heart and condemned the Prince for brutality in turning him away
    was deluded. . . . The sense of security created in nineteenth-
    century England by the predominance of the British navy in-
    duced men to rate that very security too cheaply and to exalt
    the instinct of rebellion above its legitimate station. They forgot
    the threat of disorder which was ever present with the Eliza-
    bethans. Schooled by recent events we should have no difficulty
    now in taking Falstaff as the Elizabethans took him" (p. 330).

75. Arber, p. 47.

76. See *The Oxford Classical Dictionary*, pp. 652–653.

77. In Dodge, p. 8.

78. See J. E. Spingarn, *A History of Literary Criticism in the Renais-
    sance* (New York, 1963), p. 35.

79. II, 25, 165; italics added. Cf. also II, 8: "For speech it selfe is arti-
    ficiall and made by man, . . . but speech by meeter is a kind of
    vtterance more cleanly couched and more delicate to the eare
    then prose is. . . . It is beside a maner of vtterance more eloquent
    and rethoricall then the ordinarie prose which we vse in our
    daily talke, because it is decked and set out with all maner of

fresh colours and figures, which maketh that it sooner inuegleth the iudgement of man, and carieth his opinion this way and that, whither soeuer the heart by impression of the eare shalbe most affectionatly bent and directed." Puttenham later glances at that kind of ornament "inwardly working a stirre to the mynde," not the ear, but his emphasis is always on how "we burnish our language" (II, 148).

80. Sonnet XXVIII, in Feuillerat, II, 254.
81. See *OED*.
82. Lewis, p. 469.
83. *Ibid.*, pp. 474–475.
84. *Ibid.*, p. 476.
85. See *The Oxford Classical Dictionary*, "Mimus" and "Pantomimus." Shorter but also helpful is the discussion of "mime" in *Aspects of the Drama: A Handbook*, compiled by Sylvan Barnet, Morton Berman, and William Burto (Boston, 1962), p. 229.
86. Preface to his first *Booke of Ayres* (1601); cited by Smith, II, 456.
87. *The Oxford Classical Dictionary*, "Archilochus." Also see "Catullus (1)"; "Epigram"; "Hipponax"; "Iambic Poetry, Greek"; "Iambic Poetry, Latin"; "Martial"; "Metre, Greek"; and "Metre, Latin."
88. I, 294. Webbe is translating part of George Fabricius's anthology of Horace's "Cannons or generall cautions of Poetry"; see I, 290, 416 ff.
89. See Spenser's "Letter" to Raleigh, in Dodge, p. 137, and *The Faerie Queene*, I. vii. 11; I. iv. 11–12.
90. *Ibid.*, VI. xii. 1; cf. also I. xii. 1; I. xii. 42.
91. *Ibid.*, VI. ix. 1.
92. The *OED* makes it clear that in Tudor times, both "hotchpot" (or "hotchpotch") and "gallimaufry" were almost always culinary terms. See also "Method, II, 6."
93. Lewis, p. 373.
94. *Mythology and the Renaissance Tradition in English Poetry* (Minneapolis, 1932), p. 6.
95. *Thee First Foure Bookes of Virgil his Aeneis* (1582), ed. with intro. by Edward Arber (London, 1880), pp. 100–101, 108, 114.
96. Cited by Henry Burrowes Lathrop, *Translations from the Classics into English from Caxton to Chapman, 1477–1620* (Madison, Wis., 1933), p. 131.
97. Ll. 2242, 2250, 2283–2285, in *The Poetical Works of Chaucer*, ed. F. N. Robinson (Cambridge, Mass., 1933).
98. *The Legend of Good Women*, ll. 1233–1237.

Suggestions for Further Reading

Some helpful collections of and commentaries upon Elizabethan criticism are noted at the conclusion to the previous chapter. The following studies, on the other hand, are not histories of criticism, but some successful efforts to see Tudor writers or translators reacting to contemporary critical contexts:

Bush, Douglas. *Mythology and the Renaissance Tradition in English Poetry*. Minneapolis, 1932.

Chute, Marchette. *Ben Jonson of Westminster*. New York, 1960.

————. *Shakespeare of London*. New York, 1949.

Craig, Hardin. *New Lamps for Old*. Oxford, 1960.

Doran, Madeleine. *Endeavors of Art*. Madison, Wis., 1954.

Harbage, Alfred. *Shakespeare and the Rival Traditions*. New York, 1952.

Hardison, O. B. *The Enduring Monument*. Chapel Hill, N. C., 1962.

Hunter, G. K. *John Lyly: The Humanist as Courtier*. London, 1962.

Jordan, John Clark. *Robert Greene*. New York, 1915.

Lathrop, Henry Burrowes. *Translations from the Classics into English from Caxton to Chapman, 1477–1620*. Madison, Wis., 1933.

Lewis, C. S. *English Literature in the Sixteenth Century*. Oxford, 1954.

Lucas, F. L. *Seneca and Elizabethan Tragedy*. London, 1922.

Matthiessen, F. O. *Translation: An Elizabethan Art*. Cambridge, Mass., 1931.

Pettet, E. C. *Shakespeare and the Romance Tradition*. London, 1949.

Prouty, Charles T. *George Gascoigne: Elizabethan Courtier, Soldier, and Poet*. New York, 1942.

————. *The Sources of Much Ado about Nothing*. New Haven, Conn., 1950.

White, Harold Ogden. *Plagiarism and Imitation During the English Renaissance*. Cambridge, Mass., 1935.

V

SIGNPOSTS TO ARDEN

Courtiers and Citizens at Play

Pointe forth six of the best giuen Ientlemen of this Court, and all they together, shew not so much good will, spend not so much tyme, bestow not so many houres, dayly, orderly, and constantly, for the increase of learning and knowledge, as doth the Queenes Maiestie her selfe. Yea I beleue, that beside her perfit readines, in *Latin, Italian, French,* and *Spanish*, she readeth here now at Windsore more *Greeke* euery day, than some Prebendarie of this Chirch doth read *Latin* in a whole weeke. . . . Whose onely example, if the rest of our nobilitie would folow, than might England be, for learnyng and wisedome in nobilitie, a spectacle to all the world beside.

—Roger Ascham, *The Scholemaster* (1570)

The people againe were wonderfullie rauished with the louing answers and gestures of their princesse. . . . For in all hir passage she did . . . shew hir most gratious loue toward the people in generall. . . . So that if a man would saie well, he could not better tearme the citie of London that time, than a stage, wherein was shewed the woonderfull spectacle of a noble hearted princesse towards hir most louing people, and the peoples exceeding comfort in beholding so woorthie a souereigne.

—Holinshed's *Chronicles*, An. Dom. 1559

But I shall tell yoo, Master Martin, by the mass, of a mad adventure. Az thiz Savage, for the more submission, brake hiz tree asunder, kest [cast] the top from him, it had allmost light upon her Highness hors head; whereat he startld, and the gentleman mooch dismayd. See the benignittee of the Prins; as the footmen lookt well to the hors, and hee of generositee soon calmd of himself—"no hurt, no hurt!" quoth her Highness. Which words I promis yoo wee wear all glad to heer; and took them too be the best part of the Play.

    —Robert Laneham, *A Letter . . . of . . . This Soomerz Progress, 1575.*

Gloriana's Private Theater

Elizabeth's tutor tells us that she was a spectacle of scholarship; her chief historian, that the royal touch turned England's largest city into a stage. For our present purpose, however, the most valuable kind of information is furnished by one of the humbler Tudor household officers, Robert Laneham, a rather roguish Keeper of the Council Chamber Door.[1] That any Renaissance prince was capable of making a truly majestic entry comes as no surprise. We also expect of each a "perfit readines" in several tongues. But what would Machiavelli have advised concerning the situation Elizabeth found herself in at Leicester's Kenilworth on July 11, 1575?

Returning from the hunt that Monday evening, the Queen is suddenly stayed by "a Savage man, all in ivie."[2] She recognizes this "woodwose," or wild man of the woods, as that medieval folk-personage, the Green Man, who had long contributed to the rich pageantry of the Lord Mayors' shows. And under the weedy regalia she probably perceives the courtliness of George Gascoigne. But she, too, has a role to play. The question to be asked is not "What are you up to now, George?," but something like "What would yon savage with me?" The wild man is, of course, dumbfounded. Why has he, "Ordeyned thus in savage wise for ever more to be," recently observed such splendor and beauty in the groves of Kenilworth? Oddly enough, it is Jupiter who is asked, and the classical nymph, Echo, who answers. In jangling poulter's measure, ornamented with Roman myth and British legend, Savage Man makes his own plaint, rehearses the festivities to date, and neatly underlines their Arthurian motif. Between each couplet Echo repeats the woodwose's last syllables, thus ingeniously providing him with information sufficient to evoke further exclamations of wonder, and eventually setting him up for a pun on Leicester's name:

Gifts? what? sent from the Gods, as presents from above?
Or pleasures of provision, as tokens of true love?
Eccho.   True love.
And who gave all these gifts? I pray thee *(Eccho)* say;
Was it not he who (but of late) this building here did lay?
Eccho.   Dudley.
O, Dudley, so methought: he gave himselfe and all,
A worthy gift to be received, and so I trust it shall.
Eccho.   It shall.

(I, 496)

Echo finally leads Savage Man to realize that he stands before Elizabeth of England, whereupon he immediately kneels, delivers some choice flattery, and promises that

On Thursday next (thinke I) here will be pleasant dames;
Who bet then I may make you glee, with sundry gladsome
    games.

Gascoigne's description of his own excellent device ends here. Modesty (or pride) forbids his noting an event that led to what Laneham calls the "best part of the Play." As wild men are prone to do, he overplayed his part, and that grandly savage gesture of submission could have killed his Queen. If "no hurt, no hurt!" bespeaks her "benignittee," a more romantic aspect of her character is suggested by the quickness with which she apparently returned the "mooch dismayd" Gascoigne to the make-believe he had inadvertently punctured.

It is difficult to make any sense out of what happened during Kenilworth's nineteen-day sylvan frolic unless we assume that Ascham's diligent student admired Greek but loved Malory. For contemporary educators, she is naturally the scholar's scholar. For literary critics like Puttenham, she is the poet's poet, "whose learned, delicate, noble Muse easily surmounteth all the rest that haue written before her time or since." [3] Foreign diplomats respect her as an astute friend or enemy, a damnably clever woman who often sees the international scene more clearly and steadily than most of the patriots in her Parliament and Privy Council. But there is also the Gloriana side of Elizabeth; at first the frightened girl, finally the lonely old woman, but always, like her father, willing to entertain the marvelous. As "Perfect Beautie" in her "Fortresse" of Whitehall, she is besieged by "The Four Foster

Children of Desire," among them, Sidney and Fulke Greville. As the "Beauteous Quene of second Troye," she has Envy's blocks of malice removed from her path by the Graces and Hours. From "a goodly Pond, cut to the perfect figure of a half moon" by the Earl of Hertford, Nereus and his train of Tritons salute "Faire Cinthia the wide Ocean's Empresse," and squealing Daphnes fleeing lecherous Apollos naturally beg succor from "the Queene of Chastety."

In all this romantic stuff we tend to see a wily goddess encouraging her chief priests to develop a cult, a series of elaborate rituals through which she might inspire the loyalties of self-seeking courtiers. But *Realpolitik* hardly explains other quixotic devisings that Elizabeth sponsored. The following is merely a sampling of the romantic fare presented at Court between 1572 and 1582:

> 1573–1573/4: Playes showen at Whytehall videlicet . . . Herpetulus the blew knight & perobia playde by my Lorde klintons servantes the third of January.
>
> 1573–1573/4: Heare [hair] for the wylde Men
>
> 1573–1573/4: Propertymaker Iohn Caro for mony to him due for sundry percells
>> Holly & Ivye for the play of predor . . .
>> ffyshes Cownterfete for the same . . .
>> A payle for the castell topp . . .
>> Past & paper for the dragons head . . .
>> Deale boordes for the senat howse.
>
> 1576/7: The Historie of the Solitarie knight showen at Whitehall on Shrovesundaie at night, enacted by the Lord Howardes seruauntes.
>
> 1578/9. The history of the Knight in the Burnyng Rock shewen at Whitehall on Shrovesondaie at night enacted by the Earle of Warwickes servauntes.
>
> April 1581: The Mounte, Dragon with ye fyer woorkes, Castell with ye falling sydes Tree with shyldes, hermytage & hermytt, Savages, Enchaunter, Charryott, & incydentes to theis. cc markes.[4]

Two things should be noted concerning these wondrous spectacles. First, it is the world of lusty loves and doughty deeds that at least partially replaces the more realistic and sometimes politically oriented representations previously featured at Elizabeth's Court. The Protestant Queen's first mask (Twelfth Night, 1559) presented crows, asses, and wolves dressed in the habits of cardinals, bishops, and abbots. The early years also saw courtiers decked out as astronomers, fishermen, patriarchs, barbarians, shipmen, and "swartrutters," soldiers in black armor with blackened faces, like those currently infesting the Netherlands.[5] Since Court tastes were dictated by the Queen, she must have been ultimately responsible for the knights, enchanters, dragons, and hermitages that came to supplant the more "relevant" figures. Secondly, in all the fabulous adventures enacted by the servants of Clinton, Howard, and Warwick, there was no role for Elizabeth to play. The Knight of the Burning Rock might have advanced values she was known to hold, and perhaps his "Solitarie" cousin made some flattering allusions. It seems more likely, however, that Elizabeth genuinely enjoyed romantic story for its own sake than that she went to such incredible lengths for merely practical ends.

The many knights who follow Herpetulus and his Perobia tell us that Lord Clinton's men scored a hit. The fact of the Blue Knight's popularity must in turn be explained in one of the following ways: (1) Both Queen and Court sincerely relished what strikes us as impossibly quixotic; (2) the Queen saw it as silly stuff, but realized that when Tudor myths needed bolstering, dragons and falling castles were just the thing for her impressionable courtiers; (3) the Court thought it wise to indulge Her Highness's incurably romantic disposition; (4) both Queen and Court thought such stuff absurd, but each side always assumed the other was taking it seriously. The last alternative offers a surfeit of exquisite ironies; for more than forty years neither party realized it was being gulled. The second and third, on the other hand, are suspicions always worth entertaining. By 1581 the Rose of the House of Tudor surely realized that she had withered, that even with a Platonic gloss her Beautie was not quite Perfect; seven years later, the Spanish invaders discovered the value of fiction known to be fiction but cultivated as fact. Under many a fanciful devising, it is even easier to find some lord bidding for advancement in or restoration to the royal favor. But the equally romantic deeds and writings of men like Raleigh, Sidney, and Essex cannot always be explained along such practical lines; actions that bring them out of grace are likely to be as extravagantly chivalrous as those which got them in.

The *Arcadia* was not written to humor anyone's illusions. As for the Queen, there were moments with no gallery to play to, no one but herself to please. In 1564 Sir James Melville, ambassador of Mary Queen of Scots, attempted to satisfy Elizabeth's curiosity about her cousin, even offering

> to convey her secretly to Scotland by post, clothed like a page; that under this disguise she might see the Queen, as James the Fifth had gone in disguise to France with his own ambassador, to see the Duke of Vendome's sister, who should have been his wife. Telling her, that her chamber might be kept in her absence as though she were sick; that none needed to be privy thereto, except my Lady Stafford and one of the grooms of her chamber. *She appeared to like that kind of language*, only answered it with a sigh, saying, alas, if I might do it thus.[6]

Elizabeth eventually realized that it would be far safer to "do it thus" within the nooks and crannies of her own realm. During the winter months, make-believe remained something mostly to be watched in the chambers of Whitehall, Greenwich, or Hampton Court. In the summer, however, Gloriana helped create it, turning any visitable city street or country lawn she pleased into the faraway land of Herpetulus. Whereas the descriptions of the entertainments presented at the early Court are scattered and vague, many of those offered Elizabeth during her annual progresses are quite precise. Beginning with the Queen's reception at Bristol in August, 1574, and concluding with the Harefield festivities of 1602, there are more than a dozen detailed reports of her sundry "joyfull receavinges" into country towns and the houses of her nobles, many of which were promptly published for the benefit of the Londoners back home.[7] The accounts are generally enthusiastic and filled with congratulatory praise. The songs, harangues, and gestures of every lisping nymph, lurking sibyl, and fawning satyr or woodwose were delivered to perfection. The reader can only gather that rude reality never intruded, that this most noble lord or that most courteous citizen reaped a rich harvest of royal gratitude, and that the thanks of the whole nation were certainly due the gallant deviser—who, more often than not, was also the narrator, peddling his own wares. There are too few earthy Lanehams to balance the ecstatic Gascoignes.

Of the varied romantic worlds that burgeoned amid Gloriana's presence, none outshone those conjured up by Leicester in 1575. This favorite had already been granted titles, monopolies, lands, even the grounds he was now busily enchanting, and the recurrent themes underlying the devisings with which Dudley besieged her indicate that the rising star now sought the benefactress herself. For such amorous warfare, no expense was spared; the revels are said to have cost the gem-girt lord about a thousand pounds daily.[8] To the impressionable countryfolk of Warwickshire—an eleven-year-old William Shakespeare may have been among them [9] —the splendors must have inspired a reverence akin to that with which the peasants of Calais viewed the proceedings on the Field of the Cloth of Gold, where Henry VIII and Francis I rubbed noses in high Renaissance fashion. For the Queen's flattery as much as for her protection, Dudley had numerous regiments and cannon placed in the outlying areas. His main hope, however, centered in a formidable rank of poets, each employed to fire off adulatory fragments of verse and prose at the most opportune moments: William Hunnis, Master of the Chapel; John Badger, Beadle of Oxford; George Ferrers, sometime Lord of Misrule in the Court; Richard Mulcaster, Master of the Merchant Taylors' School and formerly Spenser's headmaster; Henry Goldingham, evidently a professional pageantwright (three years later, he reappears at Norwich); and finally George Gascoigne, soldier, critic, courtier, and poet *extraordinaire,* who "did the lion's share of the writing" and whose *Princely Pleasures* (1576) is "the first complete version of any Elizabethan masque or revel." [10]

From Hunnis's "Speeches of Sibylla" on July 9 through Gascoigne's "Farewell of Silvanus" on the 27th, the Queen obligingly underwent the gamut of former fabulous story. To those who waded farther with classical and medieval myths, it must have been obvious that the shrewd Dudley was not wont to part with twenty thousand pounds without some lucrative scheme in view. And in Leicester's commission to pen part of the Kenilworth program, Gascoigne certainly saw long-desired preferment at hand, "a chance to recoup low-fallen fortunes." [11] His fellow devisers would have also welcomed royal patronage. It was no doubt recent life, as well as the old chronicles Marlowe read, that inspired Piers Gaveston's subacid commentary upon masking as machination:

> I must have wanton poets, pleasant wits,
> Musicians that with touching of a string
> May draw the pliant king which way I please.

Music and poetry is his delight.
Therefore I'll have Italian masks by night,
Sweet speeches, comedies, and pleasing shows;
And in the day when he shall walk abroad,
Like sylvan nymphs my pages shall be clad:
My men, like satyrs grazing on the lawns,
Shall with their goat feet dance an antic hay:
Sometimes a lovely boy in Dian's shape,

. . . .

Shall bathe him in a spring: and there hard by,
One like Actaeon peeping through the grove,
Shall by the angry goddess be transform'd:
And running in the likeness of an hart
By yelping hounds pull'd down, and seem to die.
Such things as these best please His Majesty.[12]

Leicester, long an intimate favorite, well knew which shows best pleased a less pliant Sovereign. Flattery couched in romantic lore might win the trick, and he had sent his poets off to the tales of Malory, Ovid, and British folklore. As Elizabeth approached the castle on Saturday, July 9, recalls Gascoigne, "*Sibylla* being placed in an arbor in the parke . . . did step out" and "prophecied unto her Highness the prosperous raigne that she should continue" (I, 486 ff.). At the main gate her arrival is seemingly heralded by gigantic pasteboard representations of trumpeters, placed in the battlements and signifying "that in the daies and reigne of King Arthure, men were of that stature; so that the Castel of Kenelworth should seeme still to be kept by Arthur's heires and their seruants" (I, 490). The porter at the gate—none other than Hercules—first offers to stay her passage but, overcome by "rare beutie and prince-lie countenance," soon surrenders both his keys and himself. The Queen now nears the lower court. Here Leicester, taking advantage of his estate's natural situation, serves up his most romantic devising. Across a pond adjacent to the castle, "being so conveyed, that it seemed shee had gone upon the water," proceeds the Lady of the Lake, attended by two nymphs (I, 491). In a forty-two-line rehearsal of Saxon and Norman invasions, the Lady explains why she has "led a lowring life in restles paine" since Arthur's departure. Elizabeth's third visit [13] has broken the enchantment and "voides the place from feare." After this benedic-

tion, the Queen makes her way over the bridge leading to the inner
court, where she is greeted with some Latin verses penned by
Mulcaster and several flourishes of drums, fifes, and trumpets.

Sunday proves relatively uneventful, but a display of fireworks
upon the water enlivens the evening.[14] On Monday, Savage Man
brandishes a branch to prove his wildness, then breaks it to signify
his newly acquired civility, and finally heralds Thursday's "gladsome games." Behind such "glee" we can again detect a serious
purpose. The "games" were to have been a mask celebrating one of
Diana's chaste nymphs, Zabeta. This "shewe," Gascoigne laments,
although "prepared and redy (every Actor in his garment) two or
three days together, . . . never came to execution. The cause
whereof I cannot attribute to any other thing than to lack of
opportunity and seasonable weather" (I, 515). Even Laneham
blames inclement elements (I, 459), but it is probable that the matter was dropped because Elizabeth got wind of its significance.
The abortive woodland show opens with Diana's mourning over
the loss of Zabeta and her prayer to Jupiter that this most loved of
all nymphs be found. Mercury restores her to Diana's train, but
Iris, Juno's messenger, is given the closing forty-six lines, strongly
admonishing the coy beauty to exchange dignified celibacy for
wedded bliss. Both Gascoigne and his patron were treading dangerous ground; Parliament had already discovered how elusive the
nymph under whom it sat could be.

The next principal devising freely draws from both Olympus
and Camelot. Returning from the hunt on Monday, July 18, Elizabeth is again stopped, this time by Triton, riding upon a mermaid
near the bridge to the inner court (I, 498 ff.). This minor deity
explains that Neptune has sent him to declare the new perils into
which the Lady of the Lake has fallen. (Shades of Hobgoblin!)
Because of his "inordinate lust," the Lady long ago enclosed
Merlin in a rock. Since that time his cousin, "Sir *Bruse sauns pitie*"
(Shades of Malory!), has sought vengeance. She is presently his
captive, awaiting the fulfillment of Merlin's prophecy that she
will be delivered only "by the presence of a better maide than
herselfe." By merely crossing the bridge, Elizabeth satisfies
Neptune, conquers the wicked Sir Bruse, and wins the loyalty of
the Lady, who floats over the pond "upon heapes of bulrushes"
to render obeisance. The show was designed to be even more "gallant," according to Gascoigne. Before the Lady's delivery, "a
Captaine with twentie or thyrtie shotte should have bene sent from

the Hearon House (which represented the Lady of the Lake's Castell)" and Sir Bruse was to have assembled like numbers upon the shore; during the evening, these two forces were to have engaged in a sea-skirmish.[15] In any case, there was time for the aquatic revelry to be concluded with the appearance of Proteus, sitting upon a dolphin twenty-four feet long and propelled by a boat underneath. So artfully contrived was this vessel that the oars resembled dolphin's fins, and within the docile creature "a consort of musicke [group of musicians] was secretely placed, the which sounded; and Protheus, clearing his voyce, sang . . . [a] song of congratulation" and then told the Queen "a pleasant tale of his deliverie, and the fishes which he had in charge." [16]

Although Gascoigne's Mask of Zabeta was countermanded, he and Leicester renewed their pursuit on the last day of Elizabeth's visit. Again the Queen's hunt is interrupted by one clad in savage guise; again the author and presenter is Gascoigne, decked out this time as Silvanus, the Roman god of the woods (I, 515 ff.). His whole realm, he reports, while flourishing under her glorious aspect, now evinces signs of decay at the prospect of her departure. To enforce his request that she remain forever in the groves of Kenilworth, Silvanus breathlessly pours out a variation of the Zabeta story. Surpassing all the nymphs of Diana's court was *"Ahtebasile,"* also known as Zabeta. This proud fair refused the most noble and worthy suitors and in her scorn metamorphosed poor *"Constance"* into "this old Oke," and "his contrarie Inconstancie into yonder Popler." Some transformations were justly done, to be sure, but the pitiful case of *"Deepedesire"* proves a most cruel exception.

> At these wordes her Majestie came by a close arbor, made all of Hollie; and whiles Silvanus pointed to the same, the principal bush shaked. For therein were placed both strange musicke, and one who was there appointed to represent Deepedesire.
>
> (I, 520)

Accompanied by his "consort of musicke," the trembling Deepedesire quavers out a message of Nature's impending travail and (except she remain) of his own certain death. With arch ambiguity, Silvanus then pleads that Elizabeth will either be a suitor unto the gods for the holly's plight or give her "gracious consent that

hee be restored to his prystinate estate" (I, 523). Upon this note
The Princely Pleasures closes.

Laneham covers less ground, but with a livelier pace. "The
Blak Prinz"—so he dubs himself—provides a witty commentary on
the misfortune that befell Savage Man, and those other splendid
events that his official duties did not prevent him from witnessing
are described in a racy and vivid style. Arthur's welcoming trumpeters, for instance, are "armonious blasterz"; Savage Man becomes "*Hombre Salvagio,* with an oken plant pluct up by the
roots in hiz hande, himself forgrone all in moss and ivy"; Gascoignes "Protheus" is turned into Arion, "that excellent and fa-
mouz muzicien, in tyre [attire] and appointment straunge, well seeming to hiz parson, ryding alofte upon hiz old freend the dolphin"
(I, 431, 436, 458). Laneham is most valuable when including royal
asides during a moment of make-believe, and some are more jocular
than "no hurt, no hurt!" When the Lady of the Lake offers *her*
realm to Elizabeth, for example, "it pleazed her Highness too thank
this Lady, and too add withall, 'we had thought indeed the Lake
had been oours, and doo you call it yourz noow? Well, we will
herein common [commune] more with yoo hereafter' " (I, 431).

In view of such facetious descriptions, we might well expect the
witty court official to wreak merry havoc upon the poets' romantic artificialities. Instead, Laneham is filled with admiration for
their most fantastic flights. Gascoigne's Device of Savage Man
was "pronounced in good meeter and matter, very wel indighted in
rime," his abortive Mask of Zabeta contained "ingenious argument,"
and the Hunnis-Ferrers-Goldingham presentation evinced "tyme,
tune, and temper . . . incomparably melodious, . . . sharpnes of
conceyt, . . . [and] lyvely delighte" (I, 437, 458–459). It is not
romantic conventions, but folk celebrations and rustic antics, that
receive continual ridicule. On Sunday, July 17, Elizabeth was entertained with country shows of a bride-ale, quintain, and morris
dances by the folk of the parish and with episodes from a Hock
Tuesday play by the men of Coventry. So ludicrous does the
narrator find the bovine bride, her loutish husband, and his
boorish cohorts, and so humorous Captain Cox, romantic antiquarian [17] and leader of the Coventry expedition, that a knowing
smirk accompanies the reporting of each performance. Those running at the quintain are betrayed by their amorous steeds or
strike the target with their heads instead of their spears (I, 445).

The Hock-day dumb show, representing the victory of English women over Danish invaders in the eleventh century, is reduced to a barnyard assault of foxes upon geese. Elizabeth seems to have enjoyed the latter, however, for she remunerated the warriors and requested that they "have it full oout" the following Tuesday. Perhaps this was Zabeta's revenge. One purpose for summer progresses was to withdraw from Court intrigue, and the Queen no doubt found these rustic revels a relaxing change from Leicester's pliant strings.

Despite Deepedesire's quavering protests, Gloriana and her train promptly removed from Kenilworth on July 27, visited no less than twenty-four estates during the following month, and arrived at Woodstock, in Buckinghamshire, on August 29.[18] Here she was welcomed by Sir Henry Lee, her official Champion and Master of the Game at the estate.[19] Although the only account of Elizabeth's thirty-six-day sojourn at Woodstock comes to us in a mutilated tract printed by Cadman in 1585,[20] enough remains to indicate that Lee offered the Queen a diet as romantic as Leicester's, but with arguments less pointed and "practical." The program in its extant form begins as one Hemetes, a hermit, interrupts two knights, Loricus and Contarenus, who have been fighting before the latter's true love, Lady Caudina. Hemetes brings all three to a bower, where Elizabeth sits, and commences his story. Once upon a time in the country of Cambia there was a mighty Duke, Occanon, whose dearest possession was his only child, Caudina, heiress to his rich realm and wooed by many worthy suitors. Contarenus, a knight "of estate but meane, but of value very greate," eventually won her love, and "in smal proces of time the seecret fires of their fancies discoured by the smoake of their desires, bewrayed this matter vnto her father long time before they woulde." [21] The crafty Duke neither rebuked his daughter nor challenged her lover, but hired an enchantress to have the knight borne through the air far from his realm. After depositing Contarenus upon "the very bounds of the *Occean* sea," the sorceress charged him to care for the blind Hemetes, promising that within seven years he would obtain his lady, and the hermit his sight. Before these miracles come to pass, however, Contarenus must "fight with the hardiest knight, and see the worthiest Lady of the world." Meanwhile the grief-stricken Caudina fled the kingdom in disguise and, "at the grate of *Sibilla*," ventured upon Sir Loricus, a knight seeking renown to gain his mistress's favor. The prophetess bade them wander together until they found a land "where men were most strong, women most fayre, the countrey most fertile, the people most wealthy, the gouernment most iust, and the Princes most worthy: so shoulde the Lady see that would content her, so should the knight heare that might comfort him." [22]

The prophecies are of course resolved by the presence of England's Elizabeth and Elizabeth's England. But Hemetes adds to this adulatory cross fire by turning to the Queen and confessing that he, too, has been under an enchantment. Once a brave knight who dearly loved the worthiest of ladies, he was blinded by Venus for seeking learning as well as beauty. Mercury brought him to Delphos, where Apollo promised his sight would be restored when "two of the most valiant knights shal fight, two of the most constant louers shal meet, and the most vertuous Lady of the world shall be there to looke on." [23] The obvious morals are consequently expounded, and the rejoicing Hemetes leads the Queen to his hermitage, actually an elaborate sylvan banqueting house sheltered by a great oak. While the hermit goes off to do his orisons, Elizabeth is entertained by "the Queen of the Fayry," who presents her with an embroidered gown. Caudina renders a speech, the "sprite" of the oak a song, and the pastoral devising concludes with the Queen's "earnest command that the whole in order as it fell, should be brought her in writing." [24]

The magical groves through which Zabeta led her often weary train continued to abound in figures and scenes as unreal as those we meet in *The Faerie Queene* or *The Countesse of Pembrokes Arcadia*. Some sang, others lectured, and occasionally the more daring begged. As the Queen entered Wanstead Garden in May, 1578, an honest country wife, prompted by Sir Philip Sidney, "came suddenly among the train, . . . crying out for justice." [25] Her only daughter, the May Lady, is being so fiercely wooed by Espilus, a shepherd, and Therion, a forester, that "bloodie controversie" must soon erupt. In the presence of majesty, however, peace is restored. The rivals vie with songs, cornets, and recorders, and Elizabeth deigns to involve herself in this pastoral *débat* by choosing the victor. In similar wise at Cowdray during August, 1591, while hunting or merely meandering about Viscount Montague's handsome estate, the Queen at divers times is suddenly stayed by a nymph, pilgrim, wild man, angler, netter, and rustic dancers with pipe and tabor (III, 90–96). Each has a little gift and well-turned compliment to offer. With a "sweet song" the nymph,

for instance, presents her with a crossbow and a paddock full of
deer; from a "delicate bowre" the royal musicians play while Elizabeth and the Countess of Kildare fire away at the enclosed
animals (III, 91).

The Bisham, Sudeley, and Rycote Entertainments of 1592 again
feature blendings of classical, medieval-romantic, and Renaissance-
pastoral worlds, each spiced with homespun realism. Upon a hill
overlooking Lady Russell's Bisham on August 21, the Queen's approach is heralded by "Cornets sounding in the Woods," at which
a woodwose appears, questioning the meaning of such "enchanted"
strains (III, 131 ff.). Like Kenilworth's Savage Man, he has been
informed by Echo that "Shee it is, and you are Shee, whom in our
dreames many yeares wee Satyres have seene, but waking could
never find any such." Accompanied by her trusty Savage, Elizabeth begins to descend the hill; halfway down they confront Pan
and two virgins, Sybilla and Isabella, "keeping sheepe, and sowing
in their samplers" (III, 132). In a pleasant dialogue these modest
bourgeois deities compare the Queen's visit to the benign Jupiter's
sojourn at the house of poor Baucis, and Sybilla plans to "entreat
her to come into the valley, that our houses may be blessed with
her presence." Last, at the foot of the hill, "Ceres with her
Nymphes, in an harvest cart, meet her Majesty" and offer up "a
crown of wheat-ears with a jewell" (III, 135). Lady Russell and
her son, Sir Edward Hoby, have attempted to step beyond Kenilworth by taking advantage of an autumnal landscape. But they
could hardly have realized that their "hockey," the feast at harvest-
home, antedates the Roman invasion of England, and that "wheat-
ears" and house-blessings belonged to the native pagan Britons
long before Ovid wrote of Baucis.

Two weeks later the harvest motif reappeared at Lord Chandos's
Sudeley Castle. Before the gates of the fortress stood an old
shepherd, who presented the Queen with a "lock of wooll, Cots-
holdes best fruite," whose whiteness of course symbolizes undefiled virginity (III, 137). This theme was in turn expanded on the
following day, when a local Daphne fled into the arms of "the
Queene of Chastety," begging protection from a lustful neighborhood Apollo. Finally, from Lord Norris at Rycote in September
and October, Elizabeth received gifts more valuable, but entertainment less fanciful (III, 168–172). Her old friend and loyal
soldier greets her in his own person and presents a fair gown. As
she walks in his garden during the ensuing week, messengers just

arrived, as it were, from Ireland, Flanders, France, and Jersey
come in with gifts from the retired general's sons and daughter:
a golden dart, for example, set with diamonds and inscribed with
the posy, "I flye onely for my Soveraigne." As Norris admits, his
make-believe is but a "rough hewen tale of souldier" compared
to "so much smooth speeches of Muses." Gloriana was perceptive
enough to see the genuine affection underneath these older-fashioned devisings, however, and though no romantic personages
haunted the Rycote groves, she honored them with many visists.[26]

In contrast to the relatively simple fare of long-trusted friends
was the elaborate reception given by Edward Seymour, Earl of
Hertford, at Elvetham in September, 1591. We cannot be sure
which poets and dramatists Hertford hired to grace the Queen's
stay. From the Elvetham festivities one song found its way into an
Elizabethan anthology, *England's Helicon* (1600), where it is
ascribed to Nicholas Breton.[27] Professor Warwick Bond long ago
claimed the entertainment as a whole, as well as the speeches at
Cowdray, Bisham, Sudeley, and Rycote, for John Lyly.[28] Regardless of whose muses Hertford employed, the reasons for the great
trouble and expense to which he went are transparent. Unlike
Norris, the Earl had lived a good portion of the reign under one
cloud or another. In the winter of 1560 Catherine Grey, great-
granddaughter of Henry VII and heiress-presumptive to the
Crown, had quietly left Whitehall, slipped down the Thames in a
barge, secretly married Hertford in his own lodgings, and returned
to Court in time for dinner.[29] The identity of the clergyman who
performed the ceremony was known only to Hertford's sister
and sole witness, Lady Jane Seymour, who died several months
later. By the following August Catherine could no longer conceal
her pregnancy. Her husband had been sent to France, whence he
was sending presents to other women of the Court, but no responses to her letters. As a last resort Catherine appealed to Leicester, then Lord Robert Dudley, who in turn revealed all to the
Queen. Within the afternoon Catherine was conveyed from Ips-
wich, where the Court was on progress, to the Tower, where she
bore a son. The young Earl was recalled from France and quartered in another suite. The guards were evidently open to bribery,
for Hertford soon offered the Queen the purely gratuitous insult
of getting Lady Catherine with a second son. For such incontinence
the Star Chamber fined him fifteen thousand pounds: "£ 5000 for
deflowering a virgin of the blood royal in the Queen's home,

£ 5000 for breaking out of quarters, and £ 5000 for repeating his wickedness." [30] More damaging was the Privy Council's action to neutralize the danger posed by prospective princes. Since Hertford could produce neither clergyman, witness, nor marriage settlement, a commission under Archbishop Parker declared the children illegitimate.[31] After seven years of imprisonment Catherine died; her husband spent almost nine years in close custody or house arrest.

Although Hertford must have been partially forgiven by 1584—a German visitor mentions him as one of the "handsome old gentlemen" attending the Queen in her great hall at Greenwich[32]—he probably saw in Elizabeth's sole visit to Elvetham an opportunity to expiate any remaining guilt. And just as Leicester had shadowed forth his wooing of Zabeta with fanciful embroidery, so Hertford approached his equally serious mission of atonement with devices passing strange. Unfortunately, as the anonymous narrator acknowledges in "The Proeme," Elvetham was "none of the Earle's chiefe mansion houses" (III, 101 ff.). It was situated in a park merely two miles in circumference. Far worse, its lack of a convenient pond seemed to rule out Kenilworth's adulatory water deities or any other attempt to capitalize upon the fact that Elizabeth, since the recent defeat of the Armada, now enjoyed a new title: Empress of the Ocean. Nevertheless, "to shew his unfained love, and loyall duetie . . . his honor with all expedition set artificers a work, to the number of three hundred, many daies before her Majestie's arrivall" (III, 101). The house was greatly enlarged; halls, bowers, galleries, and a withdrawing chamber were set up to accommodate Queen, attendant nobles, and servants; a whole set of tiled offices for the royal quartermasters was hastily erected. Finally, to offset Nature's parsimony, the Earl managed a *tour de force* in Elizabethan engineering. Between his expanded house and the newly created commissaries was constructed,

> by handy labour, a goodly Pond, cut to the perfect figure of a half moon. In this Pond were three notable grounds, where hence to present her Majestie with sports and pastimes. The first was a *Ship Ile*, of a hundred foot in length, and four-score foote broad, bearing three trees orderly set for three masts. The second was a *Fort* twentie foot square every way, and overgrown with willows. The third and last was a *Snayl Mount*, rising to foure circles of

greene privie hedges, the whole in height twentie foot, and fortie foote broad at the bottom. These three places were equally distant from the sides of the ponde, and everie one, by a just measured proportion, distant from the other. In the said water were divers boates prepared for musicke: but especially there was a pinnace, ful furnisht with masts, yards, sailes, anchors, cables, and all other ordinarie tackling, and with iron peeces; and lastly with flagges, streamers, and pendants, to the number of twelve, all painted with divers colours, and sundry devises.[33]

Having thus improved upon Nature to the point of shaping his pond to resemble fair Cynthia, not to mention the infamous crescent formation in which the Armada had sailed to destroy her,[34] the Earl then busied himself with last-minute preparations. About nine in the morning all the servants were summoned to "the chiefe thicket of the parke," where Hertford assured them that their reputation, as well as his own, would soon be at stake. Various virgins, poets, and mythological personages were then strategically deployed while the Earl and his train of two hundred posted forth to meet the Queen at Odiham Park. Early in the evening their return is stayed inside the gates by a "sooth-saying poet," who salutes Elizabeth with a "Latine Oration, in heroicall verse" (III, 104). While "Augusta" is being reminded that in her radiance all calumny disappears, six maids, representing the Graces and Hours, begin removing Envy's malicious blocks from her path. From here the "Beauteous Quene of second Troye" rides up the flower-strewn way to greet the Elvetham dignitaries. Soon after retiring to her suite, which of course looked out upon the pond, she is entertained with "a long volley of chambers" fired between the Snail Mount and Ship Isle. The first day closed with a concert and one of Thomas Morley's pavans.

On the next day Hertford set his aquatic machinery in full gear. Shortly after dinner Elizabeth is seated under a "canapie of estate" at the pond's head. Out of a bower at the other end of the water issues Nereus, followed by five Tritons, "cheerefully sounding their trumpets" (III, 110). Next appear Neptune, Oceanus, Phorcus, and Glaucus, all leading a gaily decorated pinnace, upon whose decks three virgins play Scottish jigs. Accompanying these cornettists are three others singing to a lute, as well as Neaera, "the old supposed love of Sylvanus." The rest of this "pompous array of sea-persons" remains behind the pinnace, drawing smaller boats and bearing "huge woodden squirt[s]." As the watery crew swims toward the Queen, Tritons and virgins play antiphonally, the Fort becomes invested with warriors, the Snail Mount turns into a "monster, having hornes full of wild-fire," and one of the Nereids does a "summersawt" from the Ship Isle into the water. These strange events are immediately expounded by Nereus, who has by this time conducted his train to the chair of state. "Faire Cinthia the wide Ocean's Empresse" is told that

> we Sea-gods,
> (Whose jealous waves have swallowed up your foes,
> And to your Realme are walles impregnable,)
> With such large favour seldome time are grac't:
> I from the deepes have drawen this winding flud,
> Whose crescent forme figures the rich increase
> Of all that sweet Elisa holdeth deare.
>
> (III, 112)

The theme of the succeeding lines centers in the supreme economic, biological, and political efficacy of the regal countenance. Nereus explains that the somersaulter is "gould breasted India, / . . . daunted at your sight," whose ship has turned into a fertile island "from verdure of your lookes." The snail was once an "ugly monster creeping from the South / To spoyle these blessed fields of Albion," but is now metamorphosed "By selfe same beams." For the Queen's protection, Neptune kindly raised the Fort; for her recreation, Thetis sent her "musicke maydes." Nereus then offers a jewel, betokening the "endlesse treasure" that India has bestowed on Albion before her hasty departure, and finally a song, which is first answered "dialogue-wise" by the pinnace, and secondly, "as if they had beene ecchoes," by the smaller boats.

Not content with borrowing Gascoigne's device of classical Echo, Hertford next appropriated his Savage Man. Directly after the antiphonal hymn to Eliza, the five Tritons sound, and Silvanus, attired in hairy kids' skins and goat's head, and followed by his ivy-leaved, dart-wielding attendants, intrudes upon the scene. As the woodland god delivers a "holly scutchion, wherein Apollo had long since written her praises," he confesses that "those faire beames that shoote from Majesty" have drawn him forth (III, 111, 114). His worship is interrupted by Neaera, who would descend from her pinnace if Silvanus will vow gentlemanly conduct. Her references to his former wantonness naturally evoke further insults from her musical maids, and soon the gods of wood and sea are engaged in amphibious combat, a charming battle of darts against syringes. Silvanus is eventually "duckt" and retreats to the bower at the pond's end, thoroughly frightening "a number of the contrey people, . . . [who] ran from him for feare, and thereby moved great laughter" (III, 115). Tuesday's revels are ended as Neaera presents Elizabeth with a jeweled sea fan, and the Queen christens her pinnace "The Bonadventure."

Having thus waded beyond Kenilworth to underline Albion's triumph over the Armada, the Earl retreated to Arcadia to open the third day in a pastoral vein. Gloriana is awakened by three musicians "disguised in auncient countrey attire," singing a madrigal of Coridon and Phyllida beneath her gallery window (III, 116). This is followed in the afternoon by several games of "bord and cord" (lawn tennis?) and in the evening by a sumptuous banquet in the garden. While the Court dines upon one thousand dishes served by two hundred gentlemen-caterers and one hundred torchbearers, it is entertained with another display of pyrotechnics. The monster that has been reduced to a harmless snail by an imperial glare still proves capable of setting off one hundred chambers, and the ship which was recently metamorphosed into a verdant island manages to counter with a like number. Neptune's Ocean Fortress joins in with rockets that run upon lines leading to the cursed Spanish Mount.

Since Wednesday's pastoral song had received a royal encore, Elizabeth's last day began with similar strains. Beneath her window three cornets played "fantastike dances, at the measure whereof the Fayery Quene came into the garden, dauncing with her maides about her" (III, 118). With sprightly song the Elvetham fays blessed the place "Where sweet Elisa builds her bowre," and their Queen, Aureola, offered a garland from her consort, Auberon. By royal command the delicate device was thrice repeated, but within the hour Elizabeth was making her way through heavy rain, lamenting poets, and wailing deities to her next rendezvous, the Bishop of Winchester's palace at Farnham. As she left, Hertford was assured "that the beginning, processe, and end of this his entertainment, was so honorable, she would not forget the same" (III, 121). Unfortunately the Earl was to place too much trust in the efficacy of crescent-shaped ponds, wild men, and wildfire. Several years later he was caught attempting to legitimate his "bastard" sons, and promptly returned to the Tower.[35]

Although Elizabeth's humbler subjects eventually borrowed from their betters' grandiose offerings, civic receptions were at first less fanciful, more inclined to build upon a single moral, and by means of philosophical or political rather than romantic allegory. To judge from the accounts of the Queen's "joyfull receyvings" into Coventry in 1566 and Bristol in 1574, the citizen wooed more formally and with greater recourse to old-fashioned devices. Among the personages who welcomed Elizabeth during her earliest years, we find an occasional goddess or stray nymph, but usually figures drawn from the traditional pageants of the guilds. The men of Coventry, for example, used the Corpus Christi cars of the Tanners, Drapers, Smiths, and Weavers.[36] Even Bristol, which could afford the services of a London professional, Thomas Churchyard, offered worlds no more exotic than those that could be quickly gleaned from the early Tudor morality plays, Henry VIII's mock battles, and the current Midsummer Watches and Lord Mayors' shows. When Elizabeth reaches Bristol's High Cross on August 13, she is greeted by honest English abstractions, not those that frequent the pages of Ovid. Each "excellent boy"—Fame, Salutation, "Gratulacion," and Obedient Good Will—draws his sword, Fame throws her a garland, and the first three pipe forth their best wishes in horrendous fourteeners and poulter's measures (I, 396 ff.). Time ran out, unfortunately, before Master Good Will could

> declaer indeed,
> What deep desier they have,
> To spend their goods, their lands, and lives,
> Her staet in peace to save;

but since Churchyard was the deviser as well as the narrator, every golden line is nevertheless furnished the reader.

The first day closed on a more martial note. When the Queen reached her lodgings, the three hundred soldiers who had escorted her "shot of[f] thear peeces in passyng good order," and the city artillery, composed of one hundred thirty cannon, saluted in return. Sunday brought a brief respite from such brave alarums, but the morrow opened with a two-day broil between the Fort of Peace, located "beyond the water," and certain soldiers of fortune, known collectively as "Wars." In the same dreadful verse that marked the speeches of Fame and his cohorts, Dissension first exhorted the inhabitants of Peace to take up arms, and then inspired the troops of War to assault the Fort. Despite Peace's aid, its neighboring fortress, Feeble Policy, was soon overthrown, and on the next day, though reinforced by "divers Gentilmen of good callynge from the Court, which maed the shoe very gallant," the Fort itself seemed doomed (I, 402). In desperation Peace sent one "John Robarts, of the Temple" to beg the Queen's help. Bearing "a book covered with green velvet, which uttred the whoell substance of this device," Robarts swam to the scaffolding where Elizabeth sat as spectator of honor, presented his program notes as well as a complimentary harangue, and returned to the "reoryng shot and fearful sight." By late afternoon both combatants were weary enough to allow Persuasion to "unfold what follies . . . rises in civill broyle, and what quietnesse coms by a mutual love." Peace thereupon complimented the Queen, Wars retired to the banquet hall, and Elizabeth returned to her less noisy lodgings.

Whereas Bristol offered the Queen only conventional addresses, the themes of *Gorboduc,* and a "morality in armor," Norwich greeted her in 1578 with far more elaborate homage. As the realm's second-largest city, it could muster large sums for importing knowledgeable showmen and for erecting the costly devices they recommended. According to Churchyard, he "was the fyrste that was called and came to Norwiche aboute that businesse, and remayned there three long weekes before the Courte came thither, devising and studying the best I coulde for the Citie, albeit other Gentlemen, as Maister Goldingham, Maister Garter, and others, dyd steppe in after."[37] While the professionals were busily versifying, the citizens hastily set everything in order: Streets were brushed, houses new-polished, refuse removed, roads freshly graveled, and undesirable creatures like beggars and the diseased swept from the royal path.[38] Forty junior members of the guilds were conscripted to attend the Mayor, the justices of the peace, and the aldermen; those refusing to "apparell themselves . . . all in one suit, and one sashing, in such sort as is appointed," were to forfeit forty shillings each.[39] And the Mayor, Master Robert Wood, directed that none of the Queen's retainers "shoulde be unfeasted or unbidden to dinner and supper, during the space of those six dayes" of her visit (II, 133). In view of such universal hospitality and conscientious planning, it is no wonder that Churchyard claims that Norwich "taughte and learned all the Townes and Cities in Englande a lesson, howe to behave themselves in such-like services and actions" (II, 133).

The characteristic Renaissance attention to detail, order, degree, ceremony, and rich visual display are exemplified by the huge procession that met Elizabeth outside Norwich on Saturday, July 16. First came sixty of the "most comelie yong men of the Citie," each appareled in "universall liverie." Behind them, wearing armor decorated with silks of green and white and a helmet of black velvet with a plume of white feathers, rode "Gurgunt, sometyme Kyng of Englande, whiche buylded the Castle of Norwich, called *Blanch Flowre*, and layde the foundation of the Citie" (II, 138). Next proceeded various gentlemen, wealthy citizens, civic officers, and the Lord Mayor's sword-bearer; then the Mayor, his twenty-four aldermen, and the City Recorder, all in gowns of scarlet; and finally the justices and "divers other, to keepe the people from disturbyng the array aforesayde." The royal and civic trains met at Hartford Bridge, where the Mayor presented his liege with the city sword, a silver cup containing one hundred pounds in gold, and an eloquent Latin oration. From the bridge, citizen and courtier proceeded toward the city gates. At the "Towne Close," King Gurgunt issued out of Blanch Flowre, hoping to narrate the founding of Norwich in terms much like those used by Leicester's Lady of the Lake several years before:

> Two thousand yeares welnye in silence lurking still:
> Heare, why to thee alone this service I do yelde.
>
> (II, 142)

Gurgunt had lurked a few minutes too long, however, for a brief shower prevented his explanation.

Elizabeth hastened on to St. Stephen's Street, which offered the first of Bernard Garter's pageants (II, 143 ff.). Above a stage representing the loom industries, which had made Norwich wealthy and famous, stood a sign declaring "The causes of this Commonwealth." Below this list of virtues were paintings of artisans weaving types of cloths, and upon the stage itself sixteen small girls industriously spun and knit. In their midst was a small boy, Commonwealth, proclaiming the glories of busy hands. Thus enlightened, the Queen passed on to the marketplace, where the city musicians played and "five personages apparelled like women" waited to address her. "City of Norwich," Deborah, Judith, Esther, and "Martia, sometime Queene of England" in turn offered advice gained from experience in their own respective worlds. Next on the program were ditties by Garter and Churchyard, played and sung "by the Waytes [civic instrumentalists] and best Voyces in the Citie," and one more rhymed harangue, delivered by another small boy decked out in "Turkishe fashion" (II, 183). Elizabeth then proceeded to Norwich Cathedral, where *Te Deum* was offered, and finally to her suite in the Bishop's palace.

Churchyard's devisings for Monday and Tuesday met with a success rarely granted to his sundry prodigious labors. Bursting with pride, the lovable hack confesses that for "a long season" a magnificent coach "was closely kept in secret," shaped in "such a fashion, as few men have seene: the whole whereof was covered with birdes, and naked sprites hanging by the heeles in the aire and cloudes, cunningly painted out, as thoughe by some thunder cracke they had bene shaken and tormented, yet stayed by power devine in their places, to make the more wonder and miraculous shew" (II, 184, 188). On Monday, heralded by trumpet peals, the celestial vehicle rattled through the city, pursued by the wide-eyed citizenry, marveling at its swiftness. When it halted beneath the Queen's palace window, a boy dressed as Mercury, all in blue satin and cloth of gold and with winged hat and heels, boldly leaped out, shook his serpentine rod, and declared that Jove had prepared wondrous delights for Her Majesty's recreation.

Jove's word had been gaged, and his prophet, despite "some crossing causes in the Citie," was determined to honor it. As the Queen rode "without Saint Benets Gates" on Tuesday, Churchyard therefore hastily mustered his boys, furniture, and coaches and charged off in pursuit. Before Elizabeth reached her hunting grounds in "*Gossie Parke*," Churchyard managed to intercept her with his "Shewe of Chastitie" (II, 189 ff.). The royal train is ambushed by Cupid's spangled coach and the plaints of Venus's darling. Having been banished from heaven, he and his mother fled to earth, where Venus, mocked by "a father grave and wise," promptly went mad for grief and indignation. Her son now seeks revenge and refuge in the Court. But his threats are in turn interrupted by the appearance of Dame Chastity and her maids, Modesty, Temperance, Good Exercise, and "Shamefastness," who pull him down from his golden seat and despoil him of bow, arrows, and "counterfeyte godhead and cloke." Accompanied by music, Dame Chastity belabors the moral:

> Then sith (O Queene) chast life is thus thy choyce,
> And that thy heart is free from bondage yoke,
> Thou shalt (good Queene) by my consent and voyce,
> Have halfe the spoyle; take eyther bowe or cloke.
> The bowe (I thinke) more fitte for such a one
> In fleshly forme, that beares a heart of stone
> That none can wound, nor pearce by any meane.
> Wherefore take heere the bowe, and learn to shoote
> At whome thou wilt.   (II, 192)

While Chastity and her modest maidens ride off to their realm of "Powers Divine," Cupid wanders about the forest, takes up with certain prodigals, Wantonness and Riot, is soon reduced to beggary, and comes upon the Queen "running afoote like a vagabond." Out of a nearby cave springs a Philosopher, perhaps the same solemn "father" who drove Venus mad. This stern and hardly romantic hero forestalls Cupid's flight, and rebukes him primarily for his idleness and incidentally for his pagan theology: "In Heaven is but one that rules, no other Gods there are" (II, 194). Wantonness and Riot urge Cupid not to strive against such learning, and the merrymakers exit, probably intending, as Riot puts it, "to daunce with belles a morrice [morris] through the streets" (II, 196). The Philosopher then treats Elizabeth to a sermon on the foolishness of Folly, Modesty exhorts her to continue in virtue, and Chastity's virgins return to hymn praises of the chaste life. Despite the "naked sprites" on Cupid's coach, and for all its emphasis upon rich costuming, hurried traffic, and colorful spectacle, Churchyard's muse is severely moral. Make-believe barely sugars the pill; Olympus is brought in to adorn, but never control, the world of *Everyman* or *Godly Queen Hester*. Concerning the Queen's marriage, Churchyard had sided with Elizabeth and against both quaking Deepedesire and Parliament, and despite his rather infelicitous reference to her who "beares a heart of stone," he claims that the devising "had gracious words of the Queene openly, and often pronounced" (II, 190).

Such praise seems to have inspired the hack with renewed fervor, for on the next day, as Elizabeth and the French ambassadors dined with the Earl of Surrey at Mousehold Hill, Churchyard was lurking at the "backedore" with his show of "Manhode and Dezarte" (II, 198 ff.). The entertainment was to have featured a battle with "'sworde and targette" between Good Fortune's warriors and Manhood, Favor, and Desert for the hand of Lady Beautie, but was thrice postponed and finally abandoned. Surrey's grounds, according to the despairing deviser-narrator, lacked suitable space for such a martial enterprise. He therefore shipped both cast and "shotte" back to the docks at Norwich, where they waited three hours amid approaching darkness before withdrawing. When the Queen finally arrived, Stephen Limbert, a mere schoolmaster, stole Churchyard's thunder with a well-received oration before Norwich Hospital (II, 154 ff.), while poor Thomas solaced himself with plans for the morrow. Taking no chances, Churchyard managed to obtain from the Lord Chamberlain Elizabeth's Thursday itinerary, and for the third time Beauty and her knights were properly stationed in the woods. But he also saw an opportunity to step beyond Kenilworth. Alongside the water Churchyard had a huge pit excavated, and into this "cave" of sixty feet square and four feet deep he deposited a group of musicians and a dozen water nymphs. When the Queen passed, the camouflaged canvas that concealed the company was to be suddenly drawn back, "so that . . . the earth woulde seeme to open" (II, 199). While the musicians sounded, the nymphs, clad in silks, moss, and ivy, were to have sprung forth, dancing with timbrels. But again Dame Fortune bewrayed her perversity:

> There fell suche a shoure of rayne . . . that it was a greater pastime to see us looke like drowned rattes, than to have beheld the uttermost of the shewes rehearsed. . . . But what shoulde I say of that whiche the Citie lost by this cause, velvets, silkes, tinsels, and some cloth of golde, being cutte out for these purposes, and could not serve to any great effect after? . . . He that thought he had receyved moste injurie kept greatest silence, and lapping up, among a bundle of other mysfortunes, this evil chaunce, every person quietly passed to his lodging.
>
> (II, 200–201)

Clearly Churchyard's muse should have kept withindoors. After his brief triumphs on Monday and Tuesday, darkness had forced him to dismiss his weary cast on Wednesday, while a mere orator appropriated his praise. And while he resuscitated his half-drowned water deities on Thursday, a greater rival, Henry Goldingham, scored another success with an after-dinner mask (II, 159 ff.). About the Queen's privy chamber had marched Jupiter, Juno, Mars, Venus, Apollo, Pallas, Neptune, Diana, Mercury as the presenter, Cupid, and sundry musicians and torchbearers. Speeches and gifts ranging from Jupiter's "ryding-wande of whales fin" to Cupid's golden arrow had been received "very thankfully." The hearty appreciation Elizabeth had shown to the Lord Mayor would no doubt be rendered in turn to the deviser. Churchyard, on the other hand, could only return to his employers a muddy hole and badly damaged goods. But if the hack lacked good fortune, he possessed a surplus of fortitude. The Queen would be leaving on Friday, and there was no time for lamentation. "Fearing that all . . . labour shoulde be lost," he "devised to convert the Nimphes of the water, to the Faeries on the land," quickly packed up boys and baggage, and hurried out of the city (II, 201). Since time did not permit any marvelous machinery or even a partial restoration of his nymphs' bedraggled costumes, he substituted the ludicrous for the enchanting, improvised several apposite verses, and led his company into a thicket to await Elizabeth's passage. Lest the newly converted fays miss their cues, Churchyard himself, dressed as a water sprite, emerged from the bushes to lead his boys in a dance with timbrels, making "the Queene's Highnesse smyle and laugh withall" (II, 211).

It is clear that not only Churchyard's Last Stand but the whole Norwich panorama greatly pleased Elizabeth. The city, to be sure, had never managed to give her the roles she enjoyed at Kenilworth and Woodstock in 1575. Even the Olympians did not confuse her with Zabeta or Gloriana; she remained Elizabeth of England, Commonwealth's model of careful husbandry, Gurgunt's of ancient princely qualities, Esther's answer to virtuous government, and Dame Chastity's to Wantonness and Prodigality. For her humbler subjects there was very little make-believe in any of this. Nevertheless, Bernard Garter tells us that before she rode on to Kimberley, she confessed, "I have laid up in my breast such good will, as I shall never forget Norwich" (II, 166). And among the fifteen worthies of Suffolk and Norfolk whom she knighted during her progress of 1578 was "Mayster Woodde, Maior of Norwich" (II, 225). Like Leicester and Hertford, the first citizen of England's second-largest city knew what things best pleased majesty; the strings he touched were less courtly, but the same attention to duty he admired in Elizabeth allowed him to arise "Sir Knight."

HENRY VIII'S DERRING-DO

In whatever ways Elizabeth sponsored the marvelous, whether answering Gurgunt's or Savage Man's prayers, watching Feeble Policy being overthrown, or freeing the Lady of the Lake from wicked Sir Bruse, she was herself merely wading beyond her father's greenwood and tiltyard adventures. And the pageantry from which her civic and courtly entertainers drew in order to fuse the faraway with the near at hand was itself as often incongruous marriage between the medieval and the modern. "The tradition of pageantry had its roots deep in the Middle Ages," explains E. K. Chambers, "but it made its appeal also to the Renaissance, of which nothing was more characteristic than the passion for colour and all the splendid external vesture of things; while the ranging curiosity of the Renaissance was able to stimulate into fresh life the fading imaginative energies of the past, weaving its new fancies from classical mythology, from epic and pastoral, from the explorations of history and folk-lore, no less delightfully than incongruously, into the old mediaeval warp of scripture and hagiology and allegory." [40] If Gurgunt and Martia answer to both epic and folklore, and if Judith and Esther satisfy Chambers's "hagiology," the Norwich tapestry is typically eclectic. Its worlds are, if anything, less mingled than those with which London a half century before greeted Henry VIII and his guest, the Holy Roman Emperor, Charles V. It is possible that to a few of Norwich's more ancient citizens, Churchyard's conventional fusions of pagan lore and Christian instruction brought back memories of even braver days, when all the stuff of Olympus, Arcadia, and Camelot was turned to grist for the royal mill.

The itinerary of early June, 1522, called for a few days of pastimes at Greenwich, where Henry, "the more to doo the Emperor pleasure," had "Iustes [jousts] royall," a grand "Tornay" or tournament, and several delicate masks prepared.[41] On the sixth, the two princes proceeded to London, each with a naked sword borne before him and a great company behind. The royal chronicler, Edward Hall, himself revels in the majesty of the occasion, filling page after page with sensuous description: "And when the Herauldes had appointed euery man their roume, then euery man set forwarde in ordre, richly apparelled in Clothe of gold, Tissew, Siluer, Tynsell, and Veluettes of all coloures. There lacked no massye Cheynes, nor curious Collers" (p. 637). Just outside Southwark, Sir Thomas More presents a eulogy; inside, the clergy welcome them with crosses and swinging censers. As they pass by Marshalsea, Henry obliges Charles by pardoning "a great nomber" of its prisoners. London Bridge is guarded by two hulking yet obeisant giants, Hercules, bearing a mighty club, and Samson, with the jawbone of an ass. Each of these oddly sorted companions holds up one end of "a greate Table, in the whiche was written in Golden letters, all the Emperours Stile" or titles (p. 638). In the midst of the bridge rises a castle, upon which perch Jason, Medea, a fiery dragon, and "two Bulles whiche . . . cast out fyer continually." Awaiting their majesties at "Gracious strete" is a bastille, from which Charlemagne kindly bends to offer Charles the Sword of Justice and Henry the Sword of Triumphant Victory. At "Leden halle" they discover John of Gaunt, sitting "in a rote" of a tree upon whose branches recline fifty-five figures representing his lineage, including, of course, Henry, his Queen, and her nephew, the Emperor. Cornhill sets forth two "towers embattailed," both playing music; between them sits "kyng Arthur at a rounde table," served by ten attendant kings (p. 639). The "Stockes" reflects Nature's abundance; fish, fowl, beasts, elements, planets, and stars are set in motion, while an angelic host sings and the Trinity blesses the sovereigns. And finally "Chepe," not to be outdone by sister districts, offers three spectacles. Near the "great Conduite" are more towers, each containing a damsel representing a cardinal virtue; at the "standard," another huge edifice, its pillars supported by monsters and its figures once more advertising the princes' kinship; then the "litle Conduite," revealing "a place like heauen," about which parade versifying apostles (p. 640).

Such a wealth of pictorial stimuli must have affected the average Londoner as strongly as the man who records it so enthusiastically. Within a year the irascible Humanist, Vives, would publish his contempt for those "so plain and foolish lies" about Amadis, Tristan, and Lancelot, stories so far-fetched that only "madness" finds them pleasurable, tales with "no wit in them but a few words of wanton lust." [42] Erasmus had similarly censured all medieval romances, including the Arthurian cycle, as little more than "trivial nonsense, neither true to fact nor morally helpful, not even clothed in notable language." [43] And a decade later (1534), Polydore Vergil, one of the Italian scholars Henry VIII imported to adorn his Court, even politely questioned the historicity of Brute, Britain's legendary founder.[44] But what were the carpings of hostile Humanists compared to those wondrous spectacles that burgeoned amid the city streets? What minds were disciplined enough to resist the impressions that nourished the mind's eye? Few men do not believe more than they know, and even those myths that many intelligent early Tudors would have classified as knowledge rather than belief included the "annals" furnished by Geoffrey of Monmouth (c. 1150) through Malory. Professor J. H. Hexter reminds us that "when Henry VII named his first son Arthur, he was not making a casual curtsey to a lightly held fairy story." [45] Nor were the commissioners selected by Thomas Cromwell in 1535 to assess the taxable value of monasteries a group of wide-eyed romantics. They were expected to do what Polydore had attempted the year before: uncover the truth, separate fact from fiction. Their response was to exempt a considerable sum of Glastonbury's income, for under the terms of King Arthur's will the monks were commanded to use such funds for alms.[46] In view of such contradictory evidence, one wonders whether the highly moral Humanists, from Erasmus to Ascham, would not have found medieval romance more true to fact if it had not been so false to their concept of godly conversation. It is impossible to know exactly where that always elusive "typical Englishman" would have marked off matters "true," "presumably and hopefully true," and "purely fanciful." It is equally impossible not to conclude from Hall's accounts that no Englishman worked harder to blur those lines, to make the fabled glories of yore an everyday affair, than Henry himself. What Shakespeare's Norfolk says about his liege's and Francis I's exploits on the "Field of the Cloth of Gold" might well have been said about all but the last years of Henry's triumphant reign:

> When these suns—
> For so they phrase 'em—by their heralds challeng'd
> The noble spirits to arms, they did perform

Beyond thought's compass, that former fabulous story,
Being now seen possible enough, got credit,
That Bevis was believ'd.[47]

Between 1344, when Edward III is celebrated for holding a
Round Table at Windsor,[48] and 1613, when *Bevis of Southampton*
exemplifies the incredible, English chroniclers are usually sympathetic to "former fabulous story." One case in point is the outcry
raised by Polydore Vergil's incipient historical criticism. Quite
aware that he is treading sacred ground, the Italian reveals his
skepticism as graciously as possible. Of Brute's seed he merely
asks,

> whether shall we goe, seing that all things are full of
> darcknes. Trulie ther is nothinge more obscure, more
> uncertaine, or unknowne then the affaires of the Brittons
> from the beginninge. . . . But, bie cause it is wisdom, and
> time allso requireth the same, . . . wee will, therfor,
> briefelie passe through the life of those kinges whome this
> newe historie of a sodaine . . . hathe browght forthe and
> placed in the lighte. The which thinge (albeit not alto-
> gether without indignation) yet will wee doe it, both
> havinge regarde to the time and the avoydinge of evel
> will.[49]

But the cautious Polydore had not sufficiently regarded the avoiding of ill will. His simple reminder that if Brute had ever reigned in
Albion, no annalist prior to Geoffrey of Monmouth had bothered
to note that fact, met with a crescendo of abuse among chroniclers
who were primarily loyal Englishmen and secondarily objective
historians. Richard Grafton attempts to remain dispassionate but
rests his case with the Trojan dynasty; Holinshed champions
Brute's pedigree with confidence; the learned Camden profits by
Polydore's example and proceeds with great caution.[50]

   In 1580, nine years after Elizabeth and her justices "thought
[it] good" to honor Paramore's medieval gauntlet,[51] Citizen John
Stow does not insist on the descent of Brute from Aeneas, but
stubbornly maintains the historicity of "one *Brute*, or *Brito*, King
of this Realme, which left it to his posterity." [52] As for Polydore,
he is merely another "vaine-glorious" Italian who, "to aduance his
owne Country, will not endure that any other . . . shall haue monuments of antiquity." [53] After dismissing his opponent as a man who

"with one dash of a pen, cashireth threescore Princes together," thereby displaying only "inconsiderate" judgment and "grosse errours," Stow commences his English history with the landing of the Trojans at "Totnes in Deuonshire, the yeere of the world, 2855."[54] Within the succeeding six pages we are informed of all that transpired from Brute's reign through Cymbeline's, and this is followed by a comprehensive survey of contemporary foreign events. In the year of the world 2466, for example, Joshua succeeded Moses, and thirty-one years later, "*Perseus,* the sonne of *Jupiter* and *Danaë* slew *Medusa* one of the *Gorgons.*"[55] Finally, in 1611 John Speed renews Vergil's charges concerning the silence of historians before Geoffrey; his motives, however, are more moral than scientific.

> To conclude; (by what destiny I know not) nations desire their originals from the *Troians,* yet certaine it is, that no honor from them can be brought, whose city and fame stood but for six descents. . . . So let BRITAINES . . . disclaime their BRVTE, that bringeth no honour to so renowned a Nation, but rather cloudeth their glorie in the murders of his parents, and imbaseth their descents, as sprung from *Venus* that lasciuio[u]s Adulteresse.[56]

It would seem that well into the reign of James I the fate of Brute and his kindred remained undetermined. It is therefore not surprising to find Continental tourists like Hentzner (1598) recording in their journals that London "was originally founded, as all historians agree, by *Brutus,*" or like Rathgeb (1592) noting that the University of Cambridge was established by "Cantaber, a Spaniard, in the time of Gurguntius, the son of Belinus, King of Britain, A.M. 3588 and B.C. 375 (as affirmed by the principal historians)."[57]

And if the Trojans were too firmly lodged in the hearts, and therefore the minds, of Tudor Englishmen to be displaced by Polydore's appeal to evidence, continual innovations in the practical business of soldiery did not seem to change their attitudes toward the value of Henry VIII's chivalric exercises. William Caxton concludes *The Book of the Ordre of Chyvalry* (c. 1484) with a fervent affirmation of lance and charger:

> O ye Knyghtes of Englond where is the custome and usage of noble chyualry that was used in tho dayes / . . . Allas

> what doo ye / but slepe & take ease / and ar al disordred
> fro chyualry / I wold demaunde a question yf I shold not
> displease / how many knyghtes ben ther now in Englond /
> that have thuse and thexercyse of a knyghte / that is to
> wete / that he knoweth his hors / & his hors hym / that
> is to saye / he beynge redy at a poynt to haue al thyng
> that longeth to a knyght.[58]

Almost a century later Ascham castigates "bookes [of] Cheualrie,"
whose "whole pleasure . . . standeth in two speciall poyntes, in open
mans slaughter, and bold bawdrye," and "made in Monasteries, by
idle Monkes, or wanton Chanons." [59] The reformer's scorn, however, is directed not at the honest knightly exercises Caxton recommends, but upon the books he published, filled with unnecessary sex and violence. The modern workaday military and social
structures need men able "to ride cumlie: to run faire at the tilte or
ring: to plaie at all weapons: to shote faire in bow, or surelie in
gon: to vaut lustely . . . and all pastimes generally . . . conteining
either *some fitte exercise for warre*, or some pleasant pastime for
peace," for these things are not only pretty but practical, "verie
necessarie, for a Courtlie Ientleman to vse." [60] And in the last year
of Elizabeth's reign we find Sir William Segar maintaining that his
account of the Queen's fanciful tiltyard proceedings will provide
"the meanes of aspiring vnto honour," "reasons and examples . . .
to incite our English youth." [61]

Perhaps by now we have adjusted a few expectations about the
obvious and begun to sense the dangers of accepting claims that
open with references to "the superstitious" or "the intellectually
alert" Tudor. Our general impressions must be continually reshaped
by the facts along the way. He who despises "the feyned no where
acts of Arthur of the rounde table" is the bohemian, Nashe; he
who would "dare vndertake" to praise "honest King *Arthur*" is
the no less educated Sidney; [62] and he who sends us to the tiltyard
is Cambridge's Regius Professor of Greek. When plain-spoken
Wyatt would leave Spain, and

> With spurr and sayle . . . go seke the Temis,
> Gaynward the sonne, that showth her welthi pryd;
> And to the town which Brutus sowght by dremis,[63]

he seems to be registering a fact, not decorating a sentiment. And
in the last year of the sixteenth century, Drayton sees nothing farfetched about Surrey's reasons for departing for Florence,

whither, to advance her [Geraldine's] Fame,
He travels, and in publique Justs [jousts] maintayn'd
Her Beautie peerelesse, which by Armes he gayn'd.[64]

The nonsense Sidney detects in *Astrophel and Stella*, XLI, does not appear in the sonnet's opening lines:

Having this day, my horse, my hand, my Launce
Guided so well, that I obtaind the prize,[65]

but in what follows, the silly reasons people gave to explain his victory. The tournament is quite serious; the judges, who do not realize that it was Stella's "beames, which made so faire a race," are comical. If this is merely an aristocrat propagandizing aristocratic fancies, what shall we make of Campion's song to that disdainful beauty who must, in the next world,

speak of banqueting delights,
Of masks and reuels which sweete youth did make,
Of Turnies and great challenges of knights,
And all these triumphes for thy beauties sake:
When thou hast told these honours done to thee
Then tell, O tell, how thou didst murther me.[66]

Following one of the commonest lyrical conventions, Campion directs the whole stanza toward its "surprising" conclusion: so fair —and yet so cruel. Had he sensed anything inane about the way his mistress's beauty was established, he would have been undercutting his method rather than his poem's subject. Yet in working toward his conceit, the seventeenth-century lawyer and physician gives us a sentiment that might easily have been expressed by a forlorn thirteenth-century courtier.

Since straightforward celebrations of the spirit, heroes, or exercises of chivalry appear throughout sixteenth-century literature, we must not exaggerate the amount of make-believe that went into the era's tiltyard devisings. It is easy to conclude that the more masklike and less martial the tournament became, and the more elaborate its introductions and rules, the more it must have been seen as something wholly fanciful, beautiful but irrelevant, and like the chivalry it bespeaks, too removed to operate as a vital, civilizing force. Such deductions are encouraged by at least two modern habits of thought. First, what Chambers calls the "splendid external vesture of things" is obviously never the thing itself. Secondly, we tend to be impatient with if not downright suspicious about ceremony, even humbly clothed. Presumably neither the man Philip sent to destroy England nor the man Elizabeth selected to save it was principally bent upon re-creating the days of yore, yet each honored all the fine points of medieval-romantic etiquette. "The first modern naval battle in history began with gestures out of the middle ages, out of romances of chivalry," according to Garrett Mattingly.[67] "The Captain General of the Ocean Sea hoisted to his maintop his sacred banner as a signal to engage, as Castilian commanders at sea had always done since first they sighted the Moorish galleys. And the Lord Admiral of England sent his personal pinnace, the *Disdain,* to bear his challenge to the Spanish admiral, like King Arthur sending Sir Gawain to defy the Emperor Lucius." Since England's life was at stake, it is doubtful that Howard or the crew of the *Disdain* thought their mission a "gesture" or poetic overture to the practical business of survival. It was a necessary part of the thing itself, the way wars should be won.

We have already noticed how some evolutionary historians have "evolved" the Renaissance out of existence by detecting increasingly earlier anticipations of the new beneath the old. Each "first modern" turns out to be heralded by another, and we may eventually confront Homer. If we use visual display and complicated ceremony as reflections of chivalry-known-to-be-fiction, we may similarly regress through the Middle Ages, find no time during which "modern" fancies are not in some way anticipated, and therefore conclude that chivalry-taken-as-fact never existed. At the Abbey of Wallenden in 1252, reports Matthew Paris, there was held a *tabula rotunda,* at which a knight was pierced by a lance "which had not been blunted as it ought to have been." [68] From this simple statement we may infer several things. The knight had attended this new Round Table in order to identify himself with legendary heroes and was, in a sense, playing his part. He also knew that part was not dangerous, for the rules of mimetic warfare rendered his opponent's lance relatively harmless. Finally, he was wounded because someone confused make-believe with reality. Such inferences, although true, are dangerous unless qualified. Although the champion knows he is not really one of Arthur's knights, he never doubts their authenticity; he is re-creating history, not legend. Although he knows the combat is staged, he is not jousting in tribute to a skill no longer useful, for his battle is fought long before lance and charger are outmoded as effective instruments in actual warfare. Had his passage to make-believe been challenged by some rude baron, his style of fighting would not have changed, only the point of his lance. If chivalry's true spirit is found in men fighting bravely, serving faithfully, and loving humbly, Wallenden was advancing the first, those martial exercises through which unpracticed knights could acquire necessary skills: the joust for individual combat, the tournament for full-scale battle. There were right ways to fight, serve, and love; order and ceremony to be observed. If there was any nostalgia at the Abbey, it was not because the sense of immediacy had been lost, but because each knight was humbly comparing himself to his far nobler predecessors. The unreality of the blunted lances is the unreality of any practice for the real thing. Rather than reporting make-believe, Paris tells us that men were rational enough not to risk death unnecessarily.

In the next two centuries, which lead up to the advent of the first Tudor monarch, rules and safeguards become increasingly elaborate. In his description of the jousts at Arras in 1429, for instance, Monstrelet mentions the introduction of "the tilt," on either side of which the combatants rode, thus ruling out the possibility of collision.[69] Armor was strengthened and enlarged, encasing "those taking part in the tourney in an almost impenetrable shell, from which they could barely see or do more than couch and aim their lances." [70] To offset the danger of falling in two hundred pounds of plate, the rules were again altered. One no longer sought to unhorse his adversary, but to splinter one's own lance, whose weight was decreased until it became little more than a gaily decorated brittle splinter. The *Kolbenturnier* among the Germanic kingdoms featured what must strike us as an amusing variation. Again no personal injury seems to have been intended, for the lance was used to batter off the crest that brightly decorated, and was often much larger than, the opponent's helm.[71] If we use these plumed tortoises as evidence that chivalry is near death, the reign of Henry provides its epitaph, since serious incident is now only the result of freak accident. In 1524, Hall reports (p. 674), Henry clashed against one of his dearest cronies, the Duke of Suffolk. Half-blinded by his own headpiece, the Duke failed to perceive that his liege had forgotten to lower his visor and came within inches of killing him. In similar wise, Henri II was fatally injured in a *fête d'armes* at Paris in 1559.[72] Representations of combat without horse also became far safer with the introduction of "barriers," over and about which men wielded their swords. Armor became so strong and heavy, and the contestants padded with so much underclothing, that faintings and even deaths from heat prostration are recorded.[73]

None of this sounds very heroic, to be sure; Malory records no cases of coronary thrombosis at Camelot. But would not the tortoises of the time have seen their scalding shells as an extension of Wallenden's blunted lances, an opportunity to develop accuracy without undue risk of life? As often as Henry courted the marvelous, on the day Suffolk wounded him he was honoring only the expedient: "The x. day of Marche the kyng hauyng a newe harnes made of his own deuise and fashion, suche as no armorer before that tyme had seen, thought to assaye the same at the tilte, and appointed a Iustes to serue him." [74] To judge from Hall's descriptions of the real battles waged against Scotland and France during the previous year, Henry's reasons and method for proving his armor seem more practical than pretty: "The lorde Pountdormy . . . hearyng Mountdedyer was besieged, called to him diuers . . . menne of armes and dimy launces [light horsemen armed with short-shafted lances], . . . & as they wer thither commyng by night, Thomas Palmer, capitain of the skout watche of thenglishe army them askried and skyrmished with them although they wer more in nomber . . . and slewe diuers, and two speres were broken on the brother of the lord Pountdorny, but by the swyftnes of his horse he saued himselfe" (p. 669). Also a matter of fact rather than fiction is the quixotic behavior of one of Suffolk's own officers in encouraging his troops across the River Somme: "By reason of this noyse the souldiers stayed, which ye lord Sandes perceiuyng, . . . sirs sayd he, behold what I do, and with that he toke a banner of sainct George & sayd, as many as loue the kyng of England & be true to him and to the croune, folow me, and then . . . all other persones coragiously folowed" (p. 668).

Perhaps what bothers us even more than the ceremonies and rich display of derring-do is its increasing tendency to become only a part of a far larger and patently fictional program. In other words, if the historians tell us that real as well as staged warfare was often conducted so incredibly "point-device," and that both actual and feigned combats were sometimes won with appeals to hoisted St. Georges, surely the wholly occasional narratives that men begin to invent as settings for the tournament proper represent a deliberate, fully conscious retreat from reality. Supporting this impression is the complaint of one modern historian of the tournament: Chroniclers of the fifteenth and sixteenth centuries evince a lack of technical knowledge concerning the joust, and usually pay less attention to its martial aspects than to the accompanying pageantry, music, and themes.[75] We can, for example, find some practical reasons behind the romance of the earlier—but not the later—years of Edward III's reign (1327–1377). Almost a century after Wallenden's *tabula rotunda*, Edward holds a Round Table at Windsor. Probably the same year he founds the Order of the Garter. We can also digest Stow's report that Edward even brought the glories of yore into London itself; the marketplace in Cheapside was covered with sand to aid the horses' footings, and "divers joustings" were performed for three days "betwixt Sopar's lane and the great cross." [76] Toward the end of Edward's reign, however, the flowers of knighthood exude a perfume all too exotic. Edward's concubine, Dame Alice Perrers, comes attired as the Lady of the Sun; accompanied by the nobility, "every lady leading a lord by his horse-bridle," she proceeds from the Tower to West Smithfield, where "began a great joust, which endured seven days after." [77] The spectacle of this goddess and her shameful train ostensibly honoring chivalric exercise must have sickened those old knights who had triumphed at Crécy.

But under Edward's successor, Richard II, Londoners became accustomed to bizarre processions and weird figures issuing out of the Old Palace at Westminster: fantastically appareled damsels leading fully armed knights upon silver chains; malapert courtiers strutting about in costumes whose sleeves swept the ground; pampered royal favorites, wearing all the wealth they possessed, including shoes that protruded six inches beyond the toe and whose ends were, for mobility's sake, "caught up in gold chains to the knees, or even to the waist." [78] Richard's Court was a city unto itself, feeding up to ten thousand mouths daily, importing taxes, and exporting rumors of recreations unspeakable. If the citizenry that whispered about the revelry of Richard's minions also developed odd notions concerning what "longeth to a knyght," we can hardly blame it.[79] We are well on the way to the great splendors and elaborate fictions of the fifteenth-century tournament, in which contestants don the armor of characters out of chivalric song or story, or disguise themselves as unknown champions. As Saumur in 1446, for instance, René d'Anjou stages the *Emprise de la Gueule du Dragon.* Just outside this "dragon's mouth" he erects a special gallery for the ladies of the Court, "le chasteau de la joyeuse garde" (the name, incidentally, of Sir Lancelot's castle), from which Jeanne de Laval directs the festivities.[80] Three years later René invents a pastoral setting for his shepherdly joust, *Le Pas de la Begiere.* Joyous Guard becomes a thatched cottage, and the combatants, "deux gentilz escuiers pastoureaux," who engage under a tree of honor, from which hang two shields, black and white, *tristesse* and *liesse.* In their midst we again discover Jeanne de Laval, this time as a beautiful shepherdess, "gardant ses brebiettes." [81]

To us all this may suggest the lily thrice gilded. If Wallenden's framework complements the main event and the fourteenth-century English Lady of the Sun detracts from it, the fifteenth-century French shepherdess makes us wonder where center stage really is. Are we to watch the combat or the sheep, safely grazing upon the field of honor? The narrator fancies the flock; "brebis" or lambs is too crude a term; they must be lamb*kins*, "brebiettes." Yet in the midst of this period of rich ornamentation, ritual, and cultivation of fiction-known-to-be-fiction, it is still possible to see the knight as the upholder of justice. One of the few Canterbury pilgrims whose integrity and usefulness to society remain unquestioned is Chaucer's "verray, parfit gentil knyght," his "habergeon" or coat of mail "al bismotered" from recent and very real wars. And though Chaucer frequently exhibits a keen sense of the incongruous and risible, he appears to take his champion's victories in tournaments as seriously as those in actual campaigns.

> At mortal batailles hadde he bene fiftene,
> And foughten for oure feith at Tramyssene
> In lystes thries, and ay slayn his foo.[82]

This does not mean that Chaucer had to admire Edward III's or Richard II's exotic elaborations upon chivalric exercise. The "Tale of Sir Thopas" contains a whimsical tribute to recent court customs as well as to the clichés of plot and language in earlier metrical romances.[83] It is quite likely that had Chaucer lived to see René's devisings, he could have worked them into a sequel to "Sir Thopas," yet still believed that this had nothing to do with "verray . . . knyghts."

Whether dealing with the tournament's ceremony, display, or

fictional elaborations, we are back to the problem posed in Chambers's discussion of pageantry. The Renaissance "passion for colour" and other "splendid external[s]" is quite genuine. So is that "ranging curiosity" that led men to explore classical myths, native folklore, epic "histories," and "historical" pastorals. Such discoveries Chambers sees as those "new fancies" that the Renaissance weavers worked so "incongruously" into the old medieval warp. Like Mattingly's "gestures," Chambers's terms are intended *ad hominem*, an explanation of what happened as we see events in retrospect. But did not the weavers themselves see these "new fancies" as additional knowledge to supplement old facts? In our examination of literary criticism we found very few indications of what we should call the sense of the mutually exclusive. We often discovered, on the other hand, a remarkably high tolerance for an artifice of multiplicity. If the critics happen to notice those worlds that immediately strike us as strangely mingled, or those allusions and adornments that seem so oddly variegated, they see them as essentially harmonious, the happy result of wading farther. The same negative and positive evidence is furnished by the sixteenth-century chroniclers in their descriptions of contemporary or not-too-distant devisings. An annalist like Ben Jonson's learned mentor, William Camden, is the exception. Despite the incitements of native pride and pictorial effect, he refuses to linger over the era's pageantry; his few remarks are pointed, polite, and disinterested. When Elizabeth's ambassador to Denmark presented Frederick II with the ensigns of the Order of St. George, Camden relates that the monarch "gladly suffered the Chain or Collar of Roses to be put about his Neck, and the Garter to be tied about his Leg: the rest . . . he received to lay up and keep, but refused to put them on, because they were outlandish." [84] In 1581, Sidney and his fellow Foster Children of Desire besiege Perfect Beautie's Fortress above the tiltyard at Whitehall with perfumed cannonades. The battle, which raged for two days, was colorful and conceited enough to have driven Edward Hall into an ecstasy, but Camden disdains to report more than the fact that the French ambassadors were "entertained with Tiltings performed at a vast Expense . . . to say nothing of other Courtly Sports and Pastimes, which are not so proper for an Historian to relate." [85]

Far more representative attitudes toward romantic spectacle are reflected in those who contributed to Holinshed's *Chronicles*.[86] They obviously approve of Henry VIII's escapades on May Day,

1510, when the King, "being yoong, and willing not to be idle, . . . clothed all his knights, squiers and gentlemen in white sattin" and rode off "with his bow and arrowes shooting to the wood." [87] And when the Court celebrates the forthcoming marriage of Princess Mary to the Dauphin before the French ambassadors in 1519, they not only include all of Hall's account, but use the margin to point out how "very sumptuous and of notable deuise" the pageant was (III, 633). In the Great Hall at Greenwich is placed "a rocke full of all maner of stones, verie artificiallie made," upon which stand five trees, each bearing the arms of one of the five powers in league against pagandom. The fair maiden who sits between these trees of course represents the Princess, for she has a dolphin in her lap. The lords and ladies who share the back part of the rock probably stand for the wealth of the Indies, since the women are dressed "after the fashion of Inde," and the ten knights who issue "out of a caue in the said rocke" to fight "a faire tournie" probably represent the five Christian nations and their opponents. After the warriors exit, the lords and ladies descend from the rock, dance "a great space: and suddenlie the rocke mooued and receiued the disguisors, and immediatlie closed againe" (III, 634). Whereupon Report, "apparelled in crimsin sattin full of toongs"—notice his similarity to "Rumour, *painted full of tongues*," who introduces Shakespeare's *2 Henry IV*—rides in upon his charger, Pegasus, to expound the meaning, which the annalist evidently considered too obvious to bother including.

But the men we refer to collectively as Holinshed are not always so enthusiastic. To be drawn into the romantic worlds they describe, they need an inspiring court and monarch as well as a "sumptuous deuise." If they linger fondly over Hall's accounts of Henry VIII's most fanciful doings and offer marginal salutes to both the pageantwrights and their players, they can be abrupt and sometimes even cynical in their descriptions of Edward VI's and Mary's shows. The nature of those "sundrie sights and deuises of rare inuentions, and . . . diuerse interludes" that brightened Edward's Christmas Revels of 1551–1552, for example, remain ambiguous (III, 1033). These pastimes were, after all, mere political machinations "to remooue fond talke out of mens mouths," to quiet the charges of injustice occasioned by the Lord Protector's impending execution. When the feasting and fooleries of George Ferrers were past, "wherewith the minds and eares of murmurers were meetlie well appeased, . . . it was thought now good to proceed to the execution of the iudgement giuen against the duke of Summerset." Also symptomatic is the sketchy account of Queen Mary's royal entry into London on September 30, 1553 (IV, 6–7); less than six years later, her sister's similar passage will require no fewer than nineteen folio pages.

The most explicit attitude toward display is reflected by one of the contributors to the second edition of Holinshed's *Chronicles*, probably John Stow. Practical in his refusal to be taken in by the show of things, romantic in his nostalgic desire to restore former stateliness, his description of the Duke of Brabant's reception by Antwerp in 1581 provides a good example of the honest soldier's point of view. For the precedent of peerless pageantry, he insists, we must go back to the military "triumphs" of ancient Rome, since "the beholding of a goodlie companie of men armed in goodlie armour, marching in good order . . . dooth . . . wonderfullie rauish mens minds, and driue the beholder into an astonishment, . . . filling him with a ioy and contentation surmounting all others" (IV, 467). Granted, "triumphant Rome" offered "other shewes, also . . . verie glorious and beautifull," but lacking the essence of chivalry. Granted, too, that knowledgeable moderns include gold, silver, and precious gems among things "desireable to behold." In determining which kind of pageantry most honors the prince and best delights his subjects, however, we must remember that the same people who allow adornments "passe ouer those things and stand not vpon them. But when they come to talke of faire armour, good horsses, and such other things as belong to knighthood and chiualrie: then they make such tariance vpon them, as they hold . . . that in beautie and glorie nothing is comparable to a goodlie armie" (IV, 467). Precisely because the citizens of Antwerp had to rely upon a well-ordered military display, the writer concludes, even foreign visitors agreed that their reception surpassed all others. They could not match Paris for its crowds of spectators. They offered none of that "great plentie of riches and roialties in attires of kings and queenes" so frequently seen elsewhere. They had, moreover, only six days' notice of the Duke's arrival, and therefore "could not put to making anie worke of silke, nor of gold . . . nor anie rare costlinesse of imageries, pillers, triumphall arches, or other pageants: but were constreined to make a shift with such things as they had in a readinesse aforehand of their owne store."

Here, at last, we seem to find a determined realist, crying out in a desert of "sumptuousnesse," anxious that we see how the rela-

tively colorless Antwerp affair came far closer to the greatest Roman triumphs and "such other things as belong to knighthood" than
its more lavish rivals. But having established this practical perspective in his three prefatory paragraphs, our honest soldier proceeds to
the account proper, some twenty pages that overflow with every
conceivable kind of display and a sumptuousness that is, by our
standards if not his, truly staggering. He gives us, in short, a world
we have lost, but which his first readers took for granted, a world
of "banners of silke azured with the armes of Aniou" and castle
walls "couered with tapistrie" (IV, 469). It is also a world in which
medieval traditions still prevail: "the custome required that the
states should presentlie be sworne . . . to yeeld him fealtie" (IV,
472); "And then sounding the trumpets, they made a largesse,
casting a great sort of peeces of gold and siluer among the standers
by" (IV, 474); "From this scaffold he might behold . . . three
companies of banished and condemned men in fetters, and bare-
headed, crauing mercie at his hand, which was granted vnto them"
(IV, 484). It is finally a world in which a typical city hastily dresses
up "such things as [it] had in a readinesse aforehand of [its] owne
store" and yet manages to honor a visiting prince with several
dozen speaking pictures, immediately recognizable emblems and
allegorical figures. Along his passage Brabant encounters the
Chariot of Alliance, in which ride Antwerp and her sisters, Religion ("apparelled like one of the Sybils"), Justice, Concord, Wisdom, and Force. He knows Faithfulness and Watchfulness by their
ensigns, "a pellican killing hirselfe for hir yoong birds: and . . . a
hen a brooding hir chickens" (IV, 476). In the huge portrait of
Saul he recognizes the King of Spain and in that of David, himself.
The next street figures forth Antwerp as Jonathan. And if the Duke
is not at first certain about the relevance of the elephant bearing a
castle, Neptune on a dolphin, Concord riding a sea horse, or the
pictures of Flora, Ceres, Apollo, and Hercules, explanatory verses
are either inscribed or pronounced. Nor does the narrator, who
carefully glosses these shows, seem to feel that they are at odds
with his earlier insistence upon well-armed and -ordered men. He
no doubt agrees with Antwerp's Reformed churchmen, whose
reminders to Brabant conclude his account: "we haue seene manie
commonweales florish so long as they professed chiualrie and
learning togither" (IV, 487).

Of all the Tudor chroniclers, none is more enthusiastic about the
marriage of learning and chivalry or more inclined to linger over

"new fancies" with high seriousness than Edward Hall. Students of constitutional and economic history are bound to be disappointed by *The Vnion of the Two Noble and Illustre Famelies of Lancastre & Yorke* (1548), especially as the historian passes from Richard III's "Tragical Doynges" and Henry VII's "Politique Gouernaunce" to the era of splendor that occupies almost half of his huge tome: "The Triumphant Reigne of Kyng Henry The. VIII" (pp. 374, 422, 505–868). From a chronicler always bent on illustrating how the temper of the monarch determines the temper of his time, "triumphant" means much more than "successful" or "victorious." Hall uses the word as the soldier-historian does in likening Antwerp to "triumphant Rome," as a synonym for "magnificent." We sense a sigh of relief on Hall's part as he concludes the annals of the first Tudor, whose Court was too little removed from real battles to be able to stage them. Entertainments are occasionally described or alluded to, but we usually see this "good & modest prince," this man of great "wyt & prudence" (pp. 504–505), busy about the mundane tasks of stamping out sedition or fortifying against foreign invasion. Henry VII had little leisure to be less than "politique," particularly during the first troubled years of his reign. By the turn of the century, however, house and kingdom have been set in order, Prince Arthur and Catherine of Aragon are married, and Hall's characteristic admiration commences:

> I passe ouer the wyse deuises, the prudent speches, the costly woorkes, the conninge portratures practised and set foorth in. vii. goodly beutiful pageauntes erected & set vp in diuerse places of the citie. . . . And there in the paleys [at Westminster] were suche marciall feates, suche valiaunt iustes, suche vygorous turneys, suche fierce fight at the barreyers, as before that tyme was of no man had in remembraunce. Of thys royall triumphe lord Edwarde duke of Buckyngham was chiefe chalengeour, and lorde Thomas Grey Marques dorcet was chiefe defendoure which . . . bare theim selfes so valyauntly that they obteyned great laude and honoure, both of the Spanyardes and of their countrymen.
>
> (Pp. 493–494)

Among the "wyse deuises" that Hall inexplicably passes over is one of the earliest English court masks of which we possess a full account,[88] and a summary of its plot and themes will aid us in seeing how it later served Henry VIII's turn. To celebrate the marriage of England and Spain, the nobility assembled in Westminster Hall for feasting and entertainment. Four great beasts draw a wheeled castle into the hall, pass the guests, and stop before Henry VII and his Queen. Inside the castle are eight ladies, peering through its windows; in each of its four turrets is a child, sweetly singing. Then a ship filled with masker-mariners, a lady attired like Catherine, and those two incurable romantics, Hope and Desire, "sails" down the hall and casts anchor alongside the castle. Hope and Desire summon the eight ladies: They are ambassadors from the Knights of the Mount of Love. When the ladies "utterly refuse . . . any such company," the ambassadors become even more passionate, warning that such contempt merits grievous assault. Down the hall immediately rolls the third pageant, "in likeness of a great hill or mountaine," upon which stand eight knights with banners spread. Hope and Desire report the ladies' disdain, whereupon the knights, "with much malice and courageous minde," descend from their mount, besiege the castle, win the maids, pair off with them, dance, and disappear. Arthur then initiates dancing among the royal audience, but his younger brother steals the show. While dancing with Lady Margaret, Henry, "perceiving himselfe to be accombred with his clothes, sodainly cast of his gowne and daunced in his jackett . . . in so goodly and pleasant manner, that it was to the King and Q. right great and singular pleasure." [89]

With this notable exception, the chroniclers record few revels until Henry ascends the throne. In 1509 Father's thrifty practices are discarded; amusements of a much more costly and extensive nature than Henry VII could have conceived begin to multiply. Hoarded gold fills the royal coffers, and the new monarch is anxious to prove himself the most active gentleman of Europe. His forceful, romantic, and often egocentric personality is undoubtedly the most important single factor to be considered in a study of the Court's pastimes. The spontaneous exhibitionism revealed at Arthur's marriage festivities initiates a series of events in which Henry continually assumes a leading role. Like Samuel Johnson, he is fond of "rolling his majestic frame," and it is fortunate for students of early Tudor drama that in Edward Hall he found his wide-eyed Boswell. Hall seldom misses an opportunity to illustrate how his liege, "beyng lustye, young, & coragious, greatly delited in feates of chyualrie" (p. 520). On one page alone (513) we discover Henry taking on several romantic roles: He is first "straunger knight," secretly arming for a tournament and risking death at the hands of his own courtiers; next he is one of "Robyn Hodes men," breaking into the Queen's chambers and frightening her ladies; he and his cronies habitually vanish from banquets only to return as Turks, Russians, or Germans and introduce some dancing or merriment.

As long as it allowed him to make a grand entrance and to remain center stage, Henry does not appear to have been too particular about the nature of his spectacular pastimes. And like the poets of his Court, he chose to refurbish the old rather than to attempt something entirely new. Whatever variety of pageantry he exploited—mask or mummery, courtly show, civic procession, royal joust—he invariably borrowed from both native and Continental mimetic traditions, accented their romantic-heroic motifs, blended the most disparate elements, and again like his poets, rendered each fusion more indigenous to English soil. For "classical tilts" and "pastoral tournaments" Henry had the fantastic productions of René d'Anjou and like-minded monarchs of the preceding century on which to draw. For his maskings and mummeries, there was even native precedent. The earliest mention of what were probably masks are the "ludi dominus regis" of 1347, at which eighty-four nobles disguised themselves as women, angels, dragons, peacocks, and swans to brighten Edward III's Yuletide Revels at Guildford.[90] Thirty years later, masked revelers entered Kennington Palace with musicians and torchbearers to dice, dance, and drink with Richard II and his company.[91] Back of these disguisings was the ancient tradition of folk-mumming, the Plough Monday and Christmas mummers' plays, which themselves reflect pagan celebrations of the passing seasons.[92] This tradition had already begun to take a literary turn before John Lydgate's disguisings of 1427-1430: In place of the dice game of "mumchance," we find an allegorical show expounded by a presenter.[93] With Lydgate, the dance in disguise became centered in one theme; through their presenter, the mummers, like their counterparts in the earliest morality plays, presented lessons in virtue. Finally, for civic processions and triumphs at Court Henry and his devisers could elaborate upon both English and European pageants of the fifteenth century. While England suffered from an internal unrest that was later to erupt into anarchy, France, Burgundy, and the Italian states began to vie with one another in splendor and ceremony. At these courts the dance in disguise not only worked itself into the tournament, but incorporated almost every other mimetic form then in vogue: conversations between allegorical or mythological personages, the rich display of the royal entry, even the interlude.[94] In Florence, Lorenzo de' Medici attempted to revive the old Roman triumphs; at Milan, the Duke and his bride were received with a show featuring Leonardo da Vinci's pageant of the seven planets in motion.[95] That even England, despite lengthy civil wars, had its share of triumphs, is indicated by numerous references to royal entries. Unfortunately, although the annalists assure us that the festivities were magnificent, they never offer a detailed description.

Perhaps the best examples of Henry's ability to imitate creatively are his elaborations upon the "castle-assault" device. Although the account of Arthur's and Catherine's marriage festivities contains the earliest recorded instance of its *dramatic* representation in England, carvings upon ivory caskets and figures decorating tapestries indicate that its *pictorial* delineation was familiar as early as the reign of Edward II.[96] And certainly much of the pageantry used to dramatize this theme was no novelty; by 1501 both courtier and citizen had become accustomed to animals drawing edifices adorned with maidens, singing children, and personalized virtues. For sacred as well as profane medieval writers, the siege of a castle was a natural metaphor. In a parable assigned to St. Bernard, a king commands his three daughters, Fides, Spes, and Caritas, to guard the City of Mansoul and to defend its castles, Rationabilitas, Concupiscibilitas, and Irascibilitas. An army of similarly personified virtues eventually defeats a host of vices under all the images of contemporary warfare. Shortly after St. Bernard's parable, about 1220, its secular counterpart, a representation of the siege of the Château d'Amour, was enacted in connection with the spring festivals of the Italian folk.[97] During the following decades Guillaume de Lorris and Jean de Meun altered the natures of assaults and characters in accordance with the religion of courtly love, and from the *Roman de la Rose* through the less literary Elizabethan tiltyard entertainments we discover continual reworkings of the siege of the Castle of Jealousy and the attempted liberation of Belacueil (Fair-Welcoming) by the Soldiers of Ardent Desire.

It is easy to understand why the motif was so popular among the Tudor devisers. It was first of all simple and striking; themes that depended upon symbolism and pantomime to convey their significance had to be both "readily intelligible, and yet afford opportunity for the necessary scenic display."[98] Secondly, this motif automatically included the very stuff of romance—lusty loves and doughty deeds—and in handling such matters of heroism and gallantry, even the dullest deviser could hardly have missed the chance to flatter the principal players in his show, to enrich his plot with the ceremonials of chivalry, and to adorn his dialogue with the sentiments of courtly love. With the works of de Lorris and his imitators in the bower, and the representations of Camelot in the tiltyard close by, it was just as inevitable for him to dub the sober Caritas "Dous Regart" and send a new champion into the lists. Castles could be made to stand or fall depending upon who participated in the assault and the nature of the device that followed the battle. If, for example, the charge was to be led by Henry himself and a dance of knights and ladies was next on the program, the hours of the apparently impregnable fortress were numbered. For obvious reasons, during Elizabethan sieges Fortune was kinder to frailer castles.

In the earliest battles staged at Henry VIII's Court, the castle is only incidental. The King's very first joust, for instance, is framed along the lines of a medieval *débat* between "Dame Pallas Schollers," whose castle is carried into the room, and "Dianas Knightes" (pp. 511 ff.). Hall claims that he does not know whether Diana's men won Pallas' crystal shield or Pallas' men Diana's golden spear. He does imply that on the second day, when the broil was resumed, the heat of mimetic warfare caused a momentary lapse in good sportsmanship: "his grace conceiuying, that there was some grudge, and displeasure betwene theim," suddenly curtailed the ceremonies and dismissed both parties. Upon the birth of Prince Henry the following year, royal jousts were held to honor the Queen. Again the castle is almost incidental, but the *débat* receives somewhat greater fictional elaboration. Two huge beasts, led by woodwoses, draw in a forest, amid which stands a castle. When the foresters sounded their horns, the "pageant opened on all sides" and Henry and three of his courtiers issued forth as *"Les quater Chiualers de la forrest saluigne"* (p. 517). So taken with this spectacle was one annalist that he concluded his account with a poem introducing Henry as the Tenth Worthy![99]

When it assumes primary importance, the castle usually houses ladies to be wooed rather than knights to be suddenly revealed. In a program designed to introduce a joust, in other words, it is customarily no more than a stage property, a means of making a grand entrance. As part of a mask, on the other hand, it always occupies center stage until the dance it serves to initiate has begun. At first both the siege and capitulation of Henry's castles are relatively matter-of-fact invitations to the dance. The fall of *"le Fortresse dangerus"* in 1512, for example, is quite straightforward. During the following decade, however, the Court's—or at least the annalist's—attention appears to focus less on the dance than on the increasingly spectacular methods by which fair lady is won. An especially splendid castle was erected in Cardinal Wolsey's palace in 1522. From each of its three towers flies a banner, the first portraying "iii. rent hartes," and the second and third, ladies' hands "gripyng" or "turnyng" men's hearts (p. 631). As is indicated by the "straunge names" of those who keep the castle, de Meun's Rose has acquired sixteen characteristics: Beautie, Honor, Perseueraunce, Kyndnes, Constance, Bountie, Mercie, and Pitie appear above, while below the fortress stand those intimidating virgins, Dangier, Disdain, Gelousie, Vnkyndenes, Scorne, Malebouche, and Straungenes.[100] Henry and seven courtiers, representing eight of courtly love's virtues—Amorus, Noblenes, Youth, Attendaunce, Loyaltie, Pleasure, Gentlenes, and Libertie—and "led by one all in crimosin sattin with burnyng flames of gold, called *Ardent Desire*," promptly lay siege. Amid flying dates, oranges, comfits, rose water, and Desire's brave speeches, not to mention "a greate peale of gunnes" fired outside the chamber, "Lady *Scorne* and her compaignie" are driven out, and Beautie and her sisters taken prisoner. Only after the ensuing dances do the participants reveal their identities.

Perhaps the most formal assault was conducted during the Christmas Revels of 1524-1525. Its incorporation of the elaborate rules that characterized the fifteenth-century Continental *pas d'armes* rendered it intricate enough to be considered a dance in itself. It is also an exception to the general rule that all important castles are inhabited by ladies to be wooed, for in this instance doughty deeds are not means but ends. Before the Queen at Greenwich appears a herald, one *"Chasteau Blanche,"* who announces that the King has given the Castle of Loyaltie to four maidens of his Court (p. 688). They in turn have chosen sixteen noble lords to defend it, and to that end their captain is presently raising a mount, upon which will stand a unicorn, supporting four shields. He who wishes to challenge these lords may choose his method and weapons by touching the appropriate shield: the red, for example, if he would undertake "tenne strokes at the Turnay, with the sworde, edge and poynt abated."

In addition to the blunted weapons, further safeguards were stipulated: (1) All challengers may devise any engine for the siege except "edge tole to break the house and ground"; (2) "no other weapon shalbe vsed, but such as . . . shalbe sette vp, by the saied Vnicorne"; (3) there is to be no meddling with fire "within or without, but the matches for gonnes." Despite such precautions, representation eventually merged with reality. After several skirmishes, the challengers eventually claimed that the castle Sir Thomas Wyatt and his comrades were defending "could not be wonne by sporte, but by ernest." Henry was also frustrated by the royal carpenters, too dull to follow his plans for an engine suitable for the assault. When the castle at last fell and the combatants were disarmed, a sense of earnestness still prevailed: "sodainly all the young persones without, threwe stones at them within the castle, and they at theim, and many honest men whiche threwe not wer hurt, and with muche pein thei without wer apeised, and no man knewe how nor why, this hurlyng began" (p. 690).

It should not surprise us that the introductory framework, whether designed to initiate dancing or jousting, should thus become the most important part of the show. The ostensible ends offered little opportunity for wading farther; it was upon those almost infinitely variable means that Henry and his courtiers could exercise their ingenuity. Hence the increasingly large amount of machinery that we must endure before the ladies descend or the combatants come to blows. Hence, too, our impression that the Court is more interested in how it travels than in where it is going, for the means have become ends in themselves. In June, 1512, for example, Hall tells us that his liege appointed "a solempne Iustes at Grenewiche" (p. 533). Except for noting that Henry and Sir Charles Brandon ran against Essex, Howard, and Knevet, and that "euer the king brake moste speres," the chronicler pays little heed to the battle. What catches his eye is the splendid procession that entered the tiltyard: first those beautiful ladies, clothed in red and white silk, sitting upon coursers similarly attired, yet "freated ouer with gold"; next "a fountain curiously made of Russet Sattin, with eight Gargilles spoutying Water, within [which] sat a knight armed at all peces"; then another lady, more horses, a knight carried on a litter, evidently wounded, all in black silk with silver spangles.

Slowly the procession winds its way around the yard, Henry and Brandon emerge from the fountain and litter to abide all comers, and "with great noyse of Trompettes, entered sir Thomas Kneuet in a Castle of Cole blacke, and ouer the castell was written, *The dolorous Castle*." Spectacles like this, as the patriotic annalist often points out, impressed foreign visitors as well. The Spanish ambassadors "much reioysed" to see "his grace rychely armed and decked," but after the tilt was concluded and Henry allowed them to take any trappings they desired, their joy was even greater, "for in the beginning they thought that they had bene counterfait, and not of gold" (p. 514). It is the ambassadors from Scotland, however, who ask the best questions, ones which Henry no doubt hoped would cross the minds of princes everywhere. Between the sieges of the Castle of Loyalty, the Scots "asked a gentleman which accompaignied them, if all the warre tyme the kyng and the lordes wer so mery, or had had suche ioyous pastyme, or kepte suche royall housholde, or were so well appareled: for . . . thei thought that the realme of Fraunce, is not a realme to sport with, nor to Maske with" (p. 690).

If such displays underlined Henry's wealth and health or proved, as in the example above, that he "set not by the French kyng one bene," they also served to propagandize Tudor politics. The views of statecraft spelled out on Twelfth Night, 1515, are as obvious as the thesis of Hall's history, *The Vnion of . . . Lancastre & Yorke*. King and Queen enter "a tent of clothe of golde," before which stand their defenders, four armed knights. At the sound of a trumpet four other knights rush in to attack the royal guard. Amid "a great and fearce fight" there "sodainly came oute of a place lyke a wood. viii. wyldemen, all apparayled in grene mosse, . . . with Vggly weapons and terrible visages, and there foughte with the knyghtes. viii. to. viii. & after long fighting, the armed knightes draue the wylde men out of their places, and folowed the chace out of the hall" (p. 580). By 1515 Englishmen had begun to realize that the victor of Bosworth Field had not been just another king, monarchizing for no longer than it pleased his mutinous nobility. A crown that was a football during the anarchy of the fifteenth century had once more become an absolute referee, fiercely intolerant about grandiose schemes among the players. Nevertheless, Tudor propagandists never wearied of pronouncing the doom of houses divided against themselves: disorder, anarchy, chaos, or arbitrary laws imposed by rude, uncivilized men. No noble savages resided in Tudor England, and when *Gorboduc* was presented before Henry's daughter almost fifty years later, the same message was spelled out in one of its introductory dumb shows.

Representations centered in political themes were usually less theoretical. The majority seem apposite only to the immediate international situation and include pointed references to the princes of states and church as they temporarily related to Henry's vacillating policies. Hall mentions "a disguisyng or play" presented before King and Emperor following the London reception of 1522: "theffect of it was [that] there was a proud horse which would not be tamed nor brideled, but amitie sent prudence and pollicie which tamed him, and force & puissaunce brideled him. This horse was ment by ye Frenche kyng, & amitie by the king of England & themperor" (p. 641). Four years later an old yet "goodly disguisyng" by a certain "Ihon Roo" was performed at Gray's Inn, allegedly to ridicule Cardinal Wolsey. Hall tells us that "this plaie" about the overthrow of Dissipation and Negligence by the champions of Lady Public Weal "was highly praised of all menne, sauyng of the Cardinall" (p. 719). The cycle was completed within ten months, when Henry and the French ambassadors watched a company of children, evidently directed by Wolsey, present a Latin play eulogizing the Cardinal's role in restoring the Pope to freedom and in making peace between France and England (p. 735). Even Henry's later usurpation of supreme ecclesiastical authority eventually found its way into the royal repertoire. The most amusing is the "water triumphe" of June 17, 1539, as described by Charles Wriothesley. Up the Thames to Westminster came "two barges prepared with ordinance of warre . . . one for the Bishop of Rome and his cardinalles, and the other for the Kinges Grace . . . and at the fourth course they joyned togither and fought sore; but at last the Pope and his cardinalles were overcome, and all his men cast over the borde into the Thames." [101]

Although Henry's historians seem anxious to include detailed descriptions of every princely pastime, they make only passing references to what we should label "the drama proper." Almost lost amid his lengthy accounts of the spectacular jousts and masks of 1511 is Hall's incidental acknowledgment, "There was an interlude of the gentlemen of his chapell before his grace, and diuers freshe songes" (p. 518). Similarly uninspired is his comment that just before the splendid "disguysyng" of March, 1519, "there was

a goodly commedy of Plautus plaied" (p. 597). To judge from
Hall's frequent alternations between the terms "disguysyng" and
"play" to describe a single event, however, Henry's Court drew no
hard and fast distinctions between revels and strictly dramatic performances. Even with our knowledge of what comes after, it is
often difficult to catalogue the results of that constant interaction
between play and entertainment. Shall we refer to some shows as
morality plays embellished with masks and morris dances, and
designate others as basically masks seasoned with allegorical personages and moral lessons? And how does this political interlude
differ from that symbolical pageant celebrating a recent diplomatic
victory? [102] Hall had no reason even to attempt to distinguish
between drama and devising. In the first place, the events to single
out are those that illustrate one's thesis: Henry was magnificent,
and therefore his reign was "triumphant." Hence Hall's special
emphasis upon the spectacular, whether reporting the realities of
war or the adventures staged in times of peace. If his ostentatious
King and Court occasionally happened upon a strictly dramatic
mode to reveal their splendors, and if the result was striking
enough to satisfy Hall's standards of relevance, then the annalist
inadvertently became a historian of the theater. Examples of truly
dramatic representations might also merit brief mention if they included some clever political message. But Hall is never primarily
concerned about marking milestones in the evolution of English
drama proper. Even if he recognized it as an independent form,
it was, after all, a form that had yet to prove its worth.

And so Hall carefully lingers over satin fountains and shield-
bearing unicorns, continually frustrating economic, constitutional,
and often even dramatic historians. He is only helpful when his
hero's exhibitionism takes a dramatic direction. Of far-reaching
consequence to sixteenth-century drama was Henry's introduction
of the Italian mask, in which disguised dancers freely mingle with
the audience, calling it out to share in their revelry rather than
merely dancing with their masked partners. Except for the Kennington "mumming" of 1377, English masks had hitherto followed
the old forms of masking; the spectators were entertained, but
never invited to participate.[103] Henry had already shown his penchant for novel proceedings at Arthur's wedding in 1501, when he
suddenly threw his gown aside and danced in his jacket. On the
evening of Epiphany, 1512, he again found an opportunity to take
his Court by surprise: "the kyng with a. xi. other were disguised,

after the maner of Italie, called a maske, a thyng not seen afore in Englande. . . . These Maskers came in . . . and desired the ladies to daunce, some were content, and some that knewe the fashion of it refused, because it was not a thyng commonly seen" (p. 526).

Amid such courtly innovations and elaborations, however, we must not lose sight of Henry's greatest contribution to the development of romantic traditions, his blazing the trail, as it were, to Greene's "merry *Fresingfield*," the lands of Peele's *Famous Chronicle of . . . Edward Longshankes*, or Shakespeare's Arden and Illyria. Of farther-reaching consequences than the introduction of foreign fashions was the royal willingness to entertain the wonderful, to sponsor the fantastic and faraway. If perfumed assaults upon pasteboard castles lack profound significance, they at least offer better imaginative fare than the ponderous meditations of Tudor moralists. For along with the swaggering defiances and the absurd propositions of mimetic warfare, the ransoms of "right satten" and candied missiles, came dramatizations of romantic love. As Henry, seated in his satin fountain and surrounded by spouting gargoyles, was borne to the "solempne Iustes" at Greenwich in 1512, neither he nor his bedazzled reporter was aware of what lay ahead: Leicester's Camelot, *Common Conditions*, *Cymbeline*. In the meantime Henry remained. content to play the Arcadian game, and his annalist, to sketch quite unwittingly the first vignettes of Arden. In May, 1515, Hall tells us, King, Queen, and Court rode out of Greenwich

> to take the open ayre, and as they passed by the way, they espied a company of tall yomen, clothed all in grene . . . to the number of. ii. C. Then one of them, which called him selfe Robyn hood, came to the kyng, desyring him to se his men shoote, and the kyng was content. . . . Then Robyn hood desyred the kynge and quene to come into the grene wood, & to se how the outlawes lyue. The kyng demaunded of ye quene & her ladyes, if they durst aduenture to go into the wood with so many outlawes. Then the quene sayde, that if it pleased him, she was content, then the hornes blewe tyl they came to the wood vnder shoters hil, and there was an Arber made of boowes with a hal, and a great chamber and an inner chamber very well made & couered with floures & swete herbes, whiche the kyng muche praysed. Then said Robyn hood, Sir Outlawes

brekefastes is venyson, and therefore you must be content
with such fare as we vse. Then the kyng and quene sate
doune, & were serued with venyson and wyne by Robyn
hood and his men, to their great contentacion.

(P. 582)

CITIZENS ON HOLIDAY

Adventures in the greenwood were sadly lacking during the
brief and troubled reigns of Edward VI and Mary. On February
19, 1547, one day before his coronation, the young Prince passed in
triumph through London. Henry had bequeathed to his sickly son
a realm responsive to regal splendors, and the city showed its appreciation with a wealth of display.[104] But the nine-year-old monarch had also inherited a nation disturbed by political strife and
religious controversy. It was therefore with more hope than
wisdom that the citizenry sang:

> King Edward up springeth   from puerility,
> And towards us bringeth   joy and tranquillity;
> When he waxeth weight,   and to manhood doth spring,
> He shall be without fail   of four realms the King.

For the moment, however, Ned's interest was wholly taken by the
acrobatics of a Spanish rope-dancer, despite the inspiring representations of St. George, angels, a lion, and a phoenix, or the learned
speeches advocating justice, truth, mercy, and "regality." [105] The
accounts of the Revels Office record the new Court's attempts
also to continue Henry's indoor spectacles. Masks of Moors and
Amazons highlighted the Christmas festivities of 1551–1552, and
during the following Yuletide, George Ferrers directed an elaborate
"Triumph of Venus and Mars." [106] One of Professor Feuillerat's
documents seems to sum up fairly well the standard repertoire:

> Maskes. v. One of the worthies of the grekes. Another of
> Medioxes being half deathe, half man. Another of Bagpipes.
> Another of Cattes. and another of tumblers goinge vpon
> theyre handes with theyr feete vpward. A play of the
> State of Ierland and another of childerne sett owte by M^r
> haywood & diuers other playes & pastymes—apareled fur-
> nysshed & wrought vpon within the office of the
> Revelles.[107]

Some of this fare sounds intriguing, some quite fantastic. The mask featuring the Greek worthies might have included medieval-chivalric motifs, but it seems safe to conclude that the boy-king's courtiers were wading backward and that the romantic atmosphere of Henry's derring-do was generally lacking.

Under Edward's austere sister, the last spark of the old spontaneity appears to have died and Henry's troubled spirit returned, seeking vengeance. So it must have appeared, at least, to Philip of Spain, as he entered the city with his bride on August 19, 1554. After crossing London Bridge, the first pageant to greet the Queen and her popish consort was a huge portrait of the Nine Worthies,

> whereof king Henrie the eight was one. He was painted in harnesse hauing in one hand a sword, and in the other hand a booke, wherevpon was written Verbum Dei [the Word of God], deliuering the same booke (as it were) to his sonne king Edward, who was painted in a corner by him. But herevpon was no small matter made, for the bishop of Winchester lord chancellor, sent for the painter, and not onelie called him knaue for painting a booke in king Henries hand, and speciallie for writing therevpon Verbum Dei: but also ranke traitor and villen, saieng to him that he should rather haue put the booke into the queenes hand (who was also painted there) for that she had reformed the church and religion. . . . [A]nd so commanding him to wipe out the booke and Verbum Dei too: he sent him home.[108]

During the same year Mary's Court presented the customary round of maskings: devices of Mariners, "Arcules," Venetian senators, and Turkish magistrates. We also find "A Greate Maske of Allmaynes, pylgryms and Irysshmen" at Whitehall in April, 1557.[109] For the most part, however, the decade between Henry and Elizabeth provided rather dull entertainment. Its few devisings appear to have been essentially the same kinds of shows produced in the earliest years of Henry VIII, remolded to fit the occasion and usually rendered more prosaic. We sense a compliance with precedent instead of a delight in creative imitation; traditions were being merely observed, not nourished.

If Henry's elder daughter failed to catch her subjects' imagination, his younger provided more than sufficient compensation. Intimations of that godly Queen Esther, Dame Chastity's Champion, who would later appear at Coventry, Bristol, and Norwich, were clear from the outset. More important than the numerous devices London used to flatter and edify Elizabeth during her Coronation Entry of January 14, 1559, were her sensitive and sensible responses. Many times Holinshed points out that the Queen had her chariot stopped, often asking the youthful presenters to repeat their messages so that she might not miss one word (IV, 159, 162, 164, 165, 170–171). And when the predominantly Protestant city repeated the *Verbum Dei* motif, no inquisition interrupted the joyous procession. Instead, "when hir grace vnderstood that the bible in English should be deliuered vnto hir by Truth, which was therein represented by a child: she thanked the citie for that gift, and said, that she would oftentimes read ouer that booke" (IV, 166). Being advised that Truth wished to present the book in person, she proceeded to "the little conduit in Cheape," where two mountains had been built. At the foot of the first, "cragged, barren and stonie," sat Ruinosa Respublica, mourning the decay of his commonwealth. Opposite him "stood vpright one fresh personage," Respublica Bene Instituta, amid the verdant growth of his own country. Out of a cave between these two mountain-nations issued Time,

> apparelled as an old man, with a sieth in his hand, hauing wings artificiallie made, leading a personage . . . all clad in white silke, . . . The daughter of Time. . . . And on hir brest was written hir proper name, which was Veritas, Truth, who held a booke in hir hand, vpon the which was written Verbum veritatis. . . . The queene . . . as soone as she had receiued the booke, kissed it, and with both hir hands held vp the same, and so laid it vpon hir brest, with great thanks to the citie therefore.
>
> (IV, 167–168)

The older courtiers who had once reveled it with Henry, those who had weathered Edward's purges and Mary's persecutions as well as Time's scythe, must have been disappointed to see the spectacular so harnessed to the moral. Henry would never have endured the amount of preaching that went into eighty per cent of the pageants erected by these earnest people. And lest their Queen miss the obvious meaning of any show, two giants, "Gotmagot the Albione" and "Corineus the Briton," were set up at Temple Bar with a "table" advertising "theffect of all the Pageantes which the Citie before had erected."[110] But to this ascendance of the hortatory over the adulatory Elizabeth responded magnificently. Did they "hope that thou none errour wilt support"? So she also hoped, holding up her hands to heaven and asking her people to pray God that He might give her wisdom.[111] So rapt was the citizenry with her final farewell, "Be ye well assured I will stande your good Quene," that its shouts of approval were likened by Richard Tottel to the "noyse of ordinance which the Towre shot of at her Graces entraunce." In the space of one wintry afternoon Elizabeth seems to have won her Londoners, and only nine days later Tottel gave the rest of the realm a detailed description of her actions, including "Certain notes of the Queenes Majesties great mercie, clemencie, and wisdom, used in this passage." [112] Tottel also presses the message home in his introduction, comparing the whole city to one great stage. Both he and Holinshed, who appropriated most of his tract, are quite clear that the "wonderfull spectacle" of "so worthy a Soveraigne" required a stage even larger than London.

In emphasizing the pageantry with which sixteenth-century citizens honored and instructed their monarchs, however, we must not overlook those far more frequent and equally spectacular displays that the larger cities designed for themselves: May games, Midsummer Night watches, the Lord Mayors' shows, and similar civic processions. With the exception of the mask, whose splendors eventually made financial demands often too great even for royal coffers, every form of entertainment in which the aristocracy participated found its complement among those groups we may anachronistically call the middle and lower classes. Behind most civic and courtly pastimes there is probably one common primitive source, festive observances of the passing seasons by the pagan folk. Images of deities became images of saints; Christmas revels were grafted upon the Roman Saturnalia; [113] Church and guild came to sponsor processions originally pagan in nature out of propagandistic and commercial considerations. Even the nobility's tiltyard exercise, a relatively recent "Christian" recreation, had its counterpart among the bourgeoisie. While medieval courtiers clashed in tournaments, the citizenry ran at the quintain, an object supported by a crosspiece on an upright post. John Stow notes that although his Elizabethan contemporaries no longer engage with "disarmed lances and shields . . . to practise feats of war," they still ride at a "dead mark," the "quinten," and he traces the history of this sport back to

1253, when "the youthful citizens, for an exercise of their activity, set forth a game to run at the quinten; and whoever did best should have a peacock, which they had prepared as a prize." [114] This form of bourgeois jousting evidently lacked the patronage it enjoyed under Elizabeth, for "certain of the king's [Henry III's] servants" from the Court at Westminster precipitated a riot by hooting at the citizens, who in turn "beat them shrewdly."

Stow reprehends the King's servants' actions as an affront to the "dignity of the city, and ancient privilege which they [the Londoners] ought to have enjoyed." [115] The codification of this privilege was not exactly "ancient," but the ritual with which it was observed developed into a civic display as rich and varied as the royal entry. In 1209 King John granted that the city, hitherto governed by bailiffs, should have a mayor of its own choosing, provided that the elected officer swear fealty to him or to his appointed justices as Westminster. [116] Thus was initiated a progress upon which the guilds could lavish all the pageantry customarily reserved for welcoming princes. Each year London's chief magistrate rode in pomp from the Guildhall, along the Strand, and over to Westminster. His train included the beadle or apparitor of his own trade company, his brother aldermen, various city functionaries, and, of course, divers minstrels. During the fifteenth century these annual "ridings" were replaced by water progresses; each city company had its own barge to escort the mayor-elect up to Westminster via the Thames. To these guilds also fell the responsibilities of adorning both the Midsummer Show and the more occasional royal entry. To reduce expenses, they would attempt to use the same costumes and furniture for all three processions, [117] thus making a royal entertainment differ from a civic perhaps in quantity, but never in quality.

From the very beginning, then, the ceremony and spectacle of the royal entry arose through the co-operative efforts of city and court. The earliest "riding" on record, the passage of Henry III and Eleanor of Provence in 1236, provides Stow with his first example of "triumphant shows made by the citizens of London . . . [when] the city was adorned with silks, and in the night with lamps, cressets, and other lights without number, besides many pageants and strange devises there presented." [118] When Edward I returned from his victory over the Scots in 1298, the guildsmen provided features that may have already characterized the Lord Mayors' and Midsummer shows:

Every citizen, according to their several trade, made their several show, but especially the fishmongers, which in solemn procession passed through the city, having, amongst other pageants and shows, four sturgeons gilt, carried on four horses; then four salmons of silver on four horses; and after them six and forty armed knights riding on horses, made like luces of the sea; and then one representing St. Magnus, because it was upon St. Magnus' day, with a thousand horsemen, &c.[119]

Originating in these relatively simple processions of trade guilds, marching with images of fowl, fish, and beasts symbolizing their respective crafts, over the following centuries holiday parades drew from every current form of mimetic display. Unfortunately, London's Livery Companies did not see fit to include in their records any of their contributions to these events until 1485, when the Drapers' Wardens requested "Allowaunce for the mayrys messe [a feast held by the Drapers on the day the mayor was elected] And for mynstrelles pleyers and Russhis."[120] Similarly, the first record of a Midsummer Show appears in 1504, when the Drapers' Wardens noted payment made for "xiij pageantes for mydsom' watch for the said Mair' & the Charges of the same."[121] And not until 1540 is there recorded any reference to pageants for the Lord Mayors' shows; on October 15 of that year, the Drapers entered in their books an agreement "to haue the pageaunt of theassump-con' [the Assumption, probably of Our Lady] boren befor' the mayr' from the tow' to the gild hall."[122] This entry, however, notes that the agreement was made "by a p'cydent [precedent?] in the ijd tyme of ser John Aleyn beyng mayr [1535]."

For a reference to Lord Mayors' shows before 1535 we must turn once again to the Court-oriented Edward Hall. The historian's account of the coronation of Anne Boleyn in 1533 not only indicates that pomp and ceremony had long been associated with the annual progress of London's first citizen, but also suggests that the royal entry was sometimes modeled upon it. Noting Anne's pregnancy, Henry "wrote letters to the citee of London, to prepare pagiauntes against thesame coronacion," appointed overseers to direct the solemnities, and commanded the Mayor and aldermen to fetch her from Greenwich to the Tower; the City Council in turn ordered the haberdashers to "prepare a barge for the Batchelers [junior guildsmen] with a wafter [armed, convoying vessel] and a foyst [a light galley] garnished with banners and streamers *like-wyse as they vse to dooe when the Maior is presented at West-minster* on the morowe after Symon and Iude [29 October]" (pp. 795, 798. Italics added.) If the displays with which the guilds greeted Anne are in any way "likewyse" those provided for the Lord Mayor, the latter must have been splendid indeed. On May 19 the Mayor, Sir Stephen Pecocke, his brethren, "all in Scarlet," and enough guildsmen and civic notables to occupy forty-nine additional barges were rowed down the Thames to Greenwich. From the Mayor's own vessel came the "goodly armony" of "Shalmes, Shagbushes & diuers other instrumentes," but such strains must have soon been drowned out by the procession's harbinger, "a Foyst . . . full of ordinaunce, . . . a great Dragon continually mouyng, & castyng wyldfyer, and . . . terrible monsters and wylde men castyng fyer, and makyng hideous noyses" (p. 799). Order and degree were of course carefully observed. The nautical train passed Greenwich and made a smart about-face; thus "the Maior['s] and Shiriffes officers [now went] first, and the meanest craft next, and so ascendyng to the vttermost craftes in order and ye Maior last as they go to Poules [St. Paul's] at Christmas" (p. 799). At Greenwich, the barge containing Henry's Cleopatra, and adorned with earls and bishops, joined the procession back to the Tower. The remainder of Anne's progress, through the city to Westminster, took place the week following, and as usual the streets were graced with "merueilous connyng" pageants: Mount Parnassus and the Fount of Helicon, from which "ranne aboundantly Racked Rennishe wyne"; Apollo, Calliope and four sister Muses, falcons, angels, St. Anne, the Three Graces, numerous orators and choirs; a purse of gold comes from the City Recorder, and a golden ball from Pallas, Juno, and Venus, for Anne is evidently wiser, more majestic, and beautiful than they (pp. 800–802).

The shows conjured up by London to greet Anne in 1533, or Charles V a decade before, were obviously gleaned from a large number of disparate traditions. Miracle plays and popularized hagiographies yielded Biblical characters, latter-day saints, and their roaring persecutors. It was customary for each guild to champion its patron saint; hence the appearance of figures like John the Baptist, leading their respective companies, none of which seemed unwilling to include the sacred among the more secular symbols of its profession.[123] From chivalric literature a castle came forth to cover a conduit, as well as some "medieval" champion like

Hector or Alexander to defend it; upon these edifices were also placed chanting angels and stately virgins, sometimes translated after the manner of Lydgate into cardinal virtues, or Fortune and Nature. From the era of Brute and Troynovaunt arose the awesome giant, an anonymity when he welcomed Henry V in 1415, but under Henry VIII, christened Gogmagog and eventually, through some inexplicable fission, both Gog and Magog. The psalms of David or Ovid sometimes provided the Nine Worthies with apposite sentiments, and the acme of this happy mingling was reached when a representation of the Crucifixion appeared upon a tower of a castle placed on the back of an elephant.[124]

Such fusions also characterized the spectacles presented at Continental courts and cities. In 1468 Margaret of York was married to Charles the Bold at Bruges; the wedding was celebrated with all the splendors the ceremonious Court of Burgundy could muster, and Charles's English guests no doubt returned home with new ideas. About the same time the merchants of London must have been telling their fellow citizens similar stories about the civic displays they had seen in the Low Countries. Regardless of who influenced whom, the similarities between the pageants produced in London and those that appeared in European cities become "too striking to be the result of accident." [125] Two years before Jason's fiery dragon saluted Charles V on London Bridge, prophets of the Old Testament, the Virgin Mary, the Three Magi, and a dragon, led by St. Margaret and followed by St. George, paraded down the streets of Antwerp.[126] Charles's visit, in fact, caused a change in the Drapers' schedule of pageants. On May 12 the company had decided to "renewe" its old shows for the coming Midsummer and to construct a new one "of the goldyn fflees"; when the Emperor's impending arrival was made known, the Drapers hastily canceled their contributions for the Midsummer Show and set to work adorning London Bridge.[127] Through a great stroke of fortune, their half-finished "fflees" had suddenly become topical; everyone knew that Charles V was the Grand Master of Europe's most illustrious Order of the Golden Fleece.

Interacting with the themes and characters of royal entries and Lord Mayors' shows were those featured during the festivities of Midsummer. To judge from the items registered in the accounts of the London companies, the most important civic procession throughout the first half of the sixteenth century was the Midsummer Show or Watch, annually celebrated during the last week

of June. Once a pagan pastime to usher in the longest day of the
year, it had received formal recognition as early as 1253, when
Henry III established watches in cities and borough towns.[128] Besides the inevitable minstrels, sword players, morris dancers, giants,
and "waits" or city musicians, the watch featured shows quite
similar to those we have already noticed, but probably smaller,
for its pageants were borne along by porters. The characters thus
honored occasionally suggest an affinity to the miracle play. In
1519, for example, the Skinners hired the pageant of Our Lady
and St. Elizabeth from Barking, and another of St. Thomas Becket
from St. Giles.[129] Until the last entry in 1545, agreements to sponsor the Assumption of Our Lady are frequent and indicate that
show's special popularity. An overwhelming majority of these devices are of a religious nature, but occasionally we discover what
appears to be a secular subject tucked in among the saints. In 1521
the Drapers prepared for Midsummer with "iij pagentes that is to
say / the Castyll of Werr'. / the Story of Iesse. & Saynt Iohn
Euñgelist / And also they had. A King of Moores & l [50?]
moryans in the stede of an [other] pagent." [130]

In view of the occasional nature of these summer shows rendered
continuity of theme impractical, the custom of including a passing compliment to the lord mayor or to one of London's two sheriffs became increasingly popular. The Drapers seem to have been
the first Tudors to incorporate a reference to a civic dignitary. In
1512 they not only furnished pageants of "Saynt Blythe," the Assumption, and "the Castell of were," but also honored their brother
draper, now Mayor Roger Achilly, with a representation of the
Greek worthy, Achilles.[131] During a royal entry eighty years
before, Mayor Wells had been similarly flattered when three
virgins drew wine at the three wells of virtue, but the Drapers may
not have been aware of their "borrowing." In any case, ingenious
compliments became frequent by the 1530's: a "Castle of Denham"
(and made of denim?) for Sheriff William Denham by the Iron-
mongers in 1535; another "of Monmoth" for Sheriff Humphrey
Monmouth by the Drapers in 1536; and a "Rock of Roche alum"
for the Mayor, Sir William Roche, by the Drapers in 1541.[132]
Even an apparently religious figure, St. Christopher, which appeared in the Drapers' Midsummer Show for 1534, may have been
selected in deference to Mayor Christopher Askew.[133]

In view of the watch's increasingly greater emphasis upon contemporary themes and personages, its sudden demise after 1545

seems at first inexplicable. How could displays so timely become so quickly unfashionable? One explanation is provided by the fact that as the guilds' pageants for Midsummer start to wane, those for the Lord Mayor's Day begin to wax. The watch was evidently undone by its own relevance, its principal features being readily transferred to the Mayor's Show.[134] From 1535, when the Mercers bore the time-honored pageant of the Assumption before their fellow guildsman, Sir John Allen, the Livery Companies put more and more money and creative energy into celebrating their First Citizen, his trade, and London itself. By the 1550's these glories have supplanted the watch's religious devisings; the sacred remains only in the figures of the companies' patron saints. In 1553, 1556, and 1568, for example, the Merchant Taylors' processions were led by John the Baptist, and the payment made to a certain "Mr. Grimbald" for writing the speeches for their show of 1556 is probably a reference to Nicholas Grimald, whose academic Latin play, *Archipropheta* (c. 1547), is based upon the life of John, that "Christian" prophet and saint.[135]

A more important custom appropriated from the Midsummer Show was the "conceited" compliment, a pageant that shadowed forth the name of the honored official. The Merchant Taylors spent large sums in devising an elaborate salute to their brother, Sir William Harper, on the day of his inauguration, 1561. "To answer the speches" provided by the company, one "Iohn Shutte" produced a representation of five harpers, plucking and hymning psalms of praise to God and their Lord Mayor, and the "stage directions" indicate that for his five pounds Shutte was obliged to offer his employers the best of several literary worlds:

On the toppe as a fane the Armes of the lord mayoʳ electe
on the one side thereof, And the Armes of the m'chaunt
tailloʳs on the other side thereof
Vnder in the myddest David wᵗʰ his story aboute hym
On the right side Orpheus wᵗʰ his story before
On the lefte Amphion wᵗʰ his story
On the lefte side on the ende Arions &c
On the right side of thende Topas wᵗʰ his &c
Orpheus playeng vpon his harpe, and Trees Rivers Mountaynes, as Daunsinge & harkeninge
Amphion so, wᵗʰ a Citie & the wall, a buyldinge & the stones as voluntary Ronninge to it

Arion syttinge on a Dolphyn in the sea playeng on the
harpe
Topas so, before a table of princes and eu'y [every one]
of theis to haue his posie [motto]
In all places . . . of the pageant to haue paynted the
verses of 150 psalme [136]

A group so oddly sorted should not startle us, for we have often
seen the royal entry mingling the figures of the Old Testament
with those of Greek myths. It is rather surprising, however, that in
seeking a model "Troiane Knight," whose "Learning, Conninge,
[and] witt" were "vttered at the harpe," the Merchant Taylors
should have settled upon Chaucer's Sir Thopas.

Throughout Elizabeth's reign the citizen's shows, like the courtier's jousts, became increasingly literary. In 1566 the Ironmon-
gers paid James Peele, father of the dramatist, thirty shillings for
his pains in fashioning a pageant that featured the "quiristers of
Westminster." [137] Richard Mulcaster probably earned a handsome
sum for his verses on "Roe, the swyfte in chace" and similar compliments about Sir Thomas Roe in 1568, for the total cost of the
pageant ran over three hundred pounds. In 1584 the Drapers, unable to pun upon the name of Sir Thomas Pullison, contented
themselves with a representation of the justice and integrity of his
office. We learn this not from the Drapers' records, which note
only the observance of "all other Cerimonyes vsull," but through a
German tourist, Lupold von Wedel. His four-page account includes a description of "some men . . . carrying a representation in
the shape of a house with a pointed roof painted in blue and golden
colours and ornamented with garlands, on which sat some young
girls in fine apparel, one holding a book, another a pair of scales,
the third a sceptre." [138] George Peele joined the ranks of the professional city pageantwrights during the year following. His "Device of the Pageant borne before Woolstone Dixi" is the earliest
complete Lord Mayor's Show now extant,[139] and renders homage
to Dixie through thirteen figures: a Moor, London, Magnanimity,
Loyalty, Country, Thames, Soldier, Sailor, Science, and four
nymphs. For his third civic pageant Peele also exploited the conventional complimentary conceit; in 1591 Sir William Webb was
preceded by Nature, holding a distaff and spinning a web.[140]

Although poets and dramatists like Grimald, Mulcaster, and Peele
sophisticated these shows with learned verse and strange conceits,

the guildsmen never neglected the traditional high jinks. The watch had always employed a Sultan or King of Moors and his attendant "morians" to head the procession and clear its path. The Lord Mayor's shows often replaced these swarthy harbingers with other medieval figures, ivy-clad woodwoses or savage men armed with clubs and squibs, and various devils, who had evidently strayed out of the miracles and moralities.[141] For the average spectator, the importance of Lord Mayor's Day must have been represented as much by these boisterous grotesques as by the cunning devices and learned speeches they ostensibly heralded. At least such is the impression we receive from Henry Machyn's *Diary* of 1550 to 1563, which contains the first detailed descriptions of these street scenes. On October 29, 1553, London's new Mayor, Sir Thomas White of the Merchant Taylors, was approved at Westminster, returned to the city via the Thames, and

> landyd at Banard Castyll and [in St. Paul's] chyrche-yerd dyd hevere [every] craft wher set in [array]: furst wher ij tallmen bayreng ij gret stremars [of] the Merchand-tayllers armes, then cam on [with a] drume and a flutt playng, and a-nodur with a gret f[ife?] all they in blue sylke, and then cam ij grett wodyn [armed] with ij grett clubes all in grene, and with skwybes bornyng . . . with gret berds and syd here, and ij targets a-pon ther bake . . . and then cam a duyllyll, and after cam the bachelars all in a leveray, and skarlett hods; and then cam the pagant of sant John Baptyst gorgyusly, with goodly speches; and then cam all the kynges trumpeters blowhyng, . . . and then the craftes, and then the wettes playhyng, and then my lord mayre('s) offesers, and then my lord mayre with ij good henchmen, and then all the aldermen and the sheryffes, and so to dener.[142]

Although Machyn's descriptions are usually variations upon one glorious theme, they do provide important eyewitness accounts of those items sketchily recorded in the guilds' account books. Each procession has its colorful banners and streamers, its gaily decorated craftsmen and officers and musicians, its fearsome green savages and threatening devils, and, to insure law and order, its tallmen, beadles, and whifflers. The pageants also vary but slightly. The following year Sir Thomas White yields to "master Lyons

groser [grocer]," and Machyn again sees John the Baptist, this time
"with a lyon," as well as "a gryffen with a chyld lyung in harnes." [143] Himself a merchant taylor and therefore a dealer in
what we should call dry goods, Machyn also frequently focuses
his attention on the pomp of funeral processions and, indirectly,
on the high cost of dying. Lord Chandos is interred in 1557 "with
ij haroldes of armes, and a herse of wax, and . . . iiij baners of
emages, and elmett, mantylles, and viij dosen of skochyons
[scutcheons] and iiij baner-rolles of [arms], and viij dosen of
penselles [small pennons or streamers]." [144] As a businessman,
Machyn is of course a man about town, whose eye does not
scorn the humbler, old-fashioned folk festivals. On May 30, a few
weeks after Lord Chandos is buried, he sees "a goly May-gam in
Fanch-chyrche-strett with drumes and gunes and pykes, and ix
wordes [worthies] dyd ryd; and thay had speches evere man, and
the morris dansse and the sauden [sultan], and a elevant with the
castyll, and the sauden and yonge morens [Moors] with targattes
and darttes, and the lord and the lade of the Maye." [145] Two years
later, similar revellers "had spechys rond a-bowt London" and
then gave what was probably a command performance "a-for the
Quen and the consell" at Greenwich; they included the Baptist's
father, "sant John Sacerys, with a gyant, . . . ix wordes, . . . sant
Gorge and the dragon, the mores dansse, and after Robyn Hode
and lytyll John, and M[aid Marian] and frere Tuke." [146]

"The English are very rich and are fond of pomp and splen-
dour," concluded the German nobleman, von Wedel, in 1585.[147]
But amid the pomp of these processions, let us not lose sight of
their audiences, and especially the effects such continually flowing
sensory impressions must have had upon the imagination of both
readers and writers. Chaucer's Perkyn Revelour, who

> whan ther any ridyng was in Chepe,
> Out of the shoppe thider wolde he lepe—
> Til that he hadde al the sighte yseyn,[148]

is the prototype of the humble Tudor spectator. At Anne Boleyn's
water-progress of 1533, Hall's attention momentarily shifts from
ceremonies to citizens: "But for to speake of the people that stode
on euery shore to beholde the sight, he that sawe it not would not
beleue it" (p. 800). Machyn's "grett wodyn" and red "duyllyll,"
waving clubs and casting squibs, point up the crowd's pressing

HE DID

FOR GOD
SO LOVED, *the Lord of earth and heaven*
THE WORLD, *and longed to see forgiven,*
THAT HE GAVE *in sin and pleasure mad*
HIS ONLY BEGOTTEN SON, *the greatest Gift He had:*
THAT WHOSOEVER
BELIEVETH,
IN HIM, *to take our place*
SHOULD NOT PERISH *oh, what grace!*
BUT HAVE EVERLASTING LIFE *the Righteous and the Just,*
(John 3:16) *placing simple trust* *lost in sin,* *in Him.*

DID YOU?

what startled to
...our is offered,"
...ocession was also
... garlands, out of
it to give way, for
...hat when the First
...ore than a hundred
...nts were heard from
on the river as far as

...ost as revealing as his
...onjunctions with which
...ge to its successor, and
we sense the intensity of
...ered upon the common
stimuli continually before
records seventy-three pro-
courtiers and citizens could
on flesh and walking. For all
beautiful ornament or a chal-
lenge for the ... ...e man on the street must have
recognized Nature, Scie... Country as quickly as his
friends from Sherwood Forest. Whereas Virgil's "pyth" had to be
"groaped," the allegory of holiday highlighted rather than hid its
significance. We rightly celebrate the pictorial power of artists like
Sackville, Marlowe, and Spenser their ability to give us personages and situations bigger and more intense than life itself. But
we must also realize that if such imaginative flights characterize
certain poets, the habit of mind underlying these flights was
shared by all men. Machyn is not speaking about holiday when
he casually records that on November 5, 1557, there rode through
London "a man on horsebake, ys fase toward the horses tayl, and a
wrytyng on ys hed; and he had a fryse [coarse woolen] gown,
[and] ys wyff leydyng the horse, and a paper on her h[ead, for]
horwdom the wyche he lett ys wyff to . . . dyvers men." [150]
Although this scene looks like a synopsis of an episode from *The
Faerie Queene*, it was written by the city magistrates. And although
poetry was not their primary concern, it must have seemed to them
only natural that in making an example of this pander, he should
be punished pictorially. For men like Machyn, life thus heightened
became a commonplace part of life itself. A few years later Sack-

ville began "The Induction" to *The Mirror for Magistrates*, partly inspired, no doubt, by the speaking pictures of poets as ancient as Virgil and as recent as Dante and Lydgate. For the intense imagery that goes into his personifications of Dread, Revenge, and Death, the pictorial power that marks the *Induction* as a product of the Renaissance imagination, Sackville was probably no less indebted to the city streets. This may also be said of Spenser, Shakespeare, and to a lesser extent, even Milton.

Some Glosses upon Make-believe

Despite our previous efforts to see Tudor ceremony, chivalry, and display through Tudor eyes, and for all our attempts to render intelligible the apparently quixotic programs of Henry, Elizabeth, and their subjects by references to courtiers jockeying for positions and citizens for titles, Sidney's tiltyard fiction of 1581 may still seem incredible. If this most fantastic of all sixteenth-century devisings is to make any sense whatsoever, it must be viewed against several courtly traditions.

The first is a result of the Queen's own desire to elaborate upon her father's derring-do. As Gloriana, she stepped beyond Henry's greenwood adventures, turning every visitable nook of England into Albion. About the same time, she also assumed the role of maiden besieged, who dwelt in castles similar to the ones Henry had assaulted. The creativity of this latter imitation was satisfied by shifting the show's emphasis from challenger to defender. Mimetic warfare allowed her courtiers to borrow from their grandfathers' doughty deeds, but the new ground rules dictated that their loves be more reverent than lusty and that all sieges be repulsed. In this way Elizabeth translated Henry's heroics into a martial religion, whose goddess was herself, and though her devisers' romantic rituals sometimes remained invitations to the dance or joust, they always became enticements to adore.

At first the translation proceeded slowly. In the Queen's early years we find nothing like the involved challenges and showy assaults that characterized her father's triumphs. Instead of Perfect Beautie resisting Desire's Children, we see only Elizabeth of England reviewing her citizens' musters. Holinshed tells us that on the first Sunday of July, 1559, fourteen hundred Londoners, "furnished foorth by the crafts and companies of the citie," paraded to Greenwich Park and set themselves "in battell arraie, euen as they should haue fought" (IV, 184). "For the honor and celebration" of the Earl of Warwick's marriage six years later, "a goodlie chalenge was made and obserued at Westminster at the tilt, each one six courses" (IV, 229). Warwick was Her Majesty's General of the Ordnance, and when the Queen visited his estate in 1572, he drew upon his knowledge of gunnery to stage one of the noisiest Elizabethan entertainments, a battle between his fortress and another commanded by the Earl of Oxford. Fourteen "battering-pieces" and twelve "faire chambers" were brought down from the Tower of London and "divers persons" of his shire recruited and suitably furnished.[151] Between the cannon, mortars, and an over-zealous missile-firing dragon, considerable damage was inflicted not only upon the forts, but also on the town close by.

> The fire-balles and squibbes cast upp did so flye quiet [quite] over the Castell, and into the myds of the Towne, falling downe, some on houses, some in courts and baksides, and some in the streate, . . . to the great perill . . . of the inhabitants of this Borough: and so . . . foure houses in the Towne and Suburbes were on fyre at once.
>
> (I, 320)

As Henry's Court had discovered, however, mere push of puncheon and shot of cannon were but furious clashes, signifying nothing. Chivalric exercise needed a theme of honor and renown, preferably one based upon that most essential element of romance, the prospect of gaining or defending fair lady. Indirectly, it was Elizabeth herself who provided the formula. In 1561 she improved and enclosed the tiltyard at Whitehall, which her father had constructed early in his reign; the following year she directed that the rules for courtly combat, codified by John Tiptoft a century earlier, be brought up to date.[152] To any courtier of reasonable intelligence, such obvious interest in the tournament must have suggested another avenue to royal favor, and of those who entered at this door, none appears to have been better received than the romantic gentleman sheep-farmer of Ditchley Hall, Sir Henry Lee. According to Sir William Segar, sometime Garter King-of-Arms, who wrote at the end of the reign, it was Lee who first proposed that tiltyard ceremonies be annually observed to commemorate Elizabeth's accession to the throne on November 17, 1558.

> These annuall exercises in Armes . . . were first begun and occasioned by the right vertuous and honourable Sir *Henry*

Lea, Master of her Highnesse Armorie, and now deseru-
ingly Knight of the most noble Order, who of his great
zeale, and earnest desire to eternize the glory of her
Maiesties Court, in the beginning of her happy reigne, voluntarily vowed (vnlesse infirmity, age, or other accident
did impeach him) during his life, to present himselfe at the
Tilt armed, the day aforesayd yeerely, there to performe
in honor of her sacred Maiestie the promise he formerly
made. Wherevpon the Lords and Gentlemen of the sayd
Court, incited by so worthy an example, determined to
continue that custome, and not vnlike to the ancient
Knighthood *della Banda* in *Spaine*, haue euer since yerely
assembled in Armes accordingly.[153]

Although Segar claims that the Queen's Day tilts were initiated
"in the beginning" of Elizabeth's "happy reigne," records of them,
as E. K. Chambers points out, do not commence until 1581,
shortly after Lee had become Master of the Armory.[154] Once at
Court, Loricus—for so Lee had dubbed himself at Woodstock in
1575—gained ample opportunity to work out those romantic
themes that appear in "Hemetes' Tale." Another of his offices, that
of Royal Champion, gave him additional incentive, for he would
be expected to appear not only on Queen's Day, but at tournaments
throughout the year. The most fully recorded of those entertainments in which Lee played his part was held on May 15–16,
1581. The groundwork, however, had been laid well in advance.
As the Queen returned from chapel on April 16, a small boy,
dressed in red and white, rudely stayed her passage; "without making any precise reverence at all," this "martial messenger" uttered
certain "speeches of defiance" sent by the Earl of Arundel, Lord
Windsor, and Sirs Philip Sidney and Fulke Greville, who called
themselves "The Four Foster Children of Desire."[155] In an elaborate and highly flattering cartel, these Children designated the
gallery from which Elizabeth customarily watched her tilters[156]
"The Castle or Fortresse of Perfect Beautie," and to it "layde
tytle and claime as their due by descent to belong unto them. And
uppon deniall, or any repulse from that their desired patrimonie,
they vowed to vanquishe and conquer by force who so shoulde
seeme to withstand it" (II, 313). For like Hemetes's model knight,
Loricus of Cambia, Desire has driven them to seek respite by
wandering, and having discovered that Perfect Beautie's castle is
"seated in this Realme,"

These foure I say, and say againe, thus nourished, thus
animated, thus entituled, and thus enformed, doe will
you . . . in the name of Justice, that you will no longer
exclude vertuous Desire from perfect Beautie. . . . But if
(alasse, but let not that be needful) Beautie be accompanied
with disdainful pride, and pride waighted on by refusing
crueltie, then . . . it shall be seene what knights . . . Beautie
may draw to resist a rightful title.

(II, 314-315)

Beautie's answer was not recorded, but she could hardly have
been surprised to hear of her impending ravishment. Holinshed
tells us that for three weeks prior to this proud "defie," 375 London
craftsmen had been busy at Westminster, erecting a stately pleasure
dome to banquet "certeine commissioners out of France" (IV,
434-435). And on the very day Desire's impudent offspring issued
their challenge, the Dauphin of Auvergne, the Marshall of France,
and eight other dignitaries had arrived in England to discuss a
marriage between Elizabeth and the Duke of Anjou. The theme
of Desire's quest for matchless Beautie thus underlined high matters
of state. Unfortunately, such matters—or perhaps uncompleted tiltyard machinery—occasioned several postponements from April
24, the scheduled day of conquest, and the Children were kept
burning until May 15. On this day the four challengers, heralded by
blaring trumpets, ventured out of the tiltyard stables, each dressed
in resplendent armor upon which were "comparisons and furniture
richly and bravely embrodered," and followed by ushers, pages,
yeomen, and a large body of private gentlemen (II, 315 ff.). The
nature of their quest was darkly figured forth by the "poesie, or
sentence written upon" the coats of Sidney's troupe: *Sic nos non
nobis* (Thus we do, rather than being done unto).

As the four companies passed in review under the Queen's gallery, their principal engine, a canvas-covered mount painted to
resemble an earthen bulwark, was wheeled about the yard. Upon
this "rowling trench" were two wooden cannons, two gunners, and
an ensign-bearer; within it was a goodly consort of musicians. When
the trench had reached Beautie's Fort, Desire's tiny ambassador
informed her that the present broil was needless; only obstinate
Disdain had turned Desire into Fury, a divine wrath, as was obvious
from the fact that the naturally heavy earth had risen to a mount
and was now erupting with music. The fort was next summoned
with a "delectable song," advocating complete capitulation:

Yeeld, yeeld, O yeeld, you that this fort doo hold,
Which seated is in spotlesse honors feeld,
Desire's great force no forces can withhold:
Then to Desire's desire, O yeeld, O yeeld.

(II, 318)

Hereupon preliminary assault was given by the Mount's two cannons, one firing "sweet powder" and the other, "sweet water, verie
odoriferous and pleasant," while certain footmen adjusted their
scaling ladders, ascended the "never conquered wals," and supported the perfumed cannonades with barrages of "floures and
such fansies . . . as might seeme fit shot for Desire."

The siege was suddenly interrupted by twenty-one defendants,
each making a grand entrance with servants, pages, trumpeters,
and his own speech and "mysticall invention" or conceited device.
First to enter were Sir Thomas Perot and Anthony Cooke, "both
in like armour beset, with apples and fruit, the one signifying
Adam, and the other Eve, who had haire hung all down his helmet," and their page, "arraied like an Angell," who announced
to Beautie the cause of their quest (II, 319 ff.). A frozen knight
was once enforced by Desire to behold "the sun on the earth,"
and he loyally melted in adoration. When his spirit later beheld
this sun besieged, its anguished cries roused the gods of heaven
and hell to vengeance. An angel, along with the proud parents of
humanity, were promptly dispatched to remedy this eclipse of a
light in which all rejoiced. Thomas Ratcliffe next appeared as
the Desolate Knight, a champion who had lived as a hermit for
many years until upon the body of a man slain by pirates he discovered a scroll prophesying Beautie's overthrow; he immediately
abandoned his hermitage to defend her. Then came the four
Knollys brothers, attired as the Four Sons of Despair and heralded
by a sermon from one of their pages, Mercury. After the other
defendants had similarly rendered their addresses, expounded their
devices, and marched about the yard, each in turn ran six courses
against the challengers. The ceremony seems to have been interrupted only once, when "in the middest of the running came in
Sir Henrie Leigh, as unknowne, and when he had broken his six
staves, went out in like manner againe" (II, 319).

The second day of battle opened as Desire's Chariot, drawn by
horses in red and white silk, rolled down the tiltyard (II, 327).
Within the coach sat musicians, playing "verie dolefull musike,"

and on the top, Dame Desire and her Children, "forewearied and halfe overcome." Their herald made it clear that they had chosen to resume the conflict not out of scorn for Beautie's defenders, but because they were Desire's captives and totally consumed by "flame unquenchable." And so once more "each Knight induced to win the golden fleece," this time at the tourney and barriers. But as dusk approached, a boy clad "in ash-coloured garments" and bearing a sprig of olive fell prostrate before Beautie and delivered the Children's submission:

> They acknowledge this fortresse to be reserved for the eie of the whole world, farre lifted up from the compasse of their destinie. . . . They acknowledge they have degenerated from their fosterer in making Violence accompanie Desire. . . . Therefore they doo acknowledge themselves overcome, as to be slaves to this Fortresse for ever, which title they will beare on their foreheads, as their other name is ingraven in their hearts.
>
> (II, 328–329)

In such terms Desire humbly relinquished its aspirations; Beautie was to remain Perfect, a universal light and source of common comfort. Despite their flattering impudence, the Children had not dared to extend their new doctrine of submission to the spectators in the gallery. Had the French commissioners fully explicated the martial parable, however, they would have saved Anjou a fruitless passage to England. Eight months later even the noble Duke came to realize that this Fortress was indeed "reserved for the eie of the whole world."

Approximately six months after Lee had clashed against Desire's Children as Stranger Knight, the first recorded Queen's Day Tilt was held at Westminster, where the Knight of the Crown again matched prowess with Sidney. And over the next twenty years,[157] the elaborate machinery, comparisons, and cartels that had characterized Beautie's siege continued, under the careful eye of Loricus, to pour forth in never-ending flattery. When the next recorded Queen's Day approached, a German tourist, von Wedel, made a point of returning from Scotland to watch the festivities. Having evidently joined the "many thousand spectators" who, "by paying 12 *d.* could get a stand and see the play," he notes the stately nature of these chivalric minuets:

During the whole time of the tournament all who wished to fight entered the list by pairs, the trumpets being blown at the time and other musical instruments. The combatants had their servants clad in different colours; they, however, did not enter the barrier, but arranged themselves on both sides. Some of their servants were disguised like savages, or like Irishmen, with the hair hanging down to the girdle like women, others had horse manes on their heads, some came driving in a carriage, the horses being equipped like elephants, some carriages were drawn by men, others appeared to move by themselves. . . . The costs amounted to several thousand pounds each. When a gentleman with his servant approached the barrier, on horseback or in a carriage, he stopped at the foot of the staircase leading to the queen's room, while one of his servants in pompous attire of a special pattern mounted the steps and addressed the queen in well-composed verses or with a ludicrous speech, making her and her ladies laugh. When the speech was ended he in the name of his lord offered to the queen a costly present, which was accepted and permission given to take part in the tournament.[158]

Another body of evidence indicating the avenues taken by Loricus's muse is a manuscript collection of pieces in verse and prose, long preserved at Ditchley Hall, where Lee died in 1611.[159] In it we find summaries of the challenges and speeches that prefaced and accompanied his adulatory programs. Many, unfortunately, are undated, nor can we even be sure of how many were written for Lee himself. Taken as a whole, however, their romantic conventions suggest that the much admired themes of "Hemetes' Tale" were articulated as often in suburban tiltyard as country boscage. Of the collection's thirty-one items, "The Suplicacion of the old Knight" was obviously acted out by Lee sometime after his retirement in 1590: "A Knight, disabled by age, yet once the first Celebrator of 'this Englishe holliday or rather Englandes happie day', asks the tilters to accept 'in his fathers rome this only sonne of myne', and, lest he should forfeit his tenure of the day's honouring, begs that one of them will present 'this litle' to the queen, as the yearly fine of his faith."[160] This device of the Old Knight must have been employed at least one year after Accession Day, 1590, when the fifty-seven-year-old

Royal Champion resigned his office to the Earl of Cumberland. Except for Goldwell's and Holinshed's accounts of the Foster Children's assault of 1581, only this event appears to have merited a detailed published description: George Peele's *Polyhymnia* (1590),[161] in which the dramatist's mastery of blank verse is turned to hymning the praises of the twenty-six tilters, and Segar's fuller narration in *Honor Military, and Ciuill* (1602). The ceremony took place under Elizabeth's gallery, where she sat with the "chiefest Nobilitie" and French ambassadors.[162] Accompanied by ethereal strains, a "Pauilion" of white taffeta, representing "the sacred Temple of the Virgins Vestall," rose out of the earth. Three holy maids issued forth to present the Queen with gifts from the altar. Before the temple door stood Lee's heraldic device, a crowned pillar, now symbolically "embraced by an Eglantine tree," which bore a complimentary "prayer." As the temple arose and the priestesses appeared, one "M. *Hales* her Maiesties seruant" provided the moral in song:

> My golden locks time hath to siluer turnd,
>
> . . . .
>
> My Helmet now shall make an hiue for Bees,
> And louers songs shall turne to holy Psalmes:
> A man at Armes must now sit on his knees,
> And feed on pray'rs, that are old ages almes.
>
> . . . .
>
> Goddesse, vouchsafe this aged man his right,
> To be your Beadsman now, that was your Knight.[163]

At the opposite end of the tiltyard Lee and his successor now appeared, followed by twelve pairs of combatants, each in the order of their first running of six courses. It is not surprising that Sir William, Garter King-of-Arms, should speak so solemnly about such fantasies, but George Peele, poet and commoner, seems even more serious. To capture the meaning of that clash between past and future Queen's Champions, Peele bypasses satire and irony to attempt pure epic:

> Mightie in Armes, mounted on puissant horse,
> Knight of the Crown in rich imbroderie,
> And costlie fair Comparison charg'd with Crownes,
> Oreshadowed with a withered running Vine,

As who would say, My spring of youth is past:
In Corslet gylt of curious workmanship,
Sir Henry Lea, redoubted man at Armes
Leades in the troopes, whom woorthie Cumberland
Thrice noble Earle, aucutred as became
So greate a Warriour and so good a Knight,
Encountred first, yclad in coate of steele,
And plumes and pendants al as white as Swanne,
And speare in rest, right readie to performe
What long'd unto the honour of the place.
Together went these Champions, horse and man,
Thundring along the Tylt, that at the shocke
The hollow gyring vault of heaven resoundes.[164]

When every course had been run, Lee dismounted, entered Vesta's shrine, doffed his magnificent armor, and, "at the foot of her Maiesties crowned pillar," offered up his gear with a petition that she would accept Cumberland in his stead. With his goddess's consent, the aged knight invested the new Champion in his own armor and "mounted him vpon his horse," [165]

Protesting to her princelie Majestie,
In sight of heaven and all her princelie Lordes,
He would betake him to his Oraysons:
And spend the remnant of his waining age,
(Unfit for warres and Martiall exploites)
In praiers for her endlesse happines.[166]

Having donned a black velvet robe and "couered his head (in liew of an helmet) with a buttoned cap of the countrey fashion," [167] Lee thus brought his last official extravaganza to a close. For several days he continued to go about the Court in his hermit's weeds, upon which appeared "a crowne embrodered, with a certaine motto or deuice, but what his intention therein was, himselfe best knoweth." It no doubt advertised that the hoary beadsman had once been the realm's foremost defender. It probably reiterated the allusion Lee had been so careful to include in his retirement festivities: brave Loricus, who had once charmed the Queen at Woodstock in 1575, was now become another Hemetes. As a spinner of myths, Lee had done an admirable job. Whitehall was already decorated with the shields and escutcheons used on former Accession Day tournaments,[168] and there was nothing left but to retire into his own fictions. Given these new circumstances, Malory could not have designed a fitter conclusion, nor could he have selected a more qualified successor. Two years later Philip Gawdy describes Cumberland and Essex entering the Privy Chamber, fully armed, to issue this challenge; "Uppon the xxvjth of ffebruary next . . . they will runn with all commers to mayntayn that ther M. is most worthiest and most fayrest Amadis de Gaule." [169]

Obviously Lee's retirement by no means ended the reenactments of former fabulous story. At Elizabeth's command, he continued to preside over the more important tournaments as a kind of master of ceremonies, keeping a watchful eye on the Knight of Pendragon Castle, as Cumberland called himself, and insuring that the glories of yore were decorously represented. During the last decade of her reign, the Queen's own theater was brilliantly illuminated with the feats of Robert Carey and the magnificent, self-seeking Essex. Even Francis Bacon is thought to have had a hand in these martial revels; the device of Eros and Philautia, which Essex bore in 1593, is still extant in the handwriting of Britain's forward-looking philosopher, essayist, and parliamentarian.[170] And when James I's eldest son, Prince Henry, made his first public appearance at the barriers in January, 1610, the Lady of the Lake, Merlin, and Arthur were conjured up for the occasion by England's eminent classicist, Ben Jonson.[171] Three years later the Earl of Rutland tilted on James's Accession Day, his devices or emblems painted by Richard Burbage and his motto or posy composed by Shakespeare.[172]

Nor were the fairy grounds of Albion disenchanted after Gloriana's adventures among the groves of Elvetham, Sudeley, and Rycote in the early 1590's. Part of her last summer was spent on progress, and though the "hower glasse" held by Time at Harefield was "stopped, not runninge," the deities and dairymaids of Middlesex and Buckinghamshire made their customary appeals and curtsies.[173] Halfway through James's reign, St. George is still a formidable figure; at the marriage of Princess Elizabeth in 1613, the Christian warrior delivered an Amazon queen from her captor, Mango the Necromancer.[174] Three years earlier Burbage and Rice had exchanged their parts in *Pericles* and *Cymbeline* for the roles of Amphion and Corinea, and ridden upon dolphins up the Thames to deliver London's welcome and Anthony Munday's

speeches to Prince Henry.[175] For all the New Learning that intervening decades had ushered in, James's triumphs are as variegated
as Henry VIII's. Like the first generation of Tudor courtiers and
citizens, the last freely drew upon modern, medieval, and classical
facts and fictions, and with an amazingly elastic sense of artistic
decorum, fused all times, customs, and matters. There is no evidence, in other words, to indicate that James's devisers attempted
to divorce the disparate figures and situations Henry's Court had
married and Elizabeth's domesticated.

But how are we finally to interpret the attitudes of the actors and
stagehands who hurried back and forth between the real and magical worlds of Elizabeth's realm and Gloriana's stage: Sir Philip,
lamenting the absurdities of early romantic comedy on one day,
assaulting Beautie with candied missiles on the next; Leicester and
Hertford, up to their noble necks in Court intrigue, emitting
anguished moans from holly thickets or firing off rounds of flattery
from metamorphosed island-ships; would-be poet laureates like
Gascoigne, invoking Jupiter to the tune of antic hays? Were there
smiles among the royal train when the worldly-wise Burghley welcomed the Queen to Theobalds in 1593 with "I am the poor Hermit,
your Majestie's Beadman"? [176] Did the retired statesman accent
the word "poor," hoping his patroness would realize that each of
her dozen visits had cost him between two and three thousand
pounds? Or did he grimace over "Hermit" to show his contempt
for Loricus? Or did he simply play his lines straight, either out of
respect for Elizabeth's romantic tastes, or in deference to the make-
believe that had become a traditional part of her progresses, or because he could find nothing better than this cliché to express a
genuine regard?

The most enigmatic player is the Queen herself, often surrounded by a cast of characters as oddly sorted as those she met
while descending the hillside at Bisham: Pan and his virgins, sewing
samplers; Ceres and her nymphs in a hock cart; a right courteous,
almost too chatty woodwose-satyr. Did she welcome frantic appeals from screaming Daphnes or requests to judge which maiden's
rustic wooer was more worthy? When, according to Laneham, Pan
sent "Hiz mery morrys-dauns, with theyr pype and taber" to
increase the Kenilworth revelry (I, 470), did Ascham's diligent
scholar laugh to see the Roman god of woods stealing from Sherwood Forest? If we could establish Elizabeth's attitude toward any

one of those many festive observances patronized by both native sprites and the country gods of paganism, we should probably know how she enjoyed the rest. Perhaps she first winced and then smiled at Sylvanus and Neptune holding a London muster with darts and squirts, or at the numerous medieval "salvages" who conversed with the classical nymph, Echo. Perhaps she especially enjoyed her assigned role of magical vivifier of the fields, realizing, as C. L. Barber points out, that it had "affinities with the traditional lustral visit" of the mummery lady, making her *quête* to bring the luck of the season to house and village.[177] But having recognized the affinities, was she also amused at the incongruities? For all their references to decorum, the critics offer little help. The same year that Gascoigne the woodwose brandished his club, Gascoigne the instructor of poetry warned that "to entermingle merie iests in a serious matter is an *Indecorum*." [178] As a gloss upon his own excellent devising, however, this comment leaves us no wiser than we were. To be assured that the Queen and her courtier were being wholly serious or wholly merry, we should need a note upon intermingling Greek nymphs with green men. The only other piece of critical commentary is equally ambivalent. Laneham was obviously amused at the "mad adventure" that interrupted Gascoigne's make-believe, but he thought the device itself was "pronounced in good meeter and matter, very wel indighted.'

For the few who have bothered to read these Tudor "plays," the incongruities they highlight have proved perplexing. In 1759 the antiquarian Bishop of Worcester, Richard Hurd, pacified his troubled neoclassical conscience by finding congruity in incongruity:

> If something of the Gothic romance adhered to these classical fictions, it was not for any barbarous pleasure that was taken in this patchwork, but that the artist found means to incorporate them with the highest grace and ingenuity. . . . The attributes and dresses of the deities themselves are studied with care, and the most learned poets of the time employed to make them speak and act in perfect character.[179]

Satyrs "to advantage dressed" are nevertheless satyrs, and their appearance on those grounds "still . . . kept by Arthur's heires and

their seruants" is certainly an instance of romantic "patchwork."
Professor Barber, on the other hand, insists upon the pleasure of
underlined incongruities.

> Another source of fun at entertainments, which is merely
> glanced at in the accounts of them, must have been the
> incongruity between fact and fiction, and the fun of quick
> transitions between the two. When one reads the texts of
> welcomes, . . . they often seem almost tediously solemn.
> But they were witty, or "conceited," when they were per-
> formed, by virtue of the deftness with which they extended
> actuality into make-believe. Because this dramatic dimen-
> sion was furnished by the occasion, it did not need to be
> expressed in the language of occasional verses. When
> Shakespeare puts pageantry on the stage, he makes comedy
> out of incongruity between make-believe and reality.[180]

For this delightful prospect of the real and unreal juxtaposed
for comic effects, we need at least one telltale phrase in the narrators' detailed descriptions or lengthy prefaces. It is tempting to
reconstruct the situations at Kenilworth and Elvetham with the
programs presented within *Love's Labor's Lost* and *A Midsummer Night's Dream* as our glosses. Once we equate what Shakespeare found with what he did, Gloriana's stage abounds with
clever presenters, at once acting out and undercutting their lines.
But the "occasion" faced by Leicester and Hertford was different
from Shakespeare's. For any subject, the Queen's visits must have
brought some anxiety, and for courtiers and civic officials seeking
advancement her advent was probably regarded with a seriousness
bordering on fear. Leicester's Hercules may have been a waggish household servant, and Norwich's King Gurgunt, a renowned
wit of the city. It seems unlikely, however, that either would have
risked his superior's wrath by speaking or acting out of character
with the solemn lines assigned him, by making make-believe a
"source of fun" with clever asides or whimsical gestures.

We catch the Queen laughing at three kinds of comedy. The first,
noted by von Wedel at the tiltyard in 1584, is the "ludicrous
speech" of a page in "pompous attire." The joke was intentional
and appreciated. But for us it remains ambiguous; there is little to
indicate that it drew upon perceived disparities between reality
and make-believe, or between chivalry and "horses . . . equipped

like elephants." The second kind of comedy is both unambiguous and unintentional. Both Laneham and his Queen laughed at the bumpkins who brought in their bride-ale and Hock-day dumb show. Notice, however, that no member of the Court had a part in those plays. And because Puck had not come forth to remind the Kenilworth nobility of the "folly" of its own actions, it was free to smile at the rustics with impunity. In determining which fictions the Court probably mocked, we may gain some help from that sophisticated instructor of courtiers, Puttenham. He sneers at those "midsommer pageants in London, where, to make the people wonder, are set forth great and vglie Gyants marching as if they were aliue, and armed at all points, but within they are stuffed full of browne paper and tow, which the shrewd boyes vnderpeering do guilefully discouer and turne to a great derision." [181] Only the naïve, in other words, will take such artless stuff seriously. But Puttenham's sense of the farfetched does not include the matters Leicester's own devisers exploited, for the critic is proud of that "brief *Romance* or historicall ditty" he himself has written to be sung "to the harpe in places of assembly, where the company shalbe desirous to heare of old aduentures & valiaunces of noble knights in times past, as are those of king *Arthur* and . . . Sir *Beuys* of *Southampton*, *Guy* of *Warwicke*, and others like." [182] Granted, he knows that some of his courtly audience "would peraduenture reproue and disgrace euery *Romance*." But it never occurs to him that they will scorn his subject matter. Their hostility, rather, will proceed from the mistaken notion that these brave heroes should be celebrated only "in long meeters or verses *Alexandrins*, according to the nature and stile of large histories."

The third and most Shakespearean kind of comedy furnished by Gloriana's stage seems also unintentional, an inadvertent puncturing of the make-believe created by Queen and subject. A carelessly thrown branch starts a royal mount and accidentally introduces reality, but both Elizabeth and George quickly remedy the situation and return to their sylvan frolic. Churchyard made his Queen "smyle and laugh withall" on that rainy day at Norwich, but his original script called for something more dignified; only a sudden shower obliged him to convert his water-nymphs into land-fairies, and we cannot even be sure that the conversion was intended to evoke the mirth he proudly reports. No doubt the most entertaining misadventure is noted by an anonymous witness at Kenilworth:

> There was a spectacle presented to Queen Elizabeth upon
> the water, and among others Harry Goldingham was to
> represent *Arion* upon the dolphin's backe, but finding his
> voice to be verye hoarse and unpleasant, when he was to
> perform it, he tears off his disguise, and swears he was none
> of Arion, not he, but even honest Harry Goldingham,
> which blunt discoverie pleased the Queene better than
> if it had gone through in the right way.[183]

Hoarseness hardly explains Master Goldingham's actions; perhaps
Arion had been tippling with the musicians inside his docile beast.
In any case, although Laneham wittily describes Arion "ryding
alofte upon his old freend the dolphin," and Gascoigne solemnly notes
Goldingham's "clearing his voyce," neither admits that actuality
was thus extended into make-believe. With Holofernes's and Peter
Quince's devisings before us, we naturally hope to find many men
like Honest Harry within the Queen's theater. Instead, we almost
always discover things going "through in the right way." The
incongruities between fact and fiction are rarely admitted, and even
then more by accident than deft design. The incongruities between
the literary traditions that compose the devisers' patchwork, on the
other hand, do not seem to have been sensed even by Shakespeare,
for if Bottom as Pyramus is comic and Puck always a source of
fun, the amusing fact that they inhabit the same world as the
Queen of the Amazons is never exploited.

To doubt that Elizabeth's devisers ever contrived situations that
concurrently fostered and undercut their own fictions does not, of
course, leave us with a theater essentially solemn. Writers, pro-
ducers, and actors exercised their wits in seeking greater spectacle,
brighter and more "conceited" or emblematic furniture, verses
that made the inevitable flattery sound spontaneous, and themes
that would take advantage of each estate's prospect at a given season. Sometimes these themes also exploit recent political events,
and in that special sense Barber seems quite correct about the
deliberate extension of actuality into make-believe. But in such
cases fact is introduced to complement rather than displace fiction.
Did Hertford, for example, cut part of his estate into "the perfect
figure of a half moon" to celebrate Elizabeth's virginity or her victory over the crescent-shaped Armada? Instead of fretting over
alternatives, Nereus, the Earl's presenter, simply states that she is
"Faire Cinthia the wide Ocean's Empresse." Elizabeth's chastity

is no less a fact than Philip's defeat or the moon's influence upon ocean tides; hence, history has merely provided a new instance of the myth's truth. Underlying the deviser's conceited excursions into the meaning of the moon—its moral, political, economic, and biological significances—is the sense that each part of the relationship is equally fanciful and equally real. He is earnest about these fanciful suggestions, however, because each will furnish additional evidence of his artifice and invention. To see how many ways one flattering theme could be varied must have been an enjoyable exercise for both writer and audience, but to modify the illusion with hints of the Snail Mount's silliness or Cynthia's professional virginity was a source of fun probably unperceived and certainly never used.

If we see Sidney and his fellow Children of Desire working within and elaborating upon these conventions, we shall find a similar seriousness of purpose underlying their siege of Beautie. The facts that motivated this tiltyard fiction were as varied as the literary traditions they appropriated. No doubt uppermost in Sidney's mind was a sordid political-moral-religious reality, the marriage proposed between the Queen and Anjou. Only a year earlier he had written against that "Frenchman and . . . Papist, that . . . son of a Jezabel," [184] and then found it wise to retire from Court. Upon his return, he must have decided to advertise his Protestant concerns less directly. Like every Elizabethan critic, he knew that poetry sweetened the pill, and like most Renaissance sonneteers, he was experimenting with the theme of renouncing Desire. The eloquence of the following is Sidney's own, but its ideas were commonplace:

> Thou blind mans marke, thou fooles selfe chosen snare,
> Fond fancies scum, and dregs of scattred thought,
> Band of all evils, cradle of causelesse care,
> Thou web of will, whose end is never wrought.
>
> Desire, desire I have too dearely bought,
> With prise of mangled mind thy worthlesse ware,
> Too long, too long asleepe thou hast me brought,
> Who should my mind to higher things prepare.
>
> But yet in vaine thou hast my ruine sought,
> In vaine thou madest me to vaine things aspire,
> In vaine thou kindlest all thy smokie fire.

For vertue hath this better lesson taught,
Within my selfe to seeke my onelie hire:
Desiring nought but how to kill desire.[185]

Sidney's next decision probably involved the selection of the best indirect means to spell out his concerns. How could he both instruct his prince courteously and enhance himself gloriously? This model courtier hardly needed Castiglione's instructions, for the ideals espoused by those beautiful people at Urbino several generations earlier had already become a part of him. He knew, with Lord Octavian, that "as musicke, sportes, pastimes, and other pleasant fashions, are (as a man woulde say) the floure of Courtlinesse, even so is the training and helping forwarde of the Prince to goodnesse, and the fearing him from evil, the fruite of it." [186] To assist in producing "the fruite," one must first prove himself a "floure." In Sidney's case, the "evil" was French papistry and the "fruite" English-Protestant instruction. He also knew, with Count Lewis, Castiglione's kinsman, that to become known as "the floure of Courtlinesse," a man must "set all his delight and diligence to wade in everie thing a little farther than other men" (p. 41). Most important (and to us perhaps most strange), he knew, along with every one of those highly civilized Italians, that courtliness could be as readily established and "waded farther with" in the tiltyard as in the banquet hall or council chamber. For though Castiglione's courtiers were of a culture that had always equated chivalry with a world of fantasy,[187] they were practical enough to respect chivalric exercise as one means of catching the prince's eye. Hence the author, in setting the scene for his elegant conversations, first speaks of each gentleman's striving "to shew himselfe such a one, as might deserve to bee judged worthie of so noble assembly," and begins his account of those strivings by noting their endeavors "at Tilt" and "at Tourney" (p. 19). Hence, too, the tendency of the Duchess's polite company to employ chivalric metaphors in their conversations. Stirred by Lord Gaspar's misogyny, Lord Cesar requests permission "to execute . . . this duety of a good knight, which is to defend the truth" (p. 222). Lady Emilia has already warned the insulting Gaspar that "wee will set into the field a fresher knight that shall fight with you," and dispatched Lord Julian to put "to flight so bitter an enimie" to womankind (p. 182). This envisioning of courtly accomplishments in terms of doughty deeds is later underlined by Gaspar's own query, whether "Aristotle and Plato ever daunced, or were Musitions in all their life time, or practised other feates of chivalrie" (p. 301).

We are not surprised, therefore, when Count Lewis asks the courtier who would be perfect to excel all Italians "at the Ring, and at Tilt," and stand out "amongst the best Frenchmen" in the "Tournament" and "in fighting at Barriers" (p. 41). For one of the greatest opportunities to outdo through creative imitation comes during the performance of "feates of Chivalrie in open sights," when the assets of both mind and body are displayed: "remembring the place where he is, and in presence of whom, hee shall provide before hand to be in his armour no lesse handsom and sightly than sure, and feede the eyes of the lookers on with all thinges that hee shall thinke may give a good grace, and shall doe his best to get him a horse set out with faire harnesse and sightly trappings, and to have proper devises, apt posies, and witty inventions that may draw unto him the eyes of the lookers on as the Adamant stone doth yron" (p. 96). Such means of wading farther may strike us as cheap theatricalities, but for Castiglione and his Elizabethan readers, capturing the glances of the "lookers on" was the first step to preferment and competition was keen. And if Castiglione evinces no sense of uneasiness as he passes from the courtier as "the formost to scale the walles of a battered towne" (p. 96) to the courtier as a kind of debutante in armor, it is unlikely that Sidney would have been aware of any incongruities. The Foster Children's fragrant missiles and mystical inventions were not calculated to underline the unreality of chivalry or to divorce it from any working military structure. To both challengers and defenders, the songs and scrolls and rose water, the fanciful costumes and elaborate comparisons, and all the strange business about frozen knights and "flame unquenchable" represented concomitant aspects of chivalry as a working, civilizing force. For us, nothing better documents chivalry-known-to-be-fiction than Adam and Eve in the tiltyard at Whitehall. Like Sidney, however, Perot and Cooke had taken their cue from that noble Italian soldier, Federico Fregoso, who commends "a man at armes in forme of a wilde shepeheard, or some other such kind of disguising, . . . because the minde of the lookers on runneth forthwith to imagin the thing that is offered unto the eyes at the first shew, and when they behold afterwarde a far greater matter to come of it than they looked for under that attire, it delyteth them, and they take pleasure at it" (p. 99).

With Castiglione's transfigured knight-errant before us, the antics of April and May, 1581, can be seen as the poetry of policy. Perfect Beautie looked down from her Fortresse, ready to hear the overtures. Did one wish to offer his wisdom for the secular needs of the governing class? An elaborate cartel might be instrumental in gaining an office. Or was one for the practical business of soldiery? A well-aimed sweetmeat might win a regiment.[188] Although their wooden cannons fired only "sweet powder" and other "fit shot for Desire," the toiling gunners were engaged in earnest warfare. No doubt some courtiers were, like Lee, simply seeking their own advancement; they would eventually retire to nurse wounds as mimetic as the battles they had fought. Like Sidney, however, others sought nobler goals—saving England from the French or the Pope, for example—and some of these tilters later died in actual combat for the same ends. Regardless of their very different motivations, both the selfish and selfless were equally serious about their quixotic means. In his letter concerning vile Anjou, Sidney had played the historian and philosopher, stubbornly maintaining that Elizabeth was only Elizabeth. His retreat to poetry was a mark of intellectual alertness, a realization that sometimes, even in high matters of state, the shibboleth was "Gloriana." We may call the result a highly romanticized chivalry, but it hardly developed amid a spirit of nostalgia.

As a gloss upon Desire's defeat, then, Castiglione is helpful in establishing atmosphere and attitude. Through his instructions concerning the most theatrical (and therefore the most effective) means to a single, solemn end, we come to understand what Sidney and his fellows took for granted. The stipulations that the courtier advise his prince, wade farther, and exploit the advantages of the tiltyard were all satisfied by Sidney's dramatizing his sonnets of renunciation. Probably for Sidney and certainly for us, Castiglione is also helpful in a very specific way. His treatise concludes with Master Peter Bembo's ecstatic apostrophe to Universal Beautie, "which lyeth hidden in the innermost secretes of God, lest unhalowed eyes shoulde come to the sight of it" (p. 321). In Gloriana the courtier who knew his responsibilities saw a revelation of the divine mystery, an incarnation of the Platonic Idea. Bembo

had urged all lovers to "climbe up the staires, which at the lower-
most steppe have the shadow of sensuall beautie, to the high mansion place where the heavenly, amiable and right beautie dwelleth"
(pp. 320–321). "High mansion place" was spelled out in terms of
a medieval castle, and the slow, contemplative ascent became a rude
assault by wholly sensual Desire. To gain a glimpse of this "bodi-
lesse, . . . heavenly shining beame" (p. 313) and thereby come to
"possesse beautie perfectly" (p. 306), the courtier "on fire . . .
to covet" her had been told to dismiss "the judgement of sense"
(p. 304)–apposite inspiration as one faced his forty-eight-year-old
Queen, as well as a theme with dramatic possibilities. Both the
politics of the situation and the conventions of Elizabethan mimetic
warfare dictated that Desire be defeated and the castle remain un-
scaled, and so the Foster Children represented Bembo's challenge
negatively. Other creative elements of this imitation were necessitated by transferring the Italianate Plato to the stage: all the machinery that extinguished "flame unquenchable," lance and charger
to illustrate that when physical beauty produces "fresh nourishment
to the fire," one must "raise up reason, and with her to sense [that
is, test] the fortresse of his hart" (p. 313).

No doubt Cardinal Bembo would have shuddered to see his
mysteries reduced to a rolling trench, but his friend, Castiglione,
had supplied the impetus. To the Venetian Humanist, the equation
between Elizabeth and the ineffable would have been arrant blas-
phemy, yet such an equation was bound to be made within a
theater whose final end was the acme of flattery and whose playwrights each sought, with Castiglione's blessing, to "outstage"
his rivals. The polite world of Urbino epitomized the process of
outdoing through elaboration. Its inhabitants not only told Queen
Bess's less polished courtiers where, when, before whom, and with
what to step beyond, but exemplified such doctrines in their very
manner of conversation. Behind these refined creatures stood their
reporter, himself merging and elaborating upon materials as diverse
as Cicero's *De Oratore* and Boccaccio's *Filocolo*.[189] Even the
learned Bembo, in his rhapsodic flight to Perfect Beautie's "high
mansion place," had ranged widely for his illustrations. While making this perilous journey, he assures us, our souls will be purged
by "holy fire," which "consumeth whatsoever there is mortall in
them, and relieveth and maketh beautifull the heavenly part, which
at the first by reason of the sense was deade and buried in them"

(p. 320). To strengthen his argument, he then provides a curious catalogue of those brave souls who have experienced Plato's purgatory:

> This is the great fire in the which . . . Hercules was buried on the toppe of the mountaine Oeta: and through that consuming with fire, after his death was holy and immortall.
> This is the fiery bush of Moses: The devided tongues of fire: the inflamed Chariot of Helias: which doubleth grace and happinesse in their soules that be worthie to see it.
>
> (P. 320)

Obviously this apocalyptic marriage of Greek and Hebrew worthies was not capriciously intended. For Bembo, it suffices that all these revelatory experiences somehow involved fire and ecstasy; this fact alone establishes their common, essentially Platonic nature. The earnest scholar, in short, is no more sensitive to the varied contexts of his illustrative incidents than those impious tilters who gave them an even stranger setting. And so thoroughly has he confounded disparate times and matters that we cannot be sure whether his "inflamed Chariot" belonged to the Old Testament prophet, Elijah, or to the Greek god of the sun, Helios. If such a habit of thought reminds us of the medieval clerk, emptying upon a single page his store of commonplace similarities, so much to the shame of the New Learning. Men of the Renaissance never tire of noting humanity's entrances and exits within "this wide and universal theatre," of moralizing upon each of our seven ages; they are almost obsessed by Mutability's sway. Nevertheless, they seldom exhibit an awareness of historical perspective, of the appalling irrevocability of any earlier era, and therefore our modern notion that all past events are unique combinations of irredeemable conditions seems never to have been even anticipated. Certainly neither the limping analogies of the Cardinal's sermon nor the oddly sorted casts of the Queen's devisers offer instances of the New Learning untainted by the Old "Ignorance." Despite their different interests and machinery, both parties honor fundamentally similar premises, a method that is keenly conscious of stepping beyond, but either blind to or incredibly offhand about the obstructions of times and customs it steps over.

The extent to which this method characterizes and thereby explains the peculiar strengths and weaknesses of sixteenth-century art will be the principal concern of our concluding chapter. Does the Cardinal, for example, speak for his equally learned yet poetically superior English contemporaries? Do the far better lines cast by the artificers outside the Queen's theater nevertheless reveal the same uncritical penchant to appropriate with impunity as the occasional verse faltering within it? Is the pageant's tendency to set all persons and places inside an everlasting present also found in other signs of the times, its splendid tapestries, detailed edifices, and lush frontispieces? Tudor reenactments of "former fabulous story" evince no anxiety about their relevance for a contemporary audience. Is this because both writer and viewer thought of history simply as a procession of one's Greek, Roman, Celtic, Saxon, and Norman brothers, and therefore saw no cultural barriers large enough to prevent a ready identification with any group? If so, is their undiscriminating vision shared by those dramatists, poets, and prose narrators who also treat the past? Had a reasonably well-educated Elizabethan been suddenly asked to "think Greek," would he have first thought of Homer or Heliodorus? And would he have smiled at his ancestors' medievalized Homer: the similarities between Priam's knights and Arthur's, Achilles made subject to the bright eyes of Polyxena, Hector's affair with Morgan le Fay?

Finally, to see how closely the Elizabethan entertainment anticipates the techniques of drama proper, we shall single out those elements of the devising that several playwrights retained or improved upon. About four years after Desire's siege, for instance, John Lyly waded farther with *Endymion* (c. 1585). Now Perfect Beautie is once again Cynthia, "whom none ought, or dare aduenture to loue, whose affections are immortall, & vertues infinite." [190] For the myth of Endymion's sleep and Cynthia's kiss, Lyly is indebted to Lucian and Ovid; for his balanced structure and some characters, to Plautus and Terence; we even catch glimpses of Petrarch inverted and the fairies of folklore. Central to our understanding of this allegory of love, however, is that its writer was every inch a courtier, anxious to prove how he could step beyond the Foster Children's flattering dramatization of Bembo. Most of his plot is devoted to the major characters' ascents to various rungs of the Cardinal's neo-Platonic ladder, and the mythological machinery had been popular at Court since Henry VII. In view of the fact that the world of *Endymion* came from the

Italian academies by way of an English tiltyard, we may wonder how whimsically Lyly intended his Prologue's claim that Elizabeth might find his play "ridiculous for the method, or superfluous for the matter, or for the meanes incredible," [191] But what shall we make of those other disclaimers by which Lyly, intentionally or not, puts us in a somewhat ironic situation? Having waded through so many devisings to what is like a show but unquestionably a play, we find that play introduced as "neither Comedie, nor Tragedie, nor storie [history], nor anie thing, but . . . a tale of the Man in the Moone." And having watched make-believe played so seriously, we finally discover a playwright presenting his equally serious and more realistic visions of the social fabric in terms of "Chymera, . . . a fiction," a series of mere "fancies" to which none should "apply pastimes."

Notes to Chapter V

1. See E. K. Chambers, *The Elizabethan Stage* (Oxford, 1923), I, 69.
2. George Gascoigne, *The Princely Pleasures at the Courte at Kenel-*
   woorth (London, 1576), as reprinted in Johns Nichols, *The Prog-*
   resses and Public Processions of Queen Elizabeth (London, 1823),
   I, 485-523. Laneham's *Letter* (London, n. d.), which describes the
   same affair, is also found in Nichols, I, 420-484.
3. *The Arte of English Poesie* (1589), in G. Gregory Smith, *Elizabethan*
   Critical Essays (Oxford, 1904), II, 66.
4. Albert Feuillerat, *Documents Relating to the Office of the Revels in*
   the Time of Queen Elizabeth (Louvain, 1908), pp. 193, 199, 203,
   270, 303, 345. It is doubtful that "Herpetulus," "the Solitarie
   knight," and "the Knight in the Burnyng Rock" were ever
   printed; none is referred to elsewhere than in the Accounts of
   the Office of the Revels.
5. See Frederick S. Boas, *An Introduction to Tudor Drama* (Oxford,
   1933), p. 70; and Feuillerat, pp. 94-95, 97.
6. *Memoirs of Sir James Melville of Halhill*, cited by Karl J. Holzknecht,
   The Backgrounds of Shakespeare's Plays (New York, 1950), p.
   288. Italics added.
7. Elizabeth's progresses, of course, began long before her descent on
   Bristol in 1574. Her first was through Hertford and Middlesex to
   London, five days after her accession at Hatfield on November 17,
   1558, and not a year passed without her making some visits
   among the landed nobility. Cf. Chambers, "A Court Calendar"
   (Appendix A, IV, 75-130). Since we are mainly interested in ascertaining the influence which her receptions and entertainments
   had upon contemporary dramatists, I have usually based my discussion upon nine accounts published in London no later than
   1592 (the year of Robert Greene's death) and therefore readily
   available to the city playwrights:
   (1) Bristol, 1574: Thomas Churchyard, *The Firste Parte of Church-*
       yarde's Chippes, contayning Twelve seueral Labours (London,
       1575), as reprinted in Nichols, I, 393-407.
   (2) Kenilworth, July, 1575: see n. 2 above.
   (3) Woodstock, September, 1575: an anonymous pamphlet printed,
       according to its colophon, by Thomas Cadman in 1585; sig. A,
       with title page, is missing; the work is therefore referred to by

its running headline, *The Queenes Majesties Entertainment at Woodstocke*, ed. with intro. by A. W. Pollard (Oxford, 1910).

(4) Norwich, 1578: Ber.[nard?] Gar.[ter?], *The joyfull Receyving of the Queene's most Excellent Majestie into hir Highnesse Citie of Norwich* (London, n. d.; S. R. August 30, 1578), in Nichols, II, 136–178; and Thomas Churchyard, *A Discourse of the Queenes Majesties Entertainment in Suffolk and Norfolk* (London, n. d.; S. R. September 20, 1578), partly reprinted in Nichols, II, 115–117, 128–133, 179–213, 219–225.

(5) Cowdray, 1591: an anonymous pamphlet printed by Thomas Scarlet, *The Honorable Entertainment given to her Majestie, in Progresse, at Cowdray in Sussex, by the Right Honorable the Lord Montecute* (London, 1591), in Nichols, III, 90–96.

(6) Elvetham, 1591: an anonymous tract printed by John Wolfe, *The Honorable Entertainment gieven to the Quene's Majestie, in Progresse, at Elvetham in Hampshire, by the Right Hon'ble the Earle of Hertford, 1591* (London, 1591), in Nichols, III, 101–121.

(7) Bisham, Sudeley, and Rycote, 1592: J.[oseph?] B.[arnes?], *Speeches delivered to her Majestie this last Progresse, at . . . Bissam, . . . Sudeley; and . . . Ricorte* (London, 1592), in Nichols, III, 130–143, 168–172.

8. E. S. Turner, *The Court of St. James's* (New York, 1959), p. 88.

9. *Ibid.*

10. C. T. Prouty, *George Gascoigne: Elizabethan Courtier, Soldier, and Poet* (New York, 1942), pp. 87–88, 177–178. Prouty points out that even though Gascoigne's is the first detailed description, Leicester's entertainment was not necessarily novel. Both Ferrers and Hunnis had "previously been active in court amusement, and . . . may, therefore, be logically expected to continue in the tradition which was familiar to them" (pp. 177–178). For more on these contributors, see also Chambers, IV, 61–62.

11. Prouty, p. 87.

12. *Edward II*, I. i. 51–61, 66–71, in *The Plays of Christopher Marlowe*, ed. Leo Kirschbaum (Cleveland, 1966). Less cynical are Oberon's reminiscences in *A Midsummer Night's Dream*, II. i. 148 ff.

13. Elizabeth had visited Kenilworth in 1565 and 1572; see Chambers, IV, 82, 88, and Nichols, I, 192–198, 318–321. During her second visit, according to Lord Burleigh (Nichols, I, 321), she had refused the Duke of Alençon's offer of marriage. Laneham's *Letter* is prefaced by a lengthy description of the estate's many pleasant prospects.

14. The Elizabethan fascination for fireworks appears to have been universal. The Lord Mayor's squib-casting woodwoses and the devils of mystery and morality plays would have envied the

displays at Warwick Castle on August 17, 1572. During a siege reminiscent of Henry VIII's mimetic battles, a certain dragon, appointed to safeguard an important canvas fortress, overshot one missile and set fire to the house of Henry Cowper, the town's miller. Despite valiant attempts by the Earl of Oxford, Fulke Greville, and other courtiers to extinguish the fire, the house was a total loss. On the following day the royal hat was passed, and Cowper received compensation. Cf. Nichols's extracts from "The Black Book," a manuscript account of the Queen's visit to Warwickshire (I, 309–320).

15. Nichols, I, 501–502. Gascoigne's description of the wonderful things which might have been perhaps inspired the Earl of Hertford's devisers to stage a similar naval battle at Elvetham in 1591.

16. Laneham, who enjoyed the show as much as its author, calls Proteus "Arion"; see Nichols, I, 458.

17. Laneham's account of those books Cox has "at hiz fingers endz" occupies several pages (see Nichols, I, 451–454); the diversity of these volumes points up Louis B. Wright's thesis in *Middle-Class Culture in Elizabethan England* (Chapel Hill, N. C., 1935): "Catholicity is the quality of middle-class taste that is most noteworthy" (p. 83). Laneham's list includes popular tales, jest books, dream books, plays, books of riddles, ballads, domestic literature, treatises on health, almanacs, native metrical romances, and romanticized British histories. But according to Wright, p. 85, the last "were still enjoying considerable favor, even with aristocratic readers."

18. See Chambers's "Court Calendar," IV, 91–92.

19. Lee's role as the Royal Champion is discussed in a consideration of the tiltyard entertainments below.

20. See n. 7 (3) above.

21. Pollard, p. xvi. The tale's style and sentiment places it among the numerous examples of euphuism existing prior to John Lyly's *Euphues, the Anatomy of Wit* (1579).

22. *Ibid.,* p. xix.

23. *Ibid.,* p. xxi.

24. *Ibid.,* p. xxviii. The narrator's account concludes with a "Comedy . . . acted before her Maiesty . . . vpon the 20. day of the same moneth"; see Pollard, pp. 1–32. In it Occanon and Eambia, the Fairy Queen, persuade Caudina that Contarenus must "giue place to care of Countries weale" (p. 26). Chambers (III, 402) doubts that it advocates a rejection of Leicester's suit: "It would have been dangerous matter for a courtly pen." As we have seen at Kenilworth, however, Gascoigne ventured several "dangerous" matters. Although the themes of the Woodstock entertainment

may not point back to Deepedesire and Zabeta, Elizabeth certainly
found in the Caudina story a view of celibacy as responsibility
rather than mere choice. In any case, Gascoigne, with characteristic agility, sought to exploit the favorable reception of Hemetes's
story. On January 1, 1575/6, he presented to Elizabeth as a New
Year's gift an elaborate manuscript of "The Tale of Hemetes the
Heremyte" in its English original and followed by his own translations into Latin, Italian, and French. See Prouty, pp. 90, 222–223.

25. Sidney's pastoral show, *The Lady of May*, first appeared in the
third (1598) edition of the *Arcadia*. I follow Nichols's text, II,
94–103. Though Nichols assigns its presentation to 1578, Chambers
(III, 492) believes 1579 or 1582 also possible.

26. Chambers (IV, 83 ff.) lists 1566, 1568, 1570, 1575, and 1592. Even
Leicester admitted that "a hearty noble couple are they as ever
I saw towards her Highness." It was Lady Norris who befriended
Elizabeth during Mary's reign, when she was imprisoned at Wood-
stock; see Chambers, I, 112.

27. See Chambers, IV, 66.

28. Hence his inclusion of these and other devisings in his edition of
The Complete Works of John Lyly (Oxford, 1902), I, 404–507.

29. Cf. Elizabeth Jenkins, *Elizabeth the Great* (New York, 1960), pp.
92–94, 108, 111; and Turner, pp. 83–84.

30. Turner, p. 84.

31. Jenkins, pp. 108–109.

32. *Ibid.*, p. 292.

33. III, 102. Facing III, 101, is Nichols's reproduction of the woodcut
that the printer, John Wolfe, included in one of the two editions
of 1591.

34. See Garrett Mattingly, *The Armada* (Cambridge, Mass., 1959), p.
275.

35. Turner, p. 92.

36. Chambers, I, 126.

37. II, 182. Since Churchyard and Bernard Garter, the two recorders
of the Norwich reception, are more interested in displaying their
own wares than in giving a full account in chronological sequence,
my discussion draws from both and presents each event as it
evidently took place. For the titles of their works, see n. 7 (4)
above.

38. Turner, p. 87.

39. Norwich Corporation Records, 2 Aug. 20. Eliz.; cited by Nichols,
II, 133.

40. I, 106–107.

41. Edward Hall, *The Vnion of the two noble and illustre famelies of
Lancastre & Yorke* (London, 1548), ed. Sir Henry Ellis (London,

1809), pp. 635–637. For easier reading, I have replaced Hall's tildes with m's or n's.

42. *De instructione feminae Christianae* (1523), trans. Richard Hyrde (c. 1540), as cited by J. W. H. Atkins, *English Literary Criticism: The Renascence* (London, 1955), p. 60.

43. Atkins, p. 61.

44. See *Polydore Vergil's English History*, ed. Sir Henry Ellis (London, 1846), p. 33. Ellis states that this anonymous translation was made late in the reign of Henry VIII or early in that of Elizabeth; cf. Ellis's introduction to his edition of *Three Books of Polydore Vergil's History* (London, 1844), pp. xxx–xxxi.

45. *Reappraisals in History* (New York, 1963), p. 82.

46. *Ibid.*

47. *Henry VIII*, I. i. 33–38. All citations from Shakespeare are to *The Complete Works*, ed. Peter Alexander (London, 1951).

48. R. Coltman Clephan, *The Tournament: Its Periods and Phases* (London, 1919), p. 4.

49. Ellis, p. 33.

50. Douglas Bush, *Mythology and the Renaissance Tradition in English Poetry* (Minneapolis, 1932), pp. 40–41.

51. Raphael Holinshed *et al.*, *The Chronicles of England, Scotland, and Ireland* (London, 1587), ed. Sir Henry Ellis (London, 1807–1808), IV, 261–262.

52. *Annales, or, A Generall Chronicle of England* (London, 1631), p. 6.

53. *Ibid.*, p. 7.

54. *Ibid.*, p. 8.

55. *Ibid.*, p. 18.

56. *The History of Great Britaine* (London, 1627), p. 166.

57. Paul Hentzner, *A Journey into England in the Year MDXCVIII*, trans. Richard Bentley (Edinburgh, 1881), p. 7; Jacob Rathgeb, *A True and Faithful Narrative*, in *England as Seen by Foreigners*, ed. William Brenchley Rye (London, 1865), p. 33.

58. Ed. Alfred T. P. Byles (London, 1926), pp. 122–123.

59. *The Scholemaster* (1570), ed. Edward Arber (London, 1870), p. 80.

60. *Ibid.*, p. 64. Italics added.

61. *Honor Military, and Ciuill* (London, 1602), p. 204.

62. Both in Smith, I, 188, 323.

63. "Tagus, fare well," in *The Poems of Sir Thomas Wiat*, ed. A. K. Foxwell (London, 1913), I, 57.

64. *Englands Heroicall Epistles*, in *The Works of Michael Drayton*, ed. J. William Hebel, II (Oxford, 1932), 277.

65. In *The Complete Works*, ed. Albert Feuillerat, II (Cambridge, 1922), 258.

66. *A Booke of Ayres*, XX, in *Campion's Works*, ed. Percival Vivian (Oxford, 1909), p. 17.

67. P. 278.
68. As quoted by Clephan, p. 3.
69. Francis Henry Cripps-Day, *The History of the Tournament in England and in France* (London, 1918), p. 93.
70. Clephan, p. 40.
71. *Ibid.*, p. 41.
72. *Ibid.*, p. 125.
73. *Ibid.*, p. 41.
74. Hall, p. 674.
75. Clephan, p. 85.
76. John Stow, *A Survey of London, Written in the Year 1598*, ed. William J. Thoms (London, 1876), p. 101.
77. *Ibid.*, p. 142.
78. Turner, pp. 29–31.
79. Although London eventually disapproved of the royal pastimes, at first it co-operated. The earliest detailed account of "masking and mumming" is recorded as having taken place in 1377, when one hundred thirty citizens entered Kennington Palace with musicians and torchbearers to dice, dance, and drink with the Prince and his companions. See Chambers, I, 150.
80. Cripps-Day, p. 87.
81. *Ibid.* Also interesting is J. J. Jusserand's lament, "Trop beau pour durer," in *Les Sports et Jeux D'Exercice dans L'Ancienne France* (Paris, 1901), pp. 98–99.
82. Prologue, ll. 61–63, in *The Poetical Works of Chaucer*, ed. F. N. Robinson (Cambridge, Mass., 1933).
83. See Robinson's notes, p. 845.
84. William Camden, *The History of the most Renowned and Victorious Princess Elizabeth, Late Queen of England*, trans. R. Norton (London, 1675), pp. 273–274. And perhaps "outlandish" simply means "strange" or "alien," not "fantastic" or "barbarous."
85. *Ibid.*, p. 265.
86. *The Chronicles* were actually a group project, arranged by Reginald Wolfe, an Elizabethan printer. When Wolfe died in 1573, Holinshed became the chief co-ordinator, and under his name the first edition was issued in 1577. About three years later, Holinshed died; the greatly expanded second edition of 1587 was the work of numerous contributors. See James Westfall Thompson, *A History of Historical Writing* (New York, 1942), I, 603–604: "In the second edition continuations were made down to 1586 by Stow—whose contribution forms, except for Harrison's *Description*, the most valuable part of the work—by John Hooker, Francis Thynne, and Abraham Fleming, with valuable notes and reprints of some contemporary pamphlets."

87. Ellis, III, 556.
88. From MS. Harl., No. 69, ed. Alfred T. Goodwin, *The Shakespeare Society's Papers* (London, 1844), pp. 47–51.
89. *Ibid.*, p. 50.
90. Cornelia Baehrens, *The Origin of the Masque* (Groningen, Holland, 1929), p. 2. Other sources of sources are discussed in Chambers, I, 149–155; Lee Monroe Ellison, *The Early Romantic Drama at the English Court* (Menasha, Wis., 1917), pp. 1–47; Robert Withington, *English Pageantry: An Historical Outline* (Cambridge, Mass., 1918); Boas, pp. 58–73; Enid Welsford, *The Court Masque* (Cambridge, 1927); and Glynne Wickham, *Early English Stages: 1300 to 1660* (London, 1959–).
91. Chambers, I, 150.
92. Withington, I, 4.
93. Wickham, I, 202.
94. Chambers, I, 150–151.
95. Boas, p. 61.
96. Ellison, p. 23.
97. *Ibid.*, pp. 14, 23–24.
98. *Ibid.*, p. 3.
99. Clephan, p. 118.
100. Hall does not note the eighth courtly vice; see p. 631.
101. *A Chronicle of England During the Reigns of the Tudors,* ed. William D. Hamilton (London, 1875–1877), I, 99–100.
102. See Welsford, pp. 276–277.
103. Chambers states that "this intimacy between performers and spectators differentiates the mask from the drama to the end; its goal is the masked ball, not the opera" (I, 149–150). In some of the best Elizabethan romantic comedies (e.g., Greene's *James IV* and Peele's *Old Wives' Tale*), however, an "audience" is established in the framework in order to have it mingle with and comment upon the players in the main plot. The reasons for this deliberate fusion of the worlds of actor and audience are discussed in the conclusion to Chapter VI.
104. My account is based on tracts ed. J. G. Nichols, *London Pageants* (London, 1831), pp. 42–50.
105. *Ibid.*, p. 49.
106. See Albert Feuillerat, *Documents Relating to the Revels in the Time of King Edward VI and Queen Mary* (Louvain, 1914), pp. 85, 93–96, 125.
107. *Ibid.*, p. 145.
108. Holinshed, IV, 62–63; for the most part the historian is not interested in the "gauds and pageants of pastime," the "vaine great spectacle" offered Queen Mary.

109. Feuillerat, pp. 161, 163, 166, 172, 225.
110. Richard Tottel, *The Passage of our most drad Soveraigne Lady Quene ELYZABETH through the Citie of LONDON to WESTMINSTER* (London, 1559), in John Nichols, I, 55.
111. *Ibid.*, I, 57.
112. *Ibid.*, I, 58 ff.
113. Withington, I, xviii, 13.
114. *A Survey*, p. 36.
115. *Ibid.*
116. See Withington, II, 3.
117. *Ibid.*, II, 5–10.
118. Stow, p. 36.
119. *Ibid.*, pp. 36–37.
120. *A Calendar of Dramatic Records in the Books of the Livery Companies of London: 1485–1640*, ed. Jean Robertson and D. J. Gordon (Oxford, 1954), p. 132. This valuable volume provides extracts for Midsummer shows (1504–1545), Lord Mayors' shows (1540–1640), and miscellaneous revels (1485–1639). Figures representing "-es" and "-er" have been normalized throughout my citations.
121. *Ibid.*, p. 1.
122. *Ibid.*, p. 37.
123. Withington, I, 195 ff.
124. *Ibid.*, I, 165, 195.
125. F. W. Fairholt, *Lord Mayors' Pageants* (London, 1843), p. ix.
126. *Ibid.*, p. xii.
127. Robertson and Gordon, pp. 11–12.
128. *Ibid.*, p. xiv.
129. *Ibid.*, pp. xx, 3–4.
130. *Ibid.*, p. 5.
131. *Ibid.*, p. 2.
132. *Ibid.*, pp. xxi, 26, 28, 33.
133. *Ibid.*, pp. xxi, 22.
134. *Ibid.*, pp. xxiii, xxxvii.
135. *Ibid.*, p. 40; see also Boas, p. 45.
136. *Ibid.*, pp. 43–44.
137. For the Lord Mayors' shows of 1566, 1568, and 1584, see Robertson and Gordon, pp. 45–50, 53–54.
138. *Journey Through England and Scotland*, trans. Gottfried von Bülow, in *Transactions of the Royal Historical Society* (London, 1895), p. 255.
139. David H. Horne, *The Life and Minor Works of George Peele* (New Haven, Conn., 1952), p. 154.
140. Robertson and Gordon, p: xxxvii, and Horne, p. 218.

141. Robertson and Gordon, p. xxv.

142. *The Diary of Henry Machyn, Citizen and Merchant-Taylor of London (1550–1563)*, ed. John Gough Nichols (London, 1848), pp. 47–48; letters or words in brackets or parentheses supplied by Nichols.

143. *Ibid.*, pp. 72–73.

144. *Ibid.*, p. 133.

145. *Ibid.*, p. 137.

146. *Ibid.*, p. 201,

147. P. 262.

148. "The Cook's Tale," Robinson, I (A), ll. 4377–4379.

149. Pp. 230, 253–255.

150. P. 156.

151. See the extracts from the Warwick "Black Book," in Nichols, I, 319–320.

152. Chambers, I, 140–141.

153. *Honor Military, and Ciuill*, p. 197.

154. Chambers, I, 141–142; see also Chambers's fine study of Lee's life, *Sir Henry Lee: An Elizabethan Portrait* (Oxford, 1936), p. 133. Segar himself alludes to only three tilts that took place before 1581, and none of them was on November 17: the "magnificent triumphs" of 1558 and 1571, and "an honourable Challenge" brought before the Queen on January 6, 1580, by the Earl of Arundel, who called himself Callophisus (pp. 194–195).

155. My account is primarily based on Henry Goldwell's *A briefe Declaration of the Shews, Devices, Speeches, and Inventions, . . . on the Munday and Tuesday in Whitson Weeke last, Anno 1581* (London, n. d.), in Nichols, II, 310–329. This has been supplemented by Holinshed, IV, 434–445.

156. In 1578 Gilbert Talbot mentions strolling about the tiltyard one morning "under the Gallery where her Matie useth to stande to see the runninge at tylte; where by chaunce she was"; cited by Nichols, II, 92–93.

157. In his "Court Calendar" (IV, 75–130) Chambers records only four years for which there is no evidence of a Queen's Day Tilt: 1582, 1583, 1585, 1586.

158. In *Transactions*, pp. 258–259.

159. Collated by Chambers in *Sir Henry Lee*, pp. 268–275.

160. Chambers's summary, *ibid.*, p. 269.

161. Horne, pp. 231–243.

162. Segar, pp. 197 ff.

163. *Ibid.*, pp. 198–199.

164. In Horne, pp. 232–233.

165. Segar, p. 199.

166. Peele, p. 242.
167. Segar, p. 199.
168. In 1584 von Wedel (p. 236) remarked concerning Whitehall, "We were taken into a long passage . . . which on both sides is beautifully decorated with shields and mottoes. These shields originate from tournaments which the queen orders to be held twice a year, the first on her birthday, the second when she ascended the throne. Everybody who wishes to take part must ask permission; this being granted, he offers the shield to the queen, who orders it to be hung up there."
169. *Letters of Philip Gawdy: 1579-1616,* ed. Isaac Herbert Jeayes (London, 1906), p. 67.
170. Chambers, I, 145; III, 211-214.
171. *Ibid.,* III, 393.
172. *Ibid.,* I, 148.
173. Nichols, III, 581 ff.; cf. Chambers, IV, 67, 115.
174. Chambers, I, 139.
175. *Ibid.,* I, 139-140; IV, 72.
176. Nichols, III, 241.
177. *Shakespeare's Festive Comedy: A Study of Dramatic Form and its Relation to Social Custom* (Princeton, 1959), p. 32.
178. *Certayne Notes of Instruction,* in Smith, I, 48.
179. Dialogues Moral and Political, as cited by Nichols, I, xxiv-xxvi.
180. Barber, p. 35.
181. In Smith, II, 159.
182. *Ibid.,* II, 43-44.
183. From MS. Harl. 6395; ed. Nichols, I, 458.
184. John Buxton, *Sir Philip Sidney and the English Renaissance* (London, 1965), p. 54.
185. Feuillerat, II, 322.
186. *The Book of the Courtier,* ed. W. B. Drayton Henderson, trans. Sir Thomas Hoby (London, 1956), p. 261.
187. See Francesco De Sanctis, *History of Italian Literature,* trans. Joan Redfern (New York, 1931), II, 488: "A serious feeling for chivalry—a feeling that was capable of inspiring a work like the Cid—was non-existent in Italy; and the crumbling of every religious, moral, and political feeling had left honour without a basis, bared of everything except one or two of the more superficial qualities that are brilliant rather than solid." Even in 1528, when Castiglione's work was first published, Urbino was only a "famous memorie" which the author vows "to defend . . . from mortall oblivion" (p. 186), and the prefaces to each of his four books contain nostalgic reminiscences. The Elizabethans, how-

ever, viewed their tournaments not as a memorial to, but as a legitimate continuation of this courtly world.

188. Sir Walter Raleigh's famous cloak may never have existed, but examples of courtiers who received preferment through similar devices are numerous. E. S. Turner offers a list of historical instances to illustrate that "a broad chest and a good leg, a bold glance, a well-turned compliment—all these could carry a man to the heights" (p. 74).

189. For Castiglione's diverse sources, see Thomas Frederick Crane, *Italian Social Customs of the Sixteenth Century* (New Haven, Conn., 1920), pp. 179 ff.

190. II. i. 97–98; in Bond, III, 17 ff.

191. *Ibid.*, III, 20.

Suggestions for Further Reading

There is no better way of watching courtiers and citizens at play than through the eyes of firsthand observers. Reasonably accessible editions of their reports are found in John Nichols, *The Progresses and Public Processions of Queen Elizabeth*, 3 vols., London, 1823; J. G. Nichols, *London Pageants*, London, 1831; F. W. Fairholt, *Lord Mayor's Pageants*, London, 1843; J. G. Nichols, *The Diary of Henry Machyn*, London, 1848; A. W. Pollard, *The Queenes Majesties Entertainment at Woodstocke*, Oxford, 1910; Jean Robertson and D. J. Gordon, *A Calendar of Dramatic Records in the Books of the Livery Companies of London: 1485–1640*, Oxford, 1954; Albert Feuillerat, *Documents Relating to the Office of the Revels in the time of Queen Elizabeth*, Louvain, 1908.

Perhaps a less intimidating route is to begin with Chapters V–XII of E. S. Turner's *The Court of St. James's* (New York, 1959) and then leaf through the Everyman's Library edition of John Stow's *The Survey of London* (London, 1956). Nor can one proceed very far in the histories of Hall (ed. Sir Henry Ellis, London, 1809) or Holinshed (ed. Ellis, 6 vols., London, 1807–1808) without happening upon some royal entry, mask, or other civic-princely pastime.

Indispensable reference works are provided by E. K. Chambers's *The Elizabethan Stage*, 4 vols., Oxford, 1923, and for earlier Tudors, *The Mediaeval Stage*, 2 vols., Oxford, 1903. Also valuable is Glynne Wickham's unfinished study, *Early English Stages: 1300–1660*, 3 vols., London, 1959, 1963,——.

Finally, some imaginative applications of the evidence are to be found in Lee Monroe Ellison, *The Early Romantic Drama at the English Court*, Menasha, Wis., 1917; C. L. Barber, *Shakespeare's Festive Comedy*, Princeton, 1959; Enid Welsford, *The Court Masque*, Cambridge, 1927; and Frances A. Yates, "Elizabethan Chivalry: The Romance of the Accession Day Tilts," *Journal of the Warburg and Courtauld Institutes*, XX (1957), 4–25.

VI

NOTES BEYONDE ELA

Translations and Transfigurations

Jaq. You are full of pretty answers. Have you not been acquainted with goldsmiths' wives, and conn'd them out of rings?

Orl. Not so; but I answer you right painted cloth, from whence you have studied your questions.

—*As You Like It* (III. ii. 255 ff.)

Gentlemen, so nice [fastidious] is the world, that for apparrel there is no fashion, for Musick no instrument, for diet no delicate, for playes no inuention, but breedeth sacietie before noone, and contempt before night.

Come to the Tayler, hee is gone to the Paynters, to learne howe more cunning may lurke in the fashion, then can bee expressed in the making. Aske the Musicions, they will say their heads ake with deuising notes beyonde Ela [i.e., the highest note of Guido's scale]. Enquire at Ordinaries [eating places], there must be sallets for the Italian; picktooths for the Spaniard; pots for the German; porridge for the Englishman. At our exercises, Souldiers call for Tragedies, their obiect is bloud: Courtiers for Commedies, their subiect is loue; Countriemen for Pastoralles, Shepheards are their Saintes. Trafficke and trauell hath wouen the nature of all Nations into ours, and made this land like Arras, full of deuise, which was Broade-cloth, full of workemanshippe.

Time hath confounded our mindes, our mindes the matter; but all commeth to this passe, that what heretofore hath beene serued in seuerall dishes for a feaste, is now minced in a charger for a Gallimaufrey. If wee present a mingle-mangle,

427

our fault is to be excused, because the whole worlde is become an Hodge-podge. . . .

—JOHN LYLY, Prologue to *Midas* (1592)

FOR PLAYES NO INUENTION

Unlike Gloriana's other entertainers, from Gascoigne the courtier-
poet to Churchyard the citizen-hack, John Lyly not only described
but analyzed his offerings. In 1589 the highly select audience in the
singing-room of Paul's choir was first treated to a discussion of
those social and artistic fashions that had influenced *Midas*, the play
it had come to watch. From this Elizabethan Shaw, the gentlemen
had come to expect an artful arrangement of problems, ideas, and
ideals; they received as well a staged Shavian preface. The simple,
carefully wrought native broadcloth no longer pleases the sophisticated tastes of an enlightened era. To satisfy fastidious moderns,
the tailor strives for the painter's cunning, the musician frantically
pursues ever-higher strains, and the restaurateur continually varies
his menu. The dramatist faces a worse predicament. If the creativity of other artificers also stales before noon, at least their customers do not demand different diet from a single platter. The
playwright can stay in business only by removing the old-
fashioned bill of fare, bowing to the requests of "an Hodge-
podge" world, and hashing dramatic kinds. At a time when
"inuention" must "mingle-mangle," and "deuise" replace honest
"workemanshippe," the tragicomic pastoral about King Midas
should please, but the weary deviser foresees nothing promising in
such bastard concoctions.

Despite Lyly's lengthy warnings, *Midas* still surprises us, for this
play is not so much a fusion of dramatic genres as of literary traditions. Prepared to excuse the kind of impropriety Lyly is so self-
conscious and explicit about, we encounter an indecorum never directly mentioned, a world whose frames of reference shift so
rapidly that we are never quite sure whether Midas's court resides in Ovid's Phrygia, Castiglione's Italy, Philip II's Spain, or
Elizabeth's England. As a result, although the first seven scenes
represent less than an hour of real time and are all set in the palace
gardens, the unities of time and place are, in a sense, continually
violated. And it is these disunities that characterize Lyly's kind of

theater, creating a sometime-nowhere atmosphere for both the sprightly wit and solemn cerebration of his pastel-shaded characters. To have brought the whole of *Midas* into perfect agreement with all the Renaissance notions about the proper observance of time and place, Lyly would have needed to change only a few lines. But to have made his world unified in this secondary yet more significant sense, he would have had to write an entirely different play. Although that new play might have mingled tragedy and comedy, kings and clowns, hornpipes and funerals, or taken its hero from birth to death and from Asia to Africa, it would not have moved Phrygia across Urbino, the Armada, and the Bankside.

After the manner of the *Metamorphoses* (XI, 85-193), Lyly begins the story of the golden touch and asses' ears with Bacchus's offer to Midas. The dramatist's departures from Ovid at first appear inconsequential. In the Roman myth, for example, Bacchus's gratitude is aroused by the kindly treatment his foster father, Silenus, has received at Midas's court; in Lyly, Bacchus himself has been honored, and Silenus is not even mentioned. But we need only compare Lyly's version of the offer and response to see where his interests lie and through what process he has managed to produce a work approximately sixteen times the length of its main source. Ovid is primarily interested in the results of Midas's choice; a reward is quickly offered, decided upon, requested, and granted:

> Then did the God, rejoicing in his foster-father's safe return, grant to the king the free choice of a boon, a pleasing, but useless gift. Midas, fated to make an ill use of his gift, exclaimed: "Grant that whatsoever I may touch with my body may be turned to yellow gold." Bacchus granted his prayer. . . .[1]

For Lyly, the giver must at least suggest several options and the receiver, before selecting, consider every ramification:

> *Bacchus.* All thy grounds are vineyards, thy corne grapes, thy chambers sellers, thy houshold stuffe standing cuppes: and therfore aske any thing it shalbe graunted. Wouldest thou haue the pipes of thy conducts to run wine, the vdders of thy beasts to drop nectar, or thy trees to bud ambrosia? Desirest thou to be fortunate in thy loue, or in thy victories famous, or to haue the yeres of thy life as

many as the haires on thy head? Nothing shalbe denied,
so great is *Bacchus*, so happie is *Midas*.
Mid. Bacchus, for a king to begge of a God it is no shame,
but to aske with aduise, wisdom; geue me leaue to consult:
least desiring things aboue my reach, I bee fiered with
Phaeton: or against nature, I be drowned with *Icarus:* & so
perishing, the world shal both laugh and wonder. . . .[2]

And so we must undergo seventy-five lines of choice animadversions by the three Phrygian councillors. Before Midas is resolved,
conflicting attitudes toward love and women have been argued, the
nature of religion, chastity, tyranny, loyalty, and responsibility debated at length, and classical wisdom and lore paraded. The whole
play is but an extension of its opening scene. Both character and
incident have been shaped to support theses, and it would be more
accurate to call the merry wit (or half-wit) of the pages, maids,
and barber a form of thesis relief than comic relief. Unity of
theme, if not dramatic interest, is attained by balancing the nobility's exquisite rhetoric and erudite pronouncements against their
inferiors' similar, though less solemnly expressed, concerns.
Whether their conversations are serious or frivolous, the courtly
creatures who inhabit Lyly's world all reason adroitly, speak endlessly, conclude wittily, and *do* almost nothing. The accent is on
urbanity rather than action, and we soon feel closer to the polished
Court of Urbino than a fabled kingdom in Asia Minor, to the stuff
of courtesy books than Roman myth.[3] People much like those who
sat at the feet of Elizabetta Gonzaga have, in other words, been
incorporated into Latin legend and deposited upon a London stage.

But Lyly is not content with Phrygia as a sixteenth-century
Italian city-state. We have no sooner adjusted to this equation than
he is off to Spain to vilify Philip's international politics. The first
direct indication that Midas is more than mythical king and Italian
aristocrat appears at the end of the opening scene.

Mid. Come my Lords, I wil with golde paue my court, and
deck with gold my turrets, these petty ilands neer to
Phrygia shal totter, and other kingdoms be turned topsie
turuie.

(110–112)

Throughout the play Bacchus's friend schemes to erect a "bridge of gold" leading to "Lesbos," that island in which "all my nauie could not make a breach" (III. i. 46–47), and even Apollo's sacred oracle warns that

> Vnlesse he shrinke his stretching hand from Lesbos,
> His eares in length, at length shal reach to Delphos.
>
> (V. iii. 28–29)

The shepherds near Mount Tmolus also appear pro-English. Amyntas, at least, knows that "those Ilanders are too subtil to nibble at craft, and too riche to swallowe treasure," that Midas "may as wel diue to the bottome of the sea, . . . as plod [for "plot"?] with his gold to corrupt a people so wise. And besides, a Nation (as I haue heard) so valiant, that are redier to strike than ward" (IV. ii. 40 ff.).

Although the Phrygians regard Lesbos with hatred and admiration, an occasional incident or sentiment proves them English at heart. We consequently discover that we are sometimes both looking upon and from within that proud island. When one of Midas's councillors complains, "He is more fauoured that pricks his finger with his mistres needle, then hee that breakes his launce on his enemies face" (II. i. 71–72), we know we are in the Renaissance; when Midas's daughter continues, "Let him thrust thee, *Eristus* with thy loue, into Italie, where they honour lust for a God" (98–100), we can be only in moral England. The Phrygian pages provide a lengthy catalogue of devices worn or used by fashionable Elizabethan ladies (I. ii), quibble upon terms employed by English sportsmen (IV. iii), and engage in a series of native high jinks with Motto, the royal barber, and his apprentice, Dello (III. ii; V. ii). Motto is Lyly's version of the anonymous Ovidian slave who whispers his master's secret, and may stand as well for Antonio Perez, Philip's secretary, who was banished for revealing matters of state.[4] For all his political-allegorical responsibilities, however, Motto is basically a harbinger of Robert Greene's worlds of rogues and vagabonds.

> *Motto (aside to his boy)*. May I but touch them Dello, Ile
> teach his tong to tel a tale, what villenie it is to cosen one
> of a bearde, but stand not thou nigh, for it is ods when
> he spits, but that all his teeth flie in thy face.
>
> (III. ii. 68–71)

And when the sprightly maid, Pipenetta, "chaunts it":

> 'Las! How long shall I
> And my Mayden-head lie
> In a cold Bed all the night long
> (V. ii. 50 ff.),

we realize that she is a servant to neither Phrygian, Italian, nor Spanish lady, but a lusty wench of Shoreditch.

Thus Lyly, in devising his own "notes beyonde Ela," confounds times and matters in a manner not directly noticed by his Prologue. Is the dramatist himself wiser than his spokesman appears, more aware of the incongruous threads woven into his allegedly modern "Arras"? This at first seems unlikely, for the only explicitly *dramatic* "fault . . . to be excused" is the mingling of tragedy, comedy, and pastoral. But the rest of Lyly's apology, including references to "the nature of all Nations" and "minced in a charger," may darkly anticipate his fusion of classical myth, courtly conversation, chauvinistic allegory, and earthy native scenes. His concluding paragraph would then indicate more than a mere attempt to relate the hashing of genres to the improprieties of other artisans, to find all inventors equally guilty and equally innocent as they capitulate to newfangled modes. In any case, Midas's court is located somewhere in that "whole worlde" of the Prologue's "Hodge-podge." And if Lyly has not minced very convincingly— Greene and Peele were to do better—*Midas* at least exemplifies the contemporary quest for new treatments of old themes, for inventions that would possess vitality at noon and freshness at night. In its carefree appropriation of varied sources, the play is also representative of the fare offered Gloriana during her sylvan gambols, when ancient myths were taken prisoner, forced into marriages with native medieval traditions, and made to support an odd assortment of modern, often political meanings. Although the fictions staged on the grounds of country estates are, like Lyly's, filled with classical figures and allusions, the Muses native to both worlds are more Gothic than Olympian. Lyly's role of "minglemangler" was hardly new. For our purpose, the importance of *Midas* is mainly owing to the dark hints of its Prologue. Here at last a deviser seems to be acknowledging that he will entertain a multiplicity of traditions within a single context and that he is keenly, perhaps even delightfully aware of his method's impropriety. If we have not read too much into it, the statement provides a valuable link between sixteenth- and twentieth-century literary theory and practice. The special kind of indecorum that Elizabethan critics never mention, and modern readers find so evident in so much Elizabethan literature, is finally discussed and consciously employed.

BROADE-CLOTH, FULL OF WORKEMANSHIPPE

Lyly had some reason to liken earlier English art to honest, plain broadcloth. Although Henry VIII's courtly makers were hardly the first to introduce foreign threads into the native literary fabric, they initiated a period of increasingly rapid translations, imitations, and elaborations. Hence Lyly, by 1589, could contribute to and yet sincerely lament an art much too "full of deuise." In contrasting the careful workmanship of the past to the modern chaotic "Arras," however, he overstates his case. The unclassical freedom to weave into one's tapestry as many disparate strands as possible is exercised as freely in the Middle Ages as in the Renaissance. The Tudor looms simply had more stuff available.

In the medieval and early Tudor mysteries and moralities, such fusions appear largely unintentional. It is at least difficult to know where to draw lines between absolute ignorance, partial knowledge accompanied by a disdain for considering matters too curiously, and deliberate anachronisms that were part of the playwrights' strategies. The contributors to the craft cycles, for example, invariably dramatize Biblical episodes in terms of their own society. Is this because they really saw Noah as their contemporary? Or were they careless about the differences, having discovered that making him an Englishman was the easiest way of making him human? Or was "Noah Our Neighbor" a result of carefully considered dramatic priorities, an acknowledgment that the real meanings of Scriptural incidents could not be fully realized in their own terms? If the last alternative is correct, then Noah is English because the easiest way was the only way; the dramatist yielded to an audience that demanded greater and more realistic detail than the source provided and was unable to grasp petty distinctions between everyday life in Yorkshire and that of the antediluvian Near East.

Since we cannot prove that the contributors' learning varied as greatly as their dramatic abilities, we may get farther by tempo-

rarily assuming that they were all as insensitive to incongruities as
their audiences, and then ask what kind of theater these unintentional anachronisms fostered. In the best and worst mysteries we
always find an interest in character beyond the demands of the
ostensible moral, and a desire to interlace sacred themes with homespun vignettes. Both were satisfied by the grand entrance that the
Glovers of Wakefield gave to Cain in *The Killing of Abel* (c. 1450).
The villain comes in, ploughing and shouting to his team, as well
as to his boy, "Pike-harnes."

> Io furth, Greyn-horne! and war oute, Gryme!
> Drawes on! God gif you ill to tyme!
> Ye stand as ye were fallen in swyme.[5]

Such bold elaborations upon Holy Writ are the rule; the Glovers'
Cain yields to their fellow craftsmen's *Noah*, which features a racy
domestic quarrel between the Old Testament hero and his stubborn
wife before the deluge washes away "cart," "plogh," and "many
castels." [6] Nor did the allegorical demands of the earliest moralities
preclude a similarly realistic treatment. Amid the ghostly and usually dull personifications of virtues cavort the earthy vices, quick
to offer glimpses of an England readily familiar to their audience.
In *The Castle of Perseverence* (c. 1425), Belial not only defines his
infernal activities but includes his field of operation:

> Now I sytte, Satanas, in my sad synne,
> As deuyl dowty, in draf as a drake [dragon]!
> I champe and I chase, I chocke on my chynne,
> I am boystows and bold, as Belyal the blake.
> What folk that I grope, thei gapyn and grenne.
> I-wys, fro Carlylle in-to Kent my carpynge thei take! [7]

Following the demands imposed by tradition, later writers of
moralities postulate a representative of humanity, *Infans* or *Hu-
manum Genus* or *Anima* or *Mankind*, and besiege him with the persuasions of allegorized good and evil qualities.[8] This is their common point of departure or basic fabric. With the exception of the
dignified *Everyman*, however, the threads run through the texture
at curious angles; the virtues remain fairly aloof, in the realm of
abstraction, but the vices take on flesh and strut. While the Seven
Virtues or Four Daughters of God are gaining man's soul with

stock moral instruction, how often Belial or his grandsons, Back-biter and Mischief, win the field of dramatic interest with vital language, timely references to earthly realities, and a series of sprightly antics. Belial's creator not only gives him the best lines, but is anxious about how he should first appear: "loke that he haue gunne-powder brennyn[ge] In pypys in his handis and in his eris, and in his ers, whanne he gothe to bat[tel]."[9] Less sensational spectacle is employed in *Mind, Will, and Understanding*, where *Anima* appears with little devils running in and out beneath her skirts.[10] The sad fact that evil is always easier to make exciting than good is best illustrated by *Mankind* (c. 1475), where the author's lingering by native waysides almost subverts his didactic journey. The forces of righteousness have been reduced to one forlorn character, Mercy, whose "ponderous Latinistic diction" and "sac-charine talk" are continually derided.[11] Although Mercy is granted first and last say, the world he introduces is almost completely controlled by his enemies, Mischief, New-Gyse, Now-a-days, Nought, and the devil, Titivillus. The wiles of wickedness are represented by Titivillus's merry pranks—stealing Mankind's corn and placing a board under the earth he attempts to till—and the fields of psychic warfare are located near the hamlets of Cambridgeshire:

TITYUILLUS. Forth! and espye were ye may do harme!
Take W[illiam] Fyde, yf ye wyll haue ony mo.
I sey, New-gyse, wether art thou avysyde to go?

NEV-GYSE. First I xall be-gyn at M[aster] Huntyngton
    of Sanston;
Fro thens I xall go to Wylliam Thurlay of Hanston,
Ande so forth to Pycharde of Trumpyngton:
I wyll kepe me to thes iij.[12]

These homely designs upon the native dramatic broadcloth be-speak a desire to render the abstract concrete, the unknown im-mediately recognizable. But in carrying old matter across space and time into such radically different contexts, the dramatists were bound to change that matter both in form and meaning. Whether or not they sought merely to "translate," they invariably trans-figured. If Hebrew patriarchs are to walk by faith, they must make their journeys on English roads; if archetypal man is to wrestle against fallen principalities and powers, the rulers of darkness should

at least be granted Saxon flesh and blood. Long after Henry VIII's
splendid Court introduced the Italian Renaissance into England,
native mysteries and moralities were popular among courtiers and
citizens; well into the seventeenth century, they continued to fas-
cinate country crowds. We must remember that when Polydore
Vergil questioned the historicity of Brute and Sidney proclaimed
the unities of his Italianate Aristotle, they were speaking to people
who had watched four thousand years of history unfold within
the compass of a spring day; who had seen Sir Lancelot massacring
the Innocents and the cities of Rome, Jerusalem, and Marseilles upon
tangential scaffolds; who had heard Herod swearing by Mahound
and the shepherds at the Nativity by the death of Christ.[13]

At its best, however, medieval drama exploits the traditional
anachronisms, answers to and yet surpasses its audiences' incongruous expectations. In *The Second Shepherds' Play*, for instance,
the so-called Wakefield Master gives us the customary Christians
before Christ and a characteristically Anglicized Israel. He becomes
so interested in everyday England (the landlords, weather, and
wives near "Horbery Shrogys" must have been equally oppressive)
and in the popular legend of roguish Mak, that upon first reading,
the concluding Nativity scene comes as almost a surprise. But a
closer look suggests that he used native figures and scenes as more
than shortcuts to the creation of character, atmosphere, and setting;
both represent attempts to enrich the meaning of the story and
deftly anticipate the journey to Bethlehem. While Mak takes us
and the stolen sheep to his thoroughly English wife and cottage,
the First Shepherd has been dreaming that he and his fellows "layd
vs / full nere Yngland." [14] This apparently gratuitous reference is
probably the dramatist's reminder that his method is deliberately
anachronistic; he at least knows that his vision of the past has
brought him as "full nere Yngland" as his Hebrew's dream of
future times and places. And from this point we suspect that the
play is being run according to God's time, the eternal present, in
order to celebrate the birth of the man who would later state,
"Before Abraham was, I am" (John 8:58). Our suspicions are partly
confirmed by the playwright's uses of the term "lytyll day-starne"
or day-star. It is first employed by the Third Shepherd as a tribute
to Mak's fraudulent son, the sheep in the cradle (l. 577); it next
appears in the Second Shepherd's address to God's true son, "the
Lamb . . . which taketh away the sin of the world" (John 1:29).
By blending a picaresque medieval folk tale into sacred story, the

dramatist illustrates that all men must hope with confidence and act with charity. Perhaps he was thinking of an earlier Christian teacher, who asked his audience to "add to your faith virtue" and "to godliness brotherly kindness," until "the day dawn, and the day star arise in your hearts" (II Peter 1:5, 7, 19) In any case, the play moves from hopelessness to good cheer, and from human to divine charity. The Third Shepherd, by kindly offering Mak's "son" a sixpence, uncovers his lost sheep, and immediately after all three shepherds have given the thief something far better than his just deserts, they are in turn granted a glimpse of God's greatest gift. However oddly the road to the manger may at first seem to turn, we eventually discover that the dramatist knew where he was going, and that a more direct and less homespun route would not have been so significant.

Rather than dismissing the Biblical episodes of the craft cycles, Tudor playwrights modified them to accord with changing tastes in religion and dramatic conventions. The author (or printer) of *The Historie of Jacob and Esau* (1568), for example, takes care to point out the work's modernity: it is "A newe mery and wittie Comedie or Enterlude." [15] The source is duly noted—"taken out of the xxvij. Chap. of the first booke of Moses intituled Genesis"— and the dramatist is also mindful of verisimilitude, having furnished "The partes and names of the Players who are to be consydered to be Hebrews and so should be apparailed with attire." [16] The influence of classical drama is obvious: Genesis 27 is carefully divided into acts and scenes; Ragan, Esau's talkative, wayward servant, is kin to Plautus's and Terence's wily slaves; Isaac and Rebecca no longer quarrel with clubs, but through Senecan stichomythia (e.g., I. iv). But if pagan Rome has helped to make this mystery "mery and wittie," Protestant Switzerland has made it *avantgarde*. For with the aid of Paul's glosses (Romans 9:10 ff.), this anonymous Puritan playwright has used Moses's history to propagandize Calvin's tenets of reprobation and election. The Prologue spells out the message all too explicitly, the characters remark upon Genevan justice throughout the play, and Rebecca counterplots in order that "Jacob have the blessing, whom thou [God] hast elect" (III. ii).

But neither the moral discipline of the Reformation nor the artistic discipline of the classically oriented Renaissance prevents this early Elizabethan from using racy language and meandering about the English countryside. The first stage direction has Ragan enter "with his horn at his back and his hunting staff in his hand" and leading "three greyhounds, or one, as may be gotten"; the first fifty lines are filled with Ragan's curses upon Master Esau, that insatiable hunter, off with his hounds before daybreak. From the Prologue's solemn introduction, we know that the playwright has a theological axe to grind.

> As the prophet Malachi and Paul witness bear,
> Jacob was chosen, and Esau reprobate:
> Jacob I love (saith God) and Esau I hate.

The dramatist, however, cannot fully share God's hatred, for if Geneva casts Esau as a son of perdition, England is bound to feel that "a cunning hunter, a man of the field" (Genesis 25:27) could not have been all bad. Running somewhat counter to his thesis, then, is the writer's sympathetic portrayal of Esau, the hearty sportsman:

> [*Here he speaketh to his dogs.*]
> Now, my master Lightfoot, how say you to this gear,
> Will you do your duty to red or fallow deer?
> And, Swan, mine own cur, I do think in my mind
> The game shall run apace, if thou come far behind:
> And ha, Takepart, come, Takepart, here: how say you, child,
> Wilt not thou do thy part? yes, else I am beguil'd.
> But I shrew your cheeks, they have had too much meat.
> (I. i)

So great an interest in character for its own sake and so careful an eye for homely detail make the world of *Jacob and Esau* quite similar to those of its medieval predecessors. An early fourteenth-century Yorkshireman would have relished Esau's roistering and the scatological outcries of his irked neighbors—"He is up day by day, before the crow piss" (I. ii)—though such dialogue may strike us as oddly sorted, given the play's Puritan goal. That same Yorkshireman might have foundered upon the playwright's new-fashioned stichomythia, and been baffled by his act and scene divisions, but he would have understood his rough humor, brawling, trickery, and simple narrative line. The new religion has not made Jacob, that "young man of Godly conversation," any more interesting, and though the resurrection of classical models gives the playwright new kinds of rhetoric, he still sets out the action in a series of loosely related episodes. What Calvin could not cleanse, nor Plautus shape, was that characteristic delight in lingering over native scenes, often at the cost of an abstract moral or well-structured plot.

That *Jacob and Esau* is at times so modern in matter and medieval in method should not surprise us. Men are often content to pour recent wine into old bottles, especially if new ones are beyond their reach. And once we distinguish between the playwright as thinker, a purveyor of ideas, and the playwright as playwright, we can better understand why this dramatist seems sometimes solemn and sometimes carefree in his handling of Genesis. He is earnest enough about making Israel, Rome, and merry England all serve Geneva's turn; modern thought is the result of conscious contrivance. Far less conscious are his old dramatic techniques, which fuse Israel and England; Esau the hearty Elizabethan sportsman is native life breaking through the theological machinery, something other than what the play as thought needed, something better than what the playwright as thinker intended. With the exception of Geneva, the dramatist seems no more aware of his disparate frames of reference than the great majority of his medieval precursors, and therefore we might call the methods through which he dramatizes his thought innocent, uncritical, carefree but not cavalier.

The lines between honest ignorance and subtle awareness, between conventions honored and undercut, are of course difficult to establish. The play's frequent incongruities, for example, seem deliberately accented in its resolution. All parties are reconciled and hymn God's praises; the Poet returns to underline Calvin's moral; finally, Isaac prays for "the whole clergy," Rebecca for "the Queen's majesty," Jacob for her "councillors most noble and true," and Esau for the nobility and citizenry. Since the convention of the closing compliment could have been easily satisfied by the Poet, was the playwright being facetious when he kept his Hebrews on stage to register their concerns for England's prosperity? It is more likely that he was borrowing from civic pageantry, which frequently and solemnly re-created the past in order to counsel and encourage the present. Rebecca would then suggest neither Puck nor Genesis, but Deborah, Judith, and Esther, those Jewish queens who ruled Norwich in 1578. Lyly notwithstanding, the old broadcloth was also "full of deuise," some as obviously the result of intentional patchwork as the elements of guerrilla theater in *Jacob and Esau,* or the "full nere Yngland" of the Wakefield Master. From his first stage direction advising horn and greyhounds for Ragan, on the other hand, we can be sure that the Puritan playwright had little notion of Hebrew life or attire, despite his careful advertisement on the title page.

THIS LAND LIKE ARRAS

The carefree mingling that produced such odd designs upon the Elizabethan arras was, therefore, largely an extension of medieval methods, and evinces the same syncretic habit of mind. Upon the native warp, whose threads almost invariably ran at curious angles, Tudor writers introduced an often brighter, richer, more "learned" but equally incongruous woof. Until the last decade of the sixteenth century we seldom find the New Learning inspiring more than new ornament among the poets, and rarely realized attempts at ordering action among the dramatists. And as we have already noticed at the close of our study of the era's "More Relevant Literary Theories," although the critics are quick to note many kinds of indecorum, Hobgoblin's method usually passes undetected; what immediately strikes us as a "mixed bag" is for them a kind either undiscovered or not worth mentioning. Even from the artists themselves it is difficult to infer a sense of the mutually exclusive. Spenser's quests are epic, the fashioning of "the twelve private morall vertues, as Aristotle hath devised," but he also believes in chivalry, Calvin, Ovid, and Plato, and has found in Ariosto, that mad weaver of Ferrara, the same serious spirit that permeates Homer, Virgil, and Tasso. Like the great majority of Tudor playwrights, who are as interested in wayside inns as their advertised destinations, Spenser admits that his ship has been blown off course, or warns that he must return to the rich soil that his plough has missed. Despite a plethora of classical allusions among the writers of prose fiction, there is a similarly native romantic temper. They often resemble the dramatist of *Jacob and Esau,* who achieves Seneca's stichomythia but not his structure, and seem proud of those arabesques of style or incident that only hinder their narrations. Like the biographer of *Euphues,* they lose themselves in rhetorical convolutions and tell stories that are scarcely stories, or like Greene and many other imitators of the Alexandrian romance, they stagger under the complexities of plot. What we immediately see as evidence of writing before "wrighting," they would have praised as right curious, artificial, and even classical, for was not the romantic embroidery of Heliodorus, Longus, Achilles Tatius, and Musaeus written in Homer's and Aristotle's tongue?

The wondrous workings of the Gothic Apollo are nowhere better illustrated than in the actual tapestries and kindred forms of pictorial and plastic representations that adorned Elizabethan England. From royal arras to lowly painted cloth, from the elaborate escutcheons surrounding the keyholes of country manors to the highly ornamented golden toothpicks that fashionable courtiers brought to board, from the statues of the Nine Worthies before Montacute House in Somerset to Sir Thomas Gresham's crest, the grasshopper, which he had had carved on prominent points about the roof of his Royal Exchange,[17] we find a keen interest in the visual, a fascination for the symbolical, and a remarkable insensitivity to the incongruous. These signs of the times, in short, tell much the same story as the pageantry of streets, lawns, and tiltyard, and therefore support our earlier use of Gloriana's stage as a relevant gloss upon the less occasional literature contemporary to it. First of all, the decorative arts must have reflected and in turn stimulated the imagination of artisan and audience no less than civic and courtly spectacles. The Elizabethan poet, for example, might have read the *Metamorphoses* very carefully. But in elaborating upon Ovidian figures and situations, would not his own poem or "speaking picture," as Sidney calls it,[18] have also been influenced by those dumb scenes which spoke from a nearby frieze or tapestry? Secondly, besides offering valuable links between original literary sources or traditions and their Tudor transfigurations, the Queen's designers speak even more conclusively than her devisers about the confusion between Hobgoblin and Apollo. For although it is conceivable that Elizabeth's entertainers might have sometimes facetiously fused disparate stuff to engender knowing smiles, it is hardly likely that the aristocracy would have adorned its manors for the same comic effect. Nevertheless, the architecture and interior design of the era provide numerous examples of mingle-mangles that cost their proud owners over fifty thousand pounds.

These monuments to the Gothic muse were another result of what Lyly calls "Trafficke and trauell." During Henry VIII's reign, Italian and French artificers introduced the "nature of [their]

Nations" to the simple early Tudor home. By Elizabeth's time, the Dutch craftsmen were busily stepping beyond with their versions of latest fashion. These successive invasions produced an odd patchwork of the old and new, native and Continental; "a homely English dress with Italian trimmings; a Gothic framework with Classic overlay; or Classic features treated in a Gothic manner. . . . It had the naïvety, the curious mingling of the mediaeval and classic in an atmosphere of romance, which characterize *The Faerie Queene*." [19] The wealthier Elizabethans, in other words, not only ate from minced chargers; they lived in them. Like tailors and poets and innkeepers, English builders waded farther by combining and thereby transfiguring their respective traditions. According to one modern architect, the influences brought to bear upon his sixteenth-century predecessors "emanated from sources too divergent to be capable of being perfectly welded." [20] But the notion of subordinating each rich detail to a unifying theme probably never entered the builder's mind. His client certainly seems to have been too hospitable to turn any foreign fashion out of doors; one by one they were welcomed and allowed to find a comfortable place. Indeed, both builder and owner were far too democratic, fair to the point of being undiscriminating. None of their beautiful or strange or fanciful guests was allowed to outshine another; each was granted leave to speak of his own time and country.

Hence those classic Orders that we find grafted upon native stock [21] actually reveal the same kind of "classicism" as the bits of classical lore that candy the writings of Nashe, Greene, and other university men. Rare was the playwright who could "resist dragging in references to Hector or Hannibal or Hercules, and poetry was never merely poetry but always that classical lady, 'the Muse.' A superficial classicism of this kind was one that any intelligent Londoner could acquire in a week if he settled down with a copy of Aesop's *Fables*, a handbook on mythology and an anthology of classical quotations." [22] For all the dramatists who had whole pages of Cicero and Horace by heart, Jonson was the first who reached behind the rules to grasp the principles, and therefore sought to re-create the spirit of the classics instead of simply displaying their trappings.[23] Until the very close of Elizabeth's reign, we therefore discover the builders of poems, plays, and houses all exploiting the classics in a thoroughly unclassical manner.

Yet their jarring literary and architectural overlays seem earnestly intended. To have sensed a contradiction between their own tangled and loose containments of multitudes and the unified, balanced designs of those disciplined ancients whose sentences were ever on their lips, the Elizabethans would first have had to become acutely self-conscious about their native romantic outlook. It is difficult for men of any time to consider their era's cultural and aesthetic axioms objectively, to speak of their own methods of perception as revealing peculiar habits of mind that may pass as quickly as those they recently replaced. Even today we are not prone to admit that we have been trained to see what we see. A case in point is our response to smoke-belching factories, those contaminating monsters that served as symbols of renewed hope and a return to prosperity in the films of the late 1930's. And to read social protest into the social optimism of only thirty years past, and thereby overlook the beauty of air pollution, is certainly less excusable than the curious reception Tudor England gave ancient Rome. What we have been taught to see as a case of "first come, first served" was no doubt built in the spirit of "let us appropriate whatever is fitting." Both designer and deviser thought their overlays organic, even though the only harmony we can discover is that between the oddly sorted styles of the great houses and the equally incongruous fictions staged on their lawns.

The mingled worlds represented in woodwork, inlay, plaster, glass, and even upon andirons and chimney pieces provide corroborating evidence. As architectural novelties, chimneys received great attention. At Wollaton Hall they were shaped as supporting columns; elsewhere they were fluted or "constructed in twisted, rope-like or sugar-stick design." [24] Heraldry, which played so important a part in royal entries and other civic festivities, was also given free reign in the decoration of houses. Not only was the owner's arms carved over the front door, but upon any object lacking sufficient ornament. Wherever the guest walked, an image of the family animal—fowl, beast, fish, or fabulous monster—reminded him of his host's noble lineage. One could have hardly avoided these household pets, for they appeared on the mantels of the principal chimneys, "on stone finials outside, on newel-posts inside, in the panels of a screen," and even upon the panels running across the ceilings.[25] In addition to shields of arms, ceilings were enriched by sundry flowers, birds, golden cherubim, and pendants, which hung down at set intervals,[26] while in the fireplace below, the panels on the andirons related the stories of Adam and Eve, Samson tearing down the gates of Gaza, David killing his lion, and

the Crucifixion.[27] However false a tale Shakespeare's Iachimo
bears to Posthumus, the villain does not exaggerate the splendors
of Imogen's boudoir:

> First, her bedchamber,
> Where I confess I slept not, but profess
> Had that was well worth watching—it was hang'd
> With tapestry of silk and silver; the story,
> Proud Cleopatra when she met her Roman. . . .

> The chimney
> Is south the chamber, and the chimney-piece
> Chaste Dian bathing. . . .

> The roof o' th' chamber
> With golden cherubins is fretted; her andirons—
> I had forgot them—were two winking Cupids
> Of silver, each on one foot standing, nicely
> Depending on their brands.[28]

The figures of history and legend were often drawn into an
even closer relationship upon the mantel of the fireplace. In a
chimney piece designed by Hans Holbein for the Palace of Bride-
well, for example, we find side by side scenes of a cavalry combat,
"Esther and Ahasuerus with a wreathed rondel," and medallions
of those ubiquitous medieval personages, Charity and Justice.[29]
Medallioned heads of Roman emperors, oriental potentates, and
grotesques also adorned the frieze encircling the room. For many
of his fanciful creations the Elizabethan craftsman found ample
Gothic inspiration in the pattern books of the Flemish designers.
The oval medallions of Medusa and Danaë at Charlton House, Kent,
are quite similar to two of Abraham de Bruyn's "panels of figures
and animals in grotesque ornament round a central cartouche containing a mythological scene." [30] Perhaps the most informative
imitation of de Bruyn is found on the chimney piece in the
drawing room of Boston House, Brentford. De Bruyn's pattern
book offered the artisan an oval medallion of Andromeda, surrounded by the customary fanciful figures. As if this panel were
not striking enough, the carver substituted the Sacrifice of Isaac
for Andromeda, and thus surrounded Father Abraham and his dutiful son with palm-bearing human grotesques, mermaids, leaping
dogs, and sea horses.[31]

For the most part, the wonders of Elizabethan manor houses and grounds are seen through the eyes of foreign travelers. Just as cultivated, young Englishmen continued to journey to the Continent as a part of their education, so fashionable Europeans dared the perils of the Channel to see for themselves the rumored marvels of the little kingdom, especially toward the end of the century.[32] Like their predecessor, Lupold von Wedel, they fill their journals with lengthy accounts of the elegance, comfort, beauty, and rarities surrounding those magnificent islanders; again like him, they alternate between admiration of great art and of mere curiosities, describing both with the same careful attention to detail. As tourists, they are even interested in the kind of attractions Henry Peacham catalogues in 1611 as "toyes . . . shew'd for a penny": "The caue of Merlin . . . sword of Sir Guy a Warwicke . . . Caesars wine yet i' Douer," and, of course, "Drakes ship at Detford."[33] But all are learned and relatively sophisticated men: Paul Hentzner, tutor to a German nobleman, who wrote in 1598; Jacob Rathgeb, private secretary to Frederick, Duke of Wirtemberg (1592); Thomas Platter, a doctor of medicine on vacation (1599); and John Ernest, Duke of Saxe-Weimar (1613).[34] And yet none reveals the slightest uneasiness or hint of amusement as he diligently records the superstitions his hosts advanced as truths or the grotesqueries they obviously thought beautiful.

These educated tourists are especially interested in exterior design. Not one fails to praise the ingenious devices of royal parks and private gardens. Rathgeb finds Hampton Court the most magnificent palace in the world, and the plants in its many gardens, "trained, intertwined, and trimmed in so wonderful a manner, and in such extraordinary shapes, that the like could not easily be found' (p. 18). Although he appears to have had one eye on Rathgeb's account, Platter gives a more detailed description: "There were all manner of shapes, men and women, half men and half horse, sirens, serving-maids with baskets, French lilies and delicate crenellations [battlements] all round made from the dry twigs bound together and the aforesaid evergreen quick-set shrubs, or entirely of rosemary, all true to the life, and so cleverly and amusingly interwoven, mingled and grown together, trimmed and arranged picture-wise that their equal would be difficult to find" (p. 200). Equally Gothic were the elaborate monuments that centered the park's or courtyard's curiosities. At Greenwich, where Gloriana's champions met "at set Times and Holidays to Exercise on Horseback," Hentzner admires "an old square Tower, called *Mirefleur,* supposed to be that mentioned in the Romance of *Amadis de Gaul*" (p. 33). The "Parnassus Mount" in the garden at Somerset House featured a fusion of classical legend and native allegory. Upon the Mount, John Ernest observes "Pegasus, a golden horse with wings; with divers statues, one of black marble representing the River Thames" (p. 166).

Of all classical myths, however, none seems to have been more popular than Ovid's pretty tale of Actaeon and Diana (*Metamorphoses* III, 155 ff.). Orsino uses it to open *Twelfth Night*'s series of gloriously self-annihilating, melancholic posturings, and Francis Meres draws upon the same story to launch another of his endless similes: "As Actaeon was wooried of his owne hounds: so is Tom Nash of his *Isle of Dogs*." [35] And if lustful Actaeon serves as fuel for both high-comic art and critical commonplace, we should not be surprised to find him as well among actual Elizabethan bowers. Platter discovers "a grove called after Diana" as he enters one of the gardens at Nonsuch. Water springs from a rock into a basin, and upon the basin, "portrayed with great art and life-like execution," he sees "the story of how the three goddesses took their bath naked and sprayed Acteon with water, causing antlers to grow upon his head, and of how his own hounds afterwards tore him to pieces" (pp. 195–196). But more important for our purposes are the "mottoes" Platter finds "inscribed" within "a small vaulted temple" nearby: "The goddess of chastity gives no unchaste councils, she does not council disgrace, but avenges it, they are the fruits of an evil mind and an evil spirit"; "From an unclean fountain impure springs, from an unpleasant mind a sight defiled" (p. 196). These were hardly the meanings Ovid intended, but they do tally with so many pieces of Gloriana's theater, wherein nymphs were ravished for moral or political ends. The mottoes suggested by a misunderstood Ovid epitomize the manner in which the Elizabethans rode roughshod over ancient myth, fashioning it according to the demands of their own day's burning issues and making the classics "relevant," and therefore popular, almost in spite of themselves. For if Diana resembled their Virgin Queen, who could not see in Actaeon her lustful would-be wooer, Philip II, and in his metamorphosis, the wreckage of the Armada? That, at least, is the impression one gains from the verses Hentzner finds engraved at the entrance to the park at Whitehall:

The fisherman who has been wounded, learns, though late, to beware

But the unfortunate Actaeon always presses on.
The Chaste Virgin naturally pitied:
But the powerful Goddess revenged the Wrong.
    Let Actaeon fall a prey to his Dogs,
        An Example to Youth,
    A Disgrace to those that belong to him!
    May Dian live the Care of Heaven;
        The Delight of Mortals;
    The security of those that belong to her! [36]

Among the many Gothic splendors of Elizabethan palace and
estate, apparently none outshone those of Lord Burghley's Theobalds. To cater to Gloriana's fancies, the great statesman occasionally donned an ancient beadsman's weeds, but his home remained
quite unlike a hermitage. His marvels were especially noteworthy
because he kept them indoors. In the main hall Rathgeb comes
upon a towering multicolored rock, "out of which gushes a
splendid fountain that falls into a large circular bowl or basin,
supported by two savages" (p. 44). The ceiling contains no less
than the twelve signs of the zodiac; at night one can see the stars
proper to each, while during the day the sun, "without doubt
contrived by some concealed ingenious mechanism," also performs
its course. But what he most admires is Burghley's cunning in
vying with nature: "On each side of the hall are six trees, having
the natural bark so artfully joined, with birds' nests and leaves
as well as fruit upon them, all managed in such a manner that
you could not distinguish between the natural and these artificial
trees; and, as far as I could see, there was no difference at all, for
when the steward of the house opened the windows, . . . birds
flew into the hall, perched themselves upon the trees, and began
to sing" (p. 44).

Burghley's Sovereign also had her masterpieces, but not under one roof. At Nonsuch, Ernest singles out "a carved bust said to
be an exact image of Christ" (p. 167), and at Greenwich, Platter is
impressed by "a picture of a creature half-woman and half-ox" (pp.
224–225). In 1598 Hentzner discovers at Windsor "the Horn of an
Unicorn, of about eight spans and a half in length, valued at above
£ 10,000" (p. 45). Perhaps this is the same magical horn Platter
finds the following year at Hampton Court; having "been filed
down to heal the sick," it measures only seven spans (p. 204).
In any case, the value placed upon this curio and the use to which

it was put may prepare us for Hentzner's startling description of the Chamber of Parliament in Westminster Hall: "The Seats and Wainscot are made of Wood, *the Growth of Ireland;* said to have that occult property that all poisonous animals are driven away by it; and it is affirmed for certain, that in *Ireland* there are neither Serpents, Toads, nor any other Venomous Creatures to be found" (p. 22).

Such idle lore fills the journals of these impressionable men of the world. It is important to remember, however, that the tourists were no more credulous than their hosts, and that their apparently trivial jottings form a significant index of received opinion and a valuable commentary on Lyly's statement concerning the confusion wrought by Time upon minds, and minds upon matter. Like the odd creatures that paraded along London's streets during high holiday, the elaborate decorations, statues, and queer treasures of palace, manor, and civic edifice never failed to make a silent but relentless demand upon the imagination. And imagination in turn ascended the monuments and spoke with authority, insuring that fictions would be felt as facts, and the weird properly reverenced as beautiful. What, for example, were the insane, envious, Italianate suspicions of Polydore Vergil regarding the historicity of Brute and his progeny, once a man had seen Troynovaunt's brave knights saluting his Queen, or if he daily passed the towering figures before Guildhall? Hentzner finds the latter a "fine structure," adorned by "two Giants, said to have assisted the *English* when the *Romans* made war upon them; Corinius of *Britain* and Gogmagog of *Albion*" (p. 24). Apparently antedating even this historical event is one of the artifacts Ernest singles out at Whitehall. Next to "A Moor's head of stone, the breast of metal, said to be the image of Balthasar, one of the three Kings" is "Moses in metal, perfectly black, . . . the hair standing up from the forehead like two horns; a short pointed beard, and looking somewhat gravely" (p. 165). Needless to say, the stone under Westminster's Coronation Chair was that on which "the Patriarch *Jacob* slept, when he dreamed he saw a ladder reaching quite up into Heaven" (Hentzner, p. 15).

Equally stimulating visual impressions were provided by the tapestries and painted cloths that hung in palaces, manors, inns, churches, and even in the private dwellings of the Queen's wealthiest and humblest subjects. With their usually incongruous embellishments of popular motifs, these hangings were probably more responsible for the fusions of literary traditions than any other form of design. For no less than the swiftly moving pictures of masks and pageants, they dressed up common themes with abundant pictorial detail, often romantically altering the original scenes and figures beyond immediate recognition. The Elizabethan eye thus became familiar with mythological, Biblical, and quasi-historical heroes placed in strange settings and combinations.[37] Hentzner visits Hampton Court and finds that "all the walls of the Palace shine with gold and silver," especially when the Queen receives foreign ambassadors and the tapestries are displayed (p. 47). Rathgeb is equally excited, but more explicit: "In short, all the apartments and rooms in this immensely large structure are hung with rich tapestry, of pure gold and fine silk, so exceedingly beautiful and royally ornamented that it would hardly be possible to find more magnificent things of the kind in any other place. In particular, there is one apartment belonging to the Queen, in which she is accustomed to sit in state, costly beyond everything; the tapestries are garnished with gold, pearls, and precious stones—one tablecover alone is valued at above fifty thousand crowns" (p. 18). To judge from the accounts of these foreigners, the worlds portrayed on such royal arrases were legion. According to Platter, Hampton Court itself featured "the history of Pompey" and that "of Tobias worked and embossed in gold relief"; other rooms unfolded the stories of Abraham and Lot on tapestries "golden . . . [and] immense in size" (p. 202). Among the "costly tapestries" Ernest found "worth particularizing" are two pieces in the Tower, "worked very elegantly, representing the sea-fight with the Spaniards in 1567, and the fight before Calais"; those at Theobalds, "with Roman Histories worked on them"; and Hampton Court's "several pieces, containing the story of Hagar's delivery; how Abraham is about to offer up his son Isaac; how Isaac courted, &c." (pp. 164, 167).

We cannot help wondering how Isaac's courtship was represented, but like his fellows, Ernest seldom describes a tapestry in enough detail to indicate how its theme and figures were treated. He does note that in the episodes from Genesis, "the dress, landscapes, buildings, and the like are in gold, silver, and variegated silks, so artistically worked as though they had been carefully painted with colours" (p. 167). If Abraham and Isaac played their parts in sixteenth-century dress and against a background of walled medieval towns and everyday country life, Ernest would not have bothered explaining this to his subjects in Saxe-Weimar. Extant woodcuts and other forms of design produced on both sides of the Channel rarely illustrate the ancient past in any other way. The tapestries' richness and verisimilitude strike him as exceptional, not their characteristic anachronisms. He is evidently impressed with "the history of the Creation of the World" for two reasons. First, it is extraordinarily large, composed of "several pieces." Secondly, "the Deity is always represented as three old persons in episcopal habits, with crowns on their heads and sceptres in their hands" (p. 167). The latter comment, however, does not reflect an awareness of the anachronistic; Ernest is simply struck by a peculiar kind of anthropomorphism. Similarly, when Platter admires "the history of the murder of Julius Caesar" depicted in "gold embroidered tapestry on the walls" of Hampton Court, and notes that "by the door stood three of the emperor's electors in customary dress painted in life-like fashion" (p. 202), it is quite likely that "customary" means "contemporary."

Finally, if each arras or portrait demanded that the spectator take divers times and places as a single world, the visual impressions created by juxtaposing a dozen of these independently fused worlds within one room must have been overwhelming. Although the tourists probably wrote in retrospect, their journals frequently retain the excitement of men quickly scanning rooms and hallways with eyes bedazzled by multiplicity. Hentzner stands amid Whitehall's numerous portraits and provides the same kind of rapid commentary as Henry Machyn on Lord Mayor's Day: "Queen ELIZABETH, at 16 years old. HENRY, RICHARD, EDWARD, Kings of ENGLAND; ROSAMOND; LUCRECE, a Grecian Bride, in her Nuptial Habit; the Genealogy of the Kings of ENGLAND; . . . Besides many more of illustrious Men and Woman; and a Picture of the Siege of Malta" (p. 23). A decade after Elizabeth's death, Ernest registers even greater multitudes at St. James's (pp. 161–162).

Unlike his visitors, who carefully catalogue each marvel, the Elizabethan usually takes native wonders in stride. We could hardly expect him to have done otherwise, for whether courtier or citizen, he lives, loves, and dies amid a never-ending series of pictorial stimuli. He is consequently on intimate terms with mythological paraphernalia, if not the spirit these myths celebrate, and is naturally prone to measure the ancients by their Tudor trappings. Citizen William Harrison, for example, would no doubt have insisted that his pagans were by the book and have vigorously impugned any intermediary sources. Tapestries are like interior paneling, he would have explained; they keep out unpleasant drafts. "The wals of our houses on the inner sides in like sort be either hanged with tapisterie, arras worke, or painted cloths, wherin either diuerse histories, or hearbes, beasts, knots, and such like are stained, or else they are seeled with oke of our owne, or wainescot . . . whereby the roomes are not a little commended, made warme, and much more close than otherwise they would be."[38] Harrison, of course, can afford to stress the practical worth of the cloths rather than the imaginative value of the "diuerse histories, or . . . beasts" they portrayed. But both he and his first readers would have unconsciously drawn from a common stock of imagery and easily glossed a passage like Macbeth's

> now witchcraft celebrates
> Pale Hecate's offerings; and wither'd murder,
> Alarum'd by his sentinel, the wolf,
> Whose howl's his watch, thus with his stealthy pace,
> With Tarquin's ravishing strides, towards his design
> Moves like a ghost.
>
> (II. i. 51–56)

Because figures like Witchcraft and Murder and Tarquin, surrounded by a wealth of concrete detail, are part of a world irrevocably lost, we need to think far more critically than Shakespeare's original audience, lest we lose ourselves in what were never intended to be abstractions and conclude that Macbeth's imagination was not only vibrant but sometimes farfetched. Ernest saw "Lucretia, very artistically painted," at Whitehall in 1613 (p. 160). Who is to say whether that painting, or one of its cheaper imitations, would not have told us something important about "Tarquin's ravishing strides," or explained some differences between *The Rape of Lucrece* and Shakespeare's literary models, Livy, Ovid, and Chaucer? Throughout the poem Shakespeare is thinking and relating pictorially, and when his ravished heroine seeks new means to mourn her fate,

> At last she calls to mind where hangs a piece
> Of skilful painting, made for Priam's Troy;

and a ninety-line verbal equivalent of a tapestry of medieval Troy ensues (ll. 1366 ff.).

For the most part, however, Shakespeare prefers to draw upon rather than re-create the visual arts. Whereas the narrative poet has space to imitate the artifice of the design by painting lengthy descriptions, the playwright goes directly to the figures and incidents popularized by it, seeking shortcuts to the creation of mood and character within dialogue and soliloquy. Hence Shakespeare the dramatist elaborates upon pictorial and plastic representations only when he wishes to accent splendor, and then those unusually fine ornaments provided by the magnificent estates between Stratford and London are "collated and published" as Imogen's boudoir or Christopher Sly's bedchamber. But this close attention to detail is uncharacteristic. With the eye of a verbal craftsman, yet in a spirit as practical as Harrison's, Shakespeare is quick to exploit any image with which his audience is readily familiar, and those displayed on tapestries took their places alongside others offered by nature, pastimes, and the daily round of traffic and travel. It is indeed unlikely that he was ever keenly concerned about his speaking-pictures' precise sources, or that before turning his own thoughts into his characters' conversations, he first determined that the dialogue would feature a metaphor from falconry followed by two nautical similes and an agricultural personification. Such imagery came as naturally to Shakespeare, to his audience, and to his essentially Elizabethan characters as the everyday life that supplied them.

As stuff for dialogue, then, tapestries offered Shakespeare specific pictures and general illustrations of magnificence. In the first case, it is the pictures that are important; in the second, the arrases themselves. When Falstaff, for example, calls his pitiful troops "slaves as ragged as Lazarus *in the painted cloth*, where the Glutton's dogs licked his sores" (*1 Henry IV*, IV. ii. 28–30), the italicized words serve no dramatic function; they merely footnote one of the many visual arts that treated St. Luke's story of Dives. When Richard likens the courage that shone through Salisbury's "old feeble body" to "rich hangings in a homely house" (*2 Henry VI*, V. iii. 12–13), on the other hand, it is a pictureless tapestry that provides the picture. Moreover, when the pictures are extremely important, as in Macbeth's soliloquy above, we cannot be certain that they came from tapestry and painted cloth. Borachio's comments suggest that Shakespeare was careful about his similes but not their origins: "Seest thou not . . . what a deformed thief this fashion is, how giddily 'a turns about all the hot bloods between fourteen and five and thirty, sometimes fashioning them like Pharaoh's soldiers in the reechy [smoke-blackened] painting, sometime like god Bel's priests in the old church-window, sometime like the shaven Hercules in the smirch'd [filthy] worm-eaten tapestry, where his codpiece seems as massy as his club?" (*Much Ado*, III. iii. 120 ff.). Probably such a Hercules would not have been found on any church window, but as a general rule, most figures could have appeared wherever men resorted and in every artistic medium.

We should not insist, however, that tapestries are always employed in ways that fit either of the above categories. Notice, for instance, Falstaff's answer to Mistress Quickly's charge that he has eaten her out of house, "plate and . . . tapestry": "glasses, glasses, is the only drinking; and for thy walls, a pretty slight drollery [comic picture], or the story of the Prodigal, or the German hunting, in water-work, is worth a thousand of these bed-hangers and these fly-bitten tapestries" (*2 Henry IV*, II. i. 137 ff.). Unlike the "rich hangings" Richard uses to illustrate Salisbury's resolution, the household stuff Falstaff proposes is the cheapest ornament. More important, it is seen as a series of detailed pictures. Yet none of these pictures serves as more than local color. Whereas Borachio's figures have been selected to support a thesis, the hot actions of hot bloods, Falstaff's scenes, although almost as specific, could have been replaced by any others. They simply reminded Shakespeare's audience that the Boar's Head was rapidly becoming a typical Eastcheap inn.

Finally, Shakespeare takes the arts of design as they were taken by his fellow citizens—visual equivalents of the chroniclers' annals and ministers' sermons. So poorly does Sir Nathaniel play Alexander the Great that Costard laments, "You will be scrap'd out of the painted cloth for this. Your lion . . . will be given to Ajax. He will be the ninth Worthy" (*Love's Labor's Lost*, V. ii. 570 ff.). On the less comic side is the apposite moral Pandarus attaches to the perverse world of *Troilus and Cressida*: "Good traders in the flesh, set this in your painted cloths" (V. x. 45). Like Stratford, each country town had its Chapel of the Guild of the Holy Cross, upon whose walls a boy from the nearby grammar school could see allegory and legend in fresco: The Day of Judgment, St. George and the Dragon, the Murder of St. Thomas à Becket, the Invention of the Cross, with its heroine, St. Helena.[39] Curates, magistrates, schoolmasters, and even innkeepers were evidently of Tarquin's opinion,

> Who fears a sentence or an old man's saw
> Shall by a painted cloth be kept in awe
> (*Lucrece*, 244–245),

and they accordingly besieged charges and customers with pictorial lessons. If the churches about Stratford offered figures from the Annunciation and the Adoration of the Magi, along with medieval saints and bishops, William Perrott's tavern in Rother Market featured Tobit, bidding farewell to his wife, each of course in Tudor apparel.[40] As a young man Shakespeare may also have visited William Sheldon's newly established looms at Barcheston and Bordesley—both were within a few miles of Stratford—and it is likely that he saw some of Sheldon's best tapestries at Kenilworth.[41] Once in London, there was ample opportunity to see all the bravery which the tourists recorded, and he could hardly have escaped the equally varied though less costly scenes done in oil upon cloth or canvas, for these stained or painted pictures were hung in the streets to welcome celebrities, and every dramatic company used them to advertise its plays and decorate its theater's stage and interior.[42] If Pandarus may be trusted, they even greeted the patrons of brothels. One keeper of a house of better repute (Savoy, Denham) satisfied his didactic impulse by having old men's saws worked into the water-staining on its plaster walls; still extant is a room decorated with "a series of scenes from *Exodus*, in which Moses and his followers are represented in the costume of about 1600, with texts on scrolls spouting from their mouths." [43]

Precisely because the visual arts served to advance education, incite morality, and improve commerce, their messages were on every hand, quite clear, and probably redundant. Shakespeare appears to accent this last aspect when Orlando tells Jaques, the melancholy philosopher, that his carping is commonplace: "I answer you right painted cloth, from whence you have studied your questions" (*As You Like It*, III. ii. 258 ff.). If Jaques, with his desire to "cleanse the foul body of th' infected world" (II. vii. 60), is meant to suggest some recently fashionable satirists, Orlando's lines characterize such angry young men as both wrong and unbearably trite. And when we realize that Jaques's famous speech on man's seven ages (II. vii. 139 ff.) can be glossed with designs ranging back to medieval woodcuts,[44] we must admit that Orlando's point about painted cloths is well taken. Jaques's loveless denunciation of the human condition is simply a new combination of old scenes and old cynicism. And quite unlike the situation at Elsinore, which begets Hamlet's melancholy, the actions in Arden seem designed to refute Jaques's misanthropy. Adam, "now almost fourscore" (II. iii. 71), enters hard upon the philosopher's closing moral: "Sans teeth, sans eyes, sans taste, sans every thing" (II. vii. 166). Similarly, if the play does not contradict the notion that infants are eternally "mewling and puking," it certainly shows that there is more to "honour" than "the bubble reputation." It directly disproves the sentiments of "good cousin" (Amiens, or Jaques?), who sings of "man's ingratitude" and "benefits forgot," and would have it that "Most friendship is feigning, most loving mere folly" (II. vii. 173 ff.).

If the arts of design assume such important functions within the playwright's relatively short "poems," their influence upon the narrative poets from Sackville through Spenser is almost incalculable. Except for one passage, "The Induction" to *The Mirror for Magistrates* straightforwardly unfolds a series of scenes and personifications, and the one exceptional piece (ll. 400–476) is unusual only to the extent that its pictures are set within one of the poem's larger pictures. Having successively faced Dread, Revenge, Misery, Famine, and Death, the poet finally confronts War, and for seventy-seven lines his eye rests upon that grim hero's

> targe [shield] with gashes depe and wyde.
> In mids of which, depaynted there we founde
> Deadly debate, al ful of snaky heare,
> That with a blouddy fillet [hair-band] was ybound,
> Outbrething nought but discord euery where.[45]

The pictorial power characterizing the Greek, Persian, and Roman slaughters that follow was of course Sackville's own. The *Mirror*'s other contributors also found scenes already "depaynted" and were not nearly so successful in articulating them. To establish the influence of the visual arts upon this work's imaginative verse, however, we need not contend that the rich imagery they offered was always successfully realized. Nor is it really necessary to distinguish between those scenes Sackville claims he is describing first-hand and those he feigns were already pictured; some of the former were certainly inspired by tapestries, and at least parts of the latter were his own invention. The important point is that we keep in mind our own ignorance of these rarely extant backgrounds as we attempt to gloss the poem, that we never assume its pictures were only in the mind's eye and not sometimes directly before the eye itself. "Truly, for my selfe," pleads Sidney, "*mee seemes* I see before my eyes the lost Childes disdainefull prodigality, turned to enuie a Swines dinner." [46] Only the italicized words assure us that what Falstaff calls "the story of the Prodigal" was not over Sidney's desk even as he wrote.

Of all the poets whose imaginations were quickened and shaped by these extinct arts, surely Spenser makes us most mindful of lost pictures. "A more or less agreed mythology and allegory poured in upon him from masque, pageant, tapestry, emblem, carvings, tournaments, woodcuts (and their manuscript predecessors). This provided the forms with which he found it natural to work. Some of his figures were instantly recognizable by his first readers; as if a modern poet used Father Christmas. . . . But Father Time (his name was once Saturn) is the only form common to Spenser's age and ours." [47] Like Shakespeare and Sackville, Spenser sometimes tells us that his pictures are simply descriptions of what has already been painted. In modern, colloquial terms, for example, the moral being spelled out for 171 lines of *The Faerie Queene* (III, xi, 28 ff.) is that one soon spots a playboy by his pin-ups, although the sinister aspects of Busirane and the richness of his many "tapets" suffer in such a translation. Again like Shakespeare, Spenser sometimes uses an arras as a convenient means of underlining magnificence. In the second of the *Two Cantos of Mutabilitie*, the poet finds Nature's garments too dazzling to describe, much less gaze at length upon, and even her "foot-stoole . . . / . . . richer seem'd then any tapestry, / That princes bowres adorne with painted imagery" (x, 7–9).

We can never fully compensate for our loss of so much "painted imagery," not to mention all the ideas that the artists' first readers would have automatically inferred from it. But it is often possible to reconstruct the picture on the basis of several literary reactions and partially regain its significance by extrapolating any meaning commonly assigned to it. Such a method assumes that writers as unlike as Shakespeare, Spenser, Lyly, and Harvey nevertheless spoke out of the same tradition, and that when one of them employs a fleeting and therefore difficult image, his fellows may provide fuller contexts. One of Shakespeare's oddest pictures, for instance, is presented through Don Pedro, immediately after he and Claudio have done penance at Hero's alleged tomb.

> Good morrow, masters; put your torches out;
> The wolves have prey'd; and look, the gentle day,
> Before the wheels of Phoebus, round about
> Dapples the drowsy east with spots of grey.
> (*Much Ado*, V. iii. 24–27)

The wheels of Apollo's chariot cause no problem. A reader totally unfamiliar with mythology will relate Phoebus to the sun before he has finished the passage. The "wolves" are another matter, and one not solved with any of the figurative uses of that word as itemized in *The Oxford English Dictionary*. The most we can infer from the immediate context, the thirty-three lines of scene iii, is that the image bespeaks an evil action already accomplished and that it may have something to do with the penitential epitaph from which Claudio reads: " 'Done to death by slanderous tongues / Was the Hero that here lies. . . .' " (ll. 3–4).

From these two passages, however, Shakespeare's first spectators inferred much more. Like us, they realized that the whole play deals with false report and the merry and solemn ado arising from nothing and "noting," or eavesdropping. But unlike us, many of them must also have known that slander and wolves often kept company, and they would not have missed, as we are likely to do, the importance of those pictures with which Don John represents his potential villainy: "I am trusted with a muzzle and enfranchis'd with a clog; therefore I have decreed not to sing in my cage. If I had my mouth, I would bite" (I. iii. 26 ff.). And they would consequently have relished the irony of Claudio's lines, spoken even as Don John enters to introduce his foulest slander: "Hero and Margaret have by this played their parts with Beatrice; and then the two bears [Beatrice and Benedick] will not bite one another when they meet" (III. ii. 68 ff.).

Assuming that Shakespeare did not bring to a public theater oracles to be grasped only by specialists in iconography, how much of his audience could he have counted upon to relate the "muzzle" of the first act with the "wolves" of the last? If we could discover several literal pictures depicting slander in terms of biting beasts, we could be fairly confident that even the illiterate members of the audience would have made the proper equation. Unfortunately, the only extant pictures suggesting the evils of slander come to us in the woodcuts of the emblem writers, though it is quite likely that the visual devices that preceded their moral mottoes were imitated upon painted cloths. In any case, there are four writers who use the emblem of a huge dog baying at the moon, and only Andrew Alciat seems content with a literal application; his motto, *Inanis impetus* ("A vain attack"), is followed by four Latin verses about the dog that barks at his image reflected in the moon while silent Diana, oblivious to the angry voice, moves majestically onward.[48] For Calvin's friend, Theodore Beza, however, the moon represents Christ or his ministers, who hear and "despise" the "barking" of this "scorner . . . the pointer out even of his own folly." [49] And five years later we find the English emblematist, Geffrey Whitney, expanding, revising, and combining the 1581 editions of Alciat and Beza. From Alciat he draws his motto and the first of his two six-line stanzas; he simply sets his dog to barking at its shadow in the moonlight. But it is Whitney's second stanza, a revision of Beza, that brings us closer to slander, for this picture reprehends

> those fooles which baule, and barke,
> At learned men, that shine aboue the reste:
> With due regarde, that they their deedes should marke,
> And reuerence them, that are with wisedome bleste.[50]

Finally, in 1595 Camerarius employs the same device to support a slightly different motto—"the dog despises high things"—and asks the reader, "Why carest thou for the angry thorns of a vain speaking tongue?" [51]

Given an audience nourished upon this combination of silent and speaking pictures, the Elizabethan writers could rely upon their verbal vignettes being properly glossed. Henry Green suggested long ago that the "perfect counterpart of Alciat's 164th Emblem" is Brutus's response to Cassius's tolerance of corruption: "I had rather be a dog and bay the moon / Than such a Roman" (*Julius Caesar*, IV. iii. 27-28). As an equivalent of the more malicious emblematic dogs that followed Alciat's, we may in turn suggest *Much Ado*'s preying wolf. Neither Brutus's nor Alciat's canine bespeaks detraction; it rather tells of the anger caused by frustration, of the greatness that lies outside one's grasp. The other emblematists deal with scorn, envy, and therefore malice. This is surely the kind of cur Harvey invokes when he complains of Robert Greene's desire to "counterfeit an hundred dogged Fables, Libles, Calumnies, Slaunders, Lies for the whetstone, what not, & most currishly snarle, & bite." [52] In the same vein, but even closer to *Much Ado,* are the pictures of Endymion's dream: "There portraid to life, with a colde quaking in euery ioynt, I behelde many wolues barking at thee *Cynthia,* who hauing ground their teeth to bite, did with striuing bleede themselues to death. There might I see ingratitude with an hundred eyes, gazing for benefites. . . . Trecherie stoode all cloathed in white, with a smyling countenance, but both her handes bathed in blood. Enuye with a pale and megar face . . ." (V. i. 119 ff.).

For the fullest comment upon "The wolves have prey'd," however, we must turn to a poem published only two years before *Much Ado* was acted, "The Sixte Booke of The Faerie Queene Contayning the Legend of Sir Calidore or Of Courtesie" (1596). Having watched Spenser's champions pursuing Holiness, Temperance, Chastity, Friendship, and Justice, Sir Calidore's quest for Courtesy may not at first strike us as particularly heroic. But it is soon evident that this legend has little to do with vindicating Emily Post. After seven prefatory stanzas, Spenser begins the poem proper by defining courtesy as "the ground, / And roote of civill conversation." Threatening the very fabric of society, then, and not merely good manners, is Calidore's opponent, the Blatant Beast, "a monster bred of hellishe race," and principally pictured as

> the plague and scourge of wretched men:
> Whom with vile tongue and venemous intent
> He sore doth wound, and bite, and cruelly torment.
>> (I, viii, 7–9)

All the ingratitude, treachery, and envy mentioned by Endymion and suggested in Don John are compounded in this cur until the close of the last canto, when Calidore

> tooke a muzzell strong
> Of surest yron, made with many a lincke;
> Therewith he mured up his mouth along,

And therein shut up his blasphemous tong,
For never more defaming gentle knight,
Or unto lovely lady doing wrong.
(XII, xxxiv, 2–7)

It is too much to suggest that Shakespeare had these lines in mind
when he closed *Much Ado* with Benedick's promise to "devise . . .
brave punishments" for Don John?

In concluding our study of the decorative arts as indexes of the
sixteenth-century senses of classicism, myth, history, and superstition and of "painted imagery" as a source of specific speaking-
pictures, we must admit that visual backgrounds can sometimes be
misleading. The emblem writers tell us that one woodcut may be
glossed several ways. To force any poet's image into agreement
with a single emblematist's application is therefore both bad
history and bad historical criticism. The most obvious examples of
potentially deceptive pictures, however, are those through which
the booksellers of Holborn, Paul's, and Paternoster Row recommended their products. When George Bishop printed *The Amendment of Life . . . Written by Master Iohn Taffin, Minister of the
word of God at Amsterdam* (1595), he ornamented this sermon
with a splendid frontispiece: A stag's head and two naked boys
appear in the top of the compartment; on the left is Minerva,
with an owl; on the right, Diana, half nude, with a quiver; the foot
contains the story of Actaeon's transformation, surrounded by
several indifferent conies.[53] Before interpreting the book by its
cover, we must be sure that the author or printer gave some
thought to the relationship between content and advertisement.
This appears unlikely, since the same plate was used the following
year by "J. Windet" for "T. Nun's" *A comfort against the Spaniard,* and in 1625 by "W. Stansby" for Francis Quarles's *Sions
elegies.*[54] Similarly, a representation of Pyramus and Thisbe in
Tudor apparel appears on the borders of editions of *Pierce the
ploughmans crede* (1553), Sir Thomas More's *A dialoge of comfort against tribulacion* (1553), and Geoffrey Fenton's *Monophylo* (1572); a compartment with David, Moses, and two satyrs
was used for thirty-one radically different works, from Thomas
Wilson's *The rule of reason* (1563) to Thomas Morley's *The first
booke of consort lessons* (1611); and to adorn Richard Grafton's
A chronicle at large (1569), the figure of Queen Elizabeth joined
those of Moses, Brute, and eight legendary and historical British
kings.[55]

From such designs and the treatises they ostensibly introduce we may gather several kinds of evidence. First, the pictures are never misleading in their own right. Pyramus and Thisbe in modern dress, David and his satyrs, and Elizabeth rubbing elbows with Moses and Brute are visual confirmations of the Tudor writers' frequent confoundings of times and matters. Even Bishop's frontispiece, whose top and sides roughly complement the Ovidian motif at the bottom, has its very Elizabethan conies. Secondly, the apparently arbitrary manner in which printers used the same plate for different kinds of literature suggests economic expedience rather than careful reflection. If the printer had an unusually important volume such as Grafton's to ornament, he might be willing to pay for a new woodcut, one especially designed to highlight the work's title. Certainly the figures that surround his *Chronicle* tally with Grafton's view of history as a procession of great princes. But the same printer would be more than likely to recoup his expenses by using the new woodcut repeatedly. It would therefore be absurd to infer that any Tudor reader found in the story of Pyramus and Thisbe something relevant to Langland's satire or More's religious dialogue. Indeed, of the five *extant* works it introduces, the woodcut is conceivably apposite only to Fenton's *Monophylo, a Philosophical Discourse and Division of Love.* Perhaps the printer used it with characteristic carelessness; perhaps he was pleased to find an illustration produced at least nineteen years before the fact. The same hypothesis holds for Bishop's use of Actaeon. We have noticed how easily Ovid's pretty fable was turned into a sermon against lust, and the presence of Minerva and her owl strengthens our suspicion that the whole picture was thought well suited to Taffin's sermon. But would we not be embarrassed about our speculations if a lost edition of the *Metamorphoses*, dated 1590, and with the same frontispiece, were discovered tomorrow?

Finally, even when we are fortunate enough to come upon a detailed description of a long-lost design, we cannot always be sure of the influence it exerted. What, for example, inspired George Peele's fantastic excursion into English history, that pastoral-comical-tragedy printed in 1593 as *The Famous Chronicle of king Edward the first, sirnamed Edward Longshankes, with his returne from the holy land. Also the Life of Lleuellen rebell in Wales. Lastly, the sinking of Queene Elinor, who sunck at Charingcrosse, and rose againe at Pottershith, now named Queenehith*? This curious mixture of romanticized history and legend reflects Peele's typically Elizabethan desire to include a mutiplicity of traditions within an "authoritative" frame of reference, and its most recent editor, Frank S. Hook, has ably demonstrated how the playwright used five chronicles and several pieces of folklore and balladry to produce his chauvinistic potpourri.[56] For Peele's most violent departures from the history he pretends to tell, the scenes vilifying Edward's cruel Castilian consort, Hook offers two ballads about other wicked foreign queens that Peele could have heard sung in the streets. To this we might add one of the many statues past which Peele and his audience often walked. In November, 1584, von Wedel casually records the following:

> As we went out to-day, not far from the queen's stables and opposite the square that lies before the royal palace near Westminster, a statue was shown to us hewn out of stone and fixed to the wall. It represents an English queen, who, in punishment of her tyranny, is said here to have sunk into the ground when she passed the gate. They pulled her out again and buried her, but it is said she was half burned. She kept many falcons, who were daily fed by a man's heart; the women's breasts she ordered to be cut off and given to her falcons. The statue on the wall is said to show her likeness.[57]

The resemblances between this queen of stone and Peele's Elinor are striking. But we shall never know whether the stuff he heard, saw, or read initiated the creative process; whether the ballads were modeled upon the statue or the reverse; whether there was inscribed on the statue itself a lengthy anti-Spanish epitaph, full of "historical" details, which helped the playwright improve upon the less patriotic facts of Holinshed and Grafton.

One thing is abundantly clear: Lyly's "land like Arras" was not only "full" but overflowing with "deuise." Like the genial country lords who welcomed strange guests into their hodgepodge manors, each of Gloriana's subjects, regardless of station or education, delighted in and carefully employed striking combinations of the visual to adorn his person and his possessions. Among the consequent romantic alterations and incongruous fusions, the poets and playwrights lived and moved. More gifted than their fellows, they were nevertheless recipients of common traditions and attitudes, and were equally influenced by the designs of the times. They, too, watched a civic procession and brought its color and pageantry into their lines. And surely they, too, admired the monuments of palaces, parks, and city squares, observed the mantels and ceilings of country houses, and dined, conversed, and probably even composed next to the painted cloths in city inns. In any of these places Macbeth could have seen "wither'd murder," Lorenzo found his English "Dido with a willow," and Hobgoblin filched the garland from Apollo.

Dishes for a Feaste . . . Now Minced in a Charger

Lyly's *Midas* was hardly the first literary feast composed of disparate dishes. In their tendency to underline the sameness of traditions and to ignore the original contexts of those themes and figures they wished to make modern and relevant, Renaissance writers of every persuasion appear to have been on common ground. At the close of the preceding chapter, for example, we noticed how cavalierly Perfect Beautie's tilters treated Cardinal Bembo's mystical utterances. But if the learned Venetian humanist would have shuddered to see Sidney's equation between Elizabeth and the ineffable, the Greek and Hebrew heroes he himself trampled upon in his passage to Plato's paradise might have been similarly dismayed. The odd use to which the Cardinal's philosophy was put, in other words, furnishes an excellent example of sixteenth-century poetic justice. Despite their very different ends, Bembo and his Elizabethan admirers were equally facile in manipulating their means.

This carefree association of mutually exclusive traditions characterizes not only the devisers' romantic representations, but the learned commentaries of their scholarly enemies. Detesting what they considered trivial nonsense and ribaldry, early Humanists like Erasmus, Vives, and Elyot arose as champions of factual truth and morality; [58] their sneering glances at medieval and modern Continental romances provided the Puritans with ready ammunition against later native excursions into the fanciful and amatory. Vives's manner is typical. "Ungracious books" such as "Florisand, Tristan and Celestina the bawd," along with "the hundred fables of Boccaccio," were written by "idle men," who "set all upon filth and viciousness." [59] What most incenses the educator, how-

ever, is that people "delight . . . in those things that be so plain and
foolish lies! One killeth twenty thousand himself alone, . . . another
wounded with a hundred wounds, and left dead, riseth up again,
and on the next day made whole and strong overcometh two giants.
. . . What madness is it of folks to have pleasure in these
books?" [60]

But Vives's ridicule of the impossibilities that daily occur in these
nowhere lands does not preclude some equally wondrous peregrina-
tions on his own part. To illustrate the duties of virtuous women, he
thumbs his commonplace book and passes over worlds sometimes
as fanciful as those he criticizes.

> Anna, mother unto Samuel the prophet, made with her
> own hands a linen coat for her son. The most chaste Queen
> of Ithaca, Penelope, passed the twenty years that her hus-
> band was away, with weaving. Queens of Macedonia and
> Eperus weaved garments with their own hands for their
> husbands and brethren, and fathers, and children: of which
> manner garments, King Alexander shewed some unto the
> Queens of Persia, that his mother and sisters had made.[61]

Throughout his *Instruction* Vives employs the same method, justifying each duty through a series of analogies drawn from history
and myth. No ancient spectacle escapes unmoralized, though sometimes we suspect that Vives's questionable logic is also aided by a
sincerely syncretic habit of mind. He evinces no sense of uneasiness, for instance, when he warns that modern wives should not
"loathe the name of the kitchen" because "Achilles . . . did not
disdain" such an "occupation." [62] Indeed, with so many examples at
his fingertips, he is bound to mingle traditions: Those who go
amongst the lowly in fine silks are not disciples of "poor Christ"
but "rich Pluto." [63]

Although the Renaissance scholars' universal catalogues of
knowledge may strike us as ironic, almost Swiftian, their tales were
not of tubs. The very earnest and influential Thomas Wilson informs those aspiring to *The Arte of Rhetorique* (1560) that he who
would "perswade, must needes be well stored with examples. And
therefore much are they to be commended, which searche Chronicles of all ages, and compare the state of our Elders with this
present time. . . . Yea, brute beastes minister . . . vnto vs, the
paterns and Images of diuers vertues." [64] Wilson immediately puts

theory into practice by premising faithfulness as a virtue, and then drawing from his own storehouse those patterns he believes most persuasive. Doves, cranes, and hens observe a code of loyalty; unthankfulness was punished by the Persians with death; finally, "three notable examples": Pliny's story of the grateful dragon, the tale of Fulvius's dog, and the adventures of Appian's lion.[65] Wilson allows even a "foolish tale" in order to capture an audience's attention, and admires Demosthenes's use of "a tale of *Robin Hood*" before offering the Athenians "an earnest cause." [66]

Like Vives, Wilson roams across numerous times and places to glean his kernels of instruction. As an illustration of most convincing argumentation, he provides a twenty-five-page "Epistle to perswade a yong Gentleman to mariage, deuised by Erasmus," a very feast of examples.[67] We begin with God's ordinances, proceed to Jesus's miracle at Cana, and then return to the laws of Moses. Next we consult David in the Psalms and "Plutarchus in the life of Cato." We then consider those laws favoring marriage enacted by all the Roman emperors from the time of Augustus Caesar, and the sentiments of Juvenal's epigrams. We are next asked to notice that adultery was punished by both Hebrews and Greeks. But marriage also agrees with the order of the natural world: "the houseband Tree," for instance, "doe leane with his boughes, euen as though he should desire copulation vpon the women Trees, growing round about him." [68] We must also observe "Mariage among precious stones," the union of the earth and firmament, and a number of great men who had wives: Solomon and Socrates and so on. Through such labyrinthine logic Ovid and Pliny wind their ways, both of course harnessed to the allegorical explications of the Christian Fathers. When we read of Orpheus, for example, making "soft with his pleasaunt melodie, the most harde Rockes and stones," what is the "meaning herein? Assuredly nothing els, but that a wise and well spoken man, did call backe harde harted men, such as liued abrode like beastes from open whoredom, & brought them to liue after the most holy lawes of Matrimonie." [69] The ancient fable, in other words, becomes Erasmus's trump card; through it he expects his young gentleman to "see plainly, that such a one as hath no mind of mariage, seemeth to be no man but rather a stone, an enemie to nature, a rebell to God himselfe, seeking through his owne folly, his last ende and destruction."

In view of the odd company into which Bembo introduces Hercules and Moses, Vives his Achilles, and Wilson almost every

Biblical or classical personage he discusses, it is no wonder that the less learned Tudor writers turned all ancient worthies into grist for the common mill. If Vives can contrast "poor Christ" to "rich Pluto" in a moment of high seriousness, we must not expect the Elizabethan hack to evince a knowing smile as he busily mingles Hebrews and pagans or grafts Amor onto the tradition of Christian love. Ovid's popularity continued through the sixteenth century, but usually because of the un-Ovidian uses to which he was put. Upon the title page of *Ars Amatoria*. *The Flores [Flowers] of Ouide* (1513) appears the well-known figure "of a teacher on a high seat, with a bundle of switches in his hand, addressing pupils hunched on a low form." [70] Vives takes *The Art of Love* with equal seriousness; Ovid was a "worshipful Artificer" who made "rules in God's name, and precepts of his [own] unthriftiness, a Schoolmaister of bawdry, and a common corrupter of virtue." [71] And Wilson is indignant over Ovid's commendation of the nut as the best of fruits. Like Virgil's praise of the gnat and Homer's interest in a battle of frogs, Ovid's nut is one of those "trifling causes" to be eschewed.[72] Finally, there is the Puritan Ovid, metamorphosed into agreement with Holy Writ.

Ovid as either Christian champion or subversive teacher, earnest advocate of trifles or stern lecturer quick to punish negligent students, is clearly an Ovid misunderstood. Other ancients suffered similar fates. If the Elizabethan tilter no longer wished to serve under Arthur, he was free to imitate his Roman brothers by staging lavish triumphs. His knowledge of the past was conditioned by medievalized, often debased materials that were for him as "classical" as if they had been personally presented by some Greek or Roman worthy. Upon the pages of the Latinized Greeks of the later Roman Empire he found examples of classical derring-do. His conception of Athens was often based more upon Heliodorus than Herodotus or Euripides;[73] the former's *Aethiopica* was, after all, written in Greek, and therefore authoritative as well as romantically appealing. Few Elizabethans touch upon the shining worlds of Greece and Rome without an attitude of reverence. The brightness they worship, however, is that of truth rather than beauty, and the truth usually turns out to be purely utilitarian, some practical advice on politics, warfare, gardening, ethics, or medicine. Until Jonson, even the literary people fail to bring us much closer to what Poe called "the glory that was Greece / . . . the grandeur that was Rome." It is in fact difficult to decide which writers are more insensitive, the popular playwrights who thunder over "Boreas' breath" or the gentlemen-scholars at the Inns of Court, who hold up Seneca as the acme of classical tragedy.

As if times and matters were not sufficiently confounded, additional "dishes" soon supplemented the dimly perceived worlds of Athens and Rome. Wilson's allusions to Robin Hood and Arthur reveal that although native folk tales and medieval romances were not always taken seriously, their heroes were readily familiar to well-educated men of the sixties. Editions of Malory's *Morte d'Arthur* appeared in 1485, 1498, 1529, 1557, and 1581, and the loves of *Blanchardine and Eglantine* were not only celebrated by Caxton (c. 1489) but by "P. T. G. Gent." in 1595 and 1597.[74] In 1485 Caxton published *Paris and Vienne;* a century later, "an old booke of *the xij pairs [peers] of Ffraunce* and of *Paris and Vienne*" was licensed to "T. Purfoot." [75] Although it is tempting to regard the latter edition as evidence of the old-fashioned tastes of the bourgeoisie, Purfoot no doubt found some aristocratic customers. The theme had been acted out by the Children of Westminster before the Queen and her Court in 1571–1572, when "parris wan the Christall sheelde for vienna. at the Turneye and Barryers," and during the seventies and eighties, the English nobility evidently found tales of "Herpetulus the blew knight," "the Solitarie knight," and "the Knight in the Burnyng Rock" to its sophisticated liking.[76]

Between 1560 and 1590, Gloriana's realm was inundated with the matters of Greece, Rome, Italy, Spain, and medieval England, and apparently neither courtier nor citizen expected one tradition to preclude another. The aristocratic "charger," in fact, often offers a feast more minced than the city's, and we sometimes find Whitehall looking backward while London ushers in the Renaissance. In 1581, for instance, Arthur Hall translated from the French the first ten books of the *Iliad*, and Thomas Newton presented a completed English version of Seneca's *Thebais*.[77] The same year, Barnabe Riche made an elaborate *Farewell to Militarie Profession* with nine stories, one taken from Bandello's *Novelle*, three from Giraldi Cinthio's *Gli Hecatommithi*, and five "forged only for delight." [78] Again in 1581, Thomas Watson celebrated Cupid's tyranny in the *Passionate Centurie of Loue*, a hundred eighteen-line variations upon the "sonnets" of Petrarch, Parabosco, Strozzi, and other Italian amorists.[79] Meanwhile, however, the Court was preoccupied with medieval glories. Petruccio Ubaldini presented a romantic biography of Charlemagne,[80] and in April, the Office of the Revels was industriously preparing materials for "The Mounte, Dragon with yᵉ fyer woorkes, Castell . . . & hermytt, Savages, Enchaunter, Charryot, & incydentes to theis." [81]

It is somewhat disturbing to discover our expectations thus undermined. We should prefer Homer and Petrarch in the hands of the beautiful people, and the dregs of Malory exciting the citizens. But if we allow the facts to alter our assumptions, the "wrong" directions taken by city and Court will seem more intelligible. First, although we may safely assume that a book that went through numerous editions was popular, we have no right to characterize that volume as exclusively middle class simply on the basis of its popularity. It would be safer merely to infer that the bourgeoisie *also* bought it. More important, we must resist the modern tendency to equate a penchant for faraway adventures with escapism, and escapism with a particular class. Attempting to explain the romantic elements of the Elizabethan popular stage, one of the most influential cultural historians of our time draws a misleading analogy.

> Outside of set conventions, naïve tastes do not ask for realism and credibility, as is evident from current motion-picture plays which exploit afresh the bourgeois interest in bizarre adventure. The zest for romantic other-worldliness persists more strongly than elsewhere in the appetites of those who practise in life the humdrum routine of getting and spending. Shopkeeping spectators who today gasp over the dashing heroics of a cinema actor as D'Artagnan or as a wanderer in Bali are spiritually akin to their predecessors who reveled in the acting of some Elizabethan favorite in the rôle of Guy of Warwick or the Blue Knight.[82]

Since the Accounts of the Revels Office hardly reflect the tastes of shopkeepers, we can only conclude that during those dreadfully boring years of peace, when Elizabeth played France against Spain, the nobility enlivened the "humdrum routine" of courting with incredibly "bizarre" presentations. Perhaps it would be wiser to amend the analogy and say that the zest for romantic other-worldliness usually varies from era to era, and within *some* eras from class to class. This would allow the Elizabethans an option they seem to have insisted upon exercising, the right of all men to be interested in dashing heroics. Whether we have that option today is an open question. Many an instructor of those incurable romantics, Spenser and Sidney and Shakespeare, would swear that naïve tastes ask for more, not less, realism and credibility. The forms in which the Spanish Peninsular Romance was sold to sixteenth-century English shopkeepers certainly suggest a movement from the fantastic to the everyday, and the final products are the heroics of homeliness. In 1580 the first book of Diego de Calahorra's *Espejo de principes y cavalleros* was translated by Margaret Tyler as *The Mirrour of Princely deedes and Knighthood*.[83] The Knight of the Sun and his brother, Rosicleer, sons of the great Emperor Trebetio, soon begot a numerous progeny. The next year Anthony Munday nearly outdid Gloriana's devisers at their own game, for his *Palmerin of England* (c. 1581) celebrates the sometime-nowhere reigns of Palmerin de Oliva, Emperor of Constantinople, and Frederick, King of England, when the Knight of Death and the Knight of the Savage Man pricked through dimly distant lands cluttered with griffins, giants, wizards, dragons, and enchanted castles.[84] With their rambling, almost incoherent plots, indefinite settings, shadowy characters, and often supernatural resolutions, the Palmerin adventures frequently remind us of the romances produced by the Greeks at Alexandria and at the courts of European princes throughout the Middle Ages.

But Munday and his middle-class fellows provided more than amalgamations of former fictional absurdities. They heightened the verbal embellishments of their originals with numerous conceits, often slowed down the narrative pace with lyrics, and made their worlds even more modern and courtly with echoes of euphuism, Platonism, and pastoralism.[85] Equally important is their subjection of courtly love to Elizabethan moral norms: Doughty deeds win wives, not mistresses.[86] Chivalry thus transfigured, however, is generally English, not specifically bourgeois. The major elements of Munday's Palmerin romances are common to *The Arcadia* and *The Faerie Queene:* All three freely entertain the marvelous, sometimes even the bizarre; all idealize marriage as the end of courtship; all feature a wealth of rhetorical adornment. The shopkeeping mind is better represented in Munday's successors, who expurgated not only the exquisite rituals of courtly love, but almost all romantic atmosphere. Whereas the sophisticated Elizabethan remained willing to court the faraway, to suspend disbelief in extravagances, the Palmerin annalists of the 1590's offered their readers increasingly realistic and bourgeois quests. In *Pheander the Mayden Knight*

(1595), for example, Henry Robarts maintained the traditional laments of unrequited love, the defense of the lady's beauty, the disguises, the war against infidels, and the happy conclusion. But there is no longer the machinery of magic and enchantment, and Pheander's knightly stature is somewhat diminished when, in a fit of petty jealousy, he attacks his rival with a chessboard.[87]

Finally, in Emanuel Forde's *Parismus, the Renowned Prince of Bohemia* (1598), the remaining romantic motifs are displaced by realism and modernity.[88] Forde's heroes are bourgeois princes upholding middle-class values. Since their principal quests are to protect their own lives, loves, and fortunes, they have no time for knight-errantry. If some evil descends upon their friends, they are quick and sometimes ruthless in their rescues, but strange ladies must shift for themselves. Forde's heroines are also straightforward, especially during courtship. His lovers express themselves in language befitting honest citizens rather than through the conventionally long-winded, stylized love plaint. Forde's world, in short, admits the realities of economics, hunger, fear, Time's winged chariot, and heroes whose motives are not wholly pure. Even his relatively few enchantments are usually dispossessed of an aura of mystery; genuinely supernatural occurrences are very rare, for magical creatures are likely to turn out to be quite human.[89] While the aristocracy continued to cultivate the incredible, the middle-class romance factories purged romance of all but successful ventures, exotic geography, and figures with outlandish names. It is precisely this colorless world of bourgeois derring-do, set in Bohemia but smelling of Houndsditch, that Francis Beaumont burlesques in *The Knight of the Burning Pestle* (c. 1607). The Elizabethan and Jacobean receptions and tournaments offer abundant proof that one could pass into the realms of lusty loves and doughty deeds without abandoning his intellectual respectability. To put armor on a grocer's apprentice was an entirely different matter. We must never assume that in an era of such divergent attitudes the chivalric tradition automatically invited facetious treatments. It was attractive to personalities and purposes as varied as Boiardo's, Ariosto's, Sidney's, Greene's, and Forde's. Even the waggish Harington has his solemn moments, and the most serious of all, Spenser, is least likely to be held as a representative of bourgeois tastes. That the romance of chivalry was regarded as a respectable vehicle for heroic action long after Beaumont is indicated by Milton's "Epitaphium Damonis" (1640), in which the poet figures forth his proposed Arthurian epic.

Robarts's and Forde's uses (or abuses) of the Peninsular Romance typify the Elizabethan habit of appropriating the serviceable. Whether the basic stock is recent Spanish or ancient French romance, learned Italian or innocent native drama, medievalized Roman or Alexandrian-Greek narrative, relevance dictates its pruning, and either invention of honest ignorance its grafting. If what we should call a "pure literary form" is seldom forthcoming, it is because all the Queen's subjects stand unabashed in the presence of ponderous traditions and sense no problems in gleaning the most attractive elements of each. For all their trimmed treatises on decorum, proportion, and the unities, they continue to act upon the same democratic premises that inspired Charles V's reception by London in 1522. Consequently, the theory most honored in practice is Sidney's rather casual assumption about the marriage of poetic kinds: "if seuered they be good, the coniunction cannot be hurtfull." [90] This romantic exception to Sidney's otherwise severe standards of literary excellence may reflect a resolution of his own doubts concerning the propriety of mixed materials. About the time he composed his *Apologie* (c. 1583), he was also rewriting *The Arcadia* with "matters Heroicall and Pastorall" before him, from Heliodorus to Malory to Sannazaro. Much of the equally mingled stuff of the busy seventies and eighties no doubt issued from minds far less troubled than Sidney's, but his syncretism is underlined on almost every page.

The literary feast of 1581 characterizes the abundance of varied matters that almost every year brought to hand. To see how widespread were the annual diffusions of each tradition, one need only select at random any year between 1560 and 1590 and compare the bibliographical entries provided by Professors Scott, Lathrop, and Esdaile. The movement's many facets preclude a detailed discussion, but it is important to realize how quickly each action begot a reaction. Whether we trace the provenance of a general theme, particular genre, or specific story, we rarely fail to catch something of the period's excitement and energy. Although this "coming-forthness" may often strike us as a kind of thesis-antithesis-synthesis, it was no doubt seen in terms of wading farther: translation, imitation, adaptation, and transfiguration. A writer steps beyond by elaborating upon and fusing his materials rather than reconciling them. In any case, however odd the attempt and dubious its success, the ferment is real. Nothing better illustrates the fact of the Renaissance, convinces us that the term is meaningful and not merely polite. Had that ferment been tempered by a more classical or more modern sense of decorum, perhaps a Robarts or a Forde would have written better. But it is just as likely that a Sidney or a Spenser would not have written so well. Which of us would wish that Shakespeare had been more critical in appropriating what struck him as "fitting"?

Sometimes the borrowing is obvious and the result predictable. Between Hoby's Englishing of Castiglione's *Courtier* (published 1561) and a translation of Boccaccio's *Filocolo* by "H.G." in 1567, for instance, Edmund Tilney received the framework, materials, setting, and spirit for his *Flower of Friendshippe* (1568).[91] The meeting in a garden or chamber, the selection of a presider over the company, and the discussion of set questions all characterize the social diversions of Renaissance Italy. Tilney wants us to know that he has simply "translated" his characters to an English house party, for they invite identification with their Italian prototypes. When certain gentlemen propose outdoor recreations, Master Pedro, "nothing at all lyking of such deuises, wherein the Ladies should be left out, said that he well remembered how Boccace and Countie Baltisar [Baldassare Castiglione] with others recounted many proper deuises for exercise, both pleasant and profitable, which . . . were used in the courts of Italie."[92] In subsequent discussions of the duties in marriage, however, Tilney also includes stories by other Italians and one from Margaret of Navarre's *Heptameron*.

One year after Tilney published his flowers of Boccaccio and Castiglione, Thomas Underdowne directed England's attention to a far more exotic matter, Heliodorus's *Aethiopica*. Again the borrowing is obvious, for Underdowne is neither imitating, adapting, nor fusing. He seeks to translate in the more conventional sense, and his text does full justice to Heliodorus's world of lustful pirates, inscrutable oracles, disguised princes, and nearly ravished virgins. The destinies of Theagenes and Cariclia, the naïve hero and quiveringly chaste heroine, are largely determined by a series of melodramatic escapes and incredibly fortuitous rescues. Like Heliodorus, Underdowne is not actually interested in the characters but in the number of impossible situations into which they can be driven. Like his fellow Elizabethans, who included Heliodorus in their classical canon, Underdowne appears to have taken the tale's rambling structure, spectacular and sentimental scenes, and ornate rhetoric as a fresh view of Athens.[93] The direct borrowing, faithful Englishing, and predictable results within the text itself, however, tell only half of Underdowne's story. What happens in his preface and lengthy marginalia is as startling as the adventures he accurately translates. Heliodorus must not only be a link to the ancient world, but the soul of earnest moral instruction. "The Gentle Reader" is reminded of "the losenesse of these days," and Underdowne hopes that this "most honest . . . historie of love" will not be compared with medieval tales "of like argument."

> Mort Darthure, Arthur of little Britaine, yea, and Amadis of Gaule, etc. accompt violente murder, or murder for no cause, manhoode: and fornication and all unlawful luste, friendely love. This booke punisheth the faultes of evill doers, and rewardeth the well livers. What a king is Hidaspes? What a patterne of a good prince? What happy successe had he? Contrariewise, what a leawde woman was Arsace? What a paterne of evill behaviour? What an evill end had she? Thus might I say of many other.[94]

With this obvious attempt to pacify Humanists and Puritans, Underdowne proceeds to force wholesome honey from Heliodorus's luxurious garden. The Herculean tasks of turning violence, rape, murder, and concupiscence to a good account and of simultaneously damning the antagonists' knaveries and justifying the protagonists' duplicities are mainly accomplished through edifying marginal notations. When Cariclia's mentor tricks one of his captors into killing another, for example, the "margent" salutes the "crafty devise of Calasiris to hinder the marriage of Trachinus and Cariclia, whereby all the pyrates are slaine."[95] Another deception is glossed as "a wise policie whereby Hydaspes took Philae."[96] And although the marginalia includes a prayer for the wily Cnemon's successors—"God graunt that the honestie of this heathen priest, condemne not some of our ministers"[97]—Underdowne is more interested in his strategies than their salvation. Apparently his contemporaries shared the translator's fascination, for legend has it that these moral patterns came to be regarded as a handbook of tactics.[98]

In view of the frequent transfigurations by translators proper, it is not surprising to find the self-acknowledged improvers making wholesale conversions. Frank S. Hook has already demonstrated that when a *littérateur* like William Painter, Geoffrey Fenton, or George Whetstone erected his palace of allegedly Italian pleasures, he invariably relied less on the rapid-moving narratives of Bandello than on the labored, highly adorned versions of the *Novelle* supplied by Belleforest's *Histoires tragiques* (1564–1582).[99] Like Boccaccio, Bandello had treated a form originally intended to be passed on orally as a social diversion; the Italian *novella* is therefore direct and concise, easy to read aloud, and usually told in less than ten pages. Having never shared in this tradition and writing for the public at large instead of a select circle, Belleforest could exercise his "positive genius for destroying the narrative movement of a story" with tedious expansions: lengthy, evidently sincere moralizations and lists of examples that seem to have been inserted not only to stress or "prove" his point, but to impress the reader with his vast knowledge of history and the classics.[100] A phrase in Bandello sometimes furnishes Belleforest with several pages. A mere reference to a song, amorous letter, or conversation is turned into a long lyric, four-page epistle, or an inflated harangue, sometimes by the original character but frequently from the omniscient author to his public.[101] Most remarkable is Belleforest's use of love jargon. Whether inflamed by pure love or vile lust, every wooer employs identical language.[102] Consequently, rhetoric is all-important, yet signifies nothing in terms of character delineation.

Between these two conceptions of storytelling, the tale as a swift, intriguing series of incidents or as a peg on which to hang one's own rhetorical cunning, few Elizabethans managed a middle course. The great majority, unfortunately, followed Belleforest. In an age that honored or was at least somewhat anxious about Plato's charge that poets were liars, the French Bandello provided model exercises in originality. Without fabricating, without changing a single name, incident, or place, Belleforest had waded farther by writing between Bandello's lines. He was thus indirectly adhering to a most important point in the Renaissance doctrine of imitation, one which "held that a plot should be based on historical fact or on that which custom and tradition had dignified as being the equivalent of historical fact [e.g., myth] or anything which the author might have known to have happened either at first hand or by report." [103] It was mainly Plato and his Puritan disciples who encouraged the English storyteller to take either the Italian or the French route. Like Edmund Tilney, a few followed the *novellieri*, who usually introduce their tales "within a specific setting and with explicit guarantees that what they are about to relate actually had taken place." [104] Like Fenton and Whetstone, however, most preferred Belleforest's less simple solution of telling more "truth" than is (at least for us) artistically necessary.

The preference is easy to understand. Whereas set situations or frameworks are limited, the stock of verbal embellishments and permutations of examples are infinite. Add to this the genuine delight that the era found in experimenting with a new world of words, as well as its remarkably high tolerance for aphorism and artifice, and it seems likely that the writers thoroughly enjoyed this method of pacifying Plato. Painter, for instance, was not morally obliged to attempt both the Italian and the French routes. In his dedicatory epistle to the Earl of Warwick (1566), he notes that he initially selected "the best and principal" stories of Livy, "that excellent Historiographer," and then adventured "into diuers other, out of whom I decerped [plucked out] . . . sondry proper and commendable Histories, which I may boldly so terme, because the Authors be commendable and well approued." [105] Having thus established his sources' verity, however, he also admits that he especially admires truth when it is elegant. The "friendly Reader" is told, for example, that "out of Bandello I haue selected seuen [tales], chosing rather to follow Launay and Belleforest the French Translatours, than the barren soile of his own [Bandello's] vain." [106]

The diverse twists and curious turns taken by Elizabethan prose fiction from Painter in the mid-sixties to Greene in the early nineties is therefore only partly explained in terms of Plato's rod and Belleforest's evasions. Its development also reflects an interest in manipulating words less for the sake of truth than beautiful artifice, and a desire to show how far one had stepped beyond his models to attain what Nashe called a "manifold varietie of inuention" and Lyly, the same year, "notes beyonde Ela." Through a properly imitative creativity, of course, a writer could at one time satisfy truth, cultivate the potential power of his native tongue, and do justice to his own genius. As the first Englishman to profit by Belleforest's richer soil, it is sufficient for Painter to adhere closely to his French text. Except for occasional attempts to give his stories an English flavor through prefatory remarks on contemporary native customs or by shifting his locales from France to England, Painter translates Belleforest word for word.[107] But for Fenton, whose *Certaine Tragicall Discourses* appeared the year following, it was necessary to outdo the French master. Belleforest's turgid prose undergoes additional adornment, becoming so labored and artificial that we are frequently reminded of Lyly's complex syntactical machinery.[108] Ingeniously husbanded, Bandello's "barren soile" has by 1567 already produced overripe fruit. The Italian's short sketches of clever means and intriguing ends have foundered under horrendous preachments, learned commentaries on life, and exquisite soliloquies on love. With Fenton, in other words, we begin to wonder how much longer characters will talk endlessly yet keep their personalities concealed. We yearn for some story built upon the more familiar options of plot and character, but for the next twenty years we usually find incidents used merely to set up long speeches. And if the narrators are hastening over their actions in order to develop psychology rather than sheer rhetoric, they are doing an incredibly bad job. How often we discover that unless we read the first sentence of a three-page outburst carefully, we forget whether the words are coming from the hero, heroine, her confidante, or the author himself. By the end of the speech, moreover, we are likely to have forgotten what event prompted it.

George Pettie runs true to form. By the time he erected his own *Petite Palace* (1576), the Elizabethan reader had come to expect the commendable histories of approved authors to yield new-fashioned personae being run through time-honored situations, and ancient settings burgeoning with modern topics. If Plato demanded an authoritative warp, one simply lavished his artifice upon the more interesting woof. Pettie's twelve "pretie Hystories" are therefore original graftings of the *questioni d'amore* of Boccaccio, Bembo, Castiglione, and like-minded sixteenth-century Italians upon Livy, Hyginus, Plutarch, Tacitus, and Ovid. Each is of course finally decked out in euphuistic paraphernalia and learned editorializations. Ovid's five-page fable of Minos and Scylla (*Metamorphoses*, VIII, 1–151), for example, is easily inflated into a nineteen-page treatise on the nature and influence of romantic love as revealed in its operations upon Nisus's daughter.[109] Like Fenton,

Pettie is interested neither in what happens—Ovid's incidents are
dismissed in a dozen lines and Minos is wheeled in only for the
necessary rejection of Scilla—nor even in whom it happens to, but
in the skillfulness with which his mouthpieces use their common
rhetorical handbook. His story, therefore, gets nowhere almost as
quickly as those by Lyly and early Greene: first, an editorial
comment on the infinite inconveniences of love (one page);
next, the introduction of Scilla's despairing suitor, Iphis, his overtures, and her disdainful reply, both invented by the author and
quoted at length (five pages); then Scilla's first view of Minos and
passionate soliloquy, again fully quoted (three pages); next, the
advice of her friend and her friend's friend, Pandarina, interspersed
with Scilla's responses and random editorializing (eight pages);
and finally, since Pettie's lore is nearly exhausted, Ovid's tale
(three sentences) and the author's concluding moral (two pages).

Pettie seems only partly aware of the incongruity between the
classical warp and the modern frames of reference he has woven
into it. His apology for the anachronisms within his rehearsal of
Plutarch's "Synorix and Camma" is as arch as the morals he underlines: "If this mislike you in my discourses, that I make *Camma*,
use the example of the countesse of *Salisbury* . . . and sutch who
were of far later yeeres, then the auncient *Camma* is, with the like
in divers other of the stories: you must consider that my *Camma*
is of fresher memory then any of them, and I thinke in your
judgment, of fresher hew then the fayrest of them." [110] Pettie is
probably parading his earlier advertisement that the classical legends he recounts "touch neerely divers of my nere freindes: but . . .
they are so darkely figured forth, that only they whom they touch,
can understand whom they touch." [111] If the pulpiteer can allegorize the classics to support modern instances, Pettie seems to
reason, why not the amorist? He thus gains the best of both worlds;
native flavor is introduced as the range of similes and examples is
extended. Nevertheless, he makes no excuse for Iphis' role as
Petrarchan lover or for Scilla as the chatterer of euphuisms.

Pettie's own role in the development of prose fiction is to represent a middle point between the techniques of grafting new
concerns upon a single ancient matter and of crossbreeding
several disparate traditions. Although he grounds each of his
narratives upon only one source, his superimpositions are so extensive and varied that the result might be classed among the examples of Elizabethan minglings. The following year (1577), John

Grange took even greater liberties with classical legend as a vehicle for personal artifice. *The Golden Aphroditis* is prudently set within the realm of "the *Homericall* Goddes"; its heroine, Lady Alpha Omega, is given Diana and Endymion for parents, "though the Poetes fayne the contrary"; the hero, Sir N.O., is a cousin of Hippomenes and Atalanta; and there are frequent references to Olympus and the nowhere island of Scyros.[112] For all his heavy reliance upon ancient myth, however, we soon realize that Grange has reversed Pettie's procedure. Instead of beginning with Ovid and then working in "darkely figured" modern meanings, Grange started with some recent Elizabethan scandal[113] and then invented an Ovidian world to disguise it. Mythology, in short, was Pettie's warp, his point of departure, but Grange's woof, his display of invention. Like Pettie, he is of course also bent on showing his rhetorical prowess and his vast knowledge of love's subtleties. But like Gloriana's showmen, he must have been even more proud of his work's occasional nature, its ability to make Olympus highlight an immediate and very real situation. Beneath Grange's learned effusions and under the masks of his "*Homericall* Goddes," there are brief glimpses of contemporary scenes: Lady A.O.'s manor, "most gorgeously adorned with highe poyntes, curious turrets, and fewe glasse windowes rounde about," in which "the long and weary winters night" is enlivened by singing to a lute, dancing, "cardyng . . . dycing . . . arguyng of Veneriall disputations"; a heroine who sees how "blinde bayarde hitteth the nayle on the hedde"; a rival suitor who mentions an unchaste lady back in Henry VIII's time; an editorial note on lovers who trim their beards, polish their teeth, and wash their temples with rose water; and above all, a disconsolate hero who composes his love plaint at Buxton Spa.[114] When the gods of land and sea finally enter to celebrate the lovers' nuptials, we are therefore assured that the wedding takes place somewhere in Albion, if not England.

The simultaneously faraway and near-at-hand setting of Grange's story is another characteristic of prose fiction from the seventies through the early nineties. The tale's title and argument can often be as misleading as the ostensible time and place heralded in the opening lines of the Queen's receptions and entertainments. In either case, we are never quite sure about the kind of world we are entering, nor whether it will not soon yield to another. In Robert Greene's romances, for instance, an Aethiopican-like pirate in medieval armor lifts his visor and reveals the eye and tongue of an Italian courtier; we walk about the walls of Troy and stumble upon a buskined Castiglione or sit in the Roman senate and hear old Tully rehearse his Petrarchan passion.[115] Harvey characterized such stuff as written by "the running Head, and the scribling Hand, that neuer linnes [i.e., lins, ceases] putting-forth new, newer, & newest bookes of the maker," and told Greene to "thanke other for thy borrowed & filched plumes of some little Italianated brauery."[116] Within the same paragraph of invective, however, "vile *Greene*" is also "the Ape of Euphues," an "Omnigatherum . . . a Stoarehouse of bald and baggage stuffe," and "for queasie stomackes," better than Sidney—"the Countesse of Pembrookes Arcadia is not greene inough . . . but they must haue *Greenes* Arcadia: and I beleeue most eagerlie longed for *Greenes* Fairie Queene."[117]

Harvey's censures could be easily documented. But if Greene aped and filched, so did the men he borrowed from. Only personal enmity explains why Harvey singled out Greene among a score of "new, newer, & newest" romancers, why he judged Greene's "Omnigatherums" imitative but not creative. Both the strength and weakness of the Renaissance is revealed in any one of these everyday *littérateurs*, for whom no stock is too alien, no grafting too curious, no mingling too artificial. At times it is difficult to say whether the writer's strange invention bespeaks a mind earnest and painstaking yet confused and insensitive, or perhaps careless because hurried, or simply carefree and whimsical. Caxton, for example, obviously struggled to provide a yeomanly English equivalent of Ovid's *Metamorphoses,* though the horror of the transformation of Glaucus's lovely Scylla escaped him: "incontynent she becam a monstre canyne or houndysshe barkynge whyche enclosed her and was taken by the strength of the venym."[118] Almost a century later Arthur Golding achieved a fairly straightforward and certainly clearer translation:

> In seeking where her loynes, and thyghes, and feete and ancles were,
> Chappes like the chappes of *Cerberus* in stead of them she found.
> Nought else was there than cruell curres from belly downe too ground.[119]

It remained for Thomas Lodge to pass entirely over Ovid and his Englishers to hear the story from Glaucus himself. As Thomas weeps beneath a willow on the banks of Oxford's Isis, the Greek sea god appears, places his head upon the poet's knee, and makes his own love plaint with citations from Ariosto.[120] The situation, as Douglas Bush notes, is "not wholly Ovidian." [121] It was, however, to the Elizabethan eye, which could see in Diana the Queen, in Actaeon Philip of Spain, and in Scylla the disdainful dame of the Italian sonneteers:

> *Scilla* hath eyes, but too sweete eyes hath *Scilla;*
> *Scilla* hath hands, faire hands but coy in touching;
> *Scilla* in wit surpasseth graue *Sibilla,*
> *Scilla* hath words, but words well storde with grutching;
>   *Scilla* a Saint in looke, no Saint in scorning;
>   Looke Saint-like *Scilla,* least I die with mourning.[122]

With such anachronistic drapery Ovid's one hundred fifty lines (XIII, 898–968; XIV, 1–74) are inflated into almost eight hundred.

While the groves of Oxfordshire echoed with Glaucus's Italianated bravery, Virgil's Corydon was holding forth on legal argumentation at the Inns of Court. Sometime along his varied course of studies, probably during his undergraduate days at Cambridge, Abraham Fraunce had experimented with English quantitative hexameters and contributed a version of Virgil's *Alexis (Eclogue II)*. At Cambridge he must also have been introduced to the works of the Calvinist logician, Peter Ramus, who had illustrated his principles and methods with excerpts from Ovid's *Epistles.*[123] And when Fraunce decided to become a lawyer, he found that his legal textbooks, like many of his undergraduate readings, exemplified the logic of English common law. All of these experiences seem to coalesce in the notions advanced at the outset of his *Lawiers Logike* (1588). Since "the true vse of Logike is as well apparant in simple playne, and easie explication, as in subtile, strict, and concised probation," young lawyers should read Homer, Demosthenes, Virgil, Cicero, Du Bartas, Tasso, and "that most worthie ornament of our English tongue, the *Countesse of Penbrookes Arcadia,* and therein see the true effectes of natural Logike." [124] With this introduction Fraunce then proceeds through a one-hundred-twenty-page examination of the excellent natural logic employed, for the most part, by the swains in Spenser's *Shepheardes Calender.* When "*Hobbinoll* in Aprill in his song of *Elisa*" lists the flowers which "Shall match with the faire Flowredelice," for instance, we are shown that "Disparates are sundry opposites whereof one is equally and in like manner opposed vnto many." [125] The second half of the study, on the other hand, is largely taken up with a *tour de force* of logical diagraming. Here Fraunce deals out some of his own "disparates," bringing into Westminster not only the findings of some recent English jurists, but his old version of the *Alexis:* "I haue, for examples sake, put downe a Logicall Analysis of the second *Aegloge* in *Virgill,* of the Earle of *Northumberlands* case in Maister *Plowdens* reportes, and of sir *William Stamfords* crowne plees." [126]

Fraunce's crabbed treatise may seem to bear little relationship to the concerns of the romancers of London and Whitehall. A man who makes *The Arcadia* serve "the true use of Logike" or forces Spenser's shepherds to prove the advantage of "sundry opposites" could have hardly become excited over mere greenwood adventures. Yet even this unromantic lawyer provides some insight into the contemporary scene. His rigid diagrams tell us that as late as 1588, an advocate who stands for careful reason, if nothing else, still honors the medieval containments of multitudes. Surely the marriage of Virgil and Master Plowden is no less odd than Plato in a tiltyard. Having explained the latter as sheer flattery, we confront an Elizabethan glossing the former as sheer logic. In between are the hacks and Humanists, usually taking from different dishes but equally prone to mincing. The Queen's devisers, in other words, were wading farther with and probably giving fresh impetus to a method honored by minds as unlike as Wilson's, Sidney's, Fraunce's and Greene's. Because this method is so very common, it is often difficult to interpret a romancer's fusion. Is his minglemangle simply another instance of one basic Renaissance habit of thought, or does it represent an attempt at the kind of art Lyly mentions in his Prologue to *Midas?*

Moreover, because the method always comes naturally yet is also sometimes employed artificially, it is even more difficult to document the influence of the Elizabethan entertainment upon kindred romantic forms. In 1573, for example, Gascoigne's *Adventures of Master F.J.* treated an adulterous affair, supposed to have taken place in northern England. Whether Gascoigne had an actual event in mind is not certain, but his later apology indicates that some "reuerend diuines" detected hints of scandal. It may therefore have been his fear of a libel suit as well as the predictable charges of lewdness that caused him to shift his setting from England to Italy and to change his title to *The Pleasant Fable of Ferdinando Jeronimi and Leonora de Valasco, Translated out of The Italian Riding Tales of Bartello* (1575). In 1576 Pettie advertises that his contemporaries are being "darkely figured forth," and Grange admits as much the year following. Unlike Gascoigne, however, neither was later obliged to expurgate materials, shift his locale, and invent an Italian source. In their use of "the *Homericall* Goddes" as prototypes, Grange and Pettie were perhaps profiting by more than Gascoigne's sad adventures with *Master F.J.* The feigned Bartello of 1575 was but one of Gascoigne's solutions to the problem of handling realistic matters. The same year he and his fellow devisers at Kenilworth had woven contemporary meanings into the safer warps of ancient legend and medieval romance.

Although we cannot prove that Leicester's politic fables directly inspired Pettie's and Grange's similar use of similar materials, it is quite likely that Gloriana's theater at least exerted a strong general influence upon the *littérateurs'* imaginations. They above all knew what both courtier and citizen desired in their fiction. Some hastened to provide the public with detailed accounts of the wonders that befell the Queen, and a few even helped to create those wonders. The most skillful romancers used the accounts—and perhaps personal experiences—as indexes of romantic techniques and public tastes. Whether translating, grafting, or crossbreeding, and whether electing to set their events in a land far away or near at hand, the readily familiar and the passing strange had to be eventually interwoven. Within the Queen's private theater, this mingling was largely dictated by the situation: Elizabeth had to be entertained, and her subjects knew she found former fabulous story entertaining. Within much of the romantic drama that followed these programs, however, the same simultaneous cultivation of the marvelous and the everyday becomes a conscious technique, freely chosen, and for art's sake rather than the Queen's. Since it is difficult to examine this transition from devising to drama in terms of precise borrowings, we should first notice two prose works of the eighties that directly imitate the former and occasionally anticipate the latter. They are also, incidentally, relevant to our discussion of taste, for the first is a courtier's hodgepodge and the second, a citizen's minced translation of "Greek" pastoral.

When Sidney began revising his *Arcadia* about 1582, one of the

new elements he carefully interlaced was an account of the cere-
monial jousts annually held to honor Queen Andromana of
Iberia.[127] To this "seven-night" exercise of chivalry came famous
knights from the court of Queen Helen of Corinth. Although the
Corinthians had been "in nature mutinously prowde, and alwaies
before so used to hard governours, as they knew not how to obey
without the sworde were drawne," Helen had "made her people
by peace, warlike; her courtiers by sports, learned; her Ladies by
Love, chast. For by continuall martiall exercises without bloud,
she made them perfect in that bloudy art. Her sportes were such as
caried riches of Knowledge upõ the streame of Delight. . . . So as it
seemed, that court to have bene the mariage place of Love and
Vertue, & that her selfe was a *Diana* apparelled in the garments of
Venus." [128] What seems very much like a compliment to Perfect
Beautie is immediately followed by a detailed description of the
colorful contest in which Helen's knights vanquished Andromana's.
Great attention is paid to each tilter's entrance, device, and exit: An
Iberian comes in as a wild man, "full of withered leaves," and his
impresa displaying "a mill-horse still bound to goe in one circle";
from one Corinthian's tent issues a bird, bearing "a written em-
bassage among the Ladies"; another Corinthian rides in as "the
Phoenix: the fire tooke so artificially, as it consumed the birde,
and left him to rise as it were, out of the ashes." [129] Against the
last enters an Iberian, a "fine frosen Knight, frosen in despaire,"
whose armor represented ice and "all his furniture . . . lively
answering thereto." [130] But the featured clash of arms is between
the Corinthian "*Lelius* (who was knowne to be second to none in
the perfection of that Art)" and the Iberian shepherd-knight,
Philisides, who feared his experienced opponent "would shew a
contempt of his youth." [131]

The more we hear about Helen and the champions who tilted
at the Iberian Court, the closer we seem to Whitehall in 1581, a
year or two before Sidney "imagined" this episode. Indeed, it is
only as these Arcadian events become impossibly farfetched
that we are certain they were modeled upon English realities; fiction and history merge when we compare the exotic devices invented by Sidney with those recorded by Goldwell and von Wedel.
And the description of Philisides, entering "with bagpipes in steed
of trumpets; a shepheards boy before him for a Page" and a lance
fashioned as a "shephook," surely verges upon autobiography, for
who but the Stella of Sidney's sonnets appears among the Iberian

ladies above the tiltyard as "the *Star*, wherby his course was only directed." [132] If Sidney employed this pastoral furniture during the Accession Day Tilt of 1581, he was probably acknowledging Spenser's recent tribute—*The Shepheardes Calender* had been dedicated to him in 1579—and thus encouraging an equation that Spenser would cultivate fifteen years later in the figure of Sir Calidore, the shepherd-knight of faerie. Under his Arcadian alias, Sir Henry Lee was also highly honored. In his "translation" of *Du Bartas His Divine Weekes* (1605), Joshua Sylvester finds that at the Creation, the sun's splendor resembled that of

> HARDY LAELIUS, that great GARTER-KNIGHT,
> Tilting in Triumph of ELIZA's Right. [133]

One year after Philisides was fatally wounded at Zutphen, Whitehall's glories were again delineated, but this time entirely within a pastoral framework. Angel Day's version of Longus's *Daphnis and Chloe* (1587) characterizes an Elizabethan translator at work, first drawing upon an intermediary rather than the original source, then superimposing verbal embellishments to satisfy the Renaissance doctrine of stepping beyond, next providing familiar vignettes according to native tradition, and consequently, despite similarities in plot and character, producing a work so utterly different from anything before as to make it his own creation. Curiously enough, Day's rhetorical elaborations represent a wholly unconscious return to the artificialities of the original. Although Longus's Greek, like Heliodorus's, is that of a Sophist, Day's own source, Jacques Amyot's *Les amours pastourales de Daphnis et Chloe* (1559), is "as innocent of artificialities as the lovers it depicts." [134] But Day's handling of Amyot is even freer than Belleforest's of Bandello. Whereas Amyot simply noted that Daphnis *saw* Chloe, for instance, Day's hero began "fastening his earnest lookes on her admirable beuties" and was "wholie confused by *Loue* the force whereof distilling amaine within him, had wrought to his most secret entrailes." [135] Amyot's most objective descriptions are thus expanded and made glossy; his accounts of the young lovers' sorrows are sentimentalized, and their first awakenings of passion, painted in vague, often elusive images. [136]

The purpose behind Day's innovations is quite clear. The innocent lovers, simple setting, and plain plot of Amyot's idyll invite tender, patronizing comments, exquisite displays of emotion, and glossy diction. Yet into this vague, sentimentally surcharged atmosphere Day introduces an adventitious element of hardy realism, touches of purely English country life. As Chloe's family prepares for dinner, "a mastiffe that was in the house . . . suddenly caught in his mouth a great peece of meate from the table, and," Day sadly explains, "the best and principall part of the same." [137] This incident is soon followed by Day's most arrant innovation, an excision of almost three-fourths of Amyot's Third Book and the substitution of his own pastoral flight, "The Shepheards Holidaie." Chloe bids Daphnis come to "a certaine yearly feast, euermore with great and most religious deuotion honoured among all the sheepeheards . . . of that Island, and all the territories therevnto adioyning." [138] The festival is graced by all the rustic nobility: Faustus, Philetas, "yong and gallant Thyrsis," and "auntient Titerus," each "descending out of the places most statelie of all that Island." [139]

The largest and most interesting part of the inserted episode is taken up with an eclogue praising "faire *Eliza*," which Day assigns to Meliboeus, "a graue old man," one of "the most artificial & cunning of the shepherds." [140] As if hymns to Elizabeth arising from Arcady's groves were not sufficiently incongruous, Day's artificial shepherd piles one curious mixture upon another. The world we enter remains basically a combination of fifth-century Lesbos and sixteenth-century Albion, but as Meliboeus notes, it also contains "noble worthies" and "stately knights," the "flowring state of *Rome*," "*Ida* woods and bankes of Muses nine," Minerva, Alcibiades, Charlemagne, Diana, Brute, and one King Edward.[141] And if Day's cunning old shepherd is the same person represented in Spenser's Meliboe, father-in-law to Sir Calidore, the praises of chaste nymphs and sylvan lovers have been dutifully chaunted by Sir Francis Walsingham, Secretary of State and chief of Gloriana's secret police.

An astute politician among Lesbian swains would not have made Day or any other Elizabethan *littérateur* uncomfortable. Each of the Queen's progresses saw courtiers and citizens abandoning chambers of state to don the garb of satyrs and hermits. Only the year before Deepedesire had left his holly thicket to command a regiment in the Netherlands. For deviser, narrator, or translator, Arcady was annually figured forth by the highest nobility, and when any theorist became a practicer, he too implied that such a magical place could support all times, customs, and matters.

With such fusions honored in the most fashionable circles, success awaited the writer whose charger was most artificially minced. The goal of both hack and genius was to find the right nowhere time and place, set within it as many relevant matters as possible, and adorn the whole with rhetorical bravery. Or, as Day himself confesses in his title, a microcosm of the movement, he who would surpass Ela must describe, interlace, and polish: *Daphnis and Chloe Excellently describing the weight of affection, the simplicitie of loue, the purport of honest meaning, the resolution of men, and disposition of Fate, finished in a Pastorall, and interlaced with the praises of a most peerlesse Princesse, wonderfull in Maiestie, and rare in perfection, celebrated within the same Pastorall, and therefore termed by the name of The Shepheards Holidaie.*

CUNNING . . . EXPRESSED IN THE MAKING

About one year after Lyly had gone to Pliny's bosom, Francis Beaumont brought to the Blackfriars Theatre a matter as hodge-podge as *Midas*. Unlike the Elizabethan and Jacobean devisings, it contained no shining presence under which all apparently contradictory traditions could be subsumed. Unlike Lyly's play, it revealed no anxieties concerning mingled life and mangled art. Instead, Beaumont created several worlds simply to have each grind against the others. In *The Knight of the Burning Pestle* (c. 1607), Jasper Merrythought's quest features all the machinery of romantic love-plotting and domestic intrigue, and Mistress Merrythought's, the very stuff of middle-class tragicomedy. Although both provide amusing comments on the bourgeois correlation between marriage and money, the main thrust of the playwright's gentle mockery is directed at two characters in the "audience," the Grocer and his wife, whose literary tastes instigate their apprentice's successive roles as ranting Hotspur, fearless Palmerin, Lord of the May, captain of a city regiment, and Senecan ghost. Despite the Prologue's efforts to center the action in Jasper's London adventures, Ralph the grocer-errant rides roughshod through each act, cheered on by the characters of the Induction. The foibles of Jasper's quest become clearer as the absurdities of Ralph's impinge upon them; the joke waxes as dramatic unity wanes. No play presents actors more conscious that they are acting, or makes its audience more aware that the worlds through which the characters stumble are mutually exclusive.

The invention of comedies to please the select, self-appointed intellectuals who frequented the private theaters in 1607 was relatively simple. One usually presented a merchant as a fool or miser, his goody as a slut, and his apprentice as either a clod or villain; each was then allowed to imitate his betters with feeble attempts at heroic or romantic actions. As Professor Harbage points out, Beaumont's play failed precisely because it did not adhere to the coterie formula. The bourgeoisie is not satirized with animosity; its "self-assertiveness . . . is treated as amusing rather than abhorrent."[142] Bypassing the conventional castigations of bourgeois ambitions, Beaumont uses the citizens of the Induction to express the middle class's more exotic literary tastes, and the characters in "The London Merchant" and "The Knight of the Burning Pestle" to burlesque its varied dreams of success. Taken individually, each of the three distinctly middle-class casts furnishes its own kind of comedy. But if the romantic appetites of James's humbler subjects account for the mock-heroic treatment of each plot, do they fully explain the comic interplay between the casts taken collectively, why the plots tend to mock one another? To some extent the latter "fault" is George the Grocer's. It is he who forces the Prologue to mingle Ralph with Jasper and thereby allow the discord of Merrythoughts and Moldavia. But surely neither George nor the good-natured Prologue reveals any awareness of the specious nature of such a fusion, the very point Beaumont underlines as the play goes out of control. Since the players would be true ("we intend no abuse to the city") and since George insists on relevance ("I will have a citizen, and he shall be of my own trade"),[143] there is a marriage of minds and consequently plots. The Prologue finishes his interrupted exposition, reminds the Grocer that he must look to his own additions to the play ("Ralph's part you must answer for yourself"), and the merry mixture begins.

To relish the full scope of Beaumont's fun, then, we should first note that the play not only burlesques romantic and bourgeois tastes, but also parodies a romantic and not exclusively bourgeois method. The Prologue proceeds on the principle of good business, and is therefore willing to admit any new matter as long as its contributor furnishes script and actors. In our own century he would never have seen the thematic difficulties of running one hero from the *Graustark* novels alongside another out of Horatio Alger. The playwright, on the other hand, proceeds on the princi-

ple of guilt by association: One kind of venture is bound to
qualify another, and certain multitudes cannot be seriously contained. Now Beaumont certainly realized that the technique he
parodied, if not the matters he burlesqued, was honored by courtly
devisers as well as scribbling citizens; and our suspicion that he was
subverting more than middle-class expectations is strengthened by
a preface to the play's second edition (1635).

> Gentlemen, the world is so nice in these our times, that
> for apparel there is no fashion; for music, which is a rare
> art (though now slighted), no instrument; for diet none
> but the French kickshaws that are delicate; and for plays
> no invention but that which now runneth an invective
> way, touching some particular persons, or else it is con-
> temned before it is throughly understood. This is all that
> I have to say: that the author had no intent to wrong any
> one in this comedy, but as a merry passage here and there
> interlaced it with delight, which he hopes will please all
> and be hurtful to none.[144]

It is difficult to believe that these scraps from *Midas*'s Prologue
were used by Beaumont's anonymous apologist simply as a gratuitous adornment. He seems to begin as a parodist and to conclude in
earnest. The verbal echoes would have been caught by his readers,
for *Midas* was one of the *Six Court Comedies . . . Written By the
onely Rare Poet of that Time, the Witie, Comicall, Facetiously-
Quicke, and vnparalell'd: Iohn Lilly*, which Blount issued in 1632.
These echoes, however, also further the spokesman's defense.
Through parody he seems to be inviting comparisons between these
very different yet equally unromantic comic playwrights. Like
Lyly, he implies, Beaumont faced a world excessively "nice,"
overly fashionable, and too prone to demand and then define the
limits of dramatic "invention." But having been encouraged to compare, we also discover some valid contrasts. Whereas Lyly bowed to
the fashion of his time and concocted a historical tragicomic pastoral, Beaumont turned from the early Jacobean "invective way"
and "interlaced . . . with delight." Lyly's select audience wanted
disparate traditions to be blended and made topical, and he obliged;
Beaumont's wanted savage satire and he gave them high comedy,
a facetious mingling of Bumbo Fair and the Kingdom of Cracovia.

Most important, Beaumont was attempting something quite new, truly inventive, whereas Lyly, for all his talk about "notes beyonde Ela," was capitalizing upon a kind of theater that had made him fashionable for almost a decade. In *Campaspe* (c. 1580) and in *Sapho and Phao* (c. 1581), he had inserted debates over the nature of passion, loyalty, and love into highly elaborate, artificial situations drawn from legend and myth. Designed to evoke arguments among the audience as to which lover suffered more, whose friendship was the stronger, and the like, his plays had enjoyed all the success Blount's title claims. In *Endymion* (c. 1585), his cerebral creatures had ascended to various rungs of Bembo's neo-Platonic ladder, encouraged by Cynthia's Perfect Beautie. Characteristically, however, they had done more talking than climbing. In each play extremely civilized people had gone through a ritualistic and rather repetitive performance. The mythological machinery had been popular at Court since Henry VII, and the arguments and characters familiar to courtiers since Castiglione. Although the Armada gave Lyly a new dish to include, *Midas* was basically more of the same thing, and even the now old-fashioned master must have sensed that some apology was in order.

Finally, in sounding their notes of invention, both playwrights produce discord within Arcadia, and the reasons for this may help us better understand the genuinely romantic comedies of Greene, Peele, and early Shakespeare. Beaumont's dissonance is of course intentional; he approaches his romantic materials with whimsical malice and aforethought, and allows them to clash within a world purged of sympathetic atmosphere. Lyly, on the other hand, pipes earnestly but with too much learning. Although his plays abound with romantic figures, from shepherds, foresters, and hermits to fairies, witches, and wise old wives, there are no lusty lovers or doughty doers, only resolute and witty pronouncers of courtly or academic sentiments. Shadowy, allegorical heroines are usually wooed with learned observations by scholarly abstractions, and they wander through their pleasant groves mainly to deface them with erudite theses. Although Beaumont steps inside the romantic tradition mainly to burlesque its bourgeois imitations, his mockery at least defines by negation what is proper to the world of romance. Among Lyly's surplus of characters who love to talk about love we occasionally find the faint outlines of a real lover, but his passion is kept soft and pale. In romance so rarefied, a world of gilt and pastels, flesh and blood would be indelicate, perhaps even obscene.

While Lyly was refining romance at Court and in the private theaters, the public stage was about to receive much more vital versions of Arcadia, the first successful dramatic realizations of those worlds that had for over fifteen years been greeting Gloriana. In *Friar Bacon and Friar Bungay* (c. 1591) and *James IV* (c. 1592), Robert Greene, sometime disciple of both Marlowe and Lyly, finally turned from the rant of foreign potentates and the rhetorical cunning of euphuistic courtiers to mingle the homely and exotic and thereby create an atmosphere that engenders belief in youthful love and courtship. With the advent of these fanciful yet recognizably English worlds, debates become deeds and rituals yield to exciting incidents. Casts of weary and wearisome talkers retire to watch real lovers declare their passion, endure its consequences, and eventually overcome all physical and social barriers. Lyly's witty mouthpieces are replaced by heroines who feel as well as think, lovely women wronged within a moral frame of reference, idealized through suffering rather than cerebration, and therefore fully human. Similarly, whether Greene's heroes are in love or lust, they are obviously more interested in the women they pursue than in the ideas their courtships are intended to suggest. Lyly keeps before us the artifice of balance and design; we are never tempted to take a potentially romantic episode as more than a small part of the working whole, the particular thesis that his "lovers" must dance out. Greene, on the other hand, begins with lovers in action; it is much easier to take their courtship as an end in itself, and only after a major crisis has been resolved do we find ourselves reflecting upon the meanings that have been advanced. Quite simply, Greene offers the never-smooth-running course of true love, whereas Lyly's dramatic appeal lies in the patterning of ideas represented through the pegs of character and plot. Greene points forward to soap opera; Lyly, backward to medieval and early Tudor disputations. Greene would have envied a modern director's freedom to assign the heroine's part to a woman; Lyly would have probably continued to use a bright little boy, lest emotion blur wit, or empathy with any dancer obscure the dance.

The most interesting thing about Greene's characters is that they remain vital and real, if not wholly realistic, despite the incredible events that befall them. Unlike Lyly, Greene never attempted to rarefy romance, to take from his plays the sense that anything can and probably will happen. Instead, the marvelous is multiplied and then supplemented with matters as disparate as Lyly's. Noting the "motley ingredients" of *Bacon and Bungay* and *James IV*, Tucker Brooke induced this formula: "Take a tangled love story involving rural scenes; mix with a like amount of fairy-lore or magical display; flavor with Plautine jokes, interlude devices (e.g., the Vice riding to hell on the devil's back), and classic reminiscence; color with a dash of pseudo-history; shake and serve." [145] Brooke's formula is accurately inferred: Greene's worlds abound with incredible incidents and seemingly impossible fusions. Nevertheless, we do not experience them in terms of the ingredients isolated by the formula, for the playwright usually manages to make the most oddly sorted elements homogeneous and to give all the improbabilities of romance an illusion of reality. As we shall soon see, atmosphere is both Greene's solvent and his catalyst, a sympathetic aura created by blending emotionally surcharged vignettes into an intricate series of exciting episodes and idealized relationships.

A playwright who wishes to honor romantic story cannot also reverence the unities of time and place. A skillful romancer, however, can attain a unity of mood, a spiritual wholeness, by making his lovers indigenous to their idyllic environment and giving them language that often amounts to incantation. Through such imaginative logic Greene renders the farfetched quite credible. And about one year after Greene's death, George Peele waded even farther. In *The Old Wives' Tale* (c. 1593), the real and unreal are so deftly mingled that we finally ask whether illusion lies within or without Arcadia. Within another year or two, Shakespeare marries human and fairy powers to produce his fanciful dream upon Midsummer Night (c. 1595), all the while realizing, like his Duke Theseus, that "the best in this kind are but shadows" (V. i. 210). If we take Shakespeare's best for granted and assume that the marvels of Arden and Bohemia were inevitable, it is easy to overlook the cunning of his predecessors. It was largely through Greene's and Peele's endeavors "in this kind" that the master found an audience familiar with and responsive to the mingling of noble lords with magicians and milkmaids, and could therefore freely postulate Athenian forests and enchanted islands, inhabited by fairies, lovers, monsters, and benevolent sorcerers. One of Shakespeare's earliest comedies, perhaps his first, *The Comedy of Errors* (c. 1589–1593), mainly follows the old classical lines. But his last plays are dramatized fairy tales into which are inserted problems that could not even be entertained within the realistic confines of "this-worldliness."

Matters impossibly incongruous under any other than romantic premises are happily blended. It is important to realize that when Greene and Peele unveiled their Arcadias, they were doing as much wading as Shakespeare. Genius saw fit to exploit precedents, to invent through innovating upon notes already sounded. Before the advent of Shakespeare's humble precursors, the London stage had never been graced with anything even approximating romantic atmosphere.

Potentially romantic themes had of course been dramatized long before Greene. At least two early Tudor Humanists set upon private stages plots drawn from the prose fiction of their Italian and Spanish contemporaries. Bonaccorso's *De Vera Nobilitate,* for example, relates the wooing of a beautiful Roman gentlewoman by two amorous rivals, a pleasure-loving aristocrat and a virtuous man of lowly origin.[146] But as its title indicates, the story is less a romance than a treatise on worthiness, a vehicle for the views of the heroine, her father, and her suitors concerning the true nature of nobility. About 1497, Henry Medwall dramatized the marriage problem in *Fulgens and Lucres,* the first purely secular English play. Although Medwall thus departs from Biblical themes and allegorical methods, and although he has the dramatic sense to flesh out his series of set speeches with a comic underplot in which the two rivals' servants engage in native high jinks for the favor of Lucres's handmaid, his end is as rational as Bonaccorso's, and even more didactic. The "disputacyon of noblenes," [147] not romantic love, is his real concern. To which suitor should Lucres render her obedience and worldly goods? All has been set in motion for her resolution:

> But unto the blood I will have little respect
> Where the conditions be sinful and abject.[148]

Her creator agrees, and concludes Bonaccorso's unresolved account by having his heroine choose the lowly but virtuous lover.

Medwall's is the first of many Tudor plays that remain essentially unromantic despite plots in which boys want and get girls. In *Calisto and Meliboea,* one of his contemporaries (probably John Rastell) turned Fernando de Rojaz's *Celestina* into a treatise on the importance of proper education for the young and the necessity of good laws and legislators.[149] Boy gets no more than one meeting with girl before the playwright's social and political concerns obliterate his source's romantic intrigue. It is not surprising that for all their lively incidents, language, and individualized characters, the early Tudor dramatists produced what are essentially moralities in disguise. They had little inspiration from native dramatic custom, which was romantic only in its undisciplined refusal to be yoked to the "classical" unities; heavy didacticism sweetened by boisterous merriment is not the stuff of Arcadia. Plautus and Terence, on the other hand, although full of intricate plotting, offered very little romance in the intrigues between father, son, courtesan, rival, and wily slave. The focus is always on the comedy of their errors, and in those rare cases where relationships are more than crisp and impersonal or actions not simply clever and amoral, they are hardly sentimental, tender, or otherwise idealized. It was of course possible to make Roman comedy yield either ethical statements or romantic concerns. Although the pre-Elizabethan playwrights often performed the former (for example, *Thersites*, c. 1540; *Jack Juggler*, c. 1555), there is nothing extant to indicate that the latter was ever even attempted.

During the second half of the century between Medwall and Greene, numerous translations and transfigurations of romantic fiction helped to influence the transition from comedies of instruction to those mainly for delight. It is not surprising to find the lovers celebrated in prose and poetry for hundreds of years finally brought into drama, nor difficult to understand why those who first made the effort to stage romance lost the essential element of atmosphere. What is startling is that the attempt was not made sooner, and that success came so slowly. But we must be patient with those artists who worked toward what became obvious only after they had mastered it. By 1582 the puritanical Stephen Gosson is able to complain that "the Palace of pleasure, the Golden Asse, The Oethiopian historie, Amadis of Fraunce, The Rounde Table, bawdie Comedies in Latine, French, Italian and Spanish, have been throughly ransackt to furnish the Playe houses in London." [150] Although it is unlikely that Gosson exaggerates the wealth of amorous matters that were being drawn into the dramatic repertories, the majority of these plays has perished, and in the few that have survived there are but faintly colored signposts to Arcadia. In no extant play, for instance, do we find youthful love set within a sympathetic, idealized atmosphere. About 1566 Gascoigne "ransackt" Ariosto's *I Suppositi*, wove into his translation-adaptation a contemporary English setting [151] and lengthy, sentimental speeches, excised his model's amoral mood, and set before the gentlemen of Gray's Inn his *Supposes*. Although the beautiful Polynesta is made the center of several intrigues, Gascoigne is preoccupied with the duplicities employed to gain her hand in marriage rather than showing how her heart was won. It is significant that her true love's courtship is described only in retrospect, and that although even the classical parasite and irascible old men turn out to be fundamentally decent people, the heroine was bedded before the play begins. The rest of Gosson's "bawdie Comedies" lack not only bawdy but romantic interest. Nicholas Udall's *Ralph Roister Doister* (c. 1553) sets Plautus's braggart soldier within a wholly English setting, reduces the complexities of classical plotting, and emphasizes Ralph's wooing of a virtuous widow. Like Beaumont, however, Udall uses romance as fuel for comedy; his Ralph is at once Roman braggart, medieval worthy, Petrarchan lover, and English bumpkin.

With possibly two exceptions, extant Elizabethan comedies prior to Greene and Peele do not even reveal an interest in romantic love-plotting. In E. K. Chambers's compilation of surviving plays,[152] we find continuations of medieval moralities and early Tudor interludes, Senecan tragedies, native chronicles, folk tales, domestic farces, classical comedies, dramatized courtly or academic debates, and varying amalgamations of each. The two exceptions, *Sir Clyomon and Clamydes* (c. 1570) and *Common Conditions* (c. 1575), both evince a serious interest in delineating the fortunes of real lovers, freely entertain the miraculous, and scorn the unities in honest native fashion. So diverse are the romantic materials packed into them that each could answer to Gosson's "Oethiopian historie" as well as to his "Amadis of Fraunce" and "The Rounde Table." The properties they employ are like those listed in the Accounts of the Revels Office—castles, savages, enchanters, "& incydentes to theis"—and the complex actions they portray are pointed up by Sidney's censure: "you shal haue *Asia* of the one side, and *Affrick* of the other, and so many other vnder-kingdoms, that the Player, when he commeth in, must euer begin with telling where he is, or els the tale wil not be conceiued." [153] These two plays are simply the remnants of "al the rest," against which he contrasts the lofty *Gorboduc*.

If Greene found nothing better to draw from within the drama proper,[154] his step beyond was certainly a mighty one. Although both *Sir Clyomon* and *Common Conditions* are romantic in plot, character, and theme, neither blends these elements to produce a refined, idyllic aura. All save the comic figures are assigned four-teeners, easy lines to memorize, but hardly the language of incantation and seldom known to evoke an illusion of reality. The lovers, even in their very love-making, cannot resist horrendous allusions to mythological monsters and heroes, and therefore are themselves partly responsible for the crude, unsympathetic backdrop against which they must love. In *Sir Clyomon*, Juliana offers her heart to Clamydes if he will but slay the flying serpent. The hero cannot accept without first stressing the dangers he faces:

> Ah Lady, if case these trauels should surmount, the trauels
>   whereby came
> Vnto the worthies of the world, such noble brute and fame,
> Yea though the dangers should surpasse stout *Hercules*
>   his toyle,
> Who fearing nought the dogged feend, sterne *Serbarus*
>   did foyle.
> Take here my hand, if life and limbe the liuing Gods
>   do lend,
> To purchase thee, the dearest drop of bloud my heart
>   shall spend.[155]

Equally prone to vaunts, Lamphedon of *Common Conditions* woos Clarisia in an even more grisly Senecan fashion:

> Else all the powers that sits in throne do end with cruell
>   dent
> My youthfull dayes, and after that with *Pluto* let me rayne,
> Where as the greesly Hags do rest with trebell care and
>   payne.
> And therefore Lady, here is my hande, eke faith and trouth
>   I giue.[156]

Complementing such drab fustian is the uncourtly behavior of the heroes and the unrefined sentiments of the heroines. The knights-errant are usually more interested in proving their man-hood than in winning their ladies. Clamydes slays the serpent, but before he can exchange its head for Juliana's hand, a cowardly knight-necromancer, one "Bryan sance foy," steals the prize and rides off to claim her for himself. Clamydes decides it is more

knightly to break his vow to Juliana than to fail to keep his promise
to appear in combat against Clyomon.[157] Equally unappealing are
the maids forlorn. Greene will soon cast a sentimental aura about
his lovely women by making them delicate and shy, and then having them wronged. Sabia, the rejected heroine of *Common
Conditions,* is not only indelicate but somewhat too realistic:

> Like as the Rat that once hath tast of *Rosalgar* or bayne,
> Runnes presently to some moist place to coole her poisned
>   pain:
> So I being possest (alas) through *Cupids* dierfull dent,
> Doth liue in pyning state for aye, that life is well ny spent,
> Ha sweet *Nomides* who causer art of this my griefe and
>   wo.[158]

Sweet Nomides thereupon enters in customary manner:

> Though raging stormes of winters force hath done their
>   worst to spoyle
> Though *Boreas* w[ith] his boisterous blasts doth range
> in euery soyle.

He eventually rants his way into identifying himself, is fiercely
wooed by winsome Sabia, scorns her suit, and rides off.[159]

    Such jarring notes were the natural results of these playwrights'
innocent eclecticism, their desire to make room for the new
while saving the old at any cost. They wished to profit by the
brave new artifice of the fourteener, by the recent experiments
with Senecan rhetoric, situations, and sentiments at the Inns of
Court, and by all the rich varieties of romantic story lately adapted
in prose narration and dramatized on country lawns. Even Bryan
Sans Foi is as much the classical braggart soldier as the cowardly
medieval chevalier. Perhaps the most adventitious elements are
those figures drawn from earlier native dramatic traditions, characters who are simply "also there," ingested but never incorporated.
Clarisia's crafty servant, Common Conditions, for instance, is a
mixture of the medieval Vice and the Plautine parasite. Little effort
is made to shape one role to the other, and even less to reconcile
either to the romantic design of the whole. His presence apparently reflects the customary desire to include the readily familiar, an earthy everyday. Perhaps his capricious pranks, which
dictate so much of the plotting, were also meant to replace Dame

Fortune's wheel,[160] but none of the perfidious Lady's turns could have ruined the bittersweet aura of love as effectively as his mischief-making and low humor. Subtle Shift, the wily, obscene page to both Clyomon and Clamydes, produces the same discord. Old-fashioned abstractions also make their several entrances. Providence, Jove's messenger, descends to admonish Princess Neronis against suicide, and Rumor comes in to noise Mustantius's usurpation of his brother's crown throughout Norway, Swabia, Denmark, Macedonia, the Isle of Marshes, and the rest of the play's rapidly shifting locales.[161]

In attempting to realize the world of romance, both playwrights therefore erred in almost every respect. They chose the worst possible medium of expression, mistaking the long-winded for the heroic, ranting harangues for passionate utterances. They failed to realize that dramatization necessitates selectivity, and endeavored to include every intricate twist and complex device of romantic plot and machinery. In juxtaposing court and country life, they never attempted to make them homogeneous; the first is impossibly high-flown, the second completely boorish. *Sir Clyomon*'s pastoral sequence, for example, features an all-too-realistic shepherd, Corin, conventional in name only. It is difficult to take love seriously when set against a landscape dotted with louts; we should prefer even the sometimes overly polished diction of Arcady to "Cham but vather *Coryn* the sheepheard, cham no furringer I." [162] Finally, their inclusion of native stock types like the Vice and Rumor hindered the development of an idealized atmosphere. Although these worlds hold little promise of what was to supplant them less than two decades later, we must not allow the jog trot, coarse humor, farcical actions, or Senecan-sounding lords and ladies to obscure the evidence of wading farther. Here at least are attempts to transfer the promising stuff of love and adventure to the stage, to realize the romantic spirit as an end in itself rather than using its expressions as vehicles for moral, political, or philosophical issues. Lyly's temporary vogue helped to destroy even these feeble strains of romantic invention.

When Greene and Peele began their own quests for Arcadia in the early 1580's, then, the stages of city and palace offered only two precedents for romantic comedy: Lyly's cerebral worlds of talkers about love, and lands like that of *Sir Clyomon*'s, full of real yet unconvincing lovers, struggling less against villains than old-fashioned dramatic conventions and their own inane heroics. Fortunately, they had other models, quasi-dramatic yet supraromantic, the temporary stages erected in city squares and country gardens. The occasional nature of these programs—a different lord mayor from another guild, the same Sovereign but new courtiers with fresh ideas seeking different favors—encouraged an assimilation of the latest literary fashions as well as allusions to the most recent international events. Having never stood within the tradition of drama proper and prone to capitalize upon whatever seemed *avant-garde*, this theater was flexible, experimental, and readily willing to abandon dumb shows, abstract personae, earthy mischief, and other earlier dramatic devices. Most important, since these courtly and civic displays were designed mainly to sponsor the marvelous and thereby reflect the splendor of the principal "actor," they tended to avoid the rational and didactic emphases of the interlude. While Medwall and Rastell were appropriating romantic situations to serve as bases for dignified treatises, Henry VIII was pricking through the greenwood with Robin Hood or, aided by his retainers, successfully dramatizing romance with assaults upon pasteboard castles. And while Lyly was conscripting mythological figures to illustrate neo-Platonic tenets, honest Arion bestrode his docile dolphin, Sylvanus mustered his woodland recruits, and a coy Daphne waited to pounce upon the Queen of Chastity. City street and country lawn became neutral lands under the influence of Majesty; recognizably English by their very settings, they nevertheless welcomed classical heroes, native sprites, and medieval lovers. Whatever worlds the royal conjurers postulated, they were filled not only by expatiating mouthpieces but also, as Zabeta's horse could testify, with lively actions. Aided by all the color and sound of pageantry, the imagination could amend what was lacking in these re-creations of former fabulous story.

What the theater needed was someone who could tap the rich streams of invention flowing beneath such romantic mimesis. Could the marvels of boscage and garden be transferred to a relatively bare London stage without losing their idyllic settings? Could the same multiplicity of traditions be given articulation without having one world outshout the others? Could mere words be used to evoke the spells cast by the expensive machinery at Kenilworth, Norwich, Whitehall, and Elvetham, words so cunningly contrived that they could create even within a dirty city playhouse that neither wholly native nor completely faraway atmosphere of Lee's magical Woodstock? To capitalize upon situations suggested by shrieking Daphnes, thunderstruck savage men, or an obeisant Lady of the Lake, one needed an ability to blend in the right proportions and to unify the whole through some theme other than Gloriana's perfection. Curiously enough, it was Greene, the roguish, poverty-stricken bohemian of Shoreditch, who first managed the conversion, and Peele, a professional writer of adulatory programs, who first burlesqued their specious fusions and thus heralded Beaumont's gentle mockery.

Both Greene and Peele had ample opportunities to be affected by civic and courtly entertainments. Peele not only contributed to the Lord Mayors' shows of 1585, 1588, and 1591, but presented his *Arraignment of Paris* at Court about 1584, and was on hand to describe Sir Henry Lee's retirement extravaganza of 1590. Greene's native Norwich, according to Churchyard, established a precedent for civic receptions in August, 1578. Greene received his B.A. from St. John's, Cambridge, that same year, and may have returned home to watch the festivities. As a saddler, his father probably took his place among the busy artisan-painters of the city; saddles were often painted and the painters were, in fact, originally members of the saddlers' guild.[163] It is even possible that both Greene and his father had a hand in decorating Churchyard's splendid coach. Peele's father, of course, had often contributed to London's pageants.

The earliest and clearest example of how Greene and Peele turned progresses into plays is the latter's *Arraignment of Paris*, published and probably acted in 1584.[164] In building upon one of the most popular commonplaces of Renaissance classicism, the story about Paris's choice of Venus's "beauty" over Juno's "wealth" and Pallas's "chivalry" (IV. iv. 110), Peele certainly had one eye upon courtly pastimes. Simply in terms of specific borrowings, Pallas's reference to Elizabeth as "she whom some Zabeta call" (V. i. 93) points back to the Queen's sojourn at Kenilworth in 1575, when Gascoigne invented the term "Zabeta" to celebrate that nymph superior to all other deities. Granted, the judgment motif was one of the few flattering strings Leicester's professionals had failed to touch. In comparing the techniques through which Peele created his world and the devisers theirs, however, the absence of Paris at Kenilworth is no more significant than the presence of "Zabeta" within *The Arraignment*. For the suggestion that Ate's golden ball really belonged to Elizabeth, Peele had almost a century of adulatory poems and programs on which to draw. In *The*

Grief of Joye, a gift Gascoigne presented to the Queen on New Year's Day, 1577, the courtier concludes by vowing that had Elizabeth

> sat in feeld
> When Paris judged that Venus bare the bell,
> The prize were hers, for she deserved it well.[165]

The same sentiment was presumably staged as early as 1503, when Margaret Tudor was welcomed to Edinburgh by "Paris and the Thre Deessys, with Mercure," and London set forth a similar show to celebrate Anne Boleyn's coronation thirty years later. The latter, devised by Nicholas Udall, has Paris first select Venus, then notice "a fouerthe lady now in presence," and deliver Ate's fatal fruit to Henry's Queen, along "with certain verses of great honour." [166] So common was this device in an era of classicism and flattery that Elizabeth, like her aunt and mother, was destined eventually to encounter some fawning Trojan shepherd.

Peele's real debt to the devising, then, is not to be summed up in lists of common plots, themes, and figures. It is rather reflected in the way his virtually plotless play is shaped, especially in *The Arraignment*'s heavy reliance upon song and spectacle to attain a lyrical, essentially masklike effect. How Peele first conceived an interest in what we should call "scenic effect" is difficult to say. Perhaps the Oxford undergraduate spent part of the summer of 1575 in neighboring Warwickshire and witnessed Kenilworth's marvels. But an eye for spectacle was certainly revealed four years later when the Oxford M.A. took his Homer, Ovid, Virgil, Chaucer, and Caxton in hand and commenced *The Tale of Troy*, a 485-line medievalized epitome of the *Iliad*.[167] To rehearse the whole Trojan tragedy, from Hecuba's dream to Aeneas's flight, in fewer than five hundred lines is of course impossible. But Peele seems less interested in narrating all the "facts" than in setting up a series of tableaux representing the story's most colorful scenes and then moralizing over the characters' actions. The spirit in which these pictures are conceived is partly medieval, partly modern, and therefore typically Elizabethan. The English patriot must commend his ancient sire, "the good Aneas," and curse the "traytrous" Greeks (ll. 413, 451, 478). Despite his Oxford M.A., the imaginative Elizabethan cannot resist the emotional nourishment of the *Roman de Troie;* hence those knights who "twist their Ladies coullers on their Launce" (l. 277). Finally there is the up-to-date Elizabethan, exploiting the currently fashionable pastoralism and archaic language of *The Shepheardes Calender* and dismissing his medieval commentaries to chide the unfortunate Paris with neo-Platonic proverbs. If only that fond shepherd had "discerned well, / Where the true beautie of the mind did dwell." [168]

Shortly before 1584 Peele was granted a chance to capitalize upon the research that had gone into his Trojan tableaux as well as to establish himself as a Court deviser. The Children of the Chapel were to perform before the Queen, and Peele was commissioned to make the play. How was the twenty-six-year-old would-be courtier to capture the royal eye? The answer probably came in the form of a question: What indoor winter revel could please Majesty better than a re-creation of those groves and bowers that always enchanted her summer excursions? One section of *The Tale of Troy* furnished a motif that had evidently not been set in motion since London's reception of Elizabeth's mother in 1533. This theme in turn furnished a setting, the innocent world of Ida, and therefore an opportunity to appropriate recently popular pastoral debates. Sidney had spelled the way with his contest of shepherds and foresters at Wanstead Garden in May, 1578, and the New Poet had gained admiration with similar elements the following year. All that remained for Peele was to cultivate one of *The Tale's* already luxuriant scenes and to translate pastoral description into lyric utterance and sensuous display. Both requirements were within Peele's power. His inclination to pause and sing hinders the narration of *The Tale,* and scenic effect, on or off the boards, was his forte. In June, 1583, shortly before *The Arraignment* was first performed, Peele was called to Oxford to assist in producing several shows for Count Albertus Alasco.[169] His services, like those of a modern technical director of musical comedy, included the supervision of lights, costuming, and scenery.

For a writer whose interest and abilities hardly lay, like Greene's, in the realm of complex plotting or, like Lyly's, in the skillful development of related ideas, the dramaturgy of Gloriana's private stage was naturally attractive. The devisers had frequently set forth places like Ida in terms of Albion, and entertained more through a rich variety of visual and tonal effects than with subtle philoso-

phizing or complicated narrative movement. They had also encouraged "literature" as long as it did not assume undue importance; set passages of poetry were in fact necessary to insure that
the wondrous spectacles that unfolded and the inevitable compliments would be fully understood. Above all, they offered young
Peele an essentially nondramatic theater, rarely honoring even contemporary notions concerning character in conflict. For what character development could there be when personages as apparently
different as knights, satyrs, shepherds, goddesses, and milkmaids
spoke mainly of the common affection that had brought them
forth? And what conflict could arise between characters who
argued almost solely about whose esteem was the greatest? If these
creatures came from different worlds with claims and gifts decorously varied, they were all obviously there for the same reason, as
parts of a common theme rather than an organic narrative. The
only business that tied them together, the only plot in which they
were logically associated, was not to be found within the pieces of
make-believe they advanced. The entertainment's structural unity
lay rather in the real story behind the scenes, the business of courting, the plot against the Queen.

The business of courting, of course, necessitated wading farther,
and Peele was not content merely to show how well he could
handle new poetic forms, including blank verse, or simply to expand the pastoral scenes of Kenilworth, Woodstock, and Wanstead
into a full-blown pastoral drama. One of the tableaux over which
he had lingered in *The Tale*, the happy bygone time when Flora
"deck'd the earth with yellow, blew and greene" (l. 76), could be
adapted to the devisers' most popular motif, the metamorphosis
of wood and field under Majesty's transfiguring influence. The
flattering resolution of Paris's misjudgment also lent itself to a
highly creative imitation. The swain's hitherto hurried decision for
the "fouerthe lady now in presence" could be temporarily suspended to allow the playwright to parade his knowledge of courtly
issues. Somewhat along the lines of the now fashionable Lyly, Peele
could have his characters represent the claims of power, wisdom,
and love. After matching the master with his goddesses' arguments
and assigning each of them a spectacle for good measure, he would
step beyond with a trial scene, Paris's arraignment. Into the prose-
cution's case he would work some legal terminology acquired
from his friends at the Inns of Court,[170] and the defense had only
to develop the excuse provided for Paris in *The Tale* (ll. 113–118).

By holding up the conclusion until Olympus had been consulted, he would gain a level of worship beyond which even the sycophantic Leicester and Lyly dared not venture.

Peele's reliance upon the devisers' techniques makes it difficult to discuss *The Arraignment* in terms usually applicable to the drama of the period. But before the play proper had even begun, from the moment Ate, his Senecan figurine, brandished her golden prize, Peele's first audience realized they were about to see an imitation of a re-creation. Rather than expecting a richness of character, plot, or ideas, they waited to see how the spiteful Prologue's "tragedy of Troy" would be turned into a delicate minuet of artificial situations, gorgeous display, and elaborately contrived compliments. And what they received is little more than a series of glossy vignettes, each formally introducing sets of characters and patterns of verse forms. Peele makes the artificiality of his world especially clear in the first four scenes. Since his characters are either on progresses themselves or busily preparing ceremonious receptions, their movements are largely ritualistic. Dialogue is also quite formal. Each "country god" enters in rustic pomp, describes the "store" he shall offer, and comments on the forthcoming royal entry of the three goddesses into Diana's pastoral Kingdom of Ida. Anyone fresh from Kenilworth senses that he is covering old ground and renewing recent acquaintances. Even the sentiments strike a familiar chord. Faunus assures Pomona that "a mighty person" takes delight in the simple gifts scorned by those "basely born" (I. ii. 5 ff.). And in forty-six lines of luscious description, Flora proclaims the "second spring" she has prepared and explicates the floral "devices" now burgeoning about Diana's "bower" (I. iii. 10 ff.).

Nothing characterizes Peele's theater as well as Flora's scenic proclamation and one of his own stage directions, "*An artificial charm of birds . . . heard within*" (I. ii. 97). For every line narrating action there are a dozen that define the movement with a wealth of pictorial comment. Every event appears calculated to produce a delicate song or songlike sentiment, a stately dance, or a spectacular display. As the goddesses journey along "the painted paths of pleasant Ida" (I. iv. 53), the next set of characters, Paris and Oenone, comes forth to rehearse the fabled metamorphoses of sundry lovers and to sing and pipe "Cupid's Curse." Peele fails to develop the irony implicit in their vows of affection; it is the couple's sweet "ditty," not their place in the story, that chiefly interests him. Their counterparts, Colin and Thestylis, serve the same purpose. Although Peele brings in Spenser's shepherd partly to parallel his plight with the unfortunate Oenone's, Colin is mainly used for additional exquisite sentiment. His lyrical sorrows, which completely occupy one scene (III. i), give rise to the comments of Hobbinol, Diggon, and Thenot upon the pains of love. Out of such a situation Lyly would have produced an elaborate debate concerning Cupid's power and curse. Peele bypasses learned discourse for delicate atmosphere and therefore, like many a medieval lyricist, sets the swain's anguish against his cheerful, springtime surroundings (III. ii. 9 ff.).

As we might expect from any play produced at Court during Lyly's vogue, *The Arraignment* does incorporate snatches of fashionable themes and stylized conversations. Despite her broken heart, the nymph Oenone plays a facile game of courtly, topical exchanges with Mercury (III. iv. 20 ff.), and both country gods and Olympian goddesses engage in formal banter (I. ii; II. i.). In Venus's commentary upon the hell that awaits forsworn lovers and in her punishment of scornful Thestylis (III. v.), Peele again reminds us of Lyly, balancing one character's case against another's and exploiting Petrarchan stances and attitudes. But once more the similarity soon fades: Venus finishes her sermon; the shepherds enter in pastoral state, hymning a dirge and bearing Colin's hearse; Thystelis then comes in, wooing "*a foul, crooked Churl*" with sonnet stuff, to which the shepherds respond antiphonally (III. v. 45 ff.). It is difficult to imagine Lyly ever allowing a character to die simply for visual and tonal effects. At least some further use would have been made of parallel situations, if only to encourage questions about which lover suffered more or whose guilt was greater. For Peele, it suffices to center sets of characters in a final flourish of display. "*The grace of this song is in the Shepherds' echo to her* [Thestylis's] *verse*," he explains in one of those many extremely important stage directions (III. v. 78). One senses that most of the scene, as well as the song, has been set up for this "grace." Owing to Peele's enchantment with Dame Echo, one of Gascoigne's braver Kenilworth devices, Colin's epitaph is hurried over. Nor do we again see or hear anything of Oenone, Hobbinol, Diggon, Thenot, or Thystelis. Their brief stories are momentary adornments, pretty pieces by the wayside, neither advancing the main action nor really contributing to the principal theme. "Cupid's Curse" proves a red herring; its pretty reflections are like tinsel, strung out for glitter and then removed.

Peele naturally reserved his greatest display for the series of scenes delineating Paris's judgment and trial. Although the pastoral lyricist verges at this point upon the perilous confines of narrative, the dance quickly reasserts primary importance. Despite the playwright's direction that Venus speak *"ex abrupto"* (II. i. 1), spontaneous interchange soon yields to patterned speeches; having now reached Diana's bower, the goddesses thrust and parry with slanderous couplets. Peele next conjures up some convenient thunder and lightning, wheels in Ate and her fatal fruit, and then has each goddess explicate its "posy" in identical triplets, thrice repeated. The formula is continued as each steps forth to prove her claim. Since none relates her argument to those of her peers, we get something closer to a series of independent pronouncements than real dialogue—beauty belongs to station, to love, to the mind. And though these tags are turned into verbal vignettes and showy devices in the succeeding scene, the measured steps are maintained: Juno's *"Tree of Gold, laden with diadems"* and its sumptuous description; Pallas's *"Nine Knights in armour, treading a warlike almain"* and its exciting promises; Venus's *"Helen . . . in her bravery, with four Cupids attending"* and its irresistible prospects. Upon these shows, which the humble swain finds "Able to rape and dazzle human eyes" (II. ii. 96), Peele hangs all the remaining action of his virtually plotless devising. The complimentary resolution is determined by the trial, the trial by Paris' choice, and the choice by pageantry. Like the plots which unfolded amid Kenilworth's groves, Peele's incidents seem to have been shaped to highlight mimetic display; his slight excuse for narrative movement is the logical end of a theater that continually subordinated story to show, character development to costuming.

From the moment the Prologue held up her "bane of Troy," any half-versed courtier among Peele's first audience would have been able to supply the resolution. Judgment naturally lent itself to flattery; eventually the three queens on their vernal progress would kneel before another Queen holding her winter court. When Paris made his decision, the absence of that traditional "fouerthe lady" must therefore have been singularly conspicuous. The swain's trial is Peele's only major narrative innovation, an unexpected departure from an otherwise shopworn motif. By having Jupiter, at Juno's and Pallas's "suit," arraign the shepherd on charges of partiality, Peele manages to include a touch of contemporary England, the world of legal plots and counterplots that seems to have fascinated both courtier and citizen as much as spectacle. Venus must surrender her fan as "bail" to answer the "action . . . enter'd in the court of heaven" (III. vi. 7 ff.). The trial also affords Peele chances to draw once again upon the pageantry of streets and lawns: ostentatious entrances like Pluto's, who *"ascendeth from below in his chair"* (IV. iii. 9); a stage crowded with glittering personages: an "oration" before the Olympians assembled "in Dian's grove." Finally, the arraignment scene allows the craftsman to justify his kind of theater, to defend his sensuous "senseless" world of colorful, unrelated events and sparkling, vacuous characters. Surrounded by all the rich display Peele can muster, Paris excuses himself for having been captivated by the visual:

> I was guerdoned,
> And tempted more than ever creature was
> With wealth, with beauty, and with chivalry,
> And so preferr'd beauty before them all,
> The thing that hath enchanted heaven itself.
>
> (IV. iv. 108–112)

To conclude his delicate devising, Peele once more exploits the concept of beauty's universal appeal. The theme that has already linked Ida to Olympus now brings both worlds into that of his audience. Duly impressed by Paris's defense, Jupiter's court determines that Diana is best able to judge between her peers. With the title "To the fairest" at stake, and with all parties vowing to rest by her decision, *"Diana describeth the Nymph Eliza, a figure of the Queen"* (V. i. 54). Like the goddesses' patterned pronouncements that precede and succeed it, Diana's description is a series of balanced, complimentary epithets. The *"Angeli"* of "Elyzium," that "second Troy," are ruled by one as chaste as Diana, as majestic as Juno, as wise and mighty as Pallas, and as lovely as Love's Queen. The contestants immediately realize that this superior creature is Zabeta, at whose birth Flora decked the earth, the Graces cast forth balm, and Cupid himself was blinded. Music sounds, *"Nymphs within sing,"* the Dames of Life and Destiny surrender their fatal instruments as tokens of esteem, the goddesses do obeisance, Diana finally *"delivereth the ball of gold to the Queen's own hands,"* and the theater of song and dance concludes with a characteristic wealth of flourish and poverty of subtle signification.

And as we watch what at first seemed an imitation of a reception finally turning into the thing itself, we again recall the difficulty of distinguishing between drama and devising. Our original question was whether this play is like a progress; we now ask whether this progress is really a play. Has not Peele simply brought into the Queen's theater more plot and better poetry than it usually enjoyed? Certainly within drama proper the Olympians, if they appear at all, are treated respectfully. Even Lyly, who fleshes out his treatises with masklike stuff, never handles his goddesses so cavalierly; like the rest of his characters, they at least represent important courtly opinions. Peele makes them into mere stepping-stones to Elizabeth's canopy. And if the drama before Peele often produces a classical-medieval-rustical-courtly world, the hodge-podge appears to result from an innocent confusion of times and matters, not from a calculated attempt to engender a neutral, time-less land. The inhabitants of Ida and Olympus, dancing an adulatory pavan about the Queen, is hardly an example of a *littérateur* naïvely treating the past in present terms. It is rather a conscious juxtaposition of traditions to represent the universality of affection, a reminiscence of Leicester's varied casts falling before "rare beutie and princelie countenance." If Peele has done a small thing, he has done it remarkably well.

Several years after Peele displayed his cunning at Court, Robert Greene brought to the public stage a group of equally spectacular and even more exotic devisings: *The Comicall Historie of Alphonsus King of Aragon* (c. 1588), *A Looking Glasse, for London and Englande* (with Thomas Lodge, c. 1589), and *The Historie of Orlando Furioso, One of the Twelve Peeres of France* (c. 1590). At first glance the differences between the glories of Ida as hymned by Peele, and those of Naples, Nineveh, and North Africa as ranted by Greene, seem overwhelming. Whereas Peele subordinates story to sensuous description, Greene concentrates upon heroic actions and evinces little patience with sylvan prospects. Upon further examination, however, Greene's indebtedness to the entertainment appears almost as great as Peele's. The differences are largely the result of common stimuli operating upon craftsmen with dissimilar interests and abilities. From the royal devisers each borrowed those techniques and materials best suited to his own purposes. If previous experience made it only natural for Peele to incline to the sweet piping and sentiment of Zabeta's idyllic meanderings, Greene's fascination with Marlowe's mighty lines, characters, and stages led him to gravitate toward the heroics of street and tiltyard.

In 1588 Greene informed the gentlemen readers of *Perimedes The Blacke-Smith,* one of his thirty-six "golden discourses," that although his recent efforts at tragedy had been ridiculed, he would at least continue writing narrative fiction: "I keepe my old course, to palter vp some thing in Prose, . . . although latelye two Gentlemen Poets . . . had it in derision, for that I could not make my verses iet vpon the stage in tragicall buskins, euerie worde filling the mouth like the faburden of Bo-Bell, daring God out of heauen with that Atheist *Tamburlan.*" [171] Despite his professed disdain for Marlowe's buskin in particular and the public theater in general, Greene quickly supplemented his first failure, very likely *Alphonsus,* with two endeavors almost as awkward, the *Looking Glasse* and *Orlando.* With such vengeance do all three plays undertake *Tamburlaine*'s vein that modern critics often regard them as feeble jokes. Messrs. Parrott and Ball, for example, consider *Alphonsus* "incredibly bad, so bad indeed that some have supposed it rather a parody than an imitation of Marlowe's play," while *Orlando* "seems to have been planned as a conscious burlesque. . . . It seems unlikely that so clever a man as Greene should have taken such stuff seriously." [172] We shall never know, of course, how Greene really felt about the heroic and romantic traditions he dramatized. But in Alexander Grosart's fifteen-volume edition of Greene's *Complete Works,* we rarely find the slightest inclination to burlesque. The cleverness is rather that of a man who found exploitation more profitable than ridicule. The preface to *Perimedes* suggests that like us, Greene's own contemporaries found his first effort to step beyond Marlowe wasteful and ludicrous; it also suggests, however, that they regarded the attempt as wholly serious, and Greene's reply does not bespeak the indignation of a misunderstood parodist. It is therefore likely that Greene's mistakes are those of an apprentice who isolates the most characteristic elements of his master's successes and earnestly multiplies by ten. *Richard III* reflects young Shakespeare's similar zeal to steal Kyd's and Marlowe's theatrical-rhetorical thunder.

Throughout Greene's early plays, then, we discover bombast and bathos. Tamburlaine's vaunts are echoed, inverted, accented, and almost invariably crippled as the playwright strains simply to fill out his lines. "Hark how their drummes with dub a dub do come!" [173] is probably Greene's worst; bad enough, however, is Alphonsus's more representative pleonasm:

> But see whereas *Belinus* Armie comes,
> And he him selfe, vnlesse I gesse awrie:
> Who ere it be, I do not passe a pinne,
> *Alphonsus* meanes his souldier for to be.
>
> (263–266)

And even where individual speeches do not falter, an anticlimactic note is achieved through dialogue. In the *Looking Glasse*, for example, King Rasni of Nineveh proclaims his deity while a chorus of sycophantic princes bears out the refrain: "Rasni is God on earth, and none but hee" (27, 35, 44). After Cilicia and Creet have paid their homage, poor Paphlagonia is squelched in the midst of his first line by Rasni's "Viceroyes, inough; peace, Paphlagon, no more" (46). Marlowe's forceful personalities are delineated with no greater success. Alphonsus was obviously intended as a second, even grander Tamburlaine; "Baiazet" is one of the many generals he overcomes, and the head of the Turkish confederation casually refers to "mightie *Tamberlaine*" (779, 1444). Like Marlowe's hero, Alphonsus quickly ascends from the humblest origin to a place where princes kneel at his very glance. Also reminiscent of Tamburlaine is his conviction that he is greater than Fortune, and therefore his practice of rewarding loyal followers with the very kingdoms they have helped him conquer. But having attempted to hyperbolize Marlowe's mightiest lines and most colorful incidents, Greene also adds a second epic hero, Amurack, "the Great Turk," who gives the lie to "Mahound" as insolently as Alphonsus derides Fortune. Evidently Greene failed to see that one play cannot support more than one Tamburlaine.

Even in *Alphonsus*, where Greene's debt to Marlowe is most obvious, however, there are promises of better and very different worlds to come. After penning prose romances for at least five years, the playwright could not resist emphasizing Marlowe's lusty loves at the cost of his doughty deeds, and the drama of heroic conquest is given a much stronger romantic orientation. Alphonsus assumes the disguise of a base soldier and eventually wars against the Amazons. Various kings in palmers' weeds bow in and out, and alongside the Senecan catalogues of horrors are lists of faithful lovers and beautiful ladies. Equally important is the manner in

which Greene develops the romantic elements of *Tamburlaine*'s
resolution and resolves the conflict between his two seemingly invincible epic heroes. Immediately after Alphonsus puts Amurack to
flight, the Turk's daughter, Iphigina, renders the conqueror help-
less. Not fear of battle, he confesses,

> But loue, sweete mouse, hath so benumbed my wit,
> That though I would, I must refraine from it.
>   (1598–1599)

As Iphigina consequently observes, Alphonsus seems to honor
Venus far more than Mars (1601–1603), a trait hardly applicable to Tamburlaine. Nor would Marlowe have ever allowed a
kingdom to be won through wooing of "sweete mouse."

Besides romanticizing and frequently sentimentalizing Marlowe's themes, Greene often makes a greater and different use of
spectacle and choric commentary. A technique that greatly aids the
realizing of romance in *Bacon and Bungay* and *James IV* is the interaction between worlds with antithetical values, and we discover a
clumsy employment of that technique in *Alphonsus*'s framework
and Greene's choice of Venus as Prologue:

> *After you have sounded thrise, let* Venus *be let downe*
> *from the top of the Stage, and when she is downe, say:*
>
> Poets are scarce, when Goddesses themselues
> Are forst to leaue their high and stately seates,
> Placed on the top of high *Olympus* Mount,
> To seeke them out, to pen their champions praise.
>
> .   .   .   .
>
> I, which was wont to follow *Cupids* games
> Will put in vre [use] Mineruaes sacred Art;
> And this my hand which vsed for to pen
> The praise of loue and *Cupids* peerles power,
> Will now begin to treat of bloudie *Mars*,
> Of doughtie deeds and valiant victories.
>   (1–4, 35–40)

The Nine Muses thereupon enter, Venus assures the despondent
Calliope that epic poetry shall once more burgeon, and the party

ascends to Parnassus, from which Venus initiates her "comicall historie" and, between each act, comments on past events and foretells the future. Although Oseas is not *"brought in by an Angell"* until its second scene, the *Looking Glasse* is similarly framed by comments from on high. Unlike Venus, the Hebrew prophet is unconcerned about what will next unfold below. At the end of each piece of wickedness, he rather delivers a pious lamentation underscoring the resemblances between Ninevites and Londoners and thus justifying the play's full title.

To a certain extent this showy theater had become traditional. From *Gorboduc* in the early sixties to *The Spanish Tragedy* and *Tamburlaine* in the middle eighties, drama proper exploited the symbolism of mask and dumb show, and glossed its episodes with inductions and choruses. Greene's cultivation of visual, sonic—perhaps even olfactory—effects was also partly conventional. Medieval and early Tudor devils of legend and drama almost invariably relished fire and powder, and by Greene's time both civic and courtly playwrights were crowding their stages with the pomp of pageantry. When Alphonsus entered *"with a Canapie carried over him by three Lords, hauing over each corner a Kings head, crowned"* (1453), he was simply following Tamburlaine's magnificent chariot, drawn by the "pampered Jades of Asia." Such splendor was largely imitative. In his conventional moments Greene, like the other colorful playwrights of the eighties, used spectacle to enhance a situation's majesty or horror, and consequently creates the impression that the show is indigenous to the story.

But what of Greene's less traditional moments, when he attempted to make the old machinery of framework and display serve new purposes? The plots of his first two plays, for example, sometimes seem to have been twisted to accommodate spectacle for spectacle's sake. The best illustration comes toward the end of the *Looking Glasse*. After harping on the wickedness of Nineveh for more than fifteen hundred lines, Greene once more presents its monstrous King, this time about to enjoy the wife of Paphlagonia. As a means of advancing action, the episode is greatly inflated; as a means of developing character or varying theme, it is wholly unnecessary. The scene was inserted primarily for the grandeur hinted at in its stage direction: *"A hand from out a cloud, threatneth a burning sword"* (1555). And this incident is surrounded by numerous exits and entrances which also seem "dramatic" only in the looser sense of being spectacular: Rasni is about to commit incest when his sister is suddenly *"stroken with Thunder, blacke"* (518); his Machiavellian counselor *"is swallowed"* up in *"a flame of fire . . . from beneath"* (1173); and Jonas is *"cast out of the Whales belly vpon the Stage"* (1398). Equally difficult to defend in terms of character, theme, or plot are *Alphonsus*'s most exotic displays: the conjurations of Medea, *"an enchantress,"* who raises up Homer's Calchas (869); the brazen head of holy *"Mahound,"* which belches forth flames, the rumbling of drums, and select oracles (1144 ff.). Before labeling such stuff dramatically gratuitous, however, we must admit that it furthers a supernatural and generally occult atmosphere. Perhaps Greene is anticipating the more successfully integrated black and white magic of the necromancers in *Bacon and Bungay*. What at first seems a dabbling in the sensational for its own sake may actually reflect a clumsy attempt to dramatize the magic of folk tales and medieval romance, to set upon the stage the mysterious lands of magicians and alchemists where anything can and usually does happen. This would explain the brazen head and burning sword as well as Greene's concern that his villains, unlike those in Kyd and Marlowe,[174] receive direct, supernatural chastisement.

Greene's romantic attitudes are also reflected in his employment of framework, the showy but often incongruous envelopes into which he places his letters. Something in addition to display, for instance, must have motivated the playwright's odd choice of Venus to introduce *Alphonsus*. "This absurd induction has no bearing at all upon the plot," complains Enid Welsford; it "must surely have been composed for the sake of those who, through their experience of masques and entertainments, had come to regard the entry or descent of divinities as indispensable to a dramatic performance." [175] But surely Greene could have satisfied such expectations with the descent of a more relevant divinity. How were the dramatists from whom he borrowed honoring the "experience of masques and entertainments"? Marlowe begins and ends his history of *Faustus* with a Chorus, who simply sets the opening scene and points up the concluding moral. Crafty "Machiavel" is resurrected to introduce *The Jew of Malta* and then disappears. *Tamburlaine*'s Prologue is a mere eight-line statement of purpose. Kyd's use of framework is far more extensive. The conversations between Revenge and the Ghost of Don Andrea not only introduce and conclude *The Spanish Tragedy*, but provide a running commentary upon the series of terrors that unfolds. To the extent that these dramatists' introductory characters are personalized, to the same extent their personalities are indigenous to the worlds they induct. Machiavel and Revenge, in fact, might properly be termed the patron devils of the wicked machinations that ensue. Greene's framework characters, on the other hand, although enjoying larger parts and more prominent physical situations, are frequently at odds with the values that obtain within their presentations. In Greene's first two plays the conflict is resolved when the characters in the letter are converted to the views expressed by or normally associated with the figures of the envelope: Rasni and his court turn to Oseas's and Jonas's God; Alphonsus finally proves truer to Venus than Mars. Venus's bearing upon the plot is admittedly murky. Like the other techniques Greene borrowed from the devisers, either directly or through Kyd and Marlowe, the interplay between love and martial conquest is not successfully realized. Greene manages this interplay more skillfully in his last two plays, where the tension is between love and lust, and where the hardheaded presenters or observers within the envelopes are converted to the romantic idealism of the characters within the letters.

In the third of his five plays, the *Orlando*, Greene made one last attempt to romanticize epic drama. To initiate this exploitation of Marlowe's meter and Ariosto's matter, he turned from masklike inductions to the pageantry of street and tiltyard. Marsilius, Emperor of Africa, commands each of the great princes who sue for his daughter, Angelica, to set "forth his passions how he can, / And let her Censure make the happiest man" (14–15). The proud rivals immediately explode with vaunting verbiage; each defines his kingdom, its glories, his glories, the difficulties encountered in his voyage, their resemblances to those endured by mythological heroes, and finally, like a schoolboy at a public exercise, bobbing to the rhythm of a familiar refrain, concludes with an identical couplet: "But leauing these such glories as they be, / I loue, my Lord; let that suffize for me" (34–35, 51–52, 72–73, 89–90). The spirit behind this braggadocio is certainly Marlowe, but Marlowe without balance or economy. That Greene is straining for epic effect with sweeping geographical allusions is pointed up by the nonsensical route the King of Mexico has allegedly taken to North Africa:

From thence, mounted vpon a Spanish Barke,
Such as transported Iason to the fleece,
Come from the South, I furrowed Neptunes Seas,
Northeast as far as is the frosen Rhene;
Leauing faire Voya [Volga], crost vp Danuby,
As hie as Saba [Sheba], whose inhaunsing streames
Cuts twixt the Tartares and the Russians.

(63–69)

Taken individually, each princely pronouncement suggests not only Marlowe's rhetoric, but the widespread interest in exploration that Marlowe himself exploited. Taken collectively, however, they remind us of the civic reception's artfully patterned declamations, spoken by a host of kings, queens, prophets, and goddesses stationed throughout the city to welcome Elizabeth. And like the devisers, Greene underlines the importance of the occasion through references to the faraway places these speakers represent and the love of matchless beauty that has brought them forth. Having delighted the eye with a procession of kings, the playwright tries to excite the fancy with a stream of imaginative associations delivered in language as expansive as the geography it unfolds. The *Orlando* closes on a similarly stately and formal chord, but here Greene reflects another kind of pageantry, something akin to the colorful derring-do at Whitehall. Charlemagne's famous peers are preparing to execute Angelica for her supposed infidelity when Orlando, "*a scarfe before his face*" (1328), comes forth to prove her innocence, overcomes two "Champions of the world" before being recognized, and begs "faire saint" to forgive his "causeles lunacie." *Tamburlaine*, in short, has now been set in a thoroughly chivalric key.

But if the *Orlando* exhibits a highly ceremonious and neatly structured beginning and end, its middle strikes us as a careless hodgepodge of blustering heroics and rustic slapstick. The actions are not only ridiculous in themselves, but fall out in an order almost worse than random, a plotting seemingly contrived to accent absurdity. Orlando wins Angelica by capping his rivals' couplets:

But leauing these such glories as they bee,
I loue, my Lord;

Angelica her selfe shall speak for mee.
(126–128)

When Marsilius defends his daughter's choice, the lords of Cuba, Mexico, and "the Isles" throw down their gauntlets, vowing his destruction. The Sultan of Egypt, however, retires in peace, for "their Trophees" will be, at best, "but conquest of a girle" (231). Upon this anticlimactic note the stage is cleared of all except County Sacripant, who rehearses those "tearmes" which make men "coequall with the Gods" and rebukes his page for knowing "no titles fit for dignities, / To grace his Master with Hyperboles!" (258 ff.). Had Greene wished to undercut the bombast that precedes the Count's reflections, he could hardly have accomplished it with greater facility.

Greene's own penchant for hyperbole is satisfied in Orlando. Equally furious as warrior, lover, or lunatic, the French peer seems designed to sound a depth of bathos undreamed of even by Ariosto. Unlike cowardly Sacripant, who has no use for Venus's toys, Orlando is filled with amorous longings, and bids his soldiers stand guard while he "meditate[s] vpon the thoughts of loue" and communes with the evening star (546 ff.). When he discovers Sacripant's slanderous "*Roundelayes*," celebrating the love of Medor and Angelica, he promptly "runs madding through the woods," whence his mistress is also banished, dressed only in rags. Except for the concluding scene, the remainder of the play (671–1291) offers something for almost every kind of taste, and the varied bill of fare is only barely unified through Orlando's insane adventures. But the play's alternating moods are far more puzzling than its episodic structure. Madness is first signalized with a scrap of Latin, some Senecan-English invective, and eight lines of Italian lifted out of Ariosto.[176] Accustomed to Greene's pursuit of Marlowe's and Kyd's styles, we take Orlando's outburst as straightforward heroic stuff, an earnest imitation of the device that heightens *The Spanish Tragedy*'s horrors or an anticipation of Lear's truly tragic madness. What would have served to enhance Orlando's suffering and epic stature, however, is soon sacrificed to what looks like comic effect, an anticipation neither of Shakespeare nor even Webster but of the bedlam lunacy of Massinger's Sir Giles Overreach. The famous French peer becomes a dismemberer of shepherds (708), the leader of a rustic troop armed with "*spits and dripping pans*" (881), who mistakes Angelica for a squire and knights her (924) and mistakes a bumpkin for Angelica and woos him (964 ff.).

With its solemn beginning, mischievous middle, and serious end, the *Orlando* refuses to answer to our modern desire for unity of mood, and remains partly heroic, partly farcical, and as essentially Elizabethan as those "tragical-comical-historical-pastoral" plays noted by Polonius. Behind this loose containment of multitudes we can almost hear Lyly's plaint, spoken at Paul's the year before: "At our exercises, Souldiers call for Tragedies, . . . Courtiers for Commedies, . . . Countriemen for Pastoralles." To say that Greene, at this point in his career, is not mingling very skillfully, and has no keener sense of the mutually exclusive than most of his contemporaries, is not to excuse the *Orlando*'s bad art but simply to explain its conventional method. Like every playwright, Greene realized that greatness comes through a resourceful exploitation. He wanted Marlowe's vigorous characters and resonant language, coveted Kyd's articulation of Senecan tragedy, and wished to profit by his own previous experiments with Sidney's and Lyly's romantic narratives. Above all, he sought to please every member of his audience. For the lover, "Looke on Orlando languishing in loue" (559); for the soldier, here are the twelve pillars of the chivalric world; for those with a bent for romantic intrigue, "*Enter* [two kings disguised] *like Palmers*" (1008); for the witty, there is a clownish misapplication of Petrarch (967 ff.); for the apprentice, some rough buffoonery—"*He strikes and beates him with the fiddle*" and then "*breaks it about his head*" (1121 ff.); for those who preferred more masklike spectacle, there is an unexplained fairy godmother, Melissa, who cures Orlando's madness with her magic potion, wand, musical satyrs, and ten-line Latin invocation (1127 ff.); and finally, for sterner tastes, Greene even squeezes a few repentant lines out of Sacripant before dispatching him (1255 ff.).

If Greene's attempt to include such disparate stuff epitomizes customary dramatic practice, so does his cavalier handling of his "Historie's" principal source. Both illustrate what could happen when the lofty concept of creative imitation was applied within the fiercely competitive business of making plays. In the rush to wade farther, no popular playwright was above forcing the best-known names and events of history or fiction to his own purpose. Hence, Greene's wholesale distortion of Ariosto's plot and characters is quite conventional. It is in fact likely that even before he conceived of those "get-penny" devices discussed above, he had already decided to step beyond Ariosto's treatment of love's madness by enlivening the story of Orlando, Angelica, and Medor (Cantos XXIII–XXIV, XXIX–XXX) with some of the intrigue of the Italian's previous tale of Ariodant and Genevra (Cantos V–VII).[177] It was Greene's typically wide-ranging reading, gleaning, and mingling that explain his editor's difficulty in locating one direct source for *Alphonsus* or the *Looking Glasse*[178] and make us ask whether Ariosto should actually be called the *Orlando*'s source or merely one of its several springboards. The same conventional eclecticism also helps us understand why one of the English stage's first romantic heroes is compounded of as many ingredients as the internationally culled melancholy of Shakespeare's Jaques.

Far less comprehensible than his free handling of Ariosto's narrative is Greene's apparent misunderstanding of his illustrious Italian's high-comic spirit, his failure to capitalize upon the mischievous mood that the mad weaver of Ferrara evokes throughout his motley epic. Although Ariosto's abundant laughter is sometimes blended with gravity when he considers the senseless waste of war and the political chaos of his own country,[179] the episodes that Greene treated so seriously were delivered in merriment. The quest for Angelica, out of which all of the play's noblest derring-do arises, is in the source a sustained burlesque, a study of chivalry in its underwear, which culminates in the foolish Astolfo's ascent to the Kingdom of the Moon to fetch Orlando's bottled brains. And Ariosto uses his mock-heroic heroine as a tempting morsel, a device to expose his heroes' credulity, to get them off their chargers, forget their proud vaunts and outworn codes, and discover Touchstone's truth: "as all is mortal in nature, so is all nature in love mortal in folly." Whether Christian crusader advertising lofty sentiments or pagan knight simply frothing at the mouth, each falls victim to the proud, luxurious, often materialistic and remorseless beauty, who in turn falls for the least of things, simple Medoro. But Ariosto blames neither the pursuers nor the pursued. Frailty, thy name is woman—and man! Knights must sometimes doff their armor; the lady cannot help her charms, and really never asked to be followed. In these episodes, at least, the patron saint under which both armies go forth often resembles Shakespeare's Puck.[180]

Greene's transfiguration of Angelica from a contrivance to expose human foibles to a guiltless creature, whose suffering reveals the extent of man's wickedness, heroism, and love, cannot be explained apart from the attitudes and techniques he developed as a prose romancer. Beginning with *Mamillia: A Mirrour or looking-glasse for the Ladies of Englande*,[181] for almost a decade he had been exercising with imitative permutations and combinations of several literary traditions, what we might for convenience call the schools of Lyly's *Euphues*, Castiglione's *Courtier*, Boccaccio's *Decameron*, and Sidney's *Arcadia*. So industrious were his attempts to capitalize upon every fashion that the reading tastes of London during the 1580's can be measured largely in terms of his thirty-five prose tracts. "In a night & a day would he haue yarkt vp a Pamphlet as well as in seauen yeare," remarked his friend, Nashe, "and glad was that Printer that might bee so blest to pay him deare for the very dregs of his wit."[182] Sometimes these "yark-ings" ranged outside Cupid's realm. From 1585 to his death in 1592, Greene the Protestant Patriot delivered nine timely exposures of papistical designs and underworld intrigues. Equally professional is the prodigal son stuff of Greene the Penitent, a series of eight partly autobiographical but often untrue confessions. Few of the sins Greene begs credit for can be documented; certainly his most trustworthy admission is found in *Greenes Vision* (XII, 195): "Many things I haue wrote to get money." But it is the far less personal Greene, the Moral Romancer, who reveals what he was trying to do with Angelica and prepares us for her more successful dramatic sisters, Margaret and Dorothea. The *littérateur* probably got more money for those works that rattle sabers, catch conycatchers, or offer sackcloths. When Greene the Dramatist tired of Marlowe and Kyd, however, the lessons he had learned in writing *Mamillia* and its seventeen successors also proved highly profitable.

Anyone with enough patience to retrace Greene's steps must grant that his learning came slowly, especially at first, but there is always a steady progression toward the more dramatic forms of narrative fiction. Although Harvey saw no development—the consummation was simply "vile *Greene*," that "Vice of the Stage"—his other abusive epithets are fairly accurate and may clarify the prose romancer's series of literary disciplineships: "the Ape of Euphues," "borrowed & filched plumes of some little Italianated brauery," "*Greenes* Arcadia: and . . . *Greenes* Faerie Queene."[183] First there

is Lyly's slavish imitator. Coveting the success of *Euphues: The
Anatomy of Wit* (1578), Greene waded farther about 1580 with
Mamillia. Like his master's, this is less a story than a series of digres-
sions, tirades, and letters. Although the sexes of Lyly's principal
characters are reversed, there is the same twenty-to-one ratio of set
discourses to action; [184] amid horrendous declamations, Greene almost parenthetically shifts his colorless figures from one stock
situation to another. But *Mamillia: The second part* (entered, 1583)
fleshes out Lyly's reflections with some intriguing actions. Mamillia's
unfaithful lover repents his perfidy, rebuffs a wealthy courtesan, and
is almost executed when she denounces him as a spy. Disguised as a
young gentleman, the heroine arrives in time to rescue her betrothed
with a heroic address before his judges. Although Greene was not to
purge his prose of Lyly's arabesques for several more years, the
stress on action and the romantic, often sentimental nature of the
events leading up to this novella's happy resolution must have
surprised any reader who expected just another aping of *Euphues*.

As we might expect after noting the directions in which Greene
wades with Lyly, his appropriations of "Italianated brauery" begin
with Castiglione's "utile" and end with Boccaccio's "dulci." In
Morando: The Tritameron of Love (1584), for example, both
speakers and topics are reminiscent of the Court of Urbino. Although Greene's sophisticated ladies and gentlemen are not
delineated as skillfully as Castiglione's, he is obviously more interested in his narrators than their tales, and wants us to appreciate
their witty dialogue, graceful repartee, and clever elaborations
upon the topics in question. Above all, the stories are not meant
to be told for their own sake; like those of Castiglione's courtiers,
they are intended to illustrate an edifying observation or support
an argument, and thereby show how well these refined people
can reason. The introductory situation is not a convenient framework for something more important, but the thing itself; the most
interesting parts of the letter, whether extended anecdotes or
well-spun yarns, are there to characterize the envelope.

But if *Morando* follows the *Courtier* almost as closely as the
first part of *Mamillia* imitates *Euphues*, by the time Greene
reaches *Euphues his censure to Philautus* (1587), he is no longer
interested in either Castiglione or Lyly. Despite its title, an implied avowal of membership in Lyly's school, the ratio of utterance to action found in Greene's first novella has been nearly re-

versed. And despite the *Censure*'s advertisement that its Greek and Trojan lords are debating "to discouer the perfection of a souldier" (VI, 149) and its author's reference to "Baldessars courtier" in the epistle dedicatory (VI, 152), we actually receive a very loosely related series of entertaining tales, sometimes irrelevant to the set topic and rarely serving to illustrate the collective personality of the speakers in the framework. Helenus's tale of a wise soldier, outwitted and poisoned by his queen, certainly figures forth a doubtful moral, and Ulysses's fable of treachery, fortune, and lust in Polumestor's court has nothing to do with virtues, military or otherwise. Finally, *Perimedes* (1588) and *Alcida: Greenes Metamorphosis* (1617, but entered in December, 1588) reveal the *littérateur* at last allowing his genius for romantic narrative complete freedom. Both collections are full of Arcadian elements: disguised pilgrims, dangerous voyages, the uneven course of true love, and constancy severely tested through separation and misfortune. Moreover, whereas *Euphues his censure* eventually ignores the set topic it first promises to discuss, *Perimedes* and *Alcida* employ frameworks flexible enough to be easily satisfied. The hitherto restrictive envelope may now contain any "honest and delightfull recreation" or "*diuerse* merry . . . Histories." That two of *Perimedes*'s three stories are from the *Decameron* is further evidence of Greene's conversion from Castiglione to Boccaccio. In one important area, however, Greene refused to follow his new master. Although the envelope has become a handy excuse for any kind of letter, and although neither work has an obtrusively didactic end, both are set within a moral frame of reference. None of the three erring maids in *Alcida* goes unpunished; each of the six faithful lovers in *Perimedes* is rewarded. In turning from patterned discourses to amorous adventures, Greene gained valuable experience in romantic love-plotting, an ability that later earned Nashe's tribute that for "plotting Plaies . . . he was his crafts master." [185] But the usually amoral moods of Boccaccio's witty intrigues was one "plume" Greene never "filched."

By far the most profitable of the future dramatist's narrative exercises originated in his desire to English the Greek Romance. Because his experiments with Arcadian story and framed tale at first ran concurrently, we again discover a steady progression toward simpler style and more complex narrative movement. His first romance, *Gwydonius* (1584), clearly reflects an attempt to enrich plot through the conventional accidents of fortune, but the story line repeatedly founders under an equally conventional and far less romantic plethora of diatribes, euphuistic epistles, and long-winded counsel. Aside from occasional instances of vernacular energy and a willingness to improve upon the similes of Lyly's Pliny, the only signpost to "*Greenes* Arcadia" is the exotic conclusion, in which sire and long-lost son clash in battle before recognizing one another, and the hero marries the daughter of his father's greatest enemy. And though the stylized lamentations of *Arbasto: The Anatomie of Fortune* (1584) offer little rhetorical improvement, in its rejected heroine, Myrania, we catch our first glimpse of the pathetic young women in whose plights Greene centers his last two plays. Compared to Arbasto's turgid vehemence, Myrania's simple declaration of love (III, 228) is almost persuasive. More important are those rare moments in which Greene discovers, perhaps stumbles upon, a successful evocation of mood. Notice, for example, the heroine's rescue of her lover: "*Myrania* hauing desperately atchiued this deed, she straight sought . . . to bereaue him [the jailer] of hys keyes, which after she had gotten, and conuied his carkasse into a secret place, she went in hir night gowne, accompanied only with hir maide to the prison" (III, 227). If this vignette seems rather pallid by modern standards, we should remember that in 1584 few prose writers could have communicated an atmosphere of mystery and urgency so economically.

Finally there are Greene's mature and deservedly well-known romances, in which he at last masters two important dramatic techniques. For an intricate, plausibly complicated, and swiftly moving series of events, nothing in the eighties surpasses *Pandosto: The Triumph of Time* (1588); for those deft touches that idealize action and character, no contemporary narrative quite touches the bittersweet melancholy of the reflective scenes in *Menaphon* (1589). Although neither romance attains the other's chief virtue, when Greene returned to making plays about 1591, he had only to blend each in the right proportions. *Pandosto* records Greene's decision to abandon ornate pronouncements and concentrate upon plain storytelling. The enduring popularity of this tale—by 1735 it had gone through twenty-six editions and is even alluded to, thirteen years later, in Richardson's *Clarissa* [186]—is a tribute to Greene's ability to engender narrative interest. Here is the very stuff of romance: an oracle's prophecy to be fulfilled; chastity vindicated; death by grief; an heiress lost at sea, adopted into lowly surroundings, but proving her royal blood through beauteous form, words, and deeds; assumptions of disguise and perilous voyages. For once Greene is too involved with action to pause for "eloquence," and his sentences become shorter, stronger, and far more cogent. Just as important is his facile employment of two plots. Sometimes closely intertwined, sometimes almost separated, the stories of young love and old jealousy are almost always naturally related and never speciously complicated. Since a certain "vpstart Crowe" from Stratford based *The Winter's Tale* upon it, he must also have admired Greene's artful double-plotting.

Like the dramatist, however, the romancer was seldom able to let well enough alone. In *Menaphon* Greene again overreached himself by turning Heliodorus's and Sidney's labyrinthine adventures into a seeming parody of needlessly involuted actions.[187] *Pandosto's* plot, not its language, is hyperbolized, and the result can be called a narrative only in the loosest sense. In our initial reading of *Menaphon*, for example, we can rarely relate the diverse events overflowing its pages unless we have first understood the full meaning of an introductory oracle. In this instance, unfortunately, Delphi deals only in inscrutabilities, dark hints to be immediately fathomed by the author alone, who can then preen himself as he unravels his conceits at the very end. Pirates enter and exit whenever an additional complexity is required. For the twenty years that suddenly elapse we are given only the barest warning and certainly no apology. Nor does the heroine, Sephestia, ever appear perplexed by the ages or identities of her three ardent, disguised suitors—her father, her husband, and her son.

But not all of the exercise that went into *Menaphon* failed. If Greene stepped too far with intricacy of action, with complexities that no longer delight but confound, he went just far enough in blending character with setting. Granted, the heroines of Greene's prose romances are not especially vivid, and Sephestia is no exception. We remember her only in customary terms, a combination of physical and spiritual loveliness. Why then are we more attracted to this woman than to her equally beautiful and pathetic predecessors, those sixteenth-century Pamelas whom Greene never tired of celebrating? The desire to sympathize with Sephestia and her dramatic successors stems not as much from the depth or clarity of their portrayals as from the refined, idyllic backdrops against which Greene places them.[188] Amid a usually hurried and tangled sequence of episodes he occasionally pauses for a more successful, much quieter scene, a close-up of the brave woman, her serene grief and beautiful surroundings. Except for these moments of reflection, Sephestia's plight and *Menaphon*'s sound and fury would signify very little. Through them Greene makes virtue surprisingly attractive and his heroine's situation count for more than her personality really merits. Such moments are of course as fragile as the lyrics they engender. One false move and the sentimentality we have been teetering upon becomes apparent. But this delicate balance is often managed well and sometimes brilliantly. At its very best, the lyricism of these emotionally surcharged scenes breaks into literal lyrics, as when Sephestia dandles and lullabies her "fatherless" child:

> Weepe not my wanton, smile vpon my knee,
> When thou art olde, ther's grief inough for thee.
> Mothers wagge, pretie boy.
> Fathers sorrow, fathers ioy.
> When thy father first did see
> Such a boy by him and mee,
> He was glad, I was woe:
> Fortune changde made him so,
> When he left his pretie boy,
> Last his sorowe, first his ioy.
>
> (VI, 43)

By now it should be clear that Greene's career in prose offers as helpful a gloss upon his early plays as the sources he dramatized and the dramatists he imitated. Down through the eighties we watch the principles of Sidney's art, imitation, and exercise being applied, and our curiosity about what life was like for a writer who had to earn his way is answered by a rapid output of assimilations and exploitations. Whether penitent, patriot, romancer, or dramatist, the real Greene is four personae in search of an audience, and no respecter of generic distinctions. After reading *Gwydonius* and *Arbasto*, we are not surprised to find Venus introducing a sequel to *Tamburlaine*. With Sephestia and Myrania (and perhaps even the woman Greene so often sins against in his confessional tracts) before us, his pathetic Angelica, so unlike Ariosto's, seems part of a pattern. Without reference to the techniques he mastered in *Pandosto* and *Menaphon*, it is impossible to explain the differences between the ludicrous *Orlando* and the highly successful *Bacon and Bungay*. Since both plays contain magic, spectacular effects, youthful love, patriotism, native horseplay, near-tragedy, and, of course, the suffering heroine, the latter's success is the result of the cunning with which Greene now handles the same old materials. Still sharing the popular desire to incorporate a wealth of varied matters, he nevertheless makes a tremendous improvement by mingling each more harmoniously. The buffoonery that surrounds pitiful Angelica is replaced by *Menaphon*'s idealized vignettes; Orlando's heroic vaunts yield to Lacy's gentle sentiments. The clowning and rant of Greene's first three plays are not expelled, but transferred to the chauvinistic, courtly, scheming world of Oxford, a far more realistic place, which impinges upon yet never undercuts the heroine's innocent, pastoral Fressingfield. To blend each world in convincing proportions, Greene capitalizes upon the double-plotting developed in *Pandosto;* to realize the relationship in dramatic and strikingly visual terms, he employs the magic glass of Friar Bacon.

If Greene's exercises in prose help to explain the ways in which *Bacon and Bungay* was shaped and are, therefore, some "sources" of the play's techniques, what about sources in the more conventional sense, the plots, characters, themes, and points of view he drew upon? We have already noticed that Greene is no less eclectic than his inferior or superior contemporaries, that his first two plays have no direct sources, and that his *Orlando* would have baffled Ariosto more than Marlowe. The difficulty in identifying Greene's indebtednesses for his fourth play is of another kind. Professor Collins long ago cited *The Famous Historie of Fryer Bacon*, "an old romance written probably towards the end of the sixteenth century, [but] the earliest extant edition of which is dated 1627." [189] Consequently, we cannot be certain that the play did not beget its alleged source, nor dare we even ignore the possibility that both were independently nourished by lost native legends. Such factors, however, do not render *The Famous Historie* worthless as a gloss. Although we lose a documented source and the prosaic pleasure of determining where Greene bagged his two plots, we still have a valuable context, a reliable index of what Bacon's career meant to another writer of the time. We need not ascertain who borrowed from whom, in other words, before using one author's interest as a commentary upon another's. After all, even if we could identify Greene's model, we should not automatically know why he chose it or why he treated it in a particular way. To solve such problems we must attempt to capture what was in the air about 1590, and to this end an analogue Greene may never have heard of—or even a work that *succeeded* his own—could be helpful.

Assuming that *The Famous Historie* is simply a source of information rather than a source proper, what kind of gloss does it offer? First, the Friar's anonymous biographer is not only outrageously unhistorical but wholly episodic. Although he may have drawn his collection of stories from the legends surrounding England's greatest conjurer, he nevertheless gives the impression that he began with some magical exploits and then looked for a magician, that he settled upon Bacon as a convenient causer of preconceived effects. Except for its conclusion, in which the Friar renounces his magic and turns anchorite, the chapters of this "biography" could be reordered in any other way and make as much sense. Motivated less by the concerns of venerable Plutarch than by the spirit of modern tabloid journalism, the biographer reduces Bacon's life to his magic, and makes his magic signify as many things as the number of sensational stories he has in store. Secondly, even if we restrict our study to the relatively few episodes Greene also uses and compare the supernatural reactions of the prose and dramatic Bacon to almost identical situations, we usually find magic taking on different meanings. The only theme the biographer and the dramatist have in common is magic as patriotism; both celebrate the Friar's spectacular victory over the German sorcerer, Vandermast, before the proud English court, and both relate how Bacon's admirable attempt to protect England from foreign invaders with a wall of brass was undone by the stupidity of his shiftless research assistant, Miles.[190]

In all the other scenes treated by both writers, however, the differences are more significant than the similarities. The biographer, for example, gives us magic as low comedy: Baited by one gentleman in the presence of the king and his court, Bacon retaliates by conjuring up the knight's "greasie sweetheart," a lowly "kitchen-mayde with a basting-ladle in her hand."[191] Greene's Bacon has the same sense of humor and honor, but the man he shows up is his colleague, Burden; when a devil brings in the mistress of a nearby tavern as the "booke" Burden actually studies each evening

(283 ff.), the disreputable, unacademic side of Oxford life is exposed. Whenever his Friar uses magic for something other than king and country, in fact, Greene associates it with lust or violence. He is close to the biographer's account of how two young country gentlemen, while gazing into Bacon's renowned "glasse prospectiue," saw their fathers in combat, fell to quarreling themselves, and killed one another, whereupon the penitent magician breaks his invention and returns to God.[192] The fathers of Greene's young scholars, however, have made Margaret their theme of honor, and thus reflect one of the dramatist's many strategies to link the worlds of Oxford and Fressingfield. But *The Famous Historie*'s most helpful gloss is a two-page tale of how Bacon aided an Oxfordshire gentleman in regaining his true love from a deceitful knight. As the covetous Bungay begins to perform the enforced marriage, Bacon discovers the proceedings in his glass, strikes Bungay dumb, has the bride brought to her lover, and marries them.[193] Although his version ends as happily, Greene allies Bacon with the lustful knight; he obviously wanted Margaret to face supernatural as well as merely mortal machinations. And whereas this episode served the rarely romantic biographer as just another passing illustration of Bacon's prowess, it was developed by the dramatist into the second and far better half of his play.

Finally, for the backgrounds that explain the interests of both biographer and dramatist as clearly as either writer's work explains the other's, we must look beyond strictly literary sources and analogues. In noting that the wicked Spanish Queen of Peele's *Edward I* may have been inspired by a statue outside Westminster, we spoke of backgrounds that must remain conjectural even though they were there for all men to experience; unless we can show that what any man could have seen or heard about was in fact seen or reported to the writer in question and was very much in his mind even as he sat down to work, we must be content with "possible stimuli" instead of "direct influences." Yet it is precisely these hypothetical sources of stimulation we are driven to when our literary glosses fail to solve essential problems concerning the reasons for an author's interests and attitudes. Why, for instance, was Greene so interested in magical display? To cite other works that capitalize upon the forbidden arts, from the aimless *Famous Historie* to Marlowe's artful *Faustus* (c. 1588–1592), is not to answer but enlarge the question: Why did all three writers find magic so marketable? Bearing in mind the common Elizabethan habits of treating the past in present terms and of interlacing accounts of faraway places with hints of well-known figures, let us glance at several items that may have stimulated Greene's shaping of *Bacon and Bungay*.

First, it is quite likely that Greene could have counted upon his audience to know about a contemporary conjurer just as patriotic as the medieval Bacon. In 1592, not more than a year after the play opened, Dr. John Dee, the Queen's astrologer, was defending his activities before a special board of inquiry. Amongst his many services to the Crown he listed the following. He had calmed the royal fears occasioned by the appearance of a large comet in 1577. And the same year he had taken some pains to counteract the spell cast against Elizabeth "by meanes of a certaine image of wax, with a great pin stuck into . . . the brest of it, found in Lincolnes Inn fields." Most important (for Greene, at least), when the Queen and her Privy Council came to see his library at Mortlake in 1575, he displayed his "glass so famous, and shew . . . vnto her some of the properties of it." [194] The magic that we take as spectacle for its own sake or as a structural contrivance to unify two plots did not require an Elizabethan suspension of disbelief. Even usually skeptical people like Reginald Scot admitted that of all mysteries, "the woonderous devises, and miraculous sights and conceipts made and conteined in glasse, doo farre exceed all other; whereto the art perspective is verie necessarie. For . . . you may have glasses . . . so framed, as therein one may see what others doo in places far distant; others, wherby you shall see men hanging in the aire." [195] Finally, we may ask whether Greene's imagination might not have been kindled by a fiendish visitation upon a town not more than a dozen miles from his native city, an event written up by Abraham Fleming as "A straunge and terrible Wunder wrought verie late in the Parish Church of Bongay, a Town of no great distance from the Citie of Norwich, namely the fourth of this August, . . . 1577, in a great tempest of violent raine, lightning, and thunder. . . . With the appeerance of an horrible shaped thing, sensibly perceived of the people then and there assembled." [196] On that day, Fleming declares, the devil assumed the shape of a black dog, rushed through the congregation, and "wrung the necks" of two kneeling worshipers "at one instant clene backward." For the reader who desired additional details, the printer furnished a woodcut of a black dog with large claws; for the unbeliever, Fleming invites an examination of the church door, where the marks of this creature's "talans" are yet clearly visible.

None of these items, of course, documents a relationship. The role Dee played, the magical qualities of optics Scot was forced to allow, the devil's invasion of a small Suffolk town sharing the name of Bacon's historical friend, and the fact that the villages of Fressingfield, Harleston, Beccles, and St. Margaret all lie within ten miles of Bungay and directly between Norwich and London—all such stuff that could have passed through Greene's mind may be entertained in our conjectures. Life in England offered these imaginative associations to enhance both of *Bacon and Bungay*'s plots. Since the play itself does not prove that the offer was accepted, we are left without analogues, but not necessarily without some of the intellectual baggage that could have enriched the original audience's reponses to the play.

Allowing these backgrounds to function as they surely must have in Greene's own time, simply as possible stimuli upon both maker and viewer, we may now search for evidence of the playwright's interests within his play. Certainly Greene's foremost concern is implicit in the very technique he employs to set off and eventually merge *Bacon and Bungay*'s disparate casts and values, and the literary traditions they bespeak. We cannot help noticing how often he alternates between the real yet not quite realistic world of rural Suffolk and the intensely realistic but nevertheless supernatural world of Oxford, between love-plotting and magical-plotting. In the first three scenes, for instance, we proceed from courtiers on holiday at Framlingham and Prince Edward's lust to the Oxford operators (Bacon, Beelzebub, Burden, and his "booke") to the rustics on holiday at Harleston Fair and the Earl of Lincoln's love. Each scene is given a readily identifiable setting and at least one recognizable historical personage, yet none remains on solid ground. Nothing better characterizes this mingling of the near at hand and faraway, the mundane and the marvelous, than the stage direction that follows Bacon's conjurings: *"Enter a woman with a shoulder of mutton on a spit, and a Deuill"* (288). Similarly, the countryside surrounding Greene's native city no doubt gave him those market towns, handsome wenches, and rustic festivities that he worked into his idyllic scenes. But where did he find a country girl as highly articulate, graceful, and courtly as his Margaret? And if everyday life is merely a springboard for incredibly idealized people and events, so is past history. The chroniclers speak of Edward I and Lacy, Earl of Lincoln, but not of "the Courtier tyred all in greene, / That helpt her [Margaret] handsomly to run her cheese" (146–147) nor of the Earl who turned up at Harleston Fair in

farmer's weeds to woo a "bonny damsell" for his liege. As different
as Greene's theater is from Peele's, both share this refusal to maintain a realistic atmosphere. When the locale is recognizable, an improbable event occurs; when the scene is set in a removed world,
something quite normal is sure to take place. As a result, the play's
frames of reference shift not only from scene to scene, but within
the scenes themselves.

This continual, rapid transition between real and unreal characters, actions, and places occurs too often to be accidental. If Greene
had simply sought to bring the romantic elements of earlier plays
like *Sir Clyomon* down to earth, Margaret would have found a
priest who was not a part-time necromancer. Moreover, the characters themselves are made to question their locales and the identities
of their fellow travelers, and thus anticipate the queries—and possibly the bewildered objections—of their audience. Rather than attempting to sharpen the vague outlines of his Suffolk world, for
example, Greene fosters credence by exploiting the very improbabilities of each unlikely situation, and sometimes even calls our
attention to the verbal magic of his method. The Harleston
scene (346–430), which best expresses the cunning of Greene's
making, also underlines his manipulation of language.

> *Margret.*   Whence are you, sir? of *Suffolke?* for your
>   tearmes
>   Are finer than the common sort of men.
>
> *Lacie.*   Faith, louely girle, I am of *Beckles* by,
>   Your neighbour, not aboue six miles from hence,
>   A farmers sonne, that neuer was so quaint
>   But that he could do courtesie to such dames.
>   (381–386)

Margaret might well have questioned her own fine language as
well as Lacy's, for this exchange is surrounded by "tearmes" which
at one moment smack of the barnyard and at the next of the
court or academic bower. Accompanied by Lacy, *"disguised in
countrie apparell,"* Margaret, Thomas, Joan, *"and other clownes"*
have just arrived at Harleston Fair, in Greene's own time evidently
held every St. James's Day, July 25.[197] The scene's reality is immediately established by Thomas's mundane considerations: "By
my troth, *Margret,* heeres a wether is able to make a man call his
father whorson; if this wether hold, wee shall haue hay good

cheape, and butter and cheese at *Harlston* will beare no price" (346
ff.). Through Margaret's reply, however, Greene shifts from bar-
ter of goods to exchange of hearts; and commerce, initially
agrarian, becomes amorous.

> When we haue turnd our butter to the salt,
> And set our cheese safely vpon the rackes,
> Then let our fathers price it as they please.
> We countrie sluts of merry *Fresingfield*
> Come to buy needlesse noughts to make vs fine,
> And looke that yong-men should be francke this day,
> And court vs with such fairings as they can.
>
> (352–358)

In turning from crops to courtship, Greene at least retains rural
Suffolk as his frame of reference; "hay good cheape" and "fairings"
are equally rustic expectations. But when his lovely country slut
next takes up Thomas's allusion to the weather, she belies her
humble origin and roams at will through several lands:

> *Phoebus* is blythe and frolicke lookes from heauen,
> As when he courted louely *Semele*,
> Swearing the pedlers shall haue emptie packs,
> If that faire wether may make chapmen buy.
>
> (359–362)

And Margaret's marvelous four-line journey from Harleston to
Olympus and sudden return to Suffolk's markets by way of Cad-
mus's mythical kingdom is bettered only by Lacy's immediate
flight:

> But, louely *Peggie*, *Semele* is dead,
> And therefore *Phoebus* from his pallace pries,
> And seeing such a sweet and seemly saint,
> Shewes all his glories for to court your selfe.
>
> (363–366)

Such close juxtapositions of disparate worlds reveal that like
his personae, Greene is holding holiday; the sixty-four lines succeeding Lacy's Petrarchan compliment contain a feast of facile,
unexpected excursions into several mutually exclusive matters, none
of which can be justified except by the imaginative logic of romance and the peculiar nature of his characters' environment.

Greene has set his happy company in a world that is as fluid, as
neutral, and as nowhere as the enchanted groves through which
Zabeta was currently leading her weary train. What is at first all too
real suddenly burgeons with exotic sentiment. Out of butter and
cheese it yields fairings and courtship; in "whorson" weather
Phoebus sports with Semele and vendors profit thereby. Lacy picks
up Peggy's classical reminiscence and deposes Semele in favor of
his own "saint." If Apollo's earlier love empties peddlers' packs,
his new amour also renders him the patron saint of the religion of
courtly love. Margaret again returns us to Harleston by terming
Lacy's elaborate compliment "a fairing, gentle sir, indeed" (367),
and Joan further grounds the fleeting glimpses of Olympus and the
court by re-establishing the initial equation between courtship
and commerce:

> *Margret*, a farmers daughter for a farmers sonne:
> I warrant you, the meanest of vs both
> Shall haue a mate to leade vs from the Church.
>
> (372–374)

Thomas then concludes this brief interchange by suggesting that
the party "snap off a pint of wine or two" at a nearby tavern
(379–380).

Only at this point does Greene pause to emphasize the process
by which he has created an atmosphere at once precise and in-
distinct. Margaret is puzzled by Lacy's uncommon terms, a language she herself has introduced but not consistently maintained.
The *"Beckls* man" insists that he is merely a "farmers sonne," a less
"quaint" variation of what, according to Joan, befits a farmer's
daughter. Yet Lacy's insistence upon his rustic, realistic origin
only accents his unreality for a third clown, Richard, promptly
queries, "Sirha, are you of *Beckls?* I pray, how dooth goodman
Cob? my father bought a horse of him. Ile tell you, *Marget*, a were
good to be a gentlemans iade, for of all things the foule hilding
could not abide a doongcart" (402–405). Greene is not simply
fleshing out his scene with random conversation, but again calling
our attention to the varied dishes of his feast. Lacy's courteous
"tearmes" identify him with the court and betray his unfamiliarity
with the world of Beccles, especially as that world is immediately
defined through Richard's own language. The clown's apparently
irrelevant comment about the gentlemanly horse of Beccles that
disdained his father's manure wagon suggests that the village

sometimes produced creatures in disguise. And only four lines after Richard's moral concerning the abandoned "doongcart," Margaret describes the Beccles farmer as "smelling of the Court." The relationship may be accidental, but in playing his game of swift transitions, Greene often ranges as quickly from perfumed chambers to earthy barnyards.

Drama placed on pages and examined in detail and drama set on stage to be momentarily seen and heard produce entirely different experiences, especially when the playwright is dealing in imaginative logic to foster romantic illusions. Like most Tudor dialogues of instruction, Lyly's dramatized treatises are better read than played; his witty feasts are formulas meant to be carefully analyzed, for their appeal, despite passing reflections on the nature of love, is entirely intellectual. If we bring the intense cerebration Lyly demands to *Bacon and Bungay*, we feel cheated by illogically yoked incongruities, signifying confusion. Placed on the boards where it belongs, Greene's interplay has a chance to succeed through sheer vitality of language. Owing to the various changes quickly rung on Thomas's simple allusions to weather and marketing, for instance, imagination triumphs over reason. We are far too preoccupied in following the rapid stream of associations to catalogue and analyze a particular transition. There is no time to note that it was Zeus, not Phoebus, who wooed Semele, and that courtship, Olympian or otherwise, has little to do with merchants' prices. The total effect is not confusion but fusion, a linking similar to those recorded in the journals of the German tourists who scanned the walls of Whitehall or as set down by Englishmen like Henry Machyn after being captivated by the passing wonders of a civic procession. Greene's shifts come too quickly to be weighed and found wanting; they unite to produce a neutral, "blythe and frolicke" world in which country and court, courtship and commerce, shake hands in good fellowship and respect a common patron, a god who has not been dragged in simply to bolster an argument.

But if Greene's imaginative associations and rapidly shifting frames of reference lead us to ask "Who is Margaret?" or "Where is Harleston?," we are never in doubt as to his moral tone or about his play's—and one of his time's—major themes, lust as a leaven tainting all it touches. Had Greene retained the usually amoral point of view of the Italian tales he partly imitated, Peggy would have evoked no more sympathy than a doe pursued and outwitted by a

pack of curs. Because they are carried on within a frame charged
with moral sentiment, her struggles against the machinations of
the court and the magic of Oxford become all important, eventually subordinating the patriotic contests and spectacular displays
that Greene may have borrowed from *The Famous Historie.*
In the opening scene, long before his bonny wench appears, she
and her world are idealized and the play's main theme spelled out
through the reflections of Prince Edward and his crew of courtly
roisterers. Like Harleston's verbal interplay, Ned's fifteen-line series
of classical allusions and Petrarchan clichés turns part of Suffolk
into an idyllic paradise and makes Margaret its goddess; whereas
that later scene remains "blythe and frolicke," however, Ned's
journey ends upon a somber note:

> When as she swept like *Venus* through the house,
> And in her shape fast foulded vp my thoughtes:
> Into the Milkhouse went I with the maid,
> And there amongst the cream-boles did she shine,
> As *Pallace* mongst her Princely huswiferie:
> She turnd her smocke ouer her Lilly armes,
> And diued them into milke to run her cheese:
> But, whiter than the milke, her christall skin,
> Checked with lines of Azur, made her blush,
> That art or nature durst bring for compare.
> *Ermsbie*, if thou hadst seene as I did note it well,
> How bewtie plaid the huswife, how this girle
> Like *Lucrece* laid her fingers to the worke,
> Thou wouldest with *Tarquine* hazard *Roome* and all
> To win the louely mayd of *Fresingfield.*
>
>   (74–88)

As another means of engendering a moral frame of reference,
Greene also relies upon aphorisms, introduced in moments of crisis
and made digestible through the refinement and rustic simplicity
of his vehicle. Like Belleforest and his English imitators, Peggy
continually harangues her audience, but in a manner far less obtru-
sive. Bungay's announcement that one of her lovers is "sonne to
Henry, and the prince of *Wales*" evokes only the slightest interest:
"Be what he will his lure is but for lust" (639–640). And to Lacy's
consequent confession that he has "liued disguisd to winne faire
Peggies loue," she promptly and quite simply queries, "What loue
is there where wedding ends not loue?" (733–734). This theme has

been anticipated in the opening scene, not only by Ned's "*Tarquine*" but through the "perfect plot" of his fool, Ralph: The maid for whom it is "marriage or no market" must be overcome with Bacon's "nigromaticke spels" (106 ff.). In scene ii we find those spells already in motion; the devil brings in the world of Henley's Bell Tavern and its Hostess to unmask professorial lechery at Oxford (287 ff.), and when Bacon later agrees to assist the Prince (599 ff.), his magic takes its place alongside the devices that help rather than hinder lust. By means of an inventive double-staging, Greene lets us observe Oxford observing Suffolk through the famous "glasse prospectiue" (620 ff.). While Ned curses Bacon's 180-line enveloped "commedie" and attempts to intervene,

> *Edward.*   Gogs wounds, *Bacon*, they kisse! Ile stab them.
>
> *Bacon.*   Oh, hold your handes, my lord, it is the glasse!
> (742–743)

Lacy surrenders worldly practicality and offers Peggy honorable terms.

Lacy's conversion signalizes the realistic world's first retreat and the eventual triumph of romance over the mundane considerations of station, wealth, and even male friendship. To make this breach in the operating world, Greene once again relies upon Margaret's winsomeness and unobtrusive moralizations. Gently prodded less by Peggy than her plight, the Earl of Lincoln turns from loyalty to his liege, to denouncing vile designs, to championing true love, to marriage. Nor can the breach, once made, be filled, even through Bacon's supernatural intercession. By the time Bungay is struck dumb and carried off by a devil, both lovers share their creator's moral-romantic premises. We are therefore confident that the marriage has been merely postponed, not prevented. From here on the machinery of idealism gathers momentum, and both sword and conjuration must yield. Seeking vengeance, Ned soon finds it difficult to keep afloat in young love's sea of virtue and self-sacrifice. To answer his Prince's accusations of treachery, the Earl adopts Margaret's aphoristic style, confessing that he thought her "fitter to be *Lacies* wedded wife, / Than concubine vnto the prince of *Wales*" (945–946). Ned next advances the code of male friendship, but Peggie proves such "realities" too weak and artificial to withstand the force of heterosexual love. He then falls to high-flown verbiage, the kind of stuff Greene took so seriously in his earlier plays, and she returns him god for god to underline the emptiness of splendid rhetoric. He finally appropriates academic logic—"*Ablata causa, tollitur effectus*" (998)—and Peggy assures him that she would shortly "meet her *Lacie* in the heauens." Having discovered that the premises of the operating world simply will not operate, the Prince can do no less than display his magnanimity and repent, much in the vein of the Alexander in Lyly's *Campaspe*.

Throughout the remainder of his play Greene continues to alternate between realistic and idealistic treatments of country, court, and university scenes. In King Henry's entertainment of his foreign guests, we find the courtly world as it should be; in the adventures of Ned and his jolly crew at Oxford and Framlingham, we discover courtiers freed from courtly conventions. The Oxford world is given patriotic idealization in Bacon's noble endeavors to make England invincible, but it also contains lecherous Burden, mischievous Miles, wayward students, alehouse brawling, and devouring beadles. In realizing the academic and courtly communities that surround and usually act upon Fressingfield, Greene shares much of *The Famous Historie*'s spirit and tone as well as some of its incidents. Greene's desire for spectacular effects, in fact, twice spoils his double-plotting. The magicians' contest (1109–1261) and the episode of the brazen head (1530–1660) provide showy theater but no relevant gloss upon the Suffolk story.

Except for these events, however, Greene takes pains to achieve an organic structure. We should recall, for example, that Bacon's biographer does not explain how two of his students' fathers became foes, merely that the boys killed one another after seeing their parents' quarrel through the magic glass. By making the older men rival suitors for Margaret, Greene is again able to show one world acting upon another. But in this case the interplay is reversed. The glass unfolds an Arcadian tragedy that occasions another among its audience; by outdoing Oxford in villainy, Suffolk converts Oxford's foremost operator. Finally, in resolving the theme of love and lust, Greene once more employs an interaction between country and court. When Peggy receives Lacy's disavowal of love (a trial of her constancy, of course, as she might have gathered from the letter's extremely artificial, euphuistic style), she who has hitherto championed romantic ideals decides that "all loue is lust but loue of heauens" (1869) and prepares to enter the convent at Framlingham. This is one repentance and one point of view Greene the romancer can ill afford, and he squelches both with a melodramatic entrance of courtiers, "booted and spurd" (1890). Just as he has used Margaret's innocence to convert his sophisticated world's immorality, so he concludes by employing chastened sophisticates to correct her now aberrant morality. With as many jests as explanations, Lacy and his fellows woo Margaret back to their party. Peggy confesses that "the flesh is frayle" and the roguish Earl of Sussex, that all women, "be they neuer so neare God, yet they loue to die in a mans armes" (1937 ff.). Through this facetious interplay Greene assures us that he has shaped his initially contradictory values into an essentially harmonious whole, that his basic frame is romantic as well as moral, and that within such a mingled world the long-suffering heroine may realize her concurrently realistic and idealistic dreams. Nor should Bacon's closing prophecy concerning "*Diana's* Rose" (2088) surprise us. The Queen's private theater frequently premises a time long past only to have it look forward to the blessed present. Like *James IV* and nine of his prose pieces, *Bacon and Bungay* bears Greene's favorite posy: *Omne tulit punctum qui miscuit utile dulci*. By now we should realize that when a sixteenth-century writer sought to carry off the laurels, he mixed much more than the useful and the sweet.

Greene's most unified treatment of love versus lust appears in his last play, *James IV*. Unlike her predecessors, Dorothea does not have to contend against unrelated characters and events for our interest, since the movement is centered in her plight from the beginning. Complementing this new disdain for spectacular irrelevancies is the plot's more rapid unfolding. By the end of the first scene we know exactly which way the land lies: Dorothea is married to James amid great ceremony; she and the Scottish nobility accompany her father, the King of England, and his lords to their ships; James confesses his lust for Ida, daughter to the Countess of Arran, in a long aside; Ida and her mother refuse to remain at court; and the stage is emptied of all save James and his vicious parasite, Ateukin, who immediately suggests how to exchange a bride for a mistress. With uncharacteristic economy, Greene uses less than four hundred lines to introduce all the major characters, define their values, and thus to focus upon the machinations Doll will soon face.

Part of the credit for the play's more unified structure and swifter pace should probably go to Greene's source, Giraldi

Cinthio's *Gli Hecatommithi*.[198] Whereas he had at most only the
loosely related episodes of a supernatural jest book for *Bacon and
Bungay*, in Cinthio's Third Decade he discovered ten tales about
the infidelity of wives or husbands,[199] each of which furnishes
an artfully organized, rapidly developed series of intriguing actions. Except for changing its locale and inventing the Machiavellian
Ateukin, Greene followed his source's plot and personae quite
closely. The world of Cinthio's story was nevertheless extensively
altered, for the dramatist next proceeded to blend the whole into a
period of Scottish pseudo-history. His fanciful treatment of English and Scottish annals, as Collins notes, "displays an ignorance
of which Greene must have been incapable." [200] Historical accuracy, of course, was hardly the *littérateur*'s major concern. Like
Peele's *Edward I, James IV* seems to have been founded within a
specific reign simply to provide its unhistorical events with the
emotional nourishment of a dimly perceived past. Certainly Greene
appears to have first settled upon a romantic adventure story and
only then begun seeking a convenient era in which to deposit it,
a reign that yielded a "cast" roughly similar to that of the
preconceived narrative. Such an *ex post facto* use of history
amounts to little more than name-dropping.

The important thing is that Greene knew which names to drop.
However hazy their knowledge of Scottish history, his audience
would have at least recognized James IV as the man who had
married the aunt of their beloved Queen, scandalized his own
Court with some notorious amours, and sponsored an invasion of
England. And owing to the activities of his granddaughter, Mary,
and the possibilities of her son, James VI, England had been looking northward throughout Elizabeth's reign.[201] These props were
all Greene needed to unify those themes on which he never tired
of harping: the virtue of patriotism, the evil of lust. Having exploited his audience's dislike of James IV and the contemporary
unrest concerning Elizabeth's successor, the rest of his *"Historie"*
was fashioned to meet the demands of an Italian *novella*. Rather
than have James slain at Flodden Field, as promised by the play's
title, England invades Scotland and James repents and lives. Nor
is it that first politic Tudor, Henry VII, who attacks Dunbar, but a
grief-stricken father seeking his lost child. Cities and armies fall not
in the quest for wealth or empire, but simply because a king
lusted and had to be punished; international plots and counterplots,
in short, are given a strictly romantic orientation.

Greene's zealous romanticism also explains his next, less conventional elaboration, the wading farther proclaimed in the last lines of the play's full title: *The Scottish Historie of James the fourth, slaine at Flodden, Entermixed with a pleasant Comedie, presented by Oboram King of Fayeries.* Having appropriated Cinthio to spell out preconceived themes and having twisted history to accommodate Cinthio, he finally inserted the mixture into a fantastic fairy framework. From the time he first imitated Castiglione and Boccaccio, Greene had been interested in an envelope to introduce, link, and enrich the meanings of the events within the letter or narrative proper. Except for the *Orlando*, he also exploited this technique when he turned to the stage. Both *Alphonsus* and the *Looking Glasse* are inducted by creatures who do not belong to the worlds they set in motion, but whose values come to be accepted by the principal players. With *Bacon and Bungay*, the mysterious interaction between the viewer and the world he views and partly shapes becomes even more explicit; the penitent necromancer, in fact, destroys his own "evil framework." In *James IV* Greene reverses *Alphonsus*'s interplay. Rather than having the Queen of Love set forth a world at first martial and eventually amorous, he uses a cynical, disillusioned old Scot, Bohan, to induct a devising which will justify his misanthropy. Amid his own re-creation of the bitter evidence, however, Bohan is won over to an idealistic outlook. Whereas in his first play Greene places the romantic premises within the framework and allows them to impinge upon the bellicose hero, in his last he sets them inside the drama proper, forcing the tale to backfire upon its unromantic teller.

At first Bohan is certain that by dramatizing James's wicked reign, he will silence the optimism of Oberon, King of Faerie, whose subjects' sprightly dancing has brought him up from his "*Tombe*." Why has he found "the Court ill, the Country worse, and the Citie worst of all" (64–65)?

> In the year 1520, was in Scotland a King, ouerruled with parasites, misled by lust, and many circumstances too long to trattle on now, much like our Court of Scotland this day. That story haue I set down. Gang with me to the Gallery, and Ile shew thee the same in action by guid fellowes of our country men; and then when thou seest that,

iudge if any wise man would not leaue the world if he
could.

(102–109)

The dour Scot requires short space to prove his point. Between
James's lustful asides and Ateukin's monstrous counsels, the picture of life at court is hateful enough. But a third major character
in this first scene is lovely Ida, who has obviously assumed Margaret's role as chastity's champion and aphoristic moralizer. "Because the Court is counted *Venus* net, / Where gifts & vowes for
stales are often set" (222–223), she will not postpone her departure.
James must therefore trust to the "charmes and spels" of Ateukin,
who lacks both Bacon's power and integrity. Ida makes only two
other brief appearances, each time to provide idealistic counter-
point to the wickedness rapidly engulfing Scotland. As Act II
opens, she is again inveighing against courtly vanities; happy to be
"honest poore," she sits busy at her needlework even as she lectures her English suitor, Lord Eustace, on the dignity of labor
(676 ff.). After her indignant answers to James's overtures through
Ateukin (784 ff.)—"But can his warrant keep my soule from hell?"
—Greene all but drops her from the play. Her betrothal to Eustace
(1470 ff.) allows the dramatist to illustrate the course of virtuous
love and to work in a little country show presented by "*certaine
Huntsmen and Ladies,*" a reception quite similar to that given
Elizabeth by Lord Norris at Rycote in September, 1592.[202] When
Ateukin next journeys to Arran (1931), he comes upon the lovers'
marriage "*triumph*" and realizes that all his machinations have gone
awry.

The more complex role of matronly chastity and marital loyalty
is taken by Dorothea, Greene's culmination of long-suffering
heroines and his best piece of evidence against the sordid world
Bohan is attempting to paint. As James's and Ateukin's activities
bring the inevitable destruction of Scotland into focus, the once-
faithful clergy and nobility flee the court, despite Doll's pleas
that her husband is only testing her constancy. But when in the
course of Machiavellian events Sir Bartram discovers James's warrant for Dorothea's death, she also flees, disguised as a squire.
Her flight offers Greene an opportunity he seldom bypasses,
chauvinistic display. To assassinate Dorothea, Ateukin naturally
hires a Frenchman, Jaques, who treats the King's English almost

as ruthlessly as he handles his daughter, and evokes from her a predictable sentiment: "Shall neuer French man say, an English mayd / Of threats of forraine force will be afraid" (1695–1696). Sir Cuthbert's rescue and his lady's consequent "insaciat lust" for the young "squire" afford additional romantic complications. As her father's forces surround Edinburgh, however, she reveals her identity and hastens to save her wanton husband. Political considerations are suspended as Sir Cuthbert steps before the assembled hosts, first to present an oracle and then to gloss it by producing the presumably dead Dorothea. And as she loyally pleads for James's life,

> Youth hath misled,—tut, but a little fault:
> Tis kingly to amend what is amisse
>
> (2371–2372)

Greene obscures the fact that at least seven thousand Scots have already died in battle. Like the conclusion to *Gwydonius*, in which the characters overlook even greater destruction to rejoice in the reunion of father and long-lost son, *James IV* ends in a flourish of pageantry, forgiveness, feasting, and "frolike," Greene's favorite word.

Complementing the play's sentimental denouement is the romantic drama developed within its envelope. Bohan's two sons, Slipper and Nano, forsake their father's framework retreat to adventure into the past he is currently delineating. The intrigues they discover as Ateukin's servants at first confirm the Scot's bitter philosophy, and Oberon, taking his cue from the events of Act I, conjures up four dumb shows illustrating the vanity of life (620 ff.). But the King of Faerie sees more in history than the falls of princes. When Bohan, at the conclusion to Act II, returns to his pessimistic pronouncements, Oberon reminds him of Ida's goodness. And by the end of his third dismal movement the Scot has somehow come to share the Fairy's sympathetic involvement. Equally important, he who devised the play to justify his hatred is apparently no longer certain as to its outcome, for his commentary has shifted from what has happened to what may occur (1455–1462). Finally, as the fourth of his "sad motions" is brightened by Nano's help in rescuing Doll, Bohan's paternal pride overcomes his world-weary disinterest and forces him into the role of a romantic playwright:

Ober. Beleue me, bonny Scot, these strange euents
Are passing pleasing, may they end as well.

Boh. Else say that *Bohan* hath a barren skull,
If better motions yet then any past
Do not more glee to make the fair[i]e greet.
But my small son made prittie hansome shift
To saue the Queene his Mistresse, by his speed.

(1815–1821)

It is only after we have recognized Greene's conventionality that
we can appreciate his creativity. The use of choric figures to introduce the show and to entertain the audience between major
episodes with song, dance, and moral or witty remarks was old
stuff. Even within the play proper Greene shows how much he
has borrowed from Gloriana's programs: *James IV* begins and ends
with the processions of two kings and their splendid trains;
in between we have a coronation (141), a mummery (1497 ff.),
and *"a seruice, musical songs of marriages, or a maske, or what
prettie triumph you list"* (1931). Bohan himself underlines the
traditional nature of the entertainments he and Oberon present between the acts: His "sad motions" are "interlast with merriment
and rime" simply "to beguile the time" (1455 ff.). Taking Bohan's
confession as Greene's own "naïve avowal of his motive," Miss
Enid Welsford sees him succumbing to stage tradition rather than
putting it to new uses: "The dramatists were expected to divert
their audiences with interludes of music and dancing, and their use
of the induction was a clumsy attempt to prevent these interludes
from confusing the dramatic action, while giving them at the same
time some more or less rational connection with the plot." [203] In
view of the interaction between framework and show that leads to
Bohan's conversion, it seems more likely that through *James IV*'s
interludes, Greene sought less to divert than to focus upon that
twilight land bordering the worlds of realism and romance. After
providing the appearance of historical truth, fleeting glimpses of
reality, Greene begins discarding the chroniclers' props. Realistic
effect is increasingly romanticized and finally traduced when
Oberon and his train storm the world of past history and carry
Slipper off from under James's nose (2268). Several years later a
much improved Oberon would confuse the course of human events
within a similarly magical and even more diversified world; it is not
improbable that Shakespeare saw in *James IV* the most facile

blending of the writer who invariably *"Entermixed"* or "interlast."

About the time Greene was inveighing against Stratford's "vp-start Crow," however, another dramatist was also profiting by his examples. In an age of such extensive borrowing it was only fitting that Peele, whose *Arraignment* had first suggested some of the dramatic possibilities of Gloriana's theater, should return to exploit the traditions he had partly inspired. With *Bacon and Bungay* and probably *James IV* as major sources of inspiration, Peele turned from history as a backdrop for comedy to a thoroughly romanticized history, *Edward I* (c. 1592), in which even less effort is made to conform to the political and military facts stressed by the chroniclers. In a world in which we would expect to find men defined as essentially political animals, there move characters like Ned Longshanks and his lovely Nell, oblivious to the responsibilities of state. Battles are fought in good sport; if lost, one simply falls to other revels. When the rebellious Welsh are defeated, even the fiery Lluellen bears no grudge, but retires with his band to a forest like Shakespeare's Arden: "Since the king hath put us amongst the discarding cardes, . . . everie man take his standing . . . and wander like irregulers up and down the widernesse[;] ile be . . . Robin Hood thats once, cousin Rice thou shalt be little John, and heres Frier David as fit as a die for Frier Tucke[;] now my sweet Nel if you wil make up the messe with a good heart for Maide marian and doe well with Lluellen under the greene wood trees, . . . why *plena est curia*." [204] And this completes the romantic cycle. From Edward Hall's accounts of Henry VIII's romps with Robin Hood we have progressed across the Queene's private stages, then turned to examples of her devisers' influences upon the drama proper, and finally found ourselves once again under the greenwood. From a real king playing merry outlaw we have traveled some eighty years only to discover an actor playing a king playing outlaw.

The most curious thing about these romantic re-creations is that we look in vain for a knowing smile, some evidence of the tongue in cheek that should underlie the juxtaposition of Hercules and Arthur at Kenilworth, or the fusion of Elinor de Montfort and Maid Marian in Peele, or the mixture of courtly, classical, and rustic references on the lips of Greene's Fressingfield wench. If Lyly's Prologue speaks facetiously about *Midas*'s "seuerall dishes," the play proper never smirks at the syncretic methods through which it is being created. Since every artisan in England was borrowing from all times and places (Lyly would have such common customs excuse his own "Hodge-podge"), we might expect some writer before Beaumont to parody instead of merely employ the Gothic muse. Our expectations seem to be answered in Peele's best play, *The Old Wives' Tale* (c. 1593), which mocks even as it mingles.

Ever since pre-Shakespearean drama began to receive critical attention, Peele's sprightly excursion has proved perplexing. For J. P. Collier it was "nothing but a beldam's story" with "a disgusting quantity of trash and absurdity"; after Professor Gummere's defense, it long enjoyed the reputation of being a clever satire.[205] More recently, it has been shown that most of Peele's materials lie within the tradition of native folklore, and that therefore he could not have been seeking to satirize or burlesque contemporary dramatizations of the heroic romance.[206] Had *The Old Wives' Tale* been mainly designed to deride the genre epitomized by Greene's *Orlando*, surely its actions would have been situated in a strange land and its hero have had at least one blustering encounter with the villain. Similarly, if Peele had wished to undercut the romantic-chivalric elements of his Old Wife's story, he would likely have given one of his witty pages some sarcastic comments. Instead, Gammer's little audience appears to be fascinated; only Huanebango's entrance evokes laughter.[207] Finally, there is the timely warning of Peele's most recent biographer, who notes that if the play's "confused and absurd action makes it sound like ridicule," it is "ridicule more subtle than was usual among Elizabethan playwrights. Peele was too naïve to write subtleties; his humor speaks out loud and bold."[208]

Certainly Peele's nondramatic stuff reveals no penchant for parody. Like Greene, he is strongly anti-Catholic, impossibly chauvinistic, and an extremely serious believer in British chivalry. When Elizabeth's "counter-Armada" sails for the Azores, Peele sounds *A Farewell* (1589) to its captains, who, "Under the sanguine Crosse, brave Englands badge," must leave "statelie Troynovant" to "deface the pryde of Antechrist, / And pull his Paper walles and popery downe" (4, 25, 35–36). He seems equally earnest about the tilters who clash (and the British lion that roars) throughout *Polyhymnia* (1590) and *Anglorum Feriae* (1595?). Nor does he ever waver in his trust or admiration of former fabulous story. Peele's style is admittedly careless, sometimes marked by "pleonasm and colorless adjectives."[209] In striving to invest Whitehall's

mimetic battles with epic significance, for example, he occasionally produces something as inane as *Polyhymnia*'s

> And hast they make to meete, and meete they doo,
> And doo the thing for which they meete in hast.
>
> (141–142)

The context, however, assures us that Peele was not guilty of
laughing at Gloriana's knights, but simply of writing bad poetry.
He no doubt saw these lines as heroically redundant rather than
bathetic. Such faults must be kept in mind as we examine the wit of
Peele's play. When the first character of Gammer's tale enters
with "Upon these chalky cliffs of Albion / We are arrived now
with tedious toil" (159–160), we sense the mock-heroic vein. Yet
alongside such seeming merriment we must place several earnest,
nondramatic exhortations, each honoring Albion's chalky cliffs.[210]

Even after allowing for the sincerity of Peele's worst poetry and
most heroic visions, however, we cannot get very far into his play
without sensing another kind of mischief afoot. The scenes are too
huddled, the figures come and go too abruptly,[211] and the two
plots "weave around each other with the seeming purposelessness
of a dream."[212] If such "flaws" can be justified by assuming that
Peele was only trying to realize a dream's inconsequentiality, how
are we to explain the equally huddled and equally disparate worlds
represented by the figures in the framework, who have not yet
begun to experience the Old Wife's fantasy? At the very outset,
in fact, Peele's inducters make us keenly conscious of the language
through which multiple frames of reference are being invoked, and
their verbal interplay reminds us of Margaret, Lacy, and the bumpkins at Harleston Fair. But the same technique is used for an entirely different purpose. Whereas Greene seeks to blend Fressingfield with Olympus, Oxford, and "the Court at London," Peele's
contradictory worlds are meant to jar. To fulfill the promise implicit in his subtitle, "A pleasant conceited Comedie," he avoids all
easy, graceful transitions and concentrates upon witty discords.

To this end of accenting disparities, Peele first brings into his
dark English forest some extremely courtly courtiers, the three
brisk pages, Antic, Frolic, and Fantastic. They imply that love
is indirectly responsible for their sad circumstances, since "Cupid
hath led our young master to the fair lady, . . . the only saint that
he hath sworn to serve" (14–16), and they have evidently wandered
astray while on one of their lord's amorous progresses. Although

despair has supposedly turned Frolic into a dead animal ("all amort"), the wild, lonely wood echoes to his civilized agonies: "*O caelum! O terra! O Maria! O Neptune!*" But such whimsical incongruities are nothing compared to what next occurs. Heralded by the barking of his dog,

> *Enter a smith, with a lantern and candle*

Fro. In the name of my own father, be thou ox or ass that appearest, tell us what thou art.

Smith. What am I? Why, I am Clunch the smith. What are you? What make you in my territories at this time of the night?

Ant. What do we make, dost thou ask? Why, we make faces for fear. . . .

Fro. And, in faith, sir, unless your hospitality do relieve us, we are like to wander, with a sorrowful heighho, among the owlets and hobgoblins of the forest. Good Vulcan, for Cupid's sake that hath cozened us all, befriend us as thou mayst; and command us howsoever, wheresoever, whensoever, in whatsoever, for ever and ever.

Smith. Well, masters, it seems to me you have lost your way in the wood; in consideration whereof, if you will go with Clunch to his cottage, you shall have house-room and a good fire to sit by, although we have no bedding to put you in.

All. O blessed smith, O bountiful Clunch!

Smith. For your further entertainment, it shall be as it may be, so and so.

> *Here a dog bark.*

Hark! This is Ball my dog, that bids you all welcome in his own language. Come, take heed for stumbling on the threshold.—Open door, Madge; take in guests.

> (37 ff.)

Nothing could be more real than this English Vulcan and the creature comforts he offers. The "house-room" Clunch provides and the "piece of cheese" and "pudding" his gammer presents yield a familiar sketch of Merry England, a tribute to simple, old-fashioned hospitality. But in the midst of a wild and therefore savage and cruel forest, Clunch really has no more business than the lost pages he shelters. To a realistic Elizabethan, "a good fire to sit by" in such a forbidding place was as unlikely as Greene's Pallas "amongst the cream-boles" of Suffolk. At Ball's first barking, Frolic concludes that "either hath this trotting cur gone out of his circuit, or else are we near some village, which should not be far off" (32–34). Since the play nowhere hints at a nearby village and since the Smith is amazed to find anyone within his "territories," we are led to assume that Clunch, Madge, dog, and boys are all out of their respective "circuits." The Smith's personality, moreover, is as mysterious as his cottage's setting. Like the accommodations he offers, his responses are at first appropriately rustic. But having called to our attention his dog's "own language," he notes the pages' exaggerated courtliness and wittily warns high-flown rhetoric against "stumbling on the threshold." In the passage above, he comes in speaking as a lout and ends with a line smacking of incantation: "Open door, Madge; take in guests."

If Gammer's tale is of the supernatural, then, the frame in which she resides is not much more realistic. And from the miniature courtiers' utterly artificial opening plaints through Madge's mixture of magic and folklore to both parties' farewell breakfast of bread, cheese, and ale, Peele eases or jolts us between his play's alternately fantastic and routine moods. Taken individually, none of these worlds or traditions is amusing. When combined and staged for Gloriana, they could still be taken seriously, for within her theater every player spoke in essentially similar terms. By assigning each creature of his varied cast a language and sentiment apposite to its own tradition, Peele made comic capital out of conventional methods. We may call the result a dream, but only if we allow that this dream is witty of "conceited," that it includes the envelope as well as the letter, and that a good many of its absurdities make a little more sense when viewed against contemporary romantic excursions. Even as she is about to unfold her wondrous story, for instance, Madge observes that "they that ply their work must keep good hours," sends the Smith to bed, and insists that one of the pages also retire, evidently to keep her husband warm. Hearing that Clunch is "a clean-skinned man, . . . without either spavin or windgall," Antic hastens off with a gallant *"Bona nox,* gammer" (112 ff.).

From here on the transitions and cross-commentary come even more rapidly. Madge's language first flows with the grace of fairy incantation, is next suddenly jarred by a realistic intrusion, and then becomes earthy and spasmodic.

> Once upon a time, there was a king, or a lord, or a duke, that had a fair daughter, the fairest that ever was, as white as snow and as red as blood; and once upon a time his daughter was stolen away; and he sent all his men to seek out his daughter; and he sent so long, that he sent all his men out of his land.

Fro. Who dressed his dinner, then?

Madge. Nay, either hear my tale, or kiss my tail.

Fan. Well said! On with your tale, gammer.

Madge. O Lord, I quite forgot! There was a conjurer, and this conjurer could do any thing, and he turned himself into a great dragon, and carried the king's daughter away in his mouth to a castle . . . and there he kept her I know not how long, till . . . her two brothers went to seek her. O, I forget! she (he, I would say,) turned a proper young man to a bear in the night, and a man in the day, and keeps by a cross that parts three several ways; and he made his lady run mad—Gods me bones, who comes here?

(130 ff.)

What comes forth initiates a phantasmagoric procession of strangely mixed creatures and scenes, a veritable feast of epic, romance, and native folklore, related only through pageantlike spectacle and imaginative logic. The quest for Delia, Princess of Thessaly, has brought her two brothers to Albion's chalky cliffs. Whether Peele intends their high-flown, inverted plaints to cruel Fortune as eloquence or magniloquence, epic vaunts suddenly yield to the simpler yet more mysterious terms of folk story. Erestus, the once "proper young man" Madge almost forgot to mention, now appears at his crossroads, gathering his food, "hips and haws, and sticks and straws" (168 ff.). But we have no sooner adjusted to the formulaic language of the brothers' ritualistic almsgiving than Peele springs an incredible *non sequitur* and another variety of repetition. To the knights' promises of greater gifts, Erestus's only response is an enigmatic, "Was she fair?" It is almost as if the characters in the tale have intuited the exposition of the framework, for the second brother, quite unflustered by the strange question, calmly replies by twisting Madge's earlier description of the stolen princess: "Ay, the fairest for white, and the purest for red, as the blood of the deer, or the driven snow." The verbal interplay then reverts to a simple echoing as Erestus counsels them with an "old spell" and the first brother repeats six of its eight lines.

At the brothers' departure, Peele finally uses language for straightforward soliloquy (206–225). Erestus, who is now the aged keeper at the cross by day and "the white bear of England's wood" by night, explains how he and his betrothed, Venelia, were two of Thessaly's happiest young lovers until Sacrapant, inflamed by lust and jealousy, enchanted them both. It is curious, but characteristic of Peele's cunning, that the more marvelous the deed, the more clear and direct the speech of its doer or narrator, and that the most matter-of-fact speaker in the whole play is its ghost. Equally strange (and presumably as facetious) is the next dramatic indecorum. The combined worlds of witchcraft, heroic romance, and epic madness, as represented by Thessaly, Sacrapant, and the enraged Venelia—who now "runs madding" across the stage—are given a domestic orientation with the appearance of Lampriscus. How Erestus of Thessaly ever chanced to end up in everyday rural England remains unexplained, but Peele insists upon the fact. In less than sixty lines (229 ff.) the earthy old Englishman and the enchanted young lover call each other "neighbour" a dozen times; "for charity," Lampriscus has brought the bear-man a pot of honey, and "for neighborhood or brotherhood," he would have the man-bear's help in marrying off his two undesirable daughters. More important, Peele again underlines his manipulation of language by having Lampriscus describe his elder, beautiful daughter with a mixture of fairy and folktale idiom: "Poor she is, and proud she is; as poor as a sheep new-shorn, and as proud of her hopes as a peacock of her tail well-grown" (262 ff.). We are surely meant to remember Madge's earlier description of Delia, for Erestus replies, "Well said, Lampriscus! You speak it like an Englishman."

If such echoings of rhythm and idiom suggest a mysterious influence exerted by the envelope upon its letter, the relationship is further enforced as Peele returns us to his framework audience.

No playwright prior to Beaumont seems more anxious to keep his fiction merely a fiction, for his inducters continually comment upon the characters and events that pass before them. As the stage within the stage is momentarily cleared, Frolic notes the smoothness of its play's plotting: "Why, this goes round without a fiddling-stick" (286–287). But the tale's teller can take little credit for the art of its dramatization, since she immediately misconstrues the next scene. "But soft! who comes here? O, these are the harvest-men. Ten to one they sing a song of mowing." Instead, these convivial farmers "come a-sowing," and their seed is nothing less than the "sweet fruits of love." What could have been Peele's first thoroughly realistic scene is thus allegorized and romanticized, and the casual manner in which Madge readily misidentifies the sowing mowers and their function only accents their unexpected and incongruous entrance. The joke, however, is on the harvest men as well as Madge, for the first "fruits of love" gleaned by these romantic love-plotters are the weedy, mock-heroic lovers, Huanebango and his squire, Booby. Here Peele's parody is as obvious as the old "two-hand sword" wielded by this son of the Spanish Peninsular Romance and grandson of Roman comedy's braggart soldier.[213] The knight roars off a list of those gods fit for every epic hero to swear by, catalogues the perils of any medieval champion's quest, declines some Latin to prove Delia his own, refuses Erestus's request for alms, and exits "haratantara," while Booby confesses that he rarely understands his lord's "superfantial" terms.

Peele next wheels out his villain, Sacrapant, who neatly outlines and demonstrates his infernal powers, yet woos his captive, Delia, with sentiments smacking of Petrarch (for example, 423 ff.). By now the dramatist's accented disparities have begun to tell. We were probably not meant to know exactly how to take the man who boasts of having turned himself into a dragon and then, only two lines later, provides so undragonlike a rationale for stealing a princess: "Fair Delia, the mistress of my heart" (412). To complicate the mood even further, Delia's two brothers now enter, led by Kenilworth's Dame Echo. After having them borne off by two Furies, Sacrapant resumes his autobiography, gloating over the magical fact that he will never "die but by a dead man's hand." This theme of the avenging dead is immediately picked up as Peele, now halfway through his play, at last introduces its ostensible hero, Eumenides, *the wandering knight* (503). Having received

Erestus's instruction to "Bestow thy alms, give more than all, / Till dead men's bones come at thy call" and, above all, to "dream of no rest," Eumenides promptly *"lies down and sleeps."*

After passing through so many partly everyday, partly fanciful worlds, we finally come upon one that seems thoroughly realistic, the decidedly English parish of Wiggen, Steven Loach, and the sexton. But even this detailed picture of native scenes yields the ghost of roistering Jack, over whose burial expenses his Christian brethren are disputing. And if Wiggen, the earthy "Parish Unthrift," at first chooses fit terms to express his indignation, it is not long before he sounds more like the subtle doctors of Oxford: "You may be ashamed, you whoreson scald Sexton and Churchwarden . . . to let a poor man lie so long above ground unburied. . . . *Domine opponens, præpono tibi hanc quæstionem,* whether will you have the ground broken or your pates broken first?" (525–529, 579–581). Eumenides awakens and, recalling Erestus's spell, surrenders his last pence in order that Jack's body may be properly laid to rest. Fantastic and Madge then comment upon Jack's popularity, and the "amorous harvesters" dance by to announce that now they "come a-reaping."

This time the love-plotters are correct. After Sacrapant strikes Huanebango deaf and Booby blind, the knight is paired off with Lampriscus's beautiful, shrewish daughter and his squire, with her ugly, sweet-tempered sister. The comic representatives of heroic romance are thus employed to satisfy the poetic justice demanded by the conclusion of any folk tale, and during the course of their courtships we also get snatches of nursery rhymes (634 ff.), love charms (734 ff.), a mock-Latin verse (745), and an echo of Chaucer's Parson (761–762), as well as one of Gabriel Harvey's worst English hexameters (754), a parody of Stanyhurst's Virgil (746), and some choice nonsense also found in one manuscript of Greene's *Orlando* (758–759).[214] The other sets of lovers are united just as quickly. The ghost of grateful Jack overtakes Eumenides and shows him how to break Sacrapant's spell. The brothers are freed, Delia raised, Erestus and Venelia resume their normal states, and except for Jack, who *"leaps down in the ground,"* Madge's cast exits for Thessaly, the Old Wife herself awakens to fetch a cup of ale, and her young guests prepare to go back to the world of the court. With a swiftness that has characterized each of his transitions, Peele underlines the cunning expressed throughout his making by carefully returning every creature to its proper "circuit."

CONCLUSION: TIME HATH CONFOUNDED OUR MINDES, OUR MINDES THE MATTER

Peele's facetious admixture, then, at once epitomizes and exposes the dramaturgy of an era overflowing with incongruous concoctions. So numerous and varied were the dishes every deviser "translated" into his gallimaufry that a positive identification of each would be as difficult as ascertaining all the methods and matters burlesqued in *The Old Wives' Tale.* Upon the usually romantic and invariably Gothic Elizabethan charger we find characters as disparate as Seneca's ranting tyrants, Petrarch's sweet saints. Castiglione's polished courtiers, Heliodorus's quiveringly chaste heroines, Malory's lusty heroes, and the citizens of Olympus in the guises of each. Perhaps it is now evident that we do not require an exhaustive catalogue of the traditions these playwrights appropriated in order to gain a proper feeling for their art. Our impressions will be accurate enough if we notice how representative samplings of materials were interpreted and exploited. Many of the romantic techniques Lyly, Greene, and Peele improved upon and Shakespeare mastered ultimately stem from Elizabeth's desire to go a-progressing. It was, after all, her chief priests who first set in motion worlds as mixed as the motives that inspired them. In his earliest extant piece of theater, we find Peele eagerly applying the devisers' outrageous eclecticism; by honoring their notion that Gloriana's presence justified any containment of multitudes, he came closer to staging a progress than writing a play. Dramaturgically speaking, *The Old Wives' Tale,* which comes almost a decade later, is *The Arraignment* revisited. After imitating the art of flattering programs in exercises for both Queen and Lord Mayor, Peele finally stepped beyond the romantic cycle by allowing each tradition to give the lie to its fellows. There is nothing profound or subtle about his "conceited Comedie." It was fully within the scope of any clever craftsman who, like Greene, realized the vitality offered by an interplay of unlike terms and who, like Shakespeare, had the sense and sensitivity to allow Puck to give Hobgoblin articulation. Like his reapers, Peele was only harvesting what had been so speciously sown and deftly loosing his own time's neatly packaged disparities.

The confounding of minds and matters Lyly laments and Peele parodies is probably the most important single factor in understanding the peculiar strengths and weaknesses of Tudor literature.

Lyly was of course quite correct in blaming Time for England's confused "passe." By 1589 neither tailor, innkeeper, nor writer could any longer accommodate all the fashions that were pouring into his once relatively parochial island; too much was happening too quickly, and artists in the midst of what is only afterwards recognized as a renaissance may become anxious about the future of art. Had Lyly been told that most works of the next decade would be as hodgepodge as *Midas* and even more "full of deuise," he would never have believed that a "workemanshippe" greater than that he fondly recalled was already in the making.

For us that future has already been, but we must be at least as respectful as Lyly about Time's power to confound. It is tempting to let the Elizabethans speak to us only as long as they seem willing to share our most recent concerns, and to defend their greatest artists on the grounds of relevance instead of art. Often a modern production of Shakespeare is celebrated because "it works," and in the rush to make his plays socially or politically meaningful at almost any cost, one feels somewhat stodgy about asking whether the "it" is not working against, rather than alongside, the text furnished by the playwright. Every age has somehow managed to make Shakespeare its contemporary. Had he written about 1450, the Elizabethans would have been the first to make him their own, just as they rewrote medieval history to highlight present problems or mistranslated the spirit, if not the letter, of the ancients they admired. If we are ready to smile at Puritan New England watching *Othello* turned into a "A Moral Dialogue in Five Parts, Depicting the Evil Effects of Jealousy and Other Bad Passions," [215] are we willing to contemplate the laughter of future centuries over our own penchant to substitute "Racism" for "Jealousy"? Few things change as quickly as each era's burning issues, and any Tudor who is genuinely and specifically relevant today will be a great bore tomorrow. No sixteenth-century writer sought to speak primarily to a time other than his own, and in treating concerns as ageless and human as love, death, freedom, responsibility, and war, each was influenced by contemporary habits of thought. If a survey of that time furnishes a series of writers whose abilities vary far more than the topics they treated, it also helps us understand the art through which only the best have endured.

Notes to Chapter VI

1. *Metamorphoses*, XI, 100–104, ed. and trans. by Frank Justus Miller (London, 1933).
2. I. i. 5–18, in *The Complete Works of John Lyly*, ed. R. Warwick Bond (London, 1902), III, 113 ff.
3. Lyly's debt to Italian social customs is made even clearer by Violet M. Jeffery's identification of an intermediate Italian analogue, Hieronimo Zoppio's *Mida* (1573). Most of Lyly's minor alterations of Ovid's plot and many of the debates are also found in Zoppio. See *John Lyly and the Italian Renaissance* (Paris, 1928), pp. 102–110. Zoppio, however, does not include comic scenes and low-life characters, nor does he use Ovid's fable to allegorize contemporary international politics.
4. See Bond's reproduction of Halpin's "conjectural key" to the allegory in *Midas*, III, 109–110. In making Lyly's allegory walk on all fours, however, Halpin overreaches himself; e.g., the contest in music refers to the Reformation, and Apollo is the principle of Protestant sovereignty.
5. Ll. 25–27, in Joseph Quincy Adams, *Chief Pre-Shakespearean Dramas* (Boston, 1924).
6. Adams, ll. 344–414, 534–538.
7. Adams, ll. 196–201.
8. E. K. Chambers, *The Mediaeval Stage* (Oxford, 1903), II, 155.
9. See Adams, p. 264; letters in brackets supplied by the editor.
10. Chambers, II, 156.
11. Adams, p. 304 n.
12. Ll. 495–501, in Adams; letters in brackets supplied by editor.
13. F. L. Lucas, *Seneca and Elizabethan Tragedy* (Cambridge, 1922), p. 84.
14. Adams, l. 353.
15. Facsimile of title page, reproduced in John S. Farmer, *Six Anonymous Plays (Second Series)* (London, 1906), p. 1.
16. *Ibid.*
17. See J. Alfred Gotch, "Architecture," and Percy Macquoid, "The Home," in *Shakespeare's England*, ed. Sidney Lee and C. T. Onions (Oxford, 1916), II, 69–70, 142.
18. *An Apologie for Poetrie* (c. 1583), ed. G. Gregory Smith, *Elizabethan Critical Essays* (Oxford, 1904), I, 158.

19. Gotch, II, 52.

20. Arthur Stratton, *The English Interior* (London, 1920), p. 15.

21. For examples, see Stratton, pp. 5 ff.

22. Marchette Chute, *Ben Jonson of Westminster* (New York, 1960), pp. 27–28.

23. *Ibid.*, p. 31.

24. Arthur H. R. Fairchild, "Shakespeare and the Arts of Design," *The University of Missouri Studies*, XII (1937), 3.

25. Gotch, II, 69–71.

26. *Ibid.*, II, 71–72.

27. M. Jourdain, *English Decoration and Furniture of the Early Renaissance (1500–1650)* (London, 1924), p. 284.

28. *Cymbeline*, II. iv. 66 ff., in *The Complete Works*, ed. Peter Alexander (London, 1951).

29. Jourdain, p. 20.

30. *Ibid.*, p. 23; cf. also figs. 16B, 24, 25.

31. *Ibid.*, fig. 19.

32. M. St. Clare Byrne, *Elizabethan Life in Town and Country* (New York, 1961), pp. 32–33.

33. Preface to Coryat's *Crudities* (1611), ed. William Brenchley Rye, *England as Seen by Foreigners* (London, 1865), pp. 139–140.

34. Citations from Rathgeb and Ernest are to Rye; those from Hentzer, to *A Journey into England in the Year MDXCVIII*, trans. Richard Bentley (Edinburgh, 1881); those from Platter, to *Thomas Platter's Travels in England, 1599*, trans. Clare Williams (London, 1937).

35. *Palladis Tamia, Wits Treasury* (1598), ed. Smith, II, 324.

36. Hentzner, pp. 23–24; Bentley notes the same contemporary references, p. 24 n.

37. See Douglas Bush, *Mythology and the Renaissance Tradition in English Poetry* (Minneapolis, Minn. 1932), pp. 78–81.

38. *A Description of England* (1587), ed. Frederick J. Furnivall, I (London, 1877), 235.

39. Lionel Cust, "Painting, Sculpture, and Engraving," in *Shakespeare's England*, II, 5.

40. Fairchild, p. 105.

41. *Ibid.*, p. 144.

42. *Ibid.*, p. 147.

43. Macquoid, II, 130.

44. Hardin Craig's edition of *The Complete Works of Shakespeare* (New York, 1951), p. 587, reproduces a woodcut illustrating man's seven ages that appeared in Bartholomaeus Anglicus's *De Proprietatibus Rerum* (1485). See also Henry Green, *Shakespeare and the Emblem Writers* (London, 1869), pp. 406–410.

45. Ll. 399–403, ed. Lily B. Campbell (New York, 1960).

46. *Apologie*, in Smith, I, 166–167.
47. C. S. Lewis, *English Literature in the Sixteenth Century* (Oxford, 1954), p. 356.
48. *Emblematum Libellus* (Antwerp, 1581), in Green, pp. 269–270.
49. *Icones* (Geneva, 1581), trans. Green, p. 271, who also furnishes Beza's woodcut.
50. Green, p. 270.
51. *Ibid.*
52. Gabriel Harvey, *Fovre Letters and certaine Sonnets, especially touching Robert Greene and other parties by him abused* (1592), ed. G. B. Harrison (London, 1922), p. 16.
53. See R. B. McKerrow and F. S. Ferguson, *Title-page Borders used in England & Scotland: 1485–1640* (London, 1932), pp. 173–174 and fig. 215.
54. *Ibid.*, p. 173.
55. *Ibid.*, pp. 83, 102–104, 114; figs. 80, 117, 131.
56. *The Life and Works of George Peele*, II (New Haven, Conn., 1961), 9–23.
57. "Journey through England and Scotland Made by Lupold von Wedel in the Years 1584 and 1585," trans. Gottfried von Bülow, *Transactions of the Royal Historical Society* (London, 1895), p. 257.
58. See J. W. H. Atkins, *English Literary Criticism: The Renascence* (London, 1951), pp. 60 ff.
59. *The Instruction of a Christian Woman*, trans. Richard Hyrde (1540), ed. Foster Watson, *Vives and the Renascence Education of Women* (New York, 1912), p. 58.
60. *Ibid.*, p. 59.
61. *Ibid.*, p. 46.
62. *Ibid.*, p. 47.
63. *Ibid.*, p. 76.
64. *Wilson's Arte of Rhetorique, 1560*, ed. with intro. by G. H. Mair (Oxford, 1909), pp. 190–191.
65. *Ibid.*, pp. 191–193.
66. *Ibid.*, p. 101. For Wilson, native romances as well as the folk tales of Robin Hood offer subjects for "good sport." If the rhetorician's company includes one named Arthur, he can prove his wit by dubbing "him Knight of the round Table, or els proue him to be one of his kinne, or els (which were much) proue him to be *Arthur* himselfe. And so likewise of other names, merie companions would make mad pastime" (p. 145). Unlike most Humanists, however, Wilson is rather fond of the "olde tale" and "straunge historie," even though he does not seem to take them seriously.
67. *Ibid.*, pp. 39–63.

68. *Ibid.*, p. 46.

69. *Ibid.*, p. 47.

70. Henry Burrowes Lathrop, *Translations from the Classics into English from Caxton to Chapman, 1477–1620* (Madison, Wis., 1933), p. 21.

71. Watson, p. 34.

72. Mair, p. 8.

73. See Hardin Craig, *The Enchanted Glass* (New York, 1950), pp. 213–214.

74. Cf. Arundell Esdaile, *A List of English Tales and Prose Romances Printed Before 1740* (London, 1912), pp. 23, 96–97.

75. *Ibid.*, p. 110.

76. Albert Feuillerat, *Documents Relating to the Office of the Revels in the Time of Queen Elizabeth* (Louvain, 1908), pp. 141, 193, 270, 303.

77. Lathrop, pp. 315–316.

78. Mary Augusta Scott, *Elizabethan Translations from the Italian* (Boston, 1916), pp. 43–45.

79. *Ibid.*, pp. 116–124.

80. *Ibid.*, pp. 488–489.

81. Feuillerat, p. 345.

82. Louis B. Wright, *Middle-Class Culture in Elizabethan England* (Chapel Hill, N. C., 1935), p. 619.

83. Mary Patchell, *The Palmerin Romances in Elizabethan Prose Fiction* (New York, 1947), p. 15.

84. Wright, p. 381.

85. Patchell, p. 93.

86. *Ibid.*, p. 70.

87. *Ibid.*, p. 104.

88. See the unpublished dissertation (Yale, 1948) by Justin V. Emerson, "A Study of the Prose Romances of Emanuel Forde," especially pp. 166–203.

89. *Ibid.*, pp. 171, 194, 203.

90. *Apologie*, in Smith, I, 175.

91. Scott, pp. 17–18, 20–22; cf. also Thomas Frederick Crane, *Italian Social Customs of the Sixteenth Century* (New Haven, Conn., 1920), p. 507.

92. Cited by Scott, p. 21.

93. See Samuel Lee Wolff, *The Greek Romances in Elizabethan Prose Fiction* (New York, 1912), p. 7.

94. *An Aethiopian History*, ed. W. E. Henley, intro. Charles Whibley (London, 1895), pp. 4–5.

95. *Ibid.*, p. 149.

96. *Ibid.*, p. 210.

97. *Ibid.*, p. 66.

98. *Ibid.*, p. xiv.

99. "The French Bandello," *The University of Missouri Studies*, XXII (1948), 1–185.

100. *Ibid.*, pp. 11–12.

101. *Ibid.*, pp. 12–13.

102. *Ibid.*, p. 16.

103. Charles T. Prouty, *The Sources of Much Ado about Nothing* (New Haven, 1950), p. 6.

104. *Ibid.*

105. *The Palace of Pleasure*, ed. Joseph Jacobs (London, 1890), I, 4.

106. *Ibid.*, I, 10–11.

107. See Hook, pp. 36–38.

108. *Ibid.*, p. 23.

109. "Scilla and Minos," *A Petite Pallace of Pettie His Pleasure*, ed. Herbert Hartman (New York, 1938), pp. 147–165.

110. "The Letter of G.P. to R.B. Concerning this Woorke," in Hartman, pp. 5–7.

111. *Ibid.*, p. 5.

112. *The Golden Aphroditis and Grange's Garden*, facsimile edition, intro. by Hyder E. Rollins (New York, 1939), sigs. C1–C1^v, C3^v.

113. In his study of the relationships between the "excellent narrative techniques and character portrayals" of Gascoigne's *Adventures of Master F.J.* (1573) and their degeneration in Grange and Whetstone, Charles Prouty identifies Grange's setting and suggests Catherine Bridges as his Lady Alpha Omega; see "Elizabethan Fiction," *The University of Missouri Studies*, XXI (1946), 135–150.

114. Sigs. D1, H3^v, F3^v, C4^v, K2, E4, G4^v respectively.

115. E.g., *Menaphon* (1589), *Euphues his Censure to Philautus* (1587), and *Ciceronis Amor* (1589), all discussed at the close of this chapter.

116. In this third of *Fovre Letters*, ed. Harrison, p. 37.

117. *Ibid.*, pp. 39–41.

118. *Ovyde Hys Booke of Methamorphose*, intro. by Stephen Gaselee (Oxford, 1924), p. 137.

119. *The .XV. Bookes of P. Ouidius Naso, entytuled Metamorphosis* (1567), ed. W. H. D. Rouse as *Shakespeare's Ovid* (London, 1904), XIV, 73–75.

120. *Scillaes Metamorphosis* (1589), in *The Complete Works*, ed. Edmund W. Gosse (Glasgow, 1883), I, 7, 11.

121. *Mythology*, p. 82.

122. *Works*, I, 12.

123. Lathrop, p. 121.

124. *The Lawiers Logike, exemplifying the praecepts of Logike by the practise of the common Lawe* (London, 1588) sig. B3ᵛ.

125. *Ibid.,* sig. N3.

126. *Ibid.,* sigs. Kkl–Kklᵛ.

127. Book II, Chapter 21, in *The Complete Works,* ed. Albert Feuillerat, I (Cambridge, 1912), 282–288.

128. *Ibid.,* I, 283.

129. *Ibid.,* I, 286.

130. *Ibid.*

131. *Ibid.,* I, 285.

132. *Ibid.* My attention has been drawn to the Iberian jousts by Frances A. Yates, "Elizabethan Chivalry: The Romance of the Accession Day Tilts," *Journal of the Warburg and Courtauld Institutes,* XX (1957), 4–25.

133. *The Complete Works,* ed. Alexander B. Grosart (Edinburgh, 1880), I, First Week, Fourth Day, 610–611.

134. Joseph Jacobs, introduction to his edition of Day's translation, *Daphnis and Chloe: The Elizabethan Version* (London, 1890), p. xv.

135. Cited by Wolff, *Greek Romances,* p. 242.

136. *Ibid.,* pp. 240–245.

137. Jacobs, p. 98.

138. *Ibid.,* pp. 100–101.

139. *Ibid.,* pp. 102–103, 118.

140. *Ibid.,* pp. 103, 113.

141. *Ibid.,* pp. 104–114.

142. Alfred Harbage, *Shakespeare and the Rival Traditions* (New York, 1952), pp. 107–108.

143. Induction, ll. 17, 35–36, in *English Drama: 1580–1642,* ed. C. F. Tucker Brooke and Nathaniel Burton Paradise (Boston, 1933), pp. 689–690.

144. *Ibid.,* p. 689.

145. "The Renaissance (1500–1660)," in *A Literary History of England,* ed. Albert C. Baugh (New York, 1948), p. 457.

146. See Frederick S. Boas, *An Introduction to Tudor Drama* (Oxford, 1959), p. 4.

147. Cf. facsimile of title page, in *Five Pre-Shakespearean Comedies,* ed. Frederick S. Boas (London, 1958), p. 1.

148. *Ibid.,* Part II, ll. 764–765.

149. Boas, *Introduction to Tudor Drama,* p. 9.

150. *Playes Confuted in Five Actions,* cited by Geoffrey Bullough, *Narrative and Dramatic Sources of Shakespeare,* I (London, 1961), v.

151. E.g., the Elizabethan marketing scene, III. i.

152. See his chronological abstract of plays printed or entered for

printing between 1558 and 1616; *The Elizabethan Stage* (Oxford, 1923), IV, 379–397.

153. In Smith, I, 197.

154. Certainly the comedies of intrigue, like Anthony Munday's (?) *Fedele and Fortunio. The deceites in Love* (1585) are too crisp and impersonal to have helped Greene much more than what he already had in Plautus and Terence. The genuinely romantic *Mucedorus* (c. 1588–1598), on the other hand, probably came too late; as we shall soon see, by 1585 Greene was already discovering other means of realizing high-flown stuff like *Sir Clyomon.*

155. Ed. W. W. Greg (Oxford, 1913), ll. 59–64.

156. Ed. Tucker Brooke (New Haven, 1915), ll. 667-670.

157. Greg, ll. 978 ff.

158. Brooke, ll. 732–736.

159. *Ibid.,* ll. 760 ff.

160. See Lee Monroe Ellison, *The Early Romantic Drama at the English Court* (Menasha, Wis., 1917), pp. 95, 121.

161. Greg, ll. 1196 ff., 1550 ff.

162. *Ibid.,* l. 1428.

163. Fairchild, p. 147.

164. The exact date of the performance is unknown. Since the title page claims that the play was "presented before the Queenes Maiestie, by the Children of her Chappell" and since this company is known to have acted at court on Twelfth Night and Candlemas, 1584, Brooke and Paradise *(English Drama,* p. 2) find it "probable" that *The Arraignment* was first performed on one of these occasions.

165. Cited by Felix E. Schelling, "The Source of Peele's 'Arraignment of Paris'," *MLN,* VIII (1893), 103–104.

166. From a description printed by Wynkyn de Worde and cited by T. S. Graves *"The Arraignment of Paris* and Sixteenth Century Flattery," *MLN,* XXVIII (1913), 48–49. In challenging the source alleged by Schelling, Gascoigne's "Grief of Joye," Graves wisely noted the difficulty of distinguishing sources from analogues, especially when the motif is so popular. As a result, no further claims were registered until 1924, when Miss V. M. Jeffery, refusing to acknowledge Peele as an innovator in pastoral drama, postulated Anello Paulilli's *Giuditio di Paride* (1566) as Peele's sole model for both theme and treatment; see "The Source of Peele's 'Arraignment of Paris'," *MLR,* XIX (1924), 175–187. To justify her statement that "it is impossible to imagine that Peele cannot have known the earlier Italian version of the story," she recruits a large number of "parallel" passages. But as Allan H. Gilbert, in "The Source of Peele's *Arraignment of Paris," MLN,*

XLI (1926), 36–40, soon pointed out, none of Miss Jeffery's parallels show more than "the general similarity that would naturally be found in the work of men treating the same theme under somewhat similar conditions."

167. David H. Horne, *The Life and Minor Works of George Peele* (New Haven, Conn., 1952) pp. 56, 149. For biographical comments on Peele I am almost exclusively indebted to Horne; citations from Peele's nondramatic poetry are to his edition.

168. Ll. 115–116; Horne comments that the judgment rendered by Ida's "jolly swaine" reads like a first draft of *The Arraignment*, and lists seven parallel passages (p. 150).

169. See Horne, pp. 57–64.

170. *Ibid.*, p. 70.

171. *The Life and Complete Works in Prose and Verse of Robert Greene*, ed. Alexander B. Grosart (London, 1881–1886), VII, 7–8. All citations from Greene's nondramatic works are to this edition.

172. Thomas Marc Parrott and Robert Hamilton Ball, *A Short View of Elizabethan Drama* (New York, 1958), pp. 70–71.

173. *Alphonsus*, l. 1430. All citations from Greene's plays are to *The Plays & Poems of Robert Greene*, ed. with intro. by J. Churton Collins (Oxford, 1905).

174. With the exception of *The Tragicall History of Doctor Faustus* (c. 1588–1592), probably performed after Greene's first two plays.

175. *The Court Masque* (Cambridge, 1927), p. 279.

176. Cf. ll. 685 ff. and Collins's note, I, 316.

177. See Morris R. Morrison, "Greene's Use of Ariosto in *Orlando Furioso*," MLN, XLIX (1934), 449–451. Collins (I, 217 ff.) lists Greene's more obvious departures from Ariosto.

178. See Collins, I, 75–76, 138–139.

179. See Allan Gilbert's introduction to his translation of the *Orlando Furioso* (New York, 1954), I, xxii ff.

180. Of the many persons to whom Greene at least tried to cater in his devising, only Sir John Harington, who was currently translating Ariosto's comical epic, seems to have been dissatisfied; he entitled Greene's play "Orlando foolioso." See F. J. Furnivall, "Sir John Harington's Shakspeare Quartos," NQ, Ser. 7, IX (1890), 383. In his *Orlando Furioso in English Heroical Verse* (London, 1591), Harington frequently glosses Ariosto's rollicking cantos with mock solemnity and deliberately specious reasoning. Townsend Rich, *Harington and Ariosto: A Study in Elizabethan Verse Translation* (New Haven, Conn., 1940), has shown that within the translation itself Sir John's interest waxes and wanes according to the wantonness of the original and that wherever possible he accents Angelica's foolishness, even to the point of adding lines

not suggested in the Italian (pp. 110, 130). Unlike Greene's elaborations, however, Harington's are at least within the spirit of his source; he merely underlines the nonsense that seems to have escaped the notice of both Greene and Spenser.

181. First extant edition, 1583, but entered for printing in the Stationers' Register in October, 1580.

182. *Strange Newes* (1592), in *The Works of Thomas Nashe*, ed. Ronald B. McKerrow (London, 1904–1910), I, 287.

183. *Fovre Letters*, pp. 37–39, 41.

184. In "Further Repetitions in the Works of Robert Greene," *PQ*, XVIII (1939), 73–77, C. J. Vincent reveals a number of instances in which Greene transferred sentences and sometimes passages several pages in length from one romance to another. Another method employed by the wily professional to eke out his tales, his purely fanciful additions to Pliny's lore, has been illustrated by Don Cameron Allen, "Science and Invention in Greene's Prose," *PMLA*, LIII (1938), 1007–1018.

185. *Have With You to Saffron-Walden* (1596), in *Works*, III, 132.

186. See René Pruvost, *Robert Greene et ses Romans* (Paris, 1938), p. 286.

187. That Greene smiled even as he engineered *Menaphon*'s complex events gains some support when we consider his most delightful representation of Cupid's complicated games, *Ciceronis Amor* (1589): Cornelia loves Fabius, who loves Terentia, who loves Tully (alias Cicero), whose regard for Lentulus (who also loves Terentia) forbids him to reciprocate. Fortunately, Terentia's friend, Flavia, also loves Lentulus, and Tully is able to use his oratory to defend the whole business before the Roman fathers in the last pages. Greene's sense of humor is also evident in one of *Menaphon*'s pastoral songs (VI, 138): "Thy lippes resemble two Cowcumbers faire, / Thy teeth like to the tuskes of fattest swine, / Thy speach is like the thunder in the aire: / Would God thy toes, thy lips, and all were mine."

188. See John Clark Jordan, *Robert Greene* (New York, 1915), p. 51.

189. Collins, II. 5. Since Collins's edition scholars have noticed several traditional and contemporary elements in Greene's portrayals of his necromancers and their contests in magic. In "Greene's *Friar Bacon and Friar Bungay*," *MLN*, XXXV (1920), 212–217, James Dow McCallum finds in the characterization of Vandermast a satire on Giordano Bruno of Nola, who disputed against members of the Oxford faculty in June, 1583. Percy Z. Round, in "Greene's Materials for 'Friar Bacon and Friar Bungay'," *MLR*, XXI (1926), 19–23, shows that Greene drew from, condensed, and mingled some characters and events of Bale's *Pageant of*

Popes and Holinshed's *Chronicles*. Again, Waldo F. McNeir, in "Traditional Elements in the Character of Greene's Friar Bacon," *SP*, XLV (1948), 172–179, points out that Greene borrowed from medieval romances to give his conjurer a more dignified role. Finally, in "Greene's Borrowings from his own Prose Fiction in *Bacon and Bungay*, and *James the Fourth*," *PQ*, XXX (1951), 22–29, Allan H. MacLaine shows Greene's indebtedness to his romances for conventional ideas, stereotyped descriptions, and types of plot and character. The "borrowings" MacLaine notes, however, could have been supplied by other romances of the era.

190. See William J. Thoms's edition of *The Famous Historie* in *Early English Prose Romances* (London, 1858), I, 197–198, 205–211, 216–219. Collins provides extracts in II, 6–13.

191. In Thoms, I, 196–197.

192. *Ibid.*, I, 245–247. Cf. *Bacon and Bungay*, ll. 1760 ff.

193. *Ibid.*, I, 235–237.

194. *The Compendious Rehearsall of John Dee* (1592), in *Autobiographical Tracts of Dr. John Dee*, ed. James Crossley (Manchester, 1851), pp. 17, 21.

195. *The Discoverie of Witchcraft* (1584), ed. Montague Summers (London, 1930), p. 179.

196. "The Black Dog of Bongay," an entry by "Zeus" in *NQ*, Ser. 2, IV (1857), 314. The date of Fleming's tract is not given.

197. But see Collins, II, 326.

198. The first novel of the Third Decade; Collins (II, 80–83) provides a summary.

199. See John Colin Dunlop, *History of Prose Fiction* (London, 1911), II, 192–194.

200. II, 79–80.

201. In "Greene's *James IV* and Contemporary Allusions to Scotland," *PMLA*, XLVII (1932), 652–667, Ruth Hudson makes it clear that from 1580 on, all England had its eyes upon the Scottish court. Burghley was in constant touch with agents in Edinburgh, and "the average Londoner of that time was thoroughly conversant with even the most trivial minutiae of Scottish affairs" (p. 654). Miss Hudson finds in Greene's play numerous reflections of conditions in contemporary Scotland, and in his characterization of James IV, several suggestions of James VI. Less convincing is Waldo F. McNeir's "The Original of Ateukin in Greene's *James IV*," *MLN*, LXII (1947), 376–381. McNeir identifies Ateukin's original as John Damian, an Italian adventurer, astrologer, and charlatan, to whom the historical James IV gave high offices.

202. Cf. ll. 505 ff., and Chambers, *Elizabethan Stage*, IV, 66–67.

203. *Court Masque*, p. 280.

204. Hook, ll. 1170 ff. For Peele's romantic handling of his sources and his indebtedness to Greene, which Hook characterizes as "absorption rather than copying," see pp. 16–23, 55–60.

205. Summarized by Harold Jenkins, "Peele's 'Old Wives' Tale'," *MLR*, XXXIV (1939), 177–185.

206. Gwenan Jones, "The Intention of Peele's 'Old Wives' Tale'," *Aberystwyth Studies*, VII (1925), 79–93. Miss Jones lists the folk-lore motifs on pp. 85–87 and notes that the few that are also found in medieval romance are invariably given "a folkloristic character."

207. See Fantastic's remarks, ll. 632–633. All citations are to the edition of Brooke and Paradise, in *English Drama*, pp. 23 ff.

208. Horne, p. 90.

209. *Ibid.*, p. 173.

210. E.g., *A Farewell*, l. 3; *Polyhymnia*, l. 183; *Anglorum Feriae*, l. 43.

211. See Jenkins, pp. 178 ff., who finds in this an indication of abridgement.

212. Horne, p. 90.

213. The "famous stock of Huanebango" includes both "Dionora de Sardinia" and "Pergopolineo"; see ll. 342 ff.

214. See Brooke's and Paradise's notes to these lines, pp. 32 ff.

215. See Karl J. Holzknecht, *The Backgrounds of Shakespeare's Plays* (New York, 1950), p. 431.

Suggestions for Further Reading

Helpful sketches of Tudor translators at work are to be found in Henry Burrowes Lathrop's *Translations from the Classics into English from Caxton to Chapman, 1477–1620* (Madison, Wis., 1933) and in F. O. Matthiessen's *Translation: An Elizabethan Art* (Cambridge, Mass., 1931). Mary Augusta Scott's *Elizabethan Translations from the Italian* (Boston, 1916) is still an invaluable reference work.

For the reader who wishes to know more about translations in the looser sense of "carrying-across," how foreign matters were altered, adapted, and transfigured, there are several excellent points of departure: Douglas Bush, *Mythology and the Renaissance Tradition in English Poetry*, Minneapolis, 1932; Frank S. Hook, "The French Bandello," *University of Missouri Studies*, XXII, No. 1 (1948), 1–185; Mary Patchell, *The Palmerin Romances in Elizabethan Prose Fiction*, New York, 1947; Townsend Rich, *Harington and Ariosto: A Study in Elizabethan Verse Translation*, New Haven, Conn., 1940; Samuel Lee Wolff, *The Greek Romances in Elizabethan Prose Fiction*, New York, 1912.

As glosses upon literary translations and transfigurations there are the works written upon cloth, glass, wood, and stone. What the fine arts tell us about one Tudor's poetry is well handled in Arthur H. R. Fairchild's "Shakespeare and the Arts of Design," *University of Missouri Studies*, XII, No. 1 (1937), 1–198. Additional evidence is provided in the articles of Lionel Cust, J. Alfred Gotch, and Percy Macquoid: See *Shakespeare's England*, ed. C. T. Onions, Oxford, 1916, II, 1–14, 50–73, 91–152. More specialized treatments can be found in M. Jourdain, *English Decoration and Furniture of the Early Renaissance (1500–1650)*, London, 1924, and in Arthur Stratton, *The English Interior*, London, 1920. But we must not forget how these signs of the times were seen by men of the sixteenth century; a good place to begin is William B. Rye's *England as Seen by Foreigners*, London, 1865.

Finally, there are a good many informative introductions to the lesser men who helped Shakespeare set his stage. C. F. Tucker

Brooke's *The Tudor Drama*, Cambridge, Mass., 1911, is still valuable; so is John Clark Jordan's *Robert Greene*, New York, 1915. More recent studies include M. C. Bradbrook, *The Growth and Structure of Elizabethan Comedy*, London, 1955; G. K. Hunter, *John Lyly: The Humanist as Courtier*, London, 1962; E. C. Pettet, *Shakespeare and the Romance Tradition*, London, 1949. Peele is finally receiving the attention he deserves; the third and final volume of *The Life and Works of George Peele*, gen. ed. Charles T. Prouty, should be issued by Yale University Press this year. We certainly need a new edition of Greene; the fifteen-volume edition of Alexander B. Grosart, London, 1881–1886, is difficult to obtain.

Indexes

The Notes have been indexed only for matter that warrants treatment as if it were part of the text.

Index A

Renaissance and Pre-Renaissance Authors and Works

Except for anonymous writings, all works are listed by author. For considerations of authors apart from works, see Index B.

INDEX B

Persons and Subjects

References to Biblical and mythological characters are omitted. For fictive treatments of historical persons (e.g., Richard III), see INDEX A.

DATE DUE